V&R unipress

Mamluk Studies

Volume 3

Edited by Stephan Conermann

ANNEMARIE SCHIMMEL KOLLEG
History and Society during the Mamluk Era (1250 – 1517)

Stephan Conermann (ed.)

Ubi sumus? Quo vademus?

Mamluk Studies – State of the Art

With numerous figures

V&R unipress

Bonn University Press

universitätbonn

MIX
Papier aus verantwortungsvollen Quellen
FSC® C003147

Bibliographic information published by the Deutsche Nationalbibliothek

The Deutsche Nationalbibliothek lists this publication in the Deutsche Nationalbibliografie; detailed bibliographic data are available on the Internet at http://dnb.d-nb.de.

ISBN 978-3-8471-0100-0
ISBN 978-3-8470-0100-3 (E-Book)

Publications of Bonn University Press
are published by V&R unipress GmbH.

Printed in Germany.
Printing and binding: CPI Buch Bücher.de GmbH, Birkach

Contents

Stephan Conermann
Quo vadis, Mamlukology? *(A German Perspective)* 7

Thomas Bauer
Mamluk Literature as a Means of Communication 23

Caterina Bori
Theology, Politics, Society: the missing link. Studying Religion in the Mamluk Period 57

Albrecht Fuess
Mamluk Politics 95

Syrinx von Hees
Mamlukology as Historical Anthropology 119

Thomas Herzog
Mamluk (Popular) Culture. 131

Konrad Hirschler
Studying Mamluk Historiography. From Source-Criticism to the Cultural Turn 159

Th. Emil Homerin
Sufism in Mamluk Studies: A Review of Scholarship in the Field 187

Carine Juvin
Mamluk Inscriptions 211

Paulina B. Lewicka
Did Ibn al-Ḥājj Copy from Cato? Reconsidering Aspects of Inter-Communal Antagonism of the Mamluk Period 231

Christian Müller
Mamluk Law: a reassessment 263

Lucian Reinfandt
Mamlūk Documentary Studies 285

Bethany J. Walker
What Can Archaeology Contribute to the New Mamlukology? Where Culture Studies and Social Theory Meet 311

Torsten Wollina
Ibn Ṭawq's *Taʿlīq*. An Ego-Document for Mamlūk Studies 337

Stephan Conermann

Quo vadis, Mamlukology? *(A German Perspective)*[1]

No one would contest in principle that Mamlukology forms a branch of the humanities. However, owing to the fact that the relevance of the humanities for society is not easily explained to the public, for the past two decades they have found themselves in a constant crisis of legitimization that is characterized by the fear of a university-internal marginalization on the one hand and by the attempt to fulfil the university administrations' wish for disciplinary expansion on the other. In fact, this dilemma isn't new. Following a suggestion by the National Council for Research ("Wissenschaftsrat") and the Conference of University Rectors of West Germany "Hochschulrektorenkonferenz", a project was carried out at Konstanz University from 1987 to 1990 that aimed at developing perspectives for the future of humanities. The outcome of this project was the highly remarkable memorandum *Geisteswissenschaft heute* ("The Humanities Today").[2] The high-profile and certainly competent authors of this programmatic treatise eventually came to two conclusions: 1. The humanities only have a realistic chance of surviving if they henceforth see themselves as Cultural Studies and re-position themselves accordingly within the universities. 2. The central scientific questions for these new Cultural Studies ("Kulturwissenschaft") are provided primarily by Historical Anthropology.

Let me clarify both points briefly, speaking from the view of the authors: The humanities are, according to their opinion, the "place" where modern societies acquire knowledge of themselves in a scientific form. But this knowledge is not positivist knowledge of the kind postulated in the positivist sciences, but rather knowledge that mainly undertakes tasks of orientation.[3] There are good reasons to start the necessary re-orientation of the humanities on the basis of their

1 This text is an extended and modified version of Conermann, St., Vorbemerkung: Islamwissenschaft als Kulturwissenschaft, in: St. Conermann/Syrinx von Hees (ed.): Islamwissenschaft als Historische Anthropologie. I. Historische Anthropologie. Ansätze und Möglichkeiten. Schenefeld 2007, 9–20.

2 Frühwald, W. et al., Geisteswissenschaften heute: eine Denkschrift. Frankfurt am Main 1991.

3 Cf. Frühwald et al. 1991, 39.

modern designation as a cultural science: "culture" no longer represents the subsection of a sphere of life (next to politics, law, economy and religion), but must be expanded to include the cultural whole, i.e. culture as the epitome of human productivity and human ways of life – including developments in natural sciences and elsewhere.[4] Cultural Studies structurally tend towards cultural pluralism, whereas the humanities tend towards the unity and entirety represented by the model of the one human spirit. Subjects like Mamlukology would not be lost after the re-structuring of disciplines, but would remain irreplaceable in the dialogue of disciplines whenever it is important to understand a matter from the context of its term, its history, its symbolic character or its form, i.e. philosophically, historically, linguistically, or aesthetically. The potential of Mamlukology's re-interpretation as a cultural science would then lie in the possibility to translate mere information into communication, to control and permanently demonstrate anew the understanding of the self through the other as well as of the other through the self. So borders need not necessarily separate, but may open up new horizons and promote the unanimity among those who know and those who act. The foundation of these Cultural Studies, as I have mentioned already, should be Historical Anthropology, because it is set to historicize the results of a basically ahistorical, yet essential discipline for Cultural Studies, such as descriptive ethnology, as well as to – reversely – explore the anthropological dimension of language, history and aesthetics for the benefit of the other sciences. The concern of such research would transcend the traditionally and institutionally still Eurocentric system of knowledge, and would need hermeneutics of intercultural communication (the keyword here is "hermeneutics of foreignness") and would have to retrieve regionally focused studies – like African Studies, South American Studies or in a certain sense Mamlukology – from their isolation, in order to make their findings available and productive for a general theory.[5]

So these are the two most important results of the treatise *The Humanities Today* that was published in the early 1990s. As the demanded changes in content and institutions have more or less not yet been implemented in Mamlukology as far as I can assess it,[6] it may be legitimate, more than 20 years later, to ask: What are we going to do with this document now? Two options present themselves: either we take it seriously and draw certain consequences or we discard it and continue along the same lines as before. I have decided to follow the direction suggested in the memorandum and – as far as I can – to give our Annemarie

4 Cf. Frühwald et al. 1991, 40.
5 Cf. Frühwald et al. 1991, 71.
6 A fresh impulse should give the various publications of the Annemarie Schimmel Kolleg "History and Society during the Mamluk Era (1250–1517)" (http://www.mamluk.uni-bonn.de).

Schimmel Kolleg a "kulturwissenschaftliche" direction. This decision was not only based on my socialization as a humanist and Islamic scholar interested in theories and methodology and on 20 years of professional experience with university and educational policies, but has to be seen mainly against the backdrop of the imminent and seemingly unstoppable transformation of the German university-level educational organisation into a Bachelor-Master system.

At this point I want to emphasize explicitly that I consider a thorough philological instruction a *condition sine qua non*, especially for studies of cultures of a Muslim character. Moreover, I believe that the historical critical method can still be a fruitful and proven approach of textual interpretation.[7] Yet, what matters are new objectives against the background of a new self-assessment acquired through permanent, constructive self-reflection. Whether Historical Anthropology will prove itself to be the methodical nonpareil remains to be seen.

1. Mamlukology (in Germany) – some general remarks

In his his seminal article "Die deutschen Orientalisten im 20. Jahrhundert und der Zeitgeist", the well-known German Iranist Bert Fragner put forward the following argumentation:[8] The insistence of Mamlukologist, formerly referred to as "Orientalists", to be in charge of the research on the history of the regions covered by them, is traditionally based on their ability acquired in their philological instruction to master the original sources linguistically and place them in their factual context, which is to be elaborated historico-critically and is conditional to their understanding. The term "Islam" encompasses, in the view of these scholars, the Islamic religion and the culture *thought of* as something inspired by it, characterized by it and arisen from it; it includes additionally the most important languages of this culture – Arabic, Persian, Turkish – and also the history of the so-called "Islamic world". The decipherment of these difficult texts, of which the Mamlukologist has every reason to be proud, result in a fragmentary and one-sided picture of the 'Islamic culture' – as every medievalist

7 Still the best introduction is Utzschneider, H./Nitsche, S.A. Arbeitsbuch literaturwissenschaftliche Bibelauslegung. Eine Methodenlehre zur Exegese des AT. Gütersloh 2005.

8 The following paragraph closely follows his text which has been published in Hiery, H.J. (ed.): Der Zeitgeist und die Historie. Dettelbach 2001. I replaced "Orientalisten" and "Islamwissenschaftler" with "mamlukologists". See also his "Iranistik zwischen brennender Aktualität und exotischer Abseitigkeit – Gedanken zur Positionierung eines 'kleinen' orientalistischen Faches", in: Poya, A./Reinkowski, M. (ed.), *Das Unbehagen in der Islamwissenschaft. Ein klassisches Fach im Scheinwerferlicht der Politik und der Medien.* Bielefeld 2008, 105–117.

knows. We learn a lot about the Islam as a textbook religion, the ideal literary Islam of the few well-educated – and only little of the Islam of the illiterate masses as they used to live it, i.e. of popular Islam. We find out much more about the culture of the elites than about the hybrid cultures of the people, the peasants, Bedouins and urban day labourers. This has the effect that text-fixated Mamlukologists that are unaffected by more modern methods and formulations of questions often cultivate an image of Islam that not only has little to do with the reality of Mamluk society as a whole, but moreover tempts us to misconceive the present as a perceived product of degeneration. Owing to this tradition, Mamlukology has been primarily defined in philological terms. This primacy meant that the sectors history, literature, religious history or history of philosophy were not seen as essential parts of Mamlukology but rather as accidental ones. The philological basis used to be considered as the very own art of Mamlukology, the truly essential element of that science. This understanding was based on a type of language reception which paralleled the one of the classics. The idealistic glorification of philology, which is still often romanticized today, has been a characteristic feature of Mamlukologists, and especially of German Mamlukologists, for generations. Paradoxically, it was the first 20 to 25 post-War years in which precisely this philological basic conviction of their own way of acting that led the German scholars deeply into an attitude typical of the *Zeitgeist* which dominated much more than scientific thought at the time. The focus on philology, so hard to connect to philosophy, ideology or politics, made it possible to be escapist in public whilst adhering to central scientific principles. For the first time in 20th century, the structural inclination of the so-called Orientalistic disciplines – to see the appropriate form of "pure science" in philology – coincided with a general attitude – also shared by the public – to reject categories that could be introduced from outside the particular discipline like "creation of theories", "philosophy of science" or the intrusion of elements suspected of being ideological. "Freedom from ideology" was the most popular catchphrase among Islamic scholars during the 1950s and 60s, even though it was not always expressed in public. Thus it is not surprising that especially during this time at German Universities one text edition was produced after the other. But then the unruly 1970s followed, threatening the mamlukological idyll with new ideas from the social sciences. It was generally thought that social sciences should take the place of philosophy as the leading science in the filed of the humanities. The questions why we research what became louder and was brought of bare on the subject from the outside. What was the relevance of Islamic Studies whose scholars were at a loss when faced with current political events and had no answers or explanations at all (one can just mention the Suez Canal conflict, the Palestinian Question, the fall of Mossadegh in Iran or the Algerian Crisis)? Islamic Studies and Mamlukology soon acquired the air of a supposedly remote and eccentric subject to the content of which depended on the idiosyncrasies of the respective professors. In some respects this has remained so – at least in Germany – until 9/11.

Outside Germany Edward Said's book *Orientalism* published in 1978 roused the scientific community from its intellectual slumber.[9] Vivid theoretical debates following overall methodical discussions lead everywhere to substantial re-orientations. But among Mamlukologists such a debate on principles did not take place yet. Because of the sustained refusal of many scholars to join the ongoing intensive theoretical debates there are – to paraphrase Ute Daniel – still far too many Mamlukologists

1. who think that facts speak for themselves
2. who believe that they can see how things really have been
3. who assume that their professional methods and their ability to reflect on scientific topics are more than able to match the requirements and who think that philosophical and theoretical discussions would only disturb this pre-stabilised harmony
4. who believe that their discourses let the world speak for itself in the form of history
5. who pursue the limited documented reconstructions of a pre-critically designed past
6. who see the experience of historical subjects as unquestionable proof and
7. who set themselves apart from many other distinguished scholars because of their hostility or at least their blindness towards theories and questions which have been raised from Hegel on.[10]

In my opinion, neither the humanities nor Mamlukology can be pursued on this basis any longer without losing the intellectual connections to the globalized world entirely.

2. Mamlukology as Cultural Studies

If we want Mamlukology to become a tributary of the broad river of Cultural Studies, we first have to define exactly what we mean by this term.[11] At the

9 Excellent introductions are Varisco, D. M., Reading Orientalism. Said and the Unsaid. Seattle and London 2007 and Burke, E./Prochaska, D. (ed.), Genealogies of Orientalism. History, Theory, Politica. Lincoln and London 2008.

10 Cf. Daniel, U., Kompendium Kulturgeschichte. Theorien, Praxis, Schlüsselwörter. Frankfurt 2001, 157–158.

11 The German "Kulturwissenschaften" must not be mixed up with "Cultural Studies". Cf. Nünning, A., Art. "Kulturwissenschaft", in: Nünning, A. (ed.), Metzler Lexikon Literatur-

beginning of the 21st century, the era of the fighting over methods seems to be over in most of the humanities, with Mamlukology having never really been affected by the sometimes heated academic arguments. The current "methods after methods" are eclectic and open, selecting theorems from the traditional methods and supplementing them by new ones while at the same time forming overlaps and crossovers. What all these approaches have in common is that they understand philologically oriented disciplines as Cultural Studies without forcing them to abandon their philological basis.[12] What matters is rather the networking of the various methodical approaches, their necessary "hybridisation" in the age of globalization. The debate about Cultural Studies in this context is the articulation of a paradigm shift within the humanities and as such it is certainly far more than just a fashionable trend. Ignoring this fact now will inevitably show its consequences in the future.

Under the name "cultural history", "cultural science" has been an established concept since the 18th century.[13] In the "Sattelzeit" of modern epistemology, i.e. in the years from 1880 until 1933,[14] philosophers and sociologists expressed and debated some basic ideas about what kind of knowledge about man the various disciplines could and should provide.[15] Thus, neither the concept nor the central problems of modern-day Cultural Studies are actually new. Cultural Studies and cultural history are both located on the same fundamental level, namely that of their self-conception. It is fundamental in that it entails decisions that have to be made before any scientific work can become possible in the first place – for example the decisions on which conditions have to be met by a scientific proposition in order to be accepted as "true" or correct; on what is to be considered a historical fact; or on exactly when something should be considered "explained" and the significance of the fact that explanations of historical phenomena are usually given in the form of narratively structured texts – in

und Kulturtheorie. Ansätze – Personen – Grundbegriffe. Stuttgart and Weimar 2001, 353–356. In this text, we use the term "Cultural Studies" for "Kulturwissenschaften". Works of reference are Jaeger, F./Liebsch, B. (ed.), Handbuch der Kulturwissenschaften. Bd. 1: Grundlagen und Schlüsselbegriffe. Stuttgart und Weimar 2004, Jaeger, F./Straub, J. (ed.), Handbuch der Kulturwissenschaften. Bd. 2: Paradigmen und Disziplinen. Stuttgart und Weimar 2004, Jaeger, F./Rüsen, J. (ed.), Handbuch der Kulturwissenschaften. Bd. 3: Themen und Tendenzen. Stuttgart und Weimar 2004 and Bachmann-Medick, D., Cultural Turns. Neuorientierungen in den Geisteswissenschaften. Hamburg 2006.

12 Cf. Benthien, C./Velten, H.R., Einleitung, in: Benthien, C./Velten, H.R. (ed.), Germanistik als Kulturwissenschaft. Eine Einführung in neue Theoriekonzepte. Hamburg 2002, 7–34, here 7.

13 Cf. Daniel 2001, 195–220.

14 See Koselleck, R., Über die Theoriebedürftigkeit der Geschichtswissenschaft, in: Conze, W. (ed.), Theorie der Geschichtswissenschaft und Praxis des Geschichtsunterrichts, Stuttgart 1972, 10–28.

15 Cf. Daniel 2001, 8. See also Oexle, O. G., Geschichte als Historische Kulturwissenschaft, in: Hardtwig, W./Wehler, H.-U. (ed.), Kulturgeschichte heute. Göttingen 1996, 14–40.

short: decisions on what kind of knowledge it is that is provided here and which criteria may be used in its discussion.[16] Although there are striking parallels between the method debate of the last 35 years and the intellectual discussions that took place around 1900, the matter here can't be a mere revitalization of considerations from the past which are naturally based in their context and time. Still, it is legitimate and maybe even necessary to take the writing of Friedrich Nietzsche, Max Weber, Emile Durkheim or Georg Simmel as an inspiration or even as a guideline in formulating new foundations for the self-concept of Mamlukology as Cultural Studies today.

The central element of Mamlukology as Cultural Studies is a comprehensive conception of culture:[17] as mentioned above, culture is thought of as a creative force of life as a whole, encompassing the ways of life, patterns of perception and forms of communication of the different groups, strata, sexes and classes. It is no longer believed that culture is a closed concept in which everyone can participate on an equal basis. Settlers and nomads, rural and urban dwellers, scholars and courtiers cannot be measured against the same concept of culture, since they are all bound by different living conditions and have different interests in life. The reality of life is characterized by a plurality of ways of living. This extended concept of culture comprises not only the scholarly code of values but also the world of the manifold traditions, lifestyles, needs and interests of the individuals and social groups, which are not interpretable in a single direction. In this was, the heterogeneity of life-ways and different constructions of meaning makes it possible to speak of many cultures rather than one, even within a single geographical entity. Accordingly, the cultural value is no longer measured after a European-style hierarchical pattern but in terms of the benefit and importance it has for the individual as well as for individual groups. Without absolute standards, after all, it becomes easier to perceive the plurality of cultures and their equality in status.

The task of Mamlukology as a part of the quite heterogeneous Cultural Studies is to locate itself in their broad and changing fields and frames. Of course this is not easy but what counts is that the borders of the discipline do not limit the things which can be known about a society. These borders only define the center point of our interest and give us the tools for our research, i. e. the philological and historico-critical access. But beyond this point, Mamlukology has to be open to the large offer in self-reflection which the Cultural Studies have developed in the last 125 years. For them there are no given facts but only socially relevant imaginations, the formation and selection of topics within a specific context. Mamlukology as Cultural Studies always has a hermeneutical dimension by

16 Cf. Daniel 2001, 9 – 10.

17 Here, I follow Dülmen 2001, 43.

asking what meaning human beings give and have given to things.[18] In the past Mamlukologists used to pass those questions on to others all too willingly. The nucleus of the debates within the Cultureal Studies is the understanding that theory and practical work cannot be separated from each other without paying high price for it: those who produce academic knowledge are not able to reflect self-critically on its status. Mamlukology as Cultural Studies is no recipe for an automatic generation of methodically proven knowledge in the latest fashion style. Method and result – and this is a central claim of Cultural Studies – are in a circular relation to each other. In this way they are mutually dependent. However different the linguistic games which characterize the current 'culturalistic' spectrum may be, all of them – from post structuralism to discourse analysis and contemporary hermeneutics to the linguistic turn – formulate in the respective language a central finding, namely the one of unavoidable circularity of all academic doings: whether you identify fields of subjects or contexts, whether you make causal connections, or whether you use terms or you tell stories – again and again the shape of what "comes out" later on is outlined through explicit and implicit parameters which were involved previously. Fortunately, Mamlukology as Cultural Studies implies an understanding of science which no longer requires the disciplinary rituals of safeguards, limiting, and profiling which seemed to be essential for a long time. Thus, by using a certain method, a certain way of acting, a certain vocabulary, you cannot score higher results on the same reference scale – you can only make them look different. And: you can argue about the results. This does not mean that all results are "equal before God" but you cannot derive their quality and acceptance from a certain methodical way of acting. If for some times some methodical ways of acting and some concepts had a big chance to be accepted this does not mean that the results reached through them are "more sure" but only that during that time there was a consent that results formulated in that way were accepted. Everyone is allowed (and has) to think for himself and let himself get inspired by positions and persons who seem to be convincing in creative and argumentative ways. Argumentation is important but only concerning results not methods. It is about weighing up the strong and weak points of ways of acting and not about hierarchization of "good" and "bad" approaches.

To make a long story short, Mamlukologists who understand themselves as scholars within the Cultural Studies should – to paraphrase Ute Daniel again – accept its three basic creeds which are:

1. Nothing can be understood or explained or described unless you include the meanings, the ways of perception and the sensibilities of the human beings into your understanding, description, and explaining.

18 This paragraph follows Daniel 2001, 13–15.

2. The scholars accept that they are not excluded from descriptions and explanations which they make but that they are part of them. It is basically about the visualization of their perception of the world and their self-concepts. And
3. Mamlukology as Cultural Studies understands itself as the symbolic from in which the individual and the collective debate their self-awareness within the historical process. It analyzes past epochs regarding how people perceived and interpreted themselves in those times; which material, mental, and social backgrounds influenced their worldviews and their meaningful reflections on the future.[19]

Key terms of Mamlukology as Cultural Studies are, for instance, fact/object/truth – objective/subjective – explain/understand – historicism/relativism – contingency/discontinuity or language/narrativity.[20] Fields of research are history of science, history of terms, history of discourse, history of generations, history of women and gender, history of the mundane, history of alterity, history of mentality, or simply Historical Anthropology, which leads us to the next point.[21]

3. One Possibility: Mamlukology as Historical Anthropology

Here it also makes sense first of all to think about what could generally be understood be Mamlukology as "Historical Anthropology". In other words: which epistemological and methodical preconsiderations would have to be internalized by a culture-specifically oriented Mamlukologist if he or she started to deal seriously with questions of Historical Anthropology?

Mamlukology as Historical Anthropology is basically a very wide theoretical concept which bases on approaches offered by historical sciences, philosophy, ethnography and cultural anthropology as well as by literary studies (key words are: history of mentalities, philosophical anthropology, the writing-culture debate or new historicism).[22] We want to analyse self-reflection of human beings in

19 Cf. Daniel 2001, 17–19.

20 Cf. Daniel 2001, 380–466

21 Cf. Daniel 2001, 297–379.

22 See for the following thoughts Benthien/Velten 2002, 25. Still valuable introductions are Dressel, G., Historische Anthropologie. Eine Einführung. Wien 1996, Dülmen, R. van, Historische Anthropologie. Entwicklung, Probleme, Aufgaben. Köln 2000, Maurer, M., Historische Anthropologie, in: Maurer, M. (ed.), Aufriß der Historischen Wissenschaften. Bd. 7: Neue Themen und Methoden der Geschichtswissenschaft. Stuttgart 2003, 294–387, Reinhard, W., Lebensformen Europas. Eine historische Kulturanthropologie. München 2004, Tanner, J., Historische Anthropologie zur Einführung. Hamburg 2004 and Winterling, A.

all forms of texts, for example with reference to the other or to non-human beings like animals or Gods. In the centre of the theoretical concept are all those phenomena known as human specifics like its dual division in mind and body, the proportion of urge and desire to establish self-control, the consciousness of mortality or human fantasy, creativity and emotionality. Mamlukology as Historical Anthropology is not base on the abstract of a "human being" but tries to put its analysis in concrete forms and to historicize it that is to situate its subjects in the particular cultural context. It analyses, as Max Weber called it, the human spun cultural web of meanings in the area of conflict of constancy and change, in the course of history or for concrete individual cases.

Even in historical anthropological disciplines Mamlukologists are still far away from real interdisciplinary work in the sense that the approaches and results of the research of others will neither be noticed nor taken into consideration for the own work.[23] However, historical anthropological research is only possible in an interdisciplinary way, as its subject is not limited to one discipline but is situated at the point of intersection to various fields. It is difficult, if not impossible, but maybe not absolutely necessary to distinguish between Historical Anthropology and the History of Mentalities.[24] You might define mentality as a collective, cultural overlapping attitude and world-view which includes heterogeneous concepts and ideas, but also unconscious motives of a complete epoch.[25] Mentalities have to be understood as pre-structured and generally pre-reflexive forms of knowledge of the reality. They are complex pictures of the world, just like the basic meaning of thinking and behaviour. Those effect on the systems of codes and on the aesthetic forms of expression of a culture, because mentalities express themselves through attitude, behaviour and actions as well as through symbolic forms. The History of Mentalities is mainly confined to collective processes of historical changes, long-term shifts of thinking patterns and collective forms of social self-understanding (keyword: *long durée*) as well as to serial processes of historical analyses.

Mamlukology as Historical Anthropology has a focus on the human in-

(ed.): Historische Anthropologie. Stuttgart 2006. See also the relatively new journal "Historische Anthropologie" (http://www.historische-anthropologie.uzh.ch/index.html).

23 For this passage, see Röcke, W., Ordnungen des Wissens: Altere deutsche Literatur, in: Benthien/Velten 2002, 35 – 55, here 39. Cf. Also Hees, S. von, Historische Anthropologie in der Islamwissenschaft, in: Conermann, S./Hees, S. von (ed.), Islamwissenschaft als Kulturwissenschaft – Historische Anthropologie/Menta-litätsgeschichte. Ansätze und Möglichkeiten. Schenefeld 2007, 21 – 35.

24 Useful introductions are still Raulff, U. (ed.), Mentalitäten-Geschichte. Berlin 1987 and Dinzelbacher, P. (ed.), Europäische Mentalitätsgeschichte. Hauptthemen in Einzeldarstellungen. Stuttgart 1993.

25 For an excellent definition, see Dinzelbacher, P., Zu Theorie und Praxis der Mentalitätsgeschichte, in: Dinzelbacher 1993, XV – XXXVII.

dividual, if only within its social, political or cultural references. In its centre stands the subjective part of historical experience.[26] It means the splitting of the historical view to the realisation and experience of individuals in their special and limited world, and at the same time to the retrospective of the thinking, ways of understandings, samples of meanings and other *attitudes mentalés*, which built the historical and cultural experience of the individual. The particularity of Mamlukology as Historical Anthroplogy is exactly this contradictory link between splitting and generalising of the historic view: on the one hand the interest in the subjective view of the individual to the conditions and limits of his or her world and also to the other side of these frontiers. On the other hand, there is an understanding that this kind of "ideology" is not due to a subjective way of life, but, on the contrary, is only possible in discussion with samples of thinking, ideology and forms of understandings of a certain historical time. Here one follows Kant's anthropology in a practical way, which focuses on the practically acting individual with its special possibilities of thinking and understanding, but also with its affects, moods and spirits, its imagination, dreams, memorial abilities or follies in the context of its special world. Of course, for the daily work of the Mamlukologist one has to ask for the sources. But one should not be discouraged. We have a huge amount of texts. And especially Mamlukology as Historical Anthropology is interested in each single and individual view of the world. And this is something which is poetically styled, confirmed or questioned in these texts. Therefore, these texts with their poetic singularities are very important for anthropological approaches. Literary, historiographic and even normative texts do not only repeat samples of explanation, "ideologies" or mentalities, but they reflect on them and change them, they accept them or call them into question.

Mamlukology as Historical Anthropology asks for possibilities of understanding and for the mental attitudes of man in his special world.[27] This task is achieved not within a sphere of trans-historical constants but, on the contrary, as a dialogue with contemporaneous attitudes. As a trans-disciplinary science Mamlukology as Historical Anthropology aims at explaining human expressions and ways of life, as well as the relation of man to his material surroundings but also to phenomena like time, space, death or luck. The Mamlukologists with this specialization want the historicization of what, at least since the splitting of science into the humanities and natural history, has been understood as universal: body, feelings, nature. The Mamlukology as Historical Anthropology looks for the origin and evolution of particular concepts, actions, thinking patterns and fields of meanings. The aim is not to interpret a person, a group, a

26 In this part, I follow Röcke 2002, 39–42.
27 See for these arguments Dülmen 2001, 5–9.

happening, a structure or a proceeding from the outside in a hegemonic way but to understand it from within, i.e. from the perspective of the actor or the actors. The historical anthropology approach does not inquire into the essence or the universal meaning of human being in history but into the changing multiple cultural and social particularities in time. It focuses on the historically grown speciality and eccentricity of human behaviour and excludes a uniform and closed view of men and women. It concentrates all its energies on showing the individual's dependence on nature, society and cultural tradition. History is recognized as an act made by man, and man is defined as a being determined by history. That neither means that the historical subject can act autonomously nor that he or she is completely at the mercy of uncontrollable powers. We have to describe this in-between, i.e. the scope of human acting. On the other hand, Mamlukology as Historical Anthropology accepts the multiplicities and contradictions of acting and of the historical process as a whole. This complexity that is due to many circumstances and conditions has to be described within the context of society. The Mamlukologist as a historically oriented anthropologist considers man as a being with inherent possibilities to change. He never reacts in the same way because his acting is always influenced by situations which cannot be determined in advance.

4. Summary and Conclusion

So, in short, if we Mamlukologists follow the advice from memorandum "The Humanities today" which suggested that the humanities from now on be pursued in an interdisciplinary and trans-departmental way as Cultural Studies based on Historical Anthropology, this means that Mamlukology, too, hast to be open to the implied new methods and questions. Having developed from philological roots, the subject has always dealt not only with language – sometimes even linguistics – and normative literature but also with Mamluk history and society. However, this has been done mainly and mostly in a text-hermeneutical way with occasional socio-historical tendencies. The methods used were developed within the subject itself, with many German representatives of the subject declaring the independence, and sometimes even the uniqueness, of the "cultural area" of Islam to be the only *raison d'etre* of their scientific discipline. The basic misconception behind this attitude is the assumption that the impact of Islam on the cultures in questions is so strong that it determines them entirely. This is just as misguided as to think that the occidental civilization was determined entirely by Christianity. However, it has been – and still is – a central assumption of some of the eminent scholars in the field – and is even more frequently supposed by the interested public.[28] In reality, we have to distinguish between different subject areas. In those disciplines which have already been affected by the "cultural turn", there is a fundamental paradigm shift going on at the moment. The old, narrow conception of culture – i. e. "culture" as a social dimension next to economy, politics and law – is being replaced by a broad, anthropologically based conception that, as a "finite segment of the meaningless infinity of the world process, a segment on which human beings confer meaning and significance", as Max Weber said,[29] comprises the whole of all possible objects of research in the field of the humanities. Culture is no longer thought of as an essentialized substance but as the interference, the "in-between" of a whole range of different traditions of meaning. The homogenous and holistic understanding of culture is thus replaced by a conception of the term as denoting a process of exchange and adoption subjected to a wide variety of influences including group strategies and hierarchies of power. Against the backdrop of this model, the task of research in Mamlukology is no longer detecting cultural characteristics and their supposedly autonomous development but reconstructing processes of cultural transfer between the various societies and pointing out their commonly shared histories.

Mamlukology as Cultural Studies is not aimed at removing the borders that separate the various scientific disciplines but rather at crossing them in the interest of mutual enlightenment. Mamlukology with a cultural objective takes the claim of its subjects – to be a discipline in its own right – seriously, while at the same time quite consciously embracing the interdisciplinary stimulative potential and the plurality of possibilities for new insights that are offered by contemporary approaches and discussions within the field of Cultural Studies.[30] The re-structuring of various individual branches of the humanities into an interdisciplinary association of Cultural Studies takes place against the backdrop of the general "anthropologization" if knowledge which is currently observable. Historical Anthropology, however, should be more than just history with an anthropological coloration, historical research applied to anthropological issues like family, relationship, birth, death, rituals, the history of every-day ways of life and mentalities. In the end, this is about calling into question a holistic and homogenous conception of culture and cultural identity, and even criticizing the universal assumption and claims of perception explicitly

28 Cf. Ammann, L., "Islamwissenschaften", in: Klaus E. Müller (ed.), Phänomen Kultur: Perspektiven und Aufgaben der Kulturwissenschaften, Bielefeld 2003, 71 – 96.

29 Cf. for this quotation and the following paragraph Lackner, M./Werner, M. (ed.), Der *cultural turn* in der Humanwissenschaft. *Area Studies* im Auf- oder Abwind des Kulturalismus? Bad Homburg 1999, 23 – 27.

30 For these convincing arguments, see Medick, H., Quo vadis Historische Anthropologie?, in: Historische Anthropologie 9 (2001), 78 – 92.

or implicitly contained in many of our most central ideas and concepts. Mamlukology as Historical Anthropology should contribute to extending and deepening the "anthropological turn" in the humanities through historical contextualisation and a critical "historicization". It should help to draw attention to cultural multifaceted-ness and complexity by focusing on the impurity and hybridity of a culture, the multitude of cultural overlaps, syncretism, border crossings, negotiations and conflicts as constitutive moments of historical process. Mamlukology as Historical Anthropology traces the question of the meaning of culture back to the question of the constitution and transformation of economy and power, rejecting a culturalistic reduction to question of mentality, production of meaning and culturally determined forms of expression and ways of acting in history. In several respects, it has to confront an "after-the-fact" situation: Firstly and most importantly, this applies to its particular concern with reconstructing human actions of the past, where it seeks to acknowledge and expose the elements of foreignness and the differences of past realities. These reconstructivist efforts take place in a post-positivistic, post-structuralist, post-colonial atmosphere. In this situation, the starting point for every effort towards historical reconstructions has to be the acknowledgement of the specifically culturally, linguistically and historically determined character of historical insight. It is this acknowledgement which is so particular about the so-called "cultural-turn" in the humanities over the last 25 years. After the *cultural* and the *anthropological turn*, Mamlukology, like any other discipline – whether their representatives like or not –, cannot turn back any more to the old holistic assumptions about the functioning of separate social, cultural, legal and political dimensions in history.

Literature

Ammann, L., "Islamwissenschaften", in: Klaus E. Müller (ed.), Phänomen Kultur: Perspektiven und Aufgaben der Kulturwissenschaften, Bielefeld 2003, 71 – 96.

Bachmann-Medick, D., Cultural Turns. Neuorientierungen in den Geisteswissenschaften. Hamburg 2006.

Benthien, C./Velten, H.R., Einleitung, in: Benthien, C./Velten, H.R. (ed.), Germanistik als Kulturwissenschaft. Eine Einführung in neue Theoriekonzepte. Hamburg 2002, 7 – 34.

Burke, E./Prochaska, D. (ed.), Genealogies of Orientalism. History, Theory, Politica. Lincoln and London 2008.

Conermann, St., Vorbemerkung: Islamwissenschaft als Kulturwissenschaft, in: Conermann, St./Hees, S. von (ed.): Islamwissenschaft als Historische Anthropologie. I. Historische Anthropologie. Ansätze und Möglichkeiten. Schenefeld 2007, 9 – 20.

Daniel, U., Kompendium Kulturgeschichte. Theorien, Praxis, Schlüsselwörter. Frankfurt 2001.

Dinzelbacher, P. (ed.), Europäische Mentalitätsgeschichte. Hauptthemen in Einzeldarstellungen. Stuttgart 1993.

Dinzelbacher, P., Zu Theorie und Praxis der Mentalitätsgeschichte, in: Dinzelbacher, P. (ed.), Europäische Mentalitätsgeschichte. Hauptthemen in Einzeldarstellungen. Stuttgart 1993, XV - XXXVII.

Dressel, G., Historische Anthropologie. Eine Einführung. Wien 1996.

Dülmen, R. van, Historische Anthropologie. Entwicklung, Probleme, Aufgaben. Köln 2000.

Fragner, B., Die deutschen Orientalisten und der Zeitgeist, in: Hiery, H.J. (ed.), Der Zeitgeist und die Historie. Dettelbach 2001.

Fragner, B., Iranistik zwischen brennender Aktualität und exotischer Abseitigkeit - Gedanken zur Positionierung eines 'kleinen' orientalistischen Faches, in: Poya, A./Reinkowski, M. (ed.), *Das Unbehagen in der Islamwissenschaft. Ein klassisches Fach im Scheinwerferlicht der Politik und der Medien.* Bielefeld 2008, 105 - 117.

Frühwald, W. et al., Geisteswissenschaften heute: eine Denkschrift. Frankfurt am Main 1991.

Hees, S. von, Historische Anthropologie in der Islamwissenschaft, in: Conermann, S./ Hees, S. von (ed.), Islamwissenschaft als Kulturwissenschaft - Historische Anthropologie/Mentalitätsgeschichte. Ansätze und Möglichkeiten. Schenefeld 2007, 21 - 35.

Jaeger, F./Liebsch, B. (ed.), Handbuch der Kulturwissenschaften. Bd. 1: Grundlagen und Schlüsselbegriffe. Stuttgart und Weimar 2004.

Jaeger, F./Rüsen, J. (ed.), Handbuch der Kulturwissenschaften. Bd. 3: Themen und Tendenzen. Stuttgart und Weimar 2004.

Jaeger, F./Straub, J. (ed.), Handbuch der Kulturwissenschaften. Bd. 2: Paradigmen und Disziplinen. Stuttgart und Weimar 2004.

Koselleck, R., Über die Theoriebedürftigkeit der Geschichtswissenschaft, in: Conze, W. (ed.), Theorie der Geschichtswissenschaft und Praxis des Geschichtsunterrichts, Stuttgart 1972, 10 - 28.

Lackner, M./Werner, M. (ed.), Der *cultural turn* in der Humanwissenschaft. *Area Studies* im Auf- oder Abwind des Kulturalismus? Bad Homburg 1999, 23 - 27.

Maurer, M., Historische Anthropologie, in: Maurer, M. (ed), Aufriß der Historischen Wissenschaften. Bd. 7: Neue Themen und Methoden der Geschichtswissenschaft. Stuttgart 2003, 294 - 387.

Medick, H., Qua vadis Historische Anthropologie?, in: Historische Anthropologie 9 (2001), 78 - 92.

Nünning, A., Art. "Kulturwissenschaft", in: Nünning, A. (ed.), Metzler Lexikon Literatur- und Kulturtheorie. Ansätze - Personen - Grundbegriffe. Stuttgart and Weimar 2001, 353 - 356.

Oexle, O.G., Geschichte als Historische Kulturwissenschaft, in: Hardtwig, W./Wehler, H.-U. (ed.), Kulturgeschichte heute. Göttingen 1996, 14 - 40.

Raulff, U. (ed.), Mentalitäten-Geschichte. Berlin 1987.

Reinhard, W., Lebensformen Europas. Eine historische Kulturanthropologie. München 2004.

Röcke, W., Ordnungen des Wissens: Altere deutsche Literatur, in: Benthien, C./Velten, H.R. (ed.), Germanistik als Kulturwissenschaft. Eine Einführung in neue Theoriekonzepte. Hamburg 2002, 35 - 55.

Tanner, J., Historische Anthropologie zur Einführung. Hamburg 2004.
Utzschneider, H./Nitsche, S.A. Arbeitsbuch literaturwissenschaftliche Bibelauslegung. Eine Methodenlehre zur Exegese des AT. Gütersloh 2005.
Varisco, D. M., Reading Orientalism. Said and the Unsaid. Seattle and London 2007.
Winterling, A. (ed.): Historische Anthropologie. Stuttgart 2006.

Thomas Bauer

Mamluk Literature as a Means of Communication

Pragmatic and literary communication

Every work of literature is the manifestation of an act of communication. In this respect, Mamluk literature is no different to Abbasid (or any other) literature. However, the use of literature as a means of communication changed considerably from the Abbasid to the Mamluk period. Most significantly, the courts of caliphs, princes, sultans and governors gradually lost their central role in literary communication. Instead, urban, bourgeois milieus increasingly participated in the consumption and production of literary texts. Anthologies like the *Yatīmat al-Dahr* by al-Thaʿālibī (350 – 429/961 – 1038) and its successors, the *Dumyat al-Qaṣr* by al-Bākharzī (c. 418 – 467/1027 – 1075) and the *Kharīdat al-ʿAṣr* by ʿImād al-Dīn al-Iṣfahānī (519 – 597/1125 – 1201) display an increasing number of poems written by judges, Ḥadīth scholars, grammarians, traders and craftsmen.

By the Ayyubid and Mamluk periods, this transformation was completed. Many, if not the majority, of religious scholars wrote poems and literary letters, while *udabāʾ*, the *hommes de lettres*, also had training in Quran, Ḥadīth and the law. Ibn Nubātah (686 – 768/1287 – 1366), to give just one example, was a full-time *adīb*, but nevertheless he gave lectures in which he transmitted Ḥadīth and Ibn Isḥāq/Ibn Hishām's *Life of the Prophet*. On the other hand, at least four judges are included among the eleven contributors to his *Sajʿ al-Muṭawwaq*, a work to which we will return later. I once labeled this process the "*adabization* of the *ʿulamāʾ* and the *ʿulamāʾization* of the *udabāʾ*", but even this description does not do justice to the increasing participation of traders and craftsmen in literary life to such a degree that there was even a gradual blurring of the boundaries between "high" and "popular" literature.[1] In any case, Ayyubid and Mamluk literature became bourgeois, or, to use a German term, underwent a process of *Verbürgerlichung*. Rather than serving for representation as in previous periods, literature began to serve as a means of communication between members of the

1 On these developments see Hirschler, *Written Word.*

educated middle class. It should go without saying that this development had a fundamental influence on the content and style of the literature produced during these periods.[2]

One of the consequences of this development was the use of literary texts for pragmatic communication as well as the creation of pragmatic texts in a literary guise.[3] As a result, the distinction between pragmatic and literary communication cannot be said to be exclusive. Texts may engage in both forms of communication. Before we examine the role of communication as played by literary texts, let us say a few words about the differences between pragmatic and literary communications.[4]

Pragmatic communication, the common form of everyday communication, is based on the assumption that texts accord with reality, that they claim to be true and induce a specific reaction from their hearers and readers that is based on the same shared assumptions. Appointment decrees are a typical example of pragmatic communication. They can only function if the person being appointed truly exists, if he/she truly has been given the job and if the people in his/her domain accept his/her authority. If they decide to read the decree for its literary value (provided it has any) alone and fail to take it seriously, the communication will have failed.

Literary texts, on the contrary, do not have to obey this rule. In societies in which literary texts exist, people understand that in artistic literature the convention mentioned above is not necessarily valid. Literary texts are under no obligation to conform to reality, and there is no requirement that they be true or that they be obeyed. Instead, they are expected to provide some sort of aesthetic benefit. The *convention of aesthetics* (rather than the convention of conforming to reality) is the first important difference between pragmatic and literary texts.

The presence of stylistic features not common in pragmatic texts such as rhyme, parallelism, paronomasia, metaphor, etc. is also a strong indication that a text is intended for literary communication. But this is not always the case. Most of the poems written for one's grandmother on her birthday will not generally be considered literary texts. This is not so much a judgment of the poems' quality but rather has to do with their lack of polyvalence. The *convention of polyvalence* is, according to S.J. Schmidt, the second criterion of literary communication.[5] People know that "ordinary" texts are intended to inform, instruct, ask, suggest, claim, command, etc. in a more or less unambiguous way. And hearers and readers know that they are expected to react accordingly. This is not the case for

2 Panegyrics to sultans, governors and high-ranking officials were, of course, still composed in Mamluk times, but no longer set the model for style.

3 As, e.g., didactic verse, see van Gelder, *Didactic Verse.*

4 On the difference between literary and every-day communication see Schmidt, *Grundriß.*

5 Ibid., 133.

literary texts. People may react differently to them at different times, on different occasions or while in different moods, they may have different individual interpretations and associations and they may connect them, in different ways, to their own lives and their own experiences. These different reactions are not in any way antithetical to the intention of the producer of the text and thus are not to be considered failed communication.

Following this definition of literary texts, it is obvious that most poems for grandmothers on their birthdays do not qualify as literary texts because they can hardly be understood as anything other than poems for these specific occasions. The same situation may, on the other hand, spur a poet to write a poem about old age, which even people who do not know the grandmother whose birthday gave rise to the poem's composition can find relevant. In this case, the poet intended (1) to speak to the occasion of the birthday and (2) at the same time to write a *polyvalent* text that is also of interest to other readers who may find the text interesting, rewarding and relevant for their own lives.

Occasional texts written to fulfill a purpose in the mode of pragmatic communication may also function as literary texts at the same time, as we have seen, provided they comply with the convention of polyvalence and are found to be aesthetically pleasing. In most instances texts like this are used at least twice, a good indication of their polyvalence. After fulfilling their immediate communicative mission, they are presented in a different context in which the original communicative situation is no longer relevant, or perhaps no longer even traceable. They may be published in an anthology, a *dīwān* or another type of collection meant to be read by a wider public that has no immediate connection to the communicative situation in which the text was first deployed.

This holds true even for appointment decrees. Let us take, for example, a decree in which a certain Shujāʿ al-Dīn was appointed Wālī of Ṣaydā (Sidon). The text, written by Ibn Nubātah, was issued in 743/1343 – 1344.[6] Appointment decrees are, no doubt, first and foremost pragmatic texts and as such they must conform to reality. Shujāʿ al-Dīn must be a real person, he must have actually been appointed to the position, and the people of Ṣaydā must not regard the text – beautiful as it may be – exclusively as a means of literary entertainment, rather they must react to its content and accept Shujāʿ al-Dīn as an authority. This is only one side of the text however. After it had been drafted, written and handed to the appointee, the story of the decree was not over. It lived a second life in one of Ibn Nubātah's works called *Taʿlīq al-Dīwān*, in which he collected the output of his first year working in the chancellery of Damascus. The title is typical for Ibn Nubātah, who (after his first book, *Maṭlaʿ al-Fawāʾid*) preferred titles based on the *double entendre* instead of rhymed titles. *Taʿlīq al-Dīwān* can mean "The

6 Ibn Nubātah, *Taʿlīq al-Dīwān*, 23a – 24a; see also al-Qalqashandī, *Ṣubḥ al-Aʿshā*, 12:333 – 334.

Draperies of the Chancellery" (that is, texts that are an adornment for the chancellery), or "The Appendix to the Collection of Poetry" (that is, prose texts that have to be considered as an addition to the author's poetry). Readers of this collection were not expected to have any knowledge of or any interest in Shujāʿ al-Dīn or the administration of Ṣaydā. Instead, they would read the text either as a model for appointment decrees and an aid to future clerks (in which case the decree would still remain in the sphere of pragmatic communication) or as an aesthetic text. Several criteria suggest that the text was indeed intended (along with others) to be read as a literary text. It is sophisticated, aesthetically ambitious and full of literary devices. Its length and stylistic perfection far exceed what would have been necessary for the appointment decree of a comparatively unimportant office-holder. Moreover, Ibn Nubātah included it in a volume that was explicitly linked to his *Dīwān* of poetry, a collection of clearly literary texts. We may safely assume, therefore, that the decree was meant to serve as both a pragmatic as well as literary text when Ibn Nubātah drafted it.

The other texts that will be dealt with in the following pages are even more unambiguously of an aesthetic nature. Nevertheless, there was a time when they served as a more direct means of communication between individuals. Yet even when they were addressed to a specific person, their authors had a broader public in mind. Inter-*ʿulamāʾ*-communication was, to a great extent, a public affair. *ʿUlamāʾ* and *udabāʾ* performed their communication in front of a public, who in the end were the real addressees. Their texts were part of a communicative strategy that was used by both professional and non-professional poets and prose writers to establish, strengthen and improve their social position. In the end, they played an important role in the formation of the class of *Bildungsbürger* in Mamluk towns.

Literature is still one of the least studied fields in Mamluk studies. The following pages will demonstrate that no comprehensive understanding of Mamluk society is possible without a careful and attentive study of its poetry and literary prose.

Dedication

The simplest way to use a text for the purpose of communication is to dedicate it to another person. Ever since the time of al-Jāḥiẓ, literary, scholarly, and scientific texts have been dedicated in great numbers. The dedicators expected either to receive a reward from the dedicatee, to win a patron's attention or to strengthen ties of friendship and comradeship. The last of these motives became far more important in Mamluk times than before, but many works were still dedicated to patrons or influential public figures, as Ibn Nubātah's dedications show.

Dedications are a form of paratext. Their connection to a text is loose, and in most cases there is no connection whatsoever between the content of a text and the person to whom the text is dedicated. We may assume that an author would choose a subject for his dedicated work which he expects the dedicatee to be interested in, but the work lives its own life and is fully comprehensible even if the reader is unaware of its dedication. In the published version of a text, the dedication may be considered irrelevant or even distracting so the author (or copyist) may wish to omit the name of the dedicatee in the published version of a text. Since the dedication is normally included as part of the foreword, the deletion of the dedicatee's name may necessitate larger textual modifications. A striking example from the work of Ibn Nubātah shows how an author can make a virtue out of necessity.

In the year 732/1331 the Ayyubid prince and governor of Ḥamāh, Abū al-Fidā', to whom the sultan had awarded the title al-Malik al-Mu'ayyad, died. Thanks to clever maneuvers of al-Mu'ayyad's mother, his son was installed as his successor in the same year. He was given the title *al-Malik al-Afḍal* and reigned Ḥamāh until he was deposed in 742/1341. Al-Mu'ayyad had been a gracious patron to Ibn Nubātah and was perhaps even his friend so his death and the transition of power to his son al-Afḍal was clearly an important matter for Ibn Nubātah and it has left its traces in several of his works. One of them is a brilliant *qaṣīdah*, in which he simultaneously condoles al-Afḍal for the death of his father while congratulating him on his accession to the throne.[7] To suit the occasion, Ibn Nubātah also compiled a book of advice and dedicated it to al-Afḍal. The text is preserved in two versions: the first is the version in which the text was dedicated and handed over to al-Afḍal and the second represents the text as Ibn Nubātah published it.[8] The book is now given an elaborate, *tawriyah*-based title (*Sulūk Duwal al-Mulūk*) which was lacking in the dedicatory version. Even more interesting, however, are the changes that Ibn Nubātah made in the preface. Here is a synopsis of the Arabic text of both versions:

7 See Thomas Bauer, *Der Fürst ist tot.*

8 MS Istanbul, Esad Efendi 1822 (first version); Wien, Staatsarchiv, Krafft 474; Oxford, Bodleian, Seld Superius 29 (both second version).

<table>
<tr><th>Dedicatory manuscript</th><th>Published version</th></tr>
<tr><td dir="rtl">فقد اخترت من بعض كتب علم
السياسة والتدبير ما حسُن وتركت
ما خشُن ، لأحمل ذلك إلى الخزانة
الشريفة السُلطانيّة الملكيّة الأفضليّة
خلّد الله مُلْكَ مالكها ، ورُبَّ حاملِ
فقْهٍ إلى من هو أفْقَه / والله تعالى
يزين ويحرُسُ بشُهُب سعادتهِ جانِبَ
الملكِ وأُفقَه/
بمنِّه وكرمِه</td><td dir="rtl">فقد اخترت من بعض كتب علم
السياسة والتدبير ما حسُن وتركت
ما خشُن ،لأحمل ذلك إلى خزانة من
بسط الله به على الخلق رِزْقَه /
ورُبَّ حاملِ فقْهٍ من هذا التصنيف
إلى من هو أفْقَه / والله تعالى يزينُ
بخلودِ مُلكه جانب الملك وأُفقَه /
ويُعمِّر بدوام مواهبِه ومهابته غرب
المعمور وشرقَه / بمنِّه وكرمِه</td></tr>
<tr><td>I selected from writings about conducting and managing the affairs of state what is suitable and omitted what is coarse in order to bring it to the Sublime Sultanic Princely Afḍalite Library – may God make the reign of its sovereign last forever!
“Many a time has a bearer brought knowledge to someone more knowledgeable.”[9] | May God the Exalted adorn and guard with the shooting stars of his bliss the territory of his dominion and its horizon ||

in His grace and generosity!</td><td>I selected from writings about conducting and managing the affairs of state what is suitable and omitted what is coarse in order to bring it to the library of him with whose help God extends his sustenance over the people. |
“Many a time has a bearer brought knowledge – as this book – to someone more knowledgeable.” | May God the Exalted adorn with his everlasting reign the territory of his dominion and its horizon |
and, by continually bestowing gifts and inspiring awe, make flourish the land from the west to the east ||
in His grace and generosity!</td></tr>
</table>

In the first version, the dedicatee al-Malik al-Afḍal is unambiguously identified by calling the library *Malakīyah Afḍalīyah.* The dedication is followed by a quotation from the Ḥadīth. It forms a transition to a sentence of blessing in praise of the dedicatee, which rhymes with the Ḥadīth. The whole and rather short passage (typical of Ibn Nubātah's prefaces) therefore consists of two rhymed cola.

In the second version, the author wanted to remove the reference to the dedicatee. He did not, however, omit the dedication entirely, which is longer now than it was before. Instead, Ibn Nubātah replaced the epithets of the dedicatee's library with a phrase that praises a great man who remains anonymous. This phrase ends with the word *rizqah* and thereby allows the dedicatory phrase to become part of the following series of cola that rhyme in *-qah.* At the very end, the author adds a further colon rhyming in *-qah* (*sharqah*) so that the rhyming series comes to consist of four quite elaborated cola instead of two.

9 Quotation of a Ḥadīth, see al-Ḥākim an-Nīsābūrī, *al-Mustadrak, Bāb al-ʿilm* etc.

As Ibn Nubātah's modified text shows, the identity of the dedicatee may not have been considered important when a book was intended to be distributed to a larger audience. In this case, authors like Ibn Nubātah took great pains to revise and improve the text. Of course, it is likely that a general audience may have been more important for an author than a single dedicatee. Dedications may have often been a mere strategic device to secure attention and influence.

Nothing better demonstrates this than cases in which the dedications have been changed. Ibn Nubātah did this at least once. One of his famous prose texts is a "Dispute between Sword and Pen".[10] The original version was dedicated to al-Malik al-Mu'ayyad (*al-yad al-sharīfah al-sulṭānīyah al-malakīyah al-mu'ayyadīyah*)[11], but in the year 729, while al-Mu'ayyad was still alive and his relationship with Ibn Nubātah untroubled, Ibn Nubātah dedicated the same text to the Dawādār Nāṣir al-Dīn Muḥammad b. Kawandak, praising *al-yad al-sharīfah al-ʿāliyah al-mawlawiyah al-amīriyah al-ʿālimīyah al-ʿādilīyah al-mālikīyah al-makhdūmīyah al-nāṣirīyah* instead.[12] We do not know if one or both of the dedicatees (and their contemporaries) knew about this double dedication and how they felt about it if they did. In any case, this example shows the degree to which the content of a dedicated work could be separated from its dedication.

Address

More or less all the texts which we deal with under the banner of Mamluk literature were meant to be sent to someone after their completion, whether or not the author also intended to make his text accessible to a wider public. The addressee may have been mentioned in the text and thus been included in its content or not. We will limit ourselves here to the first case and use the term "address" exclusively for those prose texts and poems in which the addressee is the subject of at least part of the text.

As far as poetry is concerned, most texts of this kind would fall under the headline *madḥ* / *madīḥ* "praise". Categories like *tahni'ah* / *hanā'* "congratulations" and *taʿziyah* / *ʿazā'* "condolence" may be considered subcategories of *madīḥ* because praise of the addressee is always a central concern in addition to the communicative purpose of congratulations, condolence etc. Few other developments were as momentous for Arabic literature as the gradual change of the social groups to which such *madīḥ* was addressed. It was still true during the

10 Ibn Nubātah, *al-Mufākharah*; see also Ibn Ḥijjah, *Khizānat al-Adab*, 2:218 – 238; van Gelder, *Conceit*, 356 – 358.

11 See the autograph version MS Escorial 548, 34b – 53b (here 47b – 48a).

12 See Ms. Berlin 8400, 65b – 70b (here 65b and 69b).

career of al-Mutanabbī that *madīḥ* poems were almost exclusively addressed to caliphs, princes, governors, generals and other high-ranking officials. Starting from the period known as the Sunni Revival, "bearers of the sword" became less important for poets and instead more and more *madīḥ* was exchanged among "bearers of the pen" themselves. To be sure, throughout the whole of the Ayyubid and Mamluk periods there were panegyric poems addressed to princes, sultans and high-ranking Mamluks and continued to be an important part of the output of major poets. Several poets had an especially close relationship with a *ṣāḥib al-sayf*, (e.g. Ibn Nubātah and al-Malik al-Mu'ayyad; Ṣafī al-Dīn al-Ḥillī and the Artuqids; Ibn Ḥajar al-ʿAsqalānī and the Rasūlids to name only a few). But even these poets composed more poems of praise for their fellow *ʿulamā'* than they did for princes and sultans.

Most authors in the Mamluk period did not even differentiate between panegyric poems for princes and members of the military establishment on the one hand and on scholars and *hommes de lettres* on the other. Both fell under the heading of *madīḥ*. The major exception was Ṣafī al-Dīn al-Ḥillī whose *Dīwān* included a chapter on *madīḥ*, which was reserved for poems on his princely patrons from the Artuqids of Mārdīn and the Ayyubids of Ḥamāh for the most part, and another chapter, which bore the rather old-fashioned title of *ikhwānīyāt*. The difference between these may have more to do with the character of the poems than the social position of the dedicatees, however. Thus we find a poem on the judge Jamāl al-Dīn Ibn al-ʿĀqūlī in the chapter of *madīḥ*, while the poems in the *ikhwānīyāt*-chapters are of a more familiar character, in some cases addressing members of the poet's own family.[13]

In his *Al-Qaṭr al-Nubātī*, Ibn Nubātah subsumes poems for al-Malik al-Mu'ayyad as well as for different *ʿulamā'* and *udabā'* under the headline "praise, gratitude, congratulations and the like" (*al-madḥ wa-l-shukr wa-l-hanā' wa-mā ashbaha dhālik*). The following is one example of these:[14]

لا عدِمنا لابن الأثير يراعاً جارياً للعُفاةِ بالأرزاقِ
كلّما ماس في المهارقِ كالغُصْـ ـنِ رأيتَ النّدَا على الأوراقِ

May we never be deprived of Ibn al-Athīr's reed, which is used to satisfy those who seek bounty!
As it moves over the sheets, swaying like a branch, dew can be seen on the leaves.

The addressee is ʿAlā' al-Dīn b. al-Athīr,[15] who was *kātib al-sirr* in Cairo from 709 to 729. He is praised in these lines for his generosity, a virtue that has always been

13 Al-Ḥillī, *Dīwān*, 1:403.
14 MS Paris, Bibliothèque nationale 2234, 159b.
15 See Ibn Ḥajar al-ʿAsqalānī, *Al-Durar al-Kāminah*, 4:15–18, where the epigram is quoted p. 17–18.

one of the main subjects of *madīḥ*. The profession of the addressee provides the main concept for the poem: the reed pen of the chancery secretary is compared to a twig, his paper to leaves, and his gifts to dew. Out of these elements Ibn Nubātah creates an elegant example of Abbasid-style *murāʿāt al-naẓīr* (harmonious choice of ideas or images[16]). The poem is a two-line epigram. As a result of the growing importance of epigrams, in the Mamluk period epigrams were also used for *madḥ* poetry more often than before. Occasionally one and the same subject was treated in two or more different forms. Ibn Nubātah, to mention just one example, composed a *qaṣīdah* and an epigram on the death of his slave girl and again made it the topic of a prose letter.[17] In the above example, the second line here lives a second life as the punch line of an epigram. Ibn Nubātah had already used it in a *qaṣīdah* of 25 lines, in which lines 20 – 21 line read as follows:

ذو يراعٍ جارٍ بفضل القضايا   واتّصالِ العُفاةِ بالأرزاقِ
كلّما ماس في المهارقِ كالغُصْـ   ـنِ رأيتَ النَدَا على الأوراقِ

Who has got a reed that brings about the benefit of his judgments und unites the seekers of sustenance with the bounty destined for them.
As it moves over the sheets, swaying like a branch, dew can be seen on the leaves.[18]

Obviously Ibn Nubātah liked the second line so much that he did not want to see it hidden in midst a longer poem and also wanted to use it as the punch line of an epigram. To accomplish this all he had to do was rewrite the preceding line, which now forms the perfect introductory line of an epigram.

On the other hand, this line would not have been suitable for the final line of a *qaṣīdah*. Rather the *qaṣīdah*'s final line connects praise of the *mamdūḥ* with the poet's self-praise:

جُودُكَ المجتدَى وأمداحِيَ الغُـ   ـرُّ كُنوزٌ تبقى على الإنفاقِ

Your generosity, the hope of many, and my brilliant praises are treasures that can never be exhausted.

Instructive as it may be to know that a line could be used both as part of a *qaṣīdah* and as the punch line of an epigram, it is even more instructive to learn that the *qaṣīdah*, from which the line is taken, was not addressed to the same person as the epigram. The *qaṣīdah* was written in praise of the *wazīr* Sharaf al-Dīn Yaʿqūb. Again, the immediate addressee is interchangeable and of less importance than the poetic *maʿnā*, which the author considers more generally relevant.

16 See W.P. Heinrichs, *EAL* 2:658 – 659.
17 See Talib, *Arabic Verse.*
18 Ms. Berlin 7811, 116a – 117a, Ms. Köprülü 1249, 120b – 121a, see also Ibn Nubātah, *Diwān*, 346.

Address and response

Poems and prose texts were addressed to a person in order to provoke a reaction. In the case of a *madīḥ* poem sent to a ruler or a person of considerably higher status, the author expected a *reward*, and in the case of texts addressed to people of similar status, the author expected a *response*. Due to the developments mentioned above, the second category became the more common case in the Mamluk period. It must have been quite detrimental to a person's career and prestige when they were not able to respond properly to an address in the form of a poem or letter. One such deplorable case was that of Badr al-Dīn b. Mālik (d. 686/1287), who, despite being a prolific scholar of grammar, prosody and rhetoric, lacked sufficient poetic talent to compose verses of his own.[19] This earned him the scorn of al-Ṣafadī, who considered Badr al-Dīn's failure as a poet significant enough to include it in his entry on him in the *Wāfī*. There he relates an anecdote according to which Badr al-Dīn tried desperately to answer a poem he had received. He struggled from morning till the afternoon prayer, but could not come up with a single line. In the end he had no other choice but to ask his neighbor to write the expected response-poem for him.[20]

The ability to take part in the literary communication of the educated class was an important signal of distinction and proof that one belonged to the elite. In a time when even many craftsmen had some sort of scholarly training, the production of sophisticated literary texts was the ultimate proof of one's membership in the class of the highbrow *ʿulamāʾ* and *udabāʾ*. Whereas the established scholar Badr al-Dīn had failed the test, a much less prominent woman was able to pass it. Once again it is al-Ṣafadī who transmits the report about an exam carried out by Shihāb al-Dīn b. Faḍl Allāh. The latter had heard that Fāṭimah, the daughter of a lumber merchant who lived in his neighborhood, possessed great poetic talents. In order to "test" her and provoke a response, he sent her a long poem that could be read as a love poem. The woman answered him with a short, seven-line poem of remarkable ambiguity. The poetess declares her inability and unwillingness to compete with Shihāb al-Dīn's poetic prowess. At the same time, some of the lines can be read as a lover's rejection. The main paradox of the poem lies, however, in the fact that Fāṭimah, by explicitly refusing to communicate, does in fact communicate and thereby gains al-Ṣafadī's (and most certainly Shihāb al-Dīn's) approval:[21]

19 On him see Simon, *Badr al-Dīn Ibn Mālik.*

20 Al-Ṣafadī, *al-Wāfī bi-l-Wafayāt*, 1:204.

21 Al-Ṣafadī, *Aʿyān al-ʿAṣr*, 4:33, see also *al-Wāfī* 23:702–704. – She may be identical with Fāṭimah bint ʿAlī, Bint Ibn (!) al-Khashshāb, a Ḥadīth scholar born in 708/1308–1309, who transmitted the *Ṣaḥīḥ al-Bukhārī*, see Ibn Ḥajar's *al-Durar al-Kāminah*, 4:264.

إن كان غرَّكمُ جَمالُ إزاري　　فالقبحُ في تلك المحاسن واري
لا تحسِبوا أني أُماثِلُ شِعْرَكم　　أنَّى تُقاسُ جَداولٌ ببِحارِ
لو عاصر الكنديُّ عَصْرَكُمُ رمى　　لكمُ عوالي راية الأشعار
أقصى اجتهادي فَهْمُ ظاهر نَظْمِكم　　لا أنَّني أُدعىَ دُعاء مُجارِي[22]
مَن قصَّرتْ عنه الفحول فحقُّه　　أن ليس يَبلغُه لحاقُ جواري
ولربّما استحسنتَ غير حقيقة　　فإذا سَفَرْتُ أشَحْتَ بالأبصار
لستُ الطَّموحَ إلى الصِّبَى من بعدما　　وضُح المشيب بلِمّتي كنهاري

If ever the glamour of my shawl has dazzled you, remember that ugliness sets fire to all those beauties.
Don't imagine that I would try to match your verses – how can a creek be compared to the sea?
If the Kindī (Imra' al-Qays) lived in our times, he would hand you the lances that bear the banners of poetry.
I do not strive to do any more than comprehend the overt meaning of your verses and I don't ask to be addressed like a competitor.
A man with whom not even the stallions/*master poets* can compete, can never truly be caught by the maiden's pursuit.
Did you not often deem beautiful what in reality did not exist? Such is me: if I were to unveil myself, you'd no doubt avert your eyes.
I no longer fancy the follies of youth now that my hair has turned white like bright daylight.

Al-Ṣafadī liked her lines and surmised that she might be a better poet than most of the men in his as well as in older times. He was especially delighted by her use of the word *jawārī* in the rhyme. It is after all very revealing to see al-Ṣafadī's scorn for a great scholar of his day on the grounds that he was not able to participate in a poetic exchange and his admiration for the daughter of a humble lumber merchant precisely because she could.

Exchange

Though only a subcategory of the preceding (and often difficult to distinguish from it), we will deal with this topic under a separate heading, which reflects Arabic terms such as *mukātabāt*, *murāja'āt*,[23] or *muṭāraḥāt*.[24] Such an exchange could consist of a poem or a letter sent to someone and answered by him or her by adhering to the same formal parameters as the original. Quite often the address consisted of a poem *plus* a letter and it would be answered in the same way. Today, scholars anxious to study these texts in their original context would

22 *Alḥān:* مُجارِ, *al-Wāfī:* فُجارِ.
23 For example al-Ṣafadī, *Alḥān* 1:41.
24 See Shihab al-Din al-Ḥijāzī, *Rawḍ al-Ādāb*, Ms. Wien, Staatsbibliothek 400, bāb 4 faṣl 2 (129b: *fī l-mukātabāt wa-l-muṭāraḥāt*).

be especially interested in those cases in which all parts of the exchange—the poetry and the prose, the address and the response—have come down to us. Unfortunately, the authors of these texts hardly shared this interest. Once more, they were convinced that the texts were of general relevance even when divorced from their original purpose. As a result, comparatively few works have come down to us in which the entirety of an exchange has been preserved; al-Ṣafadī's *Alḥān al-Sawājiʿ* being the most comprehensive and important example from the 7th/14th century.

Even Ibn Nubātah, who took great pride in his prose, divided his poetry and prose between separate works (*Sajʿ al-Muṭawwaq* being the major exception). The poet Burhān al-Dīn al-Qīrāṭī (726 – 781/1326 – 1379), who closely followed Ibn Nubātah's footsteps, may have been the first to include entire "packages" of prose-*cum*-poetry in his *Dīwān*; however not even he quotes the poems and letters written by his conversation partners.

Since both of the most celebrated poets of the 7th/14th century, Ibn Nubātah and Ṣafī al-Dīn al-Ḥillī, had a habit of separating their prose and their poetry as well as only publishing their own side of a literary exchange, it is difficult to reconstruct their literary conversations, and completely impossible for anyone who does not have access to both *Dīwāns*.

The only case of an address and its response which we can identify with certainty is the poem *Khafīf* / rhyme *ātahū* (*Dīwān Ibn Nubātah* 72 – 73, 26 lines), which bears the headline *wa-qāla jawāban li-l-Ṣafī* in the earliest manuscripts.[25] It is not difficult to find Ṣafī al-Dīn's poem that started the exchange off: it is no. 208 of his *Dīwān*, explicitly mentioning the addressee (and, of course, sharing the same rhyme and meter).

Other cases are more difficult to determine. One of them is a short poem of four lines (*Ṭawīl*, rhyme *xrī*,[26] *Dīwān Ibn Nubātah* 235) whose heading says it is "a response to al-Ṣafī al-Ḥillī". Provided that al-Ḥillī's poem displays the same rhyme and the same meter and that it is included in al-Ḥillī's *Dīwān*, there are at least two potential solutions: poems no. 238 and 281. A poem of 22 lines (*Khafīf*, rhyme *2qū*, *Dīwān Ibn Nubātah* 344 – 345) is again said to be "a response to al-Ṣafī," who is also mentioned in course of the poem. No corresponding poem can be found in al-Ḥillī's *Dīwān*. A three-liner (*Ṭawīl*, rhyme *xlū*, *Dīwān Ibn Nubātah* 413) is said to be "written on a *qaṣīdah* that was sent to him from Mārdīn". Seeing as al-Ḥillī spent a lot of time in this town and we know of no one else from Mārdīn who had relations with Ibn Nubātah, it is a good guess that the poem has something to do with al-Ṣafī al-Ḥillī. His *Dīwān*, however, provides no further

25 Ms. Berlin 7861, 125b – 126b, Ms. Köprülü 1249, 141b, see also Ibn Nubātah, *Dīwān* 72 – 73, where al-Ḥillī's first line is quoted.

26 Abbreviations in noting the rhyme scheme: *x* = any consonant; *2* = ū or ī; *3* = a,i,u.

clues. Finally, a number of other poems in either *Dīwān* could have been addressed by Ibn Nubātah to al-Ḥillī and vice versa, but neither the texts of the poems nor their headings are of any help.

The fact that in the *dīwāns* of Mamluk poets the addressee is often mentioned in the heading (more often in modern printed editions than in manuscripts) should not detract from the fact that the identity of the addressee was not a matter of importance for the poet, as is clear from many manuscripts as well as the fact that the relationship between the two most important poets of their time – Ibn Nubātah and Ṣafī al-Dīn al-Ḥillī – is so difficult to trace. For the authors themselves the identity of the addressee was obviously of less importance than it is to modern scholars.

Intertextuality – simple and complex

From the very first poems that have come down to us and until the present day, Arabic literature is characterized by a remarkably high degree of intertextuality. Countless works refer to other works, either directly or indirectly. In the Mamluk period, the main upholders of the literary arts were well-educated intellectuals and learned connoisseurs of the literature of the past as well as the present. It is no wonder then that intertextual references should permeate Mamluk literature. Several studies on Ibn Nubātah have shown that some of his most famous poems cannot be properly understood without taking into account their level of intertextuality.[27] Even a craftsman like Ibrāhīm al-Miʿmār, who could only draw on a much smaller repertoire of "classical" literature, displays the same passion for quotations and allusions as the high-brow intellectuals of his day. In his epigrams, the punch line is often based on the quotation of a popular proverb, but also quite often on al-Ḥarīrī's *Maqāmāt* or the same author's versification of the rules of grammar, *Mulḥat al-Iʿrāb*. "Classics" such as al-Mutanabbī and al-Buḥturī are used to construct points, as is *al-Qaṣīdah al-Zaynabīyah*, a popular religious poem attributed, among others, to ʿAlī b. Abī Ṭālib. The following example shows how lines on grammar can lend themselves to an amorous purpose. In line 19a of *Mulḥat al-Iʿrāb*, al-Ḥarīrī gives examples for the three kinds of definite nouns: nouns marked with the article, proper names and pronouns: مثالُهُ الدارُ وزيدٌ وأنا, "examples are *the house*, *Zayd* and *I*". In line 21a, al-Ḥarīrī explains that there are three categories of verbs: past tense, imperative

27 Al-Ghubārī, *Al-Tanāṣṣ*; Bauer, Communication; idem, *Der Fürst ist tot*.

and present/future tense. There exists no fourth. Taken together, they form the second line of a love epigram:[28]

مَتَى أرَى المحبوبَ وافَى بالهَنَا   ونحنُ في دارٍ ولا واشٍ لَنَا
أيُّ ثلاثٍ ما لهنّ رابعٌ   مثالُهُ الدارُ وزيدٌ وأنا

My beloved made me happy when we were alone together in a house where no slanderer could disturb us.
What better model of a set of three that has no fourth: the house, and Zayd, and me!

Quotations like this one are common in the Mamluk period, perhaps even more common than in earlier periods, but they do not set the Mamluk era apart from its predecessors. This may, however, be the case when we take into account more complex intertextual relations, which presuppose a dense network of intellectuals contributing to literary culture as was characteristic of the urban centres in the Mamluk empire. I will give two examples, which I refer to as "shared intertextuality" and "cross intertextuality".

Shared intertextuality

I use the term *shared intertextuality* to denote cases in which an existing text is used by two or more participants as the basis of a literary exchange. A case in point is a series of poems exchanged by al-Ṣafadī and Ibn Nubātah, for which they drew on poems by Imra' al-Qays and al-Mutanabbī.[29] The sequence was started by al-Ṣafadī at a moment when his friendship with Ibn Nubātah was troubled. To seek a reconciliation, he sent Ibn Nubātah a poem in which all the second hemistiches were taken from Imra' al-Qays's *Mu'allaqah*, while the first hemistiches were replaced by new formulations that gave new meanings to the famous second halves. This kind of quotation is called *taḍmīn*. As was to be expected, Ibn Nubātah answered him with a poem that used the same device. Nevertheless the dispute still did not come to an end because Ibn Nubātah sent both al-Ṣafadī's poem and his own response to Shihāb al-Dīn Ibn Faḍl Allāh, the chief of the Damascus chancellery (and perhaps even al-Ṣafadī's superior at that time). It appears that al-Ṣafadī felt ashamed and replied with another *qaṣīdah*; this time borrowing from a poem by al-Mutanabbī. The poem was carefully chosen: it is al-Mutanabbī's first poem to Sayf al-Dawlah. It contains a long description of Sayf al-Dawlah's tent and the pictures on its walls. Consequently,

28 Al-Mi'mār, *Dīwān*, Ms. Escorial 463, 61a; quoted also in al-Ṣafadī, *A'yān*, 1:89 and idem, *Al-Wāfī*, 6:177.

29 Al-Ṣafadī, *Alḥān*, 2:245 – 251; see also Ibn Ḥijjah, *Khizānat al-adab*, 4:131 – 134 together with further examples of similar transformations.

it is less bellicose than most of his other *sayfiyyāt* and, therefore, more appropriate for the tone of civility required to help settle a dispute between *hommes de lettres.*

Ibn Nubātah, however, had the far more difficult task. Whereas al-Ṣafadī was free to choose from any of al-Mutanabbī's 41 lines, Ibn Nubātah had to restrict himself to the lines that al-Ṣafadī had not used. Of course, al-Ṣafadī had picked out those lines that lent themselves most easily to the new purpose. He used most of the lines describing the tent and left only the battle scene to Ibn Nubātah; in addition he did not take up any of the rather martial lines from the concluding *madīḥ*. Despite the fact that the most easily transformable lines had already been used up by his colleague, Ibn Nubātah did a good job, using 21 of the remaining 25 lines. Among them are lines 30 – 31 and 37 – 38 of al-Mutanabbī's poem. Lines 30 – 31 form part of a battle scene. After mentioning lances and swords that have become tired of fighting, al-Mutanabbī describes an army over which birds of prey circle:[30]

وملَّ القنا ممّا تدُقُّ صُدُورَه   وملّ حديدُ الهند ممّا تُلاطِمُهْ
سَحابٌ مِن العِقْبانِ يَزْحَفُ تحتها   سَحابٌ إذا استسقَتْ سَقَتها صَوَارِمُهْ

30. The lances weary of your shaft-shattering and the Indian steel wearies of striking and being struck.
31. There is a cloud of eagles beneath which moves a cloud whose swords pour for them if they ask to drink.[31]

A few lines later, al-Mutanabbī links this to the praise of Sayf al-Dawlah:

لقد سلَّ سيفَ الدولةِ المَجْدُ مُعلِماً   فلا المجدُ مُخْفِيهِ ولا الضَربُ ثالِمُهْ
على عاتِقِ المَلْكِ الأغرِّ نِجادُهُ   وفي يَدِ جَبَّار السَمَواتِ قائمُه

37. Glory has drawn the Sword of the Dynasty as its warrior wearing a badge of defiance[32] so that neither glory can obscure it, nor can a stroke notch in its edge.
38. Over the shoulders of the most noble prince (the caliph) hangs its belt, and in the hand of the Compeller of the heavens rests its hilt.

It is difficult to imagine how the second halves of these verses could possibly be used in a poem of reconciliation between literati, but Ibn Nubātah could. This passage (ll. 8 – 11) of Ibn Nubātah's reply to al-Ṣafadī may illustrate how the poet managed to give them a completely different meaning indeed:

30 Al-Barqūqī, *Sharḥ*, 4:55 – 60.
31 Translation of l. 31 Hamori, *Composition*, 28.
32 Translation ibid., 54.

ولاطفَ آمالي بِسُقْيا زلالِه «سَحابٌ إذا استسقَت سَقَتها صَوَارِمُهْ»[33]
فتى المَجْدِ والأشعار تَلقى ضُروبَها «فلا المجدُ مُخْفِيهِ ولا الضَربُ ثالِمُهْ»
يقومُ لنا بالنَظْمِ جبَّارُ فِكرِهِ «وفي يَدِ جَبَّار السَمَواتِ قائمُه»
فتَعطِفُهُ من بعد ما ملَّت الوغى «وملّ حديدُ الهند ممّا تُلاطِمُهْ»

8 By pouring out cold water, a cloud complied with my wishes. Whenever they suffer thirst, its sharp ideas give them to drink.
9 He is a man of glory and poems that hit their match, so neither glory obscures him nor can the one kind (of poems) belittle him.
10 His compelling mind bestows us with his poetry, while its author rests in the hand of the Compeller of the Heavens.
11 And (his verses) deal gently with him after they weary of tumult. Even Indian steel grows weary of striking and being struck.

The passage starts with the transformation of al-Mutanabbī's line 31: the word *ṣawārim* is used now not for the sharp swords but for the addressee's sharp wit, which brings relief not to eagles, but to the poet's wishes. The word *ḍarb* from al-Mutanabbī's line 32 is reinterpreted to mean the "matching" lines, obviously alluding to the poetic exchange between both poets in which each poem is answered by a poem in the same meter and with the same rhyme, using the same intertextual device. Since his verses "matched" in terms of their quality as well, he has no reason to fear degradation. The verb *thalama*, originally meaning "making notches in a sword's edge," must now be understood metaphorically. Again, Ibn Nubātah manages to get rid of the swords.

The next line is a transformation of al-Mutanabbī's line 38, a particularly difficult case. It was easy to dispose of the caliph, but Ibn Nubātah had to keep God as *jabbār.* Still, there is another reference to swords in the word *qā'im.* Again, Ibn Nubātah managed to demilitarize his model. He introduced a second, secularized *jabbār* in the first hemistich ("compeller of his ideas"), who "brings us" (*yaqūmu lanā*) poetry. The rhyme word *qā'im* can thus be understood to refer to the one who brings the poetry and does not need to be understood in its original sense as "sword hilt".

Ibn Nubātah succeeded brilliantly in disarming al-Mutanabbī's verses three times, but he could not do away with the "Indian steel" in al-Mutanabbī's line 30. Instead, he turned al-Mutanabbī's phrase into simile: just as even Indian steel can become weary of striking, so our poems have become weary of quarrel.

Ibn Nubātah's transformation of al-Mutanabbī's poem presents a nice example of the *Verbürgerlichung* of Mamluk literature. Here al-Mutanabbī's heroic poem with all its lances, swords and blood-shed is transformed to fit the more irenic life of secretaries, poets and intellectuals.

It is interesting as well to trace the publication history of the poems. At first,

---

33 I read استسقت, instead of استسقى.

al-Ṣafadī objected to any dissemination of his first poem and the reply, probably because he did not want to shed light on his troubles with Ibn Nubātah. Later, when such personal motives were no longer a concern, he included the whole series of poems in his *Alḥān al-Sawājiʿ.* Ibn Nubātah for his part only included the Imra' al-Qays-transformation in his *Dīwān*; without quoting al-Ṣafadī's initial poem, of course.[34] Manuscripts do not even mention that the poem is a reaction to another poem, let alone that it was al-Ṣafadī who initiated the exchange.[35]

Ibn Nubātah's Mutanabbī transformation, however, is absent from his *Dīwān.* Perhaps Ibn Nubātah felt that the poem was difficult to understand without knowing its context and therefore of less general relevance. Perhaps he was also not entirely content with the result. After all, a reader who was not already aware of al-Ṣafadī's poem would not know that all the easily transformable lines had already been snatched away by al-Ṣafadī. In any case, we must be grateful to al-Ṣafadī for having preserved this specimen of intertextual virtuosity.

Cross Intertextuality

Whereas cases of *shared intertextuality* will be recognized immediately, there are other forms of intertextuality that are quite difficult for the distant observer to discern. One of these is what I call *cross intertextuality.*[36] This term shall designate cases in which author A addresses (or at least dedicates) a text t_1 to person X. Shortly after this, author B, who has knowledge of text t_1 and some sort of relation to author A, produces a text t_2, which is addressed (or at least dedicated) either to person X or someone completely different. At the same time, there is a discernible relationship between t_1 and t_2, and it was author B's intention that this relationship be obvious to author A and to the public (but not necessarily the addressee of the text himself).

Since in most cases author B does not explicitly mention the relationship of his text to that of A, the discovery of cases of cross intertextuality is often only possible with some speculation. Quite a clear example, however, may be provided by two letters in which al-Ṣafadī and Ibn Nubātah, respectively, respond to a gift in the form of camphorated apricots. The first letter was drafted by al-Ṣafadī in the name of the *nā'ib al-Shām* and addressed to the prince al-Afḍal of Ḥamāh, who had sent boxes of camphorated apricots (*mishmish kāfūrī*) to the *nā'ib* as a present. The letter must have been written between 732/1331 and 742/

34 Ibn Nubātah, *Diwān*, 392–393.

35 See Ibn Nubātah, *Diwān*, MS Ayasofya 3891, 44a–45b.

36 It is a form of what Genette called *métatextualité*, see Genette, *Palimpsestes*, 11–12.

1341, i.e. during al-Afḍal's reign. It is a masterpiece of *inshā'* and is quoted in Shihāb al-Dīn b. Faḍl Allāh's *Masālik al-Abṣār.*[37] In his letter, al-Ṣafadī uses a number of similes to describe the apricots in their boxes. They are compared to pearls, stars, honey, blossoms, balls of crystal, buttons on the garbs of trees, fire in the gardens of leaves and bullets shot by the cross-bows of the twigs. A central passage reads:

... وينهي ورود المشرّفة العالية قرينَ ما أنعم به مولانا من المشمش الكافوري فوقف عليها وقابل إحسانه بشكرٍ يُشرِقُ نُوراً * وثناءٍ يُديرُ على الأسماع كأساً كان مزاجه كافوراً * وواجه جوده بحمدٍ يتلوه منه وجه الأرض بمنثوره * وتجد الألسنة لمنظومه لذّةً تُنسي الأسماع ما قاله أبو الطيّب في كافوره * ومتّع ناظره بتلك الكوكب التي اتّسقَت من العُلَبِ في أفلاك * وتتسّقت كالدرر وما لها غير حسن الرصف أسلاك ...

... and he reports to have received the exalted letter together with the camphorated apricots bestowed on us by our patron, and that he devoted himself to it and answered his favors with a gratitude that shines brightly | and with words of praise that pass around the ears a goblet "the mixture of which is camphor" (Q 56:5), || and requited his generosity with a eulogy, which the surface of the earth will recite with its *gillyflower* / prose, | and in the poetry of which tongues will find a delight that causes the ears to forget what al-Mutanabbī said to his (patron) Kāfūr, || and made his pupil/eye enjoy these stars that are composed in their boxes [like] celestial spheres | and which are stringed like pearls though they have no string other than that they nicely joined together. ||

Obviously al-Ṣafadī takes as much pain to praise his own letter, which was apparently accompanied by a poem, as to praise al-Afḍal's gift. But why would al-Ṣafadī have spent so much effort praising his own prose and poetry in a letter to al-Afḍal, the rather sober and pious successor of Abū al-Fidā', the intellectual, instead of focusing on praising the donor as was to be expected? Two subtle allusions may suggest that there was another unspoken addressee. First, in speaking about his prose, al-Ṣafadī connects it to *al-manthūr*, which can mean "prose" as well as "gillyflower". However al-Ṣafadī was not the first to use this quite striking *tawriyah.* Some years before in 730, Ibn Nubātah published his first collection of prose, with which he hoped to demonstrate his capacity in the field of *inshā'*, and he gave it the title *Zahr al-Manthūr.* Given Ibn Nubātah's prominence, his name may have come to the mind of every informed contemporary reader when they heard this *tawriyah.*

Readers were thus prepared to understand the second allusion in al-Ṣafadī's praise of his own poetry. At first glance, there is nothing peculiar about a reference to Kāfūr al-Ikhshīdī in a letter on "camphorated" apricots. Bear in mind, however, that Ibn Nubātah had likened the prince of Ḥamāh to Sayf al-Dawlah

37 Ibn Faḍl Allāh, *Masālik al-Abṣār,* 12:484–485.

and Badr b. ʿAmmār, two of al-Mutanabbī's other patrons.[38] A comparison like this implies that the poet himself is assuming the role of a new Mutanabbī. Given this, the reader may understand al-Ṣafadī's claim as not only obliterating al-Mutanabbī's poetry, but Ibn Nubātah's as well. It is, therefore, reasonable to posit a subtext here that was addressed to Ibn Nubātah.

It is hard to believe that Ibn Nubātah was not aware of al-Ṣafadī's letter. They used to exchange their works, and if Ibn Nubātah had not received the letter from al-Ṣafadī himself, he would have got it from the court of Ḥamāh. Nevertheless as the letter was not directed to him, he could not immediately answer it. Opportunity came in the year 743.

This was a crucial year in Ibn Nubātah's life. After losing the support of the Ayyubids of Ḥamāh, he saw no other way to secure his livelihood than to enter the chancellery (*dīwān al-inshāʾ*) of Damascus. By then he was already 57 lunar years old, and having earned a reputation as a great stylist, his position as a "novice" in the *dīwān* cannot have been easy for him to swallow. He rose to the challenge by publishing his first year's output of official documents and letters under the title *Taʿlīq al-Dīwān*. This collection happens to include another letter in response to a gift of camphorated apricots. The situation parallels al-Ṣafadī's letter closely. Once again a secretary in the Damascus chancellery renowned for his stylistic competence seeks to express appreciation (probably also on behalf of the governor of Syria) for a present of camphorated apricots sent by the ruler of Ḥamāh. The protagonists, however, were different. Now it was Ibn Nubātah who wrote the letter rather al-Ṣafadī, and the addressee was no longer the Ayyubid prince al-Afḍal, but one of the Mamluk governors who succeeded the Ayyubids as commanders of the city and province of Ḥamāh. The identity of the addressee cannot be determined exactly since Ḥamāh saw three different Mamluk governors in the same year: Ṭuquztamir an-Nāṣirī[39], Alṭunbughā al-Māridānī,[40] and Yalbughā al-Yaḥyāwī (or al-Yaḥyawī).[41] The people of the city were not pleased to have received Mamluk governors in the place of Ayyubid princes. "Ṭuquztamir asked for the governorship of Ḥamāh," Ibn Qāḍī Shuhbah says, "and it was given to him. He was the first Turk to be installed as governor of Ḥamāh, and the people blamed him for that (*wa-ʿāba l-nāsu ʿalayhi dhālika*)."[42] The governor's gift of apricots sent from Ḥamāh to Damascus may have been a conscious attempt to signal continuity and therefore somewhat politically sig-

38 Ibn Faḍl Allāh, *Masālik al-Abṣār*, 19:453 (poem 675, line 30) (N.B.: Ibn Faḍl Allāh gives better versions of the early poems of Ibn Nubātah than the printed *Dīwān Ibn Nubātah*).

39 See Ibn Qāḍī Shuhbah, *Tārīkh*, 2:463–466; al-Ṣafadī, *Wāfī* 16:465–468.

40 See Ibn Qāḍī Shuhbah, *Tārīkh* 2:378–379 (gov. from Rabīʿ II until Jumādā II); al-Ṣafadī, *al-Wāfī* 9:364–365.

41 See Ibn Qāḍī Shuhbah, *Tārīkh* 2:538–540; al-Ṣafadī, *al-Wāfī* 29:41–51.

42 Ibn Qāḍī Shuhbah, *Tārīkh* 2:465.

nificant. Ibn Nubātah, for his part, may have had mixed feelings about writing a letter of thanks to the Mamluk successor of the Ḥamawī Ayyyūbids, to whom he owed so much. He refers to the gouvernor's "Turkishness" in the final passage of his letter, mentioning the "Ḥamawī's Khurāsānian unarabicness".[43] More interesting for our purposes, however, is the middle passage, which displays conspicuous parallels to al-Ṣafadī's letter:[44]

وينهي [37a] بعد ثناء وولاء : لهذا في الأسماع أزهى وأزهر ثمرة *
ولهذا في القلوب أرسى وأرسخ شجرة * ورود المشرِّف الكريم على يد
فلان بما ملأ السَمْعَ من أخبار مولانا المرتقية سرورا * والعَينَ من آثار
يده الكريمة نُورا * والفَمَ من هداياه المشمش الحموي كُؤوسَ لذّةٍ كان
مِزاجُها كافورا * فقبّل المملوك أسْطُرَهُ مستحْلِياً مَواقِعَ رشفاته * وقابله
بعوائد الشكر مستجلياً عوائد افتقاداته وصلاته * ومدّ فكره ويده فالتقط
النجوم المشرقة من هداياه وكلماته * واهتدى بتلك الهدية إلى أطيب
الفواكه وبمثلها يهتدى الحيران * وقسم أفلاك العلب وأقسم منها بمواقع
النجوم أنها من أنفس هدايا أنفس الجيران

… and he reports –
after having conveyed his praise and confirmed his loyalty:
the first one (his praise), most lavish to blossom and to bloom, will bear fruit in the ears, | and the second one (his loyalty) will plant a tree most firmly rooted and anchored in the heart ||
– to have received the distinguished letter, handed out by so-and-so, by which the news that arrived filled the ears with joy, | and the traces of his noble hand filled the eye with light; | and his presents, the camphorated apricots, filled his mouth with the goblets of delight "the mixture of which is camphor" (Q 76:5). || Thus the slave kissed its lines and found sweet the spots his lips touched, | and he requited it with his recurring thanks, which brings the benefits of his inquiries and his gifts to light, | and he spread out his mind and his hand and received radiant stars from both his presents and his words, || and he was guided by this gift to the best of fruits –such are those who guide the confused– | and he split the celestial spheres of the boxes, "swearing by the setting places of the stars" (Q 56:75) that they are the most precious presents from the most precious neighbor. ||

Anyone who reads both texts will notice several similarities between them that do not appear to occur by chance. Let me just mention the parallelisms between gift and words, and between eyes and ears, which are both pleased by the present or the letter; ears that are filled with *ladhdhah*; "light" (*nūrā*) rhyming with *kāfūrā*; and the (rather inevitable) quotation of Q 56:5. Nevertheless despite these similarities, Ibn Nubātah's letter is not an imitation of al-Ṣafadī's. Whereas al-Ṣafadī praises his own letter, Ibn Nubātah praises the letter that came from Ḥāmāh. Moreover, both letters use different similes for the apricots. While al-

43 Ibn Nubātah, *Taʿlīq al-Dīwān*, Ms. Berlin 8640, 37b.
44 Ibid., 36b–37b.

Ṣafadī tries to include as many comparisons for the fruits as possible, Ibn Nubātah confines himself nearly exclusively to comparing the apricots with the stars. As in many of his poems, Ibn Nubātah uses the technique of the *leitmotif*:[45] from the first part of the letter through to the end (neither quoted above), stars and other celestial bodies appear with different functions and meanings. The objects to which al-Ṣafadī likened the apricots – pearls, honey, blossoms, balls of crystal and buttons – are conspicuously absent in Ibn Nubātah's letter. There is only one remarkable exception: in the final portion of Ibn Nubātah's letter the apricots are said to be "perhaps colored bullets shot by the cross-bows of heaven" (*laʿalla hādhihī banādiqu qawsi l-samāʾi l-mulawwanati*).[46] This extravagant comparison is a clear echo of al-Ṣafadī's letter, in which we read, also toward the end, that the apricots seem "as if they were not bullets for the cross-bows of the twigs" (*ka-annahā lam takun li-qisiyyi l-ghuṣūni banādiqu*).[47] With his reference to *banādiq*, the most unlikely object of comparison mentioned by al-Ṣafadī, Ibn Nubātah was making it clear to the attentive reader that his letter was meant as a response.

This may be corroborated by the publication history of Ibn Nubātah's letter. Despite the fact that Ibn Nubātah published the letter shortly after it had been written in his *Taʿlīq al-Dīwān* in 743, it appears that the published version was not the same as the version that was actually sent. About seventy years later, Ibn Nubātah's letter was published again, this time by al-Qalqashandī who included it in his *Ṣubḥ al-Aʿshā*.[48] Al-Qalqashandī's version omits the beginning and one sentence from the middle of the letter, but carries on where the *Taʿlīq*-version ends and includes a description of a melon, which was obviously also part of the gift. As it is not very plausible that al-Qalqashandī added the melon-section from a different source, it is probable that Ibn Nubātah's original letter was indeed, as al-Qalqashandī's heading claims, "a response to the arrival of apricots and an Aleppine melon." Thus it seems that Ibn Nubātah must have decided to discard his description of the melon. By concentrating on a single subject (the apricots), the literary letter is not only made more focused and more concise, but it also becomes an exact counterpart to al-Ṣafadī's letter. Whatever Ibn Nubātah's intention, it is clear that Ibn Nubātah's publication decisions were governed by different principles than al-Qalqashandī's. Whereas the latter published shortened but otherwise unaltered versions of Ibn Nubātah's letters mainly to serve as models for other secretaries, Ibn Nubātah published revised versions of his letters to be read as aesthetic texts. Therefore, he did not dispose of the in-

45 See Bauer, *Der Fürst ist tot.*
46 Ibn Nubātah, *Taʿlīq al-Dīwān*, Ms. Berlin 8640, 37b.
47 Ibn Faḍl Allāh, *Masālik al-Abṣār*, 12:484.
48 Al-Qalqashandī, *Ṣubḥ al-Aʿshā*, 9:117 – 118.

troduction and the address, in which the leitmotif of the celestial bodies already appeared, but did not hesitate to revise it whenever he thought his modifications would yield a better text regardless of its original wording and purpose. For al-Qalqashandī, however, the role of the text in pragmatic communication was still a concern, while in Ibn Nubātah's *Taʿlīq* it is mainly a text's potential for literary communication that is considered important.

Al-Ṣafadī's and Ibn Nubātah's letters were published separately without any hint of their interrelation. Since it is highly improbable that a reader would come across both texts and recognize their interdependence, the authors must have felt their texts were fully comprehensible and enjoyable even without the recognition of their cross intertextuality. This is also true of another text I have written about, Shihāb al-Dīn b. Faḍl Allāh's *Hunting Urjūzah*, which forms a knot in a complex network of intertextual relations but can also be enjoyed on its own.[49]

In the case of cross intertextuality there are at least three (groups of) participants: the addressee; the unmentioned person(s) who is/are the author(s) of the referent text(s); and the general reading public. In the texts examined here, it is clearly the last group that is most important to the author while the addressee may be no more than a pretext for the text's creation. The author of the text to which the text refers was certainly important, but the text could always still be considered relevant by those who were unaware of the connection.

Paratexts

As we saw in the preceding examples, Mamluk texts were often sent, dedicated or addressed to someone. It is tempting, therefore, to draw the conclusion that the main reason for a text was to convey a message to the person to which it was sent, dedicated or addressed. Such a conclusion, however, would be rash. The occasion of a text is merely its starting point and is not necessarily its *raison d'être.* Texts live on even after the occasion has passed and the addressee has been forgotten. Especially remarkable examples are those texts that began as paratexts to other texts but continued to be considered relevant works of art even when separated from the text to which they were originally linked.

A paratext is a text that in one way or another *accompanies* the main text, commenting, interpreting, illustrating, advertising, criticizing it in order to influence the reception of the text.[50] The main contribution of Mamluk literature to other established forms of paratexts was the *taqrīẓ.*[51] In a *taqrīẓ* the author

49 See Bauer, *Dawādār's Hunting Party.*

50 See Genette, *Palimpsestes*, 10–11.

51 Rosenthal, *'Blurbs' (Taqrīẓ)*; Veselý, *Taqrīẓ*; Bauer, *Was kann aus dem Jungen noch werden.*

expresses his appreciation of a newly published work and praises its author. Rosenthal's translation as "blurb" captures well one aspect of the word's meaning, but it should be stressed that in many cases it is the author himself who is being praised in a *taqrīẓ* rather more than the work in question. Gathering *taqārīẓ* was especially important for young authors just about to make their entrance on the public stage of literature and scholarship. We know of several cases of such *debut-taqārīẓ*, in which young authors circulated the work with which they hoped to announce themselves new members of the elite *ʿulamāʾ* or *udabāʾ*, asking established scholars and *hommes de lettres* to write them a *taqrīẓ*.[52] Thus collecting *taqārīẓ* may have been a sort of initiation rite for young, aspiring authors. It may very well be the case that the practice was begun by Ibn Nubātah in his *Sajʿ al-Muṭawwaq*, a work to which we will return later.

In general, *taqārīẓ* were published as an appendix to the work they praised and with which they stand in paratextual relation. Nevertheless, even *taqārīẓ* managed to live a second life, separated from the text that gave rise to them. Rudolf Veselý mentions several examples.[53] One may add to these Ibn Nubātah's *taqrīẓ* on a *dīwān* of epigrams written by Ibn Ḥabīb. The *taqrīẓ* started out as an appendix to Ibn Ḥabīb's work but was recycled in a considerably shortened and revised version in Ibn Nubātah's collection *Zahr al-Manthūr*, in which it can hardly be read as anything other than an aesthetic text.[54]

Whereas *debut-taqārīẓ* come, as a rule, in groups, a single *taqrīẓ* may be dedicated to a work of an established author as a sign of friendship and veneration. Perhaps the most extravagant *taqrīẓ* ever written was a letter sent by Burhān al-Dīn al-Qīrāṭī to Ibn Nubātah, a text of "utmost beauty and length", as Ibn Ḥajar al-ʿAsqalānī put it.[55] The text is not called *taqrīẓ*, and it is not clear which of Ibn Nubātah's works provoked its composition.[56] Its style and content leave little doubt, however, that it was meant as a sort of epitome of a *taqrīẓ*. It is also quite clear what al-Qīrāṭī's main purpose for the composition of the work was. Unlike the case of *debut-taqārīẓ*, here was a younger and less famous *adīb*, praising an older and extremely famous colleague. With this *taqrīẓ* al-Qīrāṭī hoped to anchor himself in the tradition of his revered model, Ibn Nubātah, to strengthen bonds of friendship with him and introduce himself as a worthy representative of Ibn Nubātah's legacy.

Though even this text had a kind of pragmatic background, there can be no doubt that it was intended to be and was indeed understood as a chiefly aesthetic

52 Bauer, *Ibn Ḥabīb*, 37–41.
53 Veselý, Taqrīẓ.
54 Bauer, *Ibn Ḥabīb* 45–50.
55 Ibn Ḥajar al-ʿAsqalānī: *Inbāʾ al-Ghumr*, 1:312.
56 Probably Ibn Nubātah's *Sūq ar-Raqīq* gave the occasion, one of his last works. It is a collection of revised versions of the *nasībs* of his *qaṣīdahs*.

text. This is corroborated on several fronts. First, Ibn Ḥajar praised the text for its "extraordinary beauty" and considered it one of al-Qīrāṭī's main works. Second, it is included in Ibn Ḥijjah's selection of the works of al-Qīrāṭī called *Taḥrīr al-Qīrāṭī*. This volume is a *Best-of*, containing only those texts which Ibn Ḥijjah considered of extraordinary aesthetic value. Ibn Ḥijjah even mentions the "convention of aesthetics" in his foreword saying that, in the case of poetry, he omitted everything that is "purely meter and rhyme".[57] There was obviously no doubt on the part of Ibn Ḥajar and Ibn Ḥijjah that al-Qīrāṭī's text possessed aesthetic merit. Thirdly, the stylistic sophistication and the fact of the text's length– it covers more than 27 pages in the Berlin manuscript of *Taḥrīr al-Qīrāṭī*[58] – makes it all too clear that there is no justification in reading the text in a pragmatic way.

We may conclude, then, that even paratexts such as the *taqrīẓ*, which are the least probable candidates to be non-pragmatic texts, could be intended and understood as aesthetic texts, that they could be enjoyed as such and considered relevant and satisfying by readers who were not particularly interested in the texts and authors, which first gave rise to the composition of these texts.

Combinations

All the modes of communication described so far can also be combined. There is such a work that combines all of them together: Ibn Nubātah's miraculous (and still unedited) *Saj'al-Muṭawwaq*. The book is *dedicated* to al-Malik al-Mu'ayyad, and is also *addressed* to him. The texts by its contributors are *responses* to Ibn Nubātah's invitation. Thus the book is mostly made up of texts (letters, poems) that are the outcome of a literary *exchange*. The contributors to the work knew that several of their colleagues were composing texts for the same purpose and all contributors had to react to an earlier text by Ibn Nubātah. This is a case of *shared intertexuality*. Although we do not know precisely how the contributors interacted, we can safely assume that the whole book is the result of *cross intertextuality*. Finally, the core of the book is made up of *taqārīẓ*. As we can see, all of the modes of communicative strategies discussed so far are not only present in the book, they form the very root of it.

The story of the work goes as follows: In the year 717/1317, one year after he had arrived in Damascus, the time was ripe for Ibn Nubātah to make his entrance onto the stage of *adab*. His debut-work was an anthology entitled *Maṭla' al-Fawā'id wa-Majma' al-Farā'id*, a programmatic work about the role of the *adīb*

57 Ibn Ḥijjah al-Ḥamawī, *Mukhtaṣar Dīwān al-Qīrāṭī (= Taḥrīr al-Qīrāṭī)*, Ms. Berlin 7870, 2a.
58 Ibid., 40a – 54a (17 lines per page).

and its import.[59] Ibn Nubātah dedicated it to al-Malik al-Mu'ayyad, the prince of Ḥamāh, and at the same time invited a number of members of the civilian elite to write a *taqrīẓ* on the work with the intention of publishing the incoming texts in a separate volume. According to the autograph manuscript, the work was accomplished in 719/1319.[60] Here is a list of the contributors in the order of their appearance in *Saj' al-Muṭawwaq:*

(1) al-Shihāb Maḥmūd ibn Salmān ibn Fahd (644–725/1246–1325), Ḥanbalī judge and from 717 until his death director of the chancellery (*kātib al-sirr*) of Damascus, famous *adīb* and author of several works, especially on *inshā'* and *adab.*[61]

(2) Najm al-Dīn b. Ṣaṣrā (655–723/1257–1323), from 702 until his death Shāfi'ī chief judge of Damascus and, thus, the holder of the highest religious office in Syria. In this function he was one of the four judges in the trial against Ibn Taymiyya in 705.[62] Two of them had already died by 719. The fourth is number (4) on our list.[63]

(3) Jalāl al-Dīn al-Qazwīnī, known as Khaṭīb Dimashq, Shāfi'ī judge, preacher at the Umayyad Mosque in Damascus. He is best known as the author of *Talkhīṣ al-Miftāḥ.*[64]

(4) Kamāl al-Dīn b. al-Zamlakānī (667–727/1269–1327), one of the great representatives of Shāfi'ī jurisprudence in his time, author of several works, among them refutations of Ibn Taymiyya, for whose trial in 705 he acted as judge. He held several positions as *nāẓir* and served as *muwaqqi' al-dast* in the *dīwān al-inshā'* of Damascus. In 724 he (reluctantly) became chief judge of Aleppo. Years before he had hoped to become chief judge of Damascus instead of Ibn Ṣaṣrā. When he was eventually offered the position in 727, he died.[65]

(5) Badr al-Dīn b. al-'Aṭṭār (670–725/1271–1325), served as *nāẓir al-ashrāf* and secretary in the Damascus chancellery. His heyday, under Āqūsh al-Afram when he served as *nāẓir al-jaysh* of Syria, was already over by 719.[66]

(6) 'Alā' al-Dīn b. Ghānim (651–737/1253–1336), highly respected and influential intellectual and *adīb*, who preferred to stay in Damascus rather than accept the post of director of the chancellery (*kātib al-sirr*) in Aleppo.[67]

59 See Bauer, *Anthologien*, 85–94.
60 Ibn Nubātah, *Saj' al-Muṭawwaq*, Ms. Ayasofya 4045, 77b.
61 See al-Ṣafadī, *A'yān al-'Aṣr* 5:372–399 (here and in the following I will limit myself in general on one source).
62 See Jackson, *Ibn Taymiyyah.*
63 See al-Ṣafadī: *al-Wāfī* 8:16–18 and al-Subkī, *Ṭabaqāt*, 9:20–22 with a quotation from *al-Saj' al-Muṭawwaq.*
64 See al-Ṣafadī, *A'yān al-'Aṣr* 4:492–499.
65 See al-Ṣafadī, *A'yān al-'Aṣr* 5:106–111.
66 See al-Ṣafadī, *A'yān al-'Aṣr* 4:240–241 and idem, *al-Wāfī* 30:272–273.
67 See al-Ṣafadī, *A'yān al-'Aṣr* 3:496–502.

(7) Fakhr al-Dīn b. al-Mu'allim (660 – 725/1262 – 1325), lawyer, Koran reader, Ḥadīth scholar and *adīb*, former judge of al-Khalīl.[68]

(8) Amīn al-Dīn b. al-Naḥḥās (681 – 757/1282 – 1356) held several administrative positions in Damascus such as secretary in the *dīwān al-inshā'*.[69]

(9) Bahā' al-Dīn b. Ghānim (d. 735/1334) started his career as *kātib al-inshā'* in Ṭarābulus, became *kātib al-Darj* in Damascus and was transferred to Ṣafad as *muwaqqi'* around the time Ibn Nubātah composed *Saj' al-Muṭawwaq*. He would end up as *kātib al-sirr*, back in Ṭarābulus.[70]

(10) Sharaf al-Dīn Aḥmad b. al-Yazdī, a lesser known figure, representative of Ṭarābulus, just as Bahā' al-Dīn b. Ghānim.

(11) Jamāl al-Dīn Yūsuf b. Ḥammād al-Ḥamawī represented Ḥamāh.

Each of the contributors had some relation to *adab*, some more, others less. They were, after all, supposed to be interested in an anthology of *adab* and they had been asked to write a text that would match its literary standard. Many of them had positions in the chancellery and were trained to write sophisticated rhymed prose. Others, like Ibn Ṣaṣrā, had professions that had little to do with literature but they cultivated poetry in their free time. None of the eleven, however, was a poet of renown, let alone a professional littérateur. Most of them belonged to the upper rank of the civilian elite. Lesser known figures were included because Ibn Nubātah was keen not to restrict himself to people from Damascus and wanted to see the other towns in Syria also represented. It would be interesting to know whether the contributors knew of each other's contributions. This would be especially interesting in the case of 'Alā' al-Dīn b. Ghānim and Ibn al-Zamlakānī, who nourished a mutual hatred, a fact that obviously did not prevent Ibn Nubātah from including them both.[71]

It is quite remarkable that the young and still quite unknown Ibn Nubātah managed to entice all these famous people to compose a *taqrīẓ* for him. We know that he had directed poems and letters to them before. Some of these have been preserved, many in *Saj' al-Muṭawwaq* itself, and it is more than likely that al-Malik al-Mu'ayyad Abū al-Fidā' had a hand in it all. We do not know if there were any other VIPs who declined the invitation. After all, eleven contributors plus Ibn Nubātah himself would yield the magic number twelve.

In the end, *Saj' al-Muṭawwaq* ended up as a literary work in which thirteen people were directly involved: The author and editor Ibn Nubātah, the dedicatee Abū al-Fidā' (who himself remains silent), and the eleven *muqarriẓūn*. Their task was to write a text in rhymed prose, praising Ibn Nubātah, especially for the

68 See al-Ṣafadī, *A'yān al-'Aṣr* 5:183 – 184.
69 See al-Ṣafadī, *A'yān al-'Aṣr* 5:247 – 253.
70 See al-Ṣafadī, *A'yān al-'Aṣr* 2:5 – 12.
71 See al-Kutubī, *Fawāt al-Wafayāt*, 3:78 – 84.

achievement of his *Maṭlaʿ al-Fawāʾid*, and also to eulogize al-Malik al-Muʾayyad. Ibn Nubātah's task was to write a preface (the longest of any of his works), assemble the contributions and append what in the end is an anthology of his own poems and letters. The text is arranged in twelve chapters: the preface and one chapter for each contributor. Apart from the preface, each chapter is comprised of three sections: (1) a presentation of the contributor, (2) the contributor's *taqrīẓ*, (3) and a selection of the poem and letters Ibn Nubātah sent to the contributor.

The first chapter, on al-Shihāb Maḥmūd, may serve as an example. It is introduced by the word *al-shaykh*[72], written in thick ink to mark the beginning of a new section. The full name of the contributor comes next and is then followed by Ibn Nubātah's praise of ash-Shihāb Maḥmūd in rhymed prose (4 pages). The headline *nuskhah mā katabahū* introduces the second section: ash-Shihāb Maḥmūd's *taqrīẓ* of Ibn Nubātah and his praise of al-Muʾayyad (3 pages) in rhymed prose, concluding with a few lines of poetry. The third section is titled *nubdhah min madāʾiḥī wa-mukātabātī ilayhi* (12 pages). It starts with a poem of 33 lines "which I wrote to him this year"[73], followed by a short poem (5 lines) "which I wrote to him when he came to Damascus"[74], followed by a four-liner "which I wrote to him when he moved into the house of al-Qāḍī al-Fāḍil"[75]. The main piece is a very long and elaborate letter which "I wrote from Damascus while he was in Cairo" (6 pages), mostly praising Cairo at Damascus' expense. The next ten chapters follow this scheme closely.

Sajʿ al-Muṭawwaq became one of Ibn Nubātah's most popular works. It is preserved in even more manuscripts than *Maṭlaʿ al-Fawāʾid*, the book that spurred the composition of *Sajʿ al-Muṭawwaq*. It goes without saying that the edition of a work like this, comprising nearly all conceivable forms of literary communication and thus giving a distillation of Mamluk elite literature, is a great desideratum. The editor will, however, have to cope with a serious problem. The autograph version, which we used to describe the al-Shihāb Maḥmūd-section, is obviously not identical with the published version. The published version, which all other copies I have examined so far represent, shows a considerable amount of revision. Some of them are trivial. Instead of *nubdhah min madāʾiḥī wa-mukātabātī ilayh* Ibn Nubātah now writes *nubdhah min madīḥī* (or *madāʾiḥī*) *fīhi wa-mukātabātī ilayhi.* Several phrases in his letters are reworded (note that the letters had been sent a long time before, and some of their addressees were already dead). In the headline to the first poem to al-Shihāb Maḥmūd b. Nubātah

72 No. 1, 3, 4, 7 and 11 are called *al-shaykh*, no. 2 *sayyidunā*, the others *al-ṣadr.*

73 Ibn Nubātah, *Sajʿ al-Muṭawwaq*, Ms. Ayasofya 4045, 9a, text also Ibn Nubātah, *Dīwān*, 363.

74 Ibn Nubātah, *Sajʿ al-Muṭawwaq*, Ms. Ayasofya 4045, 10b, not in the *Dīwān.*

75 Ibid., not in the *Dīwān.*

cancels the words "which I wrote to him this year", which would have been misleading for later readers. Other changes are more drastic. Whole poems are omitted or added or transposed. In the case of al-Shihāb Maḥmūd, the second poem is omitted and another short poem "on the occasion of his arrival in Damascus" is added instead. In the case of Ibn al-Zamlakānī, the change is even more drastic. The main text by Ibn Nubātah in this section is an *'aynīyah* of 55 lines.[76] As it happened, out of his two long eulogies in praise of Ibn al-Zamlakānī it was not the *'aynīyah* that became famous. Rather it was his monumental *tā'īyah,*a poem of more than a hundred lines. Its fame is attested by Tāj al-Dīn al-Subkī, who quotes it and acclaims it, adding that the poem led many *udabā'* to write a *mu'āraḍah* of it, but that they all failed and none could match it;[77] this despite the fact that Tāj al-Dīn himself had been eulogized in one of these *mu'āraḍāt* composed by al-Qīrāṭī.[78] Ibn Nubātah did what his readers would have expected and replaced the *'aynīyah* with the *tā'īyah.*

Again we see how texts can live a second life. Poems and letters that had already fulfilled their first communicative purpose were reassembled and revised to serve as texts of literary interest for a broader public for whom the texts' original purpose was of little relevance. What is more, some of the texts gained a third life: they were revised a second time and found their way into other publications. This is, for example, the case with Ibn Nubātah's letter to al-Shihāb Maḥmūd, which Ibn Nubātah included in his anthology of prose texts called *Zahr al-Manthūr* from the year 730. The letter is presented in a slightly shortened version. It comes under the bare heading *min risālah.* Not even the name of the addressee is mentioned this time as it was considered to be irrelevant for the reader.[79]

Conclusion

After the *Sturm und Drang* with its cult of genius and the aesthetics of authentic experience, literature that was composed for a particular occasion was in a difficult position – or was not even considered to be "authentic" literature any longer. Despite Goethe's attempt to vindicate "occasional" poetry,[80] European romanticism reinforced the idea that the poet had to be a medium, who, owing to his individual sensibility, is gifted with deeper emotions and insights. The poet's

76 Ibid. 33b – 36a, see also Ibn Nubātah, *Dīwān* 297 – 299.

77 Al-Subkī, *al-Ṭabaqāt,* 9:191 – 201.

78 See Ibn Ḥijjah, *Taḥrīr al-Qīrāṭī,* Ms. Berlin 7870, 17a – 19b. Ibn Nubātah's *Tā'īyah* is in Ibn Nubātah, *Dīwān* 67 – 71.

79 Ibn Nubātah, *Zahr al-Manthūr,* Ms. Chester Beatty Library 3774, 84a – 85a.

80 See Segebrecht, *Gelegenheitsgedicht.*

task is then to reveal his individual, authentic vision of life to the public. In this understanding, there is no place for occasional poetry, which is irreconcilable with "the aesthetics of romanticism, where the notion of eternal models (...) is replaced by a passionate belief in spiritual freedom, individual creativity. The painter, the poet, the composer do not hold up a mirror to nature, however ideal, but invent; they do not imitate (the doctrine of mimesis), but create not merely the means but the goals that they pursue; these goals represent the self-expression of the artist's own unique, inner vision, to set aside which in response to the demands of some 'external' voice – church, state, public opinion, family, friends, arbiters of taste – is an act of betrayal of what alone justifies their existence for those who are in any sense creative."[81]

The romantic idea of poetry was a purely Western and modern concept (– it has its roots in the end of the 18th century –), but as with many Western concepts, it was soon considered universal. Writers in non-Western cultures were expected to write accordingly, and historians of literature applied the romantic paradigm to literatures of the past, using it to distinguish between good and bad texts and good and bad literatures. Arabic literature fared especially badly. There is not much of a romantic spirit in it, and, even worse, the bulk of it was quite obviously composed for particular occasions. Western scholars of Arabic literature were especially vexed by the fact that so much of Arabic literature is panegyric. Panegyric literature is occasional literature *par excellence* and was banned from the realm of "true" literature in the 19th century in most Western literatures. In classical Arabic literature, instead, panegyric poetry has always been a genre of highest prestige. Joseph Hell even went so far as to see in the Arab's esteem for al-Mutanabbī a "problem of the psychology of nations rather than of literary history".[82] On the other hand, Johann Jacob Reiske (1716–1774), who was still rooted in the ideas of the Enlightenment, had no problem with panegyrics and considered al-Mutanabbī one of the greatest poets ever.[83] Joseph Hell gave the following harsh verdict on al-Mutanabbī and his admirers: "No nation other than the Arabs would ever declare a professional panegyrist their greatest poet. The rest of the civilized world would never allow themselves to reckon among the great figures of world literature a poet who dedicated his talents – great as they may have been – almost exclusively to the glory – whether justified or not – of generous personalities."[84]

In the aftermath of Western domination and colonialism, Western concepts of literature found their way into the Middle East. In Ṭāhā Ḥusayn[85] al-Mutanabbī

81 Berlin, *Crooked Timber*, 57–58.
82 Hell, *al-Mutanabbi*, here 176 (translation T.B.).
83 Reiske, *Proben*.
84 Hell, *al-Mutanabbi*, 175 (translation T.B.).
85 Ḥusayn, *Maʿa l-Mutanabbī*.

hardly fared better than with Joseph Hell, and many literary scholars wasted their time sniffing out lines in which a poet "expresses true feelings" despite the fact that neither the idea of "true" (vs. false) feelings nor the concept of "expressing" one's feelings was shared by pre-modern Arabic poets and intellectuals.[86]

Arab scholars are even more critical about the Mamluk period. Its literature is equally as occasional as that of the Abbasid period, but, due to *Verbürgerlichung*, it lacks much of the former's heroism, which appealed to scholars who were interested in writing a nationalist literary history. Enough has been said about prejudices and misconceptions concerning Mamluk literature however. The present article is not intended as another defense of Mamluk literature or another state-of-the-field article.[87] Instead, it probed the different ways in which literature was used as a medium of communication among the educated in Mamluk society.

As a result we may state that occasionality (i.e. the production of texts first composed for a particular occasion) plays indeed an important role in Mamluk literature. It is, however, a different kind of occasionality than that of the panegyric poetry of earlier times. In a panegyric poem addressed to a caliph, a prince or a high-ranking officer the participants of the communication can be arranged in a triangle on the top of which is the *mamdūḥ* while the poet and the public form the two corners at the base.[88] In general, there is a strong hierarchic gap between the *mamdūḥ* on the one hand and the poet and the audience on the other. In Mamluk times, this kind of asymmetric communication is the exception rather than the rule. The occasion for which literary texts were produced was no longer prescribed by aristocrats. Instead, the *udabā'* created their own occasions. Often there was no occasion other than the mere desire to communicate. It could even happen that princes took part in an act of communication between the *'ulamā'* and *udabā'* as we have seen in the case of Ibn Nubātah's *Saj' al-Muṭawwaq*, in which the prince of Ḥamāh assumes the role of the *mamdūḥ*, which turns out, however to be only a supporting role.

The romantic rejection of occasional poetry entails a price: the marginalization of poetry.[89] It is hardly an exaggeration to suggest that literature that demands more than pure amusement – to say nothing of poetry – is of lesser social importance today than it was during most of the history of Western and Middle Eastern societies. Today whenever poetry reaches a wide audience, it is

86 See Bauer, *review: al-Afandi, al-Ghazal.*
87 See Homerin, *Reflections*, and Bauer, *Mamluk Literature*, and idem, *Post-Classical Literature.*
88 See Bauer, *Shā'ir (Poet).*
89 See Segebrecht, *Gelegenheitsgedicht*, 15, 25.

again thanks to its occasionality as in political songs, rap music, poetry slams or events like *shāʿir al-milyūn*.

The central importance of literature in the Mamluk period coincides with its high degree of occasionality. Literature, especially poetry and ornate prose, was central, it permeated every field of life and was an important medium of educated conversation. The subjects of literature were great emotions as in Ibn Nubātah's "Kindertotenlieder"[90] as well as the trifles of everyday life. Esprit, wit and elegance, even critique and provocation were held in high esteem; playfulness was enjoyed. In all these parameters, Mamluk literature has much more in common with the literature of the Enlightenment than with that of romanticism. No wonder both the Mamluk period and the Enlightenment share an interest in the pointed epigram, which became one of the most prevalent literary forms in both epochs.

As we have seen in the preceding, communication among the educated in the Mamluk period did not (only) take place in a private context. It was always also a means of distinction as well as a means of creating group identity. It, therefore, had to take place on a *stage*, at least on an imaginary stage. As we saw, many if not most poems and prose works were composed for a particular occasion. In many cases, however, the occasion is not important for the understanding of the texts. It may even be invented or manipulated, as was the case with Ibn Nubātah's letter on camphorated apricots, where he only told half the truth about the occasion. Though texts were (truly or allegedly) composed for a certain occasion, it was not the occasion that mattered, but their staging. The stage, of course, must not be taken literally (except in the case of popular literature as certain types of texts were intended for oral performance). Rather, the stage of the educated class was the book market. Thus, texts that were considered relevant beyond their use for a particular occasion were divorced from their original context, revised, adapted to new contexts and distributed in a different medium. The impulse to give a second (or third…) life to formerly occasional texts is one of the reasons why the Mamluk period was also the "Golden Age" of the anthology.[91]

It is remarkable that out of all literary epochs it was in the unromantic Mamluk age that one of the great ideals of the Romantics – the unity of life and literature – had come closer to becoming a reality than hardly ever before or after. For scholars of literature, this is a fascinating discovery. For scholars in other fields, it is a challenge. Anyone who seeks to gain a deeper understanding of Mamluk society has no choice but to take its literature – prose and poetry – into close consideration.

90 See note 27.

91 See Bauer, *Anthologien*.

Bibliography

Primary Sources

Al-Ḥākim al-Nīsābūrī, Abū ʻAbdallāh, *Al-Mustadrak ʻalā al-Ṣaḥīḥayn*. 6 vols., ed. Rājī al-Raḥamāt, Beirut 1998.
Al-Ḥillī, Ṣafī al-Dīn ʻAbd al-ʻAzīz, *Dīwān*, ed. Muḥammad Ḥuwwar, 3 vols., Amman/Beirut 2000.
Ibn Faḍl Allāh, Shihāb al-Din Aḥmad, *Masālik al-Abṣār fī Mamālik al-Amṣār*, vol. 12, ed. Ibrāhīm Ṣāliḥ, Abū Ẓaby 2002, vol. 19, ed. Yūnus Aḥmad al-Samarrā'ī, Abū Ẓaby 2003.
Ibn Ḥajar al-ʻAsqalānī, Shihāb al-Dīn Aḥmad, *Al-Durar al-Kāminah fī Aʻyān al-Mi'ah al-Thāminah*, 6 vols., Ḥaydarābād, 1929 - 1931, 2nd ed. 1392 - 1396/1972 - 1976.
Ibn Ḥajar al-ʻAsqalānī, Shihāb al-Dīn Aḥmad, *Inbā' al-Ghumr bi-Abnā' al-ʻUmr*, 9 vols., Ḥaydarābād 1396/1976.
Ibn Ḥijjah al-Ḥamawī, Taqī al-Dīn b. ʻAlī, *Khizānat al-Adab wa-Ghāyat al-Arab*, 5 vols., ed. Kawkab Diyāb, Beirut 1421/2001.
Ibn Nubātah, Jamāl al-Dīn Muḥammad, *Dīwān Ibn Nubātah*, ed. Muḥammad al-Qalqīlī, Cairo 1323/1905.
Ibn Nubātah, Jamāl al-DīnMuḥammad, *Al-Mufākharah bayn al-Sayf wa-l-Qalam*, ed. Hilāl Nājī, in: *al-Mawrid* 12/4 (1983), pp. 126 - 48.
Ibn Qāḍī Shuhbah, Taqī al-Dīn, *Tārīkh*, 4 vols., ed. ʻAdnān Darwīsh, Damascus 1977 - 1997.
Al-Kutubī, Muḥammad b. Shākir, *Fawāt al-Wafayāt*, 4 vols, ed. Iḥsān ʻAbbās, Beirut 1973 - 1974.
Al-Qalqashandī, Abū al-ʻAbbās, *Ṣubḥ al-Aʻshā fī Ṣināʻat al-Inshā*, 14 vols., Cairo 1331 - 37/ 1913 - 18.
Al-Ṣafadī, Khalīl b. Aybak, *Alḥān al-Sawājiʻ bayna al-Bādi' wa-l-Murājiʻ*, 2 vols., ed. Ibrāhīm Ṣāliḥ, Damascus 1425/2004.
Al-Ṣafadī, Khalīl b. Aybak, *al-Wāfī bi-l-Wafayāt*, ed. Helmut Ritter et al., 30 vols.,Wiesbaden, Beirut 1962 - 2010.
Al-Ṣafadī, Khalīl b. Aybak, *Aʻyān al-ʻAṣr wa-Aʻwān al-Naṣr*, 4 vols., ed. Fāliḥ Aḥmad al-Bakūr. Beirut 1419/1998.
Al-Subkī, Tāj al-Dīn ʻAbd al-Wahhāb, *Ṭabaqāt al-Shāfiʻīyah al-Kubrā*, 10 vols., ed. Maḥmūd Muḥammad al-Ṭanāḥī and ʻAbd al-Fattāḥ Muḥammad al-Ḥulw, Giza 1992.

Manuscripts

Ḥijāzī, Shihab al-Din Aḥmad Al-, *Rawḍ al-Ādāb*, Ms. Wien, Staatsbibliothek 400.
Ibn Ḥijjah al-Ḥamawī, Taqī al-Dīn b. ʻAlī, *Mukhtaṣar Dīwān al-Qīrāṭī (= Taḥrīr al-Qīrāṭī)*, MS Berlin 7870.
Ibn Nubātah Jamāl al-Dīn Muḥammad, *Zahr al-Manthūr*, MS Chester Beatty Library 3774.
Ibn Nubātah, Jamāl al-Dīn Muḥammad, *Al-Mufākharah bayn al-Sayf wa-l-Qalam*, MS Escorial 548, 34b - 53b; MS Berlin 8400, 65b - 70b.
Ibn Nubātah, Jamāl al-Dīn Muḥammad, *Al-Qaṭr al-Nubātī*, MS Paris, Bibliothèque nationale 2234.

Ibn Nubātah, Jamāl al-Dīn Muḥammad, *Dīwān*, MS Berlin 7861. MS Köprülü 1249, MS Ayasofya 3891.
Ibn Nubātah, Jamāl al-Dīn Muḥammad, *Saj' al-Muṭawwaq*, MS Ayasofya 4045.
Ibn Nubātah, Jamāl al-Dīn Muḥammad, *Sulūk Duwal al-Mulūk*, MS Istanbul, Esad Efendi 1822 (first version); Wien, Staatsarchiv, Krafft 474; Oxford, Bodleian, Seld Superius 29.
Ibn Nubātah, Jamāl al-Dīn Muḥammad, *Taʿlīq al-Dīwān*, MS Berlin 8640.
Al-Mi~mār, Ibrāhīm, *Dīwān*, MS Escorial 463.

Secondary Sources

Al-Barqūqī, ʿAbd al-Raḥmān, *Sharḥ Dīwān al-Mutanabbī*, 4 in 2 vols., Beirut 1407/1986.
Bauer, Thomas "Shāʿir (Poet): From the ʿAbbāsid period to the Nahḍa," in: *EI*[3], *vol. 12 (Supplement)*, Leiden 2004, 717 – 722.
Bauer, Thomas, "'Der Fürst ist tot, es lebe der Fürst!' Ibn Nubātas Gedicht zur Inthronisation al-Afḍals von Ḥamāh (732/1332)," in: *Orientalistische Studien zu Sprache und Literatur. Festgabe zum 65. Geburtstag von Werner Diem*, ed. Ulrich Marzolph, Wiesbaden 2011, pp. 285 – 315.
Bauer, Thomas, "'Was kann aus dem Jungen noch werden!' Das poetische Erstlingswerk des Historikers Ibn Ḥabīb im Spiegel seiner Zeitgenossen," in: *Studien zur Semitistik und Arabistik. Festschrift für Hartmut Bobzin zum 60. Geburtstag*, eds. Otto Jastrow, Shabo Talay and Herta Hafenrichter, Wiesbaden 2008, pp. 15 – 56.
Bauer, Thomas, "Communication and Emotion: The case of Ibn Nubātah's 'Kindertotenlieder'," *Mamlūk Studies Review* 7 (2003), pp. 49 – 95.
Bauer, Thomas, "In Search of 'Post-Classical Literature,'" *Mamlūk Studies Review* 11/2 (2007), pp. 137 – 167.
Bauer, Thomas, "Literarische Anthologien der Mamlukenzeit," in: *Die Mamluken. Studien zu ihrer Geschichte und Kultur. Zum Gedenken an Ulrich Haarmann (1942 – 1999)*, eds. Stephan Conermann and Anja Pistor-Hatam, Hamburg 2003, pp. 71 – 122
Bauer, Thomas, "Mamluk Literature: Misunderstandings and New Approaches," *Mamlūk Studies Review* 9/2 (2005), pp. 63 – 85.
Bauer, Thomas, "Review: al-Afandi, Majd, *al-Ghazal fī l-ʿAṣr al-Mamlūkī al-Awwal*," *Mamlūk Studies Review* 3 (1999), pp. 214 – 219.
Bauer, Thomas, "The Dawādār's Hunting Party. A Mamluk *muzdawija ṭardiyya*, probably by Shihāb al-Dīn Ibn Faḍl Allāh," in: *O ye Gentlemen. Arabic Studies on Science and Literary Culture in Honour of Remke Kruk*, eds. Arnoud Vrolijk and Jan P. Hogendijk, Leiden 2007, pp. 291 – 312.
Berlin, Isaiah, *The Crooked Timber of Humanity*, ed. Henry Hardy, London 1990.
Gelder, Geert Jan van, "Arabic Didactic Verse," in: *Centres of Learning. Learning and Location in Pre-Modern Europe and the Near East*, eds. Jan Willem Drijvers and A. A. MacDonald, Leiden 1995, pp. 103 – 117.
Gelder, Geert Jan van, "The Conceit of Pen and Sword: On an Arabic Literary Debate," *Journal of Semitic Studies* 32 (1987), pp. 329 – 60.
Genette, Gérard, *Palimpsestes. La littéreature au second degré,* Paris 1982.

Ghubārī, ʿAwaḍ Al-, "Al-Tanāṣṣ fī Shiʿr Ibn Nubātah al-Miṣrī," in: idem, *Dirāsah fī Adab Miṣr al-Islāmiyyah,* Cairo 2003, pp. 149–230.

Hamori, Andras, *The Composition of Mutanabbī's Panegyrics to Sayf al-Dawla,* Leiden 1991.

Heinrichs, Wolfhart, "Rhetorical Figures," in: Encyclopedia of Arabic Literature, ed. Julie Scott Meisami and Paul Starkey, 2 vols., London/New York 1998, 2:656–662.

Hell, Joseph, "al-Mutanabbi," *Der Islam* 25 (1939), pp. 174–179.

Hirschler, Konrad, *The Written Word in the Medieval Arabic Lands, A Social and Cultural History of Reading Practices,* Edinburgh 2012.

Homerin, Th. Emil, "Reflections on Poetry in the Mamluk Age," *Mamlūk Studies Review* 1 (1997), pp. 105–132.

Jackson, Sherman A., "Ibn Taymiyyah on Trial in Damascus," *Journal of Semitic Studies* 39 (1994), pp. 41–85.

Reiske, Johann Jacob, *Proben der arabischen Dichtung in verliebten und traurigen Gedichten aus dem Motanabbi. Arabisch und Deutsch, nebst Anmerkungen*, Leipzig 1765.

Rosenthal, Franz, "'Blurbs' (Taqrīẓ) from Fourteenth-Century Egypt," *Oriens* 27–28 (1981), pp. 177–196.

Schmidt, Siegfried J., *Grundriß der Empirischen Literaturwissenschaft,* Franfurt a.M. 1991.

Segebrecht, Wulf, *Das Gelegenheitsgedicht. Ein Beitrag zur Geschichte und Poetik der deutschen Lyrik,* Stuttgart 1977.

Ṭāhā Ḥusayn, *Maʿa l-Mutanabbī,* Cairo 1960.

Talib, Adam, "The Many Lives of Arabic Verse", in preparation.

Simon, Udo, „Badr al-Dīn Ibn Mālik," in: EI³, 2009–1, pp. 161–163.

Veselý, Rudolf, "Das *Taqrīẓ* in der arabischen Literatur," in: *Die Mamluken. Studien zu ihrer Geschichte und Kultur. Zum Gedenken an Ulrich Haarmann (1942–1999)*, eds. Stephan Conermann and Anja Pistor-Hatam, Hamburg 2003, pp. 379–385.

Caterina Bori

Theology, Politics, Society: the missing link. Studying Religion in the Mamluk Period*

When studying "religion" in the Mamluk period one faces a number of problems. Some of them are clearly spelled out in one of Emil Homerin's important contributions devoted to scholarship on Islam in the Mamluk period produced from the '40s to the very beginning of the 21st century. Homerin's article reviews literature in English, French, Arabic and German on various aspects of the religious practices and beliefs of this period.[1] A more recent monographic issue of the *Mamlūk Studies Review* edited by Johannes Pahlitzsch engages with religions in the Mamluk Sultanate by attempting at going beyond Islam.[2] In fact, Pahlitzsch's volume devotes some attention to non-Muslim attitudes towards their Muslims "partners". In the introduction, the editor points to the lack of studies on the Christian and Jewish communities of the Mamluk domains, an observation which, in turn, says something about a tendency to identify religion in the Mamluk domains with Islam.[3] More precisely, one may want to add, that even this identification needs to be qualified. It is in fact Sunni Islam which has gained the overall attention of scholars, while the doctrinal and practical dimensions of Shiʿism as well as its communitarian organization under the Mamluks still await a comprehensive treatment.[4]

In what follows, I will expressly avoid a detailed review of secondary literature

---

* The present chapter attempts at answering some questions which were raised at ZMO (Berlin) in September 2011 during the presentation of my DFG-funded project: "Islamic Pathways to Reform: the Reception of Ibn Taymiyya between the 16th-18th centuries". I would like to thank the participants for the lively discussion which took place and the issues they raised. I am also indebted to the generous help of my colleagues Frank Griffel, Livnat Holtzman, Jon Hoover and Giuseppe Cecere for reading and commenting on earlier drafts of this chapter. Needless to say, I am responsible for any shortcomings that remain in the text.

1 Homerin, *Study of Islam.*

2 See Mamluk Studies Review 13/2 (2009), *Religion in the Mamluk* Period ed. by Johannes Pahlitzsch and the articles therein by: Thomas, *Idealism*; Hunt, *Christian Arab*; Rustow, *Limits.* Much more has been published on Jews and Christians in the Mamluk period, but a review of this literature will not be carried out here.

3 Pahlitzsch, *Introduction.*

4 For now, see Winter, *Muḥhammad ibn Makkī.*

on religion in the Mamluk period. The above mentioned article by Emil Homerin offers an excellent starting point. Rather, I would like to focus on a few problematic topics which have so far received little attention in contemporary scholarship. This is probably due to their complexity, their scarce appeal to historians and the nature of the sources. I am referring to what I perceive to be a missing link between theological production and its potential social and political significance, between theologians and society at large, between ideas about God and their relevance to people's lives. But before dealing with this, it is necessary to point out briefly what are the main theoretical and methodological complexities that scholars are called at facing when dealing with the category of "religion".

Defining the Problem

One can begin with a pragmatic observation: most of the topics presented in this volume involve, or can involve, a "religious" dimension where by "religious" is here broadly meant those cultural attitudes which claim to have a connection with the divine. Thus, Sufism and Law, minorities, which are most often defined in religious terms (Christians, Jews, Shiʿis…), political power, which was always conceptualized religiously, all of these various fields of inquiry have something to do with "religion" as a system of cultural symbols.[5] This is indicative of the ubiquitous outreach of religion in medieval Middle Eastern societies. This very ubiquity, combined with the vagueness and imprecision of the concept, is a feature that makes "religion" per se as a complex object of inquiry.

Historically speaking, the idea that "religion was everywhere" implies that if we ever wanted to draw an overview of religious beliefs and practices in the Mamluk period we would have to map and define this "everywhere" (let's take it in its simplest geographical meaning: the city, the countryside, which city, and perhaps which spaces in the city, and which in the countryside and so on); then we will have to look deeply into these *milieux* and locate the "whos", the "actors"; humans and non-humans, materials (coins, buildings, books etc …) that contributed to the construction of "a religious identity" in that particular space, context and time. We will also have to decide which aspect of "religion" we would like to analyze: doctrine and theology? Rituals and practice? Individual or

5 In the new edition of the *Cambridge History of Egypt*, volume 1: *Islamic Egypt*, 640 – 1517 edited by Carl F. Petry, Cambridge: Cambridge University Press, 1998, Islam/Muslims are subsumed under the broader categories of "culture" and "society" (see, Berkey, *Culture and Society*), while Jews and Christians fall into another theoretical frame as they are treated in separate chapters devoted to non-Muslims (Wilfong, *Non-Muslim communities: Christian Communities* and Stilmann, *Non-Muslim communities: Jewish community*).

communitarian? And which confession in particulate: Islam, Christianity, Judaism? And so on and so forth ... This way of proceeding carries with itself a huge variety of topics and issues, methodological choices and theoretical trajectories, so one starts wondering if the lack of a comprehensive treatment of religion in this period may be due to the earnestness of its scholars, rather than to their deficiency.[6]

To avoid this evasive character, we could then attempt at providing a definition, for definitions fix borders to the field of inquiry and reflect methodological choices. But even definitions prove risky. As noted years ago by Melford Spiro, on one hand and from a scholarly perspective we can provide a definition of what religion is only at the end of a proper empirical investigation, on the other it is difficult to begin such an investigation without a definition that sets the borders of the inquiry. Scholars are then caught into a vicious circle.[7]

Religion as a cultural system implies a very high variety of expressions: its peculiarity resides into the gap between what a religion is as a cultural system (namely a human product socially, historically and culturally tied to specific historical circumstances) and what it claims to be (that is, the founding element of a given culture). This founding element is represented as something, or somebody that transcends the human dimension. The variety of religious expressions corresponds to the complexity and multiplicity of human experience. This is what makes it extremely hard to provide a definition of religion capable of accounting for this multiplicity.[8]

A discussion of all the scholarly attempts made at giving definitions of religion is beyond the scope of this paper, but it is important to be aware of the difficulties that this notion entails.[9] By embracing a historical approach, religion will be here considered as that human experience in which a changing and ever negotiable relationship takes place among three elements: a doctrinal/theological dimension implying a set of beliefs and doctrines, a practical dimension of faith implying a set of ritual and practices, and a social basis for beliefs and practices. This is not to say that these three elements are always there, or that they exhaust the essence of a religious phenomenon, but that historically they have usually been there according to a variety of combinations.[10]

6 See Homerin, *Study of Islam*, 1–2.
7 Spiro, *Religion*.
8 For a sound theoretical discussion of these issues, see Filoramo, *Che cos'è la religione*, 75–115.
9 See Fitzgerald, *Critique*, 91–110.
10 Filoramo, *Che cos'è la religione*, 84–88.

Overcoming Generalization: a refinement in the field

In the last fifty years, scholarship on religion under the Mamluks, more specifically scholarship on Islam, has achieved a good degree of refinement, most of all in trying to overcome excessive simplifications and generalizations.[11] The great variety and diversity of religious expressions, beliefs and practices according to different contexts, historical and social *milieu* is now being constantly underlined; the well-rooted dichotomy between popular and élite religion has been blurred, and so that between Sufis, on the one hand, and *ʿulamāʾ*, on the other. The former have been for long the claimed representatives of a stereotyped low/popular/heterodox form of religiosity; the latter, on the contrary, of a high/genuine/orthodox/ religiosity. This is a two tiered-model which is today no longer tenable.[12] The genesis and fuelling of these polarities was multiple. One can see at play a Eurocentric way of carrying out research on Islamic societies; a certain type of social anthropology that dramatized the gap between vulgar and lettered religion; and finally a scarcely critical use of literary sources reflecting merely the perspectives of *ʿulamāʾ*, some of whom actually did attempt to produce an "orthodox" discourse, where orthodoxy should be intended as a claim for right, genuine, unified belief, or set of beliefs, conceived for being one and dominant.[13]

Attention is being paid to different regions (Syria, Palestine, Hijaz and Egypt), to urban and rural contexts – the latter is especially true for Sufism[14] – and to minor centers as well,[15] although Damascus and, above all, Cairo still enjoy the lion's share.[16] In addition, the picture of the Mamluks as an elite disinterested in spiritual matters has been persuasively questioned.[17] In this regard, the engagement of the Mamluks with their adopted religion, Islam, has been examined as that of one of the many social groups that composed Mamluk society, although obviously a most powerful and visible one. In particular, as far as the elites are concerned, some topics have attracted a good deal of attention. Among these are

11 The bibliographical references of the following notes are by no means exhaustive. They are meant to provide an overview of the most widespread scholarly output on the mentioned topics.

12 On popular culture and religion in the Mamluk period see the classic Boaz, *Popular Culture*; Berkey, *Popular Preaching*; the review article by Berkey, *Popular Culture*, 133–146 and the related chapter in this book by Thomas Herzog.

13 See Knysh, *Orthodoxy.*

14 See for instance, Mayeur-Jaouen, *Compagnons*, and idem, *Maîtres*, 41–50; Gril, *Saint des villes.*

15 Garcin, *Centre musulman.*

16 Particularly focused on religious life in 13th century Damascus is Pouzet, *Damas au VIIe/XIIIe siècle.*

17 See Little, *Religion*; Haarman, *Arabic in Speech*; Berkey, *Silver Threads*; idem, *Transmission of Knowledge* and idem, *Mamluks as Muslims.*

the interaction between Mamluks and *ʿulamāʾ* as the ultimate source of normative Islam and legitimacy, and their complex dynamics of mutual dependence.[18] The urban dynamics of transmission of knowledge and religious education, both within the elite and outside it, stand at the centre of the seminal works by Jonathan Berkey for Cairo and Michael Chamberlain for Damascus.[19] The latter has the merit of having radically improved our way of reading and understanding the social significance of biographical dictionaries. Important research has been conducted on Mamluk religious policies by ways of royal patronage, public display of faith, such as monumental architecture, and *awqāf* policies; *awqāf* being a form of charity and an essential source for religious infrastructures.[20] Sufism is a field of research that continues to attract a lot of attention[21] and, finally, while the elite (*aʿyān* and *ʿumarāʾ*) have been for some decades the unchallenged protagonists of scholarship on social, cultural and religious life in the Mamluk period, recently more and more consideration is being given to ordinary people, to their lives, religious practices and beliefs, to the religious meaning of their social actions.[22] For instance, Konrad Hirschler's last book explores reading practices in Syria and Egypt in the so called Middle Period. In particular, it considers the reading activities in which non-elite groups were involved, a process which went hand-in-hand with a broader participation of these groups in the production of texts.[23] Notwithstanding the fact the acquiring and transmitting (religious) knowledge was a moral duty and a pious act itself, many of the texts in whose reading people participated were of a religious nature: Quran, *ḥadīth*, *sīrah* overall. Finally, one can mention the centrality of death in people's daily life. Recent studies highlighted the use of specific literacy forms to express emotions of distress and grievances.[24]

---

18 Lapidus, *Mulism Cities*, especially 130–142. For a critical discussion on literature on this topic produced up to the 1990s, see Humphreys, *Islamic History*, 201–208 and Yaacov Lev's recent article *Symbiotic Relations.*

19 Berkey, *Transmission of Knowledge*, and idem, *Popular Preaching.*

20 On waqfs, Amīn, *al-Awqāf wa'l-ḥayāt.* On madrasas found by Mamluks, see Berkey, *Transmission of Knowledge*, 142 ff.; on monumental architecture endorsed by the elite, Humphreys, *Expressive Intent*; Behrens-Abouseif, *Change in Function*; on *khanqas*, Alden, *Khanqah of Siryāqūs* and Fernandes, *Sufi Institution.* On Mamluk religious policies, see Berkey, *Mamluk Religious Policy.*

21 See, for instance, Geoffroy, *Le soufisme*; the more recent McGregor, Sabra, *Développement du soufisme.* For a thorough review of literature on Sufism in the Mamluk period, the chapter by Emil Homerin in this volume.

22 A good example of this type of literature is Sabra, *Poverty and Charity.*

23 Two processes Hirschler respectively refers to as "popularization" and "textualization", see Hirschler, *Written Word.*

24 Most important, Bauer, *Communication and Emotion.* For a review of literature on death, see Homerin, *Study of Islam*, 9–11.

Theology, Politics, Society: the missing link

What said up to now highlights that a good amount of sound scholarly work has been dedicated to the social history of the Mamluk period in which religious (Islamic) discourse either as an ideology, or more simpler as a source of individual and communal identity, political power, or juridical legitimacy, always plays an important role.[25] Less attention has been dedicated to doctrinal debates, and more specifically to the production of theological works in the Mamluk period. Throughout this paper, by theology I will mean all intellectual discourses about God, and not only discourses about God in the form of *kalām*.[26] When required by the context, I will specify which type of theological discourse to which I am referring. I will use the term *uṣūl al-dīn* to point to matters of theological nature at large.[27]

For the Mamluk period we lack a comprehensive and reliable overview of which books were mostly studied; what were the most widespread theological themes of discussions; to what extent *kalām* was taught in *madrasahs*, as it seems to have been in the Ayyubid period;[28] and which intellectual solutions were provided for the various debated matters. The impression that manuals and modern histories of Islamic theology convey is that theological production after al-Ghāzālī and Fakhr al-Dīn al-Rāzī was marginal, hence not worth of being considered. Accordingly, a great deal of attention has been dedicated to Muʿtazilī *kalām* and Ashʿarī rationalist theology up to the early 13th century, to the exclusion of what comes afterwards, both in the form of *kalām* and not. Quranic commentaries from the Mamlūk period is another field that has been neglected by religious historians and experts in Islamic theology.[29]

An initial crucial step should be that of mapping the mainstream theological trends of this period against which marginal developments can be fully understood. An interesting window was opened by Louis Pouzet in his rich book on religious life and structures in Damascus during the 13th century. In the initial chapter, Pouzet traces the profile of the most important Shāfiʿī experts in *uṣūl al-fiqh* of the 13th century who turned out to be influential rationalist scholars as well. Among these prominent personalities some stand out. They are Sayf al-Dīn

25 See, for instance, Rapoport, *Marriage* and the above mentioned Sabra, *Poverty and Charity*.

26 See Winter, *Introduction*, 2–4.

27 For a thoughtful discussion of these terms, Makdisi, *Ashʿarī*, 48–49.

28 Cfr. Talmon-Heller, *Islamic Piety*, 73 for *kalām* being taught in mosques, 236 for *kalām* being taught in *madrasahs*, and Griffel, *Fakhr al-Dīn al-Rāzī*, 341–343. Their conclusions are at odds with Makdisi, *Ashʿarī*, 45–46 and idem, *Rise of Colleges*.

29 An outstanding exception is Walid Saleh's study on Ibn Taymīyah's radical hermeneutics which deals with with Ibn Taymīyah's epistemological agenda in Quranic interpretation, but does not deal with theology proper, although Saleh states that the theological and hermeneutical are paramount in Ibn Taymīyah 's worldview (p. 132). Saleh, *Ibn Taymīyah.*

al-Āmidī (d. 1233), who was not only a specialist in the methodology of *fiqh*, but also a renown physician and a rationalist theologian; Ṣafī al-Dīn al-Hindī (d. 1315 or 1316), from Delhi, who was told to have indirectly (through his maternal grandfather) begun his studies with Faḫr al-Dīn al-Rāzī. He arrived in Damascus only in the second half of the 13th century, was a fervent Ashʿarī and the leading rationalist of the day. He was the teacher of the notorious *mutakallim* Ibn Wakīl (d. 1317), a committed rationalist and a man of power; and last, ʿAbd al-Ḥāmid al-Khusrūshāhī (d. 1254), a scholar of Iranian origins, who had been a direct pupil of Fakhr al-Dīn al-Rāzī. It is worth noting that both al-Āmidī and al-Khusrūshāhī were supported by the Ayyubid princes al-Muʿaẓẓam ʿĪsā (d. 1227) and his son al-Malik al-Nāsir Dāwūd (d. 1258), who offered generous patronage to the rational and philosophical sciences,[30] and that Ṣafī al-Dīn al-Hindī and Ibn Wakīl had been both, and not by chance, directly involved in Ibn Taymīyah's famous 1306 Damascene trials, which were addressed to restrain Ibn Taymīyah's relentless anti-Ashʿarī polemics.[31] In his book, Louis Pouzet looked mainly at historiography and not at doctrine, still he provides a good starting point for further research. While stressing the difficulty of building up a coherent picture of a religious and scholarly trend which he subsumes under the label of "disciplines et courants intellectualistes", and which also includes the above mentioned rationalist theologians, Louis Pouzet underlies how the major point of reference of the Ashʿarī school within 13th century damascene dialectical theology was unquestionably the famous Fakhr al-Dīn al-Rāzī (d. 1210), whose work, despite al-Rāzī never having personally been in Damascus, exerted a deep influence on many of its speculative scholars.[32] When looking at this trend the information that comes to the fore are the following: *fuqahā'* with an expertise in legal methodology (*uṣūl al-fiqh*) were often close to this intellectualizing trend; the *madhhab* who hosted speculative theologians was usually Shāfiʿī, Ashʿarism being their dominant school, as seen; notwithstanding some exceptionally violent episodes, according to Pouzet the intellectual activity of these scholars who

30 Cfr. Pouzet, *Damas au VIIe/XIIIe siècle*, 36 – 39, 201 – 204. For the Ayyubids' attitudes towards speculative sciences and their scholarly representatives, see Talmon-Heller, *Islamic Piety*, 233 – 239; Griffel, *Fakhr al-Dīn al-Rāzī*, 341 – 43; on al-Āmidī's life, read Endress, *Dreifache Ancilla*, 116 – 45 (not seen, quoted in Griffel, *Fakhr al-Dīn al-Rāzī*, 342, fn. 105).

31 In this regard, and for a profile of Ibn Wakīl, see Bori, *Ibn Taymīyah*, 148 – 150. For a short biography of Ibn Wakīl and Ṣafī al-Dīn al-Hindī, see also Jackson, *Ibn Taymiyya on Trial*, 46 – 47. Little of these two scholars has been so far edited. To my knowledge no research has been carried out on their theological input, at least in Western languages. A text by Ibn Wakīl which has gone so far unnoticed is his public dispute with Ibn Taymīyah on "praise and gratitude" (*al-shukr wa'l-ḥamd)* which is recorded by Ibn ʿAbd al-Hādī (d. 1343) in ʿAbd al-Hādī, *Al-ʿUqūd*, 95 – 116 and may reveal interesting details on the conflict-ridden relationship between the two and theological climate of the day.

32 Pouzet, *Damas au VIIe/XIIIe siècle*, 202; Griffel, *Fakhr al-Dīn al-Rāzī*, 339, 341.

leaned towards the philosophical and rational sciences was usually well received by the civil and religious arena; many of these scholars were foreigners coming from the East (of Iranian origins); some of them are described as being of Shiʿi leaning.[33] Ideally, Pouzet's methodology could be followed up including the 14th and 15th centuries and an examination of doctrinal debates. The spectrum of sources in terms of typology, time and geography may be widened in order to carry out a sociology of speculative scholars of the Mamlūk period, which very likely will also lead us to the so far neglected world of Shiʿism, and, next to it, to that of religious sectarianism and to the religious life of the minor centers of the Mamluk Sultanate.[34]

In 14th Damascus, the leading Ashʿarīs were represented by the powerful al-Subkī family, in particular al-Subkī senior (Tāqī al-Dīn d. 1355) who had been Shāfiʿī Chief Judge for a long time and a fierce opponent of Ibn Taymīyah and Ibn Qayyim al-Jawzīyah, and his son (Tāj al-Dīn, d. 1370).[35] The former was a legal scholar rather than a *mutakallim*, but still he was a convinced partisan of the Ashʿarī school. The latter was the author of the massive *al-Ṭabaqāt al-Shāfiʿīyah* which – George Makdisi masterly demonstrated many years ago – advanced a strenuous defense of *kalām* as the necessary epistemological tool to the divine and a monumental pro-Ashʿarī propaganda enterprise nicely disguised as a history of the Sḥāfiʿīs.[36] The contribution of the Subkīs to the evolution of 14th century damascene Ashʿarī *kalām* in terms of contents remains to be assessed. For the moment, it is their nervous and partisan affiliation to Ashʿarism that stands out; this partisanship was no doubt also a response to the threat posed by important contemporary traditionalist scholars like al-Dhahabī (d. 1348) and al-Mizzī (d. 1341), and by the vehement polemics of Ibn Taymīyah and Ibn Qayyim

33 Pouzet, *Damas au VIIe/XIIIe siècle*, 199 – 205. On Shiʿī theology from this period: Schmidtke, *Al-ʿAllāma al-Ḥillī*. The Research Intellectual Unity of the Islamicate World based in Freie Universität, Berlin, and directed by Sabine Schmidtke promises to explore, among various trajectories, the development of philosophy and science in the Eastern Lands of Islam (13th to 16th c. CE) and to reconstruct not only the intellectual-philosophical heritage of this period, but also the social setting of the relevant scholars and networks of scholars.

34 Nagel, *Islamic Theology*, 178 – 184, 206 – 213 provides a short description of the intellectual history of the late middle period. Judith Pfeiffer in Oxford is currently leading a five-year research project exploring the history of Islamic philosophy and theology from the 13th to 16th in the Nile-to-Oxus regions, which will hopefully help fill the gap. On a private basis, I was told that a group of Moroccan scholars is preparing publications of late Ashʿāri *kalām* works and that Heidrun Eichner started working on Ashʿarī theology of the Mamluk period.

35 For a rapid description of Tāqī al-Dīn al-Subkī works against Ibn Taymīyah and Ibn al-Qayyim, see Bori, *Ibn Taymīyah*, 155 – 169 and the introduction to Bori-Holtzman, *Scholar in the Shadow*, 20 – 24. Livnat Holtzman is preparing an article on al-Subkī' refutation of Ibn al-Qayyim, *al-Kāfiyah al-shāfiyah* entitled: "Tashbih, Hashwīyah and Takfīr: Taqī al-Din al-Subkī's Counterattack on the Later Hanbalis".

36 Makdisi, *Ashʿarī*, 57 – 80, especially 60 – 64 on the legitimacy of *kalām*.

al-Jawzīyah. As in previous period of Islamic history, theological affiliation had something to do with social and scholarly identity, with scholarly authority and prestige.

This brief overview highlights that some preliminary work in the social history of speculative theology and philosophical Ashʿarism in the late Ayyubid and early Mamluk periods (13th and first decades of 14th century) has been done on Damascus, yet we still lack a more precise idea of its doctrinal history and of what was going on in Cairo and in minor towns like Aleppo, for instance, which was an important window to the Eastern Islamic world. The later Mamluk period (second half of 14th to early 16th century) also deserves to be investigated together with any changes that this specific time lap may carry with itself. It is against the background here illustrated that any historical and doctrinal exploration of the main theological trends of the Mamluk period should move.

As far as non-kalamic theological production is concerned, recent research on the two famous Ḥanbalī scholars of the Baḥrī period, Ibn Taymīyah (m. 1328) and his pupil Ibn Qayyim al-Jawzīyah (m. 1351), has examined their theological input very seriously.[37] Yet, in this scholarship a big distance between theology, on one hand, and history/society on the other is observable. To some extent, Alexander Knysch's observation that in the Mamluk period the *ʿulamāʾ* have been studied more "in terms of their social power than with an interest in their doctrines", still proves valuable, although since then things have improved.[38]

This short review on research on theology in the (overall early) Mamluk period is functional to the central issue of the paper: the relationship between theological production and society. With regard to the necessity of exploring the positive or negative connections between theology, in its various forms, and the lives of ordinary people, some premises can be set. If we, as religious, social and intellectual historians, intend to study human expressions from a cultural and anthropological perspective,[39] one would assume that the way men conceived of God, the way they talked about Him, how they envisioned God relating to man, would also be an object of historical inquiry. There is usually little concern from the part of scholars doing intellectual history to reflect on the social or political significance that certain ideas about God may generate, or in investigating how theological beliefs were received also by the non-elite groups and if and to what

37 Michot, *Ibn Taymīyah*, presents the English translations of sixteen texts which had been previously translated and annotated by Michot in French, many of these texts deal with theological matters; Rapoport, Shahab, *Ibn Taymiyya* (see the chapters by Hoover, Ozervarli, el Omari, Holtzman); Bori, Holtzman, *Scholar in the Shadow* (see the chapters by Hoover, Qadhi, Belhaj, Anjum, Langermann, Gobillot). Hoover, *Ibn Taymiyya's Theodicy.* More references in: Hoover, *Ibn Taymiyya.*

38 Knysh, *Ibn ʿArabi*, 3.

39 See, Conermann, *Quo vadis Mamlukology?*

extent belief mattered to them.[40] The first cause that accounts for this situation is surely to be located in the difficulties posed by the sources. Doctrinal literature is usually not interested in telling us how beliefs were received by ordinary people, if they were received at all, and eventually in what forms. Moreover, theological doctrine, especially in the form of *kalām*, was especially designed for specialists to the exclusion of the non scholarly elite. A number of other sources should then be considered (chronicles, biographical dictionaries, list of books studied in madrasas, old library catalogues, manuscripts, history of religious institutions, *waqfīyāt*, anthologies, *fatwas*, poetry, sermons …) with which the ordinary scholar on Islamic theology, typically trained in philology and in the Greek philosophical tradition, may not be familiar, may not know how to read creatively or, more simply, in which he may not be interested. Similarly, and standing opposite on the other side, the historian is usually not properly trained to grasp the doctrinal meaning of complex intellectual debates or may feel a certain discomfort in embarking upon highly abstract literature on the divine. Yet, this disciplinary divide between social historians and experts in Islamic theology may not always prove helpful when exploring the place of theology in Mamlūk society. In his articles on the Ashʿarīs, George Makdisi skillfully demonstrated that a strong pro-Ashʿarī propaganda was voiced by Tāj al-Dīn al-Subkī in his *ṭabaqāt* and not in a classical theological compendium, for instance. Theology could be given voice in many different literary genres, it has been observed.[41] Some are "conventional", so to say: manuals, treatises, commentaries, glosses … and designed for the students or the experts' consumption, some are less "conventional" (anthologies, poetry, *ṭabaqāt*, *fatāwā* …) and were not always and uniquely intended for the scholarly elite. Recent research on Mamluk literature reveals a highly dynamic and vital literary world characterized, among various features, by "the blurring of boundaries between popular and educated

40 Notable exceptions are George Makdisi and the monumental work by Van Ess, *Theologie und Gesellschaft* which does not go as far as the Mamluk period though. See also Van Ess, *Flowering of Muslim Theology*, especially the introduction and chapter 4: "Theology and Human Reality: Historical Images and Political Ideas", 117–151. An attempt to reflect on this topic is el-Shamsy, *Social Construction*, 97–117, 110–113 in particular. Also Tilman Nagel makes an effort of historical contextualization, see Nagel, *Islamic Theology*, 93–100, 125–128. In pp. 241–251 he explores the relationship between Sunni and Shiʿī orthodoxy and the Islamic state admitting that: "We still lack a history of the relationship between Islamic rule and Islamic Orthodoxy" (p. 241).

41 Holtzman, *Insult*, opening paragraph. I thank the author for sharing with me prior to publication this and her other articles quoted in this chapter. Hoover, *God Acts*, 55. Hoover remarks the variety of literary genres which hosts Ibn Taymīyah's theological input as a peculiarity of Ibn Taymīyah's own production. This is certainly true. However, one wonders to what extent this tendency to transcend literacy boundaries may also reflect the cultural literary climate which will shortly be mentioned below, in addition to his personal eclectic style.

literature" and an increasing participation of the *ʿulamāʾ* in literary communication with a consequent process of *adabization* of the *ʿulamāʾ* production.[42] These findings somehow call for an interdisciplinary approach that combine social and religious history with literary studies and, at any rate, cannot be neglected when exploring the potential link between theology and society in this specific period of Islamic history.

Hence, it seems reasonable that this intellectual production, be it expressed in conventional or less conventional literary forms, be considered as a living aspect of the religious and social history of this period and that this should be done not only from a merely speculative angle, but also from the point of view of society. The main question is: is it possible to narrow down the current gap between theology and society that affects scholarship on the intellectual history of the Mamluk domains? And if it is not possible, if this gap is beyond remedy, namely if in Mamluk society abstract discourses about God (both in the form of *kalām* or not) were exclusively an academic exercise for few, elaborating highly intricate, speculative and hairsplitting views of the divine with no tie, or meaning, to the real world, would it not be crucial in order to have a more thorough view of the intellectual and social history of that period, to explore both the intellectual and social meaning for the absence of this tie?

Some Examples

In what follows I would like to provide some examples that are meant to show that we do have at least some materials for shedding light on what I have here called "the missing link". I suggest that the exploration of this connection should unfold on three levels. On one hand should stand the search for the ethical, legal and practical effects that determinate understandings of God can exert on people (example n. 1). On the other, some attention should be devolved to the potential political meanings of theological doctrines (example n. 2). And, finally, the exploration of ordinary people's attitudes to theology and belief, and how these were conveyed to them should also be an object of inquiry (example n. 3, and last paragraph). Beyond these, there may be of course other dimensions to investigate that have here remained unexplored.

The examples presented below are all taken from the life and doctrine of the famous Ḥanbalī scholar Taqī al-Dīn Aḥmad b. Taymīyah (d. 1328). Various reasons stand behind this choice. Ibn Taymīyah is far from representing the

42 Bauer, *Mamluk Literature*, in particular 108 – 111 (see page, 110, fn. 8 for further references), 130. Hirschler, *Written Word*, last chapter in particular and Holtzman, *Insult*, for Ibn Qayyim al-Jawzīyah's *al-Kāfiyah al-shāfiyah* as an example of this religious and literary climate.

mainstream theological trend of his day.[43] Yet, Ibn Taymīyah's antagonist talent, which took shape both through his activism and in his vibrant intellectual production, implies that his own theological discourse is predominantly articulated in the form of polemics. These polemics, in turn, shed light on the non-Taymīyan mainstream theology that he addressed. Thus, they shed light on the intellectual and historical environment of that historical moment. In addition, the example of Ibn Taymīyah is important here because it represents a constructive illustration that the boundaries between intellectual production and society at large were more fluid that modern scholarship has so far indicated. It may well be that Ibn Taymīyah, and with him also his pupil Ibn Qayyim al-Jawzīyah, were unique cases of theologians preoccupied to create a tangible link between their own theological beliefs and society (overcoming such a gap was in fact on both scholars' agenda), but until further research on the development on theology in Mamluk period and its reception in scholarly circles, as well as in society at large, is undertaken we will not know.

The last paragraph of this chapter goes beyond Ibn Taymīyah and embraces a broader look. It shows that, despite the *ʿulamāʾ's* concern for not letting the *ʿāmmah* access their elaborate discussions on God, also ordinary people took an interest in belief and that theological questions mattered to them as well. Thinking right about God helped acting rightly, and acting rightly was the principal source of salvation; thinking right about God provided a powerful way of making sense of life and its hardship. It was, in sum, a crucial ingredient for being a pious and good Muslim. What is meant by the *ʿāmmah* is a question that must be posed. Just as the *ʿulamāʾ* were far from being a homogeneous and uniform social group, the *ʿāmmah* was not as well.[44] In the course of this paper it will appear clear that the *ʿāmmah* were not exclusively the unlettered and uncultivated commoners, but also the non-specialist whom at times I simply called the "non-(scholarly) elite", meaning those who did not received a specific training in the sciences of *uṣūl al-dīn*, traditionalist theology or *kalām*, but still showed an interest to theological matters at large.

First Example

Jon Hoover's book on Ibn Taymīyah's ideas on theodicy shows an in depth analysis of Ibn Taymīyah's theological discourse on God's justice. Hoover's definition of Ibn Taymīyah theology as jurisprudential is penetrating. It implies that for Ibn Taymīyah *fiqh* is inclusive of theology and that Ibn Taymīyah's

43 See, Özervarli, *Qur'ānic Rational Theology*, especially 78 – 80 and el-Omari, *Ibn Taymiyya*.
44 Berkey, *Culture and Society*, 403 – 404, 409 – 411; Leder, *Postklassisch*, 289 – 312.

scholarship is to be seen as jurisprudential even when he is deeply preoccupied with specific theological questions.[45]

It may then be useful to remember Ibn Taymīyah's famous opposition to the practice of *ziyārat al-qubūr*, because of which he was last imprisoned in 1326. In the *ziyārah* debate, Ibn Taymīyah argues his views in legal terms, but the point behind the legal dispute is theological. At the centre of Ibn Taymīyah's argument about the practice of *ziyārah* is the safeguard of a direct and unmediated worship of God and the exclusivity of man's worship that must be for God alone.[46] The visitation of graves was connected to the Islamic cult of Saints, which was widely spread across every layer of society of the Zangid, Ayyubid and Mamluk periods. Joseph Meri has argued that the reasons for the formation of the cult of Saints were social and spiritual, while Richard McGregor and Daniella Talmon-Heller upheld that the formulation of the doctrines of sainthood (*walāyah*) also played an influence on the practice of *ziyārah*.[47] The cult of Saints implied recognizing the existence of God's Friends (*awliyā'*), accepting the validity of their *barakah* and believing in their superior powers as expressed in their "wondrous acts" (*karāmāt*). It is due to these faculties and to their proximity to God that visiting the graves of these outstandingly righteous people was perceived as a beneficial act, one that made the believer closer to God and that offered him the possibility of asking them for intercession. The recognition of *awliyā'* was a transversal phenomenon in Ayyubid and Mamluk societies, it was shared by the *'āmmah*, the rulers and the scholarly elite, it was widely spread within and without Ṣufī circles. The traditionalist Ḥanbalīs Ibn Qudāmah (d. 1223) and his colleague 'Abd al-Ghanī al-Maqdisī (d. 1203) acknowledged the existence of the *awliyā'* and their stature,[48] and so did Ibn Taymīyah in his *'Aqīdah al-wāsiṭīyah*[49] and in the long treatise entitled *The Criterion to discriminate between the Friends of the All Merciful and the Friends of Satan* (*al-Furqān bayna Awliyā' al-Raḥmān wa-Awliyā' al-Shayṭān*) where, as the title suggests, Ibn Taymīyah is preoccupied with defining the status and the identity of the true "Friends of God" and not with denying their existence.[50] It is the plea for mediation and intercession that was the object of Ibn Taymīyah's worries, together with the belief in the supe-

45 Hoover, *Ibn Taymiyya's Theodicy*, 18–69.

46 Rapoport, *Ibn Taymiyya's radical legal thought*, 210. On Ibn Taymīyah and *ziyārah:* Olesen, *Culte des saints*; Taylor, *Vicinity of the Righteous*, 168–194 and Meri, *Cult of Saints*, 130–138.

47 Meri, *Cult of Saints*, 70–71; Talmon-Heller, *Islamic Piety*, 207; Richard McGregor H-NET online book review of Joseph Meri.

48 See Talmon-Heller, *Islamic Piety*, 223–224.

49 Ibn Taymīyah, *La profession*, 82–83 (French translation) and 25 (Arabic text).

50 Ibn Taymīyah, *Al-Furqān*, 156–310. For a recent description and analysis of this work, see Sarrio, *Spiritual Anti-Elitism*, 275–291.

riority of the *awliyā'* to the Prophets and in the blind acceptance of their inspiration.[51]

This is not the place for delving at length on a topic, that of *ziyārah* and the cult of Saints, which has received abundant attention in secondary literature, what matters here is that Ibn Taymīyah's theoretical foundation for the legal prohibition of visiting the graves of the righteous is theological. It rests on the concepts of *tawḥīd al-ulūhīyah* and *tawḥīd al-rubūbīyah*, which consist of acknowledging that God is the only Creator and Lord of the world, and that divinity belongs to Him alone. This is a fine case where by means of *fiqh* theological doctrine was carried directly into people's life with the aim of correcting a practice that in Ibn Taymīyah's eyes undermined the absolute priority of worshipping God alone.[52]

In this sense, Ibn Taymīyah, as well Ibn Qayyim al-Jawzīyah, constitute a privileged ground for inquiry as already mentioned. In fact, for Ibn Taymīyah practice and theological principles are so closely intertwined that he tends to blur the distinction between the two. A famous statement of his goes: "Theological questions based on reports (*al-masā'il al-khabarīyah*) can be equivalent to practical questions (*al-masā'il al-ʿamalīyah*). Even though they have been called 'questions of principles' (*masā'il al-uṣūl*) and questions of branches' (*masā'il al-furūʿ*) this denomination was made up; a group of jurists and the *mutakallimūn* created this division which is now prevailingly used by *kalām* and *uṣūlī* theologians".[53]

Additionally, one may also want to mention a rather original treatise by Ibn al-Qayyim al-Jawzīyah titled *Tuḥfat al-mawdūd fī aḥkām al-mawlūd.* It is a handbook on the care of babies and infants, where chapters one to sixteen deal with practical issues: childrearing, how to name children, announcing a pregnancy and so on, while chapter seventeen elaborates on theological issues such as eschatology and predetermination. Ibn al-Qayyim is here clearly attempting to create a connection between everyday life and theological beliefs.[54] This

51 On this last point, see Ibn Taymīyah, *Al-Furqān*, 211 – 218. Ibn Taymīyah does not reject that some people are effectively inspired (*mulham, muḥaddaṯ, muḥāṭab*) – ʿUmar b. al-Khaṭṭāb being the most outstanding example of this – but he affirms that these people are not protected from error (*maʿṣūm*). It follows that there should be no blind acceptance of what they say. Especially, their "inspirations" should always be checked against the Quran and the Sunnah. If they do not comply with these sources, they should be rejected. On the possibility of accepting *ilhām* as a valid legal proof, read Michot, *Textes spirituels IX.*

52 The fact that the issue of *ziyārah* is also recalled right in the middle of a narrowly theological treatise on voluntary attributes confirms this impression. See, Hoover, *God Acts*, 71 – 73.

53 Ibn Taymīyah, *Majmūʿat Fatāwā*, 6:56. The passage is translated and discussed in Rahman, *Islamic Fundamentalism*, 142 – 144; al-Matroudi, *Ḥanbalī School*, 69 – 72; Hoover, *Ibn Taymīyah's Theodicy*, 24 – 25.

54 These and other pragmatic aspects of Ibn Qayyim al-Jawzīyah's theology are the subject of a

feature can be noticed in other writings of Ibn al-Qayyim. For instance, Irmeli Pehro who studied the genre of the so called "Prophetic medicine" observes the extent to which, when compared to any other earlier book of the genre, *al-Ṭibb al-nabawī* by Ibn al-Qayyim displays an exceptional interest in juxtaposing theological doctrines with medical theory.[55]

Second Example (and an open question)[56]

If we look closely at Ibn Taymīyah's letters from his Cairo prison, we will notice something interesting. Ibn Taymīyah sounds deeply discomforted. He insists on his loyalty to the Mamluk authorities, but keeps mentioning a connection between his case and the highest political authority (he mentions a rather mysterious *amr al-malik* or a *tuhmat al-malik*).[57] The Sultan al-Malik al-Nāṣir (d. 1341) was then very young. He was surrounded by two mentors. One was the *ustādhdār* Baybars al-Jashnakīr (d. 1310) that shortly afterwards will usurp al-Malik al-Nāṣir's throne. The sources tell us that Baybars was closely associated with the *shaykh* Naṣr al-Manbijī (d. 1319), a fervent supporter of Ibn ʿArabī and a very powerful man to which Ibn Taymīyah had written a polemical letter a few years before (in 1304).[58] One Egyptian historian, Ibn Dāwādārī (d. after 1331–1332), clearly states that Ibn Taymīyah's troubles began when he started criticizing the *Fuṣus al-ḥikam* of Ibn ʿArabī.[59] ʿAbd Allāh ibn Taymīyah, one of Taqī al-Dīn brothers, in a letter to their third brother, Zayn al-Dīn describing the trials,

---

research project currently carried out by Livnat Holtzman that will hopefully shed some light on what has here been called "the missing link". Livnat Holtzman and Birgit Krawietz are also carrying out a GIF-funded project entitled "Patterns of Argumentation and Rhetorical Devices in the Legal and Theological Works of Ibn Qayyim al-Jawzīyah" which explores the reflection of political and social issues in the writings of Ibn al-Qayyim.

55 Perho, *Al-Ǧawzīyah's contribution*, 194.

56 This example is formulated as an open question. I lacked the means and the time to develop the hypothetical connection between immanency and political power as I would have liked. Yet, the example is in the chapter because it gives an idea of what I mean by the potential political function of theology.

57 Ibn Taymīyah, *Majmūʿat Fatāwā*, 3:237, 259.

58 Ibn Taymīyah, *Majmūʿat Fatāwā*, 2: 452–479 (*Fī risālatihi ilā al-Naṣr al-Manbijī*). On al-Manbijī and al-Jashnakīr, see Ibn Dāwādārī, *Kanz al-ghurar*, 9:125, 143–144. For a list of sources, see Bori, *Ibn Taymiyya*, 152, n. 55 to which it should be added the recently published edition of the Syrian historian al-Birzālī (d. 1339), see, al-Birzālī, *al-Muqtafī*, 3:303, 306 and al-Ṣafadī, *Aʿyān*, 5:502 (on al-Manbijī); al-Ṣafadī, *Aʿyān*, 2:71–75 (on Baybars). All sources agree that Naṣr al-Manbijī, Baybars and the Mālikī judge Ibn Makhlūf were responsible for summoning Ibn Taymīyah to Egypt and testing his creed there. For a discussion of Ibn Taymīyah's letter to al-Manbijī and the events, see Knysch, *Ibn ʿArabi*, 92–96, and 87–111 for a survey of Ibn Taymīyah's critique to Ibn ʿArabī.

59 Ibn Dāwādārī, *Kanz al-ghurar*, 9:143–145.

affirms that prior to the first court meeting the *'ulamā'* had prepared themselves by studying Ibn 'Arabī's *Fuṣūṣ al-ḥikam* (*wa-qad kānū baḥathū fī tilka l-ayāmi bi-l-fuṣūṣi*).[60] The two statements seem to allude to the same circumstances, in any case both reports tell us that Ibn Taymīyah's critique of Ibn 'Arabī resulted in upsetting to the religious (and perhaps also the political) establishment.

It is plausible that Naṣr al-Manbijī took offense from Ibn Taymīyah's patronizing tone. Furthermore, by questioning his beliefs in Ibn 'Arabī, Ibn Taymīyah was certainly questioning also al-Manbijī's authority and social prestige. Yet, so far no scholar has ever attempted to go further than this. In the history of Islam, religious discourse has always been a legitimizing tool for political discourse and action, but scholarship may well go beyond this. By outlining his idea of divine transcendence may have not Ibn Taymīyah threatened a potential theological claim to political power? In other words, would it make sense to assume that a divine immanency as the monism envisioned by Ibn 'Arabī and his disciples may lend itself to a strong conceptualization of temporal power in theological terms? At the moment these are highly conjectural questions. Further research in this direction, may shed light not only specifically on the reasons why Ibn Taymīyah was tried in those years, but more broadly, on how determinate conceptualizations of the divine can be put at service of temporal interests.

Third Example

In 1306 Ibn Taymīyah was tried in Damascus on the highly academic question of *al-dhāt wa-l-ṣifāt.* His creed was discussed in three sessions and was finally declared to be in conformity with that of the Salaf. In spite of that, shortly afterwards Ibn Taymīyah was summoned to Egypt for yet another trial. The whole episode was silenced by a Sultan's decree, which was dispatched in Damascus after the Egyptian interrogations of Ibn Taymīyah. Ibn Taymīyah's 1306 trials are highly documented. We possess both the text of the *fatwā* which – according to one historian at least – created the unrest, and that of the Sultan's decree.[61] We also have Ibn Taymīyah's own memoirs of the court discussion of his creed and some letters from prison where the *shaykh al-islām* expresses his dismay towards what happened to him.[62]

60 Ibn Taymīyah, *Majmū'at Fatāwā*, 3:204.

61 For al-Nuwayrī (d. 1332), see, al-Nuwayrī, *Nihāyat*, 32:99–107 and for Ibn Dawādārī (d. 1335), see, Ibn Dawādārī, *Kanz al-ghurar*, 9:139–142.

62 Ibn 'Abd al-Hādī, *'Uqūd*, 206–248 and Ibn Taymīyah, *Majmū'at Fatāwā*, 3:163–190, translated by Jackson, *Ibn Taymiyya on Trial*, 41–85; the letters: *Majmū'at Fatāwā*, 3:211–77 of which some excerpts have been translated by Yahya Michot in: *Textes Spirituelles X*.

Belief is unquestionably at the centre of these events, yet it has been dismissed by historians as a device, namely as a ground which could be easily "twisted and distorted", or – in other words – as "the easiest means for indicting Ibn Taymīyah in court".[63] Ibn Taymīyah had been tested on his *'Aqīdah al-Ḥamāwīyah* already in 1298, but ironically enough, then and afterwards his creed was always declared to be in conformity with that of the Salaf. The subject of what follows is not an investigation of Ibn Taymīyah's 1306 – 1307 damascene and cairene trials, yet it is important to remember that both the early and the later *miḥan* (those which took place between the years 1318 and 1326), certainly mirror the power struggles that dominated Ibn Taymīyah's contemporary scholarly scene. In one of my previous works, following Michael Chamberlain perspective,[64] I constantly underlined that Ibn Taymīyah was deeply involved in the local dynamics for the control of teaching posts in Damascus. I also showed how the early trials were initiated by his fellows *'ulamā'* and not by the "central political power". The Mamluk authorities stepped in only when Ibn Taymīya's position openly threatened the public order, the public sphere and their own authority.[65] These conclusions remain valid, but are not exhaustive. What follows enriches this perspective by showing that belief played a prominent role in Ibn Taymīyah's misfortunes.

In presenting and commenting on Ibn Taymīyah's trials, the Egyptian historian al-Nuwayrī includes the fatwa that according to him caused the convocation of Ibn Taymīyah to Egypt after his interrogations in Damascus had successfully been concluded.[66] The text is a rather short and accessible exposition of Ibn Taymīyah's ideas on the Qur'ān and God's attributes. Together with its contents, it is the accessibility of the text in expressing some crucial issues of Islamic theology that is here important to highlight.[67]

63 Little, *Historical and Historiographical*, 321.

64 Chamberlain, *Knowledge*, 167 – 173.

65 Bori, *Ibn Taymiyya*, 136 – 139 (on the starting points of his trials – the pages are summed up in English in the introduction to *A Scholar in the Shadow*, 25) and Bori, *Ibn Taymiyya*, 145 – 146 for Ibn Taymīyah's attempts to control some important teaching positions in Damascus.

66 The *fatwā* has little to do with the *Fuṣūṣ al-Ḥikam* by Ibn 'Arabī. This discrepancy deserves further investigation by historians. Obviously the two Egyptian historians, Ibn Dawādarī and al-Nuwayrī, are giving their own interpretations of the trials. This suggests that there were more factors at work behind Ibn Taymīyah's 1306 – 1307 *miḥan*.

67 Al-Nuwayrī, *Nihāyat*, 32:99 – 107. The same *fatwā*, with some variants, is to be found in Ibn Taymīyah, *Majmū'at Fatāwā*, 12:235 – 245. Thanks to Jon Hoover for pointing to me the similarity between the two texts. The Nuwayrī version is longer and badly edited. The last section of the *fatwā* answering the issues on *istiwā'* and *ta'wīl* is missing from *Majmū'at Fatāwā* (corresponding to the second half of page 106 and page 107 of al-Nuwayrī). Also the description of the *mustaftī* is missing from *Majmū'at Fatāwā*. The *Majmū'at Fatāwā* version ends with the words: *hādhā lafẓ al-jawāb fī al-fityā al-miṣrīyah*. In what follows I abridge and

Al-Nuwayrī tells us that that the *fatwā* was shown to him by a student, a certain ʿAbd al-Raḥmān al-ʿAynūsī, who lived in the Cairene *madrasah* al-Nāṣirīya. One evening of the year 705AH al-Nuwayrī was himself at the Nāsirīyah together with the Mālikī judge Ibn Makhlūf (d. 1318) and the Shāfiʿī judge Ibn ʿAdlān (d. 1348), who also lived and worked in that *madrasah* as a repetitor (*muʿīd*). On that evening the student, who had taken the text directly from Ibn Taymīyah, showed it to the judges and al-Nuwayrī. By doing this, he did not mean to harm Ibn Taymīyah – explains al-Nuwayrī – but only to spread his good reputation. Next, the text of the *fatwā* is reported. In it the questioner asks about what an ordinary man must believe and follow to be a good a Muslim in regard to the Quran and its interpretation. More specifically, do the copies of the Quran (*maṣāḥif*) contain the eternal (*qadīm*) word of God? Or are they just an expression of it and not the word itself? Is this expression created or eternal? And is the word of God made of letters and sound? Or is it an attribute subsisting in Him? Do the words "The Merciful sits on his throne" (Q. 57:4) mean that He sits in reality (*ḥaqīqatan*)? And finally, is reading the Qur'ān according to its apparent meaning (*ʿalā al-ẓāhir*) without recurring to any reinterpretation of it (*ta'wīl*) enough as a belief, together with proclaiming: "I believe in it as it was revealed"? Or do people need to reinterpret the text? The plea is for the clearest and most explicative answer. In fact, the questioner declares to be "a confused man (*rajul mutaḥayyar*), totally ignorant (*lā yaʿrifu shay'an*), asking for an easy answer that can be followed".[68] It does not seem that the person is here being over polite by employing a deferential form of self-diminishment towards Ibn Taymīyah, for Ibn Taymīyah, who keeps well in mind the condition of his *mustaftī* when exposing his answers.

Ibn Taymīyah starts with providing a basic creed made of a list of statements about the Qur'ān which he concludes by saying "This all (*hādhā al-jumlah*) is enough for the Muslim as far as this topic is concerned".[69] Then, he explains that detailed debate of the matters in question has generated division in the community, that he has thoroughly discussed the topic elsewhere, and will offer only an abridged version of that discussion by taking into account the condition of the questioner (*bi-ḥasab ḥāl al-sā'il*).[70] More, he warns that the *ʿāmmah* should be left out from the submerging waters of detailed theological discussion (*al-khawḍ fī al-tafṣīl*) because this detailed knowledge generates disagreement: "It is necessary to order the *ʿāmmah* to hold to the firm statements of the texts (*al-*

paraphrase al-Nuwayrī's version, but will occasionally use the better variants of *Majmūʿat Fatāwā*.

68 Al-Nuwayrī, *Nihāyat*, 32:99.

69 Al-Nuwayrī, *Nihāyat*, 32:100.

70 Al-Nuwayrī, *Nihāyat*, 32:101.

naṣṣ)[71] and the consensus [of the Salaf], and to hold them back from going deep into the details that will cause divergences among them".

Thus, Ibn Taymīyah is here providing a simple creed for an ordinary fellow who was concerned about which correct belief would keep him a good Muslim. In this case, Ibn Taymīyah concedes to provide some details in a simplified form, but in the case of the *ʿāmmah* he suggests that argumentation should be avoided and only reliable statements from the tradition delivered. I will return to this point in the last paragraph of the chapter.

Let us now see how Ibn Taymīyah conveys this simplified theological discussion. As always, he sets himself into a *via media* (*wasaṭ*). On the one hand, he states, those who believe that the ink and sounds of Quran are eternal are wrong. Similarly wrong are those who think that memorizing the Quran is like having God known in one's hearts; that reciting it by the tongues is like having God recited by their tongues and that the written copy of the Quran equals God being written. Things[72] exist according to four different ranks: in concrete realities (*aʿyān*), in minds (*adhhān*), in tongue (*lisān*) and in fingers (*banān*), i.e in writing.[73] Concrete reality finds an expression in knowledge (*ʿilm*), knowledge is expressed by utterance (*lafẓ*) which in turn correlates to writing (*khaṭṭ*). Ibn Taymīyah is here employing these four-fold degrees of existence theory: a factual or actual existence (*ʿaynī*), a mental or intellectual existence (*ʿilmī*), an existence in words (*lafẓī*) and one in writing (*rasm*),[74] as a way of classifying and distinguishing the various material manifestations of the Quran. This is the only part of the *fatwā* where the text gets to some complexity and Ibn Taymīyah's explanation a bit convoluted. His point becomes clearer when he illustrates his stance with the Quranic verses: "Everything they did is in the ancient Scriptures" (*wa-kullun faʿalūhu fī l-zuburi*, Q. 54:52)" and "Indeed, it is mentioned in the ancient Scriptures of former people" (*wa-innahū la-fī zuburi l-awwalīna*, Q. 26:196), This last verse was traditionally brought into play as evidence for the announcement of the Quranic revelation in previous Scriptures. Ibn Taymīyah specifies that these words indeed refer to Muḥammad's prophecy and the future

71 Ibid.: *amr al-ʿāmmah bi-ḥaml ʿalā thābit bi-l-naṣṣ*; Ibn Taymīyah, *Majmūʿat Fatāwā*, 12: 237: *amr al-ʿāmmah bi-l-jumal al-thābitah bi-l-naṣṣ*. The translation follows the *Majmūʿat Fatāwā* variant.

72 Al-Nuwayrī, *Nihāyat*, 32:102 has *aʿyān*; Ibn Taymīyah, *Majmūʿat Fatāwā*, 12:239 has , *mawjūdāt*.

73 Al-Nuwayrī here has *bayān* which does not make much sense, whereas the word *banān*, "fingers, or finger tips", to point to writing (here the Quran) is recurrently used by Ibn Taymīyah in his four-fold classification of existence. Cf. Ibn Taymīyah, *Majmūʿat Fatāwā*, 2:158, 417; 6:62; 12:385 (the references are not exhaustive). An insightful discussion of Ibn Qayyim al-Jawzīyah's use of this classification and its debt to Ibn Ḥazm is to be found in Holtzman, *Elements*.

74 Cf. Ibn Taymīyah, *Majmūʿat Fatāwā*, 2:158.

descent of the Quran, but do not contain the Quran itself which was a prerogative uniquely of the Prophet of Islam. In brief, these verses are the written expression of uttered words that match a certain knowledge. They exemplify the written, uttered and intellectual degrees of existence, but not the factual existence of God's Word (i.e the Quran) in the *Zubur.* It is then absolutely necessary to distinguish between all things being in these Scriptures (as being referred to in them) and the divine Speech itself being in the ancient Scriptures. Accordingly, and here Ibn Taymīyah goes back to his initial point, establishing (*thubūt*) the Quran in people's memory, in their tongues and in the written copies of the text is not like establishing God's essence in them.

On the other hand, those upholding that the written copy of the Quran does not contain God's word, but only the ink and sounds, are equally wrong. The Quran in the *muṣḥaf* is like any other speech on paper. The speech belongs to who pronounces it first, not to who conveys it. Equally, a Prophetic tradition is the Prophet's in meaning and letters even when it is uttered by a traditionist (*muḥaddith*).

In so reasoning, Ibn Taymīyah skillfully keeps together two opposite Islamic theological trends on the nature of God's Speech as in the written copies of the Quran. The first are those who sacralized the temporal manifestation of the Quran by professing that the voice of the reciter and the ink of the copyist are not created (*laysa bi-makhlūq*); elsewhere he calls them *lafẓīyah.*[75] On this point, Ibn Taymīyah is keen on making clear that this was not the position of Aḥmad Ibn Ḥanbal. The second are those who affirmed that the written copy of the Quran is not God's Speech but only the ink and letters which are merely temporal expressions of the Speech. In this regard, Ibn Taymīyah repeats his idea that every degree of existence is characterized by its specific status (*ḥukm*), missing this basic idea equals confusion about the nature of things.

In conclusion of this first section of the discussion, and before embarking upon the second, Ibn Taymīyah provides a useful creedal statement for the questioner that sums up what he has demonstrated: "It is necessary to state that: the Quran is the uncreated word of God; the written Quran is like every written speech. It should not be professed that the ink and paper are uncreated. On the contrary, all ink and paper in the world are created. It is also to be professed that the Quran which is in the *muṣḥaf* is the uncreated word of God and the Quran which Muslim recite is the uncreated word of God".

Whether the Speech of God is made of letters and sounds is the second issue he tackles. Here again, Ibn Taymīyah sets himself right in the middle way between those who affirm and deny this position. Both are wrong. The *mutakallimūn* who affirmed the divine attributes (*al- mutakallimūn al-ṣifātīyah*)

75 For instance in Ibn Taymīyah, *Majmūʿat Fatāwā*, 12:168, 206.

professed that God's Speech is one in meaning, that the Speech is an attribute that resides in Him and that the letters and sounds were created by God and are not part of His word. Other supporters of God's attributes (*muthbitah*) opposed them and considered the Quran to be made only of human letters and sounds. This position is unacceptable. Setting himself on the way of the Salaf (as always), Ibn Taymīyah professes that Quran as the word of God is made of both letters and meaning and not only one of the two, exactly like any other speech which is never made either by only letters or by only meaning. Equally, a man who speaks and is able to articulate sounds (*nāṭiq*) is not only spirit (*rūḥ*), or body, but both of them combined together. God verily speaks with a sound that is not like the sounds of His servants for "There is nothing like God" (Q. 42:11) in essence, attributes and acts. At this point Ibn Taymīyah briefly highlights the theological trends with which he disagrees: *mutafalsifah*, Ṣābi'ah, Jahmīyah, *mutakallimat al-ṣifāt*, but he does not delve into intense polemics, nor in that powerfully detailed argumentation that characterizes most of his writings.

The last issue is that of *istiwā'* that is not to be reinterpreted nor taken according to its apparent meaning, which would imply admitting that God needs a throne and that He is confined in the sky. What God affirmed about himself is to be believed as it is. Belief in *istiwā'* is a duty, but investigating the modality is an innovation. Those who reinterpreted God's sitting (*istawā*) as possessing (*istawlā*), or in any other way, deny that God is above the sky.[76] From here the step to the problem of *ta'wīl* is a short one. Ibn Taymīyah closes his response with a blow to the supporters of *ta'wīl*. Reading the Quran according to its apparent meaning means to read it as the Salaf did (*fī 'urf salaf al-ummah*), without distorting the text and displacing its words. The Quran and the hadith are to be explained in a way that does not contradict the Salaf explanation (*tafsīr*); more, it is to be understood against the background of these authoritative texts.[77]

In the end, and as in previous theological scholarship, Ibn Taymīyah's discussion about God's Speech and the nature of the material copies of the Quran was about God's attributes. This was a classic battleground of Islamic theology, one in which scholars strove to provide an understanding of a most transcendent being, God. That of the nature of God's Speech and of its human expressions (writing, reciting, memorizing …) was a highly theoretical theological issue, but – at the same time – one which also had a direct impact on the believers' life for, after all, the Quran daily accompanied Muslims in many different human forms: chanting voices, amulets, oaths, inscriptions in public buildings and monu-

76 Hoover, *Ibn Taymiyya's Theodicy*, 54 ff. deals with this issue.

77 For Ibn Taymīyah's hermeneutical agenda, see Saleh, *Ibn Taymiyya*, in particular 144–148 for "the best way to interpret the Qur'ān".

ments, or on private tools and domestic objects, as well as in books which tangibly materialized in the ink, writing and paper of its copyists.

In sum, the nature of the Quran in its temporal forms and the preoccupation expressed in this regard to Ibn Taymīyah by the humble *mustaftī* can be taken as an illustrative example of the pragmatic reflections of theology in the society of ordinary people.[78] But there is more to say. Why is this *fatwā* significant to the purpose of this chapter? The *fatwā* presents a short summa of Ibn Taymīyah's own doctrine on the temporal manifestations of God's Speech and of the dominant views on the issue in question. But this is not the main point. The crux of the matter being that this summa is articulated in a clear and simplified way. Ibn Taymīyah elaborated ideas about God that his fellows *'ulamā'* disagreed with: he denied the legitimacy of any *ta'wīl* activity which did not conform to the Salaf, and while fully establishing the reality of God's attributes and engaging with their meaning, he also affirmed their absolute unlikeness to human attributes. Here, he explains his original position on the nature of the *muṣḥaf*, but expressly avoids the highly technical language of *kalām* and of linguistics in general (except for the short passage mentioned above). Ibn Taymīyah 's statement on "authorship" (a *ḥadīth* of the Prophet is the Prophet's even if copied or recited by someone else) and his comparison of the *maṣāḥif* to any other book, whose ink and papers are always created, are a good illustration of this attitude. In other words, in this text Ibn Taymīyah delivered his ideas in an intelligible form to an ordinary fellow, a non-specialist in the field of theology and *kalām*, who was nonetheless aware that there was a problem about the nature of the written and recited Quran. This last observation, in turn, suggests that doctrinal belief mattered to ordinary people, as well.

The *fatwā* here considered also shows that belief did not always take the literary shape of complicated and abstract academic treatises, which could be consumed only by the specialists. Doctrine could find simpler literary venues, such as creeds or short *fatāwā*, which made their consumption possible to the non scholarly elite. It is to this literature that we must turn if we want to explore which theological issues ordinary people were preoccupied with and how these issues were passed on to them. I will return to this point shortly. Before concluding this section, it is worth noting that the Sultan's decree which was sent to Damascus following the Egyptian trials confirms all these impressions. It presents corrects belief as the source of individual salvation and communal stability;[79] it tackles the sensitive issue of the spread of Ibn Taymīyah's ideas and

78 In this regard and for some practical implications of Ibn Ḥazm's distinction between the temporal, created manifestations of the Quran and the Quran as the uncreated word of God, see Holtzman, *Elements*. In her contribution, Holtzman also stresses the straightforward and pragmatic common sense that distinguishes Ibn Ḥazm's argumentation.

79 Al-Nuwayrī, *Nihāyat*, 32:112 and Ibn Dawādārī, *Kanz al-Ghurar*, 9:139–141.

insists on the prohibition of discussing theological matters in the public sphere.[80] Belief, then, mattered to the military elite, as well. Or better: a certain homogenization in beliefs mattered. Maintaining the public order was one of the Sultan's most incumbent duties. Avoiding doctrinal strife was one way of assuring order.

Theology and Ordinary People

So far, some interesting materials for reflection have emerged which can be developed into the following considerations. First, the *'ulamā'* did not like that *kalām* and the principles of religion (*uṣūl al-dīn*) be discussed in the public sphere, especially in front of, with, or even worse, by the *'āmmah*. The idea that ordinary people should be excluded from intricate theological discussion is true for the Mamlūk period, but it is not unique to it. A couple of centuries earlier the Ash'arī al-Ghazālī (d. 1111) wrote his last treatise about restraining the ordinary people from the science of *kalām* (*Iljām al-'Awāmm fī 'Ilm al-Kalām*) where he explores: "how the rationalism of the religious elite can be taught to the ordinary people without causing any damage either to their prospects of redemption in the afterlife or to their obeying the religious law that maintained societal order".[81] The famous Ḥanbalī preacher Ibn al-Jawzī (d. 1201) also embraced an elitist approach to the interpretation of God's corporeal qualifications in his treatise against anthropomorphism where he heavily reproached is Ḥanbalī colleagues for having descended to the level of the masses in their roughly literal understanding of God's attributes.[82]

A good example of this attitude for the Mamlūk period is Tāj al-Dīn al-Subkī, when in his famous *Mu'īd al-Ni'am*, while describing the activities of the *khaṭīb*, the preacher (*wā'iẓ*), the story-teller (*qāṣṣ*) and the *qāri' al-kursī*, warns that the holders of these religious posts should avoid speaking about complicated issues that the common people could not understand. In particular, the story-teller and the *qāri' al-kursī* should avoid talking about *uṣūl al-dīn*, beliefs (*'aqā'id*) and hadith dealing with God's attributes. The duty of both the story-teller and the *qāri' al-kursī* – says al-Subkī – is to recite to the commoners passages of religious literature (prophetic traditions, Quranic verses, reports from the Salaf, *tafsīr*), but while the former does it out of memory and in the streets (sitting or standing), the second reads from books, from a chair, in *madrasahs*, mosques

80 Al-Nuwayrī, *Nihāyat*, 32:112–114.

81 For a description of *Iljām* and its dating, see Griffel, *Al-Ghazālī's Philosophical Theology*, 266–274, especially 266–267 from where the quotation is taken.

82 Swartz, *Medieval Critique*, 121–122. For Ibn al-Jawzī's non-interventionism for the masses, see Hoover, *Ḥanbalī Theology*.

and Sufi convents. And since the *qāriʿal-kursī* reads from books, al-Subkī finds it appropriate also to mention which books are allowed to be read: al-Ġazālī's *Iḥyā' ʿUlūm al-Dīn,* Ibn al-Jawzī's sermons, al-Nawāwī's collection of prayers (*Kitāb al-Adhkār*) and his *Riyāḍ al-Ṣāliḥīn,* al-Subkī's own father (Taqī al-Dīn) legal defense of *ziyārat al-qubūr* and the *Supplications* (*al-Adʿiyah*) of a certain Ibn al-Imām (m. 1344).[83] al-Subkī, and many others with him, is here patently trying to exert some control on the transmission of religious knowledge.[84] In particular, theology, a sensitive and intricate discipline at the same time, is declared to belong to the realm of the experts, namely the religious scholarly elite. Almost two centuries later, Shams al-Dīn b. Ṭulūn (d. 1546) will repropose al-Subkī's view word by word[85] As already seen, even Ibn Taymīyah recommended that excessive details in theological matters for commoners should be avoided. Ironically, Ibn Taymīyah could not restrain himself and judging from his fatwa and his own activism, his attitude to sharing theology with the non-specialists seems to be more lenient than that of his colleagues.[86] Before his 1306 trials, he had already stirred up some disorders twice for discussing God's attributes. Once, in written form, on the occasion of the above mentioned *al-Fatāwā al-Ḥamawīyah* (1298) and the other, in 1291, when on a Friday, in the mosque, he sat on his *kursī* and started talking about *ṣifāt.*[87] Mosques provided an informal setting where elite and non-elite could join in reading or learning sessions. Hence, Ibn Taymīyah was guilty of having thrown into the public sphere a theological debate, and – moreover – a debate that was not well understood by his fellow *ʿulamā'*. His enduring challenge turned out to be particularly annoying to his colleagues. As remarked above, the case of Ibn Taymīyah is quite distinctive: it was part of his own agenda to draw society as a whole closer to his own understanding of God. Of course, practically speaking, such an understanding could be pragmatically enacted through teaching, writing and actively promoting correct worship. Recent research shed light on Ibn Taymīyah's theology of a personal God, a God which interacted with His world and was actively and dynamically involved in time. This God was different from the abstract and rational "creation-principle" of the *mutakallimūn*; a God whose attributes subsisted in His essence, but eternally, and apart from His volition and power.[88]

Yet, Ibn Taymīyah was not the only case of a scholar who got into trouble

83 Al-Subkī, *Muʿīd*, 132 – 134 (the list of books is to be found on page 134). For a description of these religious posts, read Berkey, *Popular Preaching*, 12 – 14.

84 Broadly, on this issue, see Berkey, *Popular Preaching* and idem, *Tradition*, 38 – 65.

85 Ibn Ṭulūn, *Naqd al-Ṭālib*, 158 – 161.

86 On Ibn Taymīyah's little elitism in this regard, see Michot, *Mamlūk Theologian Commentary*, I:171 – 172.

87 Birzālī, *Muqtafī*, 2:227.

88 Hoover, *God Acts*, especially, 56 – 61, 74.

because of openly discussing *ṣifāt*. In Damascus, the traditionist al-Mizzī (d. 1341) was thrown in prison shortly after Ibn Taymīyah's 1306 trials because of reading in the Umayyad mosque on the sensitive issue of God's being on the throne from the chapter against the Jahmīyah of the book *On human actions* (*Afʿāl al-ʿIbād*) by al-Bukhārī.[89] The viceroy al-Afram issued a decree that prohibited that belief (*ʿaqā'id*) be discussed in town. A detail is worth being highlighted though. In those days, al-Mizzī was reading the *Saḥīḥ* al-Buḫārī in the Great Mosque because of the plea for rain (*istisqā'*), it was in one of these sessions dedicated to the *Ṣaḥīḥ* that al-Mizzī switched to the *Kitāb Afʿāl al-ʿIbād*. Communal gatherings for the reading of al-Bukhārī's famous collections of Prophetic traditions was habitually part of the rituals connected to the prayer for rain (*ṣalāt al-istisqā'*) which would be then performed out of town and gathered together the *khāṣṣah* and the *ʿāmmah*, the vice-Roy, the *umarā'* and *ʿulamā'*, women and *dhimmīs* alike.[90] Again, it is the public dimension of al-Mizzī's reading that makes it acutely disturbing, together with the fact – of course – that this happened right afterwards the disorders caused by Ibn Taymīyah's trials.

In 1380 the preacher Zayn al-Dīn b. ʿUmar, who came from Damascus and worked in Cairo, at al-Azhar, was accused of anthropomorphism because of having talked about God's attributes in public. It was in fact the officer in charge of controlling the public sphere, the *muḥtasib*, that dealt with the case.[91] Fortunately, the chief Shāfiʿī judge Ibn Jamāʿah (d. 1388) came to the rescue and got Zayn al-Dīn and his son out of prison.[92]

Some years later, a fine preacher named Ibn Niqāsh (d. 1417), who talked to people, was tested various times. He is said to have ascribed to the Ḥanbalī creed (*iʿtiqād al-ḥanābilah*) in the interpretation of divine attributes.[93] Other cases may emerge from a close reading of chronicles, together with biographical dictionaries.[94] In fact, chronicles often mention cases of *zandaqah*, or of people being imprisoned because of belief, although they do not always provide details.[95]

89 Al-Hādī, *ʿUqūd*, 204 – 205; Ibn Dawādārī, *Kanz al-Ghurar*, 9:134; al-Nuwayrī, *Nihāyat*, 32:109 – 110; Ibn Kathīr, *Bidāyah*, 14:37; Birzālī, *Muqtafī*, 3:302. The *Kitab Afʿāl al-ʿIbād* mentioned by the sources is the abridged title of the [*Kitāb*] *Khalq Afʿāl al-ʿIbād* by al-Buḫārī. Cf. al-Bukhārī, *Khalq Afʿāl*, 1:80. The refutation of the Jahmīyah occupies the initial part of the book (2:6 – 62).

90 See Birzālī, *Muqtafī*, 1:543; 2:274, 390, 424; 4:353

91 Stilt, *Islamic Law*, 81 – 83.

92 Ibn Ḥajar (d. 1449), see, Ibn Ḥajar, *Inbā'*, 1:306; al-Maqrīzī (d. 1442), see al-Maqrīzī, *Kitāb al-sulūk*, 3:370; Ibn Qāḍī Shuhbah (d. 1448), see, Ibn Qādī Shuhbah, *Ta'rīkh*, 1:11.

93 Al-Sakhāwī (d. 1497), see al-Sakhāwi, *Al-Ḍaw'*, 4:170.

94 See also Hirschler, *Written Word*, 68.

95 See, for instance, Birzālī, *Muqtafī*, 1: 479, 481; 2: 277 – 278; 3:271, 282; 4: 216 (a strife between Shāfiʿis and Ḥanbalīs in Ba'albak because of *ʿaqā'id*), 416.

What does this all reveal? Why were al-Subkī and his colleagues so preoccupied about people taking an interest in theological issues? Evidently belief mattered not only to scholars, but also to the non-elite: belief was the source of individual salvation; it provided the individual with a right place in this world as well as in the next, it granted him, or her, a peaceful relationship with God. The abstract and impersonal God such as that envisaged and discussed by rationalist theologians could have hardly responded to these expectations. It was not a God ordinary people could connect to in their prayers, daily hopes or grievances. It was a God that created and pre-determined human actions, a notion that – the scholars feared – may have seriously shaken the authority of *sharīʿah* and its interpreters.[96] The concept of predetermination (*al-qaḍāʾ wa-l-qadar*) was a key tenet of Islamic theological thought, one which addressed not only the highly theoretical dimension of God's attributes, but also that of ethics and human responsibility. As for the temporal manifestation of the Quran, this is then again a topic that shows a direct link between the metaphysical, theological discussion and the practical world of the believers.[97] The *ʿulamāʾ* from the Mamluk period were well aware of the ethical and practical implications of this tenet. The disagreement and disorder the scholars feared from the *ʿāmmah* if they plunged into complex theology had something to do with the fear of losing authority. One can find evidence of this fear in the sources. Taqī al-Dīn al-Subkī dreaded the discredit of the Ashʿarīs that may originate from the circulation of Ibn al-Qayyim's militant ode, *al-Kāfiyah al-Shāfiyah.* He was concerned that if this piece of theological poetry found its way among the commoners, it would have torn the authority of the Doctors of the Law (himself first of all!). He laments: "If the Doctors of the Law and the leaders of the community are described in this way [by Ibn al-Qayyim] how can their opinion be accepted? What can the value of their *fatāwā* be, according to the Muslims? The only thing this man [Ibn al-Qayyim] wants for the commoners is to establish that there is no Muslim but him and his partisans".[98] In a very recent article, Livnat Holtzman draws our attention to a composition in verses (*manẓūmah*) that Ibn Taymīyah wrote to respond to a *dhimmī* who asked him about divine predetermination. The *shaykh al-islām* expressed his fear that belief in sheer determinism would shake the foundations of society.[99] Holtzman writes: "Ibn Taymīyah depicts a horrendous situation, in which acts of murder, highway robbery, corruption of rulers etc. will be dis-

96 I am indebted to Frank Griffel for drawing my attention to these points.

97 Holtzman, *Human Choice*, 162.

98 The passage is translated in the introduction to Bori, Holtzman, *Scholar in the Shadow*, 24.

99 Holtzman, *Human Choice*, 163 – 188 discusses the problem of predetermination and free will in Ibn Taymīyah and Ibn Qayyim al-Jawzīyah through an analysis of one of the *fiṭrah* tradition. Further literature on this topic is discussed in the footnotes 6 (p. 183) and 11 (p. 184).

missed as the outcome of God's will and predetermination".[100] In line with what just said, another answer in verses to the very same *dhimmī* question from the Shāfiʿī scholar and judge al-Qūnawī (d. 1329) was described in one biographical source as a response to "someone who meant to defame the divine law.[101] Accordingly, it is the Law and its interpreters that are invalidated by incorrect belief. No wonder certain theological ideas had to be circulated only among those who could understand them properly! The scholars were confirmed.

Yet, we have seen that theology was not only made of elitist *kalām* and that ordinary people took an interest in theological matters. It is reasonable to assume, then, that it was not in the conventional forms of complex treatises that they could access doctrine.[102] It has been convincingly demonstrated by Jonathan Berkey that, through the activity of popular preachers, religious knowledge was transmitted also to the commoners and that the *ʿulamā'* were not always happy with a transmission of religious matters they could not control nor regulate. In presenting the contents of popular preaching in the Mamluk period, Berkey draws attention to discussions relating to the "creation of the world and the theological meaning of the natural order", and to eschatological questions (death, salvation, Last Judgment), all expressed by debating hadith, often hadith *qudsī.*[103]

Furthermore, minor scholars often read to the *ʿāmmah* (*qarā'a ʿalā l-āmmati, takallama ʿalā l-ʿāmmati* are the recurrent expressions in the sources). The intensity, the modalities, and the cultural impact of these reading practices is the subject of Konrad Hirschler's last book. But one can simply flick through al-Sakhāwī to have an idea of how often reading to the commoners occurs in his big dictionary that describes the lives of 15th scholars.[104] What did these scholars,

100 Holtzman, *Dhimmi's Question.* The quotation occurs at page 36; the translation of the related passage is at page 51.

101 Holtzman, *Dhimmi's Question*, 45. Al-Qūnawī poem is translated at pp. 64–66.

102 For the elite making complex religious text available to the *āmmah* by simplifying them (in the Ayyubid period), see Talmon-Heller, *Islamic Piety*, 136–137, 248–249.

103 Berkey, *Popular Preaching*, 46–49, 52 and 77–80 for a preacher putting before his audience the complex question "whether a believer became an unbeliever (*kāfir*) by committing major sins (*kabā'ir*)" and discussing the tenets of the Muʿtazila, Qadarīyah and other rationalist schools.

104 Here is a list meant to be exemplary, but not exhaustive, of instances of scholars described as engaging in reading activities to the *ʿāmmah.* In brackets are the contents of the reading sessions, when mentioned. Al-Sakhāwī, *Al-Ḍaw'*, 1:13 (Bukhārī), 84 (Hadith), 214 (Hadith), 229 (*Ṣaḥīḥ* and *tarġīb*, i.e exhortary texts encouraging doing good, and else); 2:20 (Hadith), 81 (Saḥīḥ Buḫārī), 184, 204 ("He sat with the commoners and clarified to them many religious duties [*muhimmāt al-dīn*]; many of them greatly benefited from him"), 303 (Hadith; "Despite being Shāfiʿī, he joined the Ḥanbalis and leaned towards them in belief", he preached and advised people and wrote for them) ; 3:111 (Hadith), 117, 118, 145 (Hadith), 193; 4:35 (*al-miʿād*, probably meaning Qur'ānic exegesis, or, more broadly, typical subjects of preaching activities such as collections of traditions, accounts of the early

who were mostly preachers or *ʿulamāʾ* with minor religious posts, read to the *ʿāmmah?* Typically, they read *ḥadīth*, and many hadith did display theological contents, often of an anthropomorphic taste.[105] It is by no chance that in order to establish the contents of the preachers' sermons, among others works, Jonathan Berkey explored Ibn Taymīyah's short collection of story-tellers' *ḥadīth* (*aḥādith al-quṣṣāṣ*).[106] Clearly, then, the scholars' elitist prescriptions to keep the *ʿāmmah* away from discussing theological matters was not thoroughly successful. Of one scholar named al-ʿAlāʾ al-Shirāzī, al-Sakhāwī even tells us: "He used to read to people on the science of God's unity (*takallama ʿalā l-nāsi fī ʿilmi l-tawḥīdi*) in the most eloquent and clear way".[107]

Thus far, we have seen that the *fatwā* of Ibn Taymīyah reported by al-Nuwayrī demanded a simple and straightforward answer to a complex theological question. After all, for somebody like Ibn Taymīyah right belief was the source of right conduct and right conduct lead to salvation. Hence, people asked for simple guidance not only in practical and legal matters, but also in doctrine. We have seen that hadith and sermons delivered by preachers were a way in which many complex issues could be put into accessible words, including theology. But there are surely more literary genres that could be fruitfully investigated in this regard. If one wants to explore which roads theology took to get to the commoners and in what specifically the non-specialist audience (or readership) was interested in, one probably has to set aside the classical format of treatises, manuals and commentaries, and turn to a more accessible literary production. One such example is an anthology called *al-Kanz al-Madfūn wa-l-Fulk al-Mashhūn* (*The Buried Treasure and the Loaded Ship*) an eclectic book mixing up a myriad of very different subjects without apparent ordering criterion, and dealing with no particular topic in detail.[108] *The Buried Treasure* is attributed to a minor 14th

Muslims, exhortatory works [Cf. Berkey, *Popular Preaching*, 38–39]), 66, 140, 208, 260 (Buḫārī), 318 (he read *tarġīb* and *tarhīb*); 5:159 (he read to the commoners in his village and they trusted him); 6:70, 153 (Buḫārī), 240, 282 (Buḫārī, *Sīra*), 299, 313 (*Ḥadīth*); 7:217 (Buḫārī), 243, 248, 271 (edifying stories, *al-raqāʾiq*), 276; 8:91 (Buḫārī), 142, 171, 195, 229 (Buḫārī), 230, 245, 273 (Buḫārī, he was very fond of Ibn ʿArabī and even in his sermons he talked about him), 284, 300 (*Tafsīr al-Qurṭubī*); 9:24, 51, 195 (the two *Ṣaḥīḥ*), 10:111, 224 (*Kutub al-siyar*, *ḥadīth*, sermons), 263; 11:31 (Buḫārī). Most of the people here mentioned where preachers and in the majority of cases their reading activity is described as taking place in mosques.

105 For *Ḥadīth* as a theological literary genre, see Nagel, *Islamic Theology*, 73–82 and for a discussion of anthropomorphist *ḥadīth*, Gimaret, *Dieu*. For a sample of this kind of theological literature, see Holtzman, *Does God*, Really Laugh, 165–200.

106 Berkey, *Popular Preaching*, chap. 2 and Ibn Taymīyah, *Aḥādith al-Quṣṣāṣ*.

107 Al-Sakhāwī, *Ḍaw' al-Lāmiʿ*, 11:98 (Ibn Muḥmammad al-ʿAlāʾ al-Shirāzī, d. 1457– described as being an expert in the sciences of the Ancients [*ʿulūm al-awāʾil*]).

108 For a description of the anthology genre in the Mamluk period and the work in question see, Bauer, *Literarische Anthologien*, on this anthology in particular p. 98–106 and idem,

century scholar Yūnus al-Mālikī, or – according to the two Egyptian editions – to al-Ṣūyūṭī (d. 1505).[109] It is a work produced for an average readership who evidently had some interest in acquiring a basic cultural knowledge that covered a little of everything, but not an extensive and detailed education on one subject in particular. Among the many topics presented, *The Buried Treasure*, also deals with theology. It presents an *'aqīdah* whose title, *al-Murshidah*, promptly clarifies its aim. It is a brief text written in a simple language, a list of statements that proceeds rhythmically and that could rather effortlessly be learnt by heart. *Al-Aqīdah al-Murshidah* stresses God's omnipotence and omniscience, His freedom from creatures (*laysa 'alayhi ḥaqqun wa-laysa 'alayhi ḥukmun*) and the absolute inability of man to grasp Him.[110] Such a representation of God escapes any anthropomorphic temptation and, in turn, nurtures an image of man who cannot be but very tiny and humble in front of such a majestic alterity. Elsewhere, a set of questions is formulated on a variety of issues. What is God's purpose in showing to believers Hell [before Paradise]? Why did God create sin? Why Did God create Hell in seven levels and Paradise in eight? And why does God grant His favors to man but then restrain him from such blessings? Why did God create more unbelievers than believers? What is the purpose of creating heaven before earth? Were we initially created in Paradise?

A wide array of different answers is provided. Many of them reflect recurrent ideas in classical Islamic theology and eschatology, although here expressed in a laconic and simplified form. They tend to highlight God's power and His alterity, but also His mercy. God shows Hell before Paradise because he wants His servants to see the perfection of his power (*qudrah*). He created sin to make His servants aware of their neediness to Him, then He saved them to make them know His magnanimity, or to make Muḥammad happy by giving him the opportunity to intercede by Him. Paradise is bigger than Hell because Paradise is abundant gift (*faḍl*) while Hell is justice (*'adl*), and it is necessary that abundant gift exceeds justice. Furthermore, the numbers of unbelievers exceeds that of believers because in this way God shows that He is completely Self-Sufficient from man and his obedience to Him, and that victory comes only from Him. Finally, He created heaven before the earth as a sign that His acting is different

Mamluk Literature, 122–124. On *al-Kanz al-Madfūn* also, Hirschler, *Written Word*, 186–190 and Canova, *Pagina di al-Kanz al-madfūn*, 93–107. Canova thinks that *The Buried Treasure* is a collections of personal notes from a variety of texts.

109 Al-Suyūṭī, *Al-Kanz al-Madfūn* (a), (b), (c). I did not have the chance to vision the Beirut edition. I will refer below to the 1991 Cairo edition. Canova, *Pagina di al-Kanz al-madfūn*, 93–94 discusses in detail the problem of attribution.

110 Al-Suyūṭī, *Al-Kanz al-Madfūn* (b), 24–25: *wa-lā yulḥiquhū wahmun wa-lā yukayyifuhu 'aqlun wa-lā yanḥaṣiru fī l-dhihni wa-lā yatamaṯṯalu fī l-nafsi wa-lā yataṣawwaru fī l-wahmi wa-lā yatakayyafu fī l-'aqli wa-la tulhiquhū l-awhāmu wa-l-afkāru jalla 'an al-shabīhi wa-l-naẓīri laysa ka-miṯlihi shay'un.*

from His creatures' actions. In fact, he created the roof before the fundaments and lifted these without a support so that this is an indicator of the perfection of His power.[111] But on other occasions, the answers take up a more anecdotal and wondrous tone. For instance: "It was reported: Hell complained to God by saying: 'My Lord, I have never disobeyed you. Why did you make me a refuge only for tyrants and arrogant people?' So God replied: 'I will first show you to the Prophets and the obedient.'" This comes as an answer to the first question paraphrased above. It stresses God's mercy and the submission to Him also of non-human entities (Hell).[112]

Theology covers but a very minor part of the book, but the way it is dealt with and the topics it tackles give an idea not only of the type of readership at which *The Buried Treasure* was directed, but also of which theological issues preoccupied such readership. And these issues were far from being peripheral.[113] In asking questions about God, people asked questions about their own lives: the presence of evil, the mystery of creation, the pressing anxiety for the after-life. In finding answers, they found ways of reassuring themselves; in elaborating certain representations of God, they also defined their place in the world.

There are surely other works not uniquely devoted to theology or other literary genres from the Mamlūk period that might be explored to advance our knowledge about the place of theology in the society of ordinary people, uncultivated or urban middle class, whatever they be. Studies on literature in the Mamlūk period are finally blossoming. Thanks to the efforts of Thomas Bauer and others, Mamluk literature is no longer seen as a "post-classical" marginal phenomenon worth of little note, but as a subject that deserves full attention by itself.[114] The input and significance of poetry production in the Mamluk period is being seriously considered, and the study of theology in verses is now taking off thanks to the work of Livnat Holtzman.[115] Didactic verses, for example, were meant to teach a specific topic and using verses was meant to help memorization.[116] We know that didactic poetry was used in dogmatics as well. An

111 Al-Suyūṭī, *Al-Kanz al-Madfūn* (b), 104–106.

112 Al-Suyūṭī, *Al-Kanz al-Madfūn* (b), 104.

113 As described by Hirschler, *Written Word*, 187.

114 See, Bauer, *Mamluk Literature* and idem, *Post-Classical Literature.* For a review of Bauer and the scholarly literature on Mamluk literature period Bauer engages with see Holtzman, *Insult.* A good starting point for researching the connections between literature and religion in the Mamluk period could also be the volume edited by Jospeh E. Lowry and Devin J. Stewart, *Essays in Arabic Literary Biographies* (1350–1850), which makes available materials so far neglected.

115 For the state of the art on poetry in the Mamluk period, see the chapter by Thomas Bauer in this volume. On theology in verses, see Holtzman, *Dhimmi's Question* and the articles in footnote 118.

116 On didactic poetry: Van Gelder, *Didactic poetry*; idem, *Arabic didactic verse*, 103–117; Khulūṣī, *Didactic verse*, 498–509; Ullmann, *Muzdawiǧ-Gedicht*, 46–59.

outstanding example is Ibn Qayyim al-Jawzīyah's famous piece of didactic poetry entitled *al-Kāfiyah al-Shāfiyah fī al-Intiṣār li-l-Firqah al-Nājiyah* (or *al-Qasīdah al-Nūnīyah*), a polemical theological poem against Ash'arism that gained in time wide popularity. *al-Kāfiyah al-Shāfiyah* is not a piece designed for the *'āmmah*, but it is an important example of theological poetry.[117] The study of theology in verses from the Mamluk period is still in its infancy. Yet, it will not be surprising if among the many Mamluk manuscripts that still lie unstudied in Middle-Eastern and Western libraries more accessible theological literature in verses, or books of prayers meant to be learned and memorized by people one day emerged and thus advanced our knowledge on the place of theology in the society of the commoners.

Conclusions

Until this happens, one can be reminded that exploring the link between society and theology may be a rewarding research enterprise. This has been precisely the purpose of the present chapter where I have suggested that an attention to this link is generally missing in scholarship both on the intellectual and the socio-religious history of the Mamluk period. I tried to locate the reasons for this state of affairs and to provide a sample of materials that proves that we do not lack the resources for pursuing research in this direction. In this regard, I advocated an interdisciplinary approach where the efforts of experts in Islamic theology and historians interested in religion and society ought to merge. Making sense of this so far rather unexplored connection, even in its negative outcome, should present the advantage of making theology more meaningful to historians of society. Drawing attention to the social and political value of, at least, some theological ideas will possibly help historians interested in the religious life of the Mamluk period consider theological doctrines as a meaningful human expression.

Exploring which images of God ordinary people engaged with, which images of the divine were constructed by minor scholars for a middle-class consumption and through which literary genres; considering to what extent, and how, immanence or transcendence lent themselves to political power, why the scholarly elite was so anxious to keep the commoners far away from theology, especially in the form and contents of *kalām*, all these are questions that will make research on religious life in the Mamlūk period more thorough. After all,

117 For a close analysis of this theological poem, see Holtzman, *Insult*; Idem, *Accused of Anthropomorphism*.

intellectual history is part of the history of a given society, hence it is part of history as a whole.

Bibliography

Primary Sources

Al-Birzālī, *Al-Muqtafī 'ala kitāb al-rawḍatayn al-ma'rūf bi ta'rīkh al-Birzālī*, ed.'Umar 'Abd al-Salām al-Tadmūrī, 4 vols., Beirut: al-Maktabat al-'Aṣrīyah 2007.

Al-Bukhārī, *Khalq Af'āl al-'Ibād wa-l-Radd 'alā al-Jahmīyah wa-Aṣḥāb al-Ta'ṭīl*, ed. Fahd Sulaymān al-Fuhayd, 2 vols, Riyad: Dār Aṭlas al-Khaḍrā' li-l-nashr wa-l-Tawzī' 2005.

Ibn 'Abd al-Hādī, *Al-'Uqūd al-Durrīyah min Manāqib Shaykh al-Islām Aḥmad b. Taymīyah*, ed. Muḥammad Ḥāmid al-Fiqī, Beirut: Dār al-Kutub al-'Ilmīyah, [n.d.], reprint of the 1938 Cairene edition.

Ibn Dawādārī (d. 1335), *Kanz al-Ghurar wa-Jāmi' al-Ghurar*, 9 vols., Cairo: Deutsches Archäologisches Institut 1960 – 1992.

Ibn Ḥajar, *Inbā' al-Ghumr bi-abnā' al-'umr fī al-tarīkh*, 5 vols., Hyderabad: Maṭba'at Majlis Dā'irat al-Ma'ārif al-'Uthmānīyah 1975.

Ibn Kaṭīr, *Al-Bidāyah wa-al-Nihāyah fī al-Ta'rīkh*, 14 vols., Cairo: Maṭba'at al-Sa'ādah, 1932 – 1939.

Ibn Qāḍī Shuhbah, *Ta'rīkh Ibn Qāḍī Shuhbah*, ed. Adnan Darwich, 4 vols., Damascus: Institut Français de Damas 1977.

Ibn Taymīyah, "Al-Furqān bayna Awliyā' al-Raḥmān wa-Awliyā' al-Shayṭān," in: Ibn Taymīyah, *Majmū'at Fatāwā* 11:156 – 310.

Ibn Taymīyah, *Aḥādith al-Quṣṣāṣ*, ed. Muḥammad Ṣabbāgh, Beirut: al-Maktab al-Islāmī 1972.

Ibn Taymīyah, Taqī al-Dīn Aḥmad, *Majmū'at Fatāwā Shaykh al-Islām Aḥmad b. Taymīyah*, 37 vols., ed. 'Abd al-Raḥmān b. Muḥammad b. Qāsim, Rabāṭ: al-Maktab al-Ta'līmī al-Sa'ūdī bi-l-Maghrib 1981.

Ibn Ṭulūn, Shams al-Dīn, *Naqd al-Ṭālib li-Zaġal al-Manāṣib*, ed. Muḥammad Dahmān and Khālid Muḥammad Dahmān, Beirut: Dār al-Fikr al-Mu'āṣir 1992.

Al-Maqrīzī, *Kitāb al-sulūk li-ma'rifat duwal al-mulūk*, ed. Sa'īd 'Abd al-Fattāḥ 'Āshūr, 4 vols., Cairo: Maṭba'at dār al-Kutub 1934 – 1972.

Al-Nuwayrī, Shihāb al-Din Aḥmad b. 'Abd al-Wahhāb, *Nihāyat al-arab fī funūn al-'adab*, ed. Muḥammad 'Ulwī Shaltūt et al., 33 vols., Cairo: al-Mu'assasah al-Miṣrīyah al-'Āmmah li-l-Ta'līf wa-l-Tarjamah wa-l-Ṭibā'ah wa-l-Nashr, al-Hay'ah al-Miṣrīyah al-'Āmmah li-l-Kitāb 1964 – 1998.

Al-Ṣafadī, *A'yān al-'Aṣr wa-A'wān al-Naṣr*, ed. 'Alī Abū Zayd et al., 6 vols., Beirut-Damascus: Dār al-Fikr al-Mu'āṣir – Dār al-Fikr 1998.

Al-Sakhāwī, *Al-Ḍaw' al-Lāmi' li-Ahl al-Qarn al-Tāsi'*, 12 vols., Cairo: Maktabat al-Quds 1934 – 1936.

Al-Subkī, Tāj al-Dīn, *Mu'īd al-Ni'am wa-Mubīd al-Niqam*, ed. Muḥammad Fatḥī al-Nadī, Cairo: Mu'assasah al-'Alya' li-l-Nashr wa-l-Tawzī' 2008.

Al-Suyūṭī, ʿAbd al-Raḥmān, (a) *Al-Kanz al-Madfūn wa-l-Fulk al-Mashhūn*, Cairo: al-Maṭbaʿah al-ʿimārah, 1871

Al-Suyūṭī, ʿAbd al-Raḥmān, (b) *Al-Kanz al-Madfūn wa-l-Fulk al-Mashhūn*, Cairo: Maktabat Muṣṭafā al-Bābī al-Ḥalabī, 1991.

Al-Suyūṭī, ʿAbd al-Raḥmān, (c) *Al-Kanz al-Madfūn wa-l-Fulk al-Mashhūn*, ed. Yūnus al-Mālikī, Beirut: al-Mu'assasah al-Nuʿmān 1992

Secondary Sources

Alden, John, "The Khanqah of Siryāqūs: A Mamluk Royal Religious Foundation," in: *In Quest of an Islamic Humanism: Arabic and Islamic Studies in Memory of Mohamed al-Nowaihi*, ed. A. H. Green, Cairo: American University in Cairo Press 1984, pp. 109-122.

Amīn, Muḥammad, *Al-Awqāf wa-l-Ḥayāt al-Ijtimāʿīyah fī Miṣr: 648-923/1250-1517*, Cairo: Dār al-Nahḍah al-ʿArabīyah 1980.

Bauer, Thomas, "Communication and Emotion: The Case of Ibn Nubātah's *Kindertotenlieder*," *Mamlūk Studies Review* 7 (2003), pp. 49-95.

Bauer, Thomas, "In Search of 'Post-Classical Literature': A Review Article," *Mamlūk Studies Review* 11/2 (2007), pp. 137-167.

Bauer, Thomas, "Literarische Anthologien der Mamlukenzeit," in: *Die Mamluken. Studien zu ihrer Geschichte und Kultur. Zum Gedenken an Ulrich Haarmann (1942-1999)*, eds. Stephan Conermann and Anja Pistor-Hatam, Hamburg: EB-Verlag 2003, pp. 71-122.

Bauer, Thomas, "Mamluk Literature: Misunderstandings and New Approaches," *Mamlūk Studies Review* 9/2 (2005), pp. 105-132.

Behrens-Abouseif, Doris, "Change in Function and Form of Mamluk Religious Institutions," *Annales islamologiques* 21, (1985), pp. 73-93.

Berkey, Jonathan P., "'Silver Threads among the Coal': A Well-Educated Mamluk of the Ninth/Fifteenth Century," *Studia Islamica* 73, (1991), pp. 109-125.

Berkey, Jonathan P., "Mamluk Religious Policy," *Mamlūk Studies Review* 13/2 (2009), pp. 7-22.

Berkey, Jonathan P., "The Mamluks as Muslims: the Military Elite and the Construction of Islam in Mediaeval Egypt," in: *The Mamluks in Egyptian Politics and Society*, eds. Thomas Philipp and Ulrich Haarman, Cambridge: Cambridge University Press 1998, pp. 163-173.

Berkey, Jonathan P., "Tradition, Innovation, and the Social Construction of Knowledge in Medieval Islam," *Past and Present* 146 (1995), pp. 38-65.

Berkey, Jonathan P., *Popular Preaching and Religious Authority in the Medieval Islamic Near East*, Seattle, London: University of Washington Press 2001.

Berkey, Jonathan P., *The Transmission of Knowledge in Medieval Cairo: A Social History of Islamic Education*, Princeton: Princeton University Press 1992.

Berkey, Jonathan, "Popular Culture under the Mamluks: A Historiographical Survey," *Mamlūk Studies Review* 9/2 (2005), pp. 133-146.

Berkey Jonathan, "Culture and Society during the late Middle Ages", in: Petry, *Cambridge History*, vol. 1, pp. 375-411.

Boaz, Shoshan, *Popular Culture in Medieval Cairo*, Cambridge: Cambridge University Press 1993.

Bori, Caterina and Livant Holtzman (eds.), *A Scholar in the Shadow: Essays in the Legal and Theological Thought on Ibn Qayyim al-Ǧawzīyah*, Roma: Herder 2010.

Bori, Caterina and Livant Holtzman, "*A Scholar in the Shadow*", in: *A Scholar in the Shadow: Essays in the Legal and Theological Thought on Ibn Qayyim al-Ǧawzīyah*, monographic issue of *Oriente Moderno*, XC (2010), Roma: Herder 2010, pp. 13 – 44.

Bori, Caterina, *Ibn Taymiyya: una vita esemplare. Analisi delle fonti classiche della sua biografia*, Supplemento monografico alla Rivista di Studi Orientali 1/76, Pisa-Roma: Istituti Poligrafici Internazionali, 2003.

Canova, Giovanni, "Una pagina di al-Kanz al-madfūn sugli uomini più illustri," in: *Ultra mare. Mélanges de langue arabe et d'islamologie offerts à Aubert Martin*, ed. Frédéric Bauden, Louvain 2004, pp. 93 – 107.

Chamberlain, Michael, *Knowledge and Social Practice in Medieval Damascus, 1190 – 1350*, Cambridge: Cambridge University Press 1994.

Conermann, Stephan, *Quo vadis Mamlukology?*, (ASK Working Paper 1) http://www.mamluk.uni-bonn.de/publications.

El Omari, Racha, "Ibn Taymiyya's Theology of the Sunna through his Polemics with the Ash'arites," in: Rapoport, Ahmed, *Ibn Taymiyya*, pp. 101 – 119.

El-Shamsy, Ahmed, "The Social Construction of Orthodoxy," in: *The Cambridge Companion to Classical Islamic Theology*, ed. Tim Winter, Cambridge: Cambridge University Press 2008, pp. 97 – 117.

Endress, Gerhard, "Die dreifache Ancilla. Hemeneutik und Logik im Werk des Sayfaddīn al-Āmidī," in: *Logik und Theologie. Das Organon im arabischen und lateinischen Mittelalter*, ed. Dominik Perler and Ulrich Rudolph, Leiden: Brill 2005, pp. , 116 – 45.

Fernandes, Leonor, *The Evolution of a Sufi Institution in Mamluk Egypt: The Khanqah*, Berlin: Klaus Schwartz 1988.

Filoramo, Giovanni, *Che cos'è la religione*, Torino: Einaudi, 2007.

Fitzgerald, Timothy, "A critique of 'religion' as cross-cultural category," *Method and Theory in the Study of Religion* 9/2 (1997), pp. 91 – 110.

Garcin, Jean-Claude, *Un centre musulman de la Haute-Egypte médiévale: Qūṣ*, Cairo: IFAO 2005[2].

Geoffroy, Eric, *Le soufisme en Égypte et en Syrie sous les derniers Mamelouks et les premiers Ottomans: Orientations spirituelles et enjeux culturels*, Damascus: Institut Français des Etudes Arabes de Damas 1995.

Gimaret, Daniel, *Dieu à l'image de l'homme. Les Anthropomorphismes de la* Sunna *et leur interprétation par les théologiens*, Paris: Les Editions du Cerf 1997.

Griffel, Frank, "On Fakhr al-Dīn al-Rāzī's Life and the Patronage He Received," *Journal of Islamic Studies* 18 (2007), pp. 313 – 344.

Griffel, Frank, *Al-Ghazālī's Philosophical Theology*, Oxford: Oxford University Press 2009.

Gril, Denis, "Saint des villes et saint des champs. Étude comparée de deux vies de saints d'époque mamelouke," in: *Le saint et son milieu ou comment lire les sources hagiographiques*, eds. Rashida Chih and Denis Gril, Cairo: IFAO 2000, pp. 61 – 82.

Haarman, Ulrich, "Arabic in Speech, Turkish in Lineage: Mamluks and Their Sons in the Intellectual Life of Fourteenth-Century Egypt and Syria," *Journal of Semitic Studies* 33/1 (1988), pp. 81 – 114.

Hirschler, Konrad, *The Written Word in the Medieval Arabic Lands. A Social and Cultural History of Reading Practices*, Edinburgh: Edinburgh University Press 2011.

Holtzman, Livat, "Insult, Fury, and Frustration: The Martyrlogical Narrative of Ibn Qayyim al Jawziyah's al-Kāfīyah al-Shāfīyah," *Mamlūk Studies Review* 17 (forthcoming 2013).

Holtzman, Livnat, "Accused of Anthropomorphism: Ibn Taymiyyah's Miḥan as Reflected in Ibn Qayyim al-Jawziyya's al-Kāfīya al-Shāfīya", in: *Egypt and Syria under Mamluk Rule: Political, Social and Cultural* (working title), ed. Amalia Levanoni. (forthcoming)

Holtzman, Livnat, "Does God Really Laugh?- Appropriate and Inappropriate Descriptions of God in Islamic Traditionalist Theology," in: *Laughter in the Middle Ages and Early Modern Times*, ed. Albrecht Classen, Berlin: Walter de Gruyter 2010, pp. 165 - 200.

Holtzman, Livnat, "Elements of Acceptance and Rejection in Ibn Qayyim al-Jawziyya's Systematic Reading of Ibn Hazm," in: *The Life and Works of a Controversial Thinker*, eds. Camilla Adang, Maribel Fierro, and Sabine Schmidtke, Handbuch der Orientalistik Series, Brill: Leiden 2012 (forthcoming).

Holtzman, Livnat, "The Dhimmi's Question on Predetermination and the Ulama's Six Responses: The Dynamics of Composing Polemical Didactic Poems in Mamluk Cairo and Damascus," *Mamlūk Studies Review* 16 (2012), pp. 1 - 69 (forthcoming).

Homerin, Emil, "The Study of Islam within Mamluk Domains," *Mamlūk Studies Review* 9/1 (2005), pp. 1 - 29.

Hoover, Jon, "God Acts by His Will and Power: Ibn Taymiyya's Theology of a Personal God on His Treatise on the Voluntary Attributes," in: Rapoport, Ahmed, *Ibn Taymiyya*, pp. 55 - 77.

Hoover, Jon, "Ḥanbalī Theology," in: *The Oxford Handbook of Islamic Theology*, ed. Sabine Schmidtke, Oxford: Oxford University Press (forthcoming).

Hoover, Jon, "Ibn Taymiyya", in: *Oxford Bibliographies Online* .(http://www.oxfordbibliographies.com/view/document/obo-9780195390155/obo-9780195390155 - 0150.xml?rskey=uVNbpj&result=46&q=)

Hoover, Jon, Ibn Taymiyya's Theodicy of Perpetual *Optimism*, Leiden-New York: Brill 2007.

Humphreys, Stephan, *Islamic History: A Framework for Inquiry*, Princeton: Princeton University Press 1991.

Humphreys, Stephen, "The Expressive Intent of the Mamluk Architecture of Cairo: A Preliminary Essay," *Studia Islamica* 35, (1972), pp. 69 - 119.

Hunt, Lucy-Anne, "A Christian Arab Gospel Book: Cairo, Coptic Museum MS Bibl. 90 in its Mamluk Context," *Mamlūk Studies Review* 13/2 (2009), pp. 105 - 132.

Jackson, Sherman A., "Ibn Taymiyyah on Trial in Damascus," *Journal of Semitic Studies* 39/1 (1994), pp. 46 - 47.

Khulūṣī, Ṣafā', "Didactic verse", in: *Religion, learning and science in the 'Abbasid period*, eds. M. J. L. Young, John D. Latham, and Robert B. Serjeant, Cambridge: Cambridge University Press 1990, pp. 498 - 509.

Knysh, Alexander, "'*Orthodoxy*' and '*Heresy*' in Medieval Islam: An Essay and Reassessment," *The Muslim World* 83 (1993), pp. 48 - 67.

Knysh, Alexander, *Ibn 'Arabi in the Later Islamic Tradition. The Making of a Polemical Image in Medieval Islam*, Albany: State University of New York Press 1999.

Lapidus, Ira M., *Muslim Cities in the Middle Ages*, Cambridge: Harvard University Press 1967.
Leder, Stefan, "Postklassisch und vormodern: Beobachtungen zum Kulturwandel in der Mamlūkenzeit," in: *Die Mamlūken: Studien zu ihrer Geschichte und Kultur. Zum Gedenken an Ulrich Haarmann (1942 – 1999)*, eds. Stephan Conermann and Anja Pistor-Hatam, Hamburg: EB-Verlag 2003, pp. 289 – 312.
Lev, Yaacov, "Symbiotic Relations: Ulama and the Mamluk Sultans," *Mamlūk Studies Review* 13/1 (2009), pp. 1 – 26.
Little, Donald P., "Religion under the Mamluks," *The Muslim World* 73 (1983), pp. 165 – 181.
Little, Donald P., "The Historical and Historiographical Detention of Ibn Taymīyah" *International Journal of Middle Eastern Studies* 4 (1973), pp. 311 – 327.
Lowry, Joseph Edmund and Stewart, Devin (eds.), *Essays in Literary Biography (1350 – 1850)*, vol. 2, Wiesbaden: Harrasowitz Verlag 2009.
Makdisi, George, "Ash'arī and the Ash'arites in Islamic Religious History: Part I," *Studia Islamica* 17 (1962), pp. 37 – 80.
Makdisi, George, *The Rise of Colleges. Institutions of Learning in Islam and the West*, Edinburgh: Edinburgh University Press 1981.
Al-Matroudi, Hakim, *The Ḥanbalī School of Law and Ibn Taymiyyah: Conflict or Conciliation*, London: Routledge 2006.
Mayeur-Jaouen, Catherine, "Les Compagnons de la Terrasse, un groupe de soufis ruraux dans l'Égypte mamelouke," in: *Saints orientaux*, eds. Denise Aigle and André Vauchez, Paris: De Boccard 1995, pp. 169 – 179.
Mayeur-Jaouen, Catherine, "Maîtres, cheikhs et ancêtres: saints du Delta à l'époque mamelouke," In: *Le développement du soufisme en Égypte à l'époque mamelouke*, eds. Richard McGregor and Adam Sabra, Cairo: IFAO 2006, pp. 41 – 50.
McGregor, Richard and Sabra, Adam, *Le développement du soufisme en Égypte à l'époque mamelouke*, Cairo: IFAO 2006.
Meri, Josef W., *The Cult of Saints among Muslims and Jews in Medieval Syria*, Oxford, New York: Oxford University Press 2002.
Micho, Yahya, Textes spirituels d'Ibn Taymiyya X: "Je ne suis dans cette affaire qu'un musulman parmi d'autres". http://www.muslimphilosophy.com/it/works/ITA%20Tex spi%2010.pdf
Michot, Yahya J., "A Mamlūk Theologian Commentary on Avicenna's Risāla Aḍḥawiyya : Being a Translation of a Part of the Darʾ al-Taʿāruḍ of Ibn Taymiyya, with Introduction, Annotation, and Appendices," *Journal of Islamic Studies* 14/2 (2003), Part I, *Journal of Islamic Studies*, 14/2 (2003), pp.149 – 203 and Part II , *Journal of Islamic Studies*, 14/3 (2003), pp. 309 – 363.
Michot, Yahya, *Ibn Taymiyya against Extremism. Texts Translated, Annotated and Introduced by Yahya Michot*, Paris: Al-Bouraq 2012.
Michot, Yahya, Textes spirituels d'Ibn Taymiyya IX: "'Lumière sur lumière …'. La valeur de l'inspiration". http://www.muslimphilosophy.com/it/works/ITA-TexSpi-NS09.pdf
Nagel, Tilman, *A History of Islamic Theology. From Muhammad to the Present*, English translation from German by Thomas Thornton, Princeton: Markus Wiener Publisher 2000.

Olesen, Niels Henrik, *Culte des saints et pèlerinages chez Ibn Taymiyya (661/1263 - 728/ 1328)*, Paris: Librairie Orientaliste Paul Geuthner 1991.

Özervarli, M. Sait, "The Qur'ānic Rational Theology of Ibn Taymiyya and his Criticism of the Mutakallimūn," in: Rapoport, Ahmed, *Ibn Taymiyya*, pp. 78 - 100.

Pahlitzsch, Johannes, "Introduction," *Mamlūk Studies Review*13/2 3 - 5.

Perho, Irmeli, "Ibn al-Qayyim al-Ǧawzīyah's contribution to the Prophets' Medicine," in: *A Scholar in the Shadow: Essays in the Legal and Theological Thought on Ibn Qayyim al-Ǧawzīyah*, eds. Caterina Bori and Livnat Holtzman, pp. 191 - 210.

Petry, Carl F. (ed.), *Cambridge History of Egypt*, vol. 1, *Islamic Egypt*, 640 - 1517, Cambridge: Cambridge University Press, 1998

Pouzet, Louis,*Damas au VIIe/XIIIe siècle: Vie et structures religieuses d'une métropole islamique*, Beirut: Faculté des lettres et des sciences humaines de l'Université Saint-Joseph 1988.

Rahman, Fazlur, *A Study of Islamic Fundamentalism: Revival and Reform is Islam*, Oxford: Oneworld 2000.

Rapoport, Yossef and Shahab Ahmed (eds.), *Ibn Taymiyya and His Times*, Karachi: Oxford University Press 2010.

Rapoport, Yossef, "Ibn Taymiyya's radical legal thought: Rationalism, pluralism and the primacy of intention," in: Rapoport, Ahmed, *Ibn Taymiyya*, pp. 191 - 226.

Rapoport, Yossef, *Marriage and Divorce in Medieval Islam*, Cambridge: Cambridge University Press 2005.

Rustow, Marina, "At the Limits of Communal Autonomy: Jewish Bids for Intervention from the Mamluk State," *Mamlūk Studies Review*13/2 (2009), pp. 133 - 159.

Sabra, Adam, *Poverty and Charity in Medieval Islam: Mamluk: Mamluk Egypt, 1250 - 1517*, Cambridge: Cambridge University Press 2000.

Saleh, Walid A., "Ibn Taymiyya and the Rise of Radical Hermeneutics: An Analysis of An Introduction to the Foundations of Qur'ānic Exegesis," in: Rapoport, Ahmed, *Ibn Taymiyya*, pp. 123 - 162.

Sarrio, Diego R., "Spiritual Anti-Elitism: Ibn Taymīyah's Doctrine of Sainthood (walāya)," *Islam and Christian-Muslim Relations* 22/3 (2011), pp. 275 - 291.

Schmidtke, Sabine, *The Theology of al-'Allāma al-Ḥillī (d. 726/1325)*, Berlin: Klaus Schwarz 1991.

Spiro, Melford E., "Religion: Problems of Definition and Explanation," in: *Anthropological Approaches to the Study of Religion*, ed. Michale Banton, London 1966, pp. 85 - 126.

Stilmann, Normann A., "The non-Muslim communities: the Jewish community", in: Petry, *Cambridge History*, vol. 1, pp. 198 - 210.

Stilt, Kristen, *Islamic Law in Action. Authority, Discretion and Everyday Experiences in Mamluk Egypt*, Oxford: Oxford University Press 2011.

Swartz, Merlin, *A Medieval Critique of Anthropomorphism: Ibn al-Jawzi's Kitāb Akhbār al-Ṣifāt: A Critical Edition of the Arabic Text with Translation, Introduction and Notes*, Leiden: Brill 2002.

Talmon-Heller, Daniella, *Islamic Piety in Medieval Syria, Mosques, Cemeteries and Sermons under the Zangids and Ayyūbids (1146 - 1260)*, Leiden, Boston: Brill 2007.

Taylor, Christopher S., *In the Vicinity of the Righteous: Ziyāra and the Veneration of Muslim Saints in Late Medieval Egypt*, Leiden: Brill 1999.

Thomas, David, "Idealism and Intransigence: A Christian-Muslim Encounter in Early Mamluk Times," *Mamlūk Studies Review* 13/2 (2009), pp. 85 – 103.
Thomas, David, "Idealism and Intransigence: A Christian-Muslim Encounter in Early Mamluk Times," *Mamlūk Studies Review* 13/2 (2009), pp. 85 – 103.
Ullmann, Manfred, "Das Muzdawiğ-Gedicht," in: *Untersuchungen zur Rağazpoesie: ein Beitrag zur arabischen Sprach und Literaturwissenschaft*, Wiesbaden: Otto Harrassowitz 1966, pp. 46 – 59.

Van Ess, Joseph, *Theologie und Gesellschaft im 2. und 3. Jahrhundert Hidschra*, 6 vols., Berlin: Walter de Gruyter 1991 – 1997.

Van Ess, *The Flowering of Muslim Theology*, Cambridge: Harvard University Press 2006.

Van Gelder, Art. "Didactic poetry, Arabic", in: *EI*^{3}, http://referenceworks.brillonline.com/entries/encyclopaedia-of-islam-3/didactic-poetry-arabic-COM_26014 Last accessed: 07 October 2012.

Van Gelder, Geert Jan, "Arabic didactic verse," in: *Centres of Learning. Learning and Location in Pre-Modern Europe and the Near East*, eds. Jan Willem Drijvers and Alasdair A. MacDonald, Leiden: E.J. Brill 1995, pp. 103 – 117.

Wilfong, Terry G., "The non-Muslim Communities: Christian Communities," in: Petry, *Cambridge History*, vol. 1, pp. 175 – 197.

Winter, Stefan H., "Shams al-Din Muḥammad ibn Makki 'al-Shahīd al-Awwal' (d. 1384) and the Shiʿah of Syria," *Mamlūk Studies Review* 3 (1999), pp. 149 – 182.

Winter, Tim, "Introduction," in: *The Cambridge Companion to Classical Islamic Theology*, ed. Tim Winter, Cambridge: Cambridge University Press 2008, pp. 2 – 17.

Albrecht Fuess

Mamluk Politics

Introduction

What might the term *politics* mean in a Mamluk context? "Politics is concerned with the administration of home or city in accordance with ethical and philosophical requirements, for the purpose of directing the mass toward a behavior that will result in the preservation and permanence of the species."[1] This of course is a definition given by the well-known Mamluk scholar Ibn Khaldūn, an inevitable expert in this context. Ibn Khaldūn's definition does not represent the state of the art of the 21st century, but is familiar to a medieval Mamluk mind. Mamluk *politics* functioned in a twofold manner: The Masses (*al-raʿīyah*) were guided or trained by the *siyāsah*[2] (the policy or the guidance) of the rulers to maintain the prosperity and stability of the society. In return the ruler had to be just and security providing towards his flock or, as Ibn Nubātah points out, the duty of the king is, "to construct the world and secure law and order".[3] The main aspect of Mamluk *siyāsah* seems therefore to guide the ruler and the masses in the common goal to preserve the Muslim society as it is. In the following article five points of this interaction between ruler and flock and how it appears in contemporary research will be of special interest: 1) Legitimacy of the Mamluks 2) succession of sultans 3) financial administration 4) foreign policy 5) military.[4]

In general one can remark a growing skepticism about the notion of the Mamluk society as an exceptional case in the history of mankind. In particular, David Ayalon's assessment of the "distinct Mamluk Phenomenon"[5], coined in the seventies, has increasingly been questioned. Recent research places the

1 Ibn Khaldūn, *Muqaddimah*, 39.
2 For the term *siyāsah*, see: Bosworth et al., *Siyāsa*, 693.
3 Ibn Nubātah, *Sulūk*, Superius 29, fol. 2a here cited after: von Hees, *Guidance*, 372.
4 The focus of this presentation will thereby mainly be on scholarship of the last decade. For a discussion of the state of the art of roughly ten years ago, see: Irwin, *Western Eyes*; Conermann, *Es boomt*.
5 Ayalon, *Aspects* I & II.

Mamluk Empire in a long continuity of military slavery in the history of the Middle East and states that the Mamluk system, though having its peculiarities, was by no means the odd one out in the Muslim realm. But in judging Ayalon's views we have to contextualize him and his writings as well. When he started researching the Mamluks he was told by a leading Islamicist "Working on such a subject is similar in importance to working on the history of the Fiji Islands".[6]

Legitimacy of the Mamluks

The Mamluks came to power after their assassination of the last Ayyubid Sultan Tūrān Shāh in 1250.[7] As the Mamluk amirs seemed to have been unsure how to proceed and to consider, if as former slaves they were ripe to rule, we witness 10 years of experimentations and three months of exceptional female rule under Shajar ad-Durr, the widow of Sultan al-Ṣāliḥ Ayyūb (1240 – 1249), as "queen of the muslims" *(malikat al-muslimīn)*[8], an episode which was reconsidered some years ago by Amalia Levanoni and Sabine Soetens.[9] Then Stefan Heidemann has explained us in his "Das Aleppiner Kalifat" how the Mamluks netted free-floating Abbasid princes after the fall of Bagdad in 1258 and installed an Abbasid shadow caliph in Cairo in 1262.[10] The Abbasid caliphate became one cornerstone of the legitimacy of Mamluk amirs, but equally important for their prestige were the military victories against the mighty Mongols and the Christian Crusaders. The victory of the mostly Turkish born Mamluks against their Central Asian Mongol "cousins", let Abū Shāmah (d. 1268) say that against any (evil) thing there is a cure from its own kind, (*wa-li-kulli shay'in āfatun min jinsihi*).[11] Still, the military threat of the Mongol cousins was not banned until the vanishing of the Ilkhanate by the mid-fourteenth century. Therefore the ideology of the Mamluks was very much forged in the intellectual and military encounters against the Mongols, as Anne F. Broadbridge has shown in 2008 in her book "Kingship and Ideology in the Islamic and Mongol World", where she describes Mamluk ideology as follows: "Unlike Chingizid or later Turko-Mongol notions of kingship, however, this ideology hinged consistently and exclusively on antiquated Islamic concepts, on a vision of the Mamluk sultan as a martial Guardian of Islam and Islamic society. The Mamluks sultans used this outdated

6 Ayalon, *Mamluks*, 89.
7 Al-Maqrīzī, *Al-Sulūk*, 1/2:360.
8 Ibid, 362.
9 Levanoni, *Šağarat ad-Durr*; Soetens, *Šağarat ad-Durr*.
10 Heidemann, *Aleppiner Kalifat*.
11 Abū Shāma, *Al-Dhayl*, 208.

model because they suffered from two serious, linked problems: the institution of slavery and the lack of lineage".[12]

The second source of Mamluk military prestige was the victory against the Crusaders. Unfortunately we lack in the field of Mamluk-Crusader relations the same amount of new studies which we have for Mamluk-Mongol encounters. In the content list of fifteen years of *Mamluk Studies Review* the term crusader does not figure once. For the time being we have to content our self with the book "Mamluk and Crusaders" which was published in 2010 and contains a collection of selected articles of Robert Irwin.[13]

To know more about the ideological side of Mamluk – Crusader relations seems to be vital for the modern discussion about Islam and Christianity. Moreover, as the Mamluk scholar of the fourteenth century Ibn Taymīyah (d. 1328), so popular among contemporary Islamists, has shaped an enduring theological frame of the Mamluk *jihad* concept against Mongols and Crusaders.[14] For Ibn Taymīyah the Mamluks are God's chosen people to fight for the Muslim *ummah* the enemies of Islam. "If the Mongols would become their masters, there would be no more power in Islam."[15] It seems vital therefore to relook at Ibn Taymiyya and contextualise his writings with his personal biography. An important step in that direction was undertaken by Yossef Rapoport and Shahab Ahmad in 2011 by editing the volume "Ibn Taymiyya and his times".[16] Catarina Bori has contributed an article on "Ibn Taymiyya wa Jama'atuhu. Authority, Conflict and Consensus in Ibn Taymiyya's Circle" in the same volume.[17]

When the Mamluks expelled the last Crusaders from the Holy Land in 1291, Ibn al-Furāt praised them with the following words: "Praise be to God, the nation of the cross has fallen. Through the Turks the religion of the chosen Arabs has triumphed."[18] This brings us to the question of ethnicity. The early Mamluk army was composed of Kurds, Mongols, Kiptchaq Turks and others. Anne-Marie Eddé has shown that for Kurds ethnic bonds played an important role, but lately Reuven Amitai has called for caution in this respect, suggesting that there is "no indication that these Mongol-Mamluk amirs ever acted politically on the basis of

---

12 Broadbridge, *Kingship*, 12.

13 Irwin, *Mamlūks*. The main articles on the crusaders date thereby from the 80s and 90s. In recent years Robert Irwin published more on literary figures, firearms and the last decades of Mamluk rule.

14 Ibn Taymīyah, *Majmū'at fatāwā*. A series of French translations of the *fatwās* against Mongols is found in the journal "Le Musulman", see Michot, Textes spirituels.

15 Michot, *Textes*, (1995), 28.

16 Rapoport, Ahmed, *Ibn Taymiyya*.

17 Ibid., 23–52.

18 Ibn al-Furāt, *Tārīkh*, 8:115.

ethnic solidarity".[19] He calls for further case studies to find out more about an ethnic factor in Mamluk society. In general we can assume that the perception of ethnicity in the Mamluk Empire was certainly quite different from modern conceptions.

There was, nonetheless, a clear distinction among the Turkish, Kurdish or Mongol military lords and their Arab subjects. Although one can identify, as Ulrich Haarmann has shown, a Turkish-Arab antagonism for many periods of Muslim history,[20] Berkey has argued that it would be misleading to over-emphasize the Mamluks' alienation from native Egyptian society, because of numerous links which bound them together to Islamic culture.[21] One should acknowledge, though, that with the Mongols and subsequent central Asian nomadic waves, the Turkish element in the Muslim realm was strengthened. Julien Loiseau did lately even speak for the fifteenth century of a "Turkish century" (*"le siècle turc").*[22]

As outlined above, Mamluks had to be in the eyes of their subjects strong warriors and just and accessible rulers. Therefore they rode personally at the head of their army into battle and paraded regularly in town. Moreover they held the *maẓālim* (injustice) sessions were they would hear twice a week legal complaints of their subjects. The sultan then decided whether a case should be looked at in scrutiny by the judges in *sharīʿah* affairs or by other Mamluk officials, if worldly matters and civil administration (*siyāsah*) were concerned. And it was again Ibn Taymīyah who argued in his work *al-siyāsah al-sharʿīyah* that if the *sharīʿah* is observed, the *siyāsah* of rulers can never conflict with the *fiqh* (Islamic jursipridence) of the Islamic scholars, the *ʿulamāʾ*.[23]

But, in order to show this justice to the people the public display of the *maẓālim* session was very important. Maybe, as I have argued in a paper on the Mamluk *maẓālim*-practice in 2009, the Mamluks thought, they needed this additional legitimacy as just rulers as they had been only slaves at the beginning of their lives.[24] The Ottomans did not go public this way.

Still, how should a ruler know what is right? Well, this is written in the advice literature of the "Mirror of princes" (*naṣīhat al-mulūk*). In this context I would like to mention Paulina Lewicka's paper "What a king should care about?" On two memoranda for the son of Sultan Qalāwūn[25] and Syrinx von Hees recent article on "the guidance for kingdoms" focusing on the writings of Ibn Nubātah

19 Amitai, *Mamluks*; Eddé, *Kurdes.*

20 Haarmann, *Ideology*; See as well: Fuess, *Legends*, 141 – 152; Loiseau, *Soldiers*, (forthcoming).

21 Berkey, *Culture*, 392.

22 Loiseau, *De l'Asie centrale*, 33 – 35.

23 Bosworth et al., *Siyāsa*, 693.

24 Fuess, *Ẓulm.*

25 Lewicka, *King.*

al-Miṣrī (d. 1366), where she describes that Ibn Nubātah, despite being a devout Muslim, handed out very worldly advice to the prince of Hamah.[26] This fact earned Ibn Nubātah as well much prominence in Thomas Bauer's book "Die Kultur der Ambiguität", comparing him more than once with the sixteenth century Italian author Niccolò Machiavelli (d. 1527).[27]

Succession of sultans

Whether a sultan should be chosen on the basis of dynastic line or merit presented a very heavily disputed question in Mamluk times. However, recent publications have shed more light about the development of this issue. I therefore propose the following schedule of succession phases during the Mamluk sultanate:

Succession Phases of the Mamluk Sultanate:

1. "Law of the Turk" phase (1250 – 1310)
2. Qalāwūnid dynastic phase (1310 – 1382)
3. Mixed dynastic and meritocratic phase (1382 – 1412)
4. *Mulk ʿaqīm* – phase (regency is infertile) (1412 – 1517)

By law of the Turk (*asat al-turk*), is meant that the murderer of the old Sultan becomes the new sultan.[28] This is what happened to the Mamluk sultan Quṭuz (r. 1259 – 1260), when he was looking for recreation and went on a hunting party after the tiresome Mamluk victory against the Mongols in 1260. He was killed in his tent. "Afterwards the amirs assembled in the royal tent and amir Aqṭāy asked: 'Who did actually kill him'. Baybars replied 'I killed him', and then Aqṭāy said: 'Oh Lord. Sit down on the throne and take the (sultan's) place.'"[29] This story of a murder in the royal tent *(dihlīz)* narrated by al-Maqrīzī does highlight the problem of public accessibility of Mamluk rulers in the early period of their reign. It seems thereby that the murder in the royal tent did provide an additional legitimacy and hence the role of the *dihlīz* as theatre for royal murder or attempt of murder.[30] Until the abolishment of the institution of the *dihlīz* as royal tent under Sultan al-Nāṣir Muḥammad b. Qalāwūn (r. 1293, 1299 – 1309, 1310 – 1341), three sultans had been killed in the *dihlīz* and two further attempts on sultans' lives, one against al-Nāṣir himself, had been made there. For the benefit of survival, accessibility had to be better canalised and formalised at least to limit

26 Von Hees, *Guidance.*
27 Bauer, *Kultur,* see here especially 337 – 339 .
28 See on the "Law of the Turks" in the Early Mamluk period: Haarmann, *Regicide.*
29 Al-Maqrīzī, *Al-Sulūk*, 1/2:435 – 436.
30 See for further murders in the *dihlīz:* Fuess, *Dihlīz.*

the danger. Yehoshua Frenkel has shown that royal etiquette of the subsequent Mamluk period always had the aspect to it to distance the sultan from his peers while at court or during travel.[31] The succession of Sultan al-Nāṣir Muḥammad, one of the greatest Mamluk sultans, despite being a sultan's son, marks the beginning of the Qalāwūnid dynastic phase. After his rule nine of his sons, two grandsons and two great grandsons were to succeed him in 41 years; this line of succession came to end with Sultan Barqūq (r. 1382–1389; 1390–1399) who dared to declare himself sultan in 1382 without having a Qalāwūnid legacy. The sultans of the Qalāwūnid phase were frequently mere puppets in the hands of their powerful elder amirs, though the young sultans at times ruled independently. This was, then, a period of checks and balances between the sultans who came to power through family line and the different fractions of Mamluk emirs who drew their claim from their personal merits and accomplishments.

The Qalāwūnid dynastic phase had long been classified as era of decline and chaos due to endemic factional strives among powerful amirs. However, Jo von Steenbergen has recently shown in his book "Order Out of Chaos" that while a certain degree of disorder was prevailing, the Empire as a whole still continued to function rather well on the basis of personal networks.[32] When Sultan Barqūq finally ascended the throne in 1382, thereby bringing to an end the Qalāwūnid dynasty, he, too, tried to establish a family line, his son al-Nāṣir Faraj (r. 1399–1405; 1405–1412) trying his very best to hang on to the power for a decade, until his efforts were thwarted by the amirs. He was sentenced to death in 1412, and this meant the end of the mixed dynastic and meritocratic phase.The slogan "*al-mulk ʿaqīm*" (regency is infertile), which had been used already propagandistically against Sultan al-Nāṣir Muḥammad b. Qalāwūn at the beginning of the fourteenth century, became now commonplace.[33] The sons of Mamluk sultans could no longer aspire to real political power. They were just placed on the throne as place holder until the leading *amirs* had decided upon who should become the next real sultan from among their peers.

The exact processes behind the sultan-making of the fifteenth century are well described by Henning Sievert in his "Der Herrscherwechsel im Mamlukensultanat". According to Sievert the following three elements were important for the legitimacy of a Mamluk sultan in the fifteenth century. First of all was the official recognition through the Abbassid puppet caliph of Cairo, secondly the "Islamic" legitimacy as Muslim warrior and keeper of the Holy cities Mecca and Medina and thirdly the legitimacy as an army king ("Heerkönigslegitimation"), which was expressed through the "election of the most successful" ("Wahl des

31 Frenkel, *Public Projection*, 39.
32 Van Steenbergen, *Order.* See as well: Van Steenbergen, *New Era.*
33 Haarmann, *Arabische Osten*, 229.

Erfolgreichsten") by his peers.[34] This system was carried through to the end of the Mamluk sultanate with the exception of one young Sultan's son, i. e. Sultan al-Nāṣir Muḥammad II (r. 1496 – 1498). Already the choice of regal name was telling. al-Nāṣir Muḥammad II challenged the authority of the old emirs immediately by introducing new lighter clothing styles which were deemed inappropriate by the establishment. The old amirs soon responded by wearing even greater turbans and putting horns into it, thereby trying to resemble Alexander the great (Iskandar) who is often associated with the Dhū al-Qarnayn of the Quran. Finally the old emirs succeeded. The young sultan was killed near Giza on 31 October 1498.[35]

Sultan Qānṣūh al-Ghawrī (1501 – 1516), Sultan al-Nāṣir Muḥammad II (1496 – 1498) (Sources: Jean Jacques Boissard, Abbildungen der Türkischen Kayser und Persischen Fürsten, Frankfurt 1648, fig. 20 (Qānṣūh al-Ghawrī)/ Die Pilgerfahrt des Ritters Arnold von Harff, wie er sie in den Jahren 1496 – 1499 vollendet und durch Zeichnungen erläutert hat, Hildesheim: Olms 2004, 90. (al-Nāṣir Muḥammad II))

The sultans' sons-in-law also played an important role in determining succession. As Mamluk sultans knew that their own male offspring would probably never rule, it appears to me that they regarded their sons-in-law in some sense as their political heirs. Through marriage they established strong bonds to leading representatives of the next generation of Mamluks. We know for example that Sultan Lachin (r. 1296 – 99) was the son-in-law of the great Sultan Baybars.[36] Sultan Barsbāy (r. 1422 – 1438) was married to Princess Fāṭimah daughter of

34 Sievert, *Herrscherwechsel*, 81.
35 Fuess, *Sultans*.
36 Holt, *Crusades*, 102.

Sultan Ṭaṭar (r. 1421).[37] Sultan Qāytbāy (r. 1468 – 1496) and Aḥmad (r. 1461) the son of Sultan Īnāl were according to Ibn Taghrībirdī brothers in law,[38] but al-Sakhāwī states that Qāytbāy's wife Fāṭimah was in fact the sister of Sultan Īnāl's wife Zaynab.[39] And although the exact family bonds in most of these family networks still have to be clarified, even with the help of these few examples, one can assume that marriage networks were apparently of considerable importance in a context where male heritage was not allowed to play the leading role.

Financial administration

Agricultural income was the driving force of Mamluk economy; according to Stuart Borsch, "annual exports to the northern Mediterranean accounted for less than two percent of Egypt's GDP (...) Long-distance trade played a subordinate role in the overall development of Egypt's economy."[40] However, agriculture suffered a considerable blow in the fourteenth century as a result of the Black Deathl Stuarts Borsch's comparative study of 2005, "The Black Death in Egypt and England", offers considerable insights on the different ways that England and Egypt coped with the plague. "Where English landholders failed in their efforts to collectively confront a scarce rural labor market, Egyptian landholders triumphed brilliantly. The consequences were a disaster for Egypt's rural economy, the backbone of its economic power."[41] In the fifteenth century Egypt still suffered from this decay in agricultural output and this was vital for its lack of competitiveness with the Ottomans.

Long distant-trade revived considerably in the fifteenth century, but agriculture remained the backbone of the economy and was through the *iqṭā'* system responsible for the payment of the Mamluk soldiers. Looking at the *iqṭā'* system, Tsugitaka Sato's work "State and Rural Society in Medieval Islam" from 1997 is still the main reference on Mamluk agriculture, as it traces the fortunes of the industry through the land reforms (sg. *rawk)* of Sultan al-Nāṣir Muḥammad I.[42] In the fifteenth century former *iqṭā'* land was transformed on a large scale into *waqf* (endowment)-land.[43] Modern research has classified the growing number of *waqf* as a de-facto hollowing out of the old *iqṭā'* system, as the privatization of

37 Ibn Taghrībirdī, *Al-Nujūm*, 6:731; Popper, *History*, 4:124.
38 Ibn Taghrībirdī, *Al-Nujūm*, 7:684; Popper, *History*, 7:31.
39 Al-Sakhāwī, *Al-Ḍaw'*, 11:245.
40 Borsch, *Black Death*, 19.
41 Ibid., 113.
42 Tsugitaka, *State*.
43 For a new publication on *waqf* in the Mamluk period, see: Reinfandt, *Administration*.

the land developed fast, and at the beginning of the sixteenth century, almost half of the overall cultivatable land was already transformed into *waqf*-property.[44]

While the process in itself is undisputed, one cannot help but wonder about the rationale behind the changes driving it. Direct taxation of agricultural products of *waqf* land meant more cash for the sultans, whereas through the *iqṭāʿ* system less cash was generated for the royal treasury, as the income went to the Mamluk emirs and not the sultan. Moreover the treasury profited in the short run from sales of *iqṭāʿ* land, because an owner had to possess the land before turning it into *waqf*. By the mid-fifteenth century Mamluk sultans would learn that the successful Ottoman army was paid directly for its services. Financial reforms were mainly undertaken by the last two important sultans Qāytbāy (r. 1468 – 1496) and Qānṣūh al-Ghawrī (r. 1501 – 1516) at a time when the Ottoman threat became virulent. Daisuke Igarashi has shown in a 2009 article on "The Financial Reforms of Sultan Qāytbāy", how Qāytbāy tried to increase his cash reservoir by removing all unproductive people from the payroll, for example by letting them draw a bow to prove their military abilities.[45] In his 2009 book, Francisco Appelaniz has argued as well that Qāytbāy was looking for alternative funding for the military, as the *iqṭāʿ*-system seemed less and less appropriate for his military needs. He wanted a greater hand in the army and its financing and needed more cash for new arms like canons and firearms.[46] When Sultan Qānṣūh al-Ghawrī took office after an interregnum of five years in 1501, he seemed to continue the path outlined by Qāytbāy in financial affairs. He used extra taxation, large scale confiscations and the sales of offices.[47] In the light of this new research a question which was posed by Carl Petry already in 1994 might be answered in the affirmative: "Do all these disparate phenomena, once pieced together, reveal a budding master plan by which the *iqṭāʿ*-system would be scrapped outright once the sultan garnered the means to replace it?"[48]

Foreign policy

As already stated above, there are recent studies about Mamluk-Mongol relations, whereas for those of the Mamluks with the Crusader states and Byzantium we rely mainly on Holt's "Early Mamluk Diplomacy" from 1995.[49] Angus Stewart

44 Reinfandt, *Sultansstiftungen*, 32 – 36.
45 Daisuke, *Financial Reforms*.
46 Apellániz, *Pouvoir et finance*, 172.
47 Daisuke, *Financial Reforms*, 50.
48 Petry, *Protectors*, 208 – 209.
49 Holt, *Mamluk Diplomacy*.

wrote on the the relations of the Mamluks with the Armenian kingdom.[50] Unfortunately the only book about the Mamluks and Timurids I know of is Sulaymān al-Madanī's "Tīmūrlank fī Dimashq".[51] The relations among the Mamluks, Ottomans and Safawids are clearer to me, as I am preparing a study comparing the three Empires in different aspects of their systems of governance.[52]

After 1453 and the conquest of Constantinople, Ottoman-Mamluk relations turned sour, as the Ottomans displayed increasingly their military might. In 1464 an Ottoman envoy arrived at the Citadel in Cairo who, acting in a rude manner, openly challenged Mamluk authority: "And this was the reason for the end of the friendship between the Sultan of Egypt and the Son of 'Uthmān" states Ibn Iyās.[53] Further diplomatic quarrels arose. Infamous was the episode of the Mamluk exile of Cem, the brother of the Ottoman sultan Bāyezīd (r. 1481 – 1512). In 1481 Cem took refuge with the Mamluks. He tried to return to Ottoman territory with some troops, again sought succour with the Mamluk Sultan, and ultimately became the hostage of the pope, who received an annual payment from Bāyezīd in order to keep him. Ralph Hattox and Nicolas Vatin have both written some time ago on this episode, making use of Mamluk and Ottoman sources, respectively.[54] In recent years the Ottoman advance of 1516 and 1517 has come under scholarly scrutiny. Benjamin Lellouch in 2006 analysed the accounts of Ottoman historians of the conquest of the Mamluk Empire and the beginning of Ottoman rule in Egypt.[55] Together with Nicolas Michel he is moreover preparing an edited volume under the title: "*Conquête ottomane de l'Égypte (1517). Impacts et échos d'un événement majeur.*"[56]

Given the harsh initial stance of the Mamluks against the Crusaders one would not expect the Mamluks to conclude alliances with a Christian power, but in the second half of the fourteenth century Venice emerged as the main trading partner of the Mamluks.[57] As I have argued in an article about the Mamluks and Cyprus, I would consider the Mamluk Venetian relationship in the fifteenth century as a political, and sometimes even military, alliance.[58] Cyprus could not have been possibly subdued during the years 1424 to 1426 without active

50 Stewart, *Armenian Kingdom.*

51 Al-Madanī, *Tīmūrlank.* I have not read it myself but it was reviewed by Antrim, *Review.* The review, however, is very skeptical about the academic usefulness of the book.

52 Fuess, *Clash*, (forthcoming); For direct Mamluk-Safavid relations we have few scholarly works apart from the article of Clifford from 1993, see: Clifford, *Observations*, 245 – 278.

53 Ibn Iyās, *Badā'i'*, 2:420.

54 Hattox, *Qāytbāy's*; Vatin, *Sultan.*

55 Lellouch, *Ottomans.*

56 Michel, Lellouch, *Conquête ottomane.*

57 Fuess, *Verbranntes Ufer*, 386 – 405.

58 Fuess, *Cyprus.*

Venetian "neutrality", and when Venice inherited Cyprus in 1489 it continued to pay the annual tribute and defended Mamluk shores against Frankish piracy.[59] In the field of commerce, mutual trade agreements and commerce practices between Venice and the Mamluks led Francisco Appelaniz to speak of "une alliance politique (des Mamlouks) conclue avec Venise pour subvenir aux besoins financiers." ("a political alliance of (the Mamluks) concluded with Venice to satisfy mutual financial needs").[60]

Military

Mamluk rule cannot be understood without reference to its military. Mamluk rulers understood themselves first and foremost as soldiers. To maintain social stability, they were prepared to invest heavily in the military. By far the largest portion of the budget of the Mamluk treasury went into the military, either by direct payment, allotment of *iqṭāʿ* land or by modernizing the military infrastructure and technology.

Important work has been carried out lately on the Mamluks' military forces by Israeli scholars. In 2011 Kate Raphael has published a book on Muslim fortresses in the Early Mamluk period.[61] It is a detailed account on the architectural settings of twelve fortresses and their sites in the thirteenth century. Moreover, it provides valuable insights into the siege warfare of the period and the defensive techniques of the Mamluk sultanate vis-à-vis their Mongol and Crusader foes. As I have pointed out in my dissertation "Verbranntes Ufer" and some subsequent publications, the main aim of the Mamluks after the expulsion of the Crusaders from the Syro-Palestinian coast in 1291 was to prevent their return, and to that end they destroyed the harbours there and transferred the line of defence inland.[62] I classified this strategy as a cornerstone of the overall naval policy of the Mamluks, who acknowledged their inferiority on the seas, especially in the first 150 years of their reign. In this context Sultan Baybars wrote to Hugh III of Lusignan, the king of Cyprus: "Your horses are ships, but our ships are horses".[63] I have been recently criticized by Vasilios Christides, who has described the later Mamluk period, specifically the Mamluk expeditions against Cyprus of the 1420s and following interventions in Cypriot internal affairs to 1460, as a period of "formidable sea power". He bases his analysis on the alleged

59 Fuess, *Cyprus*, 19–21.
60 Apellániz, *Pouvoir et Finance*, 239.
61 Raphael, *Muslim Fortresses*.
62 Fuess, *Verbrannntes Ufer*; Idem, *Rotting Ships*.
63 Ibn ʿAbd al-Ẓāhir, *Al-Rawḍ*, 376–377.

size and the different ship types described in the Arabic sources.[64] However, while I am willing to re-discuss the use of the term "hydrophobic", which I employed previously in the context of Mamluk naval policy, I still would like to uphold that this active period of Mamluk naval activity, which dates roughly from 1420 to 1460, does not allow to speak of an overall Mamluk maritime success story, as the conquest of Cyprus and the attacks against Rhodes could not have happened without the complaisant neutrality of the Italian seafaring nations (especially Venice). I also would classify the descriptions of ships in contemporary Arab sources as exaggerated and relying on older passages of classical works on seafaring: one contemporary European source describes the Mamluk fleet of 1426 as consisting of better nutshells.[65] In the context of the military *furūsīyah* exercises of the Mamluk soldiers Shihab al-Sharraf discusses Mamluk furūsīyah literature in an article of *Mamluk Studies Review* from 2004.[66]

Recently Amalia Levanoni has asked, why the Mamluk auxiliary force of the *ḥalqah* was not completely disbanded when it largely fell out of use in the fourteenth century?[67] She then explains this phenomenon by the flexible function the *ḥalqah* had even in later periods. While there were the poor and untrained soldiers in the *ḥalqah,* it also included full Mamluk soldiers who might come from defeated factions of the Mamluk establishment and could be assigned to the *ḥalqah* before re-entering other army units. The *ḥalqah* even served as a tool to balance the relationship of Mamluk sultans towards their amirs. At times Mamluks of amirs were excluded from the *ḥalqah.* Therefore the *halqah* represented an important buffer zone of Mamluk military patronage.

64 Christides, *Mamluk Navy*, 371, 385.
65 Piloti, *L'Égypte*, 108–109.
66 Al-Sharaf, *Furūsīyah.*
67 Levanoni, *Ḥalqah.*

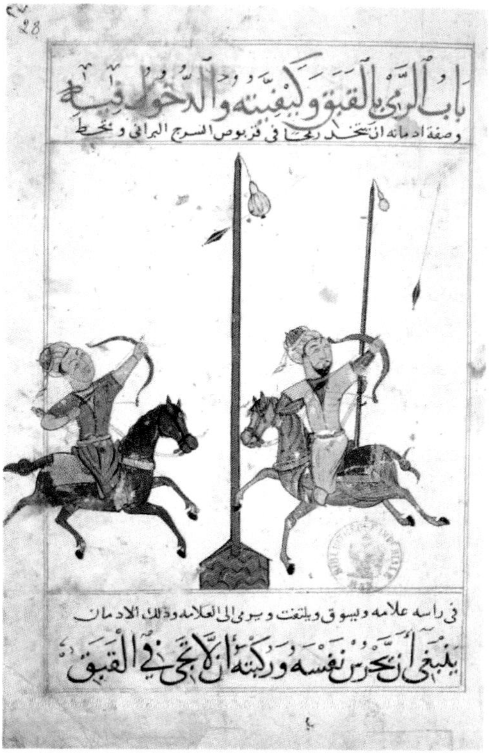

Mamluks practicing the *qabaq* (pumpkin) game, Egypt, 1470 (Source: Paris, Bibliothèque Nationale, MS Arabe 282, Ibn Akhī Khuzām, *Kitāb al-makhzūn jāmiʿ al-funūn*, fol. 28.)

Ottomans and Mamluk horseriders fighting at Marj Dābiq (1516) (Source: Khodja Efendi, *Selim nama*, Paris, Bibliothèque Nationale, supplément turc 524, fol. 159.)

For the remainder of this section, I will briefly discuss military aspects of my current research which concerns firearms and *wagenburgs.*[68] The Mamluk military downfall is often explained away by the Mamluks' refusal to use firearms. This line of interpretation can be clearly traced back to David Ayalon and his classical work "Gunpowder and Firearms".[69] He bases his affirmation especially on the Egyptian author of the 16th century Ibn Zunbul, who died in 982/1574. Ibn Zunbul cites, for example, the Mamluk amir Kurtbāy, who exclaims to the Ottoman Sultan Selīm (r. 1512 – 1520) after his capture: "How dare you shoot fire at those who profess the unity of god and the sending of Muḥammad."[70] However, Robert Irwin has already challenged the Ayalon thesis based on the fact that Ibn Zunbul is more of a literary than a historical source. Moreover, Ayalon ignored, or downplayed, the frequent reference to firearms in Mamluk sources at the beginning of the sixteenth century.[71]

Ayalon further argued that one never finds a high ranking Mamluk in the list of those who fight with firearms.[72] Of course, at the beginning of the sixteenth century no cavalry in the world fought with firearms. These arms were exclusively reserved for the infantry. Guns were simply not suited to be carried and loaded on horses at that time. It would constitute a considerable waste of money and manpower to have the highly trained professional Mamluk cavaliers leaving their bows, to descend from their horses just to take up firearms which any men could cope with after some initial training.[73] When horsemen fought at the beginning of the sixteenth century they did not use firearms.

And although Ayalon downplays the emergence of canons and firearms in the Mamluk army, canons were well known in the Mamluk Empire since the fourteenth century. Still, no signs of Mamluk guns can be traced until the Ottoman-Mamluk war of 1485 – 1491, when the Mamluks met for the first time large numbers of Ottoman Janissary musketeers in military encounters in Cilicia.[74] The immediate results of the war were the appearances of infantry units carrying guns in the Mamluk army. Ibn Iyās attributes the first use of rifles (*al-bunduq al-raṣāṣ*) to the reign of Sultan Qāytbāy (r. 1468 – 1496), during the Ottoman-Mamluk conflict of 1490, when Qāytbāy did send *awlād al-nās* and other soldiers equipped with guns to the front. After having shown in a public display to the

68 See therefore as well: Fuess, *Janissaires*, 209 – 227.

69 Ayalon, *Gunpowder.*

70 Ibn Zunbul, *Ākhirat*, 139 – 140, 217; See for Ibn Zunbul as well: Moustafa-Hamouzova, *Ottoman*, 187 – 206.

71 Robert Irwin, *Gunpowder*, 117 – 139; Petry, *Protectors*, 195.

72 Ayalon, *Gunpowder*, 69, 73.

73 Chase, *Firerarms*, 24.

74 See for the Ottoman-Mamluk war of 1485 – 1491: Har-El, *Struggle.*

sultan their newly acquired expertise, they were sent off to the North.[75] Thereafter guns are increasingly mentioned by Mamluk authors. Famous are the efforts to build infantry units using firearms like the infantry corps of black slaves by Sultan al-Nāṣir Muḥammad II (r. 1496 – 1498)[76] and the well known "*al-ṭabaqah al-khāmisah*" ("the fifth troop") under Sultan Qānṣūh al-Ghawrī (r. 1501 – 1516).[77] These efforts were modeled around the janissary troops of the Ottomans. Moreover, Miura Toru has counted 45 references to Mamluk infantry units conscribed from the residents of Damascus in the works of the Damascene historian Ibn Ṭūlūn. Although in only two cases are guns specifically mentioned, Toru argues that in that period the Mamluk army included more and more infantry elements, and guns had become a common weapon for the infantry corps.[78]

What is remarkable in this context is that successful military technology was adopted as soon as it was encountered in battle. A case in point is the *wagenburg*. The first to use these tactics were the famous Hussites in Czechia in the 1420s against German and Hungarian imperial troops. The *wagenburg* protection was essential for soldiers using the first generation of guns and cannons, as they had to be defended from attacks of the cavalry and archers of the enemy: firearms were still very slow to prepare and fire. In Middle and Western Europe gun men were usually protected by large infantry units using pikes, the famous "Landsknechte".[79]

The Hungarians used it then against the Ottomans. The Mamluks perceived the Ottoman *wagenburg* the first time in the Battle of Marj Dābiq. The Ottoman *wagenburg*, with its chained chariots, presented for the Mamluks a formidable obstacle. Ibn Ṭūlūn counted thirty wagons (*ʿarabah*) and twenty fortresses on wheels (*qalʿatun ʿalā ʿajalin*), when the Ottomans entered Damascus the autumn of 1516. He remarked that the chariots were chained together and resembled a fortified wall. For him this clearly showed the might of the Ottoman sultan, and when all canons were fired at the same time the inhabitants of Damascus thought that the sky would fall on their heads.[80]

The Mamluks apparently made use of guns and canons for defense but did not possess armed chariots in order to build a *wagenburg*. However, just after the Mamluk defeat in Syria, the new Sultan Ṭūmān Bāy tried to imitate the Ottoman

75 Ibn Iyās, *Badāʾiʿ*, 3:269.

76 Holt, *Crusades*, 198.

77 According to Ayalon the name "fifth troop" is related to the fact that its members received their payments on another day then the four usual days of payments of the Mamluk troops, Ayalon, *Gunpowder*, 71 – 83.

78 Toru, *Urban*, 170.

79 Jones, *Art of war*, 191.

80 Ibn Ṭūlūn, *Mufākahāt*, 2:30, 31, 34.

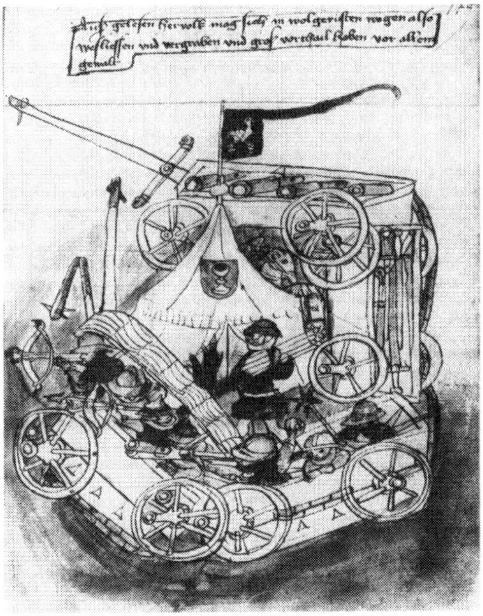

Hussite *wagenburg, 15th century* (Source: Österreichische Nationalbibliothek, Vienne Cod. 3062, in: Bert S Hall, Weapons and Warfare in Renaissance Europe. Gunpowder, Technology, and Tactics, Baltimore 1997, 109.)

tactics. He ordered that 100 chariots and canons be brought to the battlefield at al-Raydānīya, where the Mamluks waited for the Ottomans but lost another battle in January of 1517.[81] Tūmān Bāy fled, but was apprehended later and hanged in the April of 1517.[82] One has to remark in that context that the *wagenburg* was one of the most successful military technology transfers of the 15th and 16th centuries. The Safavids and Mamluks copied the Ottoman *wagenburg*. Sultan Tūmān Bay, immediately after the defeat of Marj Dābiq, and Shah Ismāʿīl ordered the construction of fifty chariots with canons after the Ottoman model that had fallen into the River Araks during the Ottoman Safavid war of 1514.[83] In 1528 the Safavid *wagenburg* was used to conquer their Eastern foe, the Uzbeks, at the battle of Cām.[84] In 1526 the Mughal Emperor Babur inflicted with the *wagenburg* a great defeat on his Indian enemies at the battle of Panipat. His military commander, a man called Muṣṭafā Rūmī, arranged the chained chariots in the "Ottoman style".[85]

81 Ibn Iyās, *Badā'i'*, 5:87, 134, 145–148.
82 Ibid., 176.
83 Bacqué-Grammont, *Les Ottomans*, 165–166.
84 Ibid., 174.
85 Babur, *Baburnama*, 323, 379.

In about a century the Hussite *wagenburg* had made its way from Central Europe to South Asia. Successful technology wanders around and is transferred. The early sixteenth century is just a case in point. It was not beyond the chivalrous sensitivities of the Mamluks to use firearms, as Ayalon has argued. The Mamluks had a military mind which was trained to defend the Empire at any cost and so they did. Therefore the problem of the Mamluks was not that they would not introduce the new weapons, but due to the scarcity of resources and other geopolitical factors they just could not obtain enough of them to compete with their great Ottoman foe.

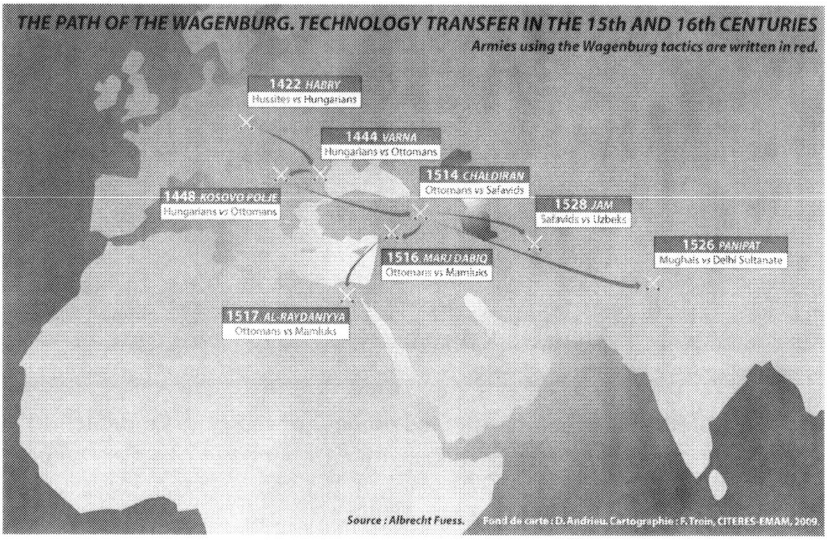

Conclusion

The last decade has witnessed a growing interest among Mamluk specialists in the Mamluk polity. There are noticeable gaps in the scholarship, but they might be closed as paradigms of research shift and new questions raised. One area of potential growth is in Mamluk-Crusader relations, which would still benefit from new impulses. For too long, the waning years of Mamluk rule received little attention. Today, however, the fifteenth and early sixteenth centuries are attracting many scholars, who are challenging traditional assumptions about Mamluk decline and decadence, and demonstrating ways in which the Mamluks were active in reforming their realm and administration in order to fulfill their duty as a ruler, i. e. preserving the status quo for their flock. That was the main aim of their policy.

Bibliography

Primary

Abū Shāmah, *al-Dhayl 'alā al-Rawḍatayn. Tarājim Rijāl al-Qarnayn al-Sādis wa-l-Sābi'*, ed. Z. al-Kawtharī, Beirut: Dār al-Jīl 1974. (Reprint from the Cairo 1947 edition)

Ibn 'Abd al-Ẓāhir, Muḥyī al-Dīn, *Al-Rawḍ al-Zāhir fī Sīrat al-Malik al-Ẓāhir*, ed. 'Abd al-'Azīz al-Khuwayṭir, Riyadh 1976.

Ibn al-Furāt, *Tārīkh b. al-Furāt*, ed. Qusṭanṭīn Zurayq and Najla 'Izz al-Dīn, Beirut: American Press 1939. (Vol. 1 contains juz' 7 and 8 of the manuscript)

Ibn Iyās, *Badā'i' al-Zuhūr fī Waqā'i' al-Duhūr*, ed. *Mohamed Mostafa*, 5 vols., *Wiesbaden: Franz Steiner 1972.*

Ibn Khaldūn, *The Muqaddimah. An Introduction to History*, trans. and introduced by Franz Rosenthal, with a New Introduction by Bruce B, Lawrence, Princeton: Princeton University Press 2005.

Ibn Nubāta, *Kitāb Sulūk Duwal al-Mulūk. Ikhtiyār*, Seld: MS Bodleiean Library, 29.

Ibn Taghrībirdī, *Al-Nujūm al-Zāhirah fī Mulūk Miṣr wa-l-Qāhirah*, 7 vols., ed. William Popper, Berkeley: University of California Press 1909 – 1936.

Ibn Taymīyah, *Majmū'at fatāwā Shaykh al-Islām Aḥmad ibn Taymīyah*, 37 vols., Riyadh 1961.

Ibn Ṭūlūn al-Dimashqī, *Mufākahat al-Khillān fī Ḥawadith al-Zamān*, ed. Mohamed Mostafa, 2 vols., Cairo: Wizārat al-Thaqāfah wa-l-Irshād al-Qawmī 1962.

Ibn Zunbul, *Ākhirat al-Mamālik al-Wāqi'ah as-Sultān al-Ghawrī ma'a Salīm al-Uthmānī*, ed. 'Abd al-Mun'im 'Āmir, Cairo: Al-Hay'ah al-Miṣrīyah al-'Āmmah li-l-Kitāb 1997.

Al-Maqrīzī, *Kitāb al-Sulūk li-Ma'rifat Duwal al-Mulūk*, ed. by M. Mustafa Ziyādah and S.A 'Ashūr, 12 in 4 vols., Cairo: Maṭba'at Lajnat al-Ta'līf wa-al-Tarjamah wa-al-Nashr 1934 – 1973.

Popper, William, *History of Egypt 1382 – 1469*, translated from the Arabic annals of Abu l-Maḥasin ibn Taghrî Birdî. *A.D*, 9 vols., Berkeley: University of California Press 1958.

Al-Sakhāwī, Shams al-Dīn Muḥammad, *Al-Ḍaw' al-Lāmi' li-Ahl al-Qarn at-Tāsi'*, ed. by Ḥusām al-Qudsī, 12 vols., Cairo 1936.

Secondary

Amitai, Reuven, "Mamluks of Mongol Origin and Their Role in Early Mamluk Political life," *Mamluk Studies Review* 12/1 (2008), pp. 119 – 138.

Antrim, Zayde G. Antrim, Review of Al-Madanī, *Tīmūrlank*, in: *Mamluk Studies Review* 7 (2003), 264 – 267.

Apellániz Ruiz de Galarreta, Francisco Javier, *Pouvoir et finance en Méditerranée pré-moderne: Le deuxième etat Mamelouk et le commerce des Epices (1382 – 1517)*, Barcelona: Consejo Superior de Investigaciones Científicas 2009.

Ayalon, David, "Aspects of the Mamluk Phenomenon, I & II," *Der Islam* 53 (1976), pp. 196 – 225; 54 (1977), pp. 1 – 32.

Ayalon, David, "The Mamluks Mainstay of Islam's Military Might", in: *Slavery in the*

Islamic Middle East, ed. Shaun E. Marmon, Princeton: Markus Wiener 1999, pp. 89–117.

Ayalon, David, *Gunpowder and Firearms in the Mamluk Kingdom. A Challenge to a Medieval Society*, London: Frank Cass 1978.

Babur, *The Baburnama. Memoirs of Babur, Prince and Emperor*, transl. by Wheeler M. Thackston, Washington: Modern Library 2002.

Bacqué-Grammont, Jean-Louis, *Les Ottomans, les Safavides et leurs voisins. Contribution à l'histoire des relations internationales dans l'Orient Islamiques de 1514 à 1524*, Istanbul: Nederlands Historisch Archaeologisch Instituut te Istanbul 1987.

Bauer, Thomas, *Die Kultur der Ambiguität. Eine andere Geschichte des Islams*, Berlin: Verlag der Weltreligionen 2011.

Berkey, Jonathan P., "Culture and Society during the late Middle Ages", in: *The Cambridge History of Egypt*, vol. 1, ed. Carl Petry, Cambridge: CUP 1998, pp. 375–411.

Borsch, Stuart J., *The Black Death in Egypt and England. A Comparative Study*, Austin: University of Texas Press 2005.

Bosworth, C.E., I.R. Netton, and F.E. Vogel, "Siyāsa," in: *EI²*, 10.

Broadbridge, Anne, *Kingship and Ideology in the Islamic and Mongol Worlds*, Cambridge: CUP 2008.

Chase, Kenneth, *Firerarms: A Global History to 1700*, Cambridge: CUP 2003.

Christides, Vasilios, "A New View on the Mamluk Navy," *Journal for Semitics* 17/2 (2008), pp. 367–393.

Clifford, W.W., "Some Observations on the Course of Mamluk-Safavi Relations (1502–1516/908–922)," part I: *Der Islam* 70/2 (1993), pp. 245–265, part II: pp. 266–278.

Conermann, Stephan, "Es boomt! Die Mamlūkenforschung (1992–2002)," in: *Die Mamlūken. Studien zu ihrer Geschichte und Kultur. Zum Gedenken an Ulrich Haarman (1942–1999)*, eds. Stephan Conermann and Anja Pistor-Hatam, Hamburg: EB-Verlag 2003, pp. 1–69.

Daisuke, Igarashi, "The Financial Reforms of Sultan Qāytbāy", *Mamluk Studies Review* 13/1 (2009), pp. 27–51.

Eddé, Anne-Marie, "Kurdes et Turcs dans l'armée ayyoubide de Syrie du Nord (1997)," in: *War and society in the Eastern Mediterranean*, ed. Yaacov Lev, Leiden: Brill 1997, pp. 225–236.

Frenkel, Yehoshua, "Public Projection of Power in Mamluk Bilād al-Shām," *Mamluk Studies Review* 11/1 (2007), pp. 39–53.

Fuess, Albrecht, "Between Dihlīz and Dār al-ʿAdl. Forms of Outdoor and Indoor Royal Representation at the Mamluk Court in Egypt," in: *Court Cultures in the Muslim World (7th–19th Centuries)*, eds. Albrecht Fuess and Jan-Peter Hartung, London: Routledge 2011, pp. 149–167.

Fuess, Albrecht, "Legends against Arbitrary Abuse: The Relationship between the Mamluk Military Elite and their Arab Subjects," in: *Towards a Cultural History of Bilad al-Sham in the Mamluk Era. Prosperity or Decline, Tolerance or Persecution?*, eds. Slim Souad, Haddad Mahmoud, Heinemann Arnim, and Meloy John L., Beirut: Ergon Verlag Würzburg 2010, pp. 141–152.

Fuess, Albrecht, "Les Janissaires, les Mamlouks et les armes à feu. Une comparaison des systèmes militaires ottoman et mamlouk à partir de la moitié du quinzième siècle," *Turcica* 41 (2009), pp. 209–227.

Fuess, Albrecht, "Rotting Ships and Razed Harbours: The Naval Policy of the Mamluks," *Mamluk Studies Review* 5 (2001), pp. 45 - 71.

Fuess, Albrecht, "Sultans with Horns. About the Political Significance of Headgear in the Mamluk Empire," *Mamluk Studies Review* 12/2 (2008), pp. 71 - 94.

Fuess, Albrecht, "Ẓulm by Maẓālim? About the Political Implication of the Use of Maẓālim Jurisdiction by the Mamluk Sultans," *Mamluk Studies Review* 13/1 (2009), pp. 121 - 147.

Fuess, Albrecht, *The Clash of Muslim Empires. Ottomans, Safavids, and Mamluks in the Sixteenth Century.*(Forthcoming)

Fuess, Albrecht, *Verbranntes Ufer. Auswirkungen mamlukischer Seepolitik auf Beirut und die syro-palästinensische Küste (1250 - 1517)*, Leiden: E. J. Brill 2001.

Fuess; Albrecht, "Was Cyprus a Mamluk Protectorate? Mamluk Influence on Cyprus between 1426 and 1517," in: *Journal of Cyprus Studies*, 11/28 - 29 (2005), pp. 11 - 28.

Haarmann, Ulrich, "Der arabische Osten im späten Mittelalter, 1250 - 1517," in: *Geschichte der arabischen Welt*, ed. Ulrich Haarmann, München: Beck 2001, pp. 217 - 263.

Haarmann, Ulrich, "Ideology and History, Identity and Alterity: The Arab Image of the Turk From The ʿAbbasids to Modern Egypt," *International Journal of Middle East Studies* 20 (1988), pp. 175 - 196.

Haarmann, Ulrich, "Regicide and the 'Law of the Turks," in: *Intellectual Studies on Islam: Essays written in Honor of Martin B. Dickson*, ed. Michel M. Mazzaoui, Salt Lake City: University of Utah Press 1990, pp. 127 - 135.

Har-El, Shai, *Struggle for Domination in the Middle East. The Ottoman-Mamluk War, 1485 - 1491*, Leiden: Brill 1995.

Hattox, Ralph S., "Qāytbāy's Diplomatic Dilemma concerning the flight of Cem Sultan (1481 - 82)," *Mamluk Studies Review* 6 (2002), pp. 177 - 190.

Hees, Syrinx von, "The Guidance for Kingdoms: Function of a "Mirror for Princes" at Court and its Representation of a Court, in: *Court Cultures in the Muslim World (7th -19th Centuries)*, eds. by Albrecht Fuess and Jan-Peter Hartung, London: Routledge 2011, pp. 370 - 382.

Heidemann, Stefan, *Das Aleppiner Kalifat (A.D. 1261): Vom Ende des Kalifates in Bagdad über Aleppo zu den Restaurationen in Kairo*, Leiden: Brill 1994.

Holt, Peter Malcolm, *Early Mamluk Diplomacy (1260 - 1290)*, Leiden: Brill 1995.

Holt, Peter Malcom, *The Age of the Crusades. The Near East from the Eleventh Century to 1517*, London: Longman 1997.

Irwin, Robert, "Gunpowder and Firearms in the Mamluk Sultanate Reconsidered," in: *The Mamluks in Egyptian and Syrian Politics and Society*, eds. Michael Winter and Amalia Levanoni, Leiden: Brill 2004, pp. 117 - 139.

Irwin, Robert, "Under Western Eyes: A History of Mamluk Studies," *Mamluk Studies Review* 4 (2000), pp. 27 - 51.

Irwin, Robert, *Mamlūks and Crusaders. Men of the Sword and Men of the Pen*, Farnham: Ashgate 2010.

Jones, Archer, *The Art of War in the Western World*, Champaign, Il.: Illinois University Press 2000.

Lellouch, Benjamin, *Les Ottomans en Égypte. Historiens et conquérants au XVIe siècle*, Louvain: Peters 2006.

Levanoni, Amalia, "Šağar ad-Durr: A Case of Female Sultanate in Medieval Islam," in:

Egypt and Syria in the Fatimid, Ayyubid and Mamluk Eras III, Proceedings of the 6th, 7th and 8th International Colloquium, Katholieke Universiteit Leuven, May 1997, 1998 and 1999, eds. Urbain Vermeulen and Jo van Steenbergen, Leuven: Uitgeverij Peeters 2001, pp. 209 - 218.

Levanoni, Amalia, "The Ḥalqah in the Mamluk Army: Why was it not dissolved when it reached its nadir?" *Mamluk Studies Review* 15 (2011), pp. 38 - 65.

Lewicka, Paulina, "What a King Should Care About: Two Memoranda of the Mamluk Sultan on Running the State's Affairs," *Studia Arabistyczne i Islamistyczne* 6 (1998), pp. 5 - 45.

Loiseau, Julien, "De l'Asie centrale à l'Égypte: le siècle turc," in: *l'Histoire du monde au XVe siècle*," ed. Patrick Boucheron, Paris: Fayard 2009, pp. 33 - 51.

Loiseau, Julien, "Soldiers Diaspora or Cairene Nobility? The Circassians in the Mamluk Sultanate," in: *Between Parallel Society and Integration: Diasporic Groups in the Eastern Mediterranean in the Late Middle Ages*, eds. Stefan Burkhardt and Georg Christ, Heidelberg: (forthcoming).

al-Madanī, Sulaymān, *Tīmūrlank fī Dimashq*, Damascus, Beirut: al-Manārah 2000.

Michel, Nicholas and Benjamin Lellouch (eds.), *Conquête ottomane de l'Égypte (1517). Impacts et échos d'un événement majeur*, Leiden: Brill (forthcoming).

Michot, Yahya J, "Textes spirituels d'Ibn Taymiyya. Mongols et Mamlūks: L'état du monde muslulman vers 709/1310 (XI - XIII)", in: *Le Musulman* 24 (1994), pp. 26 - 31; 25 (1995), pp. 25 - 30; 26 (1995), pp. 25 - 30.

Moustafa-Hamouzova, Andrea, "The Ottoman conquest of Egypt through Egyptian eyes. Ibn Zunbul's Wāqiʿat as-Sulṭān Selim khān maʿa 's-Sulṭān Ṭūmānbāy," *Archiv Orientální* 69/2 (2001), pp. 187 - 206.

Petry, Carl F., *Protectors or Praetorians? The Last Mamlūk sultans and Egypt's Waning as a Great Power*, Albany: Suny-Press 1994.

Piloti, Emanuel, *L'Égypte au commencement du quinzième siècle, d'après le traité d'Emmanuel Piloti de Crète, incipit 1420*, Cairo: Imprimerie Université Fouad Ier 1950.

Raphael, Kate, *Fortresses in the Levant. Between Crusaders and Mongols*, London: Routledge 2011.

Rapoport, Yossef and Shahab Ahmed, *Ibn Taymiyya and his times*, Oxford: OUP 2010.

Reinfandt, Lucian, "The Administration of Welfare under the Mamluks", in: *Court Cultures in the Muslim World (7th -19th Centuries)*, eds. Albrecht Fuess and Jan-Peter-Hartung, London: Routledge 2011, pp. 263 - 272.

Reinfandt, Lucian, *Mamlukische Sultansstiftungen des 9./15. Jahrhunderts. Nach den Urkunden der Stifter al-Ašraf Īnāl und al-Mu'ayyad Aḥmad Ibn Īnāl*, Berlin: Klaus Schwarz 2003.

Al-Sharaf, Shihab, "Mamluk Furūsīyah Literature and Its Antecedents," *Mamluk Studies Review* 8/1 (2004), pp. 141 - 200.

Sievert, Henning, *Der Herrscherwechsel im Mamlukensultanat. Historische und historiographische Untersuchungen zu Abū Ḥāmid al-Qudsī und Ibn Taġrībirdī*, Berlin: Klaus Schwarz 2003.

Soetens, Sabine, "Šaǧarat ad-Durr: A Comparative Study of Three Historical Sources," *Orientalia Lovaniensia Periodica* 30 (1999), pp. 97 - 112.

Stewart, Angus Donald, *The Armenian Kingdom and the Mamluks: War and Diplomacy During the Reigns of Het'um II (1289 - 1307)*, Leiden: Brill 2001.

Toru, Miura, "Urban Society in Damascus as the Mamluk Era was ending," *Mamluk Studies Review* 10/1 (2006), p. 157 - 193.

Tsugitaka, Sato, *State and Rural Society in Medieval Islam. Sultans, Muqta's and Fallahun*, Leiden: Brill 1997.

Van Steenbergen, Jo, "On the Brink of a New Era? Yalbughā al-Khāṣṣakī (d. 1366) and the Yalbughāwīyah," *Mamluk Studies Review* 15/1 (2011), pp. 117 - 152.

Van Steenbergen, Jo, *Order out of Chaos. Patronage, Conflict and Mamluk Socio-Political Culture, 1341 - 1382*, Leiden: Brill 2006.

Vatin, Nicolas, *Sultan Djem: Un prince Ottoman dans l'Europe du XVe siècle d'après deux siurces contemporaines: Vakiat Sultan Cem, Oeuvres de Guillaume Caoursin*, Ankara: Imprimerie de la société Turque d'histoire 1997.

Syrinx von Hees

Mamlukology as Historical Anthropology
State of the art and future perspectives

The field of Historical Anthropology has much to contribute to the study of Mamluk culture and society, as it offers new and stimulating questions. I see the importance of such new modes of inquiry in their communicability to non-specialists. Mamlukology as Historical Anthropology, therefore, could be more relevant to our contemporary society than traditional approaches have been, and is, moreover, appropriate for trans-cultural studies. In my contribution, I first elucidate more precisely the central concern of Historical Anthropology, highlighting the advantages of such an approach in our research as Mamlukologists. I then discuss one topic that is ideally suited to anthropological inquiry, namely, the body. In presenting the results of research on this topic by Mamlukologists, I propose other potentially rich themes for future research, discussing some of the possible ways to deal with these and similar topics, all the while emphasizing that the historical-anthropological approach is not a methodology, as such. There is a rich and growing literature on the concept of Historical Anthropology.[1] Central to the historical-anthropological approach is the study of human beings in time and space. Turning the focus on the individual, all-too-human issues like the body and senses, sexuality and love, health and illness, youth and old age, birth and death, and the like, come to the fore. The historian is concerned with exploiting the diversity of the different perceptions, conceptions and attitudes of people towards such topics, which result in different forms of behavior and conduct. Taking the body as an example, each individual has his or her own experiences with his or her body and has tried to understand these experiences through interpretations available to him or her. Developing one's own perceptions of the body, consequently, will influence the individual's way of dealing with the body. Based on the fact that reality surrounding human beings is accessible only through interpretations – that each individual creates

1 Daniel, *Kompendium*; Dressel, *Historische Anthropologie*; Goetz, *Mediävistik*; Le Goff, *Geschichtswissenschaft*; Maurer, *Historische Anthropologie*; Medick, *Quo vadis*; Reinhard, *Lebensformen*; Van Dülmen, *Historische Anthropologie*; Wulf, *Vom Menschen.*

this realty constantly anew through his or her own experiences and interpretations – the focus of historical-anthropological research is subjective. Ideally, the task of the historian is to reveal individual perceptions, emotions and the individual's space for action and negotiation.

When dealing with this task, two important issues arise. The first concerns source material. Which kinds of sources can we use to get to the individuals' ways of dealing with their world? Self-narratives like autobiographies, letters, diaries, travel accounts or testaments seem to be outstanding sources since they allow us the most direct insight into individual perceptions of life and individual modes of living.[2] Other genres that do not explicitly intend to provide a narrative of the self can and should be used for historical-anthropological questions, as well. This is possible because of our awareness that each text gives, in some way, a testimony of the author's worldview, and it is our duty to try to understand the function of this worldview. From this perspective, we are certainly not lacking in material. The second issue to be considered while trying to reveal individual perceptions and the individual space for action and negotiation is the realization that the subjective modes of thinking and feeling about the body – to continue with this example – are dependent on perceptions of the body discussed by contemporaries in various discourses. Possibilities of behavior are also dependent on their social framework. The individual can express himself only in terms of his own culture and society. We explore further these contexts below. The distinctive feature of historical-anthropological research lies exactly in this contradictory combination of partialization and generalization of the historical view. We understand that individual expressions are not just subjective attitudes towards life, in as much they are only possible, and only understandable, in the process of negotiation with those patterns of thought, worldviews, and forms of comprehension that are available to the individual.

This project of Historical Anthropology incorporates earlier, and more mature, research approaches, such as the history of daily life and the history of mentalities.[3] Because Historical Anthropology focuses on the plurality of human behavior, it excludes a uniform idea of man. It is rather the ambiguity and inconsistency of human behavior in the complexity of its cultural and social contexts that becomes evident through this approach. This fact alone makes Historical Anthropology especially relevant for our own society, putting into perspective our own conceptions and perceptions. Everyone today is able to establish a personal reference to such topics as the body, love or illness, and this communicability to non-specialists is of particular importance to me. The

2 Von Krusenstjern, *Selbstzeugnisse*; Wollina, (in this volume).

3 Dinzelbacher, *Mentalitätsgeschichte*; Goetz, *Vorstellungsgeschichte*; Kortüm, *Menschen*; Laak, *Alltagsgeschichte*.

historical view on such topics teaches us to be more aware about our own constructions of the world. At this point, it seems especially important to me that we as Mamlukologists also take up such research questions, because in this way we may be able to more effectively deconstruct the picture of an alleged uniform and foreign Islamic culture. I will now discuss the pioneering and future potential of Mamlukology as Historical Anthropology, taking up the body as a topic for examination. In fact, Historical Anthropology has only been used in very few cases as a methodological frame of reference, not only for Mamluk studies, but also for Islamic studies more generally.[4] Without a doubt, the human body constitutes one central topic of historical-anthropological research. Publications about this topic in the framework of European History are abundant.[5]

As Mamlukologists, we would like to understand how different people within Mamluk society perceived their bodies. Did some of them experience their body as a burden that one would try to ignore and get rid of as soon as possible? Would one rather try to mask one's own corporality or, on the contrary, try to accentuate it? Which forms would people use for highlighting their corporality? How far into the Mamluk texts can we read any consciousness of the body? How was the body discussed and represented? Were bodies flagellated, castigated or mutilated? Which meanings were then ascribed to such acts? Which bodies or parts of the body, on the other hand, were trimmed, well-kept and looked after? Which aspects were important, and what kind of effort was given to such activities? What about the militarily trained body? Did different body ideals exist? Which bodies were considered as beautiful, and which were perceived as repellent? How far could individuals express their feelings through the body? How was, for example, pride or dignity displayed? Who would feel shame because of his or her body, when and for what reasons? How could pain be expressed? Were there any bodily social markers? What happened with the body, according to the Mamluk imagination, in the grave; during and after the resurrection? What do we know about forms of veneration, where individual bodies or body-parts played a role? What would this imply, and how was it interpreted? Which body gestures were described, and which functions were ascribed to them?

It seems to be of fundamental importance that we pose and follow such questions if we want to take the historical-anthropological approach seriously, trying to understand the variances amongst human beings, their feelings, and spaces of action and negotiation. Until recently, such research that engages with the human body in its comprehensive dimensions of subjective feelings, ex-

4 Conermann, Hees, *Kulturwissenschaft*; Bauer, *Ambiguität.*

5 Bynum, *Körper*; Tanner, *Körpererfahrung*; Duden, *Body history*; Van Dülmen, *Körper-Geschichten*; Frei Gerlach, *Körperkonzepte*; Labouvie, *Leiblichkeit*; Le Goff, Truong *Geschichte des Körpers*; Lorenz, *Leibhaftige Vergangenheit*; Porter, *History.*

pressions, and experiences, while at the same time connecting these to different kinds of perceptions and constructions of the body available in Mamluk society, has yet to be explored by scholars. In the frame of Islamic studies, we can find some research on religious and philosophical perceptions of the human body, but none of these studies focuses on specific Mamluk texts.[6] From Denis Gril's study on the body of the Prophet in the stimulating volume *Le corps et le sacré en Orient musulman*, for example,[7] we learn how important it can be to distinguish between the different Arabic notions for the body, namely *jism*, *jasad* and *badan*. One question worth asking is how these notions developed in Mamluk times. The outstanding symbolism of the Prophet's body is also the focus of an interesting article by Brannon Wheeler.[8] How were such issues discussed by Mamluk authors? Prominent among the above-mentioned studies are those about mystic attitudes towards the body. Can we describe any specific Mamluk ideas and practices in the field of Sufi studies? It is astonishing that there are no monograph-length studies on the philosophical-theological discussions about the relationship between body and soul. Intimately connected to the understandings of the body are the topics of gender, sexuality and love. These topics have been dealt with in the framework of the pre-modern history of the Muslim world. Relevant monographs and edited volumes on these topics do exist, but they are not dedicated specifically to the Mamluk period.[9] Concerning the methodological approach, we should highlight the considerations made by Thomas Bauer about love poetry and the history of mentalities. His approach to Arabic poetry attests to the importance of literary texts, and especially of poetry as a source for historical-anthropological research that is, of course, also available for the Mamluk period. Concerning the topic of love, Robert Irwin und Everett Rowson have dealt with similar texts from the Mamluk period.[10]

In relation to these studies are works dealing with the history of women concerning issues of gender, sexuality, and love. One must keep in mind that even in this cluster of topics that receive attention in Islamic studies, as far as Mamluk studies are concerned, an academic lacunae exists. In this case, because of the available research on earlier as well as on later periods, one could imagine a future undertaking that might investigate specific Mamluk perceptions of love, as compared to other periods. Questions about the human body lead us to the

6 Bedhioufi, *Corps*; Chebel, *Corps*; Katz, *Body*; Khoury, *Body*; Kugle, *Sufis*; Mayeur-Jaouen, Heyberger, *Corps*.

7 Gril, *Corps*.

8 Wheeler, *Gift*.

9 Al-Sayyid-Marsot, *Society*; Musallam, *Sex*; Bouhdiba, *Sexuality*; Malti-Douglas, *Woman's*; Marmon, *Eunuchs*; Wright, Rowson, *Homoeroticism*; Bauer, *Liebe*; El-Rouayheb, *Homosexuality*; Babayan, Najmabadi, *Sexualities*.

10 Irwin, *'Alī al-Baghdādī*; Rowson, *Homoerotic*, 158–191.

topics of health and illness. When and for what reasons did an individual feel ill? How did one express such feelings? Which possibilities were open for the individual to regain health? How were disabilities perceived? Which bodies were considered healthy? The works of Michael Dols on the Black Death, but even more specifically on the topic of madness, are outstanding examples of research dealing with this array of questions, but again, the Mamluk period receives no attention in his research.[11]

One Mamlukological study of particular value as an example of the possibilities for an historical-anthropological approach to questions of health and illness can be seen in an article by Fedwa Malti-Douglas on the cultural meanings of blindness.[12] She works with a highly methodological consciousness, combining ideas from the history of mentalities with the structuralistic approach taken from literary study. Referring to research done in European history, she also dares to make some trans-cultural comparisons. Her main source is the biographical lexicon on blind people written by al-Ṣafadī, but she combines her findings from this text with others, like lexicography, dream literature, Quranic commentaries, literary works, proverbs and jokes. By analyzing the Arabic vocabulary, she points out that blindness was conceived of as a disability, but it was not associated with darkness, as in Western medieval texts. Blindness was described as a bodily deficit, but, unlike European sources, this deficit was not given any spiritual meaning. Taking examples from the biographies, she tries to draw conclusions concerning the daily life of blind individuals, and she shows that one important aspect that was represented in the biographies was the possible mobility for a blind person through the help of a guide. This aspect depicted blind people on the one hand as dependent, while on the other hand, integrated into society. Blindness was not darkness, but seeing with foreign eyes. One further aspect of daily life that appeared in the biographies was the discussion of eating with the blind. This was perceived as a difficult task, but can be interpreted as an integrative, socially important action. Malti-Douglas underlines the central meaning of corporality that nurtures Mamluk perceptions of blindness. Neither ruler nor prophet could be imagined with a defected body, and blindness would make the body defected. Their authority was gained from a "whole" body. Blind people, in the Mamluk texts, were thought of in connection with women. They were, in a similar way, conceived as being bodily defected, but at the same time a natural part of society. As a compensation for the loss of sight, blind people in the Western Middle Ages gained spiritual vision. Such an idea was explicitly disclaimed by Muslim authors. In the Mamluk world of perceptions, blind people were compensated with extra sexuality, and this was another

11 Dols, *Black Death*; Idem, *Majnūn.*
12 Malti-Douglas, *Mentalités.*

point that connected them to women. On the contrary, in the West, blindness was associated with castration. Blindness in the West was seen as a punishment for sexual transgressions. Mamluk texts also depicted blindness as a punishment, but in the context of religious transgression. Fedwa Malti-Douglas also discusses the meaning of blind people engaged in recitation, especially as Qur'an reciters, that points to the importance of the oral transmission of texts. She is well aware of the fact that she cannot show any development or changes of these perceptions in order to discuss how far they were specifically Mamluk. Her study is of course only a first step that captivates through its complexity. Since historical-anthropological questions have been posed so rarely, I think it is a clever way to proceed in such a synchronic fashion, concentrating on the Mamluk period, but taking into consideration as many literary genres as possible in order to explore a topic like blindness. As a future perspective, it would be of course reasonable to extend the comparison to other periods of the pre-modern Muslim world, since this will be the only way to understand the specific possibilities for a blind person in Mamluk society. Apart from this, we can of course find out more about blind individuals and blindness during the Mamluk period. For example, Malti-Douglas does use the biographical lexicon on blind people composed by al-Ṣafadī, and all the examples she provides discuss persons from pre-Mamluk times. They belong, of course, to the Mamluk world of images of blindness, but what about contemporary individuals? She also mentions that the majority of al-Ṣafadī's blind persons became blind only in their old age, but she excludes this aspect completely from her discussion. Of course, we can use additional genres to find out more about this topic. Malti-Douglas, for example, did not touch upon medical or juridical literature, or poetry. However, this example shows us how interesting such questions can be, and how rich our material is.

Dealing with such topics surrounding issues of health and illness, of course, brings into focus the role of medicine in Mamluk culture and society. The social history of medicine is a very interesting subject, and research related to this subject matter is needed in order to contextualize individual perceptions of health and illness, and more generally of the body. Some researchers have been exploring these issues specifically for the Mamluk period; one thinks, in this line, of the work of Linda Northrup on the history and function of Qalawun's great hospital; Paulina Lewicka's engagement with the figure of the Jewish doctor; and Leigh Chipman's study on the professional world of a Mamluk pharmacist.[13] One topic that is always of special interest for historians of daily life is food and eating. This topic manifests itself in connection with blind people as a social issue, since food played a major role in Mamluk perceptions of health

13 Chipman, *Pharmacy*; Behrens-Abouseif, *Fatḥ Allāh*; Lewicka, (in this volume); Northrup, *Qalāwūn's Patronage.*

and illness. Food and eating have so many layers of meaning, making it a fascinating topic. An extensive list of studies related to the culture of eating for the pre-modern Muslim world already exists. While they have produced many interesting results, they lack any specific focus on the Mamluk period.[14] One exception is the monograph by Paulina Lewicka on food and foodways of medieval Cairenes. Her focus is on the Mamluk period, showing how a new culinary culture developed during this period.[15] At one point, she discusses the etiquette for sharing the table, where she uses texts on table manners, including Mamluk works.[16] And, like Fedwa Malti-Doulgas, she refers to existing research on Western medieval texts, making trans-cultural comparative remarks possible. She points to the importance of religious prescriptions concerning table manners in Arabic-Islamic texts, underlining the perceptions that surround the relationship between host and guest. In comparison to Western texts, she tries to show that Arabic-Islamic table manners were much more concerned with respect towards the co-eaters. She highlights the importance of tradition with regard to the Arabic-Islamic table manners, concluding from this fact that they did not take over the role of courtly trendsetter, as was the case in Europe. Amalia Levanoni deals with food and food preparation, specifically in Mamluk times, in order to understand its social and political implications.[17] She discusses the distinguishing feature of possessing one's own kitchen and cooking utensils, as well as the special role of meat and sugar consumption as an indicator of wealth, which on special occasions was shared with the poor in order to illustrate and legitimize wealth and power. Like Lewicka, Levanoni discusses table manners, and comes to the same conclusion (even though referring to specific Mamluk customs) that in the Mamluk Empire it was not the court that set the model. Rather, the scholarly elite used table manners in order to distinguish themselves not only from the poor masses, but also from the ruling Mamluk military elite. Such approaches are interesting, and we can imagine many more questions about food and eating.

Concluding with a final example, questions about the body also lead us to topics connected to the stages of life – like childhood and old age – marked by physical changes of the body. Several publications have explored the issue of childhood, most of them dealing with Muslim history more generally, approaching the topic from different vantage points.[18] From my perspective, a

14 Van Gelder, *Dishes*; Gyselen, *Banquets*; Heine, *Weinstudien*; Heine, *Kulinarische Studien*; Marin, Waines, *Alimentación*; Rosenthal, *Herb*; Waines, *Caliph's Kitchen*; Zubaida, Tapper, *Culinary Cultures.*

15 Lewicka, *Food.*

16 Lewicka, *Food*, 387–454; Idem, *Shared Meal.*

17 Levanoni, *Food.*

18 Adamek, *Kleinkind*; Giladi, *Children*; Giladi, *Infants*; Glander, *Oriental Child.*

major problem arises when such a topic is discussed as "Islamic," without further clarifying time or space. Furthermore, the uncritical use of texts of various genres without consideration of their function or contexts of production compromises the results of such studies. This predicament stems from the scarcity of published research to which scholars can refer. One way out of this dilemma is to study one very specific text, like the mamlukological study by Thomas Bauer on the Kindertotenlieder by Ibn Nubātah.[19] He elucidates, in a very sensitive way, the emotional effect of a mourning poet on the premature death of his own child. The way the poet talks about his child reveals his perceptions of childhood, but also those of the intended audience in a more general meaning. The poem attests to the intimate relationship between fathers and their children. Once more, we see the special relevance of poetry for historical-anthropological questions.

In my own research, I try to approach the topic "youth", concentrating on one specific genre, namely Quranic commentaries, including those from the Mamluk period.[20] In this way I am able to demonstrate that the authors perceived the notion of *shabāb* as the ultimate phase in life, when one is in command of his full manly strength, with a fully developed beard until the age of forty. In our contemporary perceptions, on the contrary, we understand the notion "youth" to refer to a phase of change, marked by puberty. We typically mean by this the age between roughly 15 and 24. This example indicates how different our own perceptions can be, and how easy it is to misinterpret texts when using our own frameworks. We need to study very carefully the concepts behind words, the history of notions. This can be one starting point for historical-anthropological research. On the other hand, I see the importance that one should try to combine as many different textual genres in order to be able to illuminate as many aspects of a given topic as possible. The problem lies, of course, in the fact that each genre is governed by its own rules, and many of them are deeply intertwined with their own traditions. In this early stage, it seems crucial to me to concentrate on one specific time, like the Mamluk period, in order to be able to contextualize the particular texts. In my current research on the history of old age in Mamluk times, I try to appropriate this approach. I first compare the perceptions of old age in medical, religious and literary texts. Parallel to these more general perceptions, I try to understand individual possibilities of behavior in old age in connection with illness, piety, office and dignity, using biographical information about contemporaries. The historical-anthropological approach, used in this manner, is uniquely suited to combining research on the framework imposed by cultural conceptions with individual experiences and individual negotiations

19 Bauer, *Communication.*
20 Hees, *Kraft.*

with those conceptions. Mamlukology can only be enriched through such an understanding of the individual as (s)he perceives his/her own culture.

Bibliography

Adamek, Gerhard, Das Kleinkind in Glaube und Sitte der Araber im Mittelalter, Bonn 1968.

Al-Sayyid-Marsot, E.L., Society and the sexes in Medieval Islam, Malibu: Undena 1979.

Babayan, Kathryn and Najmabadi, Afsaneh, Islamicate Sexualities: Translations across Temporal Geographies of Desire, Cambridge, London: Harvard University Press 2008.

Bauer, Thomas, "Communication and Emotion: The Case of Ibn Nubātah's Kindertotenlieder", Mamlūk Studies Review 7 (2003), pp. 49–96.

Bauer, Thomas, Die Kultur der Ambiguität. Eine andere Geschichte des Islams, Berlin: Verlag der Weltreligionen im Insel Verlag 2011.

Bauer, Thomas, Liebe und Liebesdichtung in der arabischen Welt des 9. und 10. Jahrhunderts: eine literatur- und mentalitätsgeschichtliche Studie des arabischen Gazal, Wiesbaden: Harrassowitz 1998.

Bedhioufi, Hafsi, Corps et traditions islamiques: divisions ontologiques et ritualités du corps, Tunis: Noir sur Blanc 2000.

Behrens-Abouseif, Doris, Fatḥ Allāh and Abū Zakariyya. Physicians under the Mamluks, Kairo: Institut Français d'Archéologie Orientale 1987.

Bouhdiba, Abdelwahab, Sexuality and Islam, London: Routledge & Kegan Paul 1985.

Bynum, Caroline, "Warum das ganze Theater mit dem Körper? Die Sicht einer Mediävistin," Historische Anthropologie 4 (1996), pp. 1–33.

Chebel, Malek, Le corps en Islam. Paris: Presses Universitaires de France 1999.

Chipman, Leigh, The World of Pharmacy and Pharmacists in Mamlūk Cairo, Leiden: Brill 2010.

Conermann, Stephan and Syrinx von Hees (eds.), Islamwissenschaft als Kulturwissenschaft I. Historische Anthropologie – Ansätze und Möglichkeiten, Schenefeld: EB-Verlag 2007.

Daniel, Ute, Kompendium Kulturgeschichte. Theorie, Praxis, Schlüsselwörter, Frankfurt: Suhrkamp 2001.

Dinzelbacher, Peter, Europäische Mentalitätsgeschichte. Hauptthemen in Einzeldarstellungen, Stuttgart: Alfred Kröner 1993.

Dols, Michael, Majnūn: The Madman in Medieval Islamic Society, Oxford: Calrendon1992.

Dols, Michael, The Black Death in the Middle East, Princeton: University Press 1977.

Dressel, Gert, Historische Anthropologie. Eine Einführung, Wien: Böhlau 1996.

Duden, Barbara, Body History: a repertory, Wolfenbüttel: Tandem 1990.

El-Rouayheb, Khaled, Before Homosexuality in the Arabic-Islamic World, 1500–1800, Chicago: University of Chicago 2005.

Frei Gerlach, Franziska, et al. (eds.), Körperkonzepte/Concepts du corps. Interdisziplinäre Studien zur Geschlechterforschung, Münster: Waxmann 2003.

Giladi, Avner, Children of Islam. Concepts of Childhood in Medieval Muslim Society, New York: St. Martin's 1992.

Giladi, Avner, Infants, Parents and Wet Nurses: Medieval Islamic Views on Breastfeeding and Their Social Implications, Leiden: Brill 1999.

Glander, Annelies, The Oriental Child: not born in wedlock; a study of the anthropological parameters, religious motivations, and sociological phenomena of child care in Islam and Judaism, Frankfurt: Peter Lang 2001.

Goetz, Hans-Werner, "'Vorstellungsgeschichte': Menschliche Vorstellungen und Meinungen als Dimension der Vergangenheit. Bemerkungen zu einem jüngeren Arbeitsfeld der Geschichtswissenschaft als Beitrag zu einer Methodik der Quellenauswertung," Archiv für Kulturgeschichte 61 (1971), pp. 253 – 271.

Goetz, Hans-Werner, Moderne Mediävistik. Stand und Perspektiven der Mittelalterforschung, Darmstadt: Wissenschaftliche Buchgesellschaft 1999.

Gril, Denis, "Le Corps du Prophète," in: Mayeur-Jaouen, Heyberger, Le corps, 37 – 57.

Gyselen, Rika, Banquets d'Orient, Bures-sur-Yvette: 1992.

Hees, Syrinx von, "Die Kraft der Jugend und die Vielfalt der Übergangsphasen. Eine historisch-anthropoloigsche Auswertung von Korankommentaren des 10. bis 15. Jahrhunderts," in: Islamwissenschaft als Kulturwissenschaft I. Historische Anthropologie – Ansätze und Möglichkeiten, eds. Stephan Conermann and Syrinx von Hees, Schenefeld: EB-Verlag 2007, pp. 139 – 176.

Heine, Peter, Kulinarische Studien. Untersuchungen zur Kochkunst im arabisch-islamischen Mittelalter. Mit Rezepten, Wiesbaden: Harrassowitz 1988.

Heine, Peter, Weinstudien. Untersuchungen zu Anbau, Produktion und Konsum des Weins im arabisch-islamischen Mittelalter, Wiesbaden: Harrassowitz 1982.

Irwin, Robert, "ʿAlī al-Baghdādī and the joy of Mamluk sex," in: The historiography of Islamic Egypt, c. 950 – 1800, ed. Hugh Kennedy, Leiden: Brill 2001, pp. 45 – 57.

Katz, Marion, Body of text: the emergence of the Sunnī law of ritual purity, Albany (USA): State University of New York Press 2002.

Khoury, Fouad, The body in Islamic culture, London: Saqi 2001.

Kortüm, Hans-Henning, Menschen und Mentalitäten. Einführung in Vorstellungswelten des Mittelalters, Berlin: Akademie 1996.

Kugle, Scott, Sufis and saints' bodies: mysticism, corporeality and sacred power in Islam, Chapel Hill: University of North Carolina 2007.

Labouvie, Eva, "Leiblichkeit und Emotionalität: Zur Kulturwissenschaft des Körpers und der Gefühle," in: Handbuch der Kulturwissenschaften, eds. Friedrich Jaeger, et al., Stuttgart: Metzler 2004, pp. 79 – 91.

Le Goff, Jacques and Nicolas Truong, Die Geschichte des Körpers im Mittelalter, Stuttgart: Klett-Cotta, 2007.

Le Goff, Jacques, "Neue Geschichtswissenschaft," in: Die Rückeroberung des historischen Denkens. Grundlagen der Neuen Geschichtswissenschaft, eds. Jacques Le Goff, Roger Chartier, and Jacques Revel, Frankfurt: Fischer 1990, pp. 11 – 61.

Levanoni, Amalia, "Food and Cooking during the Mamluk Era: Social and Political Implications," Mamluk Studies Review 9/2 (2005), pp. 201 – 222.

Lewicka, Paulina B., "When a Shared Meal is Formalized. Observations on Arabic "Table Manners" Manuals of the Middle Ages," Studia Arabistyczne I Islamistyczne 11 (2005), pp. 96 – 107.

Lewicka, Paulina B., Food and Foodways of Medieval Cairenes. Aspects of Life in an Islamic Metropolis of the Eastern Mediterranean, Leiden: Brill 2011.
Lorenz, Maren, Leibhaftige Vergangenheit. Einführung in die Körpergeschichte, Tübingen: Diskord 2000.
Malti-Douglas, Fedwa, "Mentalités and Marginality: Blindness and Mamlūk Civilization," in: The Islamic world from classical to modern times: essays in honor of Bernard Lewis, eds. C.E. Bosworth, et al., Princeton: Darwin Press 1989, pp. 211 – 237.
Malti-Douglas, Fedwa, Woman's Body, Women's Word. Gender and Discourse in Arabo-Islamic Writing, Princeton: Princeton University 1991.
Marin, Manuela and David Waines, La alimentación en las culturas islámicas: Una colección de estudios, Madrid: Agencia Española de Cooperación Internacional 1994.
Marmon, Shaun Elizabeth, Eunuchs and sacred boundaries in Islamic society, New York: Oxford University 1995.
Maurer, Michael, "Historische Anthropologie," in: Aufriß der Historischen Wissenschaften Band 7: Neue Themen und Methoden der Geschichtswissenschaft, ed. Michael Maurer, Stuttgart: Philipp Reclam 2003, pp. 294 – 387.
Mayeur-Jaouen, Catherine and Bernard Heyberger (eds.), Le corps et le sacré en Orient musulman. (special edition of), Revue des Mondes Musulmans et de la Méditerranée 113 – 114 (2007), Aix-en-Provence: Édisud.
Medick, Hans, "Quo vadis Historische Anthropologie? Geschichtsforschung zwischen Historischer Kulturwissenschaft und Mikro-Historie," Historische Anthropologie 9 (2001), pp. 78 – 92.
Musallam, Basim, Sex and Society. Birth Control before the nineteenth century, Cambridge: Cambridge University 1983.
Northrup, Linda S., "Qalāwūn's Patronage of the Medical Sciences in Thirteenth-Century Egypt," Mamluk Studies Review 5 (2001), pp. 119 – 140.
Porter, Roy, "History of the Body," in: New Perspectives on Historical Writing, ed. Peter Brooke, Oxford: Polity 1991, pp. 206 – 232.
Reinhard, Wolfgang, Lebensformen Europas. Eine historische Kulturanthropologie, München: C.H. Beck 2004.
Rosenthal, Franz, The Herb: Hashish versus Medieval Muslim Society, Leiden: Brill 1971.
Rowson, Everett, "Two Homoerotic Narratives from Mamluk Literature: al-Ṣafadī's Lawʿat al-Shākī and Ibn Dāniyāl's Mutayyam," in: Homoeroticism in Classical Arabic Literature, eds. J.W. Wright and Everett K. Rowson, New York: Columbia University 1997, pp. 158 – 191.
Tanner, Jakob, "Körpererfahrung, Schmerz und die Konstruktion des Kulturellen," Historische Anthropologie 2 (1994), pp. 489 – 502.
Van Dülmen, Richard, Historische Anthropologie. Entwicklung, Probleme, Aufgaben, Köln: Böhlau 2000.
Van Dülmen, Richard, Körper-Geschichten. Studien zur historischen Kulturforschung, Frankfurt a.M.: Fischer 1996.
Van Gelder, Geert Jan, Of Dishes and Discourse. Classical Arabic Literary Representations of Food, Richmond: Curzon 2000.
Van Laak, Dirk, "Alltagsgeschichte," in: Aufriß der Historischen Wissenschaften Band 7: Neue Themen und Methoden der Geschichtswissenschaft, ed. Michael Maurer, Stuttgart: Philipp Reclam 2003, pp. 14 – 80.

Von Krusenstjern, Bengina, “Was sind Selbstzeugnisse? Begriffsgeschichte und quellenkritische Überlegungen anhand von Beispielen aus dem 17. Jahrhundert,” Historische Anthropologie 2 (1994), pp. 462–471.

Waines, David, In a Caliph’s Kitchen, London: Riad El-Rayyes 1989.

Wheeler, Brannon, “Gift of the body in Islam: the Prophet Muhammad’s camel sacrifice and distribution of hair and nails at his farewell pilgrimage,” Numen: International Review of the History of Religions 57/3–4 (2010), pp. 341–388.

Wright, J.W. and Everett K. Rowson (eds.), Homoeroticism in Classical Arabic Literature, New York: Columbia University 1997.

Wulf, Christoph, Vom Menschen. Handbuch Historische Anthropologie, Weinheim und Basel: Beltz 1997.

Zubaida, Sami and Richard Tapper, Culinary Cultures of the Middle East, London: I.B. Tauris 1994.

Thomas Herzog

Mamluk (Popular) Culture. The State of Research

Before trying to assess the state of research on Mamluk (popular) culture, let me briefly discuss the notions by which we construct the object of our research, i. e. "culture" and a somehow "popular" version of it. I will next present the field of research topics that this definition circumscribes and the possible sources for such research and then discuss the main contributions that European, North American, Arab, and Japanese scholars have produced in the last decades. I will conclude with some propositions for further research.

What can we understand by "culture", and how can popular culture be distinguished, if at all, from other forms of "culture"? This question is not just a ritual academic preliminary; different definitions of "culture" and "popular" are the outcome of quite different theoretical assumptions and political standpoints, and eventually lead to quite different key questions and areas of inquiry to be covered by our research.

The first definition to establish in this context is that of "culture".[1] What do we consider "culture"? The former Cambridge professor of drama, novelist, and critic Raymond Williams (1921 – 1988) states that "culture" is "one or two of the most complicated words in the English language," and this is certainly also true for German, French, and other European languages. Williams suggests two different definitions of culture that can be useful for our purpose.[2] First, "culture" might be defined as "the works and practices of intellectual and especially artistic activity", "in other words 'culture' here means the texts and practices whose principal function is to signify, to produce [...] meaning".[3] This is what many people usually understand by "culture". But Williams also proposes a much wider definition, which is to consider culture "a particular way of life, whether of a people, a period or a group".[4] Whereas this second definition of

1 The following passages are indebted to Storey, *Cultural Theory*, 1 – 14.
2 Williams, *Keywords*, 87.
3 Storey, *Cultural Theory*, 2.
4 Williams, *Keywords*, 90, cited in Storey, *Cultural Theory*, 2.

"culture" does not exclude the first one – intellectual and artistic activities are also part of the "way of life" of human societies – it is evident that the second definition ("culture as a way of life") includes a much wider range of subjects, especially those many people associated with "popular culture". Such a wide definition of "culture" is definitely opposed to any of the traditional elitist 19th- and 20th-century conceptions of culture, as proposed, for instance, by Mathew Arnold[5] or F. R. Leavis,[6] which unconsciously still exert a considerable influence even on academic discourses. It is the wide definition of "culture" I would like to use for the following considerations.

Having thus opted for a wide definition of culture as a "way of life", what should we understand by "popular culture"? The English term "popular", after having been understood as "widespread, generally accepted", was used from the beginning of the 19th century on "to designate forms of entertainment that are said to appeal to the tastes of ordinary people", for example "popular press", "popular songs", "popular music", "popular art". In this understanding, "popular" means "what is liked by many people", a quantitative definition. The problem here is to define the threshold at which something is liked by enough people to be termed "popular": 20, 30, 40, 50 % of a given population? This is indeed difficult to say and to measure, in any case for past cultures. Another widespread understanding of popular is that of the folklorists, "popular culture" being the culture that originates from the "people", that spontaneously emerges from "below", that is communal and self-made. But who are the "people"? Many of the 19th-century nationalist and romantic intellectuals who were at the beginning of the discovery of "popular culture", distinguished "rural folk" and "urban masses", only the former being the source of genuine popular culture, the latter being considered merely passive consumers of low-level commercial entertainment. What then about Mamluk rural folk and urban masses?

Both proposed definitions oppose "popular culture" to the culture of a group of relatively few persons belonging to the "high" spheres of society, to elite culture, usually defining elite culture as the "real" culture, whereas "popular" culture is understood as a category to accommodate texts and practices that fail to be "real" culture. The problem about this definition of popular culture is that those who use it generally insist that the division between "popular" and "real" culture is absolutely clear, and that it is supposedly outside historical change and

5 Conforming to the etymology of the word, Arnold understood "culture" as intimately linked to an idea of "civilization", being the contrary of "nature", which was associated with barbarism. In Arabic, by the way, one of the main terms for "culture", *thaqāfah*, is linked to the notion of being refined, cultivated, and thus shows precisely this opposition to a "natural" state of "barbarism".

6 "Culture has always been in minority keeping." Leavis, Thompson, *Culture and Environment*, 3.

historical contingency. Nevertheless the contrary is true: if we consider such eminently elite cultural phenomenon of European culture as the theater of Shakespeare, the Italian opera, or the French "film noir", we have to admit that all these cultural products began as despised amusements of the common people before finding their way to the realm of real "high" culture. Moreover, "high" and "popular" culture fluctuate not only on the diachronic level, but also the synchronic level; products of elite culture have also always been consumed by the great mass of people, by rural "folk" and "urban masses" – for instance in the realm of religion – whereas a lot of what is commonly termed "popular culture" was and is produced and/or consumed by parts of the elite.

A number of scholars belonging to the American sociological tradition – heavily influenced by the work of Pierre Bourdieu[7] – and to the British "Cultural Studies" insist therefore, in a rigorous postmodern logic, on the necessity of abolishing altogether "the binaries of 'high' and 'low', elite and popular".[8] According to them, the terms of these binaries have no essence, but exist only as relations.[9] They understand culture "as something that exists only as a process of mutual appropriation in which various practices and discourses are constantly shared between and among social groups",[10] as a dynamic process of endless circulation. They thereby try to avoid replicating ideas of cultural hierarchy and of an autonomous and self-contained elite or popular culture.[11] Nevertheless students of culture find it nearly impossible to avoid "the popular [..., the] kind of living dead to whom scholarly research 'restores the vitality'".[12] This might be especially true for scholars studying pre-modern Islamic societies, like the Mamluk one, where the distinction between *ʿāmmah* and *khāṣṣah* is omnipresent in the sources, which were mostly written by eminent *ʿulamāʾ* who expressed their normative perception of social order and affirmed the distinction between *ʿāmmah* and *khāṣṣah* that might have been a widely used pattern of understanding of society.[13] On the other hand, Jonathan Berkey argues that "in the

7 In this perception, the ultimate sense of "culture" is to make, mark, and maintain what Bourdieu calls "social distinction", the social hierarchy of the ruling elite and the ruled people.
8 Shershow, *New Life*, 2:362.
9 Shershow, *New Life*, 2:363.
10 Shershow, *New Life*, 2:363.
11 Shershow, *New Life*, 2:379.
12 Shershow, *New Life*, 2:368.
13 See Berkey, *Popular Culture*, 139. To pose the question about the existence of a distinct "popular culture" in terms of self-consciousness, as does Berkey, op. cit., 134, ("Rather, the central issue might be phrased in this way: is there a stratum of cultural activity and production that is self-consciously distinct from that of the elite, and which is produced independently from, or even in opposition to 'elite culture'?") is appealing, but does not take us very far, for in most instances we will never be able to find clear evidence of such a self-consciousness. Moreover, in many cases we find evidence that cultural products that did not

Islamic Middle East [the] distinction [between "high" and "popular" culture] is even harder to draw, since the lines separating one social group from another were, in general, more porous than they were in medieval Europe."[14]

Sharing a large number of the aforementioned concerns, I am thus quite reluctant to continue to construct an object of study called "Mamluk popular culture", but prefer to speak on first mention of Mamluk culture in general, being the "works, practices, ways of life and world views of the population of the Mamluk Empire, be these works, practices or world views intellectual or artistical or simply of everyday use, custom and tradition."[15] After describing them as thoroughly as possible, these phenomena of culture (understood as described above) might be retraced to the various social groups they occurred in. Research on the festivities of a "saint's" *mawlid*, for instance, should thus first consist of gathering and evaluating the statements in the different sources, of describing and comparing these phenomena with other phenomena of similar kinds, before assigning and thereby confining them to certain social groups. In a large number of cases, moreover, labeling cultural phenomenon "popular" obstructs a neutral view of the phenomenon and, from the beginning, introduces social biases (those from the sources and our own) to the historical research. Researching on Mamluk culture as a whole, rather than on Mamluk "popular culture", also widens the view of the realty that Mamluk culture was an affair of many different social groups, without insisting on social hierarchies.

As a concession to the critics of the abolishment of the "popular", and in order to avoid "collisions" with other contributions to this volume, I would like to signal here that the studies of Mamluk cultural phenomenon I will review in this contribution will not include those phenomena that were primarily or exclusively restricted to the intellectual or military elite, although, as we will see, "elite" cultural products may constitute an important source material when assessing various cultural phenomena that were not restricted to elite groups.

To structure the field of Mamluk (popular) culture, I propose a tripartite division of the cultural field according to the spaces in which the cultural phenomena mainly occurred. One cultural field would thus be the works, practices, and ways of life that take place outside the house and the inner family circle: in the neighborhood, on the fields, roads, streets, and squares, and in any public or

stem exclusively from the elite imitated their learned, elite counterparts (see for instance the allegations of learned authorships in "popular" *siyar*, see Herzog, *What they saw*, 27).

14 Berkey, *Popular Culture*, 135.

15 And so did for, instance, Karamustafa, *God's unruly friends* and Taylor, *Vicinity of the Righteous*, whereas B. Shoshan adopted the contrary position, see Shoshan, *Popular Culture*, 6–7, and Shoshan, *Review of Taylor's Vicinity*, 32:545–546. See also Homerin's review of Shoshan's *Popular Culture* in *MSR* 1, 175–178. See also Shoshan, *Popular Culture*, 76.

semi-public spaces[16] of Mamluk cities and countryside. A second cultural field would concern the works, practices, and ways of life that take place inside the house and within the inner family circle. Finally, the third cultural field, which is the most difficult to grasp, could be described as the world views, imaginations, and mental attitudes in people's minds in Mamluk times.

This leads me to the question of the sources. Unlike the preceding periods of Arab and Islamic history, the Mamluk era is in fact quite rich in material that historians may rely on for reconstructing cultural history. Certainly, we do not have at our disposal the vast archival or documentary sources available to European historians, but still, the Mamluk era provides us with a huge body of *waqf* documents from which a number of scholars have extracted much useful information.[17] In addition to the bulk of *waqfīyah* material that still awaits full exploitation, the Mamluk chronicles and biographical dictionaries, when used creatively,[18] can offer much of the information European historians extracted from their documentary material. Aside from the well-known chronicles and biographical dictionaries, most of them the work of eminent *ʿulamāʾ*, there is a vast array of narrative sources, many of them still unpublished or even uncatalogued, waiting for the researcher in Near Eastern and Western libraries: treatises on religious and/or political questions, on economics, collection of sermons, *ṣūfī* manuals, religious poetry, *fatwā* collections (the most widely used are those of Ibn Taymīyah and Ibn al-Ḥājj), prose literature belonging to the canonized *adab*, encyclopedic texts and anthologies, tales of all kinds, long heroic narratives mixing prose and poetry (*siyar*), texts of shadow plays (*khayāl al-ẓill*), and collections of jokes and proverbs (*amthāl*). Once studied – and there is still a long and fascinating way to go – these texts, of which only part stems from renowned or known authors (many of them are entirely anonymous), will provide us with a much more varied image of Mamluk culture than the one we have today, which is largely marked by what is normatively termed "*al-khāṣṣah*/ the elite". Last but not least, much insight into domestic and agricultural history, for instance, can still be gained from material artifacts, sources archeologists have been studying for a number of years with precious results.[19]

The research on Mamluk cultural history done in the last four decades[20] owes

16 Streets and lanes (*shawāriʿ*, *ḥārāt* and *aziqqah*) are not entirely public spaces, but semi-public ones, as the social control of the neighborhoods filtered, if not the access, so at least the behavior of foreigners to the *ḥārah*.

17 See for instance Sabra, *Poverty and Charity* or Carl Petry's numerous publications in this field, for example for his programmatic article "*A Geniza for Mamluk Studies.*"

18 For instance, as Michael Chamberlain did in his *Knowledge* and Jonathan Berkey in his *Transmission*.

19 Please see B. Walker's contribution to this volume.

20 The following passage is indebted to Clifford, *Ubi sumus*.

a lot to a (relatively small) number of social historians who described and analyzed the social groups and structures of Mamluk society. Ira M. Lapidus' 1967 groundbreaking study *Muslim Cities in the Later Middle Ages*[21] gave us, in addition to other extremely valuable insights, a model for understanding the multiform group of the *ʿulamāʾ*. In his synchronic, normative, systems perspective,[22] Lapidus understood the *ʿulamāʾ* as the major group that transmitted elite norms and values to the Mamluk society. Very much influenced by Max Weber and Talcott Parsons' normative functionalism,[23] Lapidus saw Mamluk society functioning in equilibrium due to the normative power of the political and social elites who successfully transmitted their cultural values to the whole of the society. Although Lapidus was convinced that Mamluk society was functionally integrated by the elite's normative power, entailing a consensual behavior in the lower classes that conformed to these elite values, he was by no means an advocate of a clear-cut, bipolar model of Mamluk society. He thought on the contrary that informal social networks, patronage, and clientelist networks (families, ethnic-religious factions, neighborhoods, etc.), transcended both "class" segmentation in Mamluk cities and the assumed dichotomy between city and countryside. Jean-Claude Garcin's 1976 study of the southern Egyptian provincial city of Qūṣ[24] and its intimate interwovenness with the surrounding countryside confirmed this basic view of Lapidus, and Carl F. Petry's 1981 *The Civilian Elite of Cairo in the Later Middle Ages* points out that the civilian elite did not derive from a single class or a restricted stratum, but that social mobility was a reality.[25] Finally, in the last chapter of his 1992 *The Transmission of Knowledge in Medieval Cairo*,[26] Jonathan Berkey shows that in Mamluk times religious and juridical knowledge was not confined to the cultural elite, but transcended "class" borders. In 1995, the paradigmatical change from structuralism and functionalism to dysfunctionalism in social sciences, a change that integrated Pierre Bourdieu's theory of struggle for "cultural capital",[27] reached the study of the social and cultural history of the Mamluk era with Michael Chamberlain's *Knowledge and Social Practice in Medieval Damascus, 1190–1350*. For Chamberlain, the main forces shaping society are no longer integrating and equilibrium-creating values, but a "never-ending struggle for social power and status".[28] With this assumption, Chamberlain broke up Lap-

21 Lapidus, *Muslim Cities*.
22 Clifford, *Ubi sumus*, 46.
23 Lapidus, *Muslim Cities*, VIII.
24 Garcin, *Centre musulman*.
25 Petry, *Civilian Elite*, 312.
26 A chapter entitled "Beyond the Elite: Education and Urban Society".
27 Bourdieu, *Outline*, 159–197.
28 Chamberlain, *Knowledge*, 175.

idus' conception of value-integrated social subsystems and made for to a model of social groups that constantly compete for political, economic, and cultural capital. In 2006, Jo Van Steenbergen's study *Order out of Chaos*, which focuses on the Mamluk elite's struggle for power between 1341 and 1382, joins Chamberlain's turn from a synchronic, normative, macro-sociological structure perspective to a diachronic, materialistic, micro-social, and post-structural view of Mamluk society.

Due the nature of the sources and their own intellectual training, many scholars from Lapidus to Van Steenbergen focused on the political and cultural elites, whom many of them saw as the sources of social formation and reproduction.[29] Nevertheless, we now have at our disposal quite a lot of studies on a variety of social groups, not all belonging to what might be termed the "elite", but, as Clifford complained in his 1997 contribution to *Mamluk Studies Review* (in the following: *MSR*) 1, they were described, but not "understood as components of social formation."[30] And still, as he continues, many scholars have conformed to Lapidus' functionalist and synchronic view of social integration by stasis,[31] eclipsing the possibility of diachronic social and cultural change.

Be this as it may, dichotomist concepts of Mamluk society dividing it into clearly separated spheres of *khāṣṣah* and *ʿāmmah*, elite and "people", learned and illiterate, city and countryside, etc., have by now mostly disappeared from the arena of scholarly research. In the domain of culture also, the idea of common cultural fields that transcend traditionally assumed dichotomies is emerging. Boaz Shoshan for instance, despite of his criticism of Taylor's, as he puts it, "simplistic assumption that [...] there has been just one monolithic [...] culture to which rulers and peasants, scholars and illiterate folk alike belonged,"[32] acknowledges that there may have been a "multi-directional flow of culture,"[33] that "in the final analysis, a refined approach to the history of culture should transcend the '-chtomous' view, the tendency to emphasize the dichotomy between 'high' and 'low' ", and concludes his book stating that the example of the Mamluk cult of "saints" indeed shows that there was in Mamluk culture "a

29 See Clifford, *Ubi sumus*, 53.

30 Clifford, *Ubi sumus*, 54. For a large list of these studies, some of them escaping Clifford's verdict (Petry, Irwin, Toru – see now also Toru, *Urban Society*), see Clifford, *Ubi sumus*, 54–55, notes 30–35.

31 Clifford, *Ubi sumus*, 55. Exception has to be made for J. Berkey's recent dialectical approach of social change brought about by confrontation of progressive and conservative tendencies, see Berkey, *Tradition* (these tendencies should by the way not simply be identified as "traditional = high" and "innovative = low" culture, an identification Clifford ascribes to Shoshan's *Popular Culture*). See the other studies cited by Clifford, *Ubi Sumus*, 56, note 36, namely Malti-Douglas, *Mentalités* and Lutfi, *Manners and Customs*.

32 Shoshan, *Review of Taylor's Vicinity*, 545–546.

33 Shoshan, *Review of Taylor's Vicinity*, 546.

common cultural domain consisting of shared practices and meanings, the very links between high and low cultures".[34]

As others have already mentioned,[35] quite a lot of research has been done in the last decades, beginning with Barbara Langner's still fundamental *Untersuchungen zur historischen Volkskunde Ägyptens nach mamlukischen Quellen.* Fortunately enough, a well-rooted social bias against non-elite cultural phenomenon that pervaded the works of many, but not all, old "orientalists" dealing with "popular culture" has more or less disappeared. In the Arab World, the study of folklore and folk life, which was often linked to Arab nationalism and nationalist regimes, may have a difficult position in times of religious rigorism that sees the Arab and Islamic past through a lens of *bida*ʿand decline and, decades after Edward Said's *Orientalism*, thereby perpetuates the traditional orientalist discourse of decline. Nonetheless, Arab scholars also continue to work on the non-exclusively elite cultural heritage, parts of it touching Mamlukological topics.

Surveying the research done, one becomes aware that most of the topics are related either to the first of my cultural fields – the works, practices, and ways of life that take place outside the house and the inner family circle – or to the third field, the world views, imaginations, and mental attitudes of people in the Mamluk (and, due to the effects of "longue durée", parts of the Ottoman) era. Probably due to the scarcity of sources, much less work has been done on the second cultural field, the practices and ways of life that took place inside the house and within the inner family circle. A *History of Private Life*[36] in the Arab World indeed remains to be written.

Many phenomena of the first of my cultural fields, i. e., the works, practices, and ways of life that take place outside, in public or semi-public spaces, have received interest in the last decades' research. In contrast to the socially restricted spaces of garrisons and palaces, the public and semi-public urban (and rural) spaces were the very place where diverse social groups gathered, and where "mass" cultural phenomenon had their setting. One of the prominent phenomena of this kind, which received some interest in recent research, is state rituals. Whereas court rituals that were restricted to the political and cultural elite have been the subject of quite a lot of previous scholarship,[37] staged events that involved the general public as a direct partner of ritual communication have become the focus of some research in the last two decades.

In his 1992 *Popular culture in medieval Cairo*, Boaz Shoshan describes several

34 Shoshan, *Popular Culture*, 78.

35 Berkey, *Popular Culture*; Canova, *Twenty Years.*

36 Ariès et al., *History.*

37 Holt, *Position*; idem, *Structure*; Holt, *Sultan*; Chapoutot-Remadi, *Symbolisme*; Petry, *Robing.* See now also: Van Steenbergen, *Ritual.*

"state festivals" as "an encounter between the rulers and their subjects, and in a more extended sense, between the culture of the elite and the culture of the people. This encounter helped," he continues, "to create new cultural processes."[38] Relying on Arab and European travel accounts and on Mamluk chronicles, Shoshan describes the annual festival of the "Procession of the Palanquin" (*dawarān al-maḥmil*) with a special interest in the people's contribution to the festivities, the carnivalesque elements they introduced and the authorities' repeated efforts to reduce these "abominations."[39] A second state festival Shoshan describes is the celebration of the "Plenitude of the Nile" (*wafā' al-nīl*), initiated and staged, like the "Procession of the Palanquin", by the Mamluk court, but largely joined, enriched, and transformed by the mass of ordinary Cairenes.[40] In his 2007 article in *MSR*, Yehoshua Frenkel further concentrates on several other important rituals as "public relations" measures the sultans financed to consolidate their position by "projecting their royal persona among the civil population."[41] Frenkel describes various public festivities on the occasion of military victories, investitures of sultans, the recovery of a sultan's health, the accession of a new governor, or the *rites de passage* of important court members, such as weddings, circumcisions, and funerals. Whereas all these public festivities were staged by the "state" as a means of propaganda, "the audiences at these events were not passive spectators. They participated in, and reacted to, the public displays and performances"[42] and thereby, together with the authorities, shaped the cultural phenomenon.[43] A much more *khāṣṣah*-dominated phenomenon that Frenkel discusses in his *MSR* article, which allowed only little participation of the *ʿāmmah*, was the Mamluks' "manipulation of the urban topography of the city and its public spaces for official image-making,"[44] an intense construction activity that also touched the countryside[45] and that shaped to quite an extent people's everyday life (construction of mosques, hospitals, fountains, canals, roads, bridges, walls, etc.).

In contrast to what Shoshan termed "state festivals," he deals at chapter length in his 1992 *Popular Culture in Medieval Cairo* with another festival, the Coptic

38 Shoshan, *Popular Culture*, 70. Shoshan sticks here as throughout his book to the idea of a distinct elite and popular culture, although he seems to have smoothed this view at the end of his book, see my citation above, note 34.

39 Shoshan, *Popular Culture*, 72.

40 Shoshan, *Popular Culture*, 73–74.

41 Frenkel, *Public Projection*, 40.

42 Frenkel, *Public Projection*, 51.

43 In this vein, Yasser Daoudi, a member of Jo van Steenbergen's research group at Ghent University, is at present preparing a PhD thesis under the working title "Ritual Politics: The Mamluk Sultanate (1412–1468)".

44 Frenkel, *Public Projection*, 52.

45 Frenkel, *Public Projection*, 44–45.

Nawrūz/New Year.[46] It was celebrated in Mamluk Egypt until the end of the 8th/14th ct. on the 11th of September and seems to have turned the official moral codes upside down. At Nawrūz, violence by the lowest classes of the *ʿāmmah* (called in the sources the *siflah*), sexual liberties, more or less open prostitution, and transvestitism seem to have been quite common phenomena. People used to elect a mock emir who was eventually led naked, his face besmeared with lime or flour and with a false beard, in a farcical procession around Cairo, followed by the crowd. During his procession he "visited" homes of dignitaries and officials and collected "debts," pressing them hard to pay by uttering curses, throwing mud, or even beating them. Shoshan proposes different functional explanations for this astonishing festival, following Burke, Gluckman and Bakhtin, who, despite different interpretations in detail, are united in the conviction that these "carnivalesque," rebellious rituals paradoxically enforced the social cohesion of the system and confirmed social order and norms.[47]

Another phenomenon of street life and culture that has received some scholarly interest in the last decade is violence. Whereas Boaz Shoshan in his *Popular Culture*[48] analyzes the phenomenon of street violence as one isolated from the violence of the dominant elite. James Grehan's 2003 "Street violence and social imagination in late Mamluk and early Ottoman Damascus" shows that popular protest and violence followed recognizable patterns.[49] But it was Konrad Hirschler who, in his 2007 "Riten der Gewalt," proposed a historical anthropology of violence and its forms of expression, a perspective that sees street violence not as a sort of spasmodic outburst, but as part of a normal repertoire of action on which social actors consciously relied.[50] Mainly based on chroniclers' narratives of acts of violence in Mamluk Damascus and Cairo, he develops a multifaceted and polysemantic[51] typology of these events: their spatial settings, their acoustic and visual forms, and their symbolic forms of expression. Hirschler thereby interpreted violence as a means of social and political expression and eschewed many of the sources' contemptuous view of "beastly" popular violence, which disturbed the "normal" order.

In his 2004 "Political Violence and Ideology in Mamluk Society," after a short reflection on various interpretations of the role and function of violence in

46 Shoshan, *Popular Culture*, 40 – 51, chapter 3: "The festival of Nawrūz: a world turned upside down".

47 See also Albrecht Fuess's contribution to what he terms "Freizeitverhalten/leisure time behaviour" of the coastal population in Mamluk Bilād al-Shām, Fuess, *Verbranntes Ufer*, chapter 5.

48 Shoshan, *Popular Culture*, 52 – 66, chapter 4: "The politics and moral economy of the Cairene crowd".

49 Grehan, *Street violence*. See also Wiederhold, *Legal-Religious Elite*.

50 Hirschler, Riten der Gewalt, 209.

51 Hirschler, Riten der Gewalt, 229.

Mamluk society, Daniel Beaumont concentrates on the "Lacanian *jouissance*" in assassination, torture, and execution, which at times led to a multiple "overkill" of the victims, a *jouissance* that often implicated mass crowds in huge outdoor spectacles.[52] Carl F. Petry has, in turn, assembled in the last decade quite a number of contributions on crime and (publicly staged) punishment of crime in Mamluk times, although usually not concentrating on the ritual, staged dimension.[53]

Besides "state festivals," "rebellious, carnivalesque" festivals, and the culture of urban violence, Mamluk public life was strongly marked by religious festivals, Jewish, Christian, and of course Muslim.[54] Muslim religious festivals,[55] which always involved not simply a restricted elite participation, were strongly marked by Sufism, a subject to which Emil Homerin offers a special contribution in this volume.[56] I will therefore not treat what he as a specialist of Sufism will develop much better, but simply underline that Sufism is one of the cultural phenomena in Mamluk times whose study inevitably makes one aware of the futility of the "elite/popular dichotomy," a dichotomy that in this field is usually associated with that of "orthodoxy/heresy."[57] In a recent *MSR* article, Richard McGregor[58] has lucidly revealed the persistence of these to his and my mind untenable conceptions in a number of important contributions to the research on "popular" Sufism.[59]

Religion shaped of course not only the spectacular festivals, but many aspects of public life. One of these aspects that has received some interest in the last two decades is charity and almsgiving. One of the main research works on this topic is Adam Sabra's *Poverty and Charity in Medieval Islam, Mamluk Egypt 1250–1517.* Relying on religious treatises, chronicles, travel accounts, and to quite a

52 Beaumont, *Political Violence.*

53 Petry, *Quis Custodiet*; Petry, *Al-Maqrizi's Discussion*; Petry, *Hoax*; idem, *Crime*; idem, *Sultanate's Response.* See also idem, *Criminal Underworld.*

54 There is unfortunately still quite little research in Arab and Islamic Studies in general, and in Mamluk Studies in particular, on Jewish and Christian public cultural phenomena in the Mamluk Empire, except notably Mayeur-Jaouens mémoire d'habilitation *Pélerinages d'Égypte*, (to my knowledge unpublished) and of course Langner, *Untersuchungen*, 51–55.

55 Still fundamental: Langner, *Untersuchungen*, 29–50.

56 Research into the use of public space for Sufi parading, and the impact of pilgrimage routes and visitation sites on the urban topography, has continued to develop in recent years, as R. McGregor notes in McGregor, *Problem of Sufism*, 70.

57 Homerin, by the way, makes it clear that the identification of the *'ulamā'* with orthodoxy being commonly opposed to Sufism is an anachronistic projection, see Homerin, *Sufis*, 226.

58 McGregor, *Problemof Sufism.*

59 See his discussion of theses dichotomies at work in Shoshan, *Popular Culture*; Winter, *Egyptian Society*, and Chamberlain, *Knowledge*, in McGregor, *Problem of Sufism*, 78–83. Let's notice at least some recent studies that are not explicitly or implicitly trapped in this conception of deviant/popular versus orthodox/elite religious culture: Taylor, *Vicinity of the Righteous*; Karamustafa, *God's Unruly Friends* (see here p. 9), and Berkey, *Popular Preaching.*

large extent on Mamluk *waqf* documents, Sabra develops a panorama of poverty and almsgiving, mainly in Mamluk Cairo. Sabra shows that almsgiving was a particularly prominent feature at various Muslim or interfaith holidays: *ʿashūrāʾ*, *al-mawlid al-nabawī* (and probably also on the *mawlids* of *awliyāʾ*), *ʿīd al-fiṭr, ʿīd al-aḍḥā, Nawrūz*, and various "state festivals," such as "private" occasions of the sultan and his household, etc.[60] Interestingly enough, Sabra not only remarks that death and cemeteries played an important role in the charity of common people in Cairo, but also that this example makes it clear that "in many respects the Mamluk elites differed in their acts of charity from the populace at large only in the scope of their gifts."[61]

Some of the poor who received charity in Mamluk times were begging. As Konrad Hirschler recently argued[62] in a fine addition to Lapidus', Pouzet's, Karamustafa's, Sabra's, and others' contribution to the topic, the able-bodied beggars (not the disabled who could not work) were at the fringe of marginality.[63] In another quite recent contribution, Carl F. Petry attacks his favorite crime subject from the angle of marginality. Drawing on chronicles, he addresses the image of banditry, namely of Bedouins, but also of urban gangs, criminals, and criminality in the late Mamluk Empire.[64] Another aspect of social life in Mamluk times, male homosexual behavior and feeling (or what is termed as such in modern Western discourse – the concept of "homosexuality" did not exist in the pre-modern Arab World[65]), a subject on which Khaled El-Rouayheb wrote a very instructive monograph in 2005, is a cultural phenomenon that many contemporary Arab and European scholars might situate at the fringes of marginality, although recent research of Thomas Bauer has showed that quite a large tolerance of ambiguity has characterized pre-modern Muslim and Arab societies.[66] The interest of El-Rouayheb's study, whose time frame from 1500 to 1800 touches only the very end of the Mamluk era and concentrates mainly on the Ottoman era,[67] lies not only in his developments on literary, theological, and

60 Sabra, *Poverty and Charity*, 52–55.

61 Sabra, *Poverty and Charity*, 96. On Jewish charity, although mainly pre-Mamluk, see Cohen, Mark, *Foreign Jewish.* See also Amy Singer's general study *Charity in Islamic Societies.* For Mamluk conceptions of poverty and the poor coming from various social groups, see my "Working-paper", forthcoming later this year on the website of the Annemarie-Schimmel-Kolleg, University of Bonn. On poverty and begging, although not exclusively Mamluk, see Herzog, *Figuren der Bettler.*

62 Hirschler, *Konformität.*

63 It was only in late Ottoman times, in the context of Ottoman "modernity", that they were really marginalized, see Ener, Shelter.

64 Petry, *Disruptive Others.*

65 El-Rouayheb, *Homosexuality*, 154.

66 See Bauer, *Ambiguität*, especially chapter 8: „Die Ambiguität der Lust".

67 He nevertheless treats quite a lot of Mamluk and pre-Mamluk sources in his discussion of the discourses on "homosexuality".

historiographical discourses on such behavior, but also in his description of some of its social settings: madrasahs, Sufi orders, coffeehouses, and public baths.[68]

Nevertheless and despite these inspiring studies, a comprehensive study or a collective volume on marginality (imagined and real) in the Mamluk Empire of the sort of Eugene Rogan's *Outside In*,[69] which covers different groups and aspects of marginality in the middle and late Ottoman Empire, is still a desideratum.

With the topic of male "homosexual" behavior, we have already partly left my first social and cultural field (the works, practices, and ways of life that take place outside, in public or semi-public spaces) and have entered the second field: the works, practices, and ways of life that take place inside the house and within the inner family circle. Indeed, the topic of gender in general, and of women in the Mamluk era in particular, overlaps the public, the semi-public, and the private spheres. Biographical dictionaries and (especially late) Mamluk chronicles, which were in many respects semi-memoirs or diaries,[70] contain lots of intimate information on women and their ways of living, so we now fortunately have at our disposal several studies devoted to Mamluk women and gender questions in general. For this topic, I would like to refer to the exhaustive overview article Yossef Rapoport published in 2007 in MSR.[71]

Late Mamluk semi-memoirs or diaries constitute another important source for many aspects of Mamluk domestic, even intimate life, at least for the milieus of their authors. Al-Biqāʿī's *Iẓhār al-ʿAṣr li-Asrār Ahl al-ʿAṣr*[72] and Ibn Ṭawq's *Al-Taʿlīq*, the latter having finally been published at the French Institute in Damascus in 2000, have received some interest in the last decade;[73] the research on Ibn Ṭawq's *Al-Taʿlīq* is at present ongoing with Torsten Wollina's Berlin PhD thesis due to be finished this year.[74] Nonetheless, insight into Mamluk everyday life and domestic life can also be gained from *waqf* documents, archeological research, close reading of chronicles, and works like Maqrīzī's *Khiṭaṭ*, as Sabra's description of the poor's housing,[75] clothing,[76] and wages and expenditures[77] in

68 El-Rouayheb, *Homosexuality*, 33–51. For the domain of Arab *siyar*, see also Herzog, *Geschichte und Imaginaire*, 266–271.

69 Rogan, *Outside In*.

70 See for instance Ibn Iyās, *Badāʾiʿ*, (d. 930/1524); Ibn Ṭūlūn, *Mufākahāt*, (d. 953/1546), al-Biqāʿī, *Iẓhār*, (885/1480), or Ibn Ṭawq, *Al-Taʿlīq*, (d. 915/1509). For a further discussion of this "genre", see Conermann, Seidensticker, *Some Remarks*, 126–130. See also Rapoport, *Women*, 3.

71 Rapoport, *Women*, (with biographical references).

72 Guo, *Tales*, (with biographical references).

73 Conermann, Seidensticker, *Some Remarks*, (with biographical references).

74 *Das Journal des Ahmad Ibn Tawq – ein arabisches Tagebuch.*

75 Sabra, *Poverty and Charity*, 102–109.

Mamluk Cairo proves.[78] One important domain of everyday life and domestic life, food and ways of eating, has received some interest in previous research[79] and is now amply documented by Paulina Lewicka's exhaustive monograph study *Food and Foodways of Medieval Cairenes.* In her research, which elaborates on material culture as well as cultural norms and manners related to food and its consumption, Lewicka makes use of a wide array of Fatimid, Ayyūbid, and Mamluk sources: chronicles, travelers' accounts, cookbooks, treatises of all kinds, and works of fiction and *adab.* She is thereby able to describe the eating and invitation routines and provides a quite precise view of the mainly Cairene menus of different social classes. But despite all these inspiring recent studies, a comprehensive piece of research in the style of James Grehan's *Everyday Life and Consumer Culture in 18th-Century Damascus* that treats topics like urban (public and semi-public) spaces, domestic spaces, furniture, food, and fashion is still lacking for the Mamluk era.

In the following, I would like to review some of the important recent research contributions on the third and last field of Mamluk (popular) culture, the field of the world-views, imagination, and mental attitudes. Like the first two fields, it relies partly on source material from historiography, travelers' accounts, treatises on a variety of subjects, *fatwā* collections, etc. Many of the studies I have mentioned cover simultaneously the historical "reality" of Mamluk public, semi-public, and private culture (fields 1 and 2) and the world-views these sources transmit from and/or about these cultural phenomena (field 3).[80] One important type of source for the third field is what is termed in English "literature," prose, poetry, and mixed genres,[81] a term that in Arabic terminology encompasses a broad variety of "genres."[82] When one touches upon "literature," the problematic of a dichotomist conception of "elite" and "popular" culture is entirely central, more than it is already with other source material. As Leder, Irwin, and Bauer[83] showed before Thomas Bauer's splendid, angry critique of the *Cam-*

76 Sabra, *Poverty and Charity*, 109 – 112.
77 Sabra, *Poverty and Charity*, 116 – 129.
78 Sabra here relies in fact mainly on previous research.
79 See Lewicka's discussion of previous scholarship in Lewicka, *Food*, x-xiii, and the rich bibliography. For the "diet" of the poor, see Sabra, *Poverty and Charity*, 112 – 116; for the diet and the table manners of the Mamluks, see Levanoni, *Food and Cooking.*
80 Some studies concentrate on this field, for instance Havemann, *Chronicle of Ibn Iyās*; Irwin, *ʿAlī al-Bahgadādī*; Martel-Thoumian, *Mort volontaire*; and Martel-Thoumian, *Plaisirs.*
81 "Mixed" or prosimetrical genres were widespread in Arabic literature, see Bauer, *Post-Classical Literature*, 149 and the studies he cites in note 18.
82 On the danger and inadequacy of applying European literary terminology to the field of Arabic literature, see Thomas Bauer's detailed critique of part IV of Allen, Richards, *Cambridge History* in Bauer, *Post-Classical Literature*, 148 – 151.
83 Leder, *Postklassisch*; Irwin, *Mamluk Literature*; Bauer: *Mamluk Literature.*

bridge History of Arabic Literature's volume on "Post-Classical Literature,"[84] Mamluk literature is deeply marked by the specific social shifts and conditions of literary production and communication in the "post-Abbasid" period. As James T. Monroe and Mark F. Pettigrew have argued,[85] it was probably the decline of courtly patronage beginning in the 10th century that brought about an interest in "popular," non-exclusively elite, formerly sub-literary genres, which in turn thematically and linguistically nourished the literary expression of their time and produced new genres.[86] These contacts between social and literary spheres[87] were definitely not one-way exchanges from "low" to "high," but included all sorts of intermingling exchanges. As Robert Irwin has put it, "the boundaries between high and low culture were fluid" in Mamluk times, "so much so that it hardly makes sense to speak of boundaries at all." In fact, many writers "took pride in demonstrating their command of both *fuṣḥā* and colloquial Arabic."[88] An author like Ibn Dāniyāl (ca. 1248–1310), for instance, produced respected works in refined classical Arabic as well as semi-colloquial shadow plays that treat characters who live on the margins of society. In Mamluk times, when many decisive patrons at court were of Turkish military slave origin and often did not sufficiently master the Arabic language to enjoy refined Arabic poetry, *prosimetrum*, or prose, the decline of court patronage for literary production led to a situation in which Mamluk literature was "mainly a bourgeois phenomenon."[89] Although highly educated *ʿulamāʾ*, to avoid endangering their reputations, seem not to have (openly) composed colloquial genres, some or even many of them did show a keen interest in literature produced in less educated circles. Besides the decline of court patronage at the "upper" end of literary production, it was certainly the spread of the madrasahs in Ayyūbid and Mamluk times and the accompanying access to education for large "middle-class" groups that was responsible for the emergence at the "lower" end of literary production of a literature of sons of Mamluks (like ʿAlī Sūdūn al-Bashbūghāwī), artisans (like Ibn al-Miʿmār), shopkeepers, and merchants. These groups adopted "the standards of *ʿulamāʾ* poetry [... and probably of *ʿulamāʾ* literature in general, T. H.] to a large extent [...], as the poetry of Ibn al-Miʿmār and other craftsmen shows."[90] And it was in turn in this very literature that

84 Bauer, *Post-Classical Literature.*

85 Monroe,Pettigrew, *Decline*, 161.

86 Monroe and Pettigrew concentrate mainly on pre-Mamluk *zajal* and *maqāmah* and on Ibn Danyāl's shadow plays.

87 They were considered to be strictly separated in Abbasid times, an assumption that, by the way, should also be reconsidered.

88 Irwin, *Mamluk Literature*, 18.

89 Bauer, *Post-Classical Literature*, 154.

90 Bauer, *Post-Classical Literature*, 154.

highly educated ʿulamāʾ, just like "lower" and "middle class" people, seem to have quite widely been interested in: a cultural synthesis was about to be born.

To avoid repeating what the three exhaustive and complementary "state of the art" articles presented very thoroughly in the *Mamluk Studies Review*[91] on the non-exclusively elite part of the Mamluk literary production,[92] in the following lines I will critically discuss the achievements and desiderata of scholarship on the Arab "epic" genre, the *siyar shaʿbīyah* or "popular *siyar*," a genre that the cited review articles only touched upon.

The Arabic *siyar* genre shows quite clearly the nonsense of a dichotomist view of Mamluk culture. Regarding the production of these texts, it cannot be assumed that they were the oeuvre only of illiterate storytellers. Whereas *Sīrat ʿAntara b. Shaddād* contains numerous links to the learned tradition of the pre-Islamic battle days, the *Ayyām al-ʿArab*,[93] *Sīrat al-Malik al-Ẓāhir Baybars* shows a clear interface with Mamluk learned historiography. Both *siyar* must thus have been at least partly composed by men of some education. This is most certainly also true for many texts of this genre, a genre that was extremely widespread in large parts of Mamluk society, as the numerous angry complaints of *ʿulamāʾ* prove[94] and as reports on the reading and listening of these texts in various social milieus document.[95] The language in which it was written made a narrative like *Sīrat ʿAntarah b. Shaddād* sometimes more popular in at least partially learned circles than in the milieu of the low "vulgar," as E. W. Lane's report from 19th-century Cairo shows.[96]

When scholarly work on Arabic *siyar* resumed after a long period of disinterest in the 1970s, a number of pioneering scholars engaged themselves outside the traditional methods of orientalist literature scholarship, driven by an enthusiasm to find contemporary oral witnesses of the old *siyar* narratives in an attempt at "safeguarding and conserving a cultural heritage under threat of extinction."[97] This field work led in the 1980s to the publication of a number of important contributions in Europe and in the United States, which were in

91 Homerin, *Reflections*; Irwin, *Mamluk Literature*; Bauer, *Mamluk Literature*.

92 See also Bauer, *Literarische Anthologien*, and idem, *Post-Classical Literature*. Despite Thomas Bauer's justified criticism, see also the individually valid contributions to part IV of Allen, Richards, *Cambridge History*; Reynolds, *Popular Prose*; Reynolds, *A Thousand and One Nights*; Kruk, *Sīrat*; Reynolds, *Sīrat*; Heath, *Other Sīras*.

93 See Herzog, *Wild Ancestors*, 421 – 422.

94 See Herzog, *Geschichte und Imaginaire*, 16 – 17.

95 See Herzog, *Orality*, 642 – 643.

96 Sīrat ʿAntara was written in a classical *fuṣḥā* Arabic and not really appreciated by the "vulgar". Lane, *Manners*, 409.

97 For a review and bibliography of the research on Arabic *siyar* in the 1980s and 1990s, see Canova, *Twenty Years*. Part of the presentation of the research up to the 1990s relies on Canova, *Twenty Years*.

general marked by an anthropological, folklorist, and structural approach.[98] Besides theses original works, three international conferences on *siyar shaʿbīyah* were organized in the Arab world in the decade from 1980 – 1990 (Hammamet/ Tunisia 1980, Cairo 1985, and Algiers 1990), two of them exclusively on the *Sīrat Banī Hilāl*, a *sīra* that was still performed in Tunisia and Algeria. The Arab interest in the *siyar* tradition in the 1970s and '80s may have been nurtured by political conditions, conditions that changed with the 1990s gain of Islamist ideologies, which are far less open to "folk" traditions than Arab nationalism was.[99] Besides these conferences, two reviews published special issues on oral narratives and epics in the 1980s: *Edebiyat* (1984) and *Oral Tradition* (1989).[100] In the 1990s, the efforts of documenting and safeguarding the Arabic *siyar* continued,[101] along with an increasing interest in more specifically literary aspects of the research topics: the question of oral vs. written composition and transmission,[102] narrative structures,[103] and questions of motifs and comparison with other epic traditions.[104] During the last decade, from 2000 to 2010, research on Arabic *siyar* reached a peak and marked a shift in topical interest and approach. Whereas in the 1970s and '80s one could observe a strong interest in the still orally performed *Sīrat Banī Hilāl*, research in the 1990s and during the last decade was much more concentrated on the manuscript tradition of the other late Ayyūbid and Mamluk *siyar: Sīrat ʿAntara b. Shaddād*,[105], *Sīrat Sayf b. Dhī Yazan*,[106] *Sīrat al-Zīr Sālim*,[107] and – with the most contributions – *Sīrat al-Malik al-Ẓāhir Baybars*.[108] Three collective volumes were dedicated in this decade to Arabic *siyar*, two of them exclusively to *Sīrat Baybars:* a special volume of *Oriente Moderno* (*Studies on Arabic Epics*, 2003), a collective volume (*Lectures*

98 Canova, *Egitto I*; Galley,Ayyoub, *Histoire*; Saada, *La Geste;* Conelly, *Arabic Folk;* Slyomovics, *The Merchant;* Al-Abnūdī, *Al-Sīrah*; ʿUmrān, *Al-Khaṣāʾiṣ.*

99 In that vein, ʿAbd al-Raḥmān al-Abnūdī could organize a series of radio programs that contributed to a nationwide popularity of Sīrat Banī Hilāl and its poets.

100 *Edebiyat*, see: Hickmann/Conelly, "Proceedings"; *Oral Tradition*, see: Boullata, "Arabic Oral Traditions".

101 Nacib, *Une geste*; Reynolds, *Heroic poets.*

102 Ott, *Metamorphosen*, (the book goes back to a phd-thesis from the 1990s); Gavillet-Matar, *Un manuscrit.*

103 Yaqṭīn, *Qāla al-Rāwī*; Ḥarb, *Bunyat al-Sīrah*; Heath, *Thirsty Sword*; Cherquaoui, *Pyramidal Structure*; Madeyska, *Poetics.*

104 Grech, *Indexation*; Lyons, *Arabian Epic.*

105 Heath, *Thirsty Sword*; Cherkaoui, *Roman de ʿAntar.*

106 Jayyusi, *Adventures.*

107 Gavillet Matar, *Geste de Zīr Sālim*; Herzog, *Wild Ancestors.*

108 Bohas, Guillaume, *Roman;* Bohas, Zakharia, *Sīrat al-Malik al-Ẓāhir Baybars*; Herzog, *Geschichte und Imaginaire*; idem, *Francs et commerçants*; idem, *First layer*; idem, *La Sīrat Baybars: histoire*; idem, *Kognitive Karten*; idem, *What they saw.* Guinle, *Stratégies narratives*; Vidal Luengo, *La dimensión*, see also the special volume of Arabica and Garcin, *Lecture du Roman de Baybars.*

du Roman de Baibars, 2003), and a special issue of *Arabica* on *Sīrat Baybars* (2004). In 2006 the cited volume of the Cambridge History of Arabic Literature on "Arabic Literature in the Post Classical Period" dedicated three chapters to Arabic *siyar.* As in the preceding decade, many contributions concentrated on narratological questions,[109] on the oral vs. written character of the *siyar* narratives,[110] or the language of the *siyar*,[111] whereas a number of other contributions continued the basic work of classifying the manuscript or oral traditions of the Arabic *siyar*,[112] tried to retrieve intertextual relations to other *siyar*, to the 1001 Nights tradition, or to historiography,[113] or presented lesser-known narratives of the genre.[114]

The last decade not only marked a peak in research on Arabic *siyar*, the tide of the "cultural turn" in humanities having reached Arabic and Islamic Studies, it also brought a broadening in thematic and methodological approach. A large variety of topics touching upon the content rather than the form and the structure of the *siyar* were treated in recent contributions: the figure of the hero,[115] love and desire in the *siyar* tradition,[116] gender,[117] identity and alterity,[118] symbolic representation of space,[119] symbolic interpretation of the *siyar*'s action,[120] *siyar* and mysticism,[121] conflict resolution,[122] social marginality,[123] *siyar* tradition between fiction and non-fiction,[124] and *siyar* as a phenomenon of Arab cultural memory,[125] to mention the most important ones.

Besides these questions, the problematic of the genesis of *siyar*, namely of the

109 Madeyska, *Delimitation*; Gavillet Matar, *Situation narrative*; Guinle, "Repetion"; Guinle, *Stratégies narratives.*

110 Ott, *Coffeehouse*; Jason, *Sirat 'Antar*; Guillaume, *Les scènes*; Herzog, *Orality.* For contemporary performances or adaptations of *siyar*, see Herzog, *Dernier conteur*; Slyomovics, *Ashig Ma'bad*; Depaule, *Conteurs.*

111 Lentin, *Variétés arabes.*

112 Bencheikh,Galley, *A propos d'un manuscript*; Canova, *Hilali Narratives*; Herzog, *Version chrétienne*; idem, *La Sīrat Baybars: histoire*; idem, *Geschichte und Imaginaire*, 31 – 52.

113 Cherkaoui, *Historical elements*; Norris, *'Amr b. Ma'dīkarib*; Chraibi, *Genre et narration*; Bohas, *Métrique*; Zakharia, *Genre poétique*; Herzog, *De l'historiographie.*

114 Doufikar, *Sīrat al-Iskandar*, Grant, *Sīrat Fīrūzshāh*; Lyons, *Qiṣṣat.*

115 Schippers, *Abū Zayd*; Herzog, *'Uṯmān*; Sublet, *Un héros*; Herzog, *Geschichte und Imaginaire*, 160 – 165; Guillaume, *Ya-t-il*; Cherkaoui, *Pyramidal.*

116 Slyomovics, *Ashig Ma'bad*; Ouyang, *Epical Turn.*

117 Kruk, *Princess Maymūnah*; Herzog, *Geschichte und Imaginaire*, 266 – 271.

118 Vidal-Luengo, *L'élément*; Herzog, *Francs et commerçants*; idem, *Invasions Mongoles*; idem, *Wild ancestors.*

119 Herzog, *Kognitive Karten*; idem, *Geschichte und Imaginaire*, 229 – 246.

120 Herzog, *Geschichte und Imaginaire*, 120 – 156.

121 Gril, *Du sultanat.*

122 Vidal-Luengo, *La dimensión.*

123 Herzog, *Geschichte und Imaginaire*, 254 – 273.

124 Herzog, *What they saw.*

125 Herzog, *Invasions Mongoles.*

Sīrat al-Malik al-Ẓāhir Baybars, has been attacked with a particular interest in the political and social context of origin and reception.[126] This approach tries to retrieve the social and political milieus in which the Arab *siyar* were born, transmitted, and performed and thereby place them in their original fields of power. This approach, which has up to now mainly been used for the sole case of *Sīrat al-Malik al-Ẓāhir Baybars,* is to my mind very promising and should be pursued in the study of other Mamluk *siyar.*

So, after all this research, what has to be done in the field of non-exclusively elite literature in general and *siyar* literature in particular? First of all, there is still a lot of basic philological work to do; many texts have still to be exhumed from the manuscript libraries, to be read, classified, and put in relation to each other. Many "treasures" are still to be discovered. In a second very important step, we should exploit these texts as windows onto past world-views, mentalities, and historical ways of life, as sources for cultural history. We should thereby understand texts like the Arab *siyar* as narratives that were produced and consumed not only by the simple "people," but that were shared by a great majority of social groups, and partly also by those belonging to an elite, however. Finally and perhaps most important, we should read these texts as having existed in a historical field of power relations, in which they seemed to have challenged the authorities' claim to determine moral and historical truth.[127] Thus if we work on these texts with new "culturalist" questioning like "gender," "space," "identity," and "memory," we have to do it while constantly keeping in mind the disputed character of the public space and the power relations in which these texts were written, transmitted, and performed. Let me therefore propose for further research on the Arab *siyar* and on non-elite Arab literature in general that we take inspiration from Discourse Analysis by becoming acutely conscious that all widespread, "popular" texts that existed in Ayyūbid, Mamluk, and Ottoman society, did so in a disputed social field and that they were by the very fact of their existence and widespread survival the result of negotiations in social (and political) fields of power, and marked by processes of resistance and incorporation.[128]

Insisting on the social and political context of Mamluk texts and discourses

126 Herzog, *First layer*; idem, *Geschichte und Imaginaire*, 120 – 128, 293 – 257, Garcin, *Lectures du Roman de Baybars*; Garcin, *Sīra-s et histoire*; idem, *Sīra-s et histoire – suite.* For the image of the just ruler, see Lerible, *Image*; Herzog, *Geschichte und Imaginaire*, 315 ff. For an in-depth study of the *Sīrat Baybars*' social milieu of origin and reception, see Herzog, *Geschichte und Imaginaire*, 248 – 291 (first published in Herzog, *Genese*).

127 See Herzog, *Orality*, 644 – 645.

128 Although I do not fully subscribe to the theory of hegemony brought forward by Antonio Gramsci, who seems stuck in a Marxist idea of oppressors and oppressed – again elite and people in dichotomist structure – his idea of negotiation is nevertheless inspiring; we merely have to liberate it from the strict dichotomy between top and bottom.

seems to me an equally valid approach to the sources of the other fields of Mamluk "popular" culture. Such an approach prevents us from taking the sources' statements at face value and makes us aware of the communicative context and power fields in which their textual communication originally took place. Of course, this does not mean that we should analyze every source only in terms of its social standpoint. Especially literature, but also other source types are intimately linked to esthetic conventions that are not always or predominantly socially or politically determined.

The scholarship on Mamluk culture is thus on a very good path and has integrated large ranges of the methodological and thematic enrichments that were the result of the numerous paradigmatic "turns" in humanities. If a wide range of approaches is employed in a creative and flexible manner, future research is definitely promising.

Literature

Primary Sources

Al-Abnūdī, ʿAbd al-Raḥmān, 1988, *Al-Sīrah al-Hilālīyah.* 5 vols., Cairo 1988 (reprint Cairo 2002).

Al-Biqāʿī, Burhān al-Dīn Ibrāhīm b. ʿUmar, *Iẓhār al-ʿAṣr li-Asrār Ahl al-ʿAṣr. Ta'rīḫ al-Biqāʿī*, ed. Muḥammad Salīm Ibn Shadīd al-ʿAwfī. Riyadh, al-Muḥaqqiq, 1992 – 1993.

Ibn Ṭawq, Shihāb al-Dīn Aḥmad, *Al-Taʿlīq. Yawmīyāt Shihāb al-Dīn Aḥmad b. Ṭawq (834/1430 – 915/1509). Mudhakkirāt Kutibat bi-Dimashq fī Awākhir al-ʿAhd al-Mamlūkī, 885/1480 – 908/1502*, vol. 1, (885/1480 – 890/1485), ed. Jaʿfar al-Muhājir/*Journal d'Aḥmad Ibn Ṭawq 834/1430 – 915/1509: la vie quotidienne à Damas à la fin de l'époque mamelouke édité et présenté par le Sheikh Jaafar al-Muhajer.* Volume I: 885/1480 à 890/1485, Damascus 2000.

Ibn Ṭūlūn, Muḥammad b. ʿAlī, *Mufākahāt al-Khillān fī Ḥawādith al-Zamān. Tārīkh Miṣr wa-l-Shām*, ed. Muḥammad Muṣṭafā, Cairo: Al-Mu'assasah al-Miṣrīya al-ʿĀmmah 1962 – 64.

ʿUmrān, Muḥammad, "Al-Ḫaṣā'iṣ al-Mūsīqīya li-Riwāyat al-Sīrah al-Hilālīya fī Miṣr", in: *Sīrat Banī Hilāl. Actes de la 1ere table ronde sur la geste des Bani Hilal (Hammamet 1980)*, ed. ʿAbd al-Raḥmān Ayyūb, Tunis 1989.

Yaqṭīn, Saʿīd, *Qāla al-Rāwī. Al-Bunyah al-Ḥikā'īyah fī al-Sīrah al-Shaʿbīyah*, Beirut 1997.

Secondary Sources

Allen, Roger and Richards, D.S., Cambridge History of Arabic Literature. Arabic Literature in the Post-classical Period, Cambridge: Cambridge University Press 2006.

Ariès, Philippe, Georges Duby, and Paul Veyne (eds.), History of private life. 3 vols. Cambridge (Mass.) 1987.
Bauer, Thomas, Die Kultur der Ambiguität: eine andere Geschichte des Islams, Berlin: Verlag der Weltreligionen 2011.
Bauer, Thomas, "In Search of Post-Classical Literature," Mamlūk Studies Revies 11/2 (2007), pp. 137 - 167.
Bauer, Thomas, "Mamluk Literature: Misunderstandings and New Approaches," MSR 9/2 (2005), pp. 105 - 132.
Bauer, Thomas, "Literarische Anthologien der Mamlukenzeit," in: Die Mamluken. Studien zu ihrer Geschichte und Kultur. Zum Gedenken an Ulrich Haarmann (1942 - 1999), eds. Stephan Conermann and Anja Pistor-Hatam, Hamburg 2003, 71 - 122.
Beaumont, Daniel, "Political Violence and Ideology in Mamluk Society," MSR 9/1 (2004), pp. 201 - 226.
Bencheikh, Omar and Galley, Micheline, "A propos d'un manuscript de la geste hilalienne conservée à la Bibliothèque Vaticane," Oriente Moderno 22 (2003), pp. 307 - 333.
Berkey, Jonathan, "Popular Culture under the Mamluks: A historiographical survey," MSR 9/2 (2005), pp. 133 - 146.
Berkey, Jonathan, Popular Preaching and Religious Authority, Seattle: University of Washington Press 2001.
Berkey, Jonathan, "Tradition, Innovation and the Social Construction of Knowledge in the Medieval Islamic Near East," Past and Present 146 (1995), pp. 38 - 65.
Berkey, Jonathan, The Transmission of Knowledge in Medieval Cairo: A Social History of Islamic Education, Princeton, N.J.: Princeton University Press 1992.
Bohas, Georges, "Métrique et intertextualité dans le Roman de Baybars," Arabica 51/1 (2004), pp. 3 - 32.
Bohas, Georges and Katia Zakharia, Sīrat al-Malik al-Ẓāhir Baybars Ḥasab al-Riwāyah al-Shāmīyah, Damascus: Institut Français du Proche Orient 2000.
Bohas, Georges and Jean-Patrick Guillaume, Le roman de Baybars. Actes Sud-Sindbad. Arles-Paris 1985 - 1998 (vol. 1 - 10).
Boullata, I. J., "Arabic Oral Traditions". Special volume of Oral Tradition (1989).
Bourdieu, Pierre, Outline of a Theory of Practice, Cambridge: Cambridge University Press. 1977.
Canova, Giovanni, "Hilali Narratives from Southern Arabia," Oriente Moderno 22 (2003), pp. 361 - 375.
Canova, Giovanni, "Twenty Years of studies on Arabic Epics," Oriente Moderno 22 (2003), pp. xi-xxii.
Canova, Giovanni, Egitto I: epica, Milano: 1980.
Chamberlain, Michael, Knowledge and Social practice in medieval Damascus, 1190 - 1350, Cambridge: Cambridge University Press 1994.
Chapoutot-Remadi, Mounira, "Symbolisme et formalisme de l'élite mamlûke: La cérémonie de l'accession à l'émirat," in: Genèse de l'État moderne en Méditerranée, ed. H. Bresc, Paris: 1987.
Cherkaoui, Driss, "Historical elements in Sirat Antar," Oriente Moderno 22 (2003), pp. 407 - 424.
Cherkaoui, Driss, "Le parcours du héros dans le roman de chevalerie arabe: l'exemple de 'Antar," Bulletin d'Etudes Orientales LIII - LIV (2001 - 02), pp. 75 - 104.

Cherkaoui, Driss, "The pyramidal structure in Arabic siyar: The example of Sirat ʿAntar," Al ʿUsūr al-Wusṭā 13/1 (2001), pp. 6–9.
Cherkaoui, Driss, Le Roman de ʿAntar. Perspective littéraire et historique, Paris: Présence africaine 2001.
Chraibi, Aboubakr, "Genre et narration: la difficile épopée d'al-Khamsā'," Oriente Moderno 22 (2003), pp. 541–557.
Clifford, W. W., "Ubi Sumus? Social Theory and Mamluk Studies," MSR 1 (1997), pp. 45–62.
Cohen, Mark, "The Foreign Jewish Poor in Medieval Egypt," in: Poverty and Charity in Middle Eastern Contexts, eds. Micheal Bonner, Mine Ener, and Amy Singer, New York: State University of New York Press 2003, pp. 53–72.
Conelly, Bridget, Arabic Folk Epic and Identity, Berkley 1986.
Conermann, Stephan and Tilmann Seidensticker, "Some Remarks on Ibn Ṭawq's (d. 915/1509) Journal Al-Taʿlīq, vol. 1 (885/1480 to 890/1485)," MSR 11/2 (2007), pp. 121–135.
Depaule, Jean-Charles, "Conteurs et cafés du Caire. Textes choisies," in: Lectures du Roman de Baybars, ed. Jean-Claude Garcin, Marseille: Ed. Paranthès/MMSH 2003, 201–208.
Doufikar-Aerts, Faustina, "Sīrat al-Iskandar: An Arabic Popular Romance of Alexander," Oriente Moderno 22 (2003), pp. 505–520.
El-Rouayheb, Khaled, Before Homosexuality in the Arab-islamic World: 1500–1800, Chicago: University of Chicago Press 2005.
Ener, Mine, "Getting into the Shelter of Takiyat Tulun," in: Outside In: On the Margins of the Modern Middle East, ed. Eugene Rogan, London, New York: I.B. Tauris, pp. 53–76.
Frenkel, Jehoshua, "Public Projection of Power in Mamluk Bilād al-Shām," MSR 11/1 (2007), pp. 39–53.
Fuess, Albrecht, Verbranntes Ufer: Auswirkungen mamlukischer Seepolitik auf Beirut und die syro-palästinensische Küste; (1250–1517), Leiden: Brill 2001.
Galley, M. and Ayyoub, A., Histoire des Beni Hilal et de ce que leur advint dans leur marche vers l'ouest, Paris 1983.
Garcin, Jean-Claude, "Sīra/s et histoire," Arabica 51/1 (2004), pp. 33–54.
Garcin, Jean-Claude, "Sīra/s et histoire – suite," Arabica 51/1 (2004), pp. 223–257.
Garcin, Jean-Claude, "De l'utilité changeante du Roman de Baybars," in: Lectures du Roman de Baybars, ed. Jean-Claude Garcin, Marseille: Ed. Paranthès/MMSH 2003, 115–142.
Garcin, Jean-Claude, Un centre musulman de la Haute-Egypte médiévale: Qūṣ, Cairo: Institut Français d'Archéologie Orientale 1974.
Gavillet Matar, Marguérite, La geste de Zīr Sālim d'après un manuscrit syrien, Présentation, édition et traduction annotées par Marguerite Gavillet Matar. Vol. I: présentation et édition; vol. II: traduction, Damascus: Institut français du Proche-Orient 2005.
Gavillet Matar, Marguérite, "Situation narrative et fonctions de l'extra-narratif dans les manuscrits des conteurs. L'exemple de la geste de Zīr Sālim," Oriente Moderno 22 (2003), pp. 377–398.
Gavillet Matar, Marguérite, Un manuscrit de la geste de Zīr Sālim: Présentation, édition et traduction annotées, Thèse de doctorat Université de Provence 1994, 4 vols. (Mikrofiche).

Grant, Kennet, "Sīrat Fīrūzshāh and the Middle Eastern Epic Tradition," Oriente Moderno 22 (2003), pp. 521 - 528.
Grech, R. L., Indexation de la geste des Banū Hilāl à partir de deux editions parallèles, 3 vols., Algiers 1989.
Grehan, James, Everyday Life and Consumer Culture in 18th-Century Damascus, Seattle, London: University of Washington Press 2007.
Grehan, James, "Street Violence and Social Imagination in Late-Mamluk and Ottoman Damascus (ca. 1500 - 1800)," International Journal of Middle East Studies 35/2 (2003), pp. 215 - 236.
Gril, Denis, "Du sultanat au califat universel: le rôle des saints dans le Roman de Baybars," in: Lectures du Roman de Baybars, ed. Jean-Claude Garcin, Marseille: Ed. Paranthès/ MMSH 2003, 173 - 197.
Guillaume, Jean-Patrick, "Les scènes de bataille dans le roman de Baybars: considerations sur le style 'formulaire' dans la tradition épique arabe," Arabica 51/1 (2004), pp. 55 - 67.
Guillaume, Jean-Patrick, "Y-a-t-il une littérature épique en arabe?," Revue Litérales 19 (1996), Paris: Université Paris X, pp. 91 - 107.
Guinle, Francis, Les stratégies narratives dans la recension damascène de Sīrat al-Malik al-Ẓāhir Baybarṣ, Damascus: Institut Français du Proche-Orient 2011.
Guinle, Francis, "Repetion as Narrative Strategy: Ibrāhīm's Embassies," Arabica 51/1 (2004), pp. 77 - 102.
Guo, Li, "Tales of a Medieval Cairene Harem: Domestic Life in al-Biqāʿī's Autobiographical Chronicle," MSR 9/1 (2005), pp. 101 - 121.
Ḥarb, Ṭalāl, Bunyat al-Sīrah al-Shaʿbīyah wa-Khiṭābuhā al-Malḥamī fī ʿAṣr al-Mamālīk, Beirut 1999.
Havemann, Axel, "The Chronicle of Ibn Iyās as a Source for Social and Cultural History from Below," in: Towards a Cultural History of the Mamluk Era, eds. Mahmoud Haddad et al., Beirut 2010, pp. 87 - 98.
Heath, Peter, "Other sīras and popular narratives," in: Cambridge History of Arabic Literature. Arabic Literature in the Post-classical Period, eds. R. Allen and D.S. Richards, Cambridge: Cambridge University Press 2006, pp. 319 - 329.
Heath, Peter, The thirsty sword: Sirat Antar and the Arabic Popular Epic, Salt Lake City 1996.
Herzog, Thomas, "La mémoire des invasions mongoles dans la Sīrat Baybars: Persistances et transformations dans l'imaginaire populaire arabe," in: Le Bilād al-Shām face aux mondes extérieurs. La perception de l'Autre et la représentation du souverain. Actes du Colloque international Damascus 2008, eds. Denise Aigle and Katia Zakharia, Damaskus: Institut Français du Proche Orient (forthcoming), pp. 203 - 222.
Herzog, Thomas, "'What they saw with their own eyes…' - Fictionalisation and ‚narrativisation' of History in Arab popular epics and learned historiography," in: Fictionalizing the Past, ed. Sabine Dorpmüller, Cairo: American University of Cairo Press (forthcoming), pp. 25 - 43.
Herzog, Thomas, "Orality and the Tradition of Arabic Epic Storytelling," in: Medieval Oral Literature, ed. Karl Reichl, Berlin, Boston: De Gruyter 2012, pp. 629 - 651.
Herzog, Thomas, "Figuren der Bettler," Asiatische Studien 65/1 (2011), pp. 67 - 94.
Herzog, Thomas, Imaginaire Geschichte und Imaginaire Entstehung, Überlieferung und

Bedeutung der Sīrat Baibars in ihrem sozio-politischen Kontext, Wiesbaden: Harrassowitz 2006.

Herzog, Thomas, "Romans populaires arabes: de l'historiographie au roman, du roman à l'historiographie," in: Ecriture de l'histoire entre historiographie et littérature. Actes du colloque international, Le Caire 4–6 décembre 2004, ed. Richard Jacquemond, Cairo/Aix-en-Provence 2005

Herzog, Thomas, "Wild Ancestors – Bedouins in Medieval Arabic Popular Literature," in: Shifts and Drifts in Nomad-Sedentary Relation, ed. Stefan Leder and Bernhard Streck, Wiesbaden: Reichert, 421–441.

Herzog, Thomas, "Kognitive Karten der arabischen 'āmma in ayyubidischer und mamlukischer Zeit: Szenarien der Stärke und Schwäche in „Sīrat Baibars" und „Sīrat 'Antar b. Shaddād," in: Mental Maps – Raum – Erinnerung. Kulturwissenschaftliche Zugänge zum Verhältnis von Raum und Erinnerung (Kulturwissenschaft: Forschung und Wissenschaft 1), eds. Sabine Damir-Geilsdorf, Angelika Hartmann, and Béatrice Hendrich, Münster 2005, pp. 211–235.

Herzog, Thomas, "Une version chrétienne de Sīrat Baybars: le manuscript de Wolfenbüttel," Arabica 51/1 (2004), pp. 103–120.

Herzog, Thomas, "The first layer of the Sirat Baybars – popular romance and political propaganda," MSR 7 (2003), pp. 137–148.

Herzog, Thomas, "La Sīrat Baybars: histoire d'un texte," in: Lectures du Roman de Baybars, ed. Jean-Claude Garcin, Marseille: Ed. Paranthès/MMSH 2003, 31–60.

Herzog, Thomas, "Le dernier conteur de Damas?," in: Lectures du Roman de Baybars, ed. Jean-Claude Garcin, Marseille: Ed. Paranthès/MMSH 2003, 209–229.

Herzog, Thomas, "'Uṯmān dans la Sīrat Baybars: un héros picaresque?," Oriente Moderno 22 (2003), pp. 453–463.

Herzog, Thomas, "Francs et commerçants francs à Alexandrie dans le roman de Baybars," in: Alexandrie médiévale II, IFAO, ed. Ch. Décobert, Le Caire 2002, pp. 181–194.

Herzog, Thomas, Genese, Überlieferung und Bedeutung der Sīrat Baibars in ihrem sozio-politischen Kontext/ Genèse, transmission et signification de la Sīrat Baybars dans son contexte socio-politique, German-french phd.-thesis, Universities of Halle-Wittenberg and Aix-en-Provence, Microfiche-Edition: Atelier National de Reproduction des Thèses. Lille 2002.

Hickmann, W. and B. Conelly, "Proceedings of the 'Symposium of Middle Eastern Oral Narrative'", in: Edebiyat (1984).

Hirschler, Konrad, "Konformität und Randständigkeit: Bettler im vormodernen Nahen Osten," in: Bettler, Prostituierte, Paria: Randgruppen in asiatischen Gesellschaften, eds. Anja Pistor-Hatam and Antje Richter, Hamburg-Schenefeld: EB-Verlag 2008, pp. 67–105.

Hirschler, Konrad, „Riten der Gewalt," in: Islamwissenschaft als Kulturwissenschaft I. Historische Anthropologie, eds. Stephan Conermann and Syrinx von Hees, Schenefeld: EB-Verlag 2007, pp. 205–233.

Holt, Peter Malcom, "The Sultan as Ideal Ruler: Ayyubid and Mamluk Prototypes," in: Suleyman the Magnificent and his Age: The Ottoman Empire in the Early Modern World, eds. Metin Kunt and Christine Woodhead, London 1995, pp. 122–37.

Holt, Peter Malcom, "The Structure of Government in the Mamluk Sultanate," in: The

Eastern Mediterranean Lands in the Period of the Crusades, ed. P. M. Holt, Warminster 1977, pp. 44 - 61.
Holt, Peter Malcom, "The Position and Power of the Mamluk Sultan," Bulletin of the School of Oriental and African Studies 38 (1975), pp. 237 - 49.
Homerin, Emil, "Sufis and Their Detractors in Mamluk Egypt: A Survey of Protagonists and Institutional Settings," in: Islamic mysticism contested: thirteen centuries of controversies and polemics, eds. Frederick de Jong and Bern Radtke, Leiden: Brill 1999, pp. 225 - 246.
Homerin, Emil, "Reflections on Poetry in the Mamluk Age," MSR 1 (1997), pp. 63 - 85.
Ibn Iyās, Badā'i' al-zuhūr fī waqā'i' al-duhūr. Die Chronik des Ibn Iyās, ed. Muhamed Mostafa, Cairo, Wiesbaden 1963.
Irwin, Robert, "Mamluk Literature," MSR 7/1 (2003), pp. 1 - 30.
Irwin, Robert, "'Alī al-Bahgadādī and the Joy of Mamluk Sex," in: The Historiography of Islamic Egypt (C. 950 - 1800), ed. Hugh Kennedy, Leiden 2001, pp. 45 - 57.
Jason, Heda, "Sīrat 'Antar as an Oral Epic," Oriente Moderno 22 (2003), pp. 399 - 406.
Jayyusi, Lena, The adventures of Sayf Ben Dhi Jazan, Bloomington & Indianapolis 1996.
Karamustafa, Ahmet T., God's unruly friends: Dervish groups in the Islamic later middle period, 1200 - 1550, Salt Lake City: Univ. of Utah Press 1994.
Kruk, Remke, "Sīrat 'Antara b. Shaddād," in: Cambridge History of Arabic Literature. Arabic Literature in the Post-classical Period, ed. R. Allen and D.S. Richards, Cambridge: Cambridge University Press 2006, pp. 292 - 306.
Kruk, Remke, "The Princess Maymūnah: Maiden, Mother, Monster," Oriente Moderno 22 (2003), pp. 425 - 442.
Lane, Edward William, An account of the Manners and Customs of the Modern Egyptians. Written in Egypt during the years 1833 - 35, London 1895 (Reprint The Hague and London. East-West Publications 1978).
Langner, Barbara, Untersuchungen zur historischen Volkskunde Ägyptens nach mamlukischen Quellen, Berlin: Klaus Schwarz 1983.
Lapidus, Ira M., Muslim Cities in the Later Middle Ages, Cambridge (Mass.): Harvard University Press 1967.
Leavis, F. R. and Denys Thompson, Culture and Environment, Westport, Connecticut: Greenwood Press 1977.
Leder, Stefan, "Postklassisch und vormodern: Beobachtungen zum Kulturwandel in der Mamlukenzeit," in: Die Mamluken. Studien zur ihrer Geschichte und Kultur im Gedenken an Ulrich Haarmann (1942 - 1999), eds. Stephan Conermann and Anja Pistor-Hatam, Schenefeld 2003, pp. 289 - 312.
Lentin, Jérôme, "Variétés arabes dans des manuscrits syriens du Roman de Baybars et histoire du texte," in: Lectures du Roman de Baybars, ed. Jean-Claude Garcin, Marseille: Ed. Paranthès/MMSH 2003, 91 - 111.
Lerible, Yannick,"Image du souverain et idéologie du pouvoir dans le Roman de Baybars," in: Lectures du Roman de Baybars, ed. Jean-Claude Garcin, Marseille: Ed. Paranthès/MMSH 2003, 159 - 171.
Levanoni, Amalia, "Food and Cooking during the Mamluk Era: Social and Political Implications," MSR 9/2 (2005), pp. 201 - 221.
Lewicka, Paulina, Food and foodways of medieval Cairenes: aspects of life in an Islamic metropolis of the Eastern Mediterranean, Leiden: Brill 2011.

Lutfi, Huda, "Coptic festivals of the Nile: aberrations of the past?," in: The Mamluks in Egyptian politics and society, eds. Thomas Philipp and Ulrich Haarmann, Cambridge: Cambridge University Press 1998, pp. 254 - 282.

Lutfi, Huda, "Manners and Customs of Fourteenth Century Cairene Women: Female Anarchy versus Male Sharīʿ Order in Muslim Prescriptive Treatise," in: Women in Middle Eastern History, eds. Nicki R. Keddie and Beth Baron, New Haven: Yale University Press 1991, pp. 99 - 121.

Lyons, M. C., "Qiṣṣat ʿArūs al-ʿArāʾis," Oriente Moderno 22 (2003), pp. 559 - 573.

Lyons, M. C., The Arabian epic: heroic and oral story-telling, 3 vols., Cambridge: University of Cambridge 1995.

Madeyska, Danuta, "Delimitation in early sīrah," in: Oriente Moderno 22 (2003), pp. 255 - 275.

Madeyska, Danuta, Poetics of the sira. Study of the Arabic chivalrous romance, Warsaw: Dialog 2001.

Malti-Douglas, Fedwa, "Mentalités and Marginality: Blindness and Mamlūk Civilization," in: The Islamic World from Classical to Modern Times: Essays in Honor of Bernard Lewis, ed. C.E. Bosoworth et al., Princeton: Darwin Press 1989, pp. 211 - 238.

Martel-Thoumian, Bernadette, "Plaisirs illicites et châtiments dans les sources mamloukes (fin IXe/XVe–début Xe/XVe siècle)," Annales Islamologiques 39 (2005), pp. 275 - 323.

Martel-Thoumian, Bernadette, "La mort volontaire: le traitement de suicide et du sucidé dans les chroniques mamloukes tardives," Annales Islamologiques 38 (2004), pp. 405 - 35.

Mayeur-Jaouen, Catherine, Pélerinages d'Égypte, mouleds coptes et mouleds musulmans, Unpublished mémoire d'habilitation, Paris IV-Sorbonne 2000.

McGregor, Richard, "The Problem of Sufism," MSR 13/2 (2009), pp. 69 - 83.

Monroe, James T. and Pettigrew, Mark F., "The Decline of Courtly Patronage and the Appearance of New Genres in Arabic Literature: The Case of the Zajal and the Maqāmah and the Shadow Play," Journal of Arabic Literature 34 (2003), pp. 138 - 177.

Nacib, Youssef, Une geste en fragments: contribution à l'étude de la légende hilalienne des Hauts-Plateaux algériens, Pubsud: Paris 1994

Norris, Harry T., "ʿAmr b. Maʿdīkarib al-Zubaydī, a Misunderstood Folk Hero," Oriente Moderno 22 (2003), pp. 529 - 539.

Ott, Claudia, Metamorphosen des Epos: Sīrat al-Muǧāhidīn (Sīrat al-Amīra Ḏāt-al-Himma) zwischen Mündlichkeit und Schriftlichkeit, Leiden: Universiteit Leiden 2003.

Ott, Claudia, "From the Coffehouse into the Manuscript: The Storyteller," Oriente Moderno 22 (2003), pp. 443 - 451.

Ouyang, Wen Ching, "The Epical Turn of Romance: Love in the Narrative of ʿUmar al-Nuʿmān," Oriente Moderno 22 (2003), pp. 485 - 504.

Petry, Carl F., The Criminal Underworld in a Medieval Islamic Society. Narratives from Cairo and Damascus under the Mamluks, Middle East Documentation Center: University of Chicago (forthcoming).

Petry, Carl F., "The Politics of Insult: The Mamluk Sultanate's Response to Criminal Affronts," MSR 15 (2011), pp. 87 - 117.

Petry, Carl F., "Crime in Mamluk Historiography: A Fraud Case depicted by Ibn Taghri-Birdi," MSR 10 (2006), pp. 141 - 151.

Petry, Carl F., "The Hoax of the Miraculous Speaking Wall: Criminal Investigation in

Mamluk Cairo," in: Mamluks and Ottomans: Studies in honour of Michael Winter, eds. D.J. Wasserstein and A. Ayalon, Studies in Middle Eastern History, London: Routeledge 2005, pp. 86–95.

Petry, Carl F., "Al-Maqrizi's Discussion of Imprisonment and Description of Jails in the Khitat," MSR 7/2 (2003), pp. 137–43.

Petry, Carl F., "Robing Ceremonials in Late Mamluk Egypt: Hallowed Traditions, Shifting Protocols," in: Robes and Honor: The Medieval World of Investiture, ed. Stewart Gordon, New York, Houndsmills: Palgrave 2001.

Petry, Carl F., "Disruptive others as Depicted in the Chronicles of the Late Mamluk Period," in: The Historiography of Islamic Egypt, ed. Hugh Kennedy, Leiden: Brill 2000, pp. 167–194.

Petry, Carl F., "'Quis Custodiet Custodes?' Revisited: The Prosecution of Crime in the Late Mamluk Sultanate," MSR 3 (1999), pp. 13–30.

Petry, Carl F., "A Geniza for Mamluk Studies? Charitable Trust (Waqf) Documents as a Source for Economic and Social History," MSR 2 (1998), pp. 51–60.

Petry, Carl F., The civilian elite of Cairo in the later middle ages, New Jersey: Princeton 1981.

Pickering, Michael, Popular Culture. Volume II. From Mass Culture to Popular Culture Studies, Los Angeles: Sage 2010.

Rapoport, Yosef, "Women and Gender in Mamluk Society," MSR 11/2 (2007), pp. 1–47.

Reynolds, Dwight Fletcher, "Popular Prose in the Post-Classical Period," in: Cambridge History of Arabic Literature. Arabic Literature in the Post-classical Period, eds. R. Allen and D.S. Richards, Cambridge: Cambridge University Press 2006, pp. 245–269.

Reynolds, Dwight Fletcher, "A Thousand and One Nights: a History of the Text and its Reception," in: Cambridge History of Arabic Literature. Arabic Literature in the Post-classical Period, eds. R. Allen and D.S. Richards, Cambridge: Cambridge University Press 2006, pp. 270–261.

Reynolds, Dwight Fletcher, "Sīrat Banī Hilāl," in: Cambridge History of Arabic Literature. Arabic Literature in the Post-classical Period, eds. R. Allen and D.S. Richards, Cambridge: Cambridge University Press 2006, pp. 307–318.

Reynolds, Dwight Fletcher, Heroic poets, poetic heroes: the ethnography of performance in an Arabic oral epic tradition, Ithaca: Cornell University Press 1995.

Rogan, Eugene, Outside In. On the Margins of Modern Middle East, London, New York: I. B. Tauris 2002.

Saada, Lucienne, La Geste hilalienne: version de Bou Thadi (Tunisie) / recueillie, établie et traduite de l'arabe par Lucienne Saada; récitation de Mohammed Hsini; préface de Jean Grosjean, Paris: Gallimard 1985

Sabra, Adam, Poverty and charity in medieval Islam: Mamluk Egypt, 1250–1517, Cambridge: Cambridge University Press 2000.

Schippers, Arie, "An Episode of a Hero in the Sīrat Banī Hilāl: Abū Zayd as a schoolboy," Oriente Moderno 22 (2003), pp. 347–359.

Shershow, Scott Cutler, "New Life: Cultural Studies and the Problem of the 'Popular'," in: Pickering, Popular Culture II, 361–383.

Shoshan, Boaz, "Review of C. S.Taylor's Vicinity," IJMES 32 (2000), pp. 545–546.

Shoshan, Boaz, Popular culture in medieval Cairo, Cambridge: Cambridge University Press 1996.

Singer, Amy, Charity in Islamic Societies, Cambridge: Cambridge University Press 200.
Slyomovics, Susan,"'Ashig Ma'bad (The Passion of Ma'bad). The Epic confronts Hilali History," Oriente Moderno 22 (2003), pp. 335 – 346.
Slyomovics, Susan, The Merchant of Art. An Egyptian Hilali Oral Epic Poet in Performance, Berkley: 1987.
Storey, John, Cultural Theory and Popular Culture. An Introduction. Fifth edition, Harlow: Pearson Education Ltd. 2009.
Sublet, Jacqueline, "Un héros populaire dans un espace encombré," Arabica 51/1 (2004), pp. 144 – 161.
Taylor, Christoph S., In the vicinity of the righteous: Ziyāra and the veneration of Muslim saints in late medieval Egypt, Leiden: E. J. Brill 1999.
Toru, Miura, "Urban Society in Damascus as the Mamluk Era Was Ending," MSR 10/1, pp. 157 – 191.
Van Steenbergen, Jo, "Ritual, Politics and the City in Mamluk Cairo: the Bayna l-Qasrayn as a dynamic 'lieu de mémoire', 1250 – 1382," in: Court Ceremonies and Ritual of Power in the Medieval Mediterranean, ed. Beihammer et al., (in publication).
Vidal-Luengo, Ana Ruth, "L'élément maghrébin dans Sīrat Baybars," Arabica 51/1 (2004), pp. 162 – 188.
Vidal Luengo, Ana Ruth, La dimensión mediadora en el mito árabe islámico: la Sīrat Baybars, Granada: Univ. de Granada 2000.
Wiederhold, Lutz, "Legal-Religious Elite, Temporal Authority, and the Caliphate in Mamluk Society: Conclusions Drawn from the Examination of a 'Zahiri Revolt' in Damascus in 1386," International Journal of Middle East Studies 31/2 (1999), pp. 203 – 235.
Williams, Raymond, Keywords, London: Fontana 1983.
Winter, Michael, Egyptian society under Ottoman rule, 1517 – 1798, London: Routledge 1992.
Zakharia, Katia,"Genre poétique et inter-textualité dans Sīrat al-Malik aẓ-Ẓāhir Baybars: L'exemple des trois premiers volumes," Arabica 51/1 (2004), pp. 198 – 211.
Zakharia, Katia and Bohas, Georges, Sīrat al-Malik al-Ẓāhir Baybars ḥasab al-riwāya al-shāmīya, Damascus: Institut Français du Proche Orient 2000.

Konrad Hirschler

Studying Mamluk Historiography. From Source-Criticism to the Cultural Turn

The Mamluk era with its encyclopaedic chronicles and massive biographical dictionaries is arguably the last period in Middle Eastern history for which narrative texts can claim a central position for documenting society.[1] For the subsequent Ottoman era, by contrast, documentary sources start to be available to such an extent that historiographical texts, although still of importance, are increasingly relegated to the back seat of historical inquiry. Narrative historiography played a particularly central role in modern Mamluk Studies during the 1950s and 1960s when the field gradually emerged as an independent area of academic inquiry. The work of the field's pioneers, such as D. Ayalon, relied almost exclusively on narrative historiographical texts, while documentary sources were virtually absent from this generation's ground-breaking work.[2] The next wave of scholars during what might be called the field's formative period, from the 1970s onwards, initially kept to this tradition and typically undertook their doctoral research on narrative historiographical texts. U. Haarmann and D. Little, for instance, both wrote their PhD theses on chronicles and biographical dictionaries of the earlier Mamluk period.[3]

Over the last 40 years, however, documentary sources have gradually started to play a more important role in writing Mamluk history and have, to an extent, challenged the primacy of narrative historiography. Many of the contributions to this volume, and to the preceding 2011-conference, bear testimony to this development in their discussion of numismatic, archaeological and epigraphic sources to name but a few. Arguably, it is this widening of the source basis that has to a large extent driven innovation in the study of Mamluk history in recent decades. This is evident when considering the programmatic or 'state of the art' articles in the *Mamlūk Studies Review*, the publication of which, in 1997, was a

1 Thanks are due to Stephan Conermann for organising the conference and editing this volume. This paper has greatly benefited from the vivid discussions that took place throughout the three-day conference.
2 For Ayalon's work cf. Elad, *Bibliography*,.
3 Haarmann, *Quellenstudien*; Little, *Introduction*.

crucial stepping-stone in the field's history. It is striking that most such articles over the past fifteen years have been linked to specific documentary source genres. In particular the journal's early volumes emphatically promoted the use of sources ranging from textual documents in the narrow sense of the term, via architecture to archaeological artefacts.[4] By contrast, the journal's early articles, which aimed to establish the direction of future research, hardly featured theoretical debates or methodological issues. The salient exception was W. Clifford's reflection on *Mamluk History and Social Theory*, but it is only in more recent years that overview articles have moved rather from sources to approaches and discuss questions pertaining to literature, gender studies and popular culture.[5]

The classical example for the 'discovery' of new documentary material that has significantly re-orientated the field of Mamluk Studies and driven innovation has been endowment deeds. Since the work of ʿA. Ibrāhīm, M. Amīn and U. Haarmann, to name just three, integrated such deeds into the canon of sources in the 1970s, this material has become one of the defining source genres of the field.[6] In the same vein, numismatics can now claim a considerably more central position than when the field of Mamluk Studies was forming in the 1970s. Recent work by S. Heidemann, Ḥ. Najīdī and W. Schultz has shown to what extent numismatic evidence is available and can refine our understanding of political and economic history.[7]

Archaeology is in many ways the late-comer to Mamluk Studies, as it has been and still is in so many fields of Middle Eastern history given its philological tradition. Yet the last decade has witnessed the first substantial publications dedicated to this field, especially those on sites in the southern Bilād al-Shām region by B. Walker and M. Milwright.[8] Studies on architecture and buildings within urban spaces have also seen a spectacular rise since the 1970s and remain closely linked to the name of M. Meinecke and subsequently D. Behrens-Abouseif.[9] Another documentary source genre that deserves more attention are the notes on manuscripts, such as reading notes (*muṭālaʿah*), certificates of transmission (*samāʿ*), licences for transmission (*ijāzah*), ownership statements (*tamlīk/tamalluk*, often in combination with seals), statements that praise or dispraise the text (*taqrīẓ* in the former case), verses by the copyists, and endowment attestation (*waqfīyah/taḥbīs*). The study of this material, which gained

4 Little, *Documents*; Whitcomb, *Mamluk*; Petry, *Geniza*; Bloom, *Mamluk*; Bauden, *Mamluk*; Walker, *Ceramics*.

5 Clifford, *Ubi Sumus*; Bauer, *Mamluk Literature*; Berkey, *Popular Culture*; Rapoport, *Women*.

6 Ibrāhīm, *Silsilat*; Amīn, *al-Awqāf*; Haarmann, *Endowment*.

7 Heidemann, *Renaissance*; Najīdī, *al-Niẓām*; Schultz, *Mamluk Money*.

8 Walker, *Jordan*; Milwright, *Fortress*.

9 Meinecke, *Architektur*; Behrens-Abouseif, *Cairo*.

pace in the 1990s, as exemplified in S. Leder's ground-breaking work on Damascene *samāʿāt*, represents one of the most promising developments in the field with regard to new source genres.[10]

While this diversification of sources has substantially changed the field's outlook and profile in recent decades, the sheer volume of historiographical texts ensures that they will retain an outstanding position in Mamluk Studies. Tellingly, the very first issue of the *Mamlūk Studies Review* contained L. Guo's overview article of historiographical studies.[11] In the same vein, J. v. Steenbergen's *Mamluk History and Culture (1250–1517)*-project at the University of Ghent, running between 2009 and 2014, relies predominantly on historiographical narrative texts.[12] The production of works of *ta'rīkh*, i.e. chronicles and biographical dictionaries, remained so prolific throughout the Mamluk era that this period's historiographical texts are even the main sources for some preceding eras. The chronicles of authors such as al-Maqrīzī (d. 845/1442) are indispensable for the Fatimid era, for example.[13] F. Bora's recent work on the relationship between Fatimid history and Mamluk historiography is the first work to address this issue in the detail it deserves.[14] Given this volume of *ta'rīkh*-texts and their encyclopaedic character it is no wonder that Mamluk-era chronicles were among the first texts to be taken up in the early stages of Arabic and Islamic studies in Europe. The concise universal chronicle by Abū al-Fidā' (d. 732/1331) enjoyed unrivalled, though entirely undeserved, popularity for writing the history of earlier periods as, for instance, is evident in early eighteenth-century works by J. Gagnier and A. Schulten.[15] In the Arabic-speaking lands themselves Mamluk *ta'rīkh* texts remained exceedingly popular and they even played a prominent role in the early days of the newly emerging Arabic press in the mid-nineteenth century. One example is an early Mamluk chronicle, Abū Shāma's (d. 665/1267) *al-Rawḍatayn,* which was serialised from 1858 onwards by the Beirut-based newspaper *Ḥadīqat al-akhbār,* in the hope of attracting a larger audience.[16]

The prominence of narrative historiography in modern studies is very much due to the veritable explosion that history writing experienced in Syria and Egypt from the seventh/thirteenth century onwards. The previous sixth/twelfth century can legitimately be called the 'dark century' of historical writing in the

10 Leder et al., *Muʿjam* (1996); Leder et al., *Muʿjam* (2000); cf. Görke, Hirschler, *Manuscript Notes.*

11 Guo, *Historiographic Studies.*

12 Cf. http://www.mamluk.ugent.be/.

13 Cf. for instance Lev, *State.*

14 Bora, *Representations.*

15 Gagnier, *De vita*; Schulten, *Vita.*

16 Hirschler, *Arabic Historiography,* 118–20.

area with few significant works being produced. For Northern Syria for instance, al-ʿAẓīmī's (d. after 556/1161) extremely concise chronicle is the main textual witness that we have for the early decades of this century.[17] Compared with the elaborate and sophisticated historical narratives of the Mamluk era, it is almost a euphemism to label this bare list of events a 'chronicle'. From citations in later works, especially those by Ibn al-ʿAdīm it is evident that a richer historiographical tradition existed in Syria during the fifth/eleventh and the sixth/twelfth centuries.[18] Among these were the works of authors such as Yaḥyā b. ʿAlī al-Tanūkhī Ibn al-Zurayq (d. c. 442/1051)[19], ʿAbd al-Wāḥid b. Masʿūd b. al-Ḥusayn (presumably from Maʿarrat al-Nuʿmān, fl. 527/1132–3)[20], the *qāḍī* ʿAbd al-Qāhir b. ʿAlawī (presumably from Maʿarrat Maṣrīn close to Maʿarrat al-Nuʿmān, fl. 571/1176)[21] and Abū Manṣūr Hibbat Allāh b. Saʿd Allāh (presumably from Aleppo, his son Aḥmad died in 628/1231[22]).

Hardly any biographical information on these authors is available as none of the rich biographical dictionaries of the following centuries included them. Information other than their names can only be guessed at from the citations that can be ascribed to them. It seems that their works were mostly chronicles, but only in one case, that of ʿAbd al-Qāhir, is the title of the work known, *Nuzhat al-nāẓir wa-rawḍat al-khāṭir.*[23] The subsequent explosion of historical writing is not so much a Mamluk-specific phenomenon, as we see the first inklings of change towards the end of the sixth/twelfth century in the early Ayyubid period. The cluster of works produced by Ṣalāḥ al-Dīn's courtiers ʿImād al-Dīn al-Iṣfahānī (d. 597/1201), Ibn Shaddād (d. 632/1234) and al-Qāḍī al-Fāḍil (d. 596/1200), but also by scholars such as Ibn ʿAsākir (d. 571/1176) initiated a new phase in the

17 The decline of historiography in Syria, reaching back into the 5th/11th century, was not experienced in Egypt to the same extent. The dearth of Egyptian historical writing for the Fatimid period is also very much due to the subsequent destruction of Fatimid/Ismāʿīli works.

18 The second prime source for this period's lost historiographical tradition is the biographical dictionary of Ibn ʿAsākir, *Taʾrīkh*,

19 Ibn al-ʿAdīm, *Bughyat*, 2:864; 5:2262; 6:2971; 7:3357 ('I read in the hand of ʿUmar b. Muḥammad al-ʿUlaymī, known as Ḥawāʾij Kash … who stated that he transmitted it from the hand of Ibn Zurayq, that is Abū al-Ḥasan Yaḥyā b. ʿAlī … Ibn al-Zurayq who was a scholar of history […]'); 9:3872.

20 Ibn al-ʿAdīm, *Bughyat*, for instance: 3:1299; 4:1630 ('I read … in this chronicle, year 527…'); 4:1958, 6:2699 ('the chronicle that he composed was a continuation (*dhayl*) of the *Summary* of al-Ṭabarī['s chronicle]').

21 Ibn al-ʿAdīm, *Bughyat*, for instance: 5:2421 (title), 7:5858.

22 Ibn al-ʿAdīm, *Bughyat*, 2:741 ('I got hold of a volume in the hand of … Hibbat Allāh … that contains a list of the governors of Aleppo … and he was interested in history.'). On his son cf. al-Dhahabī, *Taʾrīkh*, vol. 621–30, pp. 304–5.

23 On these authors cf. also the editor's introduction in al-ʿAẓīmī, *Taʾrīkh* and Bianquis, *Damas*, 22–32.

historiography of the region.[24] The reason for this historiographical revival have not been studied in detail, but the reestablishment of stable political structures and urban-centred courts, a process started under the Zangids, certainly contributed.

Mapping the Field of Mamluk Historiography

At first glance it might seem that the study of Mamluk historiography is well advanced and on a par with the study of early Arabic historiography. This impression is given by the coverage of the period in the three grand monographic surveys of Islamic/Arabic historiography: F. Rosenthal's *Muslim Historiography*, T. Khalidi's *Arabic Historical Thought* and C. Robinson's *Islamic Historiography*. They all follow the traditional periodisation and end their surveys at the 1517-watershed when the Ottoman conquest and the subsequent rise of Ottoman Turkish as the lingua franca purportedly introduced a new period. Whatever quibbles one might have with this periodisation, from a Mamlukoligist perspective it has proved very useful to ensure coverage of the field. This periodisation is also applied in the survey articles of Islamic/Arabic historiography such as those by S. Humphreys in the *Encyclopaedia of Islam*, L. Guo in the *The New Cambridge History of Islam* and K. Hirschler in the *Oxford History of Historical Writing*.[25] In addition, we now have a number of survey articles specifically on Mamluk-era historiography ranging from L. Guo's *Mamlūk Studies Review* article via D. Little's contribution to the *The Cambridge History of Egypt* to R. Irwin in the *Arabic Literature in the Post-Classical Period* volume.[26]

However, these surveys are deceptive to a degree because they suggest that they provide an authoritative overview even though we lack detailed studies on most historians and their works. The situation has barely changed since L. Guo remarked in 1997 that 'we continue to witness a dearth of articles, and even fewer monographs, devoted to Mamluk historians and their writings.' The only exception is obviously Ibn Khaldūn (d. 808/1406) who has been subject to an unrivalled number of studies, some of them focusing on his historical production, most notably those by ʿA. al-Azmeh and A. Cheddadi.[27] Yet even al-Maqrīzī, whose oeuvre constitutes arguably the most-cited historiographical material in current Mamluk scholarship has not been dealt with in a compre-

24 ʿImād al-Dīn, *al-Barq*. vols. 3 and 5 idem, *al-Fatḥ*; Ibn Shaddād, *al-Nawādir*. Ibn ʿAsākir, *Ta'rīkh*.

25 Rosenthal, *History*; Robinson, *Islamic Historiography*; Khalidi, *Historical Thought*; Humphreys, et al., *Ta'rīkh*; Guo, *Historiographic Studies*; Hirschler, *Islam*.

26 Guo, *Historiographic Studies*; Irwin, *Mamluk History*; Little, *Historiography*.

27 Al-ʿAzmeh, *Ibn Khaldūn*; Cheddadi, *Ibn Khaldûn*.

hensive survey. We now have a number of excellent articles on his works, many of them by F. Bauden in his *Maqriziana*-series and a special issue of the *Mamlūk Studies Review* on him, as well as an unpublished PhD-thesis on his historical outlook, but a dedicated monograph has not yet been published.[28] Moving beyond these two authors the picture becomes increasingly dire. Ibn Taghrībirdī (d. 815/1412) authored a crucial biographical dictionary of rulers, officers and scholars from 650/1248 to 855/1451, *al-Manhal al-Ṣāfī*, two chronicles of Egypt, *al-Nujūm al-Zāhirah* and *Ḥawādith al-Duhūr* and further condensations and summaries.[29] Yet the only monograph on him does not aim to comprehensively study the author as a historian and the published articles are less numerous and far less informative than those on al-Maqrīzī.[30] For most authors even substantial articles, such as S. Conermann on Ibn Ṭūlūn (d. 955/1548), are the exception. The sole period of Mamluk history writing which can now claim relatively good coverage is the early Mamluk era.[31]

In addition to the lack of focused studies on individual historians, overview articles of Mamluk-era historiography are also deceptive in another sense, namely with regard to the philological quality of editions. Students of the Mamluk era now have an unrivalled number of edited texts at their disposal. The large-scale biographical dictionaries of the like of al-Dhahabī and al-Birzālī from the eighth/fourteenth century, al-Nuwayrī's (d. 733/1333) monumental encyclopaedia *Nihāyat al-arab* and an ever increasing number of chronicles have become available in printed and digitised formats.[32] Yet, despite the crucial importance of historiographical texts, the scholarly field relies in many cases on editions that can be described as 'non-critical' at best. These editions are often outdated reprints of those produced in the late 19th/early 20th century. To return to the example of Abū al-Fidā' and his concise universal chronicle: The first complete edition of this text was published in 1870 in Istanbul without information on the manuscript used. Some four decades later the Cairene Ḥusaynīya press reissued the work with only slight amendments. Since then this

28 Bauden, Maqriziana IX; special issue: *Mamlūk Studies Review* 7/2 (2003); Dalil-Essakali, *La conception*. The closest we get to a monograph is F. Sayyid's introduction in F. Sayyid, *Le manusrit.*

29 Ibn Taghrībirdī, *Ḥawādith*; Ibn Taghrībirdī, *Al-Manhal*; Ibn Taghrībirdī, *Al-Nujūm*.

30 Sievert, *Der Herrscherwechsel*; Lajnat al-Ta'rīkh, *Al-Mu'arrikh Ibn Taghrībirdī*; Perho, *Al-Maqrīzī.*

31 Haarmann, *Quellenstudien*; Little, *Introduction*. Further monographs include for instance Guo, *Syrian Historiography*; Morray, *Ayyubid*; Hirschler, *Arabic Historiography*, on Ibn Wāṣil and Abū Shāmah.

32 Al-Dhahabī, *Ta'rīkh*; al-Birzālī, *al-Muqtafī*; al-Nuwayrī, *Nihāyat*; Digital resources such as *Maktabat al-ta'rīkh wa-al-ḥaḍāra al-islāmīya* (al-Turāth) and *al-Maktaba al-Shāmila* (freeware, http://shamela.ws/) are of increasing importance despite their emphasis on texts concerning the early Islamic period.

edition has been reprinted in different places (Baghdad [1968?], Beirut: Dār al-Kutub al-ʿIlmīyah [19??], Cairo: Dār al-Maʿārif [1998 – 1999]) without any substantial improvement.[33] This state of affairs is also driven by the fact that pre-modern historical works enjoy a popularity in the modern Middle East that is simply non-existent elsewhere. Consequently, publishing houses in Beirut, Cairo and other cities massively reprint and produce what C. Gilliot has called in his surveys of newly published source editions in the *Mélanges de l'Institut dominicain d'études orientales* 'commercial editions'. These editions routinely do not even state what manuscript(s) were used, they generally do not try to establish an overview of the known manuscripts and their critical apparatus is often rather poor.[34] Rather than aiming at a scholarly audience they are better understood as coffee-table editions for an educated lay readership that appreciates the richly decorated and splendid covers.

At the same time, the production of serious critical editions in European or US-American universities and research institutes has virtually stopped in recent decades. There are a few exceptions such as M. Rahim's wonderful edition of the final parts of Ibn Wāṣil's (d. 697/1298) chronicle covering the early Mamluk period or the long-running project of editing al-Ṣafadī's biographical dictionary.[35] That the production of editions has ground to a virtual halt or has at least significantly slowed down in US-American and European academia is also closely tied to the rise of 'performance'-driven and competitive mechanisms for financing academic research. Initiatives such as the German *Exzellenzinitative* or the British *Research Excellence Framework* have tended to undervalue 'mere' editorial work and have pushed the field at the same time towards inter-disciplinary and transregional work that leaves little room for producing editions. While initiatives like the Ghent-project and the Bonn-based *Annemarie Schimmel Kolleg for History and Society during the Mamluk Era* have been of great benefit for the field, the strings attached to their funding might be framing the field in ways that are detrimental in the long term.

Consequently, even for the canonical works such as those by al-Maqrīzī, Ibn Taghrībirdī and Ibn Khaldūn, editions are being used that fall way short of even the most basic requirements of philological scholarship. For instance, al-Maqrīzī's encyclopaedia of historical topography, his *Khiṭaṭ*, was used for some 150 years in the entirely unsatisfactory Bulāq-edition of 1853. A. Sayyid's new edition of this work has certainly improved the quality of the text, yet it still falls short of a truly critical edition.[36] For a widely used chronicle such as Ibn

33 Abū al-Fidā', *Mukhtaṣar* (1869/70); ibid. (1907).

34 For remarks on editorial techniques of Mamluk historiographical texts cf. also Guo, *Historiographic Studies*, 15 – 27.

35 Rahim, *Chronik*; al-Ṣafadī, *al-Wāfī*.

36 Bauden, *Review: Sayyid, al-Mawāʿiẓ*.

Taghrībirdī's *Nujūm* the situation is worse still. This chronicle was edited in Cairo from the 1920s onwards in a decade-long process. Although the quality of most volumes is mediocre at best, it is this edition or reprints of it that are routinely used until the present day.[37] Leaving the groundwork of editing to colleagues based at Middle Eastern universities, as has increasingly been the case in recent decades, cannot be the solution. The edition output of an individual such as ʿU. al-Tadmurī is simply awe-inspiring, including al-Dhahabī's massive biographical dictionary, Ibn Wāṣil's universal history and al-Birzālī's dictionary to name but a few.[38] However, it is evident that more reliable editions require cooperation between individual academics and institutions that are able to sustain such large projects. It is thus one of the great challenges of the field to direct more resources into activities as 'non-excellent', 'non-transregional' and 'non-innovative' as editing new sources or re-editing those editions of unsatisfactory quality. While source genres such as coins, deeds and manuscript notes have offered and will continue to offer crucial departure points for research, narrative historiography can only continue to play a central role in the field if the groundwork of offering a secure philological basis for these texts is carried out.

While such groundwork is indispensable, the exact role of historiography within the field depends on the ways in which Mamluk historiographical texts are used and what approaches have been applied for studying such texts in their own right. In the following, this article argues that historiographical texts, especially biographical dictionaries, still have a crucial role to play in fields such as social history and cultural history. Yet the potential of these texts for advancing the field can only be fully harnessed if they are seen as more than repositories of social and or cultural facts.

Approaches and Debates

The study of Mamluk historical writing started within the framework of source-critical approaches and these approaches have remained a crucial feature of the field. U. Haarmann's and D. Little's works examined – though not exclusively – their respective sources according to their source value for modern historians. Such an approach has remained a salient feature of the field and also underlies more recent work such as K. Franz's study of the process of compilation in chronicles and S. Massoud's discussion of late eighth/fourteenth-century chronicles.[39] The underlying assumption of many of these studies is that the

37 Ibn Taghrībirdī, *Al-Nujūm*.
38 Al-Dhahabī, *Ta'rīkh*; Ibn Wāṣil, *al-Ta'rīkh al-Ṣāliḥī*; Al-Birzālī, *Al-Muqtafī*.
39 Franz, *Kompilation*; Massoud, *The Chronicles*.

isolation of reports on a specific issue/event/person can bring about a better understanding of their historicity. While such questions will obviously remain at the heart of historical inquiry into any given topic, it is less obvious whether such dedicated studies will contribute a great deal to our understanding of historical works. For instance, the field of early Islamic historiography has moved on and has increasingly departed from the view of historical texts as a collection of individual reports in the *khabar* style. Rather, and especially for the texts written from the fourth/tenth century onwards, the view of these texts has shifted towards seeing them more as coherent narratives that have to be analysed as such.[40]

Certainly, the strict chronological system that prevailed in chronicles curtailed to some extent the possibilities of crafting such coherent narratives. Nevertheless, recent scholarship has become more interested in the authorial voice of chroniclers, which became more distinct and less timid not only in the introductions, but also in the main texts. This interest in the chronicler's voice included an interest in how an authorial decision was made to organise events and of how to endow them with new meanings. The increased textual room for manoeuvre allowed the chroniclers to craft texts more individually and a comparison of works that report the same events in the Middle Period suffices to show how these authors used this room. Beyond the organisation of historical works, the distinctive authorial presence also became evident in the increased use of the authorial 'I' and the intrusion of autobiographical elements into the texts. For instance, while Abū Shāma described his personal life in Damascus in detail in his wonderfully eccentric cross between a biographical dictionary, chronicle and autobiography, Abū al-Fidā' detailed his efforts to regain rule in his northern Syrian hometown of Hama. This development culminated in the late fifteenth and early sixteenth centuries in historical works that are diary-like accounts with the author repeatedly at centre-stage, such as the chronicles by Ibn Ṭawq (d. ca. 1431) and Ibn Ṭūlūn.[41]

The shift from analysing historical works in terms of narratives/authors rather than *akhbār*/compilers does not only mean that the coherency of the texts moves into focus, but also that the social context of the author takes on increasing importance. This shift has been evident in the field of Mamluk historiography, not so much as an outcome of a sustained scholarly discussion of the issue, but more because of a simple shift towards individual authors. As discussed above, the number of works that we have in this regard are still limited, but Morray's discussion of the late Ayyubid-early Mamluk transition-period

40 As reflected in Donner, *Narratives*; El-Hibri, *Reinterpreting*; Shoshan, *The Poetics*; El-Hibri, *Parable*.

41 Abū Shāmah, *al-Dhayl*; Ibn Ṭūlūn, *Mufākahat*; Ibn Ṭawq, *Al-Taʿlīq*.

biographical dictionary of Ibn al-ʿAdīm is a splendid example. By drawing from the text itself Morray is able to give a unique insight into the social and intellectual world of this scholar and thus contextualise the production of the text.

Arguably, a more important outcome of the shift towards narratives and authors is that it puts an end to the lingering discussion on the 'literarisation' of Mamluk historiography. U. Haarmann proposed this evocative term in 1969 and it has since remained a constant feature in debates on this period's historical writing. With this term Haarmann drew attention to the increasing use of the anecdote, of dialectical elements and of direct speech, as well as the authors' tendency to invent oral sources and their rigorous attempts to dedicate the same textual space to each year irrespective of the importance of the year's events.[42] B. Radtke has already drawn attention to the fact that these elements were not necessarily new, but had existed in earlier periods.[43] However, the main problem with this term is that it implied a dichotomy between literary fictional texts on the one hand and historical factual texts on the other. With the move towards narratives and authors this dichotomy is no longer a useful category for understanding the development of historical writing. The question is now rather how literary forms were changing over time, what different means authors employed and how they ascribed meaning to events. U. Haarmann's observations on the Mamluk period gain new significance because he had rightly observed that changes did take place in the way authors crafted their narratives. The recent and rich scholarship on historiography in the formative period has certainly shown that literarisation was not a new phenomenon, but U. Haarmann was right in saying that the use of the anecdote as a standard element in Mamluk historical writing was an important but under-researched phenomenon.

The Uses of Historiographical Texts

Owing to the centrality of narrative historiography, chronicles and biographical dictionaries have been used in virtually every study of the Mamluk era that has been published in recent decades. This holds true for the different fields of historical inquiry ranging from political and institutional history via cultural and intellectual history to social and economic history. In this sense the profile and outlook of these texts and their authors have proved to be highly influential well beyond the tenth/sixteenth century. To cite the two most obvious examples, the Mamlukologist biases towards urban centres as the central area of research

42 Haarmann, *Quellenstudien*, 159–83; Haarmann, *Auflösung*.
43 Radtke, *Weltgeschichte*.

and Egypt as the main region of research are both a direct reflection of the outlook of Mamluk-era authors.

Mamluk historiography is as urban-centred as a historiographical tradition might be. The authors resided almost without exception in large urban centres and the events they describe generally took place in the urban landscapes of the Mamluk realms. The seventh/thirteenth-century *History of the Fayyūm*, central to Y. Rapoport's project at Queen Mary/University of London on rural societies, is one of the rare exceptions dealing in detail with villages and villagers.[44] As much as the urban tunnel vision of al-Maqrīzī, Ibn Taghrībirdī and their like has remained influential until the present day, so did their Egypt-centred worldview. Throughout the Ayyubid and the early Mamluk periods, historical writing about the Egyptian/Syrian lands took place largely in Damascus, Aleppo and the lesser Syrian towns. Yet from the mid-eighth/fourteenth century onwards, Egypt started to supersede Syria as the main centre for the production of historical knowledge. While Syrian authors like Ibn Qāḍī Shuhbah (d. 851/1448) continued to produce historical works in the ninth/fifteenth century, it was evident that the heyday of Syrian historiography had come to an end. At the same time, the increasingly Egypt-based authors paid rather scant attention to Syrian events unless they were interlinked with events in Egypt. This Egypt- and Cairo-centrism has been reflected in the profile of modern Mamluk scholarship and it is not by chance that work challenging this regional bias is often based on new source genres such as the above-mentioned archaeological work by B. Walker and M. Milwright on southern Syria. In the same vein, the 2007-*Mamlūk Studies Review* special volume (XI/1) on the Mamluk provinces also contained a significant number of articles based on material culture.

However, the regional imbalance in modern studies has not only been addressed by the increased study of material culture, but also in historiographical studies themselves. One of the important developments that we have witnessed in recent decades in the field is that the rich tradition of Syrian historiography during the early Mamluk period has been brought to the forefront. It has been mainly the work of L. Guo that has consistently underlined the importance of the Syrian lands for producing historical works in significant numbers.[45] After the above-mentioned beginnings under Ṣalāḥ al-Dīn, a continuous trickle of works was produced by the likes of Ibn al-ʿAdīm (d. 660/1262), Sibṭ b. al-Jawzī (d. 654/

44 Al-Nābulusī, *Ta'rīkh*. For Rapoport's project see http://www.history.qmul.ac.uk/ruralsocietyislam/.

45 Most importantly Guo, *Syrian Historiography*, but also his overview article *History*. The vivacity of the Syrian historiographical tradition has now become a well-established notion, cf. Irwin, *Mamluk History*.

1256) and Abū Shāmah (d. 665/1267).[46] This culminated in the rich tradition of annalistic and prosopographical works authored by al-Yūnīnī (d. 726/1326), al-Jazarī (d. 739/1338), al-Birzālī (d. 739/1339), al-Dhahabī (d. 748/1348), al-Kutubī (d. 764/1363) and finally Ibn Kathīr (d. 774/1373).[47]

Biographical Dictionaries and Social/Cultural Histories

Rather than reflecting on how the biases of narrative historiography has shaped the modern field of Mamluk Studies – fascinating as the topic might be – the following focuses on two specific uses of narrative texts, namely in social and in cultural history. These examples are also chosen because they highlight the importance of prosopographical historiography, i.e. biographical dictionaries, for advancing our understanding of Mamluk history. These texts have tended to stand on the side-lines of reflections on historiographical practice as, for instance, in the above-mentioned survey works by F. Rosenthal, T. Khalidi and C. Robinson. This neglect starkly contrasts with the position of biographical dictionaries that are without doubt the most remarkable field of narrative history writing in Arabic, especially during the Mamluk period. It is not an exaggeration to claim that 'no other preindustrial society can claim such an abundance of information about various segments of the population'.[48] In the study of earlier periods of Middle Eastern history R. Bulliet's work has shown their usefulness as one of the main repositories for factual knowledge and W. al-Qadi has recently reiterated their peculiar profile compared with chronicles, framing them as the 'scholars' alternative history'.[49]

More pertinent to Mamluk Studies, biographical dictionaries were particularly helpful during the brief period when the field took up the challenges raised by social history or rather New Social History. New Social History reshaped the make-up of history departments and historical practice during the 1970s as it presented new questions and new methods, especially quantitative approaches. The classic in our field to stand in this tradition is evidently C. Petry's *Civilian Elite*, the first study that tapped into the potential of computer-based prosopographical research. Among the subsequent studies J. Berkey's *Transmission of*

46 Ibn al-ʿAdīm, *Zubdat* and idem, *Bughyat* (cf. Morray, *Ayyubid*); Ibn al-Jawzī, *Mir'āt*; Abū Shāmah, *Al-Dhayl* and idem, *Al-Rawḍatayn*.

47 Al-Yūnīnī, *Dhayl* (cf. Guo, *Syrian Historiography*); al-Jazarī, *Ḥawādith* not edited yet, cf. for instance MS Paris, BN arabe 6739 (*Jawāhir al-sulūk fī al-khulafā' wa-al-mulūk*); al-Birzālī, *Al-Muqtafī*; al-Dhahabī, *Ta'rīkh*; al-Kutubī, *Fawāt* and idem, *ʿUyūn*, vol. 20; Ibn Kathīr, *Al-Bidāya*.

48 Nawas, *Biography*, 112.

49 Bulliet, *Conversion*; Al-Qadi, *Biographical Dictionaries*. Cf. also Auchterlonie, *Historians*.

Knowledge must be singled out for its creative use of prosopographical data that is used here in combination with other sources, especially endowment deeds.[50] The central claim of New Social History was the possibility that social structures that determined politics and culture could be detected and analysed as objective and transpersonal patterns. However, Mamlukolgists never really warmed up to the positivist epistemology and objectivist ontology that underlay a great part of New Social History and that dominated many of the articles in 'general' (that is, predominantly European and US-American foucsed) history journals in the 1970s such as the *American Historical Review* and the *Journal of Modern History*. This reluctance in Mamluk Studies was arguably also linked to the very nature of biographical dictionaries and their focus on religious scholars. In consequence, social history in Mamluk Studies has always been linked to 'ulamology' and has thus had an inherent cultural bent lurking in the background.

New Social History experienced a spectacular demise in most fields of history from the 1980s onwards when the Cultural Turn worked its way through the different disciplines. While this demise was to some extent linked to simple fatigue following the hegemonic position and dominance that the social approach had held, the same cannot be said regarding its place within Mamluk Studies. Here, the potential of social-history approaches has not been really tapped into and still constitutes a crucial direction into which the field can move. This is especially the case as biographical dictionaries have been almost exclusively put to use for Cairo whereas the rich early Mamluk material for the Syrian towns such as Aleppo and Damascus has not been sufficiently taken into consideration.[51]

This regional bias towards Cairo is particularly problematic in the case of biographical dictionaries as it is precisely the heavily local and regional nature of these texts that make them so valuable. As they drill relatively deep into the social fabric of their local societies, they give unique insights into the lower ends of society that are often not evident from chronicles or other texts. Beyond doubt, almost all of those included were attached to the world of the religious scholar. Yet, in the local and regional dictionaries, such as Ibn al-ʿAdīm's *Bughyat al-Ṭalab* on Aleppo or al-Dhahabī's *Ta'rīkh al-Islām* on Damascus the net is cast widely and we gain insights into the world of the city's part-time scholars and low salaried groups such as the *mu'adhdhins* of minor mosques who would not appear in the grand chronicles.[52] There is one field closely linked to social history, women's history, for which Mamluk Studies has employed biographical dictionaries to some extent. This usage of biographical dictionaries was indeed

50 Petry, *Civilian Elitte*; Berkey, *Transmission*.
51 The main exception obviously being Chamberlain, *Knowledge*.
52 Ibn al-ʿAdīm, *Bughyat*; al-Dhahabī, *Ta'rīkh*.

in the framework of 'women's history', before this approach was reconfigured as Gender Studies. The main aim in such studies has thus been to show the role of women and their contribution to various fields of social activities.[53]

Beyond social history, biographical dictionaries will also prove to be a crucial resource for taking up the challenges of the Cultural Turn. This turn has made an explicit entrance into the field of Mamluk Studies, particularly in the form of Historical Anthropology. The most programmatic expression of the inroads culturalist approaches have made is the 2007-volume by S. Conermann and S. von Hees *Islamic Studies as Cultural Anthropology*, which contained several contributions touching upon the Mamluk era.[54] However, it is Th. Bauer's 2011-book *Culture of Ambiguity* which implements the programmatic claims of historical anthropology into the first large-scale study focused upon the Mamluk period.[55] The relatively slow arrival of the Cultural Turn in Mamluk Studies is a result of the field's inherent cultural bent, which characterised studies well before the 1980s. In contrast to the fields of European and American history, where the dominance of New Social History had been much stronger, Mamluk Studies had less of an impetus to turn with the same vehemence in the opposite direction.

While the uptake of such culturalist approaches has thus not been very accentuated in the field, the following will suggest that they have considerable potential to advance it, especially if applied to biographical dictionaries. One topic where biographical dictionaries can play a crucial role in cultural studies is suicide, to take just one example. Although the Qur'ān did not discuss suicide in detail, several *ḥadīth*s unequivocally condemn it as illicit and threaten the culprit with severe punishment in hell. Later scholarly discussions primarily focused upon whether funeral prayers may be spoken over somebody who ended his or her own life. Yet, suicide seemed to be as frequent in Egypt and Syria as in other regions, as indicated by the relative importance of the subject in popular works. The classical article on this issue remains F. Rosenthal's piece which, like other contemporary works, discusses the phenomenon in Islam in general. However, it shows the author's usual breadth as well as his skills in drawing together disparate material into an argumentative whole.[56] For Mamluk Studies B. Martel-Thoumian has extensively discussed the issue with a characteristic focus on late-Mamluk chronicles.[57]

F. Rosenthal argued that only an insignificant number of religious scholars

53 For instance Roded, *Women*; Afsaruddin, *Biographical Dictionaries*; Lutfi, *Al-Sakhāwī's*.

54 Conermann, v. Hees, *Islamwissenschaft*.

55 Bauer, *Ambiguität*. Bauer's argument transcends the Mamluk era, but due to the richness of Mamluk-era material and examples, it is an outstanding resource for our field.

56 Rosenthal, *On Suicide*.

57 Martel-Thoumian, *La mort*. The same focus on chronicle is evident in brief studies of the issue such as Jawād, *al-Muntaḥirūn*, who most probably used Ibn al-Fuwaṭī, *al-Ḥawādith*.

committed suicide in the premodern era.[58] More specifically, he enumerates for the Mamluk era eleven cases of suicide or attempted suicide, not very surprisingly all situated in Cairo. Of these, only two were scholars while the vast majority were leading officials or officers. This result is to a large extent driven by the fact that he predominantly used chronicles as a source basis, especially Ibn Taghrībirdī's *Nujūm* and Ibn Iyās' (d. ca. 930/1524) *Badā'i'*.[59] In Martel-Thoumian's study the number of suicide cases is larger at twenty-eight, but the focus on Cairo is again accentuated with only three cases registered beyond the city's walls. The most remarkable point is, however, that again leading officials and officers are at the centre. Scholars are virtually absent and there are no qadis, muftis or imams among those who decided to put an end to their lives.[60] For Cairo the source is not Ibn Taghrībirdī's *Nujūm*, as in F. Rosenthal, but al-Ṣayrafī's (d. 900/1495) *Inbā' al-Ḥaṣr*.[61] However, as late Mamluk chronicles were the main source basis in both cases the results have been comparable with regard to the social profile of the individuals and their regional background.

Yet, it is in the biographical dictionaries that we encounter a wider cross-section of society and learn more detail about the backgrounds of those who decided to end their lives, forms of and reasons leading to suicide, as well as contemporary perceptions and representations of and reactions to such deaths. It is not by chance that this information is almost exclusively found in the biographical dictionaries and not in chronicles, as the latter tended to focus on the highest echelons of the cultural, social and political elites. For instance, the contemporary chronicles did not report the suicide of a minor scholar in seventh/thirteenth-century Damascus who was driven to desperation by slander. Confronted with accusations and aggrieved by loss of money this blind scholar eventually hanged himself in the western minaret of the Umayyad mosque.[62] Taqī al-Dīn 'Īsā's suicide was only mentioned in one biographical dictionary and this person is entirely unknown from any other sources. Another example would be a certain al-'Izz al-Akhlāṭī who hanged himself some decades later in his lodgings in the Damascene al-'Ādilīya madrasah.[63] Again this person is unknown from any other source and a perfect example of how deeply biographical dictionaries can reach into the layers of their contemporary society.

Beyond doubt, chronicles and biographical dictionaries are not watertight

58 Rosenthal, *On Suicide*.

59 Ibn Iyās, *Badā'i'*.

60 B. Martel-Thoumian, *La mort*. Among the 28 cases there is only one definitely referring to a scholar (no. 23), a *muqri'* who hanged himself in a *madrasah*, and another case where the individual is closely linked to the scholarly world (no. 13).

61 Al-Ṣayrafī, *Inbā'*.

62 Abū Shāmah, *Al-Dhayl*, 54–5.

63 Abū Shāmah, *Al-Dhayl*, 190 (year 654/1256).

categories and many historiographical works combine annalistic chronography with lists of those noteworthy individuals who deceased in these years. Yet what is noteworthy for the Mamluk period is the surge in numbers of more or less 'pure' biographical dictionaries with a very specific regional focus. The Cairo-centric large compendia of Ibn Ḥajar (d. 852/1449) and al-Sakhāwī (d. 902/1497) are only the later expressions of a process that had begun earlier.[64] Of special interest for the present discussion are those dictionaries that focus on Syrian towns, such as the above-mentioned *Bughyat al-Ṭalab* by Ibn al-ʿAdīm on Aleppo or *Ta'rīkh al-Islām* by al-Dhahabī on Damascus. While Ibn al-ʿAdīm could easily include more than 8.000 individuals, al-Dhahabī's was able to include ten thousand biographies in his seventy-volume dictionary.[65] Of utmost interest are the final ten volumes covering the seventh *hijrī*-century (1203 – 1300), partly overlapping with the author's own lifetime. Here the Damascus-focus becomes ever more accentuated and increasingly obscure 'scholars' of his hometown make their appearance in the over 6.000 entries dedicated to this century alone. More fascinating still are the marginal biographical dictionaries that made their appearance. Staying with Damascus, this encompasses for instance Abū Shāmah's *Dhayl*, the above-mentioned eccentric cross between biographical dictionary, chronicle and autobiography. Some decades later a contemporary of al-Dhahabī, al-Birzālī (d. 739/1339), wrote a continuation of Abū Shāmah's *Dhayl*, in which he adopted the original work's mixture of some chronography and large chunks of prosopography for the following decades into the early eighth/fourteenth century. For the fifty-five years that he covered he included an impressive number of over 4,300 scholars in his biographical section.[66] The main point regarding al-Birzālī's work is again the very sharp regional focus that allowed the author to include numerous individuals on the margins of the scholarly community. Such scholars not only fell through the net of the pure chronicles, but also through those of the transregional biographical dictionaries, while they played here, in these biographical 'microhistories', a salient role. It is this richness of the material that makes such dictionaries crucial repositories for researching themes and approaches that have arisen in the framework of cultural history.

64 Ibn Ḥajar, *Al-Durar*; Al-Sakhāwī, *Al-Ḍaw'*.

65 Morray, *Ayyubid*. The number for Ibn al-ʿAdīm is estimated as only one quarter of his work has survived.

66 Al-Birzālī, *Al-Muqtafī*. On this work cf. Rouabah, *Une edition*.

Biographical Dictionaries and the Archival Turn

While narrative historiography in its prosopographical form will thus play a crucial role as a repository of information serving the interest of both the social and the cultural historian, their main role in advancing Mamluk Studies lies elsewhere. As M. Chamberlain has argued in his study of early Mamluk Damascus the relative scarcity of documentary material and the extremely rich tradition of narrative historiography should not be read primarily in terms of deficiencies and absences. Rather the task is to read this material in its own right taking into account the social logic for the survival or loss of specific genres of documents and narrative texts.[67] Certainly, historians of the Mamluk era lack the plethora of documentary material available for Latin European medieval societies, such as charters, deeds, land grants and legal proceedings. Yet it is in the biographical dictionaries that authors recorded, presented and narrated what they considered to be worthy of remembrance. There was an underlying social logic to producing and more importantly preserving these works. These societies were characterised by the limited role of formalised and inheritable ascriptions of status, while they were primarily structured by informal commitments between individuals. In consequence, individuals, families and social groups in these societies displayed a relatively weak tendency to preserve documents such as deeds and charters. It was rather in the biographical dictionaries that the civilian elites remembered their – often very recent – past with the intention of securing their future. This argument on the social utility of the genre focuses on the social function of biographical dictionaries, which is comparable with the role of documentary sources in other traditions. As much as deeds and charters were crucial in securing the transmission of elite status over generations in Latin Europe and China, biographical dictionaries bore testimony to those informal relationships between individuals that secured the stability of Middle Eastern societies.

Taking this argument one step further, I propose the consideration that biographical dictionaries also serve as the archives of the societies we are concerned with. Within these archives, members of the cultural elites in Syria and Egypt recorded what they perceived to be the structural element of their social world, i.e. the multitude of contacts, relationships and bonds between individuals that shaped and constituted their societies. If we consider biographical dictionaries to be a form of archive this allows us to take into account the 'archival turn', one of the developments within the broader field of cultural

67 Chamberlain, *Knowledge*, 1–26. For a criticism of Chamberlain's position cf. Marina, *A Petition*.

history over the last two decades.[68] This recent scholarly interest in archives considers them not only as neutral sites for research and repositories of more or less reliable factual knowledge, but also as fascinating objects of study in themselves. Basically this means a move from archive-as-source to archive-as-subject, i. e. the possibility of seeing the archive as a historical agent.[69]

This reconsideration of the archive is part of a larger movement within the humanities, especially cultural theory, and goes back, amongst others, to Michel Foucault's early writings. His *Order of Things* and *Archaeology of Knowledge* have been particularly influential. These works are still of sufficient specificity to be of some value for practicing historians and they have been central in the development of Cultural Anthropology in its literary bent. Here he repositioned the archive as a space of enunciation because '[t]he archive is first the law of what can be said, the system that governs the appearance of statements as unique events. […] It is *the system of [the statement-event's] enunciability.*'[70] In historical studies, this has been taken up in particular in post-colonial studies where it has proved to be particularly enriching for studying the production of colonial knowledge of or rather over the indigenous Other. At the same time it has also proved fruitful for medieval Europe. For instance, in her work on late medieval law and gender in England, Sh. McSheffrey has focused upon questions such as how the documents came to be archived in the first place, in whose interest they were preserved and how the documenting of particular events and processes – and not others – shapes how we conceptualise the past.[71]

Here again there is an element of Cultural History, but this time, instead of inviting us to study topics such as suicide on the basis of a different source material, it calls for a more substantial recalibration of our approach towards historiography. It asks for the interpretive practices that produced inter-subjective cultural patterns; it asks, in other words, how societies were underlain by systems of meanings that were as real and far-reaching as social structures. Applying such a perspective to the wealth of Mamluk biographical dictionaries that we have at our disposal thus allows us to ask questions that go well beyond the themes studied in social history along the lines of 'ulamology', but also beyond the 'archive-as-source' mode of cultural history. Such studies in the 'archive-as-subject' mode would allow us to understand the large number of these massive regional compendia stretching from Ibn al-ʿAdīm to al-Sakhāwī as agents in the historical process. They are thus works that were often composed because they were meant to do something, to be, at least potentially, perform-

68 The term 'archival turn' was to a large extent coined by Ann Stoler, an anthropologist-historian working on South and South-East Asia.

69 Stoler, *Archival Grain*, 44–46. Cf. also Stoler, *Colonial Archives*; Eichhorn, *Archival Genres.*

70 Foucault, *Archaeology*, 145/6.

71 McSheffrey, *Detective.*

ative. In this sense these texts coordinated the writers' and readers' meaning-making processes and oriented them towards 'shared mentally constructed spaces' where meaning was performed through the act of writing and re-performed through the act of reading.[72]

Such a recalibration translates into concrete research on various levels. Firstly, if we start to see Mamluk biographical dictionaries as agents, questions pertaining to their emergence and their genesis come to the forefront. Just like archives in the classical sense, they were structured by implicit rules of what was to be preserved, what was to be discarded and how it was to be collected. F. Bauden's work on al-Maqrizi's autograph has been ground-breaking to gain insights into the actual making of historical chronography.[73] Similar work for biographical dictionaries would greatly enhance our understanding of these works' structure, their silences and the authors' strategies of inclusion and exclusion. Autographs are not always available to give us insights into the different stages of drafting works. Yet an internal comparison of textual strategies for diachronic works such as al-Dhahabī's *Ta'rīkh* in the early periods and in the periods contemporary to the author will yield insights into authorial strategies that varied for the different periods. Especially in those instances where we have a multitude of biographical dictionaries for one period and one locality, the consideration of these texts as historical agents allows us to ask new questions about the different profiles, outlooks and strategies of these quasi-archival repositories. For instance, how did authors and readers envision social bonds of commitments, expound upon their problematic nature and focus or gloss over moments of conflict and rupture?

The enormous wealth of the Cairene prosopographical tradition in particular allows such questions to be studied in detail. Yet we also have sufficient material for other cases, such as al-Dhahabī's and Abū Shāma's dictionaries for seventh/thirteenth-century Damascus. One case-study to render the archival turn more concrete is the Ayyubid-Mamluk transition period during the early 650s/mid-1250s. Both authors covered this period in detail in their biographical works.[74] Abū Shāma was an eye-witness and was in his fifties. Al-Dhahabī reached maturity some four decades later, but it is evident that he had a very close interest in these years. Reading through these works we see that these authors constructed their archives in radically different modes. Each piece of information is embedded in a wider strategy to ascribe diverging meanings to the period's events.

In his narrative of these years, Abū Shāmah prioritised obituaries of those

72 Bazerman, *Textual Performance*, here 381.
73 Bauden, *Maqriziana I, Section 1*; idem, *Maqriziana I, Section 2*; idem, *Maqriziana II*.
74 The years covered are those between 651 and 655: Abū Shāmah, *Al-Dhayl*, 178–98; al-Dhahabī, *Ta'rīkh*, vol. 651–60, pp. 87–223.

scholars who withdrew from society and were reclusive. His information on individuals is thus largely limited to their piety, learnedness and their charitable deeds. This flow of information implies a reclusive ideal world of scholars who were hardly affected by the dramatic changes taking place around them in this period. This is carefully interwoven with information on the author himself and on his family, who appear over and again in a strikingly isolated and reclusive fashion. Tellingly, a poem for his wife is one of the two longest continuous sections in these years.[75] Compared with al-Dhahabī's work, his dictionary has considerably fewer biographies, indicating that Abū Shāmah carefully chose whom to include and whom to exclude, i. e. those who did not fit into this tranquil world of scholarly endeavours unaffected by the changes in the wider world.

However, at some points this idyllic world was disturbed and this is when Abū Shāmah turns to obituaries of the military and political elites. It is not that he was uninterested in them or that there were fewer of them compared with al-Dhahabī's work.[76] Yet these individuals appear as foreign elements, brutally interrupting the continuous flow of the text and thus of events. They are not part of the social and cultural map that Abū Shāma tried to build up, but rather they strive to undermine it, to usurp control and to monopolise resources. The leading Mamluk Baḥrī-officer and one of the main contenders for the Sultanate in the Ayyubid-Mamluk transition period, Fāris al-Dīn Aqṭay (d. 652/1254), breaks onto the scene as the one who 'suppressed the inhabitants' of Egypt and 'ruined' them.[77] Other biographies on members of the political and military elites are basically tales of court-intrigue, murder and treachery that are less skilfully narrated than in Hamlet, but not dramatically different in their bleak outlook.[78]

Al-Dhahabī included in his text all the individuals featuring in Abū Shāmah's text, but the world that emerges from these years is one that is radically different and essentially more complex. Members of the military and political elites are still usurping power and eating into the wealth of the civilian elites. Yet they are less foreign than in Abū Shāmah's archive, as their actions and dealings are set into the wider context of the emerging Mamluk society – even a Fāris al-Dīn Aqṭay can be praised as 'noble and generous'.[79] At the same time, the scholars he included cover much wider ground and, most importantly for the present ar-

75 Abū Shāmah, *Al-Dhayl*, 196 – 8.
76 Al-Dhahabī includes more than six times the number of biographies of Abū Shāma (235 and 35 respectively), but only twice as many biographies of members of the political and military elites (14 and 6 respectively).
77 Abū Shāmah, *Al-Dhayl*, 188.
78 Abū Shāmah, *Al-Dhayl*, 196.
79 Al-Dhahabī, *Ta'rīkh*, vol. 651 – 60, p. 118.

gument, are less reclusive than in Abū Shāmah's text. Rather they interact with wider society in roles such as trader, merchant, administrator, physician and notary witness. In other words the somewhat reclusive world of Abū Shāmah is here turned into one where the various groups of society interacted more closely. Al-Dhahabī envisaged the transition period to be as dramatic as Abū Shāma did, but he considered it to be less of an outside intrusion.

The example of the Ayyubid-Mamluk transition period shows how the same pieces of information in these two archives of the Damascene elites could gain entirely different meanings. These authors read the same obituaries in widely diverging ways and consequently envisaged the political and social processes in different modes. In some ways this completes the argument in my *Medieval Arabic Historiography* where I discussed the narrative modes in the two chronicles by Ibn Wāṣil and Abū Shāmah. The decisive difference in these outwardly similar chronicles was that Ibn Wāṣil saw just rule as a continuous reality in his recent past, whereas Abū Shāma was a staunch critic of his own times and situated a romanticised version of just rule in the periods of Nūr al-Dīn (d. 569/1174) and Ṣalāḥ al-Dīn (d. 589/1193) in the late sixth/twelfth century.[80] The vision put forward by these two authors concerned only the person of the ruler itself and was basically a contribution to medieval political thought. In their biographical dictionaries, by contrast, al-Dhahabī and Abū Shāmah deal with a completely different level of society. Rather than being theoretical reflections on where ideal rule was situated and how it was to be conceptualised, the biographical dictionaries focus on wider urban society. For the period discussed here, the Ayyubid-Mamluk transition period, these texts thus allow us to gain an understanding of how political processes were envisaged to unfold in society at large.

This is not to argue that these biographical dictionaries, or Mamluk historiography in general, were free-flowing texts that do not allow access to historical processes and events beyond their discursive strategies or archival modes. Rather, it is the best of cultural history that has achieved the bridging of the turn to meaning on the one hand with a dedicated interest in social processes on the other. There is no denial that to bridge this gap is difficult as social and cultural histories are to some degree incompatible. Whereas social history tends to assume that structure is prior to social action, cultural history sees the social world as constituted by the interpretive actions of the actors who made it up. In consequence, while social historians analyse hard data for revealing objective structure, their culturalist-inclined colleagues tend to focus on the inevitably interpretive practices that produced cultural patterns. However, the archival turn as outlined here and as applied to biographical dictionaries does not

80 Hirschler, *Arabic Historiography.*

forestall the possibility of continuing to use these texts for questions pertinent to social history, or political history for that matter. The main point is rather that the Cultural Turn allows us to consider Mamluk historiography, be it in its prosopographical or its chronistic form, as a richer genre of texts than either social or political history considered them to be. In other words, by moving beyond source-critical questions and seeing the texts as more than repositories of facts, narrative historiography can return to play a central role in driving the field of Mamluk Studies.

Literature

Primary Sources

Abū al-Fidā', Isma'īl, *Mukhtaṣar Ta'rīkh al-Bashar*, Istanbul: al-Ṭabā'ah al-'Āmirah al-Shāhānīyah 1286/1869 – 70.

Abū al-Fidā', Isma'īl, *Mukhtaṣar Ta'rīkh al-Bashar*, 2 vols., Cairo: al-Maṭba'a al-Ḥusaynīya al-Miṣrīya 1907.

Abū Shāmah, 'Abd al-Raḥmān, *al-Dhayl 'alā al-Rawḍatayn* (edited under the title: *Tarājim rijāl al-qarnayn al-sādis wa-al-sābi'*), ed. M. al-Kawtharī, Beirut: Dār al-Jīl 1974. (reprint Cairo 1947)

Abū Shāmah, 'Abd al-Raḥmān, *Kitāb al-Rawḍatayn fī Akhbār al-Dawlatayn al-Nūrīyah wa-l-Ṣalāḥīyah*, ed. I. al-Zaybaq, 5 vols., Beirut: Mu'assasat al-Risālah 1997.

Al-'Aẓīmī, Muḥammad, *Ta'rīkh Ḥalab*, ed. Ibrāhīm Za'rūr, Damascus 1984.

Al-Birzālī, al-Qāsim, *Al-Muqtafī 'alā Kitāb al-Rawḍatayn li-Abī Shāmah*, ed. 'U. 'A. Tadmūrī, 4 vols., Beirut/Ṣaydā: Al-Maktaba al-'Aṣrīya 2006.

Al-Dhahabī, Muḥammad, *Ta'rīkh al-Islām wa-Wafayāt al-Mashāhīr wa-l-A'lām*, ed. 'U. 'A. Tadmūrī, 52 vols., Beirut: Dār al-Kitāb al-'Arabī 1987 – 2000.

Al-Jazarī, Muḥammad, *Ḥawādith al-Zamān*, MS Paris, BN arabe 6739 (*Jawāhir al-sulūk fī al-khulafā' wa-al-mulūk*)

Al-Kutubī, Muḥammad, *Fawāt al-Wafayāt wa-l-Dhayl 'alayhā*, ed. I. 'Abbās, 5 vols., Beirut 1973 – 4.

Al-Kutubī, Muḥammad, *'Uyūn al-Tawārīkh*, ed. F. al-Sāmir and 'A. Dā'ūd, vol. 20, Baghdad: Wizārat al-i'lām 1980.

Al-Nābulusī, Abū 'Uthmān, *Ta'rīkh al-Fayyūm wa-Bilādihī*, ed. B. Moritz, Cairo: Al-Maṭba'ah al-Ahlīyah 1899.

Al-Nuwayrī, Aḥmad, *Nihāyat al-Arab fī Funūn al-adab*, 33 vols., Cairo: Wizārat al-Thaqāfah 1923 – 2002.

Al-Ṣafadī, Khalīl, *al-Wāfī bi-l-Wafayāt*, eds. H. Ritter et al., 30 vols., Istanbul 1931 – 97.

Al-Sakhāwī, Muḥammad, *al-Ḍaw' al-Lāmi' fī Ahl al-Qarn al-Tāsi'*, ed. Ḥ. al-Qudsī, 12 vols., Cairo: Maktabat al-qudsī 1934 – 6.

Al-Ṣayrafī, 'Alī, *Inbā' al-Ḥaṣr bi-Abnā' al-'Aṣr*, ed. Ḥ. Ḥabashī, Cairo: Dār al-Fikr al-'Arabī 1970.

Al-Yūnīnī, Mūsā, *Dhayl Mir'āt al-Zamān*, 4 vols., Hayderabad: Maṭba'at Majlis Dā'irat al-Ma'ārif al-'Uthmānīyah 1954–61.
Ibn al-'Adīm, 'Umar, *Zubdat al-Ḥalab min Ta'rīkh Ḥalab*, ed. Sāmī Dahhān, 3 vols., Damascus: al-Ma'had al-Faransī 1951–68.
Ibn al-'Adīm, 'Umar, *Bughyat al-Ṭalab fī ta'rīkh Ḥalab*, ed. Sāmī Zakkār, 12 vols., Beirut: Dār al-Fikr 1988.
Ibn al-Jawzī, Sibṭ, *Mir'āt al-zamān fī ta'rīkh al-a'yān*, vol. 8, Hayderabad: Maṭba'at Majlis Dā'irat al-Ma'ārif al-'Uthmānīyah 1951–2.
Ibn 'Asākir, 'Alī, *Ta'rīkh Madīnat Dimashq*, ed. 'U. al-'Amrawī, 80 vols., Beirut: Dār al-Fikr 1995–8.
Ibn Ḥajar, Aḥmad, *Al-Durar al-Kāminah fī A'yān al-Mi'ah al-Thāminah*, ed. M. Jād al-Ḥaqq, 5 vols., Cairo: Dār al-Kutub al-Ḥadītha 1966–7.
Ibn Iyās, Muḥammad, *Badā'i' al-Zuhūr fī Waqa'i' al-Duhūr*, ed. M. Muṣṭafā, Cairo/Wiesbaden: Steiner, vol. 1–2 1972–5, vol. 3–5 1960–63².
Ibn Kathīr, Ismā'īl, *Al-Bidāyah wa-l-Nihāyah fī al-Ta'rīkh*, eds. 'Alī N. Aṭawī et al., 14 vols., Beirut 1985.
Ibn Shaddād, Yūsuf, *Al-Nawādir al-Sulṭānīya wa-l-Maḥāsin al-Yūsufīya*, ed. J. al-Shayyāl, Cairo: Dār al-Miṣrīyah li-l-Ta'līf wa-l-Tarjamah 1964.
Ibn Taghrībirdī, Yūsuf, *Al-Manhal al-Ṣāfī wa-l-Mustawfī ba'da al-Wāfī*, eds. M. Amīn and S. 'Āshūr et al., 13 vols., Cairo: Dār al-Kutub wa-l-Wathā'iq al-Qawmīyah 1984–2009.
Ibn Taghrībirdī, Yūsuf, *Al-Nujūm al-Zāhirah fī Mulūk Miṣr wa-l-Qāhirah*, ed. F. Shaltūt et al., 16 vols., Cairo: Maṭba'at Dār al-Kutub al-Miṣrīyah 1929–72.
Ibn Taghrībirdī, Yūsuf, *Ḥawādith al-Duhūr fī Maḍā al-Ayyām wa-l-Shuhūr*, ed. W. Popper, 4 vols., Berkeley: University of California Press 1930–42.
Ibn Ṭawq, Aḥmad, *Al-Ta'līq: Yawmīyāt Shihāb al-Dīn Aḥmad b. Ṭawq [Journal d'Aḥmad Ibn Ṭawq], 834–915/1430–1509*, ed. J. al-Muhājir, 4 vols., Damascus: al-Ma'had al-Faransī li-l-Dirāsāt al-'Arabīyah 2000–02.
Ibn Ṭūlūn, Muḥammad, *Mufākahat al-Khillān fī Ḥawādith al-Zamān*, ed. M. Mostafa, 2 vols., Cairo: al-Mu'assasat al-Miṣrīyah al-'Āmmah 1962–4.
Ibn Wāṣil, Muḥammad, Kitāb al-Ta'rīkh al-Ṣāliḥī: Sīrat al-Nabī wa-l-Anbīyā' wa-l-Khulafā' wa-l-Mulūk wa-Ghayruhum, ed. 'Umar 'Abd al-Salām Tadmurī, Ṣaydā/Beirut: al-Maktabah al-'Asrīyah 2010.
'Imād al-Dīn, Muḥammad, *Al-Barq al-Shāmī*, ed. Muṣṭafā al-Ḥayyārī/Fātiḥ Ḥusayn, vol. 5, Amman: Mu'assasat 'Abd al-Ḥamīd Shūmān 1987.
'Imād al-Dīn, Muḥammad, *Al-Fatḥ al-Qussī fī al-Fatḥ al-Qudsī*, ed. C. de Landberg, Leiden: Brill 1888.

Secondary Sources

Al-'Azmeh, 'Azīz, *Ibn Khaldūn: An Essay in Reinterpretation*, Budapest: Central European University Press 2003².
'Abd al-Laṭīf, Ibrāhīm 'Alī, "Silsilat al-Wathā'iq al-Ta'rīkhīyah al-Qawmīyah. Majmū'at al-Wathā'iq al-Mamlūkīyah I: Wathīqat al-Amīr Ākhūr Kabīr Qarāqujā al-Ḥasanī," *Majallat Kullīyat al-Ādāb/Bulletin of the Faculty of Arts* 18 (1956), pp. 183–251.

Afsaruddin, Asma, "Islamic Biographical Dictionaries: 11th to 15th Century," in: *Encyclopedia of Women & Islamic Cultures*, vol. 1, Methodologies, Paradigms and Sources, ed. S. Joseph, Leiden: Brill 2003, pp. 32–36.

Al-Qadi, Wadad, "Biographical Dictionaries as the Scholars' Alternative History of the Muslim Community," in: *Organizing Knowledge: Encyclopaedic Activities in the Pre-Eighteenth Century Islamic World*, ed. G. Endreß, Leiden: Brill 2006, pp. 23–75.

Amīn, Muḥammad, *Al-Awqāf wa-al-Ḥayāt al-Ijtimāʿīyah fī Miṣr, 648–923/1250–1517*, Cairo: Dār al-Nahḍah al-ʿArabīyah 1980.

Auchterlonie, Paul, "Historians and the Arabic Biographical Dictionary: Some New Approaches," in: *Islamic Reflections, Arabic Musings: Studies in Honour of Professor Alan Jones*, eds. R.G. Hoyland and P.F. Kennedy, Cambridge 2004: Gibb Memorial Trust, pp. 186–200.

Bauden, Frederic, "Mamluk Era Documentary Studies: The State of the Art," *Mamlūk Studies Review* 9/2 (2005), pp. 15–60.

Bauden, Frederic, "Maqriziana I: Discovery of an Autograph Manuscript of al-Maqrīzī: Towards a Better Understanding of His Working Method, Description: Section 1," *Mamlūk Studies Review* 7/2 (2003), pp. 21–68.

Bauden, Frederic, "Maqriziana I: Discovery of an Autograph Manuscript of al-Maqrizi: Towards a Better Understanding of His Working Method: Description: Section 2," *Mamlūk Studies Review* 10/2 (2006), pp. 81–139.

Bauden, Frederic, "Maqriziana II: Discovery of an Autograph Manuscript of al-Maqrīzī: Towards a Better Understanding of His Working Method, Analysis," *Mamlūk Studies Review* 12/1 (2008), 51–118.

Bauden, Frederic, "Maqriziana IX: Should al-Maqrīzī Be Thrown Out with the Bath Water? The Question of His Plagiarism of al-Awḥadī's Khiṭaṭ and the Documentary Evidence," *Mamlūk Studies Review* 14 (2010), pp. 159–232.

Bauden, Frederic, "Review: Sayyid, A., *Al-Mawāʿiẓ wa-l-Iʿtibār*," *Mamlūk Studies Review* 11 (2007), pp. 169–76.

Bauer, Thomas, "Mamluk Literature: Misunderstandings and New Approaches," *Mamlūk Studies Review* 9/2 (2005), pp. 105–32.

Bauer, Thomas, *Die Kultur der Ambiguität: eine andere Geschichte des Islams*, Berlin: Verlag der Weltreligionen 2011.

Bazerman, Charles, "Textual Performance: Where the Action at a Distance Is," *JAC: A Journal of Composition Theory* 23/2 (2003), pp. 379–96.

Behrens-Abouseif, Doris, *Cairo of the Mamluks: A History of the Architecture and its Culture*, London: I.B. Tauris 2007.

Berkey, Jonathan, "Popular Culture under the Mamluks: A Historiographical Survey," *Mamlūk Study Review* 9 (2005), pp. 133–46.

Berkey, Jonathan, *The Transmission of Knowledge in Medieval Cairo: A Social History of Islamic Education*, Princeton (NJ): Princeton University Press 1992.

Bianquis, Thierry, *Damas et la Syrie sous la domination fāṭimide*, Damascus: Institut Français de Damas 1987–9.

Bloom, Jonathan, "Mamluk Art and Architectural History: A Review Article," *Mamlūk Studies Review* 3 (1999), pp. 31–58.

Bora, Fozia, Mamluk Representations of late Fatimid Egypt: The Survival of Fatimid-Era

Historiography in Ibn al-Furāt's Tarīkh al-Duwal wa-l-Mulūk (History of Dynasties and Kings), unpublished Ph.D. dissertation, University of Oxford 2010.

Bulliet, Richard, *Conversion to Islam in the Medieval Period: An Essay in Quantitative History*, Cambridge (MA): Harvard University Press 1979.

Cheddadi, Abdesselam, *Ibn Khaldûn revisité*, [Casablanca?]: Les Editions Toubkal 1999.

Chamberlain, Michael, *Knowledge and Social Practice in Medieval Damascus, 1190 - 1350*, Cambridge: Cambridge University Press 1994.

Clifford, Winslow, "*Ubi Sumus?* Mamluk History and Social Theory," *Mamlūk Studies Review* 1 (1997), pp. 45 - 62.

Conermann, Stephan and Syrinx von Hees, *Islamwissenschaft als Kulturwissenschaft, 1: Historische Anthropologie - Ansätze und Möglichkeiten*, Schenefeld/Hamburg: EB-Verlag 2007.

Dalil-Essakali, Mohyeddine, *La conception de histoire dans l'oeuvre d' al-Maqrizi (1364 - 1442)*, PhD-thesis, Univ. of Bordeaux 1990.

Donner, Fred, *Narratives of Islamic Origins: The Beginnings of Islamic Historical Writing*, Princeton: Darwin Press 1998.

Eichhorn, Kate, "Archival Genres: Gathering Texts and Reading Spaces", *Invisible Culture. An Electronic Journal for Visual Culture* 12 (2008) (The Archive of the Future / The Future of the Archive), http://www.rochester.edu/in_visible_culture/Issue_12/eichhorn/eichhorn.pdf [accessed 27/10/2011].

Elad, Amikam, "A Bibliography of Works by David Ayalon," in: *Studies in Islamic History and Civilization in Honour of Professor David Ayalon*, ed. M. Sharon, Leiden: Brill/Jerusalem 1986, pp. 13 - 18.

El-Hibri, Tayeb, *Parable and Politics in Early Islamic History: the Rashidun Caliphs*, New York: Columbia University Press 2010.

El-Hibri, Tayeb, *Reinterpreting Islamic Historiography. Harun al-Rashid and the Narrative of the 'Abbasid Caliphate*, Cambridge: Cambridge University Press 1999.

Foucault, Michel, *The Archaeology of Knowledge*, trans. A.M. Sheridan Smith, Abingdon: Routledge, 2002.

Franz, Kurt, *Kompilation in arabischen Chroniken. Die Überlieferung vom Aufstand der Zanǧ zwischen Geschichtlichkeit und Intertextualität vom 9. bis ins 15. Jahrhundert*, Berlin/New York: Walter de Gruyter 2004.

Gagnier, John, *De vita, et rebus gestis Mohammedis*, Oxford: Theatrum Sheldonianum 1723.

Görke, Andreas and Konrad Hirschler, *Manuscript Notes as Documentary Sources*, Beirut/Würzburg: Ergon 2011.

Guo, Li, "History Writing," in: *The New Cambridge History of Islam*, vol. 4, Islamic Cultures and Societies to the End of the Eighteenth Century, ed. R. Irwin, Cambridge: Cambridge University Press 2010, pp. 444 - 57.

Guo, Li, "Mamluk Historiographic Studies: The State of the Art," *Mamlūk Studies Review* 1 (1997), pp. 15 - 43.

Guo, Li, *Early Mamluk Syrian Historiography. Al-Yunini's Dhayl mir'at al-zaman*, Leiden: Brill 1998.

Haarmann, Ulrich, "Auflösung und Bewahrung der klassischen Formen arabischer Geschichtsschreibung in der Zeit der Mameluken," *Zeitschrift der Deutschen Morgenländischen Gesellschaft* 121/1 (1971), pp. 46 - 60.

Haarmann, Ulrich, "Mamluk Endowment Deeds as a Source for the History of Education in Late Medieval Egypt," *Al-Abḥāth* 28 (1980), pp. 31 – 47.

Haarmann, Ulrich, *Quellenstudien zur frühen Mamlukenzeit*, Freiburg i. Br.: Schwarz 1969.

Heidemann, Stefan, *Die Renaissance der Städte in Nordsyrien und Nordmesopotamien*, Leiden: Brill 2002.

Hirschler, Konrad, "Islam: The Arabic and Persian Traditions, Eleventh-Fifteenth Centuries," in: *Oxford History of Historical Writing*, vol. 2, 400 – 1400, ed. S. Foot and C. Robinson, Oxford: Oxford University Press 2012, pp. 267 – 86.

Hirschler, Konrad, *Medieval Arabic Historiography: Authors as Actors*, London: Routledge 2006.

Humphreys, R.S. et al. (1998), "Ta'rīkh", in: *EI²*, 10:271 – 302.

Irwin, Robert, "Mamluk History and Historiography," in: *Arabic Literature in the Post-Classical Period*, ed. Roger Allen and Donald S. Richards, Cambridge: Cambridge University Press (2006), pp. 159 – 70.

Jawād, Muṣṭafā, "Al-Muntaḥirūn fī al-Jāhilīyah wa-l-Islām," *Al-Hilāl* 42 (1934), pp. 475 – 9.

Khalidi, Tarif, *Arabic Historical Thought in the Classical Period*, Cambridge: Cambridge University Press 1994.

Lajnat al-Ta'rīkh bi-l-Majlis al-Aʿlā li-Riʿāyat al-Funūn wa-l-Ādāb wa-l-ʿUlūm al-Ijtimāʿīyah, *Al-Mu'arrikh Ibn Taghrībirdī, Jamāl al-Dīn Abū al-Maḥāsin Yūsuf, 813 – 874 H.: Majmūʿat abḥāth*, Cairo: al-Hay'ah al-Miṣrīyah al-ʿĀmmah li-l-Kitāb 1974.

Leder, Stefan, Yāsīn M. al-Sawwās, and Ma'mūn al-Ṣāgharjī, *Muʿjam al-Samāʿāt al-Dimashqīyah. Les certificats d'audition à Damas. 550 – 750/1155 – 1349*, Damascus: IFD 1996.

Leder, Stefan, Yāsīn M. al-Sawwās, and Ma'mūn al-Ṣāgharjī, *Muʿjam al-Samāʿāt al-Dimashqīya – Ṣūwar al-Makhṭūṭāt. Recueil de documents fac-similés des certificats d'audition à Damas. 550 – 750/1155 – 1349*, Damascus: IFD/Deutsches Archäologisches Institut 2000.

Lev, Yacov, *State and Society in Fatimid Egypt*, Leiden: Brill 1990.

Little, Donald, "Documents as a Source for Mamluk History," *Mamlūk Studies Review* 1 (1997), pp. 1 – 14.

Little, Donald, "Historiography of the Ayyubid and the Mamluk Epochs," in: *The Cambridge History of Egypt*, vol. 1, Islamic Egypt 640 – 1517, ed. C.F. Petry, Cambridge: Cambridge University Press 1998, pp. 412 – 44.

Little, Donald, *An Introduction to Mamlūk Historiography: An Analysis of Arabic Annalistic and Biographical Sources for the Reign of al-Malik an-Nāṣir Muḥammad ibn Qalā'ūn*, Wiesbaden: Steiner 1970.

Lutfi, Huda, "Al-Sakhāwī's Kitāb al-Nisā' as a Source for the social and economic History of Muslim Women During the Fifteenth Century A.D.," *Muslim World* 71 (1981), pp. 104 – 24.

Marina, Rustow, "A Petition to a Woman at the Fatimid Court (413 – 414 a.h./1022 – 23 c.e.)," *Bulletin of the School of Oriental and African Studies* 73 (2010), pp. 1 – 27.

Martel-Thoumian, Bernadette, "La mort volontaire: le traitement du suicide et du suicidé dans les chroniques mameloukes tardives," *Annales Islamologiques/Ḥawliyāt Islāmiyah* 38/2 (2004), pp. 405 – 35.

Massoud, Sami, *The Chronicles and Annalistic Sources of the early Mamluk Circassian Period*, Leiden/Boston: Brill 2007.

McSheffrey, Shannon, "Detective Fiction in the Archives: Court Records and the Uses of Law in Late Medieval England," *History Workshop Journal* 65 (2008), pp. 65 – 78.

Meinecke, Michael, *Die mamlukische Architektur in Ägypten und Syrien (648/1250 bis 923/1517)*, Glückstadt: Augustin 1992.

Milwright, Marcus, *The Fortress of the Raven: Karak in the Middle Islamic Period (1100 – 1650)*, Leiden: Brill 1998.

Morray, David, *An Ayyubid Notable and His World. Ibn al-ʿAdim and Aleppo as Portrayed in His Biographical Dictionary of People Associated with the City*, Leiden: Brill 1994.

Najīdī, Hamūd, *Al-Niẓām al-Naqdī al-Mamlūkī*, Alexandria: Mu'assasat al-Thaqāfah 1993.

Nawas, John, "Biography and Biographical Works," in: *Medieval Islamic Civilization: An Encyclopaedia*, ed. J. M. Meri, New York: Routledge, vol. I, pp. 110 – 12.

Perho, Irmeli, "Al-Maqrīzī and Ibn Taghrī Birdī as Historians of Contemporary Events," in: *The Historiography of Islamic Egypt (c.950 – 1800)*, ed. H. Kennedy, Brill: Leiden 2001, pp. 107 – 20.

Petry, Carl F., "A Geniza for Mamluk Studies? Charitable Trust (Waqf) Documents as a Source for Economic and Social History," *Mamlūk Studies Review* 2 (1998), pp. 51 – 60.

Petry, Carl F., *The Civilian Elite of Cairo in the Later Middle Ages*, Princeton (NJ): Princeton University Press 1981.

Radtke, Bernd, *Weltgeschichte und Weltbeschreibung im mittelalterlichen Islam*, Stuttgart: Steiner 1992.

Rahim, Mohamed, *Die Chronik des ibn Wāṣil: Ǧamāl ad-Dīn Muḥammad ibn Wāṣil Mufarriǧ al-Kurūb fī Aḫbār Banī Ayyūb*, Wiesbaden: Harrassowitz 2010.

Rapoport, Yossef, "Women and Gender in Mamluk Society–An Overview," *Mamlūk Studies Review* 11 (2007), pp. 1 – 45.

Robinson, Chase, *Islamic Historiography*, Cambridge: Cambridge University Press 2003.

Roded, Ruth, *Women in Islamic Biographical Collections. From Ibn Sa'd to Who's Who.* Boulder, London: Lynne Rienner 1994.

Rosenthal, Franz, "On Suicide in Islam," *Journal of the American Oriental Society* 66/3 (1946), pp. 239 – 59.

Rosenthal, Franz, *A History of Muslim Historiography*, Leiden: Brill 1968[2].

Rouabah, Muriel, "Une édition inattendue: le Ta'rīh d'al-Birzālī," *Arabica* 57/2 – 3 (2010), pp. 309 – 18.

Sayyid, Fu'ād, *Le manuscrit autographe d'al-Mawaʿiẓ wa-al-iʿtibār*, London: Mu'assasat al-Furqān li-l-Turāth al-Islāmī 1995.

Schulten, Albert, *Vita Et Res Gestae Sultani, Almalichi Alnasiri, Saladini … Nec non Excerpta ex Historia Universali Abulfedæ*, Lugduni Batavorum: Luchtmans, van der Mijn 1732.

Shoshan, Boaz, *The Poetics of Islamic Historiography: Deconstructing Ṭabarī's History*, Leiden: Brill 2005.

Sievert, Henning, *Der Herrscherwechsel im Mamlukensultanat: historische und historiographische Untersuchungen zu Abū Ḥāmid al-Qudsī und Ibn Taġrībirdī*, Berlin: Klaus Schwarz 2003.

Stoler, Ann, "Colonial Archives and the Arts of Governance. On the Content in the Form," in: *Refiguring the Archive*, eds. C. Hamilton et al., London: Kluwer Academic Publishers 2002, pp. 83 – 100.

Stoler, Ann, *Along the Archival Grain: Epistemic Anxieties and Colonial Common Sense*, Princeton (NJ): Princeton University Press 2009.

Schultz, Warren, Mamluk Money from Baybars to Barquq: A Study Based on the Literary Sources and the Numismatic Evidence, unpublished PhD dissertation, University of Chicago 1995.

Walker, Bethany, "From Ceramics to Social Theory: Reflections on Mamluk Archaeology Today," *Mamlūk Studies Review* 14 (2010), pp. 109 – 57.

Walker, Bethany, *Jordan in the Late Middle Ages: Transformation of the Mamluk Frontier*, Chicago: Middle East Documentation Center 2012.

Whitcomb, Donald, "Mamluk Archaeological Studies: A Review," *Mamlūk Studies Review* 1 (1997), pp. 97 – 106.

Digital resources

Maktabat al-ta'rīkh wa-al-ḥaḍāra al-islāmīya (al-Turāth, Amman, various editions, http://www.turath.com/)

Al-Maktaba al-Shāmila (freeware, http://shamela.ws/)

Th. Emil Homerin

Sufism in Mamluk Studies: A Review of Scholarship in the Field[1]

The late Dr. Annemarie Schimmel composed a number of seminal works on Islamic mysticism, yet unbeknownst to many was her pioneering work on the Mamluks. In 1943, Schimmel published "Kalif und Ḳādī im spätmittelarterlichen Ägypten"[2] and later, in 1965, a broad survey entitled "Some Glimpses of the Religious Life in Egypt during the Later Mamluk Period."[3] There, Dr. Schimmel noted that the Mamluks saw themselves as protectors of the faith while, at the same time, the Mamluk sultans manipulated the largely ceremonial caliphs for their own political ends. Dr. Schimmel also touched upon important religious events and rituals, including the celebration of the Prophet's birthday and lesser *mawlids* of various saints. This then led to her brief account of Sufism in the Mamluk period, in which she mentioned several institutions, particularly the *khānqāh* and the *zāwiyah*, and the more important Sufi orders. Dr. Schimmel added that Sufi doctrines and practice could be controversial at times, leading to protracted disputes, as was the case with debates on the teachings of Ibn al-ʿArabī (d. 637/1240) and Ibn al-Fāriḍ (d. 632/1235).

Prior to Dr. Schimmel's survey, very little had been written specifically on Sufism in Mamluk domains. A few earlier articles on saints and Sufism referenced the Mamluk period,[4] and there were occasional studies devoted to particular Sufis, such al-Shaʿrānī (897–936/1423–1519).[5] A few essays and monographs on Sufi masters living in Mamluk times appeared in the 1960s and 1970s, especially on Ibn ʿAṭā' Allāh (d. 709/1309),[6] but it was the early and insightful

1 Portions of this essay were drawn from my earlier article Homerin, *Study of Islam.*
2 Schimmel, *Kalif und Ḳādī.*
3 Schimmel, *Glimpses.* For a later German version see Schimmel, *Sufismus.* Also see the observations on Sufism in the Mamluk age published around the same time in ʿĀshūr, *Al-Mujtamaʿ.*
4 See Goldziher, *Cult of Saints*; Massignon, *Documents*; Goitein, *Jewish Addict*; and Ḥusayn, *Bayna al-Tashayyuʿ.*
5 Surūr, *al-Taṣawwuf al-islāmī.*
6 Al-Ghunaymī, *Ibn ʿAṭā' Allāh*; Nwyia, *Ibn ʿAtā' Allāh (m. 709/1309)*; Danner, *Spiritual aphormism*, and Danner, *Book of wisdom.* Also see Mackeen, *Rise of the Shādhilī.*

study by Dr. Schimmel that assessed the terrain and mapped the way for later research. In fact, several of her opinions remained standard in Mamluk studies until quite recently, including her characterization of the religious life of the Mamluk military elite:

> The impression that we get from the later sources is that neither the Mamluk Sultans themselves nor the *amirs* who rose from among them had any interest in spiritual things. Only a comparatively small number of them had sufficient knowledge of literary, or at least grammatically correct, Arabic.[7]

Nevertheless, in her article Dr. Schimmel went on to recount the pious behavior of individual Mamluks and their extensive financial support for men of religion, including scholars, Sufis, and saints.[8] Indeed subsequent research by Louis Pouzet and P.M. Holt revealed that, since the beginning of the Mamluk dynasty, sultans and amirs were often tied to Sufis and their orders, as we see in the case of the early Mamluk sultan Baybars (r. 658–76/1260–77) and his Sufi contemporary Khaḍir b. Abī Bakr al-Mihrānī, (c. 623–76/1226–1277). In separate articles, Pouzet and Holt described and analyzed in some detail the entwined relations between the two figures, which began in 661/1263, when Khaḍir foretold Baybars' future victories.[9] Thereafter, Baybars made Khaḍir's his personal spiritual advisor; the sultan built a *zāwiyah* for him in Cairo near the mosque of al-Ḥusayn and, later, endowed Khaḍir with other *zāwiyahs* in Jerusalem, Damascus, Baᶜalbakk, Ḥamāh, and Ḥimṣ to house him and his many followers during their travels. Some of Baybars' senior amirs and other officials grew uneasy with Khaḍir's influence over the sultan, and the contemporary chronicler, ʿIzz al-Dīn b. Shaddād (d. 684/1285) remarked: "[Baybars] gave him a free hand in his kingdom inasmuch as he had jurisdiction, and no one had jurisdiction over him."[10]

According to accounts, Khaḍir used his position to persecute Jews and Christians throughout the empire. He demolished a church near Jerusalem and took part in the murder of a priest there. Khaḍir and his men also ransacked a synagogue in Damascus, burned the Torah scrolls, and installed *miḥrāb*s, while in Alexandria, he converted the Greek Orthodox church believed to house the head of John the Baptist into a *madrasah.* In the end, Khaḍir's excesses and rumored sexual improprieties led senior Mamluk amirs to bring charges against him, and following an investigation, Baybars imprisoned Khaḍir for the rest of

7 Schimmel, *Glimpses*, 356.
8 Ibid., 356–65, 376–79, 381.
9 Pouzet, *Ḫaḍir Ibn Abi Bakr al-Mihrānī*; and Holt, *Early Source*; also see Ashtor, *Scheich Ḫiḍr*; Thorau, *Lion*, 225–29, and Drory, *Meʿalilot.*
10 Ibn Shaddād, *Taʾrīkh*, 274; Holt, *Early Source*, 34. Also see Ibn Shaddād, *Taʾrīkh*, 58–60, 272–74, and Ibn Dawādārī, *Kanz*, 8:220–24.

his life, but not before Khaḍir's last prediction that Baybars would die within days of his shaykh's death, which he did.

In addition to functioning as spiritual advisors, Sufis of the Mamluk period often served as saintly figures as Dr. Schimmel also noted in her survey article. Venerated by elites and commoners alike, saints and their cults became popular topics of Mamluk studies in the 1970s and early 80s, as we see in the work Ernest Bannerth,[11] Jean-Claude Garcin,[12] Su'ād Māhir,[13] and Yūsuf Rāghib,[14] all of whom compiled detailed studies of individual Sufi saints, their shrines, and their followers. A second major area staked out by Dr. Schimmel was the various institutions where Sufis lived and worked, the *khānqāhs*, *ribāṭs*, and *zāwiyahs*, which were the focus of study by scholars at this same time, and most notably by Leonor Frenandez,[15] Doris Behrens-Abouseif[16], and several others[17], including 'Abd al-Raḥmān Abū Rās who wrote a useful study on the position of the *shaykh al-shuyūkh.*[18]

About twenty years after Dr. Schimmel's article, a somewhat revisionist and influential survey of Mamluk religious life was published by Donald P. Little. In "Religion Under the Mamluks," Little argued that Muslim identity and faith inspired many Mamluk military actions against the Mongols, Crusaders, and Shi'is, and this also led to lavish Mamluk patronage of mosques, *madrasahs*, *khānqāhs*, and *zāwiyahs*, and the many religious personnel who served them.[19] Naturally, economic and political motives were involved in Mamluk support of Islam and its institutions. The *waqfs* also financially benefitted the Mamluks' families, and control of the *waqfs* gave the Mamluks extensive influence over the religious establishment, a power that sultans were not about to cede to their puppet caliphs.[20] While the Mamluks supported Sufi establishments, including the *zāwiyahs* and *khānqāhs*, the Mamluks also patronized wandering mendicants and dervishes, though they were careful to suppress individuals or groups who posed a threat to civil authority. This was particularly the case for Qalandars and dervishes of the Aḥmadīyah-Rifā'īyah with their outlandish dress and bizarre behaviors, as well as their close relationship with the Mongols, arch-

11 E.g., Bannerth, *Wallfahrtsstätten*; and Bannerth, *Stifter.*
12 E.g., Garcin, *Saints*; and Garcin, *Histoire.*
13 Māhir, *Masājid.*
14 Rāghib, *Essai*; and idem, *Al-Sayyida Nafisa.*
15 Fernandes, *Foundations*; idem, *Zāwiya*; idem, *Variations*; idem, *Foundation of Baybars*; and especially idem, *Evolution.*
16 Behrens-Abouseif, *Change*; and idem, *Takiyyat.*
17 E.g., Ibrāhīm, *Zāwiya*; Williams, *Khānqāh of Siryāqūs*; Blair, *Saints.*
18 Abū Rās, *Shaykh al-Shuyūkh.*
19 Little, *Religion.*
20 Ibid., 168–75.

enemies of the Mamluks.[21] In his assessment of religion under the Mamluks, Little concluded:

> Out of religious conviction and personal piety in some instances but also with an acute sense of their own welfare, the Mamluks strove to keep diverse religious forces in Egypt and Syria in a state of equilibrium. In such circumstances, Islam undeniably flourished.[22]

This was certainly the case in Syria as demonstrated by Louis Pouzet in his ground-breaking study of Damascus in the 7th/13th century, published a few years after Little's survey.[23] Pouzet examined Muslim religious life there and, with regards to Sufism, he found that some Muslims in Damascus undertook ascetic and mystical practices, both individually and collectively. Pouzet referred to several families prominent in Sufism whose members held the prestigious office of *mashyakha al-shuyūkh*. Despite occasional controversies, usually between supporters of Ibn al-ʿArabī and his detractors, such as Ibn Taimīyah, Sufism remained an important element in spiritual lives of many Muslims of the period.[24]

As these and other studies attest, Mamluk studies began to come of age in the 1980s, and additional fine scholars substantially contributed to the field, including David Ayalon,[25] Ulrich Haarman,[26] and Carl Petry[27] to name a few. Then in the 1990s, the study of Mamluk domains reached a critical mass, as evidenced by the appearance of the first issue of *Mamlūk Studies Review*, edited by Bruce Craig at the University of Chicago, which began to publish annually articles and book reviews relevant the Mamluk period, and to compile an extensive bibliography of sources. In addition, articles and reviews on the Mamluks continued to appear in other journals and edited volumes, including the proceedings of the International Colloquium on the History of Egypt.[28] The 1990s also witnessed the beginning of an on-going reassessment of earlier scholarship and opinions. Of particular importance to Sufism was further study and analysis of the education, social make-up, and occupations of the *ʿulamāʾ*, or the class of religious professionals. A more nuanced view of the *ʿulamāʾ* began to prevail over long-standing and simplistic dichotomies such as Sufi vs. jurist. Indeed, research

21 Ibid., 175–80, also see Karamustafa, *God's unruly friends*, esp. 51–56, and al-Qūnawī, *al-Ṣūfīyah al-Qalandarīyah.*
22 Little, *Religion*, 181.
23 Pouzet, *Damas.*
24 Ibid., 207–338. Also see Pouzet, *Prises.*
25 For a bibliography of Ayalon's work, see Amitai, *David Aylon.*
26 For a bibliography of Haarman's work, see Conermann, *Ulrich Haarman.*
27 See (Petry), *Bibliography.*
28 *Egypt and Syria in the Fatimid, Ayyubid and Mamluk Eras. Proceedings.* Multiple volumes and editors.

revealed that a qualified religious scholar might, at various times, serve in the Mamluk bureaucracy, the legal system, or in any number of other religious occupations. Certainly, the jurists and legal scholars claimed to be guardians of the *sharīʿah* and *sunnah*, and so came to hold substantial moral authority and influence. Yet, beyond the legal system, members of the *ʿulamāʾ* worked as prayer leaders and preachers, readers of religious texts, spiritual advisors, and professors and teachers of various subjects ranging from the Quran and Hadith, to law and ritual, theology and mysticism. Generally the *ʿulamāʾ* were in a position both to guide the life of the community as well as to legitimize the Mamluk dynasty, and they were often viewed by medieval Mamluk society as the custodians of religious knowledge, exemplars of normative behavior, and, at times, repositories of spiritual power (*barakah*).[29]

Clearly, Sufis were respected members of the religious class. Although some Qalandars and wondering dervishes could go to extremes, Islamic mysticism remained central to Mamluk religious life, though early, scholarship in the 1980s and early 90s tended to view Sufis as on the margins of "orthodox" Muslim life. In a thoughtful article entitled "'Orthodoxy' and 'Heresy' in Medieval Islam: An Essay in Reassessment", Alexander Knysh reviewed the use and general misuse of these terms in scholarship on Islam. He pointedly concludes that:

> Eurocentric interpretive categories, when uncritically superimposed on Islamic realities, may produce serious distortions. Thus such distinctly Christian concepts as "orthodoxy" and "heresy" foster a tendency to disregard the intrinsic pluralism and complexity characteristic of the religious life of the Muslim community, leaving aside significant and sometimes critical "nuances." In order to escape these shortcomings, one should try to let Islamic tradition speak on its own terms, to let it communicate its own concerns, its own ways of articulation and interpretation of religious phenomena.[30]

This range and diversity of Muslim religious belief in the Mamluk period is readily apparent in Knysh's subsequent book *Ibn al-ʿArabi in the Later Islamic Tradition.*[31] There, Knysh followed controversies involving Ibn al-ʿArabī and his thought throughout the medieval Islamic world, and several chapters focus on events in the Mamluk period. He notes at the outset that while the *ʿulamāʾ* have been studied extensively in terms of their social power and status, there has been less attention to "their intellectual concerns, doctrinal disagreements and factional differences."[32] Following a survey of Ibn al-ʿArabī's life and thought, and

29 See Lapidus, *Muslim Cities*, esp. 107 – 15, 130 – 41; Petry, *Civilian elite*, esp. 220 – 72, 312 – 25; Berkey, *Transmission*, 1 – 43, 60, and Chamberlain, *Knowledge*, 69 – 90, 176 – 78.
30 Knysh, *Orthodoxy*, esp. 62 – 63.
31 Knysh, *Ibn ʿArabī.*
32 Ibid., 3.

early biographical accounts of him, Knysh proceeds to analyze carefully the polemical tradition that formed against him.

Particularly authoritative for later generations have been numerous writings by the Hanbalī jurist and theologian Ibn Taymīyah (d. 728/1328) and his students, who stressed the primacy of the *sharī'ah* over any sort of metaphysical speculation. Ibn Taymīyah asserted that beliefs in mystical union with the divine and monism undermine the essential distinction between God and His creation, which was the true basis of monotheistic religion. Thus he stridently condemned any mystical writings and their authors, whom he believed were infected with the unity of being. To him, their teachings encouraged deviation from God's truth, which could only be found in the Quran, the *sunnah* of Muhammad, and codified in the divine law.[33] Ibn Taymīyah vigorously denounced Ibn al-ʿArabī's teachings, especially those found in the latter's *Fuṣūṣ al-Ḥikam*, which appeared to pervert God's literal message. Such allegorical exegesis by Ibn al-ʿArabī and others posed a grave danger to religion and society.[34] Further, their malignant doctrines had been spread in elegant forms such as the verse of Ibn al-Fāriḍ, and so their negative effects upon the Muslim community were devastating.[35] Ibn Taymīyah condemned any claims to sainthood on behalf of such heretics as a mockery of the religious law that was so necessary for proper communal life. As a result, compromise or accommodation was impossible, and Ibn Taymīyah declared that refutation of the monists was comparable to holy war against the Mongols.[36]

Ibn Taymīyah's refutations became the foundation for later polemics and public controversies that periodically arose in Mamluk domains. However, Ibn al-ʿArabī had many supporters among the *'ulamā'* and the ruling class. A number of Muslim scholars, including Jalāl al-Dīn al-Suyūṭī (d. 911/1505), argued that statements made by Ibn al-ʿArabī and other saints of God could be reconciled with the Quran and *sharī'ah* via allegorical interpretations. Therefore, Muslims should venerate them, not declare them infidels, though their difficult and obscure writings should be restricted to qualified scholars of religion.[37] What emerges from a study of the Ibn al-ʿArabī controversy is the fact that people on both sides of the dispute cut across the various classes and divisions of the *'ulamā'*. Therefore, the debates and participants involved should not be reduced to static polarities like orthodoxy vs. heterodoxy or legists vs. mystics, which mask the ambiguity and ambivalence at the heart of the matter. Further, such controversies conclusively show that for Islam in Mamluk domains, beliefs and doctrine mattered. As Knysh concludes:

33 Ibid., 87–111.

34 Regarding Ibn Taymīyah's position on Quranic exegesis in general see Calder, *Tafsir*.

35 Also see Memon, *Popular Religion*, esp. 24–46; Ansari, *Criticism*, and Schallenbergh, *Intoxication*.

36 Knysh, *Ibn 'Arabī*, 50, 62, 96–99. Also see Homerin, *Sufis*, esp. 231–35.

37 Knysh, *Ibn 'Arabī*, 113–40; 201–23.

> Like other contested theological issues, Ibn al-ʿArabī's legacy served as a convenient rallying point for various religio-political factions vying for power and supremacy. While no universal *ijmāʿ* has ever been reached on the problem of Ibn al-ʿArabī's belief/unbelief, local campaigns to either vindicate or condemn him show that a relatively effective machinery was created by the *ʿulamāʾ* for defining and formulating an authoritative position on a given doctrinal issue.[38]

Finally, it should be stressed that nearly all of the antagonists and protagonists in the Ibn al-ʿArabī debate, accepted and practiced Sufism in various degrees and forms. As was the case with Ibn al-ʿArabī, particular Sufis and their beliefs might be the target of censure, but many other aspects of Sufism were acceptable to most Muslims. The *ʿulamāʾ* were not polarized between mystics and non-mystics so much as they exhibited a range of opinion regarding mystical experiences and practice, their content and value, relative to other types of authoritative sources. Even Ibn Taymīyah accepted Sufism provided it was grounded in the literal message of the Quran and the prophetic *sunnah*.[39] Perhaps more telling was the fact that the conservative Mālikī scholar Ibn Khaldūn (d. 808/1406) enumerated Sufism as one of "the legitimate sciences that originated in Islam" (*min-a l-ʿulūmi l-sharʿīyati l-hadīthati fī l-millati*). During the Mamluk period, elites and commoners alike sought the blessings of saintly shaykhs, and Sufi ceremonies were regularly attended by Muslims of all social classes. In fact, *ṣūfī* was a legitimate occupational category in *waqf* deeds. Not surprisingly, jurists and others criticized those who used the Sufi profession as a means to accrue large sums of money. Yet such behavior was inappropriate to any religious office, and this was not a critique of Sufis, in particular, but of the *ʿulamāʾ* class, in general.[40]

Clearly, mysticism was a vital part of Islam in the Mamluk age and, as I noted earlier, this has been the focus of fruitful study for several decades. French scholars, including Paul Nwyia,[41] Jean-Claude Garcin,[42] and Denis Gril,[43] have been quite active in the field, producing a number of fine articles and monographs, while others, including Victor Dannor,[44] Mary Ann Khoury Danner,[45] Elmer Douglas,[46] and Éric Geoffroy[47] have also contributed translations along with studies of important Sufi texts from the period. Many of these and other specialized studies

38 Ibid., 273–74.
39 Homerin, *al-Ṣūfīyah*, and Schallenbergh, *Intoxication*, 460–63.
40 Homerin, *Sufis*. For more on Ibn Khaldūn's views of Sufism, also see Perlman, *Ibn Khaldūn*; ʿAbd al-Qādir, *Ibn Khaldūn wa-l-Taṣawwuf*, and, more recently, McGregor, *Sufism*.
41 E.g., Nwiya, *Ibn ʿAṭāʾ Allāh*, and idem, *Tarîqa*.
42 E.g., Garcin, *Centre*, and a collection of his essays idem, *Espaces*.
43 E.g., Grill, *Source*, and idem, *Risāla*.
44 Danner, *Spiritual aphormism*, and idem., *Book of wisdom*.
45 Al-Iskandarī, *Key*.
46 Douglas, *Mystical teachings*.
47 Al-Iskandarī, *Laṭāʾif*.

inform the best current introduction to the topic, *Le Soufism en Égypte et en Syria* by Éric Geoffroy. Though Geoffroy's ostensible focus is the later Mamluk and early Ottoman periods, this encyclopedic work covers much of the Mamluk centuries. He begins by situating Sufism within its larger social, political, and religious contexts, and he pays particular attention to the importance of the prophetic model and notions of saintliness in shaping Sufi traditions.[48] Geoffroy then examines the important roles played by scholar-Sufis, charlatan Sufis, and the shaykhs and Sufis of the *zāwiyahs* and *khānqāhs*. He finds the *zāwiyah* to have been especially important for the teaching and training of Sufis, while he regards the *khānqāh* as a more impersonal semi-political institution.[49]

Subsequent to Geoffroy's survey, I examined the Mamluk *khānqāh's* particular religious function in my article "Saving Muslim Souls: the *Khānqāh* and the Sufi Duty in Mamluk Lands."[50] Based on a study of *waqf* deeds, religious tracts on death and afterlife, and other sources, I discovered that the Mamluk *khānqāh* served primarily as a chantry, where Sufis prayed for their founder's earthly and heavenly benefit. *Khānqāh* endowment deeds explicitly mandate that the Sufis employed there were to perform a daily communal ritual called *ḥuḍūr*. This ritual included reciting specific prayers and Quranic passages, considered by al-Qurṭubī (d. 681/1273), al-Suyūṭī, and other scholars of the period, to be the most efficacious for attaining divine favor in this world and the next, and especially helpful for reducing the severity and length of the deceased's purgatorial punishment in the grave.[51]

We find, then, that students studied to be Sufis in the *zāwiyahs*, and only later did some of them eventually work as professional Sufis in the *khānqāhs* where affiliation to a specific order was not mandatory. In *Le Soufism en Égypte et en Syria*, Geoffroy goes on to review these forms of affiliation among various Sufi groups and their major representatives in Syria and Egypt, with a comparison to those of other regions, and their mutual influences.[52] This is followed by an analysis of several prominent Sufi types including the ascetic, the practicing scholar, the inspired illiterate shaykh, the accomplished master, the mad mystic, and finally, the *malāmatī* or blame-seeker.[53] Unfortunately, on this latter topic, Geoffroy did not have access to the fine study by Ahmet T. Karamustafa, *God's Unruly Friends: Dervish*

48 Geoffroy, *Soufism*, 1–144. Two more recent introductions to the subject by Manṣūr, *al-'Aqā'id*, and idem, *at-Taṣawwuf* are anti-Sufi polemics of little scholarly value.

49 Geoffroy, *Soufism*, 145–87.

50 Homerin, *Saving*.

51 Ibid., 74–83. Also see Little, *Nature*; Rachida, *Zâwiya*; Rizq, *Khānqāwāt*, and Pahlitzsch, *Concern*.

52 Geoffroy, *Soufisme*, 189–281.

53 Ibid., 283–360.

Groups in the Islamic Later Middle Period, 1200 – 1500.[54] There, Karamustafa argues that the radical renunciation and social deviance that characterize these individuals resulted largely from their belief that Muslim society was an obstacle to salvation in the world to come. These antinomian mendicants similarly rebelled against the more established Sufi orders and institutions, which they regarded as unacceptable compromises with worldly life.[55]

Geoffroy next surveys some of the doctrinal debates of the period, including those on permissible forms of *dhikr* and *samāʿ*, the belief/disbelief issues regarding Ibn al-Fāriḍ, Ibn al-ʿArabī and monism, and the value of mystical inspiration.[56] As Geoffroy makes clear, in the face of such controversies, the various lines of Sufi initiation among the *ʿulamāʾ* were crucial to harmonizing mystical inspiration and practice with social propriety and law. Further, due to the support of the sultan Qaytbay and, subsequently, the Ottoman Sultan Selim I, Ibn al-ʿArabī and his doctrine gained wider acceptance. Geoffroy argues convincingly that during the Mamluk period, Sufism's success derived, in part, from its ability to adapt to a plurality of conditions and needs, from those of the religious elite to those of illiterate peasants. As such, Sufism proved to be a fundamental and dynamic part of medieval Muslim life, socially, culturally, and, above all, religiously.[57]

In his concluding remarks, Geoffroy draws attention to the work of Boaz Shoshan regarding the place and popularity of Sufism in medieval Egypt. Shoshan takes up this and other themes in his book *Popular Culture in Medieval Cairo.*[58] He highlights the importance of the Sufi orders to congregational life and calls attention to the sermons of popular Sufi shaykhs. Shoshan examines in some detail the sermons of Ibn ʿAṭāʾ Allāh, the celebrated 14th century Shādhilī Sufi master, who preached that faith and repentance where the foundation of religious life. Ibn ʿAṭāʾ Allāh warned his audiences against Satan and sins, and urged them to perform regularly their prayers and other required religious duties, and to visit the tombs of the saints.[59] Recently, Shoshan returned to Sufi sermons from the Mamluk period as a way to gauge religious sensibilities and practices prevalent at the time, including visiting the graves and blessing the prophet Muhammad for religious merit. Shoshan frequently found stories of famous Sufis and their miracles in many sermons as well as references to Sufi practices, especially *dhikr.*[60] In the Quran, believers are advised to remember God often, and Sufis developed recollection into

54 Karamustafa, *God's Unruly Friends*, esp. 25 – 56. For a further contribution to this topic, see Frenkel, *Notes.*
55 Karamustafa, *God's Unruly Friends*, 17 – 23, 97 – 102.
56 Geoffroy, *Soufisme*, 361 – 503.
57 Ibid., 505 – 10.
58 Shoshan, *Culture.*
59 Ibid., 9 – 22.
60 Shoshan, *Sermons.*

a spiritual practice of meditation on God that might lead to mystical experiences, including ecstasy. *Dhikr* became a corner stone of many Sufi orders, and even conservative scholars, including Ibn Taymīyah, recognized its value if properly performed. In a recent article, Gino Schallenbergh examines the positions of Ibn Taymīyah's student, Ibn Qayyim al-Jawzīyah (d. 751/1350) on *dhikr* and the related and more public ritual of *samāʿ*. Ibn Qayyim praised the many benefits of *dhikr*, in the form of a private recollection and invocation of God, yet he was uneasy when *dhikr* led to displays of weeping and ecstasy. But far worse was *samāʿ*, the public gathering too listen to poetry and songs, even of a religious nature, which he believed would surely lead Muslims to sin and possible damnation.[61]

Religious conservatives also fretted over the veneration of the prophet Muhammad, which was quite popular in the Mamluk era. Indeed on the day commemorating Muhammad's birth, the *Mawlid al-Nabī*, poets often recited verse praising the Prophet and recounting his life's stories and miracles. This aspect of the Mamluk *Mawlid* has been discussed by Fāris Aḥmad al-ʿAllāwī in his book *ʿĀ'ishah al-Bāʿūnīyah al-Dimashqīyah*. ʿĀ'ishah al-Bāʿūnīyah (d. 922/1516) was a noted Sufi scholar and prolific poet who composed a number of works praising Muhammad. In his book, al-ʿAllāwī provides a useful survey of the history of celebrating the Prophet's birthday, and an overview of the *mawlid al-nabī* genre of prose and poetry.[62] Among this poetry, the *Burdah* by the Egyptian poet Muhammad al-Būṣīrī (d.c. 696/1297), has a special place as the most celebrated poem ever composed in Arabic.[63]

Al-Būṣīrī's *Burdah,* ʿĀ'ishah al-Bāʿūnīyah's *mawlids*, and other poems praising the Prophet draw attention to the devotional spirit that was pronounced in Sufism during the Mamluk period, and here, again, poetry helps to gauge Muslim religious concerns. Sufi verse composed during Mamluk period has been touched upon by several scholars including ʿAlī Ṣāfī Ḥusayn who noted that this poetry ranged from the refined verse of professional poets to the vernacular prayers of pilgrims. Further, much of this religious verse has a homiletic character and often revolves around the mystical themes of love and union with God and, of course, devotion to the prophet Muhammad.[64] Unfortunately, the works of many Sufi poets of the Mamluk period remain in unedited manuscripts, though some of the poetry by ʿĀ'ishah al-Bāʿūnīyah has been edited and published over the last several years.[65] In addition to several of her *mawlids* men-

61 Schallenbergh, *Invocation.*

62 Al-ʿAllāwī, *ʿĀ'isha*, 63–94, and see Homerin, *Review: al-ʿAllāwī, ʿĀ'ishah.* Also see Kaptein, *Festival*, 44–75.

63 Sperl, *Qasida 50*, 2:388–411, 470–76; and Stetkevych, *Mantle Odes*, esp. 70–150.

64 Ḥusayn, *Al-Adab.* Also see Ḥaydar, *Madkhal*, and more recently, Homerin, *Poetry.*

65 Al-Bāʿūnīyah, *Badīʿīyah*, and another edition by ʿAzāwī, *Al-Badīʿīyah.* Also see al-Bāʿūnīyah, *Al-Qawl.*

tioned above, an edition of her *dīwān* entitled *Fayḍ al-Faḍl wa-Jamʿal-Shaml* was recently edited and published.[66] This work contains over 370 poems on Sufi themes ranging from love and longing to intoxication and union, and some of these poems were probably recited during *samāʿ* sessions. Several scholars are currently working on the life and work of ʿĀʾishah al-Bāʿūnīya, and I hope that similar energy will be focused on many other Sufi poets of the Mamluk period.[67]

One related topic that has seen considerable study over the last twenty years is sainthood in Islam, reflecting a prominent trend in the study of religion in general, and several works in the 1980s undertook the comparative study of sainthood with contributions on Muslim saints, as scholars of Islam approached the subject with new interest.[68] As for Sufi saints in the Mamluk period, groundbreaking work was done by Jean-Claude Garcin, who studied relations between popular saints and Mamluk amirs, as well as the various types of Sufi saints and their miracles, particularly in context of the needs of the rural masses.[69] As I noted earlier, also of importance has been the pioneering work on saints, shrines, and pilgrimage by Ernest Bannerth, Suʿād Māhir, and Yūsuf Rāghib, whose efforts laid the foundations for more recent contributions on the subject. For instance, Catherine Mayeur-Jaouen has carried out extensive research on one of Egypt's greatest Sufi saints, Aḥmad al-Badawī (d. 675/1276),[70] and a number of articles and books have appeared during the last twenty years on other Mamluk saints and Sufis, including the work of Helena Hallenberg on Ibrahim al-Dasūqī (d. 696/1296),[71] my work on Ibn al-Fāriḍ's saintly fortunes during the Mamluk period,[72] and Richard McGregor's studies of the Wafāʾī Sufi Order and its founders, Muhammad Wafāʿ (d. 765/1363), and his son ʿAlī (d. 807/1405).[73]

While such studies chart the fortunes of individual Sufis during the Mamluk period, there have been several excellent anthologies addressing various aspects of Sufism and sanctity during the Mamluk Period. *Saints orientaux*, edited by Denise Aigle, features articles by Éric Geoffroy on the hagiography (*adab al-manāqib*) and typology of saints from the Mamluk period, by Mayeur-Jaouen on

66 ʿArār, *Dīwān*. Unfortunately, this edition contains many errors and discrepancies; see my review forthcoming in *Mamlūk Studies Review*.
67 See al-Rabābiʿah, *ʿĀʾishah*; and Homerin, *Emanations*; idem, *Living Love*; idem, *Sufi Biography*, and idem, *ʿĀʾishah*.
68 Brinner, *Prophet*; Sanneh, *Saints*; Denny, *God's Friends*, and more recently Meri, *Etiquette*. Also see Gramlich, *Wunder*; Chodkiewicz, *Sceau*; Smith, *Manifestations*.
69 Garcin, *Saints*; and idem., Histoire.
70 Mayeur-Jaouen, *al-Badawī*, esp. 161–506.
71 Hallenberg, *Ibrāhīm al-Dasūqī*; idem., *Sultan*, and idem., Theme.
72 Homerin, *Arab Poet*, esp. 1–75; idem., *Domed Shrine*; and idem., *ʿUmar ibn al-Fāriḍ*
73 McGregor, *Sanctity*. Also see his *New Sources*; idem., *Being*; idem., *Medieval Saint*, and idem., *Existential Dimension*.

a group of rural Sufi saints associated with al-Sayyid al-Badawī who spread Islam in the Egyptian Delta, and by Denis Gril on the importance of miracles (*karamāt*) as evidence for Sufism's prophetic heritage.[74] Miracles are the subject of a second volume edited by Aigle, *Miracle et Karāma*, which contains further engaging articles, which occasionally touch on the Mamluk period; Geoffroy reviews the ambiguous position of some Sufis regarding evident and hidden miracles, while Mayeur-Jaouen provides a lively discussion of the relationships between animals, miracles, and Muslim saints with several examples from the Mamluk period.[75]

Concern with hagiography, miracles, and intercession is also apparent in *Le Saint et son milieu* edited by Rachida Chih and Denis Gril. In his article, Gril compares the lives of an urban saint with one from the rural areas, while Mayeur-Jaouen examines saintly ideals in light of practical realities.[76] In her study of shaykhs in the lineage of Ibrahim al-Matbūlī (d. 880/1475) at the end of the Mamluk and beginning of the Ottoman eras, Mayeur-Jaouen finds that there was always a need to strike a balance between the concrete realities involved with supporting a *zāwiyah*, and the requirements of maintaining religious comportment (*wara*ʿ). This need was especially acute when shaykhs interacted with their Mamluk and Ottoman benefactors, whether at banquets and similar occasions, when receiving their gifts, or when seeking favors on behalf of the peasants, who depended on the shaykhs for intercession with both God and the ruling elite.[77] The volume *Miracle et Karāma* also contains important articles by Geoffroy and McGregor on sainthood among the Shādhilī Sufis,[78] and several additional articles on al-Shādhalī and his order in Mamluk lands are to be found in an anthology entitled *Une voie soufi dans le monde: la Shādhiliyya*, edited by Éric Geoffroy.[79] Relevant articles include Youssef Ziedan's reflections on Shādhilī buildings and manuscripts in Alexandria, Denis Gril's study of the teachings of Ibn ʿAṭā' Allāh based on one of his disciples, Richard McGregor's analysis of the impact of Ibn al-ʿArabī's thought on Muhammad Wafāʿ, and Geoffroy's examination of mystical experience, mystical doctrines, and their expression among medieval Shādhilīyah.[80]

In yet another collection on Sufism in the Mamluk period, again published by the French Institute in Cairo, *Le développement du soufisme en Égypte à l'époque*

74 Geoffroy, *Hagiograpie*; Mayeur-Jaouen, *Les Compagnons*, and Gril, *Le miracle.*
75 Geoffroy, *Les Mystiques*, and Mayeur-Jaouen, *Miracles.*
76 Gril, *Saint des villes.*
77 Mayeur-Jaouen, *Le Cheikh.*
78 Geoffroy, *L'élection*; and McGregor, *Concept of Sainthood.*
79 Geoffroy, *Une voie.*
80 Ziedan, *The Legacy*; Gril, *L'enseignement*; McGregor, *Akbarian;* and Geoffroy, *Entre ésotérisme.*

mamlouke, editors Richard McGregor and Adam Sabra have grouped the articles based on topics.[81] In "Sufism in the City and Countryside," we find a substantial review essay by Garcin regarding the study of Sufis, their orders and institutions in Mamluk society, while Mayeur-Jaouen examines various Sufi orders in the Nile Delta and their importance to rural life and society.[82] Denis Gril once again visits Qūṣ to study the Sufi networks there, while Tamer el-Leithy examines the predominant role of Sufis in violence against Coptic Christians, particularly in the same region of Upper Egypt. In her detailed study, el-Leithy argues that throughout the Mamluks' rule and their domains, Sufis, through their sermon's and writings, often spurred on "unauthorized moral actions" against Copts, recent converts to Islam, churches and monasteries, and immoral practices, such as the sale of wine, in order to realign and regulate religiously mixed communities more along Muslim lines.[83]

Another section of the volume focuses on "Varieties of Sainthood," as Adam Sabra deftly probes issues of illiteracy and learning among "every day saints" ministering to Egypt's merchants, artisans, and the poor, particularly in the figure of ʿAlī al-Khawwāṣ (d. 939/1532) as seen through the eyes of ʿAbd al-Wahhāb al-Shaʿrānī (897 – 936/1493 – 1565). As the Mamluk dynasty gave way to the Ottomans, Cairo was reduced to a provincial capital, and learned scholars seeking patronage and position frequently turned to Istanbul. Perhaps for this reason, Sufi masters among the artisan class rose to prominence, including ʿAlī al-Khawwāṣ, who is also the subject of the following study by Éric Geoffroy who notes that the illiteracy of this and other saints was often regarded by others as a sign, not of ignorance, but of spiritual receptivity and power to assist fellow Muslims in troubled times. By contrast, Richard McGregor then considers ʿAlī Wafāʾ's very learned notions of sainthood in light of the thought of Ibn al-ʿArabī, and similarly finds important eschatological dimensions here, too.[84]

Le développement du soufisme en Égypte à l'époque mamlouke also contains articles on the occult and dream interpretation, Sufi influence on Jewish mystics, and several contributions on the visitation of Sufi shrines in Cairo's al-Qarāfah cemetery. May Al-Ibrashy reviews several pilgrimage guides written during the Mamluk period to catalog and trace the development of the cemetery and itineraries for visiting the saints there, while Tetsuya Ohtoshi consults some of the same sources to gauge Sufi elements and influences on pilgrimage practices.[85] Finally, Muhammad Abū al-ʿAmāyim examines and catalogs the area encompassing the Mosque of Jāhīn (d. 954/1547), one of Qaybay's Mamluks, who later

81 McGregor, Sabra, *Le développement.*
82 Garcin, *Les soufis*, and Mayeur-Jaouen, *Maîtres.*
83 Gril, *Le soufisme*; and El-Leithy, *Sufis.*
84 Sabra, *Illiterate*; Geoffroy, *Grande figure*; and McGregor, *Conceptions of the Ultimate Saint.*
85 Al-Ibrashy, *Cairo's Qarafa*, and Ohtoshi, *Tasawwuf.* Also see Ohtoshi, *Manners.*

devoted himself to the Sufi life in a Khalwātī mosque and khānqāh overlooking the Qarāfah.[86]

These recent studies on tombs, saints, and shrines add to several earlier works that took a more comprehensive view of the saints and Sufis in terms of cemeteries and shrines important during the Mamluk Period. Christopher Taylor in his book *In the Vicinity of the Righteous* maps the sacred geography of Cairo in the Mamluk period to recount the etiquette of pilgrimage (*ziyārah*) to shrines in order to receive the divine blessings emanating from the tombs of holy persons.[87] Taylor also reviews the long-standing debate between those Muslims, including Ibn Taymīyah, who held saint cults to be a form of idolatry, and the larger Muslim majority who have believed that the saints are God's special friends whose prayers are answered on behalf of believers.[88] Taylor argues persuasively that the saints and their cults played vital roles within medieval Islam, in general, and in Mamluk Cairo, in particular, as they combined "unifying elements of universal significance with considerable diversity in local expression."[89]

Complementing Taylor's study is Josef Meri's book, *The Cult of the Saints Among Muslims and Jews in Medieval Syria.* Meri describes the spiritual topography of the region visited by those who sought *barakah*, the sacred blessing or charisma possessed by holy people, places, and relics, which Meri observes "was spiritual, perceptual, and emotive, rather than conceptual."[90] Meri offers a number of insightful sections on women devotees, individual saints, types of talismans, and such practices as seeking cures, rain, and repentance.[91] Meri also considers the proliferation of various types of shrines and other sacred sites in the 6th-7th/12th-13th centuries, and he ascribes this growth, in part, to the decline of Abbasid central authority and the need by their various local successors for religious legitimation as protectors and patrons of Islam and its holy places. The spread of Sufism and its orders also nurtured the growth of shrines and the cult of the saints, which were a central part of popular religious life among Muslims, Christians, and Jews of the medieval Near East. But by popular he does not mean "low" or "heterodox" but normative as "devotees from all walks of life… sought to reaffirm their faith, chart their sacred pasts, and derive relief from illness and adversity."[92]

Meri's study reaffirms a general conclusion reached by many of the scholars

86 Al-ʿAmāyim, *Minṭaqat.*
87 Taylor, *Vicinity*, 1–79.
88 Ibid., 168–218. Also see Olesen, *Culte des saints.*
89 Ibid., 226.
90 Meri, *The Cult*, 1–58, 103–119.
91 Ibid., 163–213.
92 Ibid., 249–87.

considered in this essay. Namely that a two-tier model of religion with a high faith of a literate elite above the vulgar superstitions of the masses is an inaccurate and misleading description of religion in the Mamluk period. We should recall that while the Quran and *sunnah* provide the foundation for Islamic belief and practice, they still allow for a wide array of regional and cultural interpretation and expression. Further, as Sunni Islam lacks an official earthly religious authority after the Prophet Muhammad, local custom may not oppose normative Islam so much as determine it. The consensus of a community, its tradition, certifies correct belief and practice to a great extent, and this appears to have been the case in Mamluk domains, where Sufism, both in thought and practice, was an essential element of society, especially in matters of literature, culture and, above all, religion.

It should be noted, too, that recent studies of the mystical dimensions of Islam in the Mamluk period cover all Mamluk domains, including Egypt, Syria, Palestine, and the Hijaz, while important studies on the 'ulamā', saints, and Sufis in Cairo have their able counterparts in Damascus and elsewhere.[93] A similar result is found when we view this research in terms of urban-rural relations, with studies of Sufism in Alexandria, Cairo, Jerusalem, and Damascus, finding their rural complements.[94] Another positive trend in recent research is a familiarity among many Mamluk scholars with related scholarship involving other regions and religions, especially, Christianity and Judaism, which allows for a comparative perspective in terms of both subject matter and methodology. I am also encouraged by the fact that a number of scholars have used manuscripts for their research, bringing new sources and light to their areas of interest. There are hundreds, if not thousands, of unpublished manuscripts composed during the Mamluk period related to Sufism and other topics awaiting careful study, and I urge students and scholars in the field of Mamluk studies to consider editing and publishing some of this important material.[95]

Though publishers in western countries may be hesitant to publish edited volumes of Arabic texts, e-books may be an exciting and viable alternative in these cases. In fact, electronic media have become increasingly useful, if not essential, to contemporary research and publishing in many fields, including Mamluk studies, as we see, for example, at the Middle Eastern Documentation Center at the University of Chicago, which now publishes *Mamlūk Studies Review* online, while offering additional on-line services including an extensive bibliography of Mamluk sources, an encyclopedia of Mamluk studies, and other

93 E.g., Ephrat, *Sufism*, 4–18; Frenkel, *Notes*; Geoffroy, *Les milieux*; and Abū Zayd, *al-Taṣawwuf.*

94 E.g., Mayeur-Jaouen, *Les Compagnons* and idem, *Maîtres*; Gril, *Le soufisme*; El-Leithy, *Sufis*; Ephrat, *Sufism*; and Frenkel, *Notes.*

95 E.g. Homerin, *Love & Life*

valuable resources.[96] This continued support by the University of Chicago, together with that from other intuitions, such as the French Institute in Cairo, and, now, the Annemarie Schimmel Kolleg of the University of Bonn, has significantly enhanced research in Mamluk studies. This, in turn, should lead to new discoveries and insights that will inform our scholarship and, perhaps, dramatically enhance how we view Sufism and Islam in the Mamluk domains.

Literature

Primary Sources

Al-Bāʿūniyya, ʿĀ'ishah, *Badīʿiyah al-Fatḥ al-Mubīn fī Madḥ al-Amīn*, ed. Ḥasan Muḥammad al-Rabābiʿah, Amman: Wizārat al-Thaqāfah, 2008.

Al-Bāʿūniyya, ʿĀ'ishah: *al-Qawl al-Ṣaḥīḥ fī Takhmīs Burdah al-Madīḥ*, ed. Ḥasan Muḥammad al-Rabābiʿah, Amman: Wizārat al-Thaqāfah 2009.

Ibn Dawādārī, Abū Bakr b. ʿAbdallāh, *Die Chronick des Ibn ad-Dawādārī. Achter Band: Der Bericht über die frühen Mamluken*, ed. Ulrich Haarman, Freiburg: Deutsches Archäologisches Institut Kairo 1971. (how many volumes does this edition has; one; this is volume 8)

Ibn Shaddād, ʿIzz al-Dīn, *Ta'rīkh al-Malik al-Ẓāhir*, ed. A. Ḥuṭayṭ, Wiesbaden: Franz Steiner 1983.

Al-Iskandarī, Ibn Aṭā' Allāh, *Laṭā'if al-Minan*, trans. Éric Geoffroy, *La sagesse de maīstres*, Damascus 1995.

Al-Iskandarī, Ibn Aṭā' Allāh, *The Key to Salvation*, trans. Mary Ann Khory Danner, Cambridge: Islamic Texts Society 1996.

Secondary sources

ʿAbd al-Qādir, Maḥmūd, "Ibn Khaldūn wa-l-Taṣawwuf al-Islāmī (732 – 808 H./1332 – 1405 M.)," *Majalla Kulliyyah al-Ādāb, Jāmiʿat al-Qāhirah* 26 (1964), pp. 89 – 112.

Abū Rās, ʿAbd al-Raḥmān, *Shaykh al-Shuyūkh bi-l-Diyār al-Miṣrīyah fī al-Dawlatayn al-Ayyūbīyah wa-l-Mamlūkīyah*, Cairo: Maktabah ʿĀlam al-Fikr 1987.

Abū Zayd, Munā Aḥmad, "al-Taṣawwuf fī al-Iskandarīyah fī al-Qarn al-Sābiʿ," *Ibdāʿ* 19/4 (2002), pp. 31 – 40.

Al-ʿAllāwī, Fāris Aḥmad, *ʿĀ'isha al-Baʿūnīyah al-Dimashqīyah*, Damascus: Dār Muʿadd li-l-Ṭibāʿa wa-l-Nashr wa-l-Tawzīʿ 1994.

Al-ʿAmāyim, Muḥammad Abū, "Minṭaqat Masjid Jāhīn al-Khalwātī: Minṭaqat Taṣawwuf Qadīmah," in: McGregor, Sabra, *Le développement*, 1 – 31 (Arabic).

96 See: http://mamluk.uchicago.edu/

Amitai, Reuven, "David Ayalon, 1914 - 98," *Mamlūk Studies Review*, vol. 3 (1999), pp. 1 - 12.

Ansari, Abdul Haq, "Ibn Taymiyah's Criticism of Sufism," *Islam and the Modern Age* August (1984), pp. 147 - 56.

ʿArār, Mahdī Asʿad, *Dīwān Fayḍ al-Faḍl wa-Jamʿal-Shaml*, Beirut: Dār al-Kutub al-ʿIlmīyah 2010.

Ashtor, Eliyahu, "Scheich Ḫiḍr: Ein Beitrag zur Geschichte der Juden in Damaskus," *Wiener Zeitschrift für die Kunde des Morgenlandes* (1937), pp. 227 - 230.

ʿĀshūr, Saʿīd ʿAbd al-Fattāḥ, *Al-Mujtamaʿal-Miṣrī fī ʿAṣr Sulāṭīn al-Mamālīk*, Cairo: Dār al-Nahḍah al-ʿArabīyah 1962.

ʿAzāwī, ʿĀdil and ʿAbbās Thābit (eds.), *al-Badīʿīyah wa-Sharḥuh: al-Fatḥ al-Mubīn fī Madḥ al-Amīn*, Damascus: Dār Kinān 2009.

Bannerth, Ernest, *Islamische Wallfahrtsstätten Kairos*, Wiesbaden: O. Harrassowitz 1973.

Bannreth, Ernest, "Über den Stifter und Sonderbrauch der Demirdāšiyya-Sufis in Kairo," *Wiener Zeitschrift für die Kunde des Morgenlandes* 62 (1969), pp. 116 - 132.

Behrens-Abouseif, Doris, "Change in Function and Form of Mamluk Religious Institutions," *Annales islamologiques* 21 (1985), pp. 73 - 93.

Behrens-Abouseif, Doris, "The Takiyyat Ibrahim al-Kulshani in Cairo," *Muqarnas* 5 (1988), pp. 43 - 60.

Berkey, Jonathan, *The Transmission of Knowledge in Medieval Cairo: A Social History of Islamic Education*, Princeton; Princeton University Press 1992.

Blair, Sheila S., "Sufi Saints and Shrine Architecture in the Early Fourteenth Century," *Muqarnas: An Annual on Islamic Art and Architecture* 7 (1990), pp. 35 - 49.

Brinner, William, "Prophet and Saint: The Two Exemplars," in: *Saints and Virtues*, ed. John Stratton Hawley, Berkeley: University of California Press 1987, pp. 36 - 51.

Calder, Norman, "Tafsir from Tabari to Ibn Kathir," in: *Approaches to the Quran*, eds. G.R. Hawting and Abdul-Kader A. Shareef, London: Routledge 1993, pp. 101 - 40.

Chamberlain, Michael, *Knowledge and Social Practice in Medieval Damascus, 1190 - 1350*, Cambridge: Cambridge University Press 1994.

Chodkiewicz, Michael, *Le Sceau des saints*, France: Gallimard 1986.

Conermann, Stephan, "Ulrich Haarman, 1942 - 1999," *Mamlūk Studies Review* 4 (2000), pp. 1 - 25.

Danner, Victor, "The Life and Works of Ibn ʿAṭā' Allāh," in: idem, *Spiritual Aphorisms, (Kitāb al-Ḥikam)*, pp. 1 - 14.

Danner, Victor, *Ibn ʿAṭā' Allāh: The Book of Wisdom*, New York: Paulist Press 1978.

Danner, Victor, *Ibn ʿAṭā' Allāh's Spiritual Aphorisms*, trans., Leiden: E.J. Brill 1973.

Denny, Frederick M., "God's Friends: the Sanctity of Persons in Islam," in: *Sainthood*, eds. Richard Kieckhefer and George D. Bond, Berkeley: University of California Press 1988, pp. 69 - 97.

Douglas, Elmer H., *The Mystical Teachings of al-Shadhili*, trans., Albany: State University of New York Press 1993.

Drory, Joseph: "Meʿalilot sheiḥ Hider ʿAluf ha-yishmaʿelim,'" in: *Meḥarim be-ʿaravit ʿuvtarbut ha-ʿislam*, ed. Binyamin Abrahamov, Bar-Ilan University 2000 - 2001, pp. 37 - 49.

Ephrat, Daphna, "Sufism and Sanctity: The Genesis of the *Wali Allah* in Mamluk Jerusalem and Hebron," in: *Mamluks and Ottomans: Studies in Honour of Michael Winter*, eds. David Wasserstein and Ami Ayalon, New York: Routledge 2006, 4 - 18

Éric Geoffroy, "Les milieux de la mystique musulmane à Alexandrie aux XIIIe et XIVe siècles," in: *Alexandrie médiévale 2*, ed. Christian Décobert, Cairo: Institut français d'archéologie orientale 2002, 169 - 80.

Fernandes, Leonor E., "The Foundation of Baybars al-Jashankir: Its Waqf, History, and Architecture," *Muqarnas* 4 (1987), pp. 21 - 42.

Fernandes, Leonor E., "The Zāwiya in Cairo," *Annales islamologiques* 18 (1982), pp. 116 - 121.

Fernandes, Leonor E., "Three Ṣūfī Foundations in a 15th Century Waqfiyya," *Annales islamologiques* 17 (1981), pp. 141 - 156.

Fernandes, Leonor E., "Two Variations of the Same Theme: The Zāwiya of Ḥasan al-Rūmī, the Takiyya of Ibrāhīm al-Ǧulšānī," *Annales islamologiques*, vol. 21 (1985), pp. 95 - 111.

Fernandes, Leonor E., *The Evolution of a Sufi Institution in Mamluk Egypt: The Khanqah*, Berlin: Klaus Schwartz 1988.

Frenkel, Yehoshua, "Notes Regarding Sufism in Mamluk *Bilād aš-Šām*," in: *Egypt and Syria in the Fatimid, Ayyubid and Mamluk Eras*, eds. Urbain Vermeien and Kristof D'Hulser, Leuven: Uitgeverij Peeters 2007, pp. 487 - 496.

Garcin, Jean-Claude, "Deux saints populaires du Caire au début du XVIe siècle," *Bulletin d'études orientales* 29 (1977), pp. 131 - 143.

Garcin, Jean-Claude, "Histoire et hagiographie de l'Égypte musulmane à la fin de l'époque mamelouke et au début de l'époque ottoman," in: *Hommages à la mémoire de Serge Sauneron (1927 - 1976), II: Égypte post-pharaonique*, Cairo: Institut français d'archéologie orientale 1979, 287 - 316.

Garcin, Jean-Claude, "Les soufis dans la ville mamelouke d'Égypt. Historie du soufisme et historie globale," in: McGregor, Sabra, *Le développement*, pp. 11 - 40.

Garcin, Jean-Claude, *Espaces, pouvoirs, et ideologies de l'Egypte medieval*, London: Variorum Reprints 1987.

Garcin, Jean-Claude, *Un centre musulman de Haute Egypte médiévale: Qūṣ*, Cairo: Institut français d'archéologie orientale du Caire 1976.

Geoffroy, Éric (ed.), *Une voie soufi dans le monde: la Shādhiliyya*, Paris: Maisonneuve and Larose 2005.

Geoffroy, Éric, "Entre ésotérisme et exotérisme, les Shādhilis, passeurs de sens (Égypte-xiii-xv siècles)," in: idem, Une voie, pp. 117 - 129.

Geoffroy, Éric, "Hagiograpie et typologie spirituelle," in: *Saints orientaux*, ed. Denise Aigle, Paris: De Boccard 1995, pp. 83 - 98.

Geoffroy, Éric, "L'élection divine de Muhammad et ʿAli Wafā (VIIIe/XIVe s.) ou comment la branche wafāʾī s'est détachée de l'arbre *šādilī*," in: *Le Saint et son milieu*, ed. Rachida Chih and Denis Gril, Cairo: Institut français d'archéologie orientale 2000, pp. 51 - 60.

Geoffroy, Éric, "Les Mystiques musulmans face au miracle," in: *Miracle et karāma*, ed. Denise Aigle, Turnhout 2000, pp. 301 - 316.

Geoffroy, Éric, "Une grande figure de saint *ummī:* le cheikh ʿAlī al-Khawwās (m. 939/1532)," in: McGregor, Sabra, *Le développement*, pp. 169 - 76

Geoffroy, Éric, *Le Soufism en Égypte et en Syria*, Damascus: L'Institut français d'études arabes de Damas 1995.

Al-Ghunaymī al-Taftazānī, Abū l-Wafā', *Ibn 'Aṭā' Allāh al-Sakandarī wa-Taṣawwufuhu*, Cairo: Maktaba al-Anjlū al-Miṣrīyah 1969.

Goitein, Shelomo Dov, "A Jewish Addict to Sufism in the Time of the Nagid David II Maimonides," *Jewish Quarterly Review*, (n.s.) 44/1 (1953), pp. 37–49.

Goldziher, Ignaz, "The Cult of the Saints in Islam," *The Muslim World* 1 (1911), pp. 302–312.

Gramlich, Richard, *Die Wunder der Freunde Gottes*, Wiesbaden: Steiner Verlag 1987.

Gril, Denis, "L'enseignement d'Ibn 'Atā' Allāh al-Iskandarī d'après le témignage de son disciple Rāfi' Ibn Shāfi'," in: Geoffroy, *Une voie*, pp. 93–106.

Gril, Denis, "Le miracle en islam, criere de la saintete?" in: *Saints orientaux*, ed. Denise Aigle, Paris: De Boccard 1995, pp. 69–81.

Gril, Denis, "Le soufisme en Égypte au début de l'époque mamelouke d'après le *Waḥīd fī sulūk ahl al-tawḥīd* de 'Abd al-Ġaffār Ibn Nūh al-Qūṣī (m. 708/1308)," in: McGregor, Sabra, *Le développement*, pp. 51–74.

Gril, Denis, "Saint des villes et saint des champs: étude comparée de deux vies de saints d'époque mamelouke," in: *Le Saint et son milieu*, ed. Rachida Chih and Denis Gril, Cairo: Institut français d'archéologie orientale 2000, pp. 61–82.

Gril, Denis, "Une source inédite pour l'histoire du *taṣawwuf* en Égypte au VIIe/XIIe siècle," *Livre du Centenaire de l'IFAO: 1880–1980*, Cairo: Institut français d'archéologie orientale 1980, pp. 441–58.

Gril, Denis, *La Risāla de Ṣafi al-Dīn Ibn Abi al-Manṣūr Ibn Ẓāfir*, Cairo: Institut français d'archéologie orientale 1986.

Hallenberg, Helena, "The Sultan Who Loved Sufis: How Qaytbay Endowed a Shrine Complex in Dasūq," *Mamlūk Studies Review* 4 (2000), pp. 147–66.

Hallenberg, Helena, "The Theme of Light and Illumination in Stories Concerning Ibrāhīm al-Dasūqī," in: *The Middle East – Unity and Diversity, Second Nordic Conference on Middle Eastern Studies*, eds. Heikki Palva and Knut S. Vikør, Copenhagen: Nordic Institute of Asian Studies 1993, pp. 115–122.

Hallenberg, Helena, *Ibrāhīm al-Dasūqī (1255–1296): A Saint Invented*, Helsinki: Academia Scientiarum Fennica 2005.

Ḥaydar, 'Alī, *Madkhal ilā Dirāsat al-Taṣawwuf: al-Shi'r al-Ṣūfī fī al-Qarn al-Sābi' al-Hijrī wa-l-'Aṣr al-Mamlūkī al-Awwal wa-l-'Aṣr al-'Uthmānī*, Damascus: Dār al-Shumūs li-l-Dirāsāt wa-l-Nashr 1999.

Holt, Peter Malcolm, "An Early Source on Shaykh Khaḍir al-Mihrānī," *Bulletin of the School of Oriental and African Studies* 46 (1983), pp. 33–49.

Homerin,Th. Emil, "Review: Al-'Allāwī, Fāris Aḥmad, *'Ā'isha al-Ba'ūnīyah al-Dimashqīyah*, Damascus: Dār Mu'add li-l-Ṭibā'a wa-l-Nashr wa-l-Tawzī' 1994," *Mamlūk Studies Review* 6 (2002), pp. 191–93.

Homerin, Th. Emil, "'Ā'isha al-Bā'ūniyya," in: *Essays in Arabic Literary Biography: 1350–1850*, ed. J.E. Lowry and D.J. Stewart, Wiesbaden: Harrassowitz Verlag 2009, pp. 21–27.

Homerin, Th. Emil, "Arabic Religious Poetry: 1200–1800," in: *The Cambridge History of Arabic Literature: The Post-Classical Period*, ed. Roger Allen and Donald Sidney Richards, Cambridge: Cambridge University Press 2006, pp. 74–86.

Homerin, Th. Emil, "Ibn Taymīyah's *al-Ṣūfīyah wa-l-fuqarā'*," *Arabica* 32 (1985), pp. 219–44.

Homerin, Th. Emil, "Saving Muslim Souls: the *Khānqāh* and the Sufi Duty in Mamluk Lands," *Mamlūk Studies Review* 3 (1999), pp. 59 – 83.

Homerin, Th. Emil, "The Domed Shrine of Ibn al-Fāriḍ," *Annales islamologiques* 25 (1991): pp. 133 – 138.

Homerin, Th. Emil, "The Study of Islam within Mamluk Domains," *Mamlūk Studies Review* 5/2 (2005), 1 – 30.

Homerin, Th. Emil, "'Umar ibn al-Fāriḍ, a Saint of Mamluk and Ottoman Egypt," in: *Manifestations of Sainthood in Islam*, ed. Grace Smith and Carl W. Ernst, Istanbul: Isis Press 1993, pp. 85 – 94.

Homerin, Th. Emil, "Writing Sufi Biography: The Case of 'Ā'isha al-Bā'ūniyya (d. 922/1517)," *Muslim World* 96/3 (2006), pp. 389 – 99.

Homerin, Th. Emil, *Emanations of Grace: The Mystical Verse of 'Ā'isha al-Bā'ūniyya*, Louisville, KY: Fons Vitae 2011.

Homerin, Th. Emil, *From Arab Poet to Muslim Saint*, 2nd ed., Cairo: American University in Cairo Press 2001.

Homerin, Th. Emil, *The Wine of Love & Life: Ibn al-Fāriḍ's al-Khamrīyah and al-Qayṣarī's Quest for Meaning*, edited Arabic text with an analytical English introduction and translation, Chicago: Middle East Documentation Center 2005.

Homerin, Th. Emil: "Living Love: The Mystical Writings of 'Ā'isha al-Bā'ūniyya," *Mamlūk Studies Review* 7/1 (2003), pp. 211 – 34.

Homerin, Th. Emil: "Sufis & Their Detractors in Mamluk Egypt: A Survey of Protagonists and Institutional Settings," in: *Islamic Mysticism Contested*, ed. Frederick De Jong and Bernd Radtke Leiden: E.J. Brill 1999, pp. 225 – 47.

Ḥusayn, 'Alī Ṣāfī, *al-Adab al-Ṣūfī fī Miṣr fī al-Qarn al-Sābi' al-Hijrī*, Cairo: Dār al-Ma'ārif 1964.

Ḥusayn, Muḥammad Kāmil, "Bayna al-Tashayyu' wa-Adab al-Ṣūfīyah bi-Miṣr fī 'Aṣr al-Ayyūbīyīn wa-l-Mamālīk," *Majallat Kullīyat al-Ādāb, Jāmi'at al-Qāhirah* 16/2 (1954), pp. 45 – 72.

Ibrāhīm, Layla 'Alī, "The Zāwiya of Saiẖ Zain ad-Dīn Yūsuf in Cairo," *Mitteilungen des Deutschen Archäologischen Instituts, Abteilung Kairo* 34 (1978), pp. 79 – 110.

Al-Ibrashy, May, "Cairo's Qarafa as Described in the *Ziyara* Literature," in: McGregor, Sabra, *Le développement*, pp. 269 – 98.

Kaptein, Nicolaas Jan Gerrit, *Muhammad's Birthday Festival: Early History in the Central Muslim Lands and Development in the Muslim West until the 10th/16th Century*, Leiden: E.J. Brill, 1993.

Karamustafa, Ahmet, *God's Unruly Friends*, Salt Lake City: University of Utah Press 1994.

Knysh, Alexander, "'Orthodoxy' and 'Heresy' in Medieval Islam: An Essay in Reassessment," *Muslim World* 83 (1993), pp. 48 – 67.

Knysh, Alexander, *Ibn al-'Arabī in the Later Islamic Tradition*, Albany: State University of New York Press 1999.

Lapidus, Ira M., *Muslim Cities in the Later Middle Ages*, Cambridge: Cambridge University Press 1967.

El-Leithy, Tamer, "Sufis, Copts and the Politics of Piety: Moral Regulation in Fourteenth-Century Upper Egypt," in: McGregor, Sabra, *Le développement*, pp. 75 – 120.

Little, Donald P., "Religion under the Mamluks," *Muslim World* 73 (1983), pp. 165 – 81.

Little, Donald P., "The Nature of *Khānqāhs*, *Ribāṭs*, and *Zāwiyas* under the Mamlūks," in:

Islamic Studies Presented to Charles J. Adams, eds. Wael B. Hallaq and Donald P. Little, Leiden: E. J. Brill 1991, pp. 91 - 106.

Mackeen, A.M. Mohamed. "The Rise of al-Shādhilī (d. 565/1258)," *Journal of the American Oriental Society* 91/4 (1971), pp. 477 - 486.

Māhir, Su'ād, *Masājid Miṣr wa-Awliyā'uhā al-Ṣāliḥūn*, 5 vols., Cairo: al-Majlis al-A'lā li-l-Shu'ūn al-Islāmīyah 1971 - 1983.

Manṣūr, Aḥmad, *al-'Aqā'id al-Dīnyah fī Miṣr al-Mamlūkīyah bayn al-Islām wa-l-Taṣawwuf*, Cairo: al-Hay'ah al-Miṣrīyah al-'Āmmah li-l-Kitāb 2000.

Manṣūr, Aḥmad, *al-Taṣawwuf wa-l-Ḥayāt al-Dīnīyah fī Miṣr al-Mamlūkīyah*, Cairo: al-Maḥrūsah li-l-Nashr wa-l-Khidmah al-Ṣaḥafīyah wa-l-Ma'lūmāt 2002.

Massignon, Louis, "Documents sur certains waqfs des Lieux saints de l'Islam principalement sur le waqf Tamimi à Hébron et sur le waqf tlemcénien Abû Madyan à Jérusalem," *Revue des études islamiques*, vol. 19 (1951), pp. 73 - 120.

Mayeur-Jaouen, Catherin, "Maîtres, cheikhs et ancêtres: saints du Delta à l'époque mamelouke," in: McGregor, Sabra, *Le développement*, pp. 41 - 50.

Mayeur-Jaouen, Catherine, "Le Cheikh scrupuleux et l'emir genereux a travers les *Akhlāq matbūliyya* de Šaranī," in: *Le Saint et son milieu*, eds. Rachida Chih and Denis Gril, Cairo: Institut français d'archéologie orientale 2000, 83 - 115.

Mayeur-Jaouen, Catherine, "Les Compagnons de la Terrasse, un groupe de soufis ruraux dans l'Égypte mamelouke," in: *Saints orientaux*, ed. Denise Aigle, Paris: De Boccard 1995, pp. 169 - 80.

Mayeur-Jaouen, Catherine, "Miracles des saints musulmans et regne animal," in: *Miracle et karāma*, ed. Denise Aigle, Turnhout 2000, pp. 577 - 606.

Mayeur-Jaouen, Catherine, *al-Sayyid al-Badawī, un grand saint de l'islam égyptien*, Cairo: Institut français d'archéologie orientale 1994.

McGregor, Richard and Adam Sabra (eds.), *Le développement du soufisme en Égypte à l'époque mamlouke*, Cairo: Institut français d'archéologie orientale 2005.

McGregor, Richard J. A., "Being and Knowing According to an 8th/14th Century Cairene Mystic," *Annales Islamologiques* 36 (2002), pp. 177 - 196.

McGregor, Richard J. A., "New Sources for the Study of Sufism in Mamluk Egypt," *Bulletin of the School of Oriental and African Studies* 65 (2002), pp. 300 - 322.

McGregor, Richard J. A., "The Existential Dimension of the Spiritual Guide in the Thought of 'Alī Wafā' (d. 807/1404)," *Annales islamologique* 37 (2003), pp. 315 - 327.

McGregor, Richard J. A., *Sanctity and Mysticism in Medieval Egypt: The Wafā' Sufi Order and the Legacy of Ibn Arabi*, Albany: State University of New York Press 2004.

McGregor, Richard J. A.: "A Medieval Saint on Sainthood," *Studia Islamica* 95 (2002), pp. 95 - 108.

McGregor, Richard J.A., "The Concept of Sainthood According to Ibn Bāḫilā a Šādilī Shaykh of the 8th/14th Century," in: *Le Saint et son milieu*, eds. Rachida Chih and Denis Gril, Cairo: Institut français d'archéologie orientale 2000, pp. 33 - 50.

McGregor, Richard, "Akbarian Thought in a Branch of the Egyptian Shādhiliyya," in: Geoffroy, Une voie, pp. 107 - 115.

McGregor, Richard, "Conceptions of the Ultimate Saint in Mamluk Egypt," in: McGregor, Sabra, *Le développement*, pp. 177 - 188.

McGregor, Richard, "The Problem of Sufism," *Mamlūk Studies Review* 13/2 (2009), pp. 69 - 83.

Memon, Muhammad Umar, *Ibn Taymīyah's Struggle against Popular Religion*, The Hauge: Mouton 1976.

Meri, Josef W., "The Etiquette of Devotion in the Islamic Cult of the Saints," in: *The Cult of the Saints in Late Antiquity and the Early Middle Ages*, eds. J.D. Howard-Johnson and Paul Antony Howard, Oxford: Oxford University Press 1999.

Meri, Josef W., *The Cult of the Saints Among Muslims and Jews in Medieval Syria*, Oxford: Oxford University Press 2002.

Nwiya, Paul, *Ibn ʿAṭā' Allāh (m. 709/1309) et la naissance de la confrérie šāḏilite*, Beirut: Dar al-Mashriq 1972.

Nwiya, Paul, *Ibn Atâ Allah et la tarîqa shâdiliya*, Beirut 1986.

Ohtoshi, Tetsuya, "Tasawwuf as Reflected in the *Ziyāra* Books and the Cairo Cemeteries," in: McGregor, Sabra, *Le développement*, pp. 299 – 329.

Ohtoshi, Tetsuya, "The Manners, Customs, and Mentality of Pilgrims to the Egyptian City of the Dead: 1100 – 1500 A.D." *Orient: Report of the Society for Near Eastern Studies in Japan* 29 (1993), pp. 19 – 44.

Olesen, Niels Henrik, *Culte des saints et pelerinages chez Ibn Taymiyya*, Paris: P. Geuthner 1991.

Pahlitzsch, Johannes, "The Concern for Spiritual Salvation and *Memoria* in Islamic Public Endowments in Jerusalem (XII – XVI c.) as Compared to the Concepts of Christendom," in: *Egypt and Syria in the Fatimid, Ayyubid and Mamluk Eras III*, eds. Urbain Vermeien and Kristof D'Hulser, Leuven: Uitgeverij Peeters 2005, pp. 327 – 44.

Perlman, M., "Ibn Khaldūn on Sufism," *Biblioteca Orientalis* 17 (1960), 222 – 223.

Petry, Carl F., *The Civilian Elite of Cairo in the Later Middle Ages*, Princeton: Princeton University Press 1981.

(Petry, Carl,) "A Bibliography of Carl F. Petry's Publications," *Mamlūk Studies Review* 14 (2010).

Pouzet, Louis, "Ḫaḍir Ibn Abi Bakr al-Mihrānī, šayḫ du sultan mamelouk al-Malik aẓ-Ẓāhir Baibars," *Bulletin d'études orientales* 30 (1978), pp. 173 – 83.

Pouzet, Louis, "Prises de position autour du 'samâʿ' Orient musulman au VIIe/XIIIe siècle," *Studia Islamica* 57 (1983), pp. 119 – 134.

Pouzet, Louis, *Damas au VIIᵉ/XIIIᵉ siècle: vie et structures religieuses d'une metrople islamique*, Beirut: Dār al-Mashriq 1988.

Al-Qūnawī, Abū l-Faḍl Muḥammad b. ʿAbd Allāh, *al-Ṣūfiyyah al-Qalandariyah: Tārīkhuhā wa-Fatwā Shaykh al-Islām Ibn Taymiyah fīhā*, Beirut 2002.

Al-Rabābiʿa, Ḥasan Muḥammad, *ʿĀ'ishah al-Bāʿūniyyah: Shāʿirah*, Irbid/Jordan: Dār al-Hilāl li-l-Tarjama 1997.

Rachida, Rachida Chih, "Zâwiya, sâha et rawda: développement et rôle de quelques institutions soufies en Égypte," *Annales islamologiques* 31 (1997), pp. 49 – 60.

Rāghib, Yūsuf, "Al-Sayyida Nafisa, sa légende, son culte et son cimetiere," *Studia Islamica* 44 (1976), pp. 61 – 86.

Rāghib, Yūsuf, "Essai d'inventaire chronologiques des guides a l'usage des pèlerins du Caire," *Review des études islamiques* 41 (1973), pp. 259 – 80.

Rizq, ʿĀṣim Muḥammad, *Khānqāwāt al-Ṣūfiyah fī Miṣr*, 2 vols., Cairo: Maktabat Madbūlī, 1997.

Sabra, Adam, "Illiterate Sufis and Learned Artisans: The Circle of ʿAbd al-Wahhāb al-Shaʿrānī," in: McGregor, Sabra, *Le développement*, pp. 153 – 68.

Sanneh, Lamin, "Saints and Virtues in African Islam," in: *Saints and Virtues*, ed. John Stratton Hawley, Berkeley: University of California Press 1987, pp. 144 - 67

Schallenbergh, Gino, "Intoxication and Ecstasy: Sufi Terminology in the Work of Ibn al-Qayyim al-Ǧawzīya," in: *Egypt and Syria in the Fatimid, Ayyubid and Mamluk Eras IV*, eds. Urbain Vermeien and Kristof D'Hulser, Leuven: Uitgeverij Peeters 2005, pp. 459 - 74.

Schallenbergh, Gino, "The Invocation of God (*dhikr*) and Audition (*samā'*) in the Spirituality of Ibn Qayyim al-Jawziyya (d. 751/1350)", in: *Egypt and Syria in the Fatimid, Ayyubid and Mamluk Eras IV*, eds. Urbain Vermeien and Kristof D'Hulser, Leuven: Uitgeverij Peeters 2010, pp. 355 - 68.

Schimmel, Annemarie, "Kalif und Ḳādī im spätmittelarterlichen Ägypten," *Die Welt des Islam* 24 (1942), pp. 1 - 128.

Schimmel, Annemarie, "Some Glimpses of the Religious Life in Egypt during the Later Mamluk Period," *Islamic Studies* 4 (1965), pp. 353 - 92.

Schimmel, Annemarie, "Sufismus und Heiligenverehrung im spätmittelarterlichen Ägypten," in: *Festscrift für W. Caskel*, ed. Erich Graf, Leiden: E.J. Brill 1968, pp. 274 - 89.

Shoshan, Boaz, "Popular Sufi Sermons in Late Mamluk Egypt," in: *Mamluks and Ottomans: Studies in Honour of Michael Winter*, eds. David Wasserstein and Ami Ayalon, London and New York: Routledge 2006, pp. 106 - 113.

Shoshan, Boaz: *Popular Culture in Medieval Cairo*, Cambridge: Cambridge University Press 1993.

Smith, Grace Martin and Carl W. Ernst (eds.): *Manifestations of Sainthood in Islam*, Istanbul: Isis Press 1993.

Sperl, Stefan: "Qasida 50", in: *Qasida Poetry in Islamic Asia and Africa*, eds. Stefan Sperl and Chistopher Shackle, 2 vols., Leiden: E.J. Brill 1996, vol. 2, pp. 388 - 411.

Stetkevych, Suzanne P., *The Mantle Odes*, Bloomington: University of Indiana Press 2010.

Surūr, Ṭāhā 'Abd al-Bāqī, *al-Taṣawwuf al-Islāmī wa-l-Imām al-Sha'rānī*, Cairo: Maktabat Nahḍat Miṣr wa-Maṭba'atuhā 1952.

Taylor, Christopher S., *In the Vicinity of the Righteous*, Leiden: E.J. Brill 1999.

Thorau, Peter, *The Lion of Egypt*, trans. Peter Malcolm Holt, London: Longman Group 1992.

Williams, John Alden: "The Khānqāh of Siryāqūs: A Mamluk Royal Religious Foundation," in: *In Quest of an Islamic Humanism*, ed. Arnold H. Green, Cairo: American University Press 1984, pp. 111 - 114.

Ziedan, Youssef, "The Legacy of the Shādhiliyya in Alexandria: Buildings and Manuscripts," in: Geoffroy, *Une voie*, pp. 63 - 71.

Carine Juvin

Mamluk Inscriptions

Epigraphy is certainly one of the most remarkable features of the Mamluk period. Inscriptions on monuments and objects participate in the unprecedented amount of written documents produced under the rule of this sultanate. Inscriptions covered the thousands of monuments that were built or restored in Cairo and all over the Mamluk territory, while calligraphy was often preferred to figural decoration on the objects. Monumentality was favored for scripts in the same way it was for architecture. One recent researcher – Vlad Atanasiu – rightly spoke about "Hypercalligraphy" or "calligraphic phenomenon" for the Mamluk period.[1]

This rich material is an important part of the memory of the Mamluk sultanate. In the first chapter of her book *Cairo of the Mamluks*, Doris Behrens-Abuseif[2] links historiography and architecture, both being intended as memorials. She quoted al-Sakhāwī who considered that reading about the life of a Muslim was like visiting him. One should also remember of the Meccan historian al-Fāsī (1379–1429?) who used inscriptions (on monuments and especially tombstones) as sources for his biographical entries. Monumental inscriptions embody ideally this link between monument and memory. They provide the name of the founder, his titles and function, a date, and the purpose of the monument, though many scholars are puzzled at some inscriptions on buildings stipulating a function which differs from the one stipulated in the *waqfīyah!*[3] Monumental inscriptions also testify to the piety of the founder and to his social status, occasionally to his literary taste, or commemorate a special historical event.[4]

1 Atanasiu, *Hypercalligraphie.*

2 Behrens-Abuseif, *Cairo*, 7.

3 One example is the mosque of Qaytbay in the northern cemetery (1472–74), a *madrasah* according to epigraphy but a *jāmiʿ* according to the *waqfīyah.*

4 An example is the inscription on the Cistern of Yaʿqūb Shāh al-Mihmāndār in Cairo, near the Citadel, dated 901/1495–96, commemorating a victory over the Ottomans: van Berchem, *CIA*, *Egypte*, 3: 547–554, n° 364. See also Rogers, *Inscription*, 737–38.

As such, inscriptions are important documents for historians as well as art historians, from a diachronic point of view – as far as they provide dates – but also from a social, political, cultural or aesthetic point of view. This material – together with data from early and medieval Islamic periods – has held the attention of scholars since the nineteenth century. It started to be methodically and extensively published by the founder of Arabic epigraphy, Max van Berchem, with the first volume of the *Matériaux pour un Corpus Inscriptionum Arabicarum (CIA)*, issued in 1894.[5] Additional volumes of the *CIA* and other important publications appeared during the course of the previous century by M. Sobernheim, E. Herzfeld, L.A. Mayer, G. Wiet, Heinz Gaube and others.[6] One should also mention the works in Arabic by ʿAlī Pāshā Mubārak,[7] Ḥasan ʿAbd al-Wahhāb[8] or Muḥammad A. Talas.[9]

Continuing the collection planned by Max van Berchem, the *Répertoire chronologique d'épigraphie arabe (RCEA)* tried throughout the decades to gather in chronological order all these scattered documents. Then, supervised by Ludvik Kalus and sponsored by the Max van Berchem foundation, this became the *Thesaurus d'épigraphie islamique*, regularly enriched, and now available on the web. Unfortunately, as a result of the enormous task and the reduced team involved in the project, mainly with regards to the inscriptions on objects, it is not up-to-date.[10] More recently new epigraphic data projects focusing on one geographical area have been undertaken in order to supplement these earlier data:

- the AUC project, under direction of Bernard O'Kane, named *Documentation of the Inscriptions in the Historic Zone of Cairo*,[11] has recorded with pictures every inscription on every monument up to 1800, including religious inscriptions that may have been neglected by the CIA.[12] Its publication – in DVD format or on the web – is still pending, but it is already at the disposal of researchers' queries.

5 Van Berchem, *CIA*, *Egypt*, vol. 1 – 3.

6 Sobernheim, *CIA*, *Syrie du Nord*; Herzfeld, *CIA*, *Syrie du Nord*, vol. 1 – 2; van Berchem, *CIA*, *Syrie du Sud*, vol. 1 – 3; Wiet, *Matériaux*. El-Hawary et al., *CIA*, *Arabie*; Mayer, *Saracenic Heraldry*; Gaube, *Inschriften*.

7 Mubārak, *Al-Khiṭāṭ*.

8 ʿAbd al-Wahhāb, *Tārīkh*.

9 Talas, *al-Athār* and *Mosquées*.

10 Besides, for the moment, the online data base does not include Arabic inscriptions from Syria and Iran, which were recorded in the *RCEA*. Inscriptions from Iran are of some interest for Mamluk studies, offering comparisons with the Ilkhanids and other mongol/turcoman dynasties.

11 Sponsored by he Egyptian Antiquities Program of the American Reasearch center in Egypt (ARCE) and AUC.

12 Van Berchem, *CIA*, *Egypte*, 1:11 indicates that especially for the end of the sultanate, not all quranic quotations were read or verified, particularly those on domes and minarets.

- an additional *Corpus Inscriptionum Arabicarum Palaestinae* has been undertaken by Moshe Sharon, a former disciple of Gaston Wiet from the late 1960's. It surveys the whole western Palestine (to the Jordan) and the north Sinaï, thus completing the CIA, which only dealt with Jerusalem. The first volume was issued in 1997. Five volumes have been published since then, including photographs.
- More recently, a program surveying medieval inscriptions in Damascus was in progress, carried out by Jean-Michel Mouton (Ecole Pratique des Hautes Etudes, Paris). And finally, since the 1980's, various publications on Mamluk architecture provided more information and photographic data, as well as general remarks on epigraphy.[13]

Here are the major works concerning the registration and publication of the inscriptions, textually or "photographically", which is of course the basis of any research. As already noted, the situation for the inscribed objects is even more fragmentary, and the researcher has to rely on many catalogues of collections, sale catalogues and articles. Nevertheless the different volumes of the *Catalogue général du Musée Arabe du Caire*[14] remain an important and valuable introduction to the world of Mamluk inscribed objects.

Let us now consider the use made of all this data. The monumental works of the *Corpus Inscriptionum Arabicarum* (*CIA*) or the *Catalogue général du Musée Arabe du Caire* provide us with far more than texts of inscriptions. Their erudite comments, listings and indexes constituted a solid ground for later scholar studies. Van Berchem in his introduction to the first volume of *CIA*, *Egypte*,[15] considered that the interest of epigraphy resides in three aspects: paleography (we will briefly return to this point), philology – this is a subject (language, level of language, faulty language, vocabulary) that would certainly need to be undertaken – and, last but most importantly, history (Van Berchem omitted there the importance of religious content). He also underlined their repetitive nature, reflecting endlessly two major concepts: divine mightiness and political absolute power. It should be pointed out, however, that inscriptions reflect only the concerns of the ruling class: sultans, amirs and to a lesser extent civilian elites, and they hardly provide comprehensive documents for a social history. Nevertheless, they still could be scrutinized with closer attention.

More recently, Mamluk inscriptions in themselves have not really been the

13 Salam-Liebich, *Architecture*; Burgoyne, *Mamluk Jerusalem*; Sadek, *Mamlukische Architektur*; and even more recently Behrens-Abuseif, *Cairo*; Idem, *Minarets*. One should also add two publications focused on inscriptions: al-Shihābī, *Inscriptions*, and Bizri, *Calligraphy*.

14 Wiet, *Catalogue* (*Objets en cuivre*); Idem, *Catalogue* (*Lampes*); David-Weill, *Catalogue* (*bois*); Wiet, *Catalogue* (*Inscriptions*).

15 Van Berchem, *CIA*, *Egypte*, 1:III – V.

subject of many specific studies.[16] A few inscriptions and their historical meaning have been studied in short articles by art historians like Oleg Grabar who wrote about the Quranic inscriptions in Qaytbay's funerary complex in the Northern Cemetery in Cairo,[17] or by historians like Reuven Amitai and Denise Aigle on some inscriptions of Baybars in the Bilād al-Shām.[18] Finally how have inscriptions been used recently by researchers in the Mamluk field? I will just mention two examples amongst recent works, the subject of which could induce the further use of inscriptions as sources/documents.

First, the book by Adam Sabra, *Poverty and Charity in Medieval Islam: Mamluk Egypt:*[19] considering the charitable institutions founded by sultans or high officials, one would expect to find there some epigraphic references. Only one mention is made of an inscription[20] in a *zāwiyah* founded in 781/1379 for a Sufi shaykh, who received the *laqab* of *khādim al-fuqarā' wa-l-masākīn*. Strangely enough, Sabra does not compare it to similar titles (*kahf/kanz/abū al-fuqarā' wa-l-masākīn*) used for sultans or amirs and found in many inscriptions.[21] Nor is there any mention of these titles in the first two chapters devoted to theories of poverty in medieval Islamic Middle east. No thoughts are put forward about the existence, context and meaning of these titles on monuments.

Another example is the remarkable book by Anne Broadbridge, *Kingship and Ideology in the Islamic and Mongol Worlds.*[22] Kingship and ideology are amongst the issues that can also be addressed through the titles (*alqāb*) of sultans, widely spread on inscriptions on both monuments and objects. In her introduction, Anne Broadbridge makes the following preliminary remark after having delineated her investigation as focusing on expressions of kingship and sovereignty not towards an internal audience but toward other sovereigns:

> "This study also relies in part on coins, inscriptions and to a much lesser degree, deeds for pious endowments… Although these items often expressed rulers' ideas of kingship, they tended to address the internal audiences of subjects, not the external audiences of other rulers."[23]

16 With the exception of the publication on Tripoli's mamluk inscriptions: Bizri, *Calligraphy.*

17 Grabar, *Inscriptions*, 465–68. Reprinted in: Grabar, *Culture*, 2:271–275.

18 Amitai, *Remarks*, 45–53; Aigle, *Inscriptions*, 96:87–115.

19 Sabra, *Poverty.*

20 Ibid., 28–29, note 133 and 134

21 Van Berchem, *CIA*, *Egypte*, 1: n° 26; 2: n°205, 218, 251, 278, 297, 301, 305, 325, 329, 344, 374; *RCEA* n° 4895, 5801, 5839, 5945, 5995, 764 004, 781 001, 788 040, 788 042, 800 008.

22 Broadbridge, *Kingship.*

23 Broadbridge, *Kingship*, 4.

This consideration can be discussed as follows: if monumental inscriptions were an internal "public projection of power,"[24] one wonders if this was the only addressed audience of the inscriptions on monuments and prestigious objects. Many foreign travelers, merchants and dwellers were found in Cairo or in other cities like Damascus; there were annual arrivals of embassies in the capital, which were sometimes the occasion of official visits to some monuments or districts of the city and also the occasion of exchange of gifts, amongst which certainly figured inscribed objects. So did they address only an internal audience? Then, the author explains that her study "mentions those sources when they add to an overall understanding of the ideologies." Finally, it appears that only very general references to inscriptions are found in footnotes,[25] relating back to number references in the RCEA, without any precise remark on them except in only one case.[26]

Mamluk *alqāb* have been comprehensively studied by Van Berchem in the *CIA* on Egypt, and then by Hasan al-Basha,[27] using both textual sources and epigraphy. Still, a closer examination of inscriptions could provide additional evidence for the use of titles and for the precise issue of ideologies of kingship. One such inscription may be that on an exceptional object that was kept for a long time in a private collection and reappeared in 1998 on the Art market. It was then purchased by the Doha Museum of Islamic Art. This is a huge metal tray measuring more than one meter in diameter with a weight of no less than 17 kg[28] (fig. 1[29]). It is the largest Mamluk metal tray known until now, with a highly refined decoration, perhaps originally highlighted with silver inlays, which makes it a particularly costly and meaningful work of art. Of note, metalwork inlaid with silver and gold was highly prized by the Mamluk sultans and their amirs, and was extensively inscribed with their long titles. As Metzada Gelber, from the Tel Aviv University, has already commented in an article on metal objects:

> "Metalwork was more central to the lives of Muslims in the Middle Ages than our modern western eyes are accustomed to seeing [...] a tool in the hands of ambitious rulers [...] Thus, these should not be perceived as merely ornamented objects, but

24 Frenkel, *Projection*, especially 44–45.

25 Broadbridge, *Kingship*, 31 note 16, 38 note 56, 148 note 46, 166, note 132, 171 note 12, 188 note 106.

26 A *laqab* of sultan Khalil is briefly discussed, Broadbridge, *Kingship*, 45 note 87.

27 Al-Bāshā, *al-alqāb*.

28 Inv. no. MW.35.1998. The diameter is 108.6 cm precisely. Allan, *Metalwork Treasures*, 90–95, n°29.

29 I would like to thank Dr Aisha al-Khater, Director of the Doha Museum of Islamic Art, who graciously allowed me to reproduce images of this tray, as well as Michelle Walton and Marc Pelletreau.

> rather as a major document attesting to medieval Islamic culture, illuminating the events of the period and reflecting the society that produced them."[30]

This tray can be used as a case study showing how historians too often dismiss inscribed objects and how art historians sometimes focus their study on stylistic or iconographic questions, failing to give a deeper insight into the meaning of inscriptions. It bears the titles of the sultan al-Malik al-Nāṣir Muḥammad b. Qalāwūn, displayed and repeated on different parts of the surface: medallions with spectacular radiating script, rectangular cartouches in alternatively kufic and thuluth script, and a discontinuous inscribed band along the diameter of the tray. This last element, owing to its length, is of special interest. It contains the longest titulature known for this sultan, even compared to preserved monumental inscriptions. The inscriptions of the tray were read one century ago first by Sobernheim,[31] then included in the *RCEA*,[32] and again published by James W. Allan in a book dedicated to the collection of metalwork in the Doha Museum.[33] Allan focused on the decoration, insisting on the abundance of delicately designed phoenixes and lotuses, these *chinoiseries* motives being considered as a mongol influence through the circulation of textiles and other artefacts (fig. 2). He emphasizes the idea of kingship conveyed by these motifs in the Mongol world, but he does not try to link them with the inscription, the content of which he doesn't comment upon at all. The external circular band gives the longest list of titles, as follows:

> "'izzun li-mawlānā l-sulṭāni l-maliki l-nāṣiri l-'ālimi [al-'āmili?] l-'ādili [al-ghāzī?] l-mujāhidi l-murābiṭi l-muthāghiri l-mu'ayyadi l-manṣūri sulṭāni l-islāmi wa-l-muslimīna muḥyī l-'adli fī l-'ālamīna munṣifi l-maẓlūmīna min-a l-ẓālimīna qātili l-kafarati wa-l-mushrikīna mubīdi l-ṭughāti wa-l-mutamarridīna ḥāmī ḥawzati l-dīni sulṭāni l-'arabi wa-l-'ajami awḥādi mulūki al-zamāni māliki riqābi l-umami sulṭāni l-shāmi wa-l-'irāqi wa-l-yamani khādimi l-ḥaramayni l-sharīfayni nāṣiri l-'isābati l-muḥammadīyati munshī'i l-dawlati l-'abbāssīyati nāṣiri l-dunyā wa-l-dīni muḥammadi bni l-maliki l-manṣūri qalāwūn."[34]

30 Gelber, *Reflections*, 72.

31 Sobernheim, *Gefässinschriften*, 179.

32 *RCEA*, n°5855

33 Allan, *Metalwork Treasures*, 90–95 n°29. This object was also previously mentioned or published in Migeon et al., *Exposition*, 34, n°194 bis; Migeon, *Manuel*, 2:205; Wiet, *Catalogue (Objets en cuivre)*, 27 n°24 and 204 n°197 and in the sale catalogue Drouot, *Paris 1998*, n°6

34 "Glory to our lord the sultan, the victorious king, the learned, the just, (the conqueror), the holy warrior, the defender, the protector of frontiers, the one fortified by God, the victorious, sultan of Islam and the Muslims, reviver of justice in the worlds, righting the oppressed against the oppressors, slayer of infidels and polytheists, annihilator of the oppressors and rebels, protector of the domain of religion, sultan of Arabs and non-Arabs, first of the kings of the earth, controller of the destinies of nations, sultan of Syria (Bilād al-Shām) and Iraq and Yemen, servant of the two noble holy sanctuaries, giving victory to the people (clan) of

Comparisons with the other known objects bearing inscriptions in the name of Muḥammad b. Qalāwūn,[35] or the remaining monumental inscriptions[36] reveal the special character of this one: most of the inscriptions on objects are reduced to a few common *alqāb* which are at the beginning of the inscription. Then follow usual titles related to the religious ideas of jihad, the fight against the infidels (Franks or Mongols), in correlation with the guardianship of the *ummah*, hence the association with the Abbasid caliph, and the insistence on their guardianship of the Hejaz holy cities. Two titles refer to the idea of justice and a fair ruler. Other titles deal with the idea of prior sovereignty amongst other rulers. On the Doha tray the list is quite exhaustive, almost redundant. Actually all of these titles can be found in other inscriptions of previous Mamluk sultans, or even earlier, but such a long list of titles is unique in the case of Muḥammad b. Qalāwūn and rare in earlier occurrences. One can question the reasons why and how these long and infatuated titles were chosen in one precise place and time, especially as far as claims for territories inside or outside the Mamluk sultanate are concerned. On the Doha tray, Muḥammad b. Qalāwūn is proclaimed "*sulṭān al-shām wa-l-ʿirāq wa-l-yaman.*"[37] Very few inscriptions contain such territorial claims exceeding the frontiers of actual Mamluk sovereignty: they are found earlier in only two inscriptions in the name of the sultans Qalāwūn and Khalīl.[38] Another even earlier example is a late Ayyubid inscription in the citadel of Busra, in the name of al-Ṣāliḥ Najm al-Dīn Ayyūb, dated 647/1249, in which he is proclaimed *malik al-hind wa-l-sind wa-l-yaman.*[39]

The claim for sovereignty over the Yemen is a rather common move, the Rasulids being the usual rivals notably in the Holy cities of the Hejaz. But the mention of *malik al-ʿirāq* on the Doha tray is particularly interesting. This is the only known occurrence of such a claim, with one exception: that on the large *tiraz* band on the façade of the Qalāwūn's *qubbah-madrasah* in Bayn al-Qasrayn, where al-Nāṣir Muḥammad's father is called "*sulṭān al-ʿirāqayn wa-l-miṣrayn.*" It was built in 683–685H/1284–85, at a time when Mamluk-Mongol relations

Muhammad, secretary of the abbasid state, the victorious of the world and religion, Muhammad son of the victorious king Qalāwūn"

35 For a list of these objects, see Wiet, *Catalogue (objets en cuivre)*, 27 and Ward, *Brass*.

36 *RCEA* n° 5059, 5061, 5079, 5100, 5111, 5135, 5146, 5147, 5160, 5161, 5162, 5166, 5213, 5266, 5267, 5318, 5319, 5320, 5344, 5365, 5386, 5398, 5401, 5427, 5450, 5559, 5587, 5654, 5821, 5925, 5932, 5933.

37 There is another inscription in the name of Muḥammad b. Qalāwūn on a tray sold at Sotheby's, *London 1985*, n° 109, which was not included in the list by Rachel Ward. The picture in the sale catalogue does not allow to verify the reading of the inscription published in the caption, this reading being incomplete. It contains a long list of *alqāb*, amongst which are: "*sulṭān al-ʿarab wa-l-ʿajam wa-l-turk wa-l-daylām ṣāḥib al-diyār al-miṣr wa-l-bilād [al-shām] wa-l-qilāʿ [al-ṣāhilīyah wa-l-diyār [bakir]...*"

38 *RCEA* n° 4852 and 4895.

39 *RCEA* n° 4308.

were quite conflictual and the Ilkhanids weren't yet converted to Islam. The claim for sovereignty over Iraq, the land of the Abbasid caliphate, was regarded as a duty and a challenge to Ilkhanid legitimacy.[40]

Ghazan's conversion to Islam and, moreover, the peace established in 1323 brought to a turning point the relationship between the two sultanates. Sovereignty over Iraqi territories was no longer debated. For instance, Fakhrī in his *Tārīkh Salāṭīn al-Mamālīk*, gives, for the year 701H/1301 – 1302, a list of the then ruling kings in which Muḥammad is defined as "*sulṭān al-diyār al-miṣrīya wa-l-shāmīya*" while the Ilkhanid Ghazan is mentioned as "*ṣāḥib al-ʿajam wa-l-ʿirāq wa-l-rūm wa-l-diyārbakir.*"[41] In addition, contemporary Mamluk historical sources usually mention Abū Saʿīd as "*malik al-ʿirāq*" or "*malik al-ʿirāqayn wa-khurāsān*" next to "*malik al-ṭaṭar.*"[42]

The international context changed at the end of Muḥammad b. Qalāwūn's reign. This is a carefully studied period in Anne Broadbridge's book.[43] After Abū Saʿīd's death in 736H/1335, a struggle ensued over the establishment of a new sovereign in Iraq and Iran, which led a search for Muḥammad's military support or recognition. According to Shams al-Dīn al-Shujāʿī in his *Tā'rīkh al-malik al-nāṣir muḥammad*, in the year 741H/1341, Shaykh Ḥasan and Ḥajjī-Taghay, rulers of Baghdad and Diyarbekir, asked for an army with which to conquer Iraq in Muḥammad's name, in return for the promises of coins minted and sermons delivered in his name, and ruling over Baghdad as Muḥammad's governors. The coins were presented officially a few months later, just before Muḥammad died.[44] Then, as established Anne Broadbridge, the Mamluk chancery developed an ideology of kingship, the seniority in rule, centered on two concepts: senior sovereign / patron of other kings and supreme guardian of Islam.[45]

The Doha tray – although it is not dated – appears to be a fascinating illustration of this particular context: its lengthy inscription enumerates all the titles associated with the idea of seniority in rule. Actually, this insistence on the superiority of one prince or king, and his *primus inter pares* quality was not new, it was indeed a kind of usual 'routine' in the practice of the Chanceries. Here, it is particularly emphasized. Moreover, it contains a claim for sovereignty over Iraq which could only take place after the death of the last great Ilkhanid Abū Saʿīd.[46]

40 On this matter see Broadbridge, *Kingship*, chapters 2 and 3.

41 Al-Fakhrī, *Tārīkh*, 96.

42 Al-Nuwayrī, *Nihāyat*, 33:22, 41, 199, 231; al-Fakhrī, *Tārīkh*, 172, 175, 191.

43 Broadbridge, *Kingship*, 138 – 145.

44 Al-Shujāʿī, *Tārīkh*, 98 – 99; and Broadbridge, *Kingship*, 144 – 45.

45 Broadbridge, *Kingship*, 138.

46 It may also be interpreted as a filial reference to al-Nāṣir Muḥammad's father, Qalāwūn, taking over his claim over the Iraq, inscribed on the façade of Qalāwūn's madrasah, a place that al-Nāṣir Muḥammad restored and used for official ceremonies.

The use of Mongol kingship-connoted motives like the phoenixes, lotuses and peonies even reinforce metaphorically this appropriation. It is noteworthy that these sino-mongol motives show an unusually refined design, which does not appear on any other object related to Muḥammad b. Qalāwūn.[47]

It is also interesting to compare Muḥammad's titles on the tray with those of Abū Saʿīd inscribed on an equally huge metalwork. This is the famous *Nisan tası*, preserved in Rumi's Mausoleum in Konya, the base and basin of which are in the name of the Ilkhanid sultan.[48] Little Ilkhanid metalwork has survived, this is the only one in the name of Abū Saʿīd together with one spherical incense-burner now in the Bargello Museum.[49] Its lengthy and large inscription has numerous common features with Muḥammad's titles on the Doha tray:

> "ʿizzun li-mawlānā l-sulṭāni l-aʿẓami māliki riqābi l-umami sulṭāni l-ʿarabi wa-l-ʿajami l-ʿālimi l-ʿādili fī l-ḥukmi ẓilli l-muslimīna muḥī l-ʿadli fī l-ʿālamīna qāmiʿi l-ṭughāti wa-l-mutamarridīna rukni l-islāmi wa-tāji l-anāmi ʿalā l-dunyā wa-l-dīni bahāduri khāni l-mu'ayyadi bi-l-ta'yyīdi l-sulṭāni l-aʿẓami abū saʿīdi l-muntasifī li-l-mazlūmīna min-a l-ẓālimīna wa-nāsiri l-millati wa-l-ḥaqqi [wa] al-dīni hāmī l-ghuzāti wa-l-mujāhidīna l-sulṭāni ʿalā l-dunyā wa-l-dīni khalada mulkuhu."

The use of Persian/Iranian titles by the Mamluks and, more largely, the connections between Mamluk and Ilkhanid (and other Iranian dynasties) titles is another interesting subject to be studied more carefully. Qalqashandī mentions some Iranian titles like *shāhinshāh, sulṭān al-ʿarab wa-l-ʿajam, Iskandar al-zaman* amongst Mamluk sultans' titles used in the Chancery.[50] On the other hand, he does not mention *mālik riqāb al-umam* though it is found in several Mamluk sultans' titles[51] and is a very common one for Persian rulers like the Ilkhanids or rulers of Fars.

The question of the specific choice and the arrangement of titles in inscriptions – especially monumental ones – would also require a closer examination. For instance, on the Doha tray, the sovereignty over Egypt (*ṣāḥib al-diyār al-miṣrīyah*) is omitted. Was it taken for granted in its special context? It seems

47 A direct Chinese influence is possible, see for instance a Chinese lacquer with similar motives reproduced in Kadoi, *Islamic Chinoiserie*, 55, fig. 2.12. For a comparison with similar phoenixes on an Iranian metalwork, see a basin in the V&A, London, inv. no. 546–1905, published in Melikian-Chirvani, *Islamic Metalwork*, 202–205.

48 It measures 95 cm in diameter. The lid was added later and bear the name of Shah Sultan, a muzaffarid governor of Shiraz since 755/1354, as identified by Melikian-Chirvani, *Islamic Metalwork*, 139, note 56. It was fully published by Baer, *Nisan Tası*,1–46 and Baer, *Turco-mongol*, 19–24.

49 Museo Nazionale del Bargello, inventory number: Depositi 6, published in: Wiet, *Catalogue (Objets en Cuivres)*, 197 n° 157, and Spallanzani, *Metalli*, 155, fig. 40.

50 Qalqashandī, *Ṣubḥ*, 6:126–128; about the use of Persian titles, see also al-Bāshā, *al-Alqāb*, 237, 275, 354, 362, 421.

51 van Berchem, *CIA*, *Egypte*, 2: n° 74–95 ; 3: n° 205–206–382–385–390.

difficult to define precise criteria. On another of Muḥammad b. Qalāwūn's metalwork, a smaller tray, *ṣāḥib al-diyār al-miṣrīyah* is mentioned,[52] while on some other monumental inscriptions, it can be also mentioned or omitted.[53]

In the case of the Doha tray, one wonders what was its destination and use? Was it only dedicated to an "internal audience" or was it deliberately used in a diplomatic context? Both from a stylistic and epigraphic point of view,[54] it can be plausibly ascribed to the very end of al-Nāṣir Muḥammad's reign, between 1335 and 1341, when no important building program was undertaken by the sultan in Cairo. Would this tray be the receptacle of a 'monumental' inscription, listing territory and an overall sovereignty claim? This very special object should all the same be considered as a relevant document for the end of Muḥammad's reign and could have been used for that purpose by Anne Broadbridge.

Speaking about destination and use of inscriptions leads to another question, that of their legibility either because of their high, remote location or their intricate script. This question has puzzled many researchers. Regarding quranic quotations on religious monuments, as Wheeler Thackston has already noted:

> "The Qur'an, in and on a mosque provides the viewer with a message and focus of meditation. It may incidentally be ornamental or decorative, but a Qur'anic inscription has value in and of itself"[55].

Thus, it does not need to be readable. Its mere presence is of a symbolic and immaterial nature. A comparable remark could be made about the decrees, often rapidly carved at the entrance of or inside a mosque.[56] Their often illegible script is particularly striking if compared to other inscriptions. On one hand, they were displayed at passers-by's eye level, which means: in order to be seen. On the other hand, wasn't it also the easiest way (and place) to carve them? Admitting that they were intended to be seen, were they also intended to be read? Or they may have been only material reminders – if necessary – of a decree that had been orally proclaimed. It may be also that the act of writing it on stone aimed at giving the appearance of a long-lasting efficiency which the decrees – often tax abrogation – actually rarely achieved.

Going back to the quranic quotations, the familiarity of Muslims with a minimal education in Arabic and with the quranic text allowed them to recite mentally a whole passage from only a few words. Moreover, as claimed by Irene

52 See note 37.

53 *RCEA* n° 4852 and 4895.

54 If compared to other metalworks like a smaller tray made for amir Kaybughā Дajjī, governor of Gaza between 1335 – 1336 and 1338 – 1339 (sold at Sotheby's, *London 1999*, n° 71) and two trays made for sultan Ismāʿīl (1342 – 1345), published in: Staacke, *Metalli*, 92 – 94, n° 11, and sale catalogue Paris 1908, n° 338.

55 Thackston, *Calligraphy*, 43 – 53.

56 For gathered published examples, see Sauvaget, *Décrets*, (a;b;c) and Wiet, *Décrets*, 128 – 143.

Bierman in her study on Fatimid inscriptions,[57] "the critical element is the range of expectation." It means that a few quranic quotations or even the sovereign's titles were expected to be found on some buildings and objects and could then be easily reconstituted. As Irene Bierman stated: "The context made the content expected."[58]

The content of religious inscriptions, slightly neglected one century ago, has gained new interest in the last decades. A database referencing quotations of quranic verses and religious inscriptions on monuments had been considered but was never created. A first attempt was carried out by Erica Dodds and Shereen Khairallah using the then published material (around 4000 inscriptions all around the Islamic world, including many Mamluk monuments).[59] One of their conclusions, which has been confirmed by the Documentation project of the AUC in Cairo,[60] is that there seems to be no precise rule for the choice of quranic verses used in monuments. Nevertheless, one wonders why should there be a precise rule? And, besides, the range of quranic verses used for a mosque entrance, a *miḥrāb*, a *minbar* or a mosque lamp is actually rather reduced if compared to the whole Qur'an. They are more often appropriate to the function of the building, or part of the building or piece of furniture. So that again, as Bierman said "The context made the content expected" and made the reading easier. Anyway, this remark on the absence of a rule, suggesting a deliberate epigraphic program opens the field to further research.

Inscriptions can also reflect the literary environment in Mamluk society. Examples have already been published, such as the quotations of the al-Ḥarīrī's *Maqāmāt* in the mausoleum of Sunqur al-Saʿdī in Cairo,[61] the pious poem in the *wikālah* of Qaytbay near al-Ḥākim,[62] or the use of al-Buṣīrī's *Burda* in the mausoleum of Qurqumas in the Northern cemetery.[63] Other occurrences exist on objects: anonymous poetic verses appear – in a repetitive way – on some metalwork, often difficult to date precisely. They have been published by J. Allan, S.

57 Bierman, *Writing Signs*, 24 – 27.

58 Ibid, 27.

59 Dodds, Khairallah, *Image*. On this topic, see also Thackson, *Calligraphy*; Hillenbrand, *Qur'anic*, 171 – 184; Gaube, *Grundriss*, for its chapter on epigraphy, with tables containing alphabetical list of Arabic phrases and a numerical list of quranic quotations.

60 As reported in Behrens-Abuseif, *Cairo*, 97, and idem, *Minarets*, 72 – 79.

61 First published in ʿAbd al-Raḥman, *Adab al-Maqāmāt*, 59 – 83 and again in Behrens-Abuseif, *Cairo*, 169.

62 Van Berchem, *CIA*, *Egypte*, 3: 494 – 495, n°325.

63 Behrens-Abuseif, *Cairo*, 311 and note 23. Al-Buṣīrī's *Burda* became increasingly popular in Egypt during the 15th century, as suggested by a number of luxurious manuscripts and architectural use also illustrated by an inscribed wooden ceiling in the Museum of Islamic Art in Cairo, inv. nr. 11686.

Melikian-Chirvani or more recently by D. Behrens-Abouseif.[64] More exceptionally, a poetic verse can be attributed to an author: this is the case on a unique Mamluk ceramic vase in the Louvre museum.[65]

Religious or poetic inscriptions are also commonly found on tombstones. Unfortunately, Mamluk tombstones from Egypt and the Bilad al-Sham seem rather rare if compared to those of earlier centuries.[66] It raises several questions: did a change occur in funerary practice? More plausibly, is it the result of the use of a more fragile material (limestone instead of marble in the case of Egypt)? Was there a discrimination in the preservation of these medieval tombstones, due to their lesser quality? Anyway, this funerary material from the Mamluk period – now enriched by the recent publications of Meccan tombstones[67] – still await an in-depth study, comparable to that of Diem and Schöller on earlier Arabic epitaphs,[68] which stops at the end of the 12th century.

I will conclude with the formal aspect of inscriptions that have received less attention from scholars. This question of course concerns the art historian initially. It covers their situation within space, their density, their distribution, their size, shape or style, if they are more or less legible, their ornaments, their relations with calligraphy in manuscripts or with theoretical writings on the art of script,[69] and their relation with other geographical areas. The question of the making of inscriptions (who thought them out, who designed them?) will most probably never be precisely answered, due to the lack of documentation.[70] We know that calligraphers could come from different backgrounds (civilian or military elite) and could have different activities. Nevertheless, with regard to the sultan's inscriptions, the influence of chancery practice is obvious. It has already been pointed out that, especially during the reign of al-Nāṣir Muḥammad b.

64 Melikian-Chirvani, *Cuivres*, 99–133; Allan, *Mamluk Metalwork*, 38–43; Allan, *Mamluk Metalwork II*, 156–164; Behrens-Abouseif, *Veneto-Saracenic*, 147–172; Behrens-Abouseif, *Lidded Tray*, 173–185; see also Curatola, *Eredità*, cat. n° 174, 176, 178, 180, 181. I recently published one metalware from the Musée Calvet in Avignon see Cavalier, *Fastueuse Egypte*, 136 n°77.

65 Inventory number MAO 638. Its inscription has been recently reexamined by Abdallah Cheikh-Moussa and published in Makariou, *Islamic Art*, 292–294.

66 Wiet, *Catalogue (stèles funéraires)*, 6:228–251; 8: n° 2850, 2854, 3089, 3100, 3117, 3118, 3140, 3132, 3155, 3157, 3159; 10:42–69, 114–138, 177–178.

67 Mainly al-Khalīfa et al, *Aḥjār*. For a brief overview see also Juvin, *Calligraphy*.

68 Dieṃ Schöller, *Living*.

69 On this matter see important overviews by Gacek: *Al-Nuwayrī's classification*, 126–130 and idem, *Arabic scripts*, 144–49.

70 The only reliable occurrence is a signature by Muḥammad b. Bilik al-Muḥsinī, supervisor of the building work of Sultan Hasan's mosque and also a calligrapher, whose career is known through historical sources, see: Kahil, *Sultan Hasan Complex*, 124, 152, 169–181. Another mention of a calligrapher in a monumental inscription is made in Amitai, *Arabic Inscription*, 116–117, but the name of the so-called calligrapher is curiously introduced by "*bi-rasm*", and the reading cannot be verified on the illustration. This identification seems dubious.

Qalāwūn, the long vertical strokes, with their repetitive rhythm, closely follow the model of the *ṭughrā* – the sultan's ornamented signature in official documents like *manāshīr* – that we know only from Qalqashandī.[71] It is particularly obvious in the radiating inscriptions already seen on the Doha tray. The *ṭughrā* style is even more notable in the royal inscriptions of the Delhi Sultanate.

Another epigraphic device also appears on an object in the name of al-Nāṣir Muḥammad b. Qalāwūn. On the large metal stand, now in the Islamic Art Museum in Cairo,[72] on its top tray, the sultan's *ism*, Muḥammad, is placed apart in a more prominent position inside a central medallion (fig. 3). Al-Nāṣir Muḥammad also used this feature on some of his coins (and before him Baybars II) and latter sultans sometimes followed his example.[73] This device reminds of the chancery practice of *elevatio* – "honorific elevation" – which separates a word – often the name of a king – in order to enhance it. This practice originated in China and was adopted by the Mongols;[74] its use by Mamluk chancery is not recorded as far as I know, but a similar sort of *elevatio* can be seen in sultan Sha'bān's *ṭughrā*, depicted in Qalqashandī's manual, where *Sha'bān* and *Ḥusayn*, his father's *ism*, are retrieved from the base line and 'elevated', intertwined with the elongated verticals.[75]

To conclude, this paper is only a brief survey of the field of inscriptions in the Mamluk period. Its aim was to offer some ideas about registration, content and the visual aspect of epigraphy. The registration programs more or less recently undertaken now make the handling of this rich material easier and will enable extensive research. Beyond the apparent redundance and repeated formulae of Mamluk epigraphy, many slight variations need to be scrutinized and properly analyzed. Many questions are still to be asked about Mamluk inscriptions and Mamluk inscriptions, might shed some light on many questions.

71 Qalqashandī, *Ṣubḥ*, 13:165 – 66.
72 Inventory number. 139. See Wiet, *Cuivres*, 14 – 18.
73 Balog, *The Coinage*, plate VII, fig. 175 a/b and plate IX, fig. 230 to 234.
74 See Ménage, *Constituent Elements*, 282 – 304 and Gallop, *Elevatio*, 41 – 57.
75 Qalqashandī, *Ṣubḥ*, 13:166, also reproduced in: Blair, *Islamic Calligraphy*, 340, fig. 8.10.

Illustrations

Fig. 1. Tray in the name of Muḥammad b. Qalāwūn, after 1335. Qatar, Doha, Museum of Islamic Art, inv. no. MW.35.1998. (Photo courtesy of Museum of Islamic Art, Qatar.

Fig. 2. Detail of the same tray, with chinoiserie motives. (Photo courtesy of Museum of Islamic Art, Qatar).

Fig. 3. Plate of a metal stand in the name of Muḥammad b. Qalāwūn, 1327 – 28. Cairo, Museum of Islamic Art, inv. no. 139 (After Gaston Wiet, *Catalogue (Objets en Cuivres)*.

Bibliography

Primary Sources

Al-Fakhrī, Baktash, Tārīkh Salāṭīn al-Mamālik. Or Beiträge zur Geschichte der Mamlukensultane, ed. K.V. Zetterstéen, Leiden 1919.

Al-Nuwayrī, Nihāyat al-Arab fī Funūn al-Adab, ed. Muṣṭafā Ḥijāzī, 33 vols., Cairo 1997.

Al-Shujāʿī, Shams al-Dīn, Tārīkh al-Malik al-Nāṣir Muḥammad b. Qalawūn al-Ṣāliḥī wa-Awlādihi, ed. Barbara Schäfer, Wiesbaden 1977.

Qalqashandī, Aḥmad b. ʿAlī, Ṣubḥ al-Aʿshā fī Ṣināʿat al-Insha', vol. 6, 13, Cairo, 2006.

Secondary Sources

ʿAbd al-Raḥman, Fahmī Muḥammad, "Bayna Adab al-Maqāmah wa-Fann al-ʿImārah fī al-Madrasa al-Sa'dīyah (Qubbat Ḥasan Ṣadaqa)," *Bulletin de l'Institut d'Egypte* 3 (1970 – 71), pp. 59 – 83.

ʿAbd al-Wahhāb, Ḥasan, *Tārīkh al-Masājid al-Atharīyah (allatī Ṣallā fīhā Farīḍat al-Jumʿah Ḥaḍrat Ṣāḥib al-Jalālah al-Malik al-Ṣāliḥ Fārūq)*, Cairo 1946.

Aigle, Denise, "Les inscriptions de Baybars dans le Bilad al-Šam. Une expression de la légitimité du pouvoir," *Studia Islamica* 96 (2003), pp. 87 – 115.

Allan, James, "Later Mamluk Metalwork II: A Series of Lunch-boxes," *Oriental Art* 17/2 (1971), pp. 156 – 164.

Allan, James, "Later Mamluk Metalwork: A Series of Dishes," *Oriental Art* 15/1 (1969), pp. 38 – 43.

Allan, James, *Metalwork Treasures from the Islamic Courts*, Doha: Museum of Islamic Art 2002.

Amitai, Reuven, "An Arabic Inscription at al-Subayba (Qalʿat Namrud) from the Reign of Sultan Baybars," *Israel Antiquities Authority Reports* 11 (2001), pp.109 – 123.

Amitai, Reuven, "Some remarks on the inscription of Baybars at Maqam Nabi Musa," *Mamluks and ottomans, studies in honour of Michael Winter*, eds. D. J. Wasserstein and A. Ayalon (2006), pp. 45 – 53.

Atanasiu, Vlad, Hypercalligraphie. Le phénomène calligraphique à l'époque du sultanat mamluk (Moyen-Orient, XIIIe – XVIe siècle), unpublished Ph.D. dissertation, Ecole Pratique des Hautes Etudes Paris 2003.

Baer, Eva, "The Nisan Tası. A Study in Persian-Mongol Metalware", *Kunst des Orients* 9/1 – 2 (1973 – 74), 1 – 46.

Baer, Eva, "Turco-mongol motives on the Nisan Tası," *IVe congrès international d'art turc*, Aix-en-Provence, Université de Provence 1976.

Balog, Paul, *The Coinage of the Mamluk Sultans of Egypt and Syria*, New York: 1964.

Al-Bāshā, Ḥasan, *al-Alqāb al-Islāmīyah fī al-Tārīkh wa-l-Wathā'iq wa-l-Athār*, Cairo 1978.

Behrens-Abouseif, Doris, "A Late Mamluk Lidded Tray with Poetic Inscriptionss," in: *The Aura of Alif. The Art of Writing in Islam*, ed. J.W. Frembgen, Munich: 2010, pp. 173 – 185.

Behrens-Abouseif, Doris, "Veneto-Saracenic Metalware: A Mamluk Art," *Mamluk Studies Review* IX/2 (2005), pp. 147 – 172.

Behrens-Abouseif, Doris, *Cairo of the Mamluks. A History of the Architecture and its Culture*, London: I.B. Tauris 2007.

Behrens-Abouseif, Doris, *The Minarets of Cairo: Islamic Architecture from the Arab Conquest to the End of the Ottoman Empire*, London: I.B. Tauris 2010.

Berchem, Max van, *CIA, deuxième partie: Syrie du Sud*, vol. 1 (Cairo 1922) Jérusalem "Ville", Cairo 1922; vol. 2, Jérusalem "Haram", Cairo 1927; vol. 3, Planches, Cairo 1920.

Berchem, Max van, *Matériaux pour un Corpus Inscriptionum Arabicarum (CIA), première partie:* Egypte, vol. 1 (Cairo 1894); vol. 2 (Cairo 1900); vol. 3 (Cairo 1903).

Bierman, Irene, *Writing Signs. The Fatimid public Text*, Berkeley: University of California Press 1998.

Bizri, Amine (ed.), *Islamic Calligraphy in Architecture. Islamic Monuments Inscriptions in the City of Tripoli during the Mamluk period*, Tripoli 1999.

Blair, Sheila, *Islamic Calligraphy*, Edinburgh University Press: 2006.

Broadbridge, Anne, *Kingship and Ideology in the Islamic and Mongol Worlds*, Cambridge: Cambridge University Press 2008.

Burgoyne, Michael H., *Mamluk Jerusalem: An Architectural Study*, London 1987.

Carine, Juvin, "Calligraphy and Writing Activities in Mecca during the Medieval Period

(Twelfth-Fifteenth Centuries)," *Proceedings of the Seminar for Arabian Studies* 43 (2013). [*Forthcoming]*.
Cavalier Odile (ed.), *Fastueuse Egypte*, (Avignon, musée Calvet, 2011.
Curatola, Giovanni (ed), *Eredità dell'Islam: Arte islamica in Italia*. Venice, Palazzo Ducale 1993 - 1994.
David-Weill, Jean, *Catalogue général du musée Arabe du Caire. Les bois à épigraphes jusqu'à l'époque mamlouke*, Cairo 1931.
Diem, Werner and Schöller, Marco, *The Living and the Dead in Islam: Studies in Arabic Epitaphs*, Wiesbaden: Harrassowitz 2004.
Dodds, Erica and Khairallah, Shereen, *The Image of the Word. A Study of Quranic Verses in Islamic Architecture*, Beirut 1981.
Frenkel, Yehoshua, "Public Projection of Power in Mamluk Bilād al-Shām," *Mamluk Studies Review* 11/1 (2007), pp. 39 - 53.
Gacek, Adam, "Al-Nuwayrī's classification of Arabic scripts," *Manuscripts of the Middle East* 2 (1987), pp. 126 - 130.
Gacek, Adam, "Arabic scripts and their Characteristics as Seen through the Eyes of Mamluk Authors," *Manuscripts of the Middle East* 4 (1989), pp. 144 - 49.
Gallop, Annabel Teh, "Elevatio in Malay Diplomatics," *Annales Islamologiques* 41 (2007), pp. 41 - 57.
Gaube, Ernst, *Grundriss der Arabischen Philologie*, Wiesbaden: Reichert 1982.
Gaube, Heinz, *Arabische Inschriften aus Syrien*, Wiesbaden/Beirut 1978.
Gelber, Metzada, "Reflections on Metal," *Assaph* 8 (2003), pp. 71 - 84.
Grabar, Oleg, "The inscriptions of the Madrasah-Mausoleum of Qaytbay," *Near-Eastern Numismatics, Iconography, Epigraphy and History. Studies in Honor of Georges C. Miles*, ed. D. Kouymjian, Beirut 1974.
Grabar, Oleg, *Islamic Visual Culture 1100 - 1800, vol. 2, Constructing the Study of Islamic Art*, Hampshire: Ashgate Publishing Limited 2006.
El-Hawary, Hasan M., Gaston Wiet, and N. Elisséeff (eds.), *Matériaux pour un Corpus Inscriptionum Arabicarum, quatrième partie, vol.1/1, Arabie. Inscriptions et monuments de La Mecque, Haram et Ka'ba*, Cairo: IFAO 1985.
Herzfeld, Ernst, *Matériaux pour un Corpus Inscriptionum Arabicarum, deuxième partie: Syrie du Nord. Inscriptions et monuments d'Alep, vol. I - II*, Cairo 1954 - 55.
Hillenbrand, Robert, "Qur'anic Epigraphy in medieval Islamic Architecture," *Revue d'Etudes Islamiques (Mélanges Dominique Sourdel)* LIV (1986), 171 - 184.
Kadoi, Yuka, *Islamic Chinoiserie. The Art of Mongol Iran*, Edinburgh 2009.
Kahil, 'Abdallah, *The Sultan Hasan Complex in Cairo, 1357 - 1364. A Case Study in the Formation of Mamluk Style*, Beirut 2008.
Al-Khalīfah, Khalīfah b. 'Abd Allāh, 'Abd Allāh b. Sulaymān Hadlaq, and 'Abd al-'Azīz b. Fahd Nafīsah et al., *Aḥjār al-Maʿlāh al-Shāhidiyya bi-Makkah al-Mukarramah*, Riyad 2004.
Makariou, Sophie (ed.), *Islamic Art at the Musée du Louvre*, Paris, Musée du Louvre/ Hazan, 2012.
Mayer, Leo. A., *Saracenic Heraldry: a Survey*, Oxford 1933.
Melikian-Chirvani, A.S., "Cuivres inédits de l'époque de Qa'itbay," *Kunst des Orients* VI/2 (1969), pp. 99 - 133.

Melikian-Chirvani, A.S., *Islamic Metalwork from the Iranian World, 8 - 18th Centuries*, London 1982.
Ménage, Victor Louis, "On the Constituent Elements of Certain Sixteenth Century Ottoman Documents," *Bulletin of the Society of Oriental and African Studies* 48/2 (1985), pp. 282 - 304.
Migeon, Gaston, Max van Berchem, and M. Huart (eds.), *Exposition des Arts musulmans: Catalogue Descriptif*, Paris: Union Centrale des Arts Décoratifs 1903.
Migeon, Gaston, *Manuel d'art musulman, vol. 2, Les Arts plastiques et industriels*, Paris: 1907.
Mubārak, ʿAlī Pāshā, *Al-Khiṭāṭ al-Jadīdah al-Tawfīqīyah*, Cairo: Bulaq 1306/1888 - 89.
RCEA. Répertoire Chronologique d'Epigraphie Arabe, vol. 1 - 18, Cairo: IFAO,1931 - 1991.
Rogers, J. Michael, "The Inscription of the Cistern of Yaʿqūb Shāh al-mihmāndār in Cairo," *Fifth International Congress of Turkish Art*, ed. Géza Fehér, Budapest 1978, pp. 737 - 38.
Sabra, Adam, *Poverty and Charity in Medieval Islam: Mamluk Egypt, 1250 - 1517*, Cambridge: Cambridge University Press 2001.
Sadek, Mohamed-Moain, *Die Mamlukische Architektur der Stadt Gaza*, Berlin 1991.
Salam-Liebich, Hayyat, *The Architecture of the Mamluk City of Tripoli*, Cambridge MA 1983.
Sauvaget, Jean, "Décrets mamelouks de Syrie," *Bulletin des Etudes Orientales* (a) 2 (1932b); (b) 3 (1933); (c) 12 (1947 - 48).
Al-Shihābī, Qutaybah, *Inscriptions of Damascus Monuments - Nuqūsh al-Kitābīyah fī Awābid Dimashq*, Damascus: 1997.
Sobernheim, Moritz, "Arabische Gefässinschriften von der Austellung islamischer Kunst in Paris (1903)," *Zeitschrift des Deutschen Palestina-Vereins* 28 (1905), pp.176 - 205.
Sobernheim, Moritz, *Matériaux pour un Corpus Inscriptionum Arabicarum, deuxième partie: Syrie du Nord*, Cairo 1909.
Spallanzani, Marco, *Metalli islamici a Firenze nel Rinascimento*, Florence 2010.
Staacke, Ursula, *I metalli mamelucchi del periodo bahri*, Palerme 1997.
Talas, Muḥammad Asʿad, *Al-Athār al-Islāmīyah wa-l-Tārīkhīyah fī Ḥalab*, Damascus 1957.
Talas, Muḥammad Asʿad, Les mosquées de Damas/ d'après Yousof ibn ʿAbd el-hadi, Damas, Institut Français, 1943.
Thackson, Wheeler M., "The Role of Calligraphy," in: *The Mosque: History, Architectural Development and Regional Diversity*, eds. Martin Frishman and Hasan-Uddin Khan, London 1994, pp. 43 - 53.
Ward, Rachel, "Brass, Gold and Silver from Mamluk Egypt: Metal Vessels made for al-Nasir Muhammad," *Journal of the Royal Asiatic Society* 14 (2004), pp. 59 - 73.
Wiet, Gaston, "Décrets mamlouks d'Egypte," *Eretz-Israel* 7 (1963), pp. 128 - 143.
Wiet, Gaston, *Catalogue général du musée Arabe du Caire: stèles funéraires*, Cairo 1939 - 1942), vol. 6, 8, 10.
Wiet, Gaston, *Catalogue général du musée Arabe du Caire. Lampes et bouteilles en verre émaillé*, Cairo 1929.
Wiet, Gaston, *Catalogue général du musée Arabe du Caire. Objets en cuivre*, Cairo 1932.
Wiet, Gaston, *Catalogue général du musée de l'Art islamique du Caire. Inscriptions historiques sur pierre*, Cairo 1971.
Wiet, Gaston, *Matériaux pour un Corpus Inscriptionum Arabicarum, deuxième partie: Syrie du Sud, tome troisième: Index général*, Cairo 1949.

Sale catalogues

Sotheby's 1985: *Islamic Works of Art, Carpets and Textiles*, Sotheby's, London, 16th-17th April 1985.

Paris 1908: *Collection de Mr. O. Homberg, Catalogue des Objets d'Art et de Haute Curiosité Orientaux et Européens: Faïence de Damas, Rhodes, Solimania, Boukhara etc. (...)*,Georges Petit, Paris, 1908.

Sotheby's 1999: *Arts of the Islamic World*, Sotheby's, London, 22th April 1999.

Drouot 1998: *Art arabe des collections du Comte de Toulouse-Lautrec*, Hôtel Drouot, Paris, 25th september 1998.

Paulina B. Lewicka

Did Ibn al-Ḥājj Copy from Cato? Reconsidering Aspects of Inter-Communal Antagonism of the Mamluk Period

Medieval Islamic society was not excessively friendly to Christians and Jews. Categorized as *ahl al-dhimma*, they had little chance to break away from the degraded status that the non-Muslim communities suffered in Dār al-Islām. However, the significance of the religious affiliation of the *dhimmīs* varied considerably from place to place and at different times, and their situation differed accordingly. For the major part of the Middle Ages[1] Muslims generally did not manifest an exceedingly repressive or prejudiced attitude towards non-Muslims. Unfavorable circumstances increased inconspicuously during the Ayyubid period and gathered momentum under the Mamluks, when inter-communal antagonisms, relatively mild in previous epochs, suddenly intensified. With Muslims' anti-*dhimmī*, particularly anti-Christian, emotions growing faster and deeper than ever, yesterday's neighbors, close even if different, turned into the enemies. Increased hostility towards non-Muslims haunted the region throughout the Mamluk period, manifesting itself in a variety of ways.

Not surprisingly, the *dhimmī* communities have attracted significant attention from contemporary scholars, which has resulted in a considerable number of studies dealing with many crucial aspects of the non-Muslims' existence within Islamic society. Among these works, studies related to the Mamluk period form an important part. The anti-*dhimmī* propaganda and politics, violence, discrimination, conversion, as well as the minorities' situation in general were particularly frequently discussed – enough to mention works by scholars such as Moshe Perlmann, Eliyahu Ahstor [Strauss], Donald P. Little, Urbain Vermeulen, Mark Cohen, Donald Richards, Huda Lutfi, Linda Northrup, Johannes Pah-

1 When used to cover the specific period of Islamic history, the term "Middle Ages" raises doubts, if only because it designates a period of European history. In the present essay the term is used for the sake of convenience and it refers roughly to the period between the rise of Islam and the Ottoman occupation of the Arabic-Islamic world, which time frame basically corresponds to the European understanding of the Middle Ages.

litzsch,[2] Tamer el-Leithy (whose exhaustive *Coptic Culture and Conversion* deserves a special place among these works),[3] Shaun O'Sullivan, Febe Armanios and Bogaç Ergene, Marina Rustow, Ray Mouawwad, André Nassar,[4] or Michael Winter.[5] At the same time, Max Meyerhof, S.D. Goitein, C.E. Bosworth, Moshe Perlmann, Donald Richards, Carl Petry, Johannes Pahlitzsch, Ahmad Hutait and Jørgen S. Nielsen[6] focused their research on the non-Muslim bureaucrats and physicians, the two groups of the non-Muslim professionals who occupied very special positions in Islamic society. Seth Ward and Benjamin O'Keeffe discussed attitudes of Muslim theologians toward the issue of constructing and repairing churches and synagogues in Dar al-Islām.[7] The studies of Thomas F. Michel, David Thomas and Walid Saleh[8] differ from the above works in that they do not discuss day-to-day problems of particular religious communities. However, these authors' analyses of theological issues reveal an important context behind the nature of Muslim-Christian and Muslim-Jewish relations. The critical editions and translations of the major anti-*dhimmī* texts published by M. Belin,[9] Karl Vilhelm Zetterstéen,[10] Richard Gottheil,[11] Moshe Perlmann,[12] Claude

2 Perlmann, *Anti-Christian Propaganda*; Ashtor, *History*. Many thanks to Prof. Yaacov Lev for turning my attention to this study. Idem, *Isolation*; Little, *Coptic Conversion*; and idem, *Coptic Converts*; idem, *Communal Strife*; Vermeulen, *Rescript*; Cohen, *Jews*; Richards, *Dhimmi Problems*; Lutfi, *Coptic Festivals*; Northrup, *Muslim-Christian Relations*; Pahlitzsch, *Mediators*.

3 El-Leithy, *Coptic Culture*; and idem, *Sufis*.

4 O'Sullivan, *Coptic Conversion*; Armanios, Ergene, *Christian Martyr*; Rustow, *Limits*; Mouawwad, *Christian Martyr*; Nassar, *Situation*.

5 Although Michael Winter's *Society and Religion* does not focus on the question of religious minorities in the Mamluk period, it includes interesting remarks on al-Shaʿrānī's (1492–1565) attitude to Christians and Jews, see ibid.

6 Meyerhof, *Jewish Physicians*; Goitein, *Medical Profession*; Bosworth, *Religious Dignitaries*; and idem, *Protected People*; Perlmann, *Position of Jewish Physician*, 315–19; Richards, *Coptic Bureaucracy*; Petry, *Copts*; Pahlitzsch, *Ärzte ohne Grenzen*; Hutait, *Position*; Nielsen, *Participation*, 3–12.

7 Ward, *Construction*; idem, *Taqī al-Dīn al-Subkī*; idem, *Ibn al-Rif'a*; O'Keeffe, *Aḥmad ibn Taymiyya*.

8 Michel, *Muslim Theologian's Response*; Thomas, Ebied, *Muslim-Christian Polemic*; Thomas, *Christian Voices*; and idem, *Idealism*; idem, *Christian-Muslim Misunderstanding*; Saleh, *Sublime*; idem, *In Defence*; idem, *Muslim Hebraist*. Many thanks to Prof. Linda Northrup for turning my attention to these studies.

9 A *fatwa* by Ibn al-Naqqāsh (d. 1362) translated by Belin, *Fetoua relative*, 478–81; now also available as Ibn al-Naqqāsh, *Al-Madhammah*, edited by Sayyid Kisrawī and published in a volume titled *Manhaj al-Ṣawāb* (251–327).

10 The anonymous chronicle edited by Zetterstéen, *Beiträge*, includes two anti-*dhimmī fatwas* (pp. 88–92). The author of one of them is apparently unknown; the author of the other is "a certain person" (*shakhṣ*), named Ṣāfī al-Dīn Aḥmad al-Kharazī.

11 Gottheil, *Answer*, includes a translation of Ibn al-Wāṣitī's (d. 1312) *Radd*. Also Gottheil, *Dhimmis*, which includes Gottheil's edition and translation of a document referring to the fate of the churches and synagogues of al-Fusṭāṭ in the years 846–860 A.H.

Cahen,[13] Denis Gril[14] and Sayyid Kisrawī[15] provided scholars with a source material the value of which cannot be overestimated. Without their contributions, any attempt to discuss the situation of religious minorities and the inter-communal tension of the Mamluk period would have proven a much more laborious, perplexing and thorny undertaking.

Although S.D. Goitein's monumental and unique *Mediterranean Society*[16] covers, above all, the Fatimid and Ayyubid periods, its value for the studies of the social history of Egypt and Syria of the Mamluk epoch cannot be ignored. This brings to mind a number of other studies – such as those by Gary Leiser, Jonathan Berkey, Hava Lazarus-Yafeh, Michael Chamberlain, or Yohanan Friedmann[17] – which, although not necessarily focused on the issue of religious minorities or inter-communal relations, include a number of interesting comments and clues referring to these questions. In this context, the crucial works by A.S. Tritton and Antoine Fattal[18] that long time ago paved the way for studies on inter-faith and inter-communal relations within the Islamic domains should by no means be neglected.

All these works have contributed significantly to the understanding of the atmosphere, phenomena, processes and events that occurred in the socio-religio-political arena of the Mamluk state. However, although so many aspects of the inter-communal relations of the epoch have already been studied, the rationale behind the increased Muslim-*dhimmī* antagonism still remains unclear. In order to show how many questions are still to be addressed, how much is still to be explained and how many possible approaches are to be applied, I will look at the phenomenon from the "rabbit's perspective," using one short account as a demonstration model. The account deals with a microcosm of minority within a minority: the *dhimmī* physicians who, apart from being vulnerable to regular oppression and discomforts which they shared with their co-religionists, from

12 Perlmann, *Asnawi's Tract*, includes an edition of a treatise by al-Asnawī (d. 1370), *Al-Kalimāt.*

13 Cahen, *Histoires Coptes*, where partial edition of al-Nābulusī's (d. 1261) *Tajrīd* is included. Aspects of al-Nābulusī's *Tajrīd* are also discussed in: Catlos, *To Catch a Spy.*

14 Gril, *Une émanaute*, includes partial edition and translation of *Al-Waḥīd fī Sulūk Ahl al-Tawḥīd*, a treatise written by Ibn Nūh al-Qūṣī (d. 1308). Aspects of Ibn Nūh al-Qūṣī's treatise are also discussed in el-Leithy, *Sufis.*

15 Sayyid Kisrawī is an editor of Ibn al-Durayhim's (d. 1361) *Manhaj al-Ṣawāb*; the volume also includes Ibn al-Naqqāsh's *Al-Madhammah* (see above, n. 9).

16 Goitein, *Mediterranean Society.*

17 Leiser, *Madrasa*; Berkey, *Transmission*; idem, *Religious Policy*; idem, *Mamluks*; Lazarus-Yafeh, *Neglected Aspects*; Chamberlain, *Knowledge*; Friedmann, *Tolerance.*

18 Tritton, *Caliphs*; Fattal, *Statut legal.*

time to time also fell victims to various additional regulations aimed specifically at them.[19]

This account was written by Ibn al-Ḥājj al-ʿAbdarī (d. 737/1336–7), an uncompromising Mālikī scholar from Maghreb who resided in Cairo in the first half of the 14th century and who today is one of the favorite authors of historians dealing with the social issues of the Mamluk epoch. Alert to the slightest symptoms of alien, non-Islamic influences, Ibn al-Ḥājj produced a book that reflected his anger at the ignorant Cairene society which did not follow his idea of the proper Islamic behavior.[20] As Muslims' carefree relations with non-Muslims were among the most serious concerns of Ibn al-Ḥājj, a significant part of the book was devoted to unmasking Christians' and Jews' dark sides and discouraging Muslims from contacting non-Muslims in all spheres of life.

In this context, the issue of health care was particularly annoying, if only because in the Near East of the Mamluk epoch Christians and Jews still constituted a significant group (if not a prevailing one) among the medical practitioners.[21] In effect, Muslims were quite often cured by non-Muslims who, as physicians, were masters of life and death of Muslims and, moreover, were aware of weak sides and the most intimate problems of their Muslim patients. In other words, in their relations with the non-Muslim doctors, Muslims were a subjective body – as is usually the case with patients. Moreover, the non-Muslim doctors, often rich and respected, and sometimes also influential, practiced professions for which Muslims were not quite fit and which they could hardly perform, if only because a religious-juridical career was much more attractive to Muslims than the medical one.[22] This special status of the *dhimmī* doctor, and the attributes it entailed, inclined Muslims to interpret his position as a manifestation of the non-Muslims' superiority. The situation provoked tension, all the more so because the religion of Islam stipulated that the non-believers be humbled. In the tense atmosphere of the Mamluk epoch one had little chance to ignore this point, their *Weltanschauung* notwithstanding. "Do not honor them after God has humiliated them and do not trust them after God deemed them

19 This special treatment was applied, above all, to *dhimmī* scribes, secretaries and other officials who had insight into, and control over, the finances of the Muslims.

20 Ibn Ḥājj, *Al-Madkhal*.

21 For a more detailed discussion of the question of the *dhimmīs*' predominance in medicine in the pre-Mamluk period see Lewicka, *Non-Muslim Physician*, forthcoming.

22 Ibn al-Ukhūwah, a Cairene author of the 13th-14th centuries, must have had good reasons to lament that "in many towns [in Egypt] there were no physicians other than those from the *ahl al-dhimma*" and that one could not find Muslims engaged in medical practice because they "flocked to the study of *fikh*, and especially to matters involving disputes and controversies" and, consequently, "filled the towns with jurists pronouncing *fatwas*." Ibn al-Ukhūwah, *Maʿālim*, 254.

untrustworthy and do not make them closer because God moved them away"[23] – this simple commandment, attributed to ʿUmar b. al-Khaṭṭāb and persistently repeated by radical religionists, quite accurately reflects the spirit of the propaganda to which Muslims were subjected.

It should be of no surprise, therefore, that the cross-cultural aspect of medicine was one of the reasons that made Ibn al-Ḥājj devote an entire chapter of his treatise to demonstrating that a non-Muslim physician could not effectively cure Muslim patients simply because he was conditioned to hate Muslims and not to help them. Moreover, his hostility towards Muslims was incurable. This seemed to be a logical consequence of what Ibn al-Ḥājj apparently believed in deeply – namely, that one of the fundamental principles of the *dhimmīs*' religion stipulated that giving good advice to Muslims equaled apostasy.[24] In a passionate attempt to warn Muslims about the danger to which they were exposed, Ibn al-Ḥājj denounced the *dhimmīs* as those who deliberately "took over the control of medicine, ophthalmology and accounts in order to harm/destroy Muslims."[25]

But, interestingly, not all Muslims were targets of this long-ranged conspiracy. According to Ibn al-Ḥājj, simple and insignificant people were not likely to fall victim to the perfidy of the *dhimmīs*.[26] The strategic objective of the *dhimmī* physicians was to destroy intellectual and religious elite of Islam, and the entire activity of *dhimmī* physicians was subservient to this objective.[27] So even if their medical advice happened to be correct, they gave it only with this evil objective in mind. In other words, by correctly diagnosing the illness and applying a proper therapy, the *dhimmī* physicians did not mean to cure their Muslim patients, but to gain prestige and position so as to be able to organize efficient annihilation of the *ʿulamāʾ* and other pious Muslims.[28] However, judging from Ibn al-Ḥājj's story of an anonymous Jewish doctor murdering his noble Muslim patient,[29] it seems that efficient annihilation of the Muslim elite could be achieved by much simpler means.

Participating in these sophisticated conspiratorial activities was not the only evil deed of the *dhimmīs*. The other was that they drank, the natural consequence

---

23 See, for example, Zetterstéen, *Beiträge*, 86; Al-Asnawī in Perlmann, *Asnawi's Tract*, 8; Ibn al-Naqqāsh, *Al-Madhammah*, 271; Ibn al-Naqqāsh in Belin, *Fetoua*, 428; O'Keeffe, *Aḥmad ibn Taymiyya*, 76.
24 See Ibn Ḥājj, *Al-Madkhal*. 4:107.
25 Ibn Ḥājj, *Al-Madkhal*, 4:113, 115. The idea that "medicine, ophthalmology and accounts are in the hands of infidels who this way can cause detriment to bodies and property of Muslims" was also expressed by Ghāzī Ibn al-Wāṣitī and Ibn Durayhim in their anti-*dhimmī* treatises; see below, pp.10-11.
26 Ibn Ḥājj, *Al-Madkhal*, 4:109.
27 See Ibn Ḥājj, *Al-Madkhal*, 4:109.
28 Ibn Ḥājj, *Al-Madkhal*, 4:108–9.
29 Ibn Ḥājj, *Al-Madkhal*, 4:110.

of which was that sometimes a non-Muslim doctor saw his patients and prescribed them medicines in an inebriated state. Not being sober he did not know what was said to him, nor what he prescribed, or what was really wrong with the patient.[30] Sober or drunk, the non-Muslim physicians harmed Muslims. Strangely enough, some people sought their advice nonetheless, which to Ibn al-Ḥājj was particularly irritating and difficult to understand.[31] In an attempt to cure this situation, Ibn al-Ḥājj appealed to the people not to have so much respect for the infidels' diplomas (*al-ijāzāt bi-ṣinā'at al-ṭibb*) and frequent Muslim doctors and ophthalmologists, who were better.[32]

Now, how can we read a record such as this? Certainly, one key is not enough to solve the puzzle. In fact, the text Ibn al-Ḥājj produced begs for a psychobiography of its author, if only because the analysis of his childhood and his early emotional experiences is essential for understanding his adult disposition, motivations and way of thinking. However, we know virtually nothing about his mother or father;[33] we know nothing about his relations with his siblings or cousins; we know nothing about the environment in which he was reared; we know nothing about what he went through as a child. With these elements missing, understanding his emotional growth becomes impossible. Moreover, knowing very little, if anything, about Ibn al-Ḥājj's family, personal, and societal relations, we cannot understand how these elements interacted with one another and with the spirit of the times in which he lived. In other words, the psychobiography of Ibn al-Ḥājj cannot be done.[34]

Under such circumstances, applying psychoanalytical techniques to Ibn al-Ḥājj's literary output may provide an interesting solution. In fact, a need for this kind of research was already noticed by Jonathan Berkey who, while commenting on "many male medieval jurists'" concern with "the preservation of sexual boundaries and the avoidance of illicit dalliances" observed that "their fears on this score are often intriguing, and would amply reward a psychological analysis."[35] Indeed, psychoanalytical techniques might prove helpful in explaining all the "horrible abominations" conjured by Ibn al-Ḥājj's "fertile imagination – or possibly his keen eye."[36]

The significance of psychoanalytic knowledge for our understanding of the individual in society was indicated as early as in the 1930's by Franz Alexander,

30 Ibn Ḥājj, *Al-Madkhal*, 4:114–15.

31 Ibn Ḥājj, *Al-Madkhal*, 4:114–15.

32 Ibn Ḥājj, *Al-Madkhal*, 4:111; also quoted by Perlmann, *Position of Jewish Physicians*, 318.

33 For the codes for infancy and early childhood see Barry III, Paxson, *Infancy*.

34 Generally, psychobiography cannot be done without very detailed personal data. Thus, the best subject is a recent historical figure; cf. Lawton, *Primal Psychotherapy*.

35 Berkey, *Tradition*, 56.

36 Berkey, *Tradition*, 56–7.

who pointed out the necessity of combining the historical-cultural-economic understanding of social situations with the knowledge of emotional mechanisms according to which individuals react to their social situation.[37] Application of psychoanalytical concepts within sociological theorizing about the individual was also advocated in the 1980's by Robert Golding who stressed the significance of the fundamental postulate of psychoanalytic thought, namely that the individual inhabits two worlds – "an outer world of the present in which men and women contend with the routines and pressures of daily existence," and "an inner psychic world which refers back to the repressions and frustrated desires of the past"[38] and indicated that without admitting the existence of an unconscious life, "our view of the individual remains too simple."[39]

While arguing that "psychoanalysis can enhance our understanding of the way in which the individual is formed by and through culture," Golding stressed that "it also cautions us against making simple generalizations about the impact of culture upon the person, showing that the individual never submits himself unequivocally to its demands and interdicts."[40] Moreover, almost fifty years earlier Franz Alexander warned that the attempt to substitute such generalizations as 'cultural patterns' for the specific details of the environmental influences upon the individual actually found in each particular case is not permissible.[41] Obviously enough, the psychological mechanisms determining every individual's reaction to the social situation, and thus underlying group behavior, cannot be disregarded for, as Golding put it, "the relationship between individual and society is complex, tense and contradictory and psychoanalysis can show us why."[42]

True, while considering Ibn al-Ḥājj's particular disposition, it is perhaps worth remembering that apart from culture patterns acquired during the socialization process there are also certain emotional experiences of one's child-

37 Alexander, *Psychoanalysis*. Alexander demonstrated that neurotic mechanisms, such as projections, aggravate those emotional tensions between individuals, classes, and nations that exist on the sociological basis of their clashing interests.

38 Golding, *Freud*, 557.

39 "...imprisoned in the very assumptions we should be questioning"; Golding, *Freud*, 560.

40 Golding, *Freud*, 545.

41 "'Cultural patterns'" is a generalization of certain types of behavior which are typical in certain groups. But we know that the individual differences can be enormous within the same civilization." Alexander, *Psychoanalysis*, 795; Franz Alexander wrote his article soon after Ruth Benedict's *Patterns of Culture* had been published (1934), when the debate over her theses must have been very lively.

42 "I shall argue that what psychoanalysis reveals about the workings of the unconscious not only helps to clarify the mechanisms by which society enters into the individual but also challenges our most basic assumptions about what it means to be conscious"; Golding, *Freud*, 547.

hood.[43] The nature of these experiences is determined not only by culture but also by extremely individual factors such as the specific family situation, which may result in ill-digested infantile hostilities and resentments against members of this family. These, in turn, may at some point be replaced with an aggressive antisocial behavior.[44] For Lloyd deMause, the pioneer of psychohistory, parenting practices and child abuse are absolutely crucial for historical explanation and understanding of both individual behavior and social events. Indeed, the history of childhood is a nightmare in which children are killed, abandoned, beaten, terrorized and sexually abused, and in which empathy toward their needs seems to have hardly existed. The further back in history one goes, the more likely that all kinds of drastic child abuse can be observed.[45] To neglect this track in analyzing Ibn al-Ḥājj's disagreement with the world would be a mistake. This, by the way, should also be valid for many radical theologians and religionists in general, whose number significantly increased in Egypt and Syria at that time. After all, as members of the same psychoclass as Ibn al-Ḥājj, they emerged out of the same style of childrearing and, as such, shared not only this psychoclass's collective childhood experiences but also the psychic conflicts resulting from them.[46]

43 Which are, by the way, "the most important factors in personality formation"; Alexander, *Psychoanalysis*, 794.

44 See Alexander, *Psychoanalysis*, 783, 795. Most of the otherwise innumerable studies devoted to the history of childhood and child rearing in medieval Islam were written by Avner Giladi; see, for example, Giladi, *Children* (the bulk of the material included in this book had been previously published in various journals).

45 Psychohistory derives many of its concepts from areas that are ignored by conventional historians as shaping factors of human history. According to psychohistorians, a study of childhood is basic for the understanding of individuals and elemental social events, since it is in childhood that much of the groundwork for our future emotional development is created. Human behavior has its ultimate origins in childhood, infantile, birth and pre-birth traumas which are the primal reasons why events happen. Psychohistorians suggest that social behavior such as crime and war may be a self-destructive re-enactment of earlier abuse and neglect; that unconscious flashbacks to early fears and destructive parenting could dominate individual and social behavior. In a study of the ultimate origins of history, deMause goes even further – he believes that those origins can have their beginnings in the psychological environment of the womb. DeMause's theories have been criticized for being insufficiently supported by credible research; the idea of psychoanalysing the subjects after the fact was also questioned. See, above all, DeMause, *Foundations* and idem, *Emotional Life*, both available on the Web page of the Association for Psychohistory, http://www.psychohistory.com/htm. For more on this area of research see also other publications available on the same site; see also, for example, *Clio's Psyche*, a scholarly journal published by the Psychohistory Forum; *Primal Psychotherapy WebPages*, http://primal-page.com/psyhis.htm.

46 The concept of psychoclass is key to deMause's thought. It emerges out of a particular style of childrearing and child abuse at a particular period of a society's development. Another key psychohistorical concept is that of *group fantasy*, which deMause regards as a mediating force between a psychoclass's collective childhood experiences (and the psychic conflicts emerging therefrom), and the psychoclass's behavior in politics, religion and other aspects

Psychohistory reduces all of its subject matter to psychological motives but history cannot really be reduced to psychohistory, just as psychological motives are not guided exclusively by pre-birth, birth, infantile and childhood traumas. After all, there are also genes, there are memes, and there is an interaction between them. In this puzzle, genes are probably the dominant component.[47] But patterns of culture matter, too, and the inner psychic word of any social individual is far from being free of their impact. In other words, there is more to Ibn al-Ḥājj's compulsive visions than experiences of his early childhood and disorders related to them. If we put these aside, we are left with Ibn al-Ḥājj who was a product of the time, place and society in which he happened to live, a product of the patterns of culture, norms, values, ideas, stereotypes, symbols, and practices that surrounded him and that were instilled into his mind not only "through the profound and subtle influences of the family"[48] but also through the later socialization process and experiences of everyday life. All these,[49] while being a part of the outer world of the present, were responsible for what was happening in the inner psychic world of Ibn al-Ḥājj. With this outer world of the present, Ibn al-Ḥājj's inner world was at odds. Ibn al-Ḥājj did not accept the outer world and rebelled against it with his words.

In this context, Ibn al-Ḥājj's text on non-Muslim doctors provokes countless questions related to the multi-dimensional historical context in which it was produced, such as: in which way were the socio-political circumstances responsible for the image of the *dhimmī* physicians Ibn al-Ḥājj pictured? In what ways was Ibn al-Ḥājj's way of thinking expressive or illustrative of the social, political, cultural and intellectual climate in which he lived? What aspects of the prevailing mentality informed the development of his views? The present paper

of social life. According to his "psychogenic theory of history," it is neither "economic class" nor "social class" but "psychoclass" – shared childrearing modes – that is the real basis for understanding motivation in history; see DeMause, *Foundations*, ii. As far as religious radicals are concerned, interesting clues regarding motives behind their behavior are to be found in: Voland, Schiefenhövel, *Biological Evolution.*

47 According to Prof. Bogusław Pawłowski, genes' responsibility for the level of aggression amounts to fifty per cent, the circumstances/situational perspective contributes further eleven per cent, while other factors remain difficult to define; it is probably in the remaining 39 per cent where one can find the impact of individual experience such as various kinds of trauma; see Pawłowski, *Złe zachowanie*, 6–7. Be that as it may, not much space is left for free will and self determination.
See also, for example, Van den Berghe, *Racism*, 21–33, where the roots of human prejudice are discussed.

48 See Golding, *Freud*, 555: "Freud shows how deeply the individual is embedded in culture, how, through the profound and subtle influences of the family, culture establishes itself within and suffuses even the most hidden corners of the mind (…). Yet Freud is well aware of the price we must pay for our reluctant entry into culture."

49 Cf. the idea of *habitus* as re-elaborated by Pierre Bourdieu.

addresses just one aspect of this context – it is an attempt to understand how the outer world was responsible for Ibn al-Ḥājj's belief in the conspiracy of non-Muslim doctors arranging annihilation of their Muslim patients. To answer this question, however, one should probably first contemplate another: did his suspicions and fears correspond with the views and emotions of other members of the linguistic community to which he belonged?

* * *

In fact, when we consider the increasing inter-communal tension of the Mamluk period and the intensified propaganda designed to incite Muslims against non-Muslims, we should not be surprised that the presumed predominance of Christians and Jews in medical practice could become a source of a serious confusion and, in fact, a serious social dilemma. It is quite possible that under such circumstances the non-Muslim medical practitioners were scrutinized in a particularly thorough way – if only to use their possible lapses as a good pretext for accusing them of malpractice or of anti-Muslim activity. This means, in turn, that if there indeed occurred any instances of pathological medical procedures carried out by non-Muslim doctors, such as deliberate attempts to poison or kill their Muslim patients, Ibn al-Ḥājj would not be the only one to see through them.

Interestingly, the literary expressions documenting such concerns are relatively limited. In fact, the quality and quantity of the Mamluk-period references to alleged deliberate malpractices of the Christian or Jewish physicians can compete neither with the charges put forward by Ibn al-Ḥājj, nor with the quantity or quality of other anti-*dhimmī* accusations, particularly those pointing to evil intentions, mean tricks and harmful anti-Muslim activity of Christian and converted civil servants. Some of the rather few records involving denunciation of *dhimmī* doctors are to be found in the treatise titled *Radd ʿalā Ahl al-Dhimmah wa-Man Tabiʿahum*. Better known as "An Answer to the *Dhimmis*", it was written in the early 1290-ties by Ghāzī b. al-Wāṣitī (d. 1312).[50] In its form, Ibn al-Wāṣitī's treatise represents a relatively typical collection of more or less fantastic accounts of incidents in the history of *dhimmī*-Muslim relations from the time of the Prophet to Ibn al-Wāṣitī's own days. Obviously enough, these accounts were chosen so as to confirm the excellence and superiority of Muslims on the one hand and to demonstrate mediocrity, inferiority and dishonesty of non-Muslims on the other.

One of these accounts includes the story of Saladin's secretary al-Qāḍī al-Fāḍil and Moses Maimonides, the philosopher, the head of the Jewish community of

50 Transl. by Gottheil, see above, p. 2, n. 11. On Ghāzī Ibn al-Wāṣitī see also Nemoy, *Scurrilous Anecdote*, 188.

al-Fusṭāṭ and, at the same time, the famous physician. According to the story, Maimonides confidentially advised al-Qāḍī al-Fāḍil never to visit a Jewish doctor, arguing that Jews are allowed to kill anyone who does not observe the Sabath. Al-Qāḍī al-Fāḍil, moved by the warning, immediately forbade Jews to practice medicine.[51] This story develops, in a way, the warning rhyme which is to be found earlier in the treatise, and which informs the reader that Christians and Jews "have gone out as physicians and as scribes, in order to steal [Muslims'] souls."[52] The same words were, by the way, used later by Ibn al-Ḥājj[53] and by a Shāfi'ī scholar Ibn ad-Durayhim (d. 1361) in his anti-*dhimmī* treatise titled *Manhaj al-Ṣawāb fī Qubḥ Istiktāb Ahl al-Kitāb.*[54] In the case of Ibn ad-Durayhim, the rhyme was preceded by a short comment which seems to have been a paraphrased version of a remark ascribed to Imām ash-Shāfi'ī and quoted in a number of the Mamluk-era treatises on prophetic medicine (*al-ṭibb al-nabawī*):[55] "and I wondered, how Muslims could, despite soundness of their minds and power of their thought, surrender themselves to Jewish doctors and their goods to Christian bureaucrats and thus give power to their enemies over themselves and their riches."[56]

Of course, there were many other authors who recognized the problem related to the inter-religious context of the patient-doctor relation. But although most of these authors were fervent theologians, none of them went as far as to accuse non-Muslim physicians of conspiring to kill or harm their Muslim patients. Ibn Taymīyah (d. 1328), from whom a more extreme standpoint could rather be expected, was surprisingly mild in this regard. In one of his *fatwas* he just stated that "a Muslim was allowed to seek medical advice from the unbeliever provided this unbeliever could be trusted, and provided there was no probability of some dirty tricks being involved, such as [gaining] sovereignty or superiority over

51 Gottheil, *Answer*, 430; the story provoked a contemporary scholar to accuse Ghāzī Ibn al-Wāṣitī of anti-Semitism; see Nemoy, *Scurrilous Anecdote*, 188 – 92. The fragment is also mentioned by Ashtor (Strauss), *Social Isolation*, 91.

52 Gottheil, *Answer*, 427.

53 Ibn Ḥājj, *Al-Madkhal*, 4:115; see above, p. 5.

54 Al-Durayhim, *Manhaj*, 200; the fragment (quoted from the British Library Ms. Or. 9264) is mentioned by Richards, *Coptic Bureaucracy*, 380, n. 35.

55 For references to treatises on prophetic medicine (*al-ṭibb al-nabawī*) see below, p. 12.

56 Al-Durayhim, *Manhaj*, 200. According to the authors of treatises on prophetic medicine, Imām al-Shāfi'ī, who considered medicine one of the most noble fields of knowledge (after the science which distinguishes between what is *ḥalāl* and what is *ḥarām*), reportedly lamented about how much of this science had been lost by Muslims, and used to say: "they lost one third of human knowledge and entrusted it to Jews and Christians." Al-Shāfi'ī's conclusion was simple and sad: "People of the Book have dominated us in medicine." See, for example, Al-Dhahabī, *Al-Ṭibb*, 228; Al-Suyūṭī, *Ṭibb*, trans. Thomson, 129 (also in trans. Elgood, 128 – 9); Ibn Ṭūlūn, *Al-Manhal*, 11.

Muslims."[57] Ibn Taymīyah's followers did not try to be more radical than their teacher.[58] Al-Dhahabī (d. 1348), a scholar "Shāfiʿī in law and Ḥanbalī in dogma" and Ibn Mufliḥ (d. 1361), a Ḥanbalī scholar from Damascus, referred to the problem by quoting various statements ascribed to Aḥmad b. Ḥanbal (d. 855). According to these quotations, Ibn Ḥanbal recommended that a Muslim patient should ignore the advice of the non-Muslim doctor if it included elements that were forbidden or that prevented him from fulfilling his religious duties. Ibn Ḥanbal was also to maintain that "to drink a medicine from the polytheist (*mushrik*) was repugnant," and that a Muslim was not allowed to use *dhimmī* medications if their contents were not known. This was because one could never be sure whether a *dhimmī* had not added some poisonous or unclean things to his medicament. These recommendations, included in the treatises on the prophetic medicine that al-Dhahabī and Ibn Mufliḥ composed, can also be found in the works written by later Mamluk-epoch authors of this genre, such as as-Suyūṭī and Ibn Ṭulūn.[59]

Although the language of recommendations ascribed to Ibn Ḥanbal is far from the insistent suspicion that radiates from the text of Ibn al-Ḥājj, it reflects, in fact, a similar fear of the non-Muslim doctors and of the danger to which the latter might expose Muslims. In fact, the message these recommendations carried was very basic: beware of those who are not from among yourselves.[60] As such, these naturally protective though biased warnings were not very much different from the Jewish fear that non-kosher parts of animals might be used in medicinal syrups and ointments. As an anonymous Hebrew translator of a medical work by John of Damascus (ca. 675 – 749) wrote in the introduction to his translation: "These [gentile] doctors do not distinguish between impure and

57 Cf. also his "in the fields which did not depend on religion, such as medicine or accounts, benefiting from the works of unbelievers and hypocrites in worldly matters was allowed"; Ibn Taymīyah, *Majmūʿat*, 2/4:70 – 71.

58 Interestingly, Ibn Qayyim al-Jawzīyah (d. 1350), probably the most renowned of Ibn Taymīyah's followers, did not discuss the question at all.

59 Al-Dhahabī, *Al-Ṭibb*, 224; Al-Muqaddasi, *Al-Ādāb*, 2:428 – 430; Al-Suyūṭī, *Ṭibb*, trans. Thomson, 126 – 7 (also in trans. Elgood, 126 – 7); Ibn Ṭūlūn, *Al-Manhal*, 289. I have not been able to identify the original source of these quotations. Cf. a discussion in Perho, *Prophet's Medicine*, 117 – 18.

60 As such, it harmonized with the original division into Muslims and Others that dated back to the very beginnings of the Islamic community and that is reflected in a number of Quranic verses, such as: 5:51: "O believers! take not Jews and Christians as friends: they are friends of each other. Whoso of you makes them his friend is one of them. God guides not the people of the evildoers"; 3:118: "O believers, do not take for your intimates outside yourselves; such men spare nothing to ruin you; they yearn for you to suffer…; 60:1: "O you who have believed, do not take My enemies and your enemies as allies, extending to them affection while they have disbelieved"; 4:144: "O you who have believed, do not take the disbelievers as allies instead of the believers. Do you wish to give Allah against yourselves a clear case?"

pure [forbidden and allowed] and in most of their (...) mixtures they mix all kinds of insects and wine and unclean meat, and they put in tallow and blood. In consequence no Jewish patient escapes soiling and consuming the forbidden."[61] As Shem Tov of Tortosa observed in the middle of the 13th century, turning to Christian doctors and putting oneself in their hands constituted transgression of the commandments of the rabbis.[62] Indeed, according to Rabbi Judah (d. 188 or 219 CE), chief compiler and editor of the *Mishnah*, "even a scar over the puncture caused by bleeding should not be healed by them."[63]

Interestingly, the pragmatism of the 13th- and 14th-century Islamic theologians, who allowed their co-religionists (however reluctantly) to seek medical advice from the unbelievers, contrasted with the approach of the famous Egyptian sufi of the 15th and 16th centuries, ʿAbd al-Wahhāb al-Shaʿrānī (d. 1565), whose views in this regard were much more strict: he maintained that if a Muslim physician was not available, one should endure the ailment patiently rather than go to a *dhimmī* physician. The motivation behind his philosophy was even more interesting: al-Shaʿrānī feared that should the non-Muslim physician succeed in curing his Muslim patient, the latter would have a warm regard for him, and this Islam proscribed.[64] However, while deeply believing that his religion recommended hatred of Christians and Jews, al-Shaʿrānī never considered the possibility of anti-Muslim conspiracy on the part of non-Muslim doctors. Nevertheless, the idea reappeared in the 16th century in the writings of a Ḥanafite scholar Sinān al-Dīn al-Amūsī known as al-Wāʿiẓ al-Makkī (d. 1591), whose accusations against non-Muslim physicians seem to resemble very much those expressed some 250 years earlier by Ibn al-Ḥājj.[65]

If we now move back to the pre-Mamluk epoch we notice that, as in later times, there are not too many records documenting denunciation of non-Muslim doctors in the Arab literature. Nevertheless, they exist. One of these few examples is included in Ibn al-Fuwaṭī's (d. 1323) obituary of Muḥyī al-Dīn Abū

61 See Shatzmiller, *Jews*, 121.
62 Shatzmiller, *Jews*, 121.
63 Babylonian Talmud: Tractate ʿAbodah Zarah, Folio. 27a, Gemara,http://www.come-and-hear.come/carah/zarah_27.html.
64 Al-Shaʿrānī, *Lawāʾiḥ*, 238; idem, *Al-Baḥr*, 164–5, printed on the margin of *Lawāʾiḥ al-Anwār*. Besides, according to al-Sha'rānī, the physician was an intermediary between the patient and God and naturally an unbeliever could not fulfill that function; see a discussion in Winter, *Society*, 283, 285–6, and the references therein.
65 As I was not able to consult the original, I have used Strauss's summary of al-Amūsī's text; see Ashtor (Strauss), *Social Isolation*, 93. In the 18th century Muṣṭafā b. Muḥammad al-Wāridānī, "one of the *ʿulamāʾ* of the Ottoman state," as the editor of his work called him, also disagreed with the idea that a *dhimmī* doctor might cure a Muslim patient; this opinion referred particularly to Jews who were "the most hostile towards the believers" and who "considered it legal to shed their blood, and waylaid for them, and had it as their duty to harm them"; see Al-Wāridānī, *Al-Nahy*, 117–18.

ʿAbd Allah Muḥammad b. Yaḥyā b. Faḍlān (d. 631/1233–4), a Shāfiʿī *faqīh*, an *ʿālim*, a teacher in the Niẓāmīyah and Mustanṣirīyah *madrasahs* in Baghdad, *qāḍī al-quḍāt*, supervisor in *dīwān al-ḥisbah*, supervisor of *waqfs* of *madrasahs* and *ribāṭs*, supervisor of the ʿAdūdī hospital and, what is most important here, supervisor of the *dīwān* for émigrés/*jizya* (*dīwān al-jawālī*),[66] or a bureau which dealt with collecting taxes from non-Muslims.[67]

According to Ibn al-Fuwaṭī, having assumed the latter position, Ibn Yaḥyā b. Faḍlān wrote to the Abbasid caliph an-Nāṣir a lengthy letter regarding the taxes collected form *ahl al-dhimma*. In the letter, which can be classified as an early example of the anti-*dhimmī* text, Ibn Yaḥyā b. Faḍlān pointed out that there were doctors who, while belonging to *ahl al-dhimma*, enjoyed significant profits. This was because they frequently visited the houses of the rich and important people, who paid these doctors more than they were entitled to and, moreover, presented them with expensive seasonal gifts. All this was apart from what those people invested in therapy, which spoiled both their temperaments and bodies. Besides, being totally incompetent, these doctors were in fact serial killers:

> A young man from them, who read no more than ten sections from *Masāʾil* of Ḥunayn,[68] and five sections from a booklet for ophthalmologists,[69] wears a nice dress and a big turban and sits on the bench in the street or bazaar so that everybody can see him; having a box with some eye powder with him, and a box with some other medicament, he once harms somebody's body, and at other time he applies something in the eye of somebody else, and kills (*fa-yaftiku*) from the early morning till the evening. Then in the evening he goes to his place, carrying with him his eye-powder box which is filled with scraps (*qurāḍah*). And once he is known and has his clientele, he starts to cruise the streets and enter people's houses.[70]

Another 13th-century example of this kind of thinking can be found in a work of al-Jawbarī, a Syrian dervish, alchemist and an author of a specialized work on fraudulent practices. Some parts of his manual, which is titled *Kashf al-Asrār*, deal with Jews as medical charlatans as well as physicians and, apart from offensive adjectives, include also information on how they kill their non-Jewish

66 On the meaning of the term *jawālī* see Cahen, *Djawālī*.

67 Al-Fuwaṭī, *Al-Ḥawādith*, 37–40 (the annal for 631).

68 That is, most probably, *Masāʾil fī al-Ṭibb li-l-Mutaʿallimīn* ("Questions on Medicine for Beginners") by Ḥunayn b. Isḥāq (d. c. 873 or 877), a "sort of catechism" for beginner doctors written in the form of questions (*masāʾil*) and answers; see Pormann, Savage-Smith, *Islamic Medicine*, 68.

69 Most probably, Ibn Yaḥyā b. Faḍlān meant here *Tadhkirat al-Kaḥḥālīn* ("Memorandum Book for Oculists") by ʿAli b. ʿIsā al-Kaḥḥāl (the 10th century), one of the most widely-read ophthalmological manuals; see Pormann, Savage-Smith, *Islamic Medicine*, 65.

70 The letter is briefly mentioned by Al-Dhahabī, *Tārīkh*, vol. 631–640 h., 83–4.

patients whenever they have a chance.[71] When we move back further in time, we find that one of the very few examples of associating *dhimmī* physicians with dishonest practices in the Abbasid literature is a certain al-Kaskarī, a physician from 10th-century Baghdad, who in his *Compendium* (*Kunnāsh*) refers to Jewish doctors from Kufa as being "fond of using falsehood and deceit."[72] However, al-Kaskarī, who gives one example of these doctors' dishonesty, does not accuse them of deliberate harming or killing his Muslim patients.[73]

Taken altogether, that is not much. The reason behind such an insignificant number of accounts linking religion or ethnicity with alleged pathological intentions or conspiracy of physicians in Arab literature may be caused by the fact that religion was never part of medical discourse in the pre-Mamluk culture. Medical errors or charlatan practices were not generally associated with religious denomination and belonging to a denomination was not used either to confirm or to question a doctor's professional competence. Quite possibly, this approach prevailed in Mamluk times.[74] Be that as it may, the intensified anti-*dhimmī* propaganda – focused on Christian/Copt and convert bureaucrats and on *dhimmīs* in general – seems to have spared non-Muslim physicians, although

71 Al-Jawbarī, *Al-Mukhtār*, 28–9. The fragment is quoted and discussed by Perlmann, *Position of Jewish Physician*, 317; also Pormann, *Physician*, 220–21.

72 See Pormann, *Physician*, 211–12.

73 See a discussion of this fragment by Pormann, loc. cit. (some of Pormann's conclusions seem far-fetched, though).

74 In a way, this was similar to the general Byzantine approach which, judging by the Byzantine literary output, seems to have been devoid of religious or ethnic bias (although an image of the greedy and incompetent doctor, as well as of the doctor-poisoner was not unknown to the Byzantine reader). This, however, is not to say that the patient-doctor relation in Byzantium had nothing to do with religion, or that religion was never used in medical discourse. It was; but religious denomination was apparently not used either to confirm or to question a physician's professional competence. The authors of the 7th-century hagiographic texts report that many physicians are negligent, cannot even make a proper diagnosis, and often make the patient's condition worse. They are only interested in the victim's money and their expensive and elaborate preparations turn out to be useless, while the healing saints, who ask for no compensation, are able to work wonders with the most paltry substances – such as candle wax form their own shrines. In other words, the rivalry was between ordinary doctors who were quite often helpless and ineffective, sometimes greedy and incompetent, and the saint who, capable of miraculous healing, cured the very diseases that doctors proclaimed incurable (see Baldwin, *Beyond the House Call*, 17; Kazhdan, *Image*, 46, 48; Duffy, *Byzantine Medicine*, 38:24). In the 10th-12th centuries this fundamental opposition was still valid; nevertheless, there is no sharp contempt for, or animosity against, ordinary (as opposed to saint) doctors; the secular physicians were less effective, but they were in no way villains (see Kazhdan, *Image*, 46, 48). The 15th-century satire *Mazaris' Journey to Hades* presents doctors not only as greedy and incompetent, but also as killers and vampires (Baldwin, *Beyond the House Call*, 16). However, it seems that these images, too, were devoid of religious or ethnic bias. For a discussion of the Jewish doctors' position in Byzantium see Scharf, *Universe.*

some aspects of the professional activity of the latter must have seriously bothered religious scholars.

Infrequent as they are, such accusations are nevertheless there, for there are always people who are more passionate than others. But which one of them inspired Ibn al-Ḥājj? Was it prejudiced and coarse al-Jawbarī, was it educated, zealous and prejudiced Ibn Yaḥyā Ibn Faḍlān, or equally prejudiced Ghāzī b. al-Wāṣitī? Or was it still someone else?

What is intriguing, the number and quality of accusations against foreign doctors conspiring to kill their patients grow as we cross the border of the linguistic and religious community to which Ibn al-Ḥājj belonged, and browse through literary output produced by Western Christians. Ironically enough, their emotions and thoughts in this respect were strikingly similar to those of Ibn al-Ḥājj, whose frame of mind seems to have been much closer to that of the officials of the Latin Church than to that of his fellow-Muslims.

It is not obvious how popular this way of thinking was among the Franks, but many seemed to believe that the non-Frankish physicians such as Jews, Samaritans, Saracens and Syrians would poison "all their leading men in the country,"[75] while others were convinced that no one should consult a Muslim physician or take any medicine that he prescribed.[76] In 1322 the council of Valladolid condemned Jews and Muslims who "under the guise of medicine, surgery or apothecary commit treachery with much ardor and kill Christian folk when administrating medicine to them."[77] These are just some examples out of many.

Moreover, from the early 13th century on, the European ecclesiastical and secular legislation against specifically Jewish medical practitioners started to multiply, reflecting increasing suspicion about Jewish doctors deliberately attempting to poison Christians.[78] For instance, a Castilian code from the 13th century prohibited "any Christian from receiving medicine (...) made by a Jew, although he may obtain it on advice of a knowledgeable Jew as long as it is prepared by a Christian fully aware of its content."[79] In the mid-15th century the Inquisition Tribunal at Briançon forced a Jewish doctor to confess that Jews "have it as a part of their customs that their doctors do not heal any [Christian]

75 See the addition of the Old French translator of the chronicle of William of Tyre, in: *L'estoire de Eracles empereur et la conqueste de la terre d'outremer*, in: *RHC, Historiens occidentaux*, I.2, p. 879; quoted by Conrad, *Usama Ibn Munqidh*, XLV.

76 See Cypriot statutes of the 13th century, *Constitutiones nicosiensis*, c. xxiv; ed. by Joannes Dominicus Mansi, *Sacrorum conciliorum nova et amplissima collection* (Florence, etc., 1759–98), XXVI, col. 314; quoted in Conrad, *Usama Ibn Munqidh*, XLV–XLVI.

77 The statement was repeated word for word in 1335 at Salamanca; see Coureas, *Reception*, 218.

78 See Shatzmiller, *Jews*, 85

79 See Shatzmiller, *Jews*, 87.

but rather kill as many of them as they can."[80] The stress and fear did not fade away as time went by. According to a 16th-century German author, "the Jews who pretend to be doctors .... cruelly torture Christians, when they kill them secretly, or when they cheat them."[81] Now, who cribbed from whom, and why? As it often is the case with the Mediterranean,[82] this time, too, traces seem to lead to Rome.

> "Concerning those Greeks (...)" – wrote Cato to his son Marcus – "They are a most iniquitous and intractable race, and you may take my word as the word of a prophet, when I tell you, that whenever that nation shall bestow its literature upon Rome it will mar everything; and that all the sooner, if it sends its physicians among us. They have conspired among themselves to murder all barbarians with their medicine; a profession which they exercise for lucre, in order that they may win our confidence, and dispatch us all the more easily. They are in the common habit, too, of calling us barbarians, and stigmatize us beyond all other nations, by giving us the abominable appellation of Opici.* I forbid you to have anything to do with physicians."[83]

The view of Cato the Elder (234 – 149 BC), according to whom Greek doctors conspired to kill off the Romans,[84] resulted from his confessed disdain for everything Greek, and particularly for non-Roman scientific medicine which, as a innovation coming from Greece, started to supplant good, old, domestic, herbal healing. However personal, Cato's stance on foreign doctors' hostile intentions apparently had attributes of timelessness and universality. Having discovered that it fitted perfectly with his own "sentiments of a gradual decline of Rome under the corrupting influence of Greece,"[85] many years later Pliny (23 – 79 CE) quoted Cato's words – under the heading of "The opinions entertained by the

80 See Shatzmiller, *Jews*, 86. The European obsession, in fact hysteria, about Jews' plans to annihilate Christianity (Muslims were also said to have been involved) reached its climax in 1321, when they were accused, together with lepers, of poisoning the French Christians. The number of Jews and lepers who fell victim, individually and collectively, to acts of popular and jurisdictional "justice" was exceedingly high. For discussion of the events of 1321 see, for example, Barber, *Lepers*, 1 – 17; Nirenberg, *Communities*, 93 – 124; for the accusations against, and massacres of, the Jews during the Black Death see Dols, *Comparative*; Nirenberg, *Communities*, 231 – 49. Interestingly, neither this kind of charges, nor this way of persecution of minorities, ever occurred in the Muslim society (save the case of the 11th-century al-Andalus).

81 See Shatzmiller, *Jews*, 85.

82 Although such a generalization may provoke criticism; for discussion on the "Mediterranean" as a (controversial) field of research, see Horden, Purcell, *Mediterranean*; I am grateful to Prof. Stephan Conermann for turning my attention to this article.
* The Opici or Osci were an ancient tribe of Italy, settled in Campania, Latium, and Samnium. From their uncivilized habits the name was long used as a reproachful epithet, equivalent to our words "bumpkin," "clodhopper," or "chawbacon" (the translator's footnote).

83 Pliny, *Natural History*, xxix:7.

84 For other examples of Romans who realized that doctors could not only be greedy but were also able to kill a patient see Baldwin, *Beyond the House Call*, 15 – 16, 19.

85 Nutton, *Murders*, 43.

Romans on the ancient physicians" – in his *Historia Naturalis.*[86] Moreover, he gave them additional value and strength by using Cato's authority to support, and confirm the correctness of, his own views on Greek doctors and their medicine. Included in the chapter "Evils attendant upon the practice of medicine" of *Historia Naturalis*, Pliny's judgment was so uncompromising that it made a contemporary scholar call it "the most sustained, influential, and potentially devastating attack on doctors and their medicine ever mounted."[87] But the story of Cato's and Pliny's black PR campaign mounted against foreign physicians conspiring to harm or annihilate their Roman patients did not end in ancient Rome.

As *Historia Naturalis* was held in high esteem in the Middle Ages and the Renaissance, and its countless manuscript and printed copies were distributed all over Europe in a long, continuous flow, Cato's and Pliny's prejudiced image of a hostile outsider doctor must have become familiar to an enormously broad, multi-generation audience. As such, it must have influenced perceptions and behavior of many, who consequently adjusted it to particular circumstances of their own times and places. This is not to say that Ibn al-Ḥājj read and imitated Roman authors. Rabbi Judah the Prince, who was a key leader of the Jewish community during the Roman occupation of Judea, and whose opinion regarding the heathen doctors was equally unfavorable (though much more concise),[88] probably did not imitate Cato or Pliny, either – even though his erudition and close contact with the Roman culture could facilitate him the access to their writings.

However, it is quite possible that the biased labels of Roman origin, which may constitute the earliest recorded examples of this trope, contributed to various revivals of fear of outsider doctors.[89] Judging by the literary evidence, the concept of conspiracy of foreign physicians determined to kill off the community in which they lived and which depended on their services is one of those motifs which, having settled into timeless types, constituted a repertoire of stock images transmitted in all types of literature within a relatively broad culture

86 See above, n. 83.
87 Nutton, *Murders*, 43.
88 See above, p. 12.
89 At the same time, it should be kept it mind that the circumstances in which the two Roman authors and Ibn al-Ḥājj wrote down their accusations were, in a way, similar: as Vivian Nutton observes while commenting on Cato's and Pliny's prejudice, it is hardly surprising that there should be some adverse comment at the invasion of eager foreigners if we consider the fact that ninety-three per cent of doctors recorded over three centuries on inscriptions from Rome and Italy bear non-Roman, and usually Greek names (Nutton, *Murders*, 44). In this context, one should probably have also some understanding for Ibn al-Ḥājj who, while being not less xenophobic than the two famous Romans, just like them could not stand the fact that his own people were entrusting their health and life to the mercy of outsider doctors.

circle (although Europe was in this respect apparently more productive than other areas).[90] This may be an interesting concern, if only because we usually look for similarities in a much narrower space and time and tend to forget that the society of the Mamluk state was as heir not only of the Ayyubid/Abbasid period, but also of the pre-Islamic civilizations and non-Islamic cultures. In a way, Ibn al-Ḥājj was a child of them all.

In a way, Ibn al-Ḥājj just reproduced the idea which had been verbalized by so many before him and which continues to be circulated in our own times.[91] It should be kept in mind, however, that the occurrence and persistence of such a phenomenon would probably be not possible without a support of some atavistic tracks in human thinking related to elements such as fear of poisonous food items, concern with one's health as well as prejudice against, and suspicion about, the stranger. This means, in other words, that the *topos* transmitted by Ibn al-Ḥājj resulted not only from the influences of the culture patterns of his times, but also from the lessons of the remote past that, transmitted from generation to generation, informed his – as well as Cato's – way of thinking.

* * *

Recognizing Ibn al-Ḥājj's role as a sophisticated link in a long chain of transmitters of literary memes may constitute a step forward towards the understanding of the multi-dimensional context behind indignation, suspicions and accusations, so typical for his account of non-Muslim physicians (and, in fact for his entire treatise as well). The problem with interpreting his text, however, is that apart from including a *topos*, it represents a complicated combination of overlapping truths, half-truths and untruths[92] related to the cultural climate and social mood typical for the circumstances of his daily life and, as social psychologists would say, for the particular "situational perspective." Anti-*dhimmī* prejudice, discrimination, negative stereotypes, distrust and hostility stirred up by religious propaganda of the epoch fused here into a complicated puzzle with the fear of doctors' incompetence, uncertainty regarding their intentions, anxiety about the incapacity of medicine in general, the long record of medical

90 Cf. al-Azmeh, *Barbarians*, 5.

91 For example, in the 1930's Nazis issued a prohibition against Jewish physicians attending to German patients (see Fritzsche, *Life*, 129). In South Africa, where the first segregation laws were introduced in the late 1940's, a black doctor could not even dare to think of attending to a white patient. The most extreme example of an obsession with "alien" medical saboteurs is of course Stalin's belief in the Jewish Doctors' Plot, a construct of a pathological mind that in the years 1948 – 1953 resulted in a bloody harvest in the Soviet Union (for an in-depth study of the problem see Brent, Naumov, *Stalin's Last Crime*).

92 Joosse, *Pride*, 137 – 8.

errors and quack swindles as well as the time-honored tradition of blaming the doctor.[93]

To distinguish what in Ibn al-Ḥājj's account is an archetypal pattern, what is a stock image, what is an ill-digested infantile resentment, what is the dictate of his superego, what is his projection, what is a compulsive vision, what is his creation and what in his account is true is, for many reasons, a thorny task. Ibn al-Ḥājj was not only more straightforward and impulsive, but also more disturbed than others. The voices he heard were louder, the pictures he saw were clearer and more insisting. He perceived the world in his own intense way and it is not impossible that sometimes he saw things that others could not. With the torments of his "almost a childhood" imprinted firmly on his mind and discreetly indicating to him the way, he was increasingly suspicious and violently alert to social issues for which others would not care much. He tended to obsessively search for conspiracy and to voice accusations. He projected upon others all he hated and feared, and all he did not accept in himself. At the same time, formed by and through the culture that surrounded him, he understood the outer world according to the prevailing system of values.

The psychological profile of Ibn al-Ḥājj notwithstanding, he was an eyewitness to, and participant in, a major social, cultural and mental transformation which was taking place in the region at that time and his book, categorized as an anti-innovation treatise, attests to that process. As this transformation did not spare the issue of health care, Ibn al-Ḥājj's account constitutes probably the most graphic picture of how Graeco-Arabic medicine, once free of theology and religion, was drawn into a trap of religious antagonism and became a subject of manipulation and an instrument of anti-*dhimmī* campaign.

An insignificant number of textual examples of similarly vehement and dogged Muslim tirades against *dhimmī* physicians might suggest that Ibn al-Ḥājj's account was just another expression of his own xenophobic *Weltanschauung* and, as such, was not representative for the social mood and cultural climate of his times. In this context, however, it is probably worthwhile to keep in mind that in Mamluk Cairo the *shaykh* Ibn al-Ḥājj was highly respected as a pious, ascetic, learned man, and that when he died at the age of 80 ("or more"), his funeral at the Cairene Qarāfa cemetery was attended by crowds.[94] True, as far as common Muslims' attitude to non-Muslim medical practitioners is concerned, it is very likely that – to paraphrase the words of two contemporary scholars – religious piety and social sensitivity notwithstanding, for the des-

93 Considering the fact that from a medical point of view the medicine practiced in the Mamluk epoch – be it Galenic, be it Galenic-Prophetic, be it popular/folk – did not make much sense, such an attitude should not be surprising.

94 Al-Sullāmī, *Al-Wafayāt*, 1:4; Al-Maqrīzī, *Al-Sulūk*, 3:224–5 (the annal for 737).

perate patient it mattered little whether a healer was Muslim, Christian, or a Jew, as long as he or she could, or claimed to be able to, heal the sick.[95]

But the instinct of survival and a common sense were one thing, and the religious leadership and policy-making was another. As for the *'ulamā'* and the members of the Mamluk elite, various developments on the socio-religio-political arena show that his way of thinking, however radical it may seem today, was not really distant from reality. The list of these developments range from the introduction of medical education into the madrasa, thus making this education inaccessible to non-Muslims,[96] to the announcements of decrees prohibiting Christians and Jews to practice medicine. One such edict was issued by the Mamluk government in 755/1354 and the other in 852/1448.[97] The *waqfīyah* for Qalāwūn's hospital, a document dating back to 685/1286, is also worth mentioning in this context, for it was even more drastic: one of its provisions not only specified that non-Muslims were not to be employed in this institution, but that they were not to be treated there, either[98] (the similarity of these prohibitions – however few – to the European ecclesiastical and secular legislation forbidding

95 Cf. Gadelrab, *Medical Healers*, 386, and Shatzmiller, *Jews*, 122–3. The existence and persistence of such an approach is suggested by a number of sources. For example, Ibn al-Ḥājj in the 14th century and al-Sha'rānī in the 15th-16th centuries (see above, pp. 5-6 and 13) criticized their contemporary brothers-in-religion for consulting the non-Muslim physicians. In the 16th century, Dāwūd al-Anṭākī, "the last great Arab physician," as Doris Behrens-Abouseif calls him, explained in the introduction to his *Tadhkirah* "that he decided to practice and teach medicine in Egypt after he saw that the *fakīh* who was the source of religious sciences would run to the lowest Jewish physician when it came to medical care" (Behrens-Abouseif, *Image*, 339). Nevertheless, the question of the Muslim patients' attitude to non-Muslim medical practitioners still requires detailed research.

96 The beginnings of this process seem to have coincided with the reign of al-Malik al-Ashraf, the Ayyubid ruler of Damascus (1229–1237). It was under his rule that medicine, as a subject to be taught, was introduced to the *madrasah* – first, it seems, to the *madrasah* founded by Muhadhdhab al-Dīn 'Abd al-Rahīm b. 'Alī, known as ad-Dakhwār (d. 628/1230, the renown physician of the epoch and the supervisor of physicians in Egypt and Syria), then to other *madrasahs* in Syria and Iraq. This process coincided with al-Ashraf's elimination of rational philosophizing from the Damascene *madrasahs* as well as with his patronage of religious institutions and the study of *hadith*, *tafsīr* and *fiqh*; for the list of *madrasahs* in which medicine was taught see, for example, Al-Nu'aymī, *Al-Dāris*, 2:127–38; Ibrahim, *Practice*; for a short discussion on *madrasah* as a medical college see Leiser, *Medical Education*, 56–8; for a concise discussion regarding al-Malik al-Ashraf's politics on *'ulūm al-awā'il* see Humphreys, *From Saladin*, 208–14. For a more detailed discussion on the social and cultural aspects of the introduction of medicine into the *madrasah* curricula see Lewicka, *Medicine*, forthcoming.

97 Al-Maqrīzī, *Al-Sulūk*, 4:203 (prohibition of 755/1354); Taghrī Birdī, *Al-Nujūm*, 384 and Al-Sakhāwī, *Al-Tibr al-Masbūk*, 2:89 (prohibition of 852/1448); the latter prohibition is mentioned by Perlmann, *Position of Jewish Physician*, 319 and idem, *Anti-Christian Propaganda*, 861.

98 Ibn Ḥabīb, *Tadhkirat*, 1:367, lines 294–7; many thanks to Prof. Linda Northrup for turning my attention to this document; see also Northrup, *Qalāwūns's Patronage*, 127.

Christians to use medical services of Muslims or Jews[99] is as intriguing as the Ottomans' lack of concern for these kinds of regulations[100]). The biased though relatively inconspicuous references to *dhimmī* doctors as inserted in the treatises on prophetic medicine, anti-*dhimmī* literature and other types of records testify to this tendency in thinking.

And this is probably one of the most precious elements of the literary production of Ibn al-Ḥājj: whatever exaggerations it may include, and whatever caution it requires from the reader, its author was able to transmit individual and social emotions that in the case of more 'regular' and more formal historical records are usually less clearly exposed. As such, the value of his work as a textual embodiment of the *Zeitgeist* is unique, the doubtful reliability of his references to anti-Muslim conspiracy, and to many other "events" notwithstanding.

Unveiling some fragments of the sophisticated, multilayered context of Ibn al-Ḥājj's suspicions, accusations and fears only partly explains his account concerning non-Muslim physicians and is by no means sufficient to make it fully explicable and clear. Too many elements are still missing, too many questions remain unanswered. We still do not exactly know exactly in which way the local circumstances were responsible for the image of the *dhimmī* physicians that Ibn al-Ḥājj pictured. What was their situation in Egypt and Syria in the Mamluk period? Did the radicalization of Islam and the escalation of general anti-*dhimmī* sentiment affect the medical culture? In which way did medicine become involved in politics and religion? Did the inter-communal tension affect Muslims' attitudes toward non-Muslim doctors? Did the atmosphere of denunciation and repression affect doctor-patient confidentiality? Did Ibn al-Ḥājj's suspicions and fears correspond, in any way, to the popular sentiment? Or, which is even

99 See canons of the Synods of Barcelona of 1243 and 1354 that tell the clergy to warn their parishioners not to call Jewish doctors or inform them that Jewish doctors should approach a Christian patient only in the presence of a Christian doctor "lest a fraud be committed in their soul and body"; see canons 100 and 101 in: Hillgarth, Silano, *Compilation*, 135–7; and Shatzmiller, *Jews*, 188, n. 42. For a detailed discussion on Western Christian ecclesiastical and secular legislation referring to this issue see Shatzmiller, *Jews*, 85–100; see also above, p. 16, and the references therein. Cf. also Canon XI of the Quinisext Council (the Council in Trullo) held in 692 under emperor Justinian II: "Let no one in the priestly order nor any layman eat the unleavened bread of the Jews, nor have any familiar intercourse with them, nor summon them in illness, nor receive medicines from them, nor bathe with them; but if anyone shall take in hand to do so, if he is a cleric, let him be deposed, but if a layman let him be cut off"; available, for example, at Fordham University Internet History Sourcebooks Project ed. by Paul Halsall, http://www.fordham.edu/halsall/basis/trullo.asp.

100 According to Uriel Heyd, the Ottoman sultans permitted the Jewish physicians to treat non-Jewish patients; see Heyd, *Moses Hamon*, 153. The only limitation to the Jewish physicians' practice was probably the 1574 *ferman* which ordered that a vacant position among the court doctors could be filled only by a Muslim; this was explained by the fact that the number of Jewish physicians at court was higher than that of Muslims; see Shefer, *Physicians*, 117.

more intriguing, did Ibn al-Ḥājj's suspicions and radical views, while being the product (partially at least) of external circumstances, influence these circumstances as a kind of "feedback"? Or, in other words, did they contribute to popularization of prejudice and institutionalization of discriminatory ideas?

But the important, yet unanswered, questions do not refer only to the medical culture of the Mamluk state. The question of increasing inter-communal antagonism is even less clear. Why did the inter-communal affairs evolve the way they did? What was responsible for converting the religious Other into the hateful enemy? What was the nature of relations within the "Mamluk elite–theologians–civilian population" triangle and what was each group's share in events, processes and phenomena which occurred in the socio-religious arena of the Mamluk epoch? In which way did the Muslims' image of the world, their system of values and of stereotypes govern their behavior towards non-Muslims?

These are probably the most important questions that an account such as that of Ibn al-Ḥājj provokes. They suffice to demonstrate how complex the issue of inter-faith relations is, how many contexts and dimensions a text such as his involves, how much there is to explore, and how much can be done in this area of studies. However, as an area of research, the problem of inter-communal and inter-faith relations is even more challenging – its non-uniform and interdisciplinary nature makes it possible to consider it in the context of such disciplines as sociobiology,[101] evolutionary psychology,[102] evolutionary biology, social psychology[103] and various branches of anthropology, all of which attempt to explain prejudice, stereotype, discrimination, etc. by investigating general correlations between social behavior, social evolution, selection pressure, genetic evolution, psychological traits, learning and biology. Creatively synthesized and innovative, these disciplines cannot fully explain particular historical events, processes or phenomena. Yet, they provide us with instruments and clues that can help us look at the past from a variety of perspectives and, in turn, to

101 Sociobiology investigates social behaviors, such as mating patterns, territorial fights, or pack hunting. It argues that just as selection pressure led to animals evolving useful ways of interacting with the natural environment, it led to the genetic evolution of advantageous social behavior. However, sociobiologists tend to content that genes play an ultimate role in human behavior and that psychological traits can be explained by biology rather than a person's social environment.

102 Evolutionary psychologists argue that much of human behavior is the output of psychological adaptations that evolved to solve recurrent problems in human ancestral environments.

103 For clues regarding the social-psychological approach see, for example, Stephan, Stephan, *Intergroup Relations*; Zimbardo, *Lucifer Effect*; Stets, Burke, *Identity Theory*; Clarke, *Social Theory*. Also Tajfel, *Social Psychology*.

create a multi-dimensional picture of it.[104] The significance of psychoanalytical concepts has already been stressed.

This idea may be unpopular, but in studies of certain aspects of history eclecticism seems to be a reasonable choice. So we probably should not reject it totally; it may be an interesting path, particularly if we believe that similarities between societies are fundamental for understanding human life in general and that differences are important only in the context of those similarities. After all, the societies, communities, cultures and individuals we deal with were not very much different from the rest of humanity, with which they share a variety of psychological traits, mechanisms, techniques of behavior and other outcomes of the evolution. The society of the Mamluk state was not an isolated microcosm, either – so to understand the text of Ibn al-Ḥājj, that was used here as a demonstration model, we should probably not neglect the extra-Mamluk world.

Bibliography

Primary Sources

Al-Asnawī, Jamāl ad-Dīn ʻAbd ar-Raḥīm, *Al-Kalimāt al-Muhimmah fī Mubāsharat Ahl al-Dhimmah*, in: Moshe Perlmann, "Asnawi's Tract against Christian Officials," *Ignaz Goldziher Memorial Volume*, Part II, ed. by Sámuel Löwinger, Alexander Scheiber and Joseph Somogyi, Jerusalem 1958, pp. 180 – 197.

Al-Dhahabī, Muḥammad b. Aḥmad, *Al-Ṭibb al-Nabawī*, Beirut: Dār Iḥyā' al-ʿUlūm 1990.

Al-Dhahabī, Muḥammad b. Aḥmad, *Tārīkh al-Islām wa-Wafayāt al-Mashāhīr wa-l-A'lām*, Beirut: Dār al-Kitāb al-ʿArabī 1998, vol. *Ḥawādith wa-Wafayāt 631 – 640 H.*

Ibn al-Wāṣitī, Ghāzī, *Radd ʿala Ahl al-Dhimmah wa-Man Tabiʿahum*, transl. by Richard Gottheil, "An Answer to the Dhimmis," *Journal of the American Oriental Society* 41 (1921), pp. 383 – 457.

Ibn al-Durayhim, ʻAlī b. Muḥammad, *Manhaj al-Ṣawāb fī Qubḥ Istiktāb Ahl al-Kitāb*, in: *Manhaj al-Ṣawāb fī Qubḥ Istiktāb Ahl al-Kitāb li-l-Shaykh al-Imām Abī-l-Ḥasan ʻAlī b. Muḥammad b. al-Durayhim, wa-yalīhi Al-Madhammah fī Istiʿmāl Ahl al-Dhimma li-l-Shaykh al-Imām Abī Amāmah Muḥammad b. ʿAlī b. an-Naqqāsh*, ed. by Sayyid Kisrawī, Beirut: Dār al-Kutub al-ʿIlmiyya 2002, 30 – 250.

Ibn al-Fuwaṭī, Kamāl al-Dīn, *Al-Ḥawādith al-Jāmiʿah wa-l-Tajārub al-Nāfiʿah fī al-Mi'ah al-Sābiʿah*, Beirut: Dār al-Fikr al-Ḥadīth 1987.

Ibn al-Ḥājj Al-ʻAbdarī, Muḥammad b. Muḥammad, *Al-Madkhal ilā Tanmiyat al-Aʿmāl bi-Taḥsīn al-Niyyah*, 4 vols., Cairo: Al-Maṭba'a al-Miṣriyya bi-l-Azhar 1929.

104 In other words, they may help us understand what really happened. As for "finding ideas in different places" and being "open to new ideas wherever they come from and adapting them to one's purposes," see Burke, *History*, 189. See also Førland, *Ideal Explanatory Text*; and idem, *Mentality.*

Ibn al-Ukhūwah, Muḥammad b. Muḥammad b. Aḥmad al-Qirshī, *Kitāb Ma'ālim al-Qurbah fī Aḥkām al-Ḥisbah*, ed. Muḥammad Maḥmūd Sha'bān, Cairo: al-Hay'ah al-Miṣrīyah al-'Āmmah li-l-Kitāb 1976.

Ibn an-Naqqāsh, Muḥammad b. 'Alī, *Al-Madhammah fī Isti'māl Ahl al-Dhimma*, in: *Manhaj al-Ṣawāb fī Qubḥ Istiktāb Ahl al-Kitāb li-l-Shaykh al-Imām Abī-l-Ḥasan 'Alī b. Muḥammad b. al-Durayhim, wa-yalīhi Al-Madhammah fī Isti'māl Ahl al-Dhimma li-l-Shaykh al-Imām Abī Amāmah Muḥammad b. 'Alī b. an-Naqqāsh*, ed. by Sayyid Kisrawī, Beirut: Dār al-Kutub al-'Ilmiyya 2002, 251 – 327.

Ibn Ḥabīb, al-Ḥasan b. 'Umar, *Tadhkirat al-Nabīh fī Ayyām al-Manṣūr wa-Banīh*, ed. Muḥammad M. Amīn, 3 vols., Cairo: Maṭba'at Dār al-Kutub 1976.

Ibn Mufliḥ al-Muqaddasi, Shams al-Dīn, *Al-Ādāb al-Shar'īyah*, ed. Shu'ayb al-Arna'ūṭ and 'Umar al-Qayyām, 2 vols., Beirut: Mu'assasat al-Risālah 1999.

Ibn Nūh al-Qūṣī, 'Abd al-Ghaffār, *Al-Waḥīd fī Sulūk Ahl at-Tawḥīd*, partially ed. and transl. by Denis Gril, "Une émanaute anti-chrétienne à Qūṣ au début du viiie/xive siècle," *Annales Islamologiques* 16 (1980), 241 – 274.

Ibn Rāfi' al-Sullāmī, *Al-Wafayāt*, ed. al-Maktabah al-Shāmilah (CD), 2 vols., Beirut 1982.

Ibn Taghrī Birdī, Abū al-Maḥāsin, Jamāl al-Dīn Yūsuf, *Al-Nujūm al-Zāhirah fī Mulūk Miṣr wa-l-Qāhirah*, 12 vols., Cairo: al-Hay'ah al-Miṣrīyah al-'Āmmal li-l-Ta'līf wa-l-Nashr 1971.

Ibn Taymīyah, Taqī al-Dīn Aḥmad, *Majmū'at al-Fatāwā li-Shaykh al-Imām Taqī al-Dīn Aḥmad b. Taymīyah al-Ḥarrānī*, ed. 'Āmir al-Jazzār and Anwar al-Bāz, 20 vols., Beirut: Dār Ibn Ḥazm 2011.

Ibn Ṭūlūn al-Dimashqī, Shams al-Dīn, *Al-Manhal al-Rawī fī al-Ṭibb al-Nabawī*, ed. Zuhayr 'Uthmān al-Ja'īd, Beirut: Dār Ibn Zaidūn 1996.

Al-Jawbarī, Zayn al-Dīn, *Kitāb al-Mukhtār fī Kashf al-Asrār*, n.p., n.d.

Al-Maqrīzī, Taqī al-Dīn Aḥmad, *Kitāb as-Sulūk li-Ma'rifat Duwal al-Mulūk*, ed. by Muḥammad 'Abd al-Qādir 'Aṭā, 8 vols., Beirut: Dār al-Kutub al'Ilmiyya.

Al-Nābulusī, 'Uthmān b. Ibrāhīm, *Tajrīd Sayf al-Himmah li-Istikhrāj Ahl al-Dhimma*, in: Claude Cahen, "Histoires Coptes d'un cadi médiéval (extraits du *Kitāb tadjrīd saïf al-himma li'stikhrādj mā fī dhimmat al-dhimma* de 'Uthmān b. Ibrāhīm an-Nābulusī," *Bulletin de l'Institut français d'archéologie orientale* 59 (1960), pp. 133 – 150.

Al-Nu'aymī al-Dimashqī, 'Abd al-Qādir, *Al-Dāris fī Tārīkh al-Madāris*, 2 vols., Damascus 1948.

Pliny (the Elder), *The Natural History*, trans. John Bostock, London: Taylor and Francis 1855.

Al-Sakhāwī, Shams al-Dīn Muḥammad b. 'Abd al-Raḥmān, *Kitāb al-Tibr al-Masbūk fī Dhayl al-Sulūk*, eds. by Labībah Ibrāhīm Muṣṭafā and Najwā Muṣṭafā Kāmil, 4 vols., Cairo: Maṭba'at Dār al-Kutub wa-l-Wathā'iq al-Qawmīyah 2002 – 7.

Al-Sha'rānī, 'Abd al-Wahhāb, *Al-Baḥr al-Mawrūd fī al-Mawāthiq wa-l-'Uhūd*, printed on the margin of al-Sha'rānī, *Lawā'iḥ*.

Al-Sha'rānī, 'Abd al-Wahhāb, *Lawā'iḥ al-Anwār al-Qudsīyah fī Bayān al-'Uhūd al-Muḥammadīyah*, Cairo: Al-Maṭba'a al-Maymanīyah 1321/1903 – 4 (Princeton Library copy).

Al-Suyūṭī, Jalāl ad-Dīn, *Ṭibb al-Nabī*, transl. by Cyril Elgood, "Tibb-ul-Nabbi or Medicine of the Prophet," *Osiris* 14 (1962), pp. 33 – 192; transl. by Ahmad Thomson, *As-Suyuti's Medicine of the Prophet*, London: Ta-Ha Publishers 1994.

Al-Wāridānī, *Al-Nahy 'an al-Isti'ānah wa-l-Istinṣār fī Umūr al-Muslimīn bi-Ahl al-Dhimmah wa-l-Kuffār*, ed. Ṭāhā Jābir Fayyāḍ al-'Alwānī, Judda: Maktabat al-Manhal 1983.

Secondary Sources

Ahmad Hutait, "The Position of the Copts in Mamluk Administration – the Example of Sharaf ad-Dīn al-Nashū," in: Haddad et al., *Towards a Cultural History*, pp. 29–40.

Ahstor (Strauss), Eliyahu, *The History of Jews in Egypt and Syria under the Rule of the Mamluks*, 2 vols., Jerusalem 1944–1951. (in Hebrew)

Alexander, Franz, "Psychoanalysis and Social Disorganization," *The American Journal of Sociology* 42/6 (1937), pp. 781–813.

Armanios, Febe and Ergene, Bogaç, "A Christian Martyr under Mamluk Justice: The Trials of Ṣalīb (d. 1512) according to Coptic and Muslim Sources," *The Muslim World* 96 (2006), pp. 115–44.

Ashtor (Strauss), Eliyahu, "The Social Isolation of Ahl adh-Dhimma," in: *Études orientales á la mémoire de Paul Hirschler*, ed. O. Komolós, Budapest 1950, pp. 73–94.

Azmeh, Aziz Al-, "Barbarians in Arab Eyes," *Past & Present* 134 (1992), pp. 3–18.

Baldwin, Barry, "Beyond the House Call: Doctors in Early Byzantine History and Politics," *Dumbarton Oaks Papers* 38, *Symposium on Byzantine Medicine* (1984), pp. 15–19.

Barber, Malcolm, "Lepers, Jews and Moslems: the Plot to Overthrow Christendom in 1321," *History* 66/216 (1981), pp. 1–17.

Barry, Herbert III and Leonora M. Paxson, "Infancy and Early Childhood: Cross-Cultural Codes," *Ethnology* 10/4 (1971), pp. 466–508.

Behrens-Abouseif, Doris, "The Image of the Physician in Arab Biographies of the post-Classical Age," *Der Islam* 66/2 (1989), pp. 331–43.

Belin, M., "Fetoua relatif à la condition des zimmis, et particulièrement des Chrétiens, en pays musulmans, depuis l'établissement de l'Islamisme, jusqu'au milieu de VIIIe siècle de l'Hégire," *Journal Asiatique*, 4eme serie, XVIII (Novembre-Décembre 1851), pp. 415–514; XIX (Février-Mars 1852), pp. 97–138.

Benedict, Ruth, *Patterns of Culture*, New York: Houghton Mifflin 1934.

Berkey, Jonathan P., "Mamluk Religious Policy," *Mamlūk Studies Review* 13/2 (2009), pp. 7–22.

Berkey, Jonathan P., "The Mamluks as Muslims: The Military Elite and the Construction of Islam in Medieval Egypt," in: *Mamluks in Egyptian Politics*, eds. Thomas Philipp and Ulrich Haarmann, Cambridge: Cambridge University Press 1998, pp. 163–73.

Berkey, Jonathan P., "Tradition, Innovation, and the Construction of Knowledge in the Medieval Near East," *Past and Present* 146 (1995), pp. 38–65.

Berkey, Jonathan P., *The Transmission of Knowledge in Medieval Cairo: A Social History of Islamic Education*, Princeton, N.J.: Princeton University Press 1992.

Bosworth, C.E., "Christian and Jewish Religious Dignitaries in Mamlūk Egypt and Syria: Qalqashandī's Information on Their Hierarchy, Titulature, and Appointment," *International Journal of Middle East Studies* 3/1 (1972), pp. 59–74; *IJMES* 3/2 (1972), pp. 199–216.

Bosworth, C.E., "The 'Protected Peoples' (Christians and Jews) in Medieval Egypt and

Syria," *Bulletin of The John Rylands University Library of Manchester* 62 (1979/1980), pp. 11 - 36.

Brent, Jonathan and Naumov, Vladimir P., *Stalin's Last Crime - The Plot Against the Jewish Doctors, 1948 - 1953*, New York: HarperCollins Publishers 2003.

Burke, Peter, *History and Social Theory*, New York: Cornell University Press 2005.

Cahen, Claude, "Histoires Coptes d'un cadi médiéval (extraits du Kitāb tadjrīd saïf al-himma li'stikhrādj mā fī dhimmat al-dhimma de 'Uthmān b. Ibrāhīm an-Nābulusī," *Bulletin de l'Institut français d'archéologie orientale* 59 (1960), pp. 133 - 50.

Cahen, Claude, "Djawālī," *Encyclopaedia of Islam*, 2nd edition, Leiden: Brill 1960 - 2005, 12 vols., vol. II.

Catlos, Brian, "To Catch a Spy: The Case of Zayn al-Dīn Ibn Dukhān," *Medieval Encounters* 2 (1996), pp. 99 - 113.

Chamberlain, Michael, *Knowledge and Social Practice in Medieval Damascus, 1190 - 1350*, Cambridge: CUP 2002.

Clarke, Simon, *Social Theory, Psychoanalysis and Racism*, Houndmills: Palgrave Macmillan 2003.

Cohen, Mark, "Jews in the Mamlūk Environment: The Crisis of 1442 (A Geniza Study)," *Bulletin of the School of Oriental and African Studies* 47/3 (1984), pp. 425 - 48.

Conrad, Lawrence I., "Usama Ibn Munqidh and Other Witnesses to Frankish and Islamic Medicine in the Era of Crusades," in: *Medicine in Jerusalem Throughout the Ages* (*Ha-Refu'ah bi-Yerushalayim le-doroteha*), eds. Zohar Amar, Efraim Lev, and Joshua Schwartz, Tell Aviv 1999, pp. xxvii-lii.

Coureas, Nicholas, "The Reception of Arabic Medicine on Latin Cyprus: 1200 - 1570," in: *Egypt and Syria in the Fatimid, Ayyubid and Mamluk Eras, VI*, eds. Urbain Vermeulen and Kristof D'hulster, Leuven: Peeters 2010, pp. 215 - 24.

DeMause, Lloyd, *Foundations of Psychohistory*, New York: Creative Roots 1982, available from: http://www.psychohistory.com/htm.

DeMause, Lloyd, *The Emotional Life of Nations*, New York: Karnac Books 2002, available from: http://www.psychohistory.com/htm.

Dols, Michael W., "The Comparative Communal Responses to the Black Death in Muslim and Christian Societies," *Viator* 5 (1974), pp. 269 - 88.

Duffy, John, "Byzantine Medicine in the Sixth and Seventh Centuries: Aspects of Teaching and Practice," *Dumbarton Oaks Papers* 38, *Symposium on Byzantine Medicine* (1984), pp. 21 - 27.

Fattal, Antoine, *Le statut légal des non-musulmans en pays d'Islam*, Beyrouth: Imprimerie catholique 1958.

Førland, Tor Egil, "Mentality as a Social Emergent: Can the 'Zeitgeist' Have Explanatory Power?" *History and Theory* 47/1 (2008), pp. 44 - 56.

Førland, Tor Egil, "The Ideal Explanatory Text in History: A Plea for Ecumenism," *History and Theory* 43/3 (2004), pp. 321 - 340.

Fritzsche, Peter, *Life and Death in the Third Reich*, USA: Harvard UP 2008.

Gadelrab, Sherry Sayed, "Medical Healers in Ottoman Egypt, 1517 - 1805," *Medical History* 54/3 (2010), pp. 365 - 386.

Giladi, Avner, *Children of Islam: Concepts of Childhood in Medieval Muslim Society*, Basingstoke and London: Macmillan 1992.

Goitein, S. D., "The Medical Profession in the Light of the Cairo Geniza Documents," *Hebrew Union College Annual* 34 (1963), pp. 177 – 94.

Goitein, S. D., *A Mediterranean Society: The Jewish Communities of the Arab World as Portrayed in the Documents of the Cairo Geniza*, 5 vols., Berkeley: UCP 1967 – 88.

Golding, Robert, "Freud, Psychoanalysis, and Sociology: Some Observations on the Sociological Analysis of the Individual," *The British Journal of Sociology* 33/4 (1982), pp. 545 – 560.

Gottheil, Richard, "An Answer to the Dhimmis," *Journal of the American Oriental Society* 41 (1921), pp. 383 – 457.

Gottheil, Richard, "Dhimmis and Muslims in Egypt," *Old Testament and Semitic Studies in Memory of William Rainey Harper* II, pp. 351 – 414.

Gril, Denis, "Une émanaute anti-chrétienne à Qūṣ au début du viiie/xive siècle," *Annales Islamologiques* 16 (1980), pp. 241 – 74.

Haddad, Mahmoud and Arnim Heinemann, and John L. Meloy (eds.), *Towards a Cultural History of the Mamluk Era*, Würzburg: Ergon 2010.

Heyd, Uriel, "Moses Hamon, Chief Jewish Physician to Sultan Süleymān the Magnificent," *Oriens* 16 (1963), pp. 152 – 170.

Hillgarth, Jocelyn N. and Giulio Silano, "A Compilation of the Diocesan Synods of Barcelona (1354): Critical Edition and Analysis," *Mediaeval Studies* 46 (1984), pp. 78 – 157.

Horden, Peregrine and Nicholas Purcell, "The Mediterranean and 'the New Thalassology," *The American History Review* 111/3 (2006), pp. 722 – 40.

Humphreys, R. Stephen, *From Saladin to the Mongols: the Ayyubids of Damascus, 1193 – 1260*, Albany: State University of New York Press 1977.

Ibrahim, Mahmood, "Practice and Reform in Fourteenth-Century Damascene Madrasahs," MSR 11/1 (2007), pp. 69 – 83.

Joosse, N. Peter, "Pride and Prejudice, Praise and Blame: 'Abd al-Laṭīf al-Baghdādī's Views on Good and Bad Medical Practitioners," in: *O Ye Gentlemen: Arabic Studies on Science and Literary Culture in Honour of Remke Kruk*, eds. Jan P. Hogendijk and Arnoud Vrolijk, Leiden: Brill 2007, pp. 129 – 41.

Kazhdan, Alexander, "The Image of the Medical Doctor in Byzantine Literature of the Tenth to Twelfth Centuries," *Dumbarton Oaks Papers* 38, *Symposium on Byzantine Medicine* (1984), pp. 43 – 51.

Lawton, Henry, *The Primal Psychotherapy Page*, http://primal-page.com/psyhis.htm.

Lazarus-Yafeh, Hava, "Some Neglected Aspects of Medieval Muslim Polemics against Christianity," *The Harvard Theological Review* 89/1 (1996), pp. 61 – 84.

Leiser, Gary, "Medical Education in Islamic Lands from the Seventh to the Fourteenth Centuries," *Journal of the History of Medicine and Allied Sciences* 38 (1983), pp. 48 – 75.

Leiser, Gary, "The Madrasa and the Islamization of the Middle East: The Case of Egypt," *Journal of the American Research Center in Egypt* 22 (1985), pp. 29 – 47.

El-Leithy, Tamer, "Sufis, Copts, and the Politics of Piety: Moral Regulation in Fourteenth-Century Upper Egypt," in: *Le développement de soufisme en Égypte a l'époque mamelouke*, ed. Richard McGregor and Adam Sabra, Cairo: IFAO 2006, pp. 75 – 119.

El-Leithy, Tamer, Coptic Culture and Conversion in Medieval Cairo: 1293 – 1524 A.D., PhD dissertation, Princeton University (N.J.) 2005, Ann Arbor (Mich.): UMI, impr. 2006.

Lewicka, Paulina B., "Medicine for Muslims? Islamic Theologians, Non-Muslim Physicians, and the Medical Culture of the Mamluk Near East," *ASK Working Paper 03*, Bonn, July 2012.

Lewicka, Paulina B., "The Non-Muslim Physician in the Muslim Society: Remarks on the Religious Context of Medical Practice in Medieval Near East," in: *Proceedings of the 25th Congress of L'Union Européenne des Arabisants et Islamisants*, Leuven: Peeters, forthcoming.

Little, Donald P., "Communal Strife in Late Mamluk Jerusalem," *Islamic Law and Society* 6/1 (1999), pp. 69–96.

Little, Donald P., "Coptic Conversion to Islam under the Baḥrī Mamlūks, 692–755/1293–1354," *BSOAS* 39/3 (1976), pp. 552–69.

Little, Donald P., "Coptic Converts to Islam during the Baḥrī Mamluk Period," in: *Conversion and Continuity: Indigenous Christian Communities in Islamic Lands – Eighth to Eighteenth Centuries*, ed. Michael Gervers and Ramzi Jibran Bikhazi, Toronto: Pontifical Institute of Medieval Studies 1990, pp. 263–88.

Lutfi, Huda, "Coptic Festivals on the Nile: Aberrations of the Past?" in: *The Mamluks in Egyptian Politics and Society*, eds. Thomas Philipp and Ulrich Haarmann, Cambridge: Cambridge University Press 1998, pp. 254–82.

Meyerhof, Max, "Mediaeval Jewish Physicians in the Near East, from Arabic Sources," *Isis* 28/2 (1938), pp. 432–460.

Michel, Thomas F. (ed./trans.), *A Muslim Theologian's Response to Christianity: Ibn Taymiyya's Al-Jawab Al-Sahih*, Delmar, N.Y.: Caravan Books 1984.

Mouawwad, Ray "Christian Martyrs in Tripoli in the Mamluk Era," in: Haddad et al., *Towards a Cultural History*, pp. 31–41.

Nassar, André "The Situation of Christians in Damascus and Aleppo," in: Haddad et al., *Towards a Cultural History*, pp. 41–75.

Nemoy, Leon, "A Scurrilous Anecdote Concerning Maimonides," *The Jewish Quarterly Review* 62/3 (1972), p. 188–92.

Nielsen, Jørgen S., "The Participation of Christians and Jews in the Ayyubid and Mamluk State: A Historiographical Reflection," in: Haddad et al., *Towards a Cultural History*, pp. 3–12.

Nirenberg, David, *Communities of Violence: Persecution of Minorities in the Middle Ages*, Princeton: PUP 1998.

Northrup, Linda, "Muslim-Christian Relations during the Reign of the Mamluk Sultan al-Manṣūr Qalāwūn, (A.D. 1278–1290)," in: *Conversion and Continuity: Indigenous Christian Communities in Islamic Lands, Eighth to Eighteenth Centuries*, eds. Michael Gervers and Ramzi Jibran Bikhazi, Toronto: Pontifical Institute of Mediaeval Studies 1990, pp. 253–62.

Northrup, Linda, "Qalāwūns's Patronage of the Medical Sciences in Thirteenth-Century Egypt," *MSR* 5 (2001), pp. 119–140.

Nutton, Vivian, "Murders and Miracles: Lay Attitudes towards Medicine in Classical Antiquity," in: *Patients and Practitioners: Lay Perceptions of Medicine in Pre-Industrial Society*, ed. Roy Porter, Cambridge: CUP 1985, pp. 23–53.

O'Keeffe, Benjamin, "Aḥmad ibn Taimiyya: Mas'alat al-Kanā'is (the Question of Churches)," *Islamochristiana* 22 (1996), pp. 53–78.

O'Sullivan, Shaun, "Coptic Conversion and the Islamization of Egypt," *MSR* 10/2 (2006), pp. 65–79.

Pahlitzsch, Johannes, "Ärzte ohne Grenzen. Melkitische, jüdische und sarmatische Ärzte in Ägypten und Syrien zur Zeit der Kreuzzüge," in: *Gesundheit – Krankenheit. Kulturtransfer medizinischen Wissens von der Spätantike bis in die Frühe Neuzeit*, ed. Florian Steger, Kay Peter Jankrift, Köln, Weimar, Wien: Böhlau Verlag 2004, pp. 101–19.

Pahlitzsch, Johannes, "Mediators Between East and West: Christians Under Mamluk Rule," *MSR* 9/2 (2005), pp. 31–47.

Pawłowski, Bogusław "Złe zachowanie jest dobre," *Gazeta Wyborcza* 5–6 stycznia 2011 (*Gazeta na Święto*), pp. 6–7.

Perho, Irmeli, *Prophet's Medicine: A Creation of the Muslim Traditionalist Scholars*, Hesinki: Finnish Oriental Society 1995.

Perlmann, Moshe, "Asnawi's Tract against Christian Officials," in: *Ignaz Goldziher Memorial Volume*, Part II, ed. Sámuel Löwinger, Alexander Scheiber and Joseph Somogyi, Jerusalem 1958, pp. 172–208.

Perlmann, Moshe, "Notes on Anti-Christian Propaganda in the Mamlūk Empire," *BSOAS* 10/4 (1942), pp. 843–861.

Perlmann, Moshe, "Notes on the Position of Jewish Physicians in Medieval Muslim Countries," *Israel Oriental Studies* 2 (1972), pp. 315–19.

Petry, Carl "Copts in Late Medieval Egypt," in: *The Coptic Encyclopedia*, 8 vols., ed. Atiya Aziz, New York: Macmillan 1991, vol. 2, pp. 618–35.

Pormann, Peter E. and Savage-Smith, Emilie, *Medieval Islamic Medicine*, Washington, D.C.: Georgetown University Press 2007.

Pormann, Peter E., "The Physician and the Other: Images of the Charlatan in Medieval Islam," *Bulletin of the History of Medicine* 79/2 (2005), pp. 189–227.

Richards, Donald S., "Coptic Bureaucracy under the Mamluks," in: *Colloque international sur l'histoire du Caire. 27 mars–5 avril 1969*, ed. Ministry of Culture of the Arab Republic of Egypt, Cairo: General Egyptian Book Organization 1972, pp. 373–81.

Richards, Donald S., "Dhimmi Problems in Fifteenth-Century Cairo: Reconsideration of a Court Document," *Studies in Muslim-Jewish Relations* 1 (1993), pp. 127–63.

Rustow, Marina, "At the Limits of Communal Autonomy: Jewish Bids for Intervention from the Mamluk State," *MSR* 13/2 (2009), pp. 133–59.

Saleh, Walid, "'Sublime in its Style, Exquisite in its Tenderness': The Hebrew Bible Quotations in al-Biqāʿī's Qurān Commentary," in: *Adaptations and Innovations*, ed. Tzwi Langermann and Josef Stern, Leuven: Peeters 2007, pp. 331–46.

Saleh, Walid, "A Muslim Hebraist: Al-Biqāʿī's Bible Treatise and His Defence of Using the Bible to Interpret the Qur'ān," *Speculum* 83 (2008), pp. 629–54.

Saleh, Walid, *In Defence of the Bible: A Critical Edition and an Introduction to al-Biqāʿī's Bible Treatise*, Leiden: Brill 2008.

Scharf, Andrew, *The Universe of Shabbetai Donnolo*, New York: Ktav 1976.

Seth Ward, *Construction and Repair of Churches and Synagogues in Islamic Law: A Treatise by Taqī ad-Dīn ʿAlī b. ʿAbd al-Kāfī al-Subkī*, Yale University Thesis 1984.

Shatzmiller, Joseph, *Jews, Medicine, and Medieval Society*, Berkeley: UCP 1994.

Shefer, Miri, "Physicians in Mamluk and Ottoman Courts," in: *Mamluks and Ottomans: Studies in Honour of Michael Winter*, eds. David Wasserstein and Ami Ayalon, London: Routledge 2006, pp. 114–22.

Stephan, Walter G. and Cookie W. Stephan, *Intergroup Relations*, Boulder, CO: Westview Press1996.

Stets, Jan E. and Peter J. Burke, "Identity Theory and Social Identity Theory," *Social Psychology Quarterly* 63/3 (2000), pp. 224 - 237.

Tajfel, Henri, "Social Psychology of Intergroup Relations," *Annual Review of Psychology* 33 (1982), pp. 1 - 39.

Thomas, David and Rifaat Ebied, *Muslim-Christian Polemic during the Crusades: The Letter from the People of Cyprus and Ibn Abī Ṭālib al-Dimashqī's Response*, Leiden: Brill 2005.

Thomas, David, "Christian Voices in Muslim Theology," *Jerusalem Studies in Arabic and Islam* 36 (2009), pp. 357 - 79.

Thomas, David, "Christian-Muslim Misunderstanding in the Fourteenth Century: The Correspondence between Christians in Cyprus and Muslims in Damascus," in: Haddad et al., *Towards a Cultural History*, pp. 13 - 30.

Thomas, David, "Idealism and Intransigence: A Christian-Muslim Encounter in Early Mamluk Times," *MSR* 13/2 (2009), pp. 85 - 103.

Tritton, Arthur S., *The Caliphs and Their Non-Muslim Subjects. A Critical Study of the Covenant of 'Umar*, London: Humphrey Milford Oxford University Press 1930.

Van den Berghe, Pierre L. "Racism, Ethnocentrism and Xenophobia: in Our Genes or in Our Memes?" in: *In-group/Out-group Behaviour in Modern Societies: An Evolutionary Perspective*, eds. Kristian Thienpont and Robert Cliquet, Brussels: NIDI CBGS Publications 1999, pp. 21 - 33.

Vermeulen, Urbain, "The Rescript of al-Malik al-Ṣāliḥ against the Dhimmīs (755 A.H./ 1354 A.D.)," *Orientalia Lovaniensia Periodica* 9 (1978), pp. 175 - 84.

Voland, Eckart and Wulf Schiefenhövel, *The Biological Evolution of Religious Mind and Behavior*, Berlin, Heidelberg: Springer Verlag 2009.

Ward, Seth, "Ibn al-Rif'a on the Churches and Synagogues of Cairo," *Medieval Encounters* 5/1 (1999), pp. 70 - 84.

Ward, Seth, "Taqī ad-Dīn al-Subkī on Construction, Continuance, and Repair of Churches and Synagogues in Islamic Law," in: *Studies in Islamic and Judaic Traditions II: Papers Presented at the Institute for Islamic -Judaic Studies, Center for Judaic Studies, University of Denver*, eds. William M. Brinner and Stephen D. Ricks, Atlanta: Scholars Press 1989, pp. 169 - 188.

Winter, Michael, *Society and Religion in Early Ottoman Egypt. Studies in the Writings of 'Abd al-Wahhāb al-Sha'rānī*, New Brunswick and London: Transaction Books 1982.

Zetterstéen, Karl Wilhelm, *Beiträge zur Geschichte der Mamlūkensultane in den Jahren 690 - 741 der Higra nach arabischen Handschriften*, Leiden: Brill 1919.

Zimbardo, Philip, *The Lucifer Effect: Understanding How Good People Turn Evil*, New York: Random House 2007.

Christian Müller

Mamluk Law: a reassessment

The renewed interest in Mamluk studies also touches crime, punishment and justice in the Mamluk empire. These historical phenomena are mainly seen from the angle of the sultan's politics,[1] a question of 'Islamic justice',[2] deviant behaviour,[3] etc. None of these studies, however, poses the question of law from a larger sociological point of view: How did Mamluk law, if it existed, function? Then, what was law's impact on society in general? Current scholarship presents the sultan's position as limited by power struggles within the military elite but above 'law'[4], a law that hardly exists as a sociological factor. Studies on Islamic law, on the other hand, deal mainly with legal theory and doctrine that was not directly linked to Mamluk social and political history.[5] A major difficulty is certainly to explain whether and how Islamic law, the only major legal referent known for Mamluk society, functioned as applied 'law' in society, not as abstract doctrine. For this I analyze an *understudied source type*, original legal documents from the Mamluk period. This allows for a bottom-up perspective on legal practices – which contrasts with the top-down perspective of historiographical sources.

Secondly, this article discusses historical facts concerning a potential 'Mamluk law' from the *sociological perspective* as a 'legal system'. The notion of a legal system, developed by Joseph Raz as a specific form of normative system,

1 Petry, *Politics of Insult*, and idem, *Quis Custodiet Custodes*; Martel-Thoumian, *Pouvoir et justice*.
2 Lange, *Justice*.
3 Martel-Thoumian, *Plaisirs illicites*, and *idem*, *Voleurs et assassins*; or the cases cited in Havemann, Chronicle of Ibn Iyās.
4 Haarmann, *Geschichte*, 252 – 7.
5 Despite its title "*Islamic Law in Action. Authority, Discretion, and Everyday Experiences in Mamluk Egypt*", Kristen Stilt's book marks no exception. Her claim that "[d]aily life … was governed by both the doctrine produced by the jurists and the policy decisions of the sultan, two distinct and mutually dependent bases of authority", p. 37, remains dissociated from the description of the Cairine market-inspector's actions, pp. 73 – 202, where she rarely cites Muslim jurists, and if so, indifferently to periods and law-schools.

implies not only a set of interlocked norms, here *fiqh*-doctrines and/or state regulations, but also its institutions (primary organs), e.g., courts of law, legal experts and executive agents. The sociological function of a legal system is to regulate and stabilize certain inter-human relations and to sanction transgressions.[6] As a consequence of this approach, law is more than a set of legal norms. Therefore, we distinguish in what follows between 'Law' – in capital letters – as a legal system and 'law(s)' – as legal norms. In this perspective, 'Islamic law', the jurists' interpretation (*fiqh*) of the Divine Commands to the Muslim community (*sharīʿah*), is a set of legal norms, not a legal system. The constitution of Islamic law-norms as part of a Mamluk legal system is the topic of this article.

Did Mamluk Law Exist?

Before answering the question how Islamic law constituted Mamluk Law, a first step is to ask whether such a Law existed at all. Most studies on crime and punishment, the *muḥtasib* or other judicial institutions, the sultan's role etc., touch on aspects of law in the Mamluk period without posing the question of a legal system. Notwithstanding, the primary organs of a legal system, *qāḍī*-courts of law, legal experts (*muftīs*) and executive agents (*muḥtasib, mutawallī*), are attested in various sources. These actors were not considered to apply Islamic law for two reasons: the scarcity of authentic documents in the absence of Mamluk court-archives, and more important, the scholarly approach to Islamic norms of law as developed by Muslim jurists since early on (*fiqh*). During most parts of the 20th century scholars were convinced that *fiqh* was first of all an unchanging deontology, characterized by a profound theory-praxis-dichotomy, which was not applied except in very limited fields.[7] Seen from such an angle, the existing works of Mamluk jurists did not necessarily control the legal system of their time. However, things changed for both aspects, the availability of legal documents and the approach to Islamic law. The edition of Mamluk documents has progressed considerably during the last 25 years, adding new sources to the few available *waqfīyāt*-documents from Cairo, deeds from St Catherine and early editions of the Ḥaram-corpus discovered in 1974.[8] The European project "Islamic Law Materialized" studies the correlation between Arabic legal documents and the jurists' law. From the Mamluk period, its database CALD contains ca

6 Raz, *Practical Reason.*
7 Against this position cf. Johansen, *Muslim fiqh.*
8 Cf. for a survey Conermann, Reinfandt, *Anmerkungen*, esp. 180–7 and bibliography.

1200 edited and non-edited deeds with more than 1700 documents.[9] Studies of Islamic law in general increasingly include aspects of its application and legal change.[10] This study on Mamluk Law follows three steps, establishing:

1) the importance of *fiqh*-norms for the actions of Mamluk *qāḍī*-courts (using legal documents),
2) the predictability of practised *fiqh*-norms, as part of the total set of valid *fiqh*-norms (via types of juridical literature)
3) its character as a legal system (by means of sociological approach)

Legal Documents and *fiqh*-Norms in Mamluk *qāḍī*-Jurisdiction

As in other societies, Mamluk jurisdiction produced legal documents that notarized court decisions and subjective rights of the concerned parties. The existing original documents are the relics of judicial practice. Earlier seen as a practice contradicting Islamic law,[11] recent studies demonstrate how the *qāḍī*, or his deputy (*nā'ib*), used documents in trials – and did so by respecting *fiqh*-rules of oral attestation as legal proof.[12] Any legal document was signed by at least two witnesses, never by the contracting parties. In case of litigation or the necessity to constitute legal proof on the basis of a document, i. e., after the death of a debtor or his prolonged absence, the *qāḍī* summoned the witnesses to perform orally the attestation (*adā' al-shahādah*) (rendering attestation) to the document's content, an attestation a witness had accepted (*taḥammul al-shahādah*) when writing the *shahādah*-notation and his name below the attested text.

Had the *qāḍī* accepted the witnesses as 'honourable', and this was the judge's responsibility as part of the proof-procedure, the proof by attestation (*bayyinah*) was performed and the facts were established as legally valid (*thubūt*). The judge then could pass a sentence (*ḥukm*) if the claimant demanded this. Marginal annotations on documents presented in court-claims from Mamluk Jerusalem confirm these different stages, i. e. accepting a document as basis for a claim (*da'wah*), the evaluation of the witnesses' honourability (*'adālah*) upon the oral attestation, the attestation to the completion of the 'establishment of facts' (*thubūt*) and the judge's ratification with his call for attesting to court procedures. The *qāḍī*-documents summarize oral performances that correspond to *fiqh*-rules. Any court-authenticated document could be used in other cities

9 Started in 2009, the project "Islamic Law Materialized: Arabic legal documents (8th to 15th century)", acronym ILM, ERC AdG2008, n° 230261, lasts five years until 2013. For its mid-term report, see http://www.ilm-project.net/en/.
10 Cf. Masud et al., *Islamic Legal Interpretation*, and Masud et al., *Dispensing Justice in Islam.*
11 Cf. Tyan, *Le notariat*; Schacht, *Introduction.*
12 Müller, *Écrire pour établir.*

without the renewal of witness attestations, contrary to an 'ordinary' witness document that lacked the quality of legal proof (*bayyinah*). These court-procedures were administrative routines, used alike by all *qāḍīs* in the Mamluk state. They are described in notarial manuals (*shurūṭ*-literature) and in *adab al-qāḍī*-literature. In practice, each city had its group of professional witnesses, who worked with the *qāḍī*-court and to whom persons went for attestations in legal affairs.[13]

With the reconstruction of these oral court-procedures that precede notarisation, i.e., of the *thubūt*-procedure, a major argument against the mainly theoretical character of *fiqh* lapses. On the contrary, judicial practice illustrates the importance of *fiqh*-rules for a functioning Mamluk Law. Substantive *fiqh*-norms also influenced Mamluk notarial practice, as the following example illustrates: According to certain rules, a buyer may cancel a valid contract unless he has seen the object (*khiyār al-ru'yah*). As a consequence, sale documents usually notarise the situation 'after' the buyers view and his knowledge of the acquired object.[14] Thus excludes the legal right of rescission, and the written document, beyond a contract deed, guarantees the property right of the buyer.

Another argument against a functioning *qāḍī*-jurisdiction in criminal cases concerns the fact that Islamic law limits his authority to cases that were presented to him with the facts (*accusatio*-competence). The *qāḍī* should not investigate crime (*inquisitio*-competence) that was hidden to him, even if he had a suspicion.[15] Once more, legal documents illustrate how *qāḍī*-jurisdiction worked, this time by a close collaboration with Mamluk officials: In injury and homicide-cases, Mamluk officials were at the origin of trials and presented claimants and defendants to the *qāḍī*-court, who, in turn, notarized to the legal facts establishing the legal rights of the concerned persons. Penalties inflicted by Mamluk authorities or the *qāḍī*-court (in form of *taʿzīr*) to combat crime or offences were not part of these documents.[16]

Mamluk legal documents reflect this *institutional collaboration* between officials and the *qāḍī*-court, whose specific role consisted in safeguarding the subjective rights of persons and institutions. One way to do so was to issue authenticated written documents. In addition, we should not forget that any heritage case passed by the *qāḍī*-court since all debts and assets had to be confirmed in order to proceed with the liquidation of the heritage. The con-

13 For a reconstruction of judicial practices and the role of court-witnesses in Mamluk Jerusalem, see Müller, *Der Kadi und seine Zeugen* .

14 Cf. Rāghib, *Actes de vente d'esclaves,* 2:62–6. The standard formula "*baʿd al-naẓar wa-l-maʿrifah*" is used in more than a hundred documents throughout the Mamluk period, cf. the unpublished database CALD (Comparing Arabic Legal Documents) of the ILM-project.

15 On this Johansen, *Verité et torture*, 136.

16 See the case studies in Müller, *Crimes without Criminals?*.

servation of legal titles in longer terms was effected by judicial procedures called '*isjāl*' and '*tanfīdh al-ḥukm*', often found in *waqf*-documents. They consisted in 're-registering' the authentication of a former judge or in the rendering applicable of a sentence of a former judge. Differences between these procedures were grounded in *fiqh*-norms.[17]

As a result, existing legal documents show how (certain) *fiqh*-rules determine the Mamluk *qāḍī*-jurisdiction and practice. A first answer to the question on Mamluk Law then is the following: Mamluk Law existed at least in those fields of law which concern legal documents issued and used by *qāḍī*-courts, that is, marriage and divorce, heritage, commercial transactions and *waqf*, as well as injury and homicide cases. The certification of legal documents by the *qāḍī*-courts was no marginal phenomenon. In fact it touched all layers of the population, as is illustrated by some 400 estate inventories drawn up in Jerusalem over just five years at the end of the 14th century: Mamluk administration systematically set up estate-inventories for dead or dying persons in the form of witness documents that served to execute inheritance by the *qāḍī*-court. This means that Islamic law – as practised in the Mamluk *qāḍī*-courts – was a major factor in society. Before dealing with Mamluk Law and its institutions from a broader historical perspective, we need to introduce paradigms that allow us to analyse Islamic law under the aspect of its application as Law.

Predictability of Law: valid and applied *fiqh*-rules

If Mamluk *qāḍīs* applied Islamic law-rules, which we may now safely assume, then the new question is: How can *fiqh*-norms, known for their variety or even contradictory content, become predictable in jurisdiction? The Law requires predictable norms in order to stabilize society. Any unreasoned change of norm-content has a touch of the arbitrary which undermines the Law's authority.[18]

From early on, Muslim scholars discussed and interpreted God's Commands (*sharī'ah*) from a legal perspective. This legal reasoning became known as *fiqh* (originally: 'understanding'), commonly translated as Islamic law. As a result of a century-old tradition that was grounded in the example of the Prophet Muḥammad and the practice of the early Muslim community and some of their leaders, literary sources of a juridical norm-system go back to the mid-2nd/8th century. Two centuries later, the hermeneutical principles of this legal inter-

17 I am currently preparing an article on these aspects of procedure in *qāḍī*-documents. See also Reinfandt, *Mamlukische Sultansstiftungen*, 113–123, referring to occurrences in his text edition.

18 Legal reasoning is the prerogative of Law's primary organs, the legal experts. This does not imply that all subjects understand or participate in this reasoning.

pretation of the Sacred Commands were defined in the *uṣūl al-fiqh*, later commonly accepted to legitimize the set of legal norms that constituted the doctrine of each law-school (*madhhab*). The legal doctrines of a *madhhab*, collected by the 8th/14th centuries in specific manuals, however do not constitute a set of 'laws' in a modern sense where a law constitutes a general norm, whose application to a case is ruled by secondary norms. The school-doctrines formed part of a much larger casuistic system of legal norms, each of them legitimized separately by legal reasoning. Of primary importance to a legal norm in *fiqh* was its rooting in Islam's sacred normativity and legal tradition, not its easy handling within hierarchically organized norm-levels. By differentiating cases and specified norms, Muslim jurists adapted their reasoning to emerging fields of law. This said, *fiqh* was a multidimensional intellectual enterprise that included the development of hermeneutical principles, the systematisation of transmitted norms, enlarging methods of norm-interpretation and creating transversal concepts. The multidimensionality of juridical thinking did not end with a 'formative period', as the writings of Mamluk jurists illustrate (see below).

As noted repeatedly, *fiqh* methodology allows for multiple solutions to the same or, nearly the same, case. Thomas Bauer situates this within a larger context as 'culture of ambiguity'.[19] Muslim jurists considered the same phenomenon not exactly as ambiguity, but as 'diversity' (*ikhtilāf*) with God's blessing, which means that different legal norms are valid and fulfill equally the requirement of Islam's Sacred Law. Then, how could Mamluk Law be based on *fiqh*, as a set of legal rules 'in diversity', and fulfill the requirement of predictability for Law that regulated social and economic relations in society? In other words, how could *fiqh* be transformed into a coherent and congruent set of legal norms? The answer lies in our perspective on *fiqh* norms: The norms produced by legal thinking and which were transmitted as part of 'Islamic law' were, taken as a whole, not free from contradictory results. This does, however, not imply that all those norms were equally applied as Mamluk laws.

In order to assess the predictability of Islamic law norms within Mamluk Law, we need to change the perspective from norm-production, the creation of valid rules within juridical reasoning, towards norm-application and its mechanisms. In other words, we need to look at Islamic law-norms from the perspective of subjective rights, as determined for example by legal documents. Law is predictable, when the holder of a deed can reasonably expect to obtain his notarized right, even in the case of litigation or death. It is also predictable if the *qāḍī*'s decision in cases of conflicting rights remains within the boundaries of the law and establishes a legal title that creates a new situation.[20]

---

19 Bauer, *Kultur der Ambiguität*, 157–182.

20 I. e. the claim of the leaseholder's heirs to complete the term of a long-term lease and the

The predictability of law at the level of court decisions depends on a preselection of legally practised norms that may be part of a wider set of theoretically existing, valid *fiqh*-rules.[21] Several factors, external and internal to *fiqh*, render Mamluk Law predictable and provide a judge with sufficient reasons to choose among the practised norm and to disregard other, equally valid *fiqh*-norms. This norm-selection was not determined by legal hermeneutics (*uṣūl al-fiqh*). Among the historical mechanisms that shaped practised Mamluk Law (in contrast to valid Islamic law) are the training of jurists in law-colleges (*madāris*) and the evolution of legal thinking within the *madhhab*. Other factors concern the state nominations of judges belonging to all four *madhhabs* to specific fields of law. In Mamluk times, school-doctrine determined many rules and judges were bound to apply the doctrine.[22] As explained before, Islamic law-norms applied to restricted cases, not to concepts of a generalized nature as in codified law. This meant that legal-norms fixed by doctrine applied only to restricted cases and, as a consequence, school-doctrine covered important parts of practised norms, not its totality. Until now, no text has been identified as authoritative 'Mamluk law', if such a law-book ever existed. The only way for us to learn more about the practised norms is to study the activities of those jurists who applied this law. The analysis of legal curriculum at law-colleges (*madāris*) illustrates which texts were important for legal training.[23] The link between practised law in courts and teaching activities at law-colleges is reflected in assignments on posts as professors and as judges.[24] A third aspect of legal practice concerns the contemporary legal literature: juridical hand-books, commentaries, responsa and notarial-manuals.

Mamluk Legal Literature and Practised *fiqh*-Rules

The distinction between valid and practised *fiqh*-rules that results from the application of Islamic law opens a new research-field that we may designate as '*fiqh-norms in the Mamluk empire*'. How to identify the relevant sources within the huge body of *fiqh*-literature? The first consideration concerns the chrono-

foundations claim to terminate the contract with the leaseholder's death, Ḥaram no, 334, cf. Müller, *Settling Litigations*, 51.

21 On the distinction between valid (justified), practised and endorsed mandatory norms see Raz, *Practical Reason*, 80 (the dimension of mandatory norms).

22 Rapoport, *Legal Diversity*, and Wiederhold, *Remarks on Mālikī Judges*.

23 For law-colleges in Damascus, see al-Nuʿaymī, *Al-Dāris*.

24 See for a first approach (on religious teaching) Pouzet, *Damas au VIIe/XIIIe*, 149–205.

logical and regional origin of a *fiqh*-work, a second its content, and a third its authority-level within the juridical discourse at various periods.[25]

As a preliminary assessment of juridical texts produced in the Mamluk empire by work titles, Brockelmann's *Geschichte der Arabischen Litteratur*, published between 1937 and 1943, reveals more than a hundred authors and a large variety of juridical texts, most of them still in manuscript form.[26] However, Brockelmann's regional and chronological classification cuts across his periodisation, as he considers Ayyubid and early Mamluk scholars among the 'post-classical period' and their successors among the 'period of decline'.[27] The mobility of scholars within the Islamic world, where legal thinking followed schools of law, not political boundaries, poses another problem for the identification of a *faqīh* as a Mamluk jurist. An example of the difficulty in qualifying a person as "Mamluk jurist" or in attributing him to the Mamluk state-apparatus is the mālikite scholar Ibn Farḥūn (d. 799/1397) who travelled in Egypt and Syria and became *qāḍī* in Medina, where he died. In fact, a legal scholar was, first of all, a scholar of *fiqh* and its valid norms. He is a 'Mamluk jurist' in those parts of his production that concern practised norms in connection with applied law. Since it is mainly those texts that have been carefully preserved and/or recopied during the centuries, any text written for the specific necessities of the period only had a chance to survive if it contained elements that were of a general interest for later generations.[28] This may be a reason why Mamluk collections of practised norms, if they existed, did not survive or were not designated as such.

The 'distinction by content' examines various text-types of Mamluk legal literature, covering the hermeneutical approach to sacred origins (*uṣūl al-fiqh*), the systematic exposition of juridical norms (*furūʿ*), and detailed studies of specific problems that mobilized all levels of juridical argumentation, often called *risālah*[29], or less exhaustive treatment by a *fatwā*. The re-writing of juridical concepts in Mamluk times included the development of 'differentiations' (*furūq*) between similar norms and technical principles (*qawāʿid*)[30]. Mamluk

25 Cf. Johansen, *Legal Literature.*

26 Cf. Brockelmann, *Geschichte der Arabischen Litteratur* [GAL]. The number of jurists' would increase if recent manuscript catalogues were included.

27 *GAL* 1:474–81, 1:496–505 (post classical period) mentions 3 Ḥanafite, 1 Mālikite, 4 Shāfiʿite and 1 Ḥanbalite jurists, and *GAL* 2:94–131, S2:86–131 (period of decline) refers to 38 Ḥanafite, 5 Mālikite, 60 Shāfiʿite and 17 Ḥanbalite jurists. Add to this works, whose authors figure among historiography (i.e. al-ʿAynī *GAL* 2:65 no 6, with 1:478 no 1b) or Quranic studies (i.e. al-Kāfiyağī, *GAL* 2:138 f. no 9).

28 Ibn Farḥūn's *Tabṣirat al-ḥukkām*, is an essential work on judicial competences among various state agents, but it is not specifically "Mamluk".

29 I.e. al-Suyūṭī's treaty on whether the sultan could convert a public pass-way to an *iqṭāʿ*, to name a work of practical importance, *GAL* 2:194 no 176.

30 Examples are the Mālikite al-Qarāfī (d. 1285) with his "*al-Furūq*" (*GAL* 1:481 no 1), and the

authors continued to write works on *uṣūl al-fiqh* where differences with 'classical works' lay in details. Prolific writers composed works in various fields of juridical thinking. Certain *furū*ʿ-works exempted, most of these writings concern the norm-production of valid *fiqh*-rules and do not concern directly the selection of practised norms.[31]

The distinction according to 'authority-level' among *furū*ʿ-works[32] that were part of the juridical tradition of each law-school, provides a provisional (theoretical) tool to distinguish between valid non-practised and valid practised *fiqh*-norms. We assume that rules that contemporary jurists discuss and comment on belonged to the practised norms, whereas other, non-mentioned rules were disregarded. However, legal literature only reports legal norms, never renders them authoritative, as a law-text would (see below). In the absence of set state-law and since we do not dispose of authoritative texts of applicable *fiqh*-norms as with the Ottoman *kanūn-name* for Egypt, the identification of authoritative norm-collections passes by the criteria of juridical discourse among Mamluk jurists.

If commentaries on a handbook in substantive law (*furū*ʿ) are a yardstick by which to measure its authority, then various early Mamluk works were important: Highly appreciated by contemporary jurists, Nawawī's *Minhāj al-Ṭālibīn* (composed in 669/1270) was commented on and summarized more than 18 times during the Mamluk period.[33] It surpassed the earlier Shāfiʿite compendium by Abū Shujāʿ (d. 593/1196), *al-Taqrīb*, with three Mamluk commentaries.[34] These works reflect the preponderance of the Shāfiʿīte law-school in Mamluk Egypt and Syria, whereas the other three law-schools produced fewer Mamluk commentaries. The most prominent work for the Ḥanafites was *al-Hidāyah Sharḥ al-Bidāyah* by the Transoxanian jurist al-Marghīnānī (d. 593/1196), with at least four Mamluk commentaries[35], the *Kanz al-Daqā'iq* by the Iranian Nasafī

Ḥanbalite Ibn Rajab (d. 1393), *Qawāʿid al-Fiqh* (*GAL* S2:130), both works are edited. Cf. Heinrichs, *Qawāʿid*, idem, *Structuring*.

31 Future studies may reveal to what extent *furūq*, *qawāʿid* and Mamluk *uṣūl*-concepts contributed to elaborate new valid and practised *fiqh*-norms.

32 Johansen, *Legal literature*.

33 *GAL* 1:496–8, S1:680–1. The *Minhāj* was a summary of the *Muḥarrar* of al-Rāfiʿī, who lived in Qazwīn and died in 623/1226, *GAL* 1:493.

34 *GAL* 2:492.

35 *GAL* 1:466–7, S1:644–5, cites among other commentaries and glosses at least ten commentaries from the Mamluk period, not all from Egypt or Syria. First printed Cairo 1326/1908 in 4 vols., a Mamluk commentary was composed by al-Khabbāzī (d. 691/1292), *GAL* 1:477; another by Akmal al-Dīn M. al-Bābartī (d. 1384), *al-ʿInāyah*, first printed Calcutta 1831, *GAL* 1:466 f., S2:89, reprinted Cairo 1970 on the margin of *Sharḥ Fatḥ al-Qadīr* by Ibn al-Humām (d. 861/1457), *GAL* 1:467, 2:91. On al-ʿAynī's commentary cf. *GAL* 2:66 no 11.

(d. 710/1310),[36] and the 7th-8th/13–14th-century handbook *Tuḥfat al-Mulūk* with at least one Mamluk commentary and contradicting indications of authorship.[37] The Egyptian Khalīl (d. 767/1364) composed a summary (*Mukhtaṣar*) on Mālikite norms that served as basis for later Maghrebi-commentators.[38] A Mamluk commentary by al-Suyūṭī' (d. 911/1505) exists.[39] The Ḥanbalite handbook *al-ʿUmdah* by Muwaffaq al-Dīn b. Qudāmah (d. 620/1223) is cited with one commentary.[40] The nowadays-famous Ḥanbalite scholars Ibn Taymīyah (d. 728/1328)[41] and Ibn Qayyim al-Jawzīyah (d. 751/1350)[42] gave new impulses to their law-school, but did certainly not dominate Ḥanbalite teaching at their time.[43] Juridical handbooks may collect a school doctrine from a hermeneutical perspective (universally accepted norms) or from a practical point of view (practised norms). They are distinct from law-codices, since they functioned within a casuistic norm-system where the significance of a rule is determined by its range and the profoundness of interpretation. Most of the cited authors of an authoritative 'handbook' also wrote extensive works on substantive law (*furūʿ*).[44]

As mentioned before, juridical rationality according to the sacred principles of interpreting Divine Commands (*uṣūl al-fiqh*) permeated *fiqh*-rules throughout centuries. In the Mamluk period (7th-10th/13th-16th centuries), this formulation of transmitted legal norms had reached a stage when Muslim jurists considered that a certain body of *fiqh*-norms were sacred and would not change by further legal reasoning. These norms belonging to the schools' doctrine varied from one school to another in details, due to hermeneutical differences.

36 *GAL* 2:251, commentaries mostly in eastern countries, but also in Mamluk territory, cf. al-ʿAynī *GAL* 2:66 no 14.

37 GAL 1:478, with al-ʿAynī, *Minḥat al-Sulūk*, 10, where the editor summarizes attributions to the *Tuḥfah*'s author: ʿAbd al-Qāḍir al-Qurashī (d. 770), *Jawāhir al-Muḍīyah*, names Muḥammad b. Abī Bakr b. ʿAbd al-Muḥsin as author of the *Tuḥfat al-Mulūk* in 10 chapters, Ḥajjī Khalīfah has Muḥammad b. Abī Bakr Ḥasan al-Rāzī, but also indicates as possible author (*qīla*) a Shams al-Dīn Muḥammad b. Tāj al-Dīn Ibrāhīm al-Tawqānī – referred to as Muḥammad b. Ibrāhīm al-Qawqānī in one of the mss. of the *Minḥat al-Sulūk* as author of the *matn*. The edition of the *Tuḥfat al-Mulūk*, has as author Muḥammad b. Abī Bakr b. ʿAbd al-Qādir al-Rāzī (d. 666), contradicting the statement that the author finished this work in Rabīʿ I 761 (!), *ibid.*, al-Rāzī, *Tuḥfat*, 1:285. For the same name attribution, see Ṣāliḥīyah, *al-Muʿjam al-Shāmil*, 3:7. It may well be that two works by different authors bore the title *Tuḥfat al-Mulūk*.

38 *GAL* 2:102 f., first printed in Paris 1844/52.

39 *GAL* 2:194 no 178n.

40 *GAL* 1:503 no 25; to this add the commentary by Ibn Taymīyah, *GAL* S2:125 no 132. The author's extensive work *al-Muqniʿ* inspired several commentaries, *GAL* S1:688.

41 *GAL* 2:125–7, S2:124–5.

42 *GAL* 2:127–9, S2:126–8.

43 On Ibn Taymīyah's limited influence before the 19th century cf. el-Rouayeb, From Ibn Ḥajar al-Hayrami.

44 Cf. al-Nawawī, *Rawḍat al-Ṭālibīn*, *GAL* 1:543 no 50c, with several glosses, Ibn Qudāmah, *al-Muqniʿ*, *GAL* 1:503 no 1.

When the Mamluk sultans invested judges of the four Sunnite law-schools in the capital and in provincial centres, the emerging 'literature of dissent' (*ikhtilāf*) summarized and compared these dogmatic differences, or tried to explain them at a theoretical level.[45]

When it comes to identifying the *fiqh*-rules practised in Mamluk Law, the notary-manuals (*kutub al-shurūṭ*) provide important indications since legal documents have to comply with practised norms in order to resist judicial litigation. Existing legal documents on inheritance, marriages and economic transactions (sales, location), correspond in their formulation to model-documents given in the manuals.[46] Since manuals offer models in other fields of law, like in injury or homicide cases, for divorce etc., we may assume that there also the jurists' law applied and that the *shurūṭ* manuals cover a range of practised law-norms. Three manuals of the Mamluk period are easily accessible: al-Asyūṭī, *Jawāhir al-'Uqūd* (completed 865/1461),[47] Muḥammad al-Jarawānī (approx. 788/1386), *al-Kawkab al-Mushriq*,[48] and al-Nuwayrī (d. 733/1333), *Nihāyat al-Arab*[49]. When *shurūṭ*-manuals provide legal explications, they usually give the practised solution. The latest, al-Asyūṭī, explains cases of dissent between the law-schools by citing the authoritative opinion.[50]

As the philosophy of law distinguishes between norm-creation and norm application, we identify the body of Muslim jurists as interpreters of a Islamic normativity – in changing form throughout the early centuries. They transmitted and selected valid *fiqh*-norms according to legal hermeneutics. Mamluk jurists applied among all valid *fiqh*-norms those that were practised at their time: The variety of legal literature should not obscure the fact that legal doctrines of the four law-schools were solidly based. The selection of practised norms was partially fixed by legal school dogma, partially subject to juridical interpretation and partially the result of state intervention in the appointment of judges from a specific law-school to certain fields of law.

An example for selecting a practised *fiqh*-norm among various valid *fiqh*-rules by Mamluk Law concerns the inheritance by cognate relatives other than parents, sisters and agnatic aunts, the (*dhawū l-arḥām*): According to Mamluk

45 For the latter see al-Kāfiyağī, *al-Faraḥ wa-l-Surūr*, 143–184; *GAL* 2:138 no 9.
46 Cf. for the Mamluk period already Little, *Documents*, 102.
47 Edition Cairo 1955.
48 Brockelmann situates the author in Iran, *GAL* S2:271. However, both versions of the *Kawkab al-Mushriq* edited by S. Saghbini in two text-columns, correspond to Mamluk judicial practice, cf. i. e. al-Jarawānī, *al-Kawkab al-Mushriq*, 307, or 334 (on *isjāl*). Only a meticulous comparison with Iranian and Mamluk documents allows to decide on the geographical origin of each version.
49 Al-Nuwayrī, *Nihāyat al-Arab*, 9:1–160.
50 I.e. al-Asyūṭī, *Jawāhir al-'Uqūd*, 2:221 f., on dissent among the four law-schools on blood-money.

legal practice these 'cognates' are excluded from succession to the benefit of the public treasury (*bayt al-māl*). The application of this legal norm is confirmed by more than 400 estate-inventories that often list the treasury, never cognates, as heir. As a consequence, escheat-estates become a major source of revenue for the state.[51] Among contemporary *fiqh*-manuals, opinions diverge: al-Nawawī explains that at the basis the Shāfiʿite law-school (*aṣl al-madhhab*) excluded cognates: parts exceeding those of legal heirs, the agnates and any liberator's family, went to the public treasury. Was the public treasury unorganized (*lam yantaẓim amr bayt al-māl*), posterior jurists then attributed exceeding parts to the cognates.[52] Historically, the legal practice to disinherit the cognates corresponds with the developed Mamluk administration and its 'bureau of escheat-inheritances' (*dīwān al-mawārīth al-ḥashrīyah*). The *Mukhtaṣar* by the Mālikite Khalīl contains the norm which excludes the cognates.[53] The Ḥanafite manual *Tuḥfat al-Mulūk* however states the opposite: the public treasury inherits beyond the legal parts only if no cognates exist.[54] In his commentary *Minḥat al-Sulūk Sharḥ Tuḥfat al-Mulūk*, al-ʿAynī (d. 855/1451) does not explicitly comment on this phrase, but explains in his chapter on cognates that Shāfiʿites and Mālikites did not consider them as legal heirs, contrary his own school, the Ḥanafites (*lanā*).[55] He explains the preference for cognates with the fact that some of the legal heirs (*aṣḥāb al-furūḍ*) become, for the rest of the heritage, cognates, as for example the closest cognate the daughter.[56] As a consequence, any surviving daughter would inherit the rest of her parents' estate, not Public treasury. This was definitely not the practised norm in Jerusalem at the end of the 14th century, since Public treasury inherited in three out of 57 cases together with one or several daughters of the defunct:[57] Mamluk law adopted the doctrine of the Shāfiʿite school for the case of a functioning Public treasury of an Islamic state. However, if the sultan wished to change the legal norm, he could appoint Ḥanafite judges over inheritance cases: They would rule according to their school-doctrine in favor of cognate heirs.

51 Cf. Müller, *Der Kadi und seine Zeugen*, chapter 5.4.
52 Al-Nawawī, *Minhāj al-Ṭālibīn*, 180. One of the four reasons to inherit is "*islām*", which is the reason why the Public treasury is included, cf. *ibid.*
53 Ḫalīl, *Muḫtaṣar*, 308, l. 10.
54 Rāzī, *Tuḥfat al-Mulūk*, 1:266. The legal position corresponds to Schacht, *Introduction*, 170.
55 *Minḥat al-Sulūk*, 448.
56 Ibid., 463.
57 Cf. Ḥaram-documents nos. 169, 464 and 771ṯ, cf. Little, *Catalogue*, 83, 124 and 222.

Islamic Law as Mamluk State Law?

With the importance of *qāḍī*-jurisdiction, based on applied *fiqh*-norms, it is difficult to uphold the idea that Mamluk society functioned without Law. Since we may therefore suppose that *fiqh*-norms were part of such a Law, the question is to what extent practised Islamic law constituted Mamluk Law. The philosopher of law Joseph Raz identifies criteria that determine whether a given 'system of norms' corresponds to a 'legal system' and to its functionality. Such an approach helps to answer two questions: Does the norm-system 'practised Islamic law' fulfill the law-sociologically required conditions of a legal system? If so, what about its status within Mamluk state Law that included institutions dominated by the military and political elite?

Any 'legal system' constitutes an institutionalized system, where 'primary organs' control a) the creation of legal norms and b) the norm-applying procedures. Both spheres, norm-creation and norm application, may be controlled by different 'primary organs', like law-giving agencies on the one hand and jurists, attorneys, judges on the other.[58] In Mamluk times, judges were nominated by the state and received a salary, professional witnesses were paid for their work as notaries by the concerned parties, and executive agents belonged to administrative services.

A major character of legal systems is that they are 'open', meaning that "they maintain and support other forms of social groupings. Legal systems achieve this by upholding and enforcing contracts, agreements, rules and customs of individuals and associations, [...], and so on."[59] Practised Islamic law did fulfill this requirement, which distinguishes its norm-system from deontology. Muslim jurists developed a three-level scale that measured the legal validity of contracts and agreements as 'valid' (*ṣaḥīḥ*), 'defective' (*fāsid*) or 'void' (*bāṭil*). Authentic legal documents of the Mamluk period indicate the 'shariatic validity' (*ṣaḥīḥan sharʿīyan*) of legal actions, like a contract or the judge's sentence. This illustrates that Islamic law-norms operated as an open system of norms. A different aspect of legal systems, sanction-mechanisms for breaching the law,[60] does not only include punishment, be it discreditory (*taʿzīr*) or a *ḥadd*-punishment: in civil cases, the judge's decision to invalidate a contract, a bequest or a foundation could have dramatic consequences for the concerned parties.[61] These

58 Raz, *Practical reasons*, 123 ff. on institutionalized systems.

59 Raz, *Practical reasons*, 153

60 On this aspect from a philosophical perspective, see Raz, *Practical reasons*, 154 – 162.

61 Following the judicial invalidation of a bequest that liberated the slaves, these were sold in the market, cf. Little, *Court Records*, 30 – 35 (edition of Ḥaram document no 650, with l. 6 invalidation, l. 20 – 26 rightful sale).

elements of an open and sanctioning system concern the internal functioning of Islamic law-norms as a legal system.

Two other criteria set by Raz concern the status of Islamic law within Mamluk Law as a whole: legal systems have to be 'comprehensive' and require 'supreme authority.[62] In fact, Islamic law is '*comprehensive*' as a legal system in the sense that it "claim[s] authority to any type of behaviour".[63] However, this "does not entail that legal systems have and other systems do not have authority to regulate every kind of behaviour."[64] And "[it] should also be remembered that an action is regulated by a norm even if it is merely permitted by it."[65] Thus the fact that *fiqh*-norms do only regulate certain fields of law, and that other institutions also have authority to regulate human behaviour, does not hurt Raz's criteria to be comprehensive. Muslim jurists assumed this claim throughout history.

Law's claim of '*supreme authority*', as a weak, but essential condition for legal systems,[66] may help to identify the status of the jurists' law (*fiqh*) within the broader frame of a, still hypothetic, Mamluk Law, with Islamic normativity (*sharīʿah*) as supreme legal authority. The Mamluk sultan exercised the highest, absolute political power as head of the state. From a constitutional point of view, the Abbasid shadow-caliph invested the sultan by diploma (*ʿahd*). The caliph himself was legally the head of the Muslim community.[67] In these letters of assignment, the Sultan figures as Protector of Islam, not as a lawgiver (*shāriʿ*).[68] The constitutional theory of al-Qarāfī distinguishes the legal implications of prophetic actions in the function of a) messager, b) mufti, c) judge and d) head of state (*imām*), and thus provides legitimacy to the Sultan's actions based on public interest.[69] The legal discussion on *siyāsah sharʿīyah*, the ruler's "governance in accordance with *sharīʿah*,"[70] illustrates that the claim of supreme authority of Divine law existed, and this independently of historical reality. It may be doubted that Ibn Taymīyah's views on *fiqh*, drawing also on public interest and utility, as part and parcel of *sharīʿah* including other sources for attaining the

62 Raz, *Practical reasons*, 150–2.
63 Raz, *Practical reasons*, 150 f.
64 Ibid., 151.
65 Ibid.
66 It "means that every legal system claims authority to regulate the setting up and application of other institutionalized systems by its subject community", Raz, *Practical reasons*, 151 f.
67 Qalqashandī cites some letters of assignments to Mamluk sultans, idem, *Ṣubḥ*, 10:111 ff. On Qalāwūn's *ʿahd*, idem, *Ṣubḥ* 10:118; see L. Northrup, *From Slave to Sultan*, 172–6.
68 For the mandate to uphold *al-sharʿ al-sharīf* and the scholars' role to furnish evidence of the *sharīʿah*, mentioned in the assignment of the Sultan al-Malik al-Mu'ayyad Abī al-Naṣr, see *Ṣubḥ* 10:126.
69 Jackson, *Prophetic Action*, 74 and 76 f.
70 See Vogel, *siyāsa*. For Ibn Taymīyah's concept of *siyāsah sharʿīyah* in detail cf. Johansen, *Perfect Law*.

public good,[71] became legal mainstream at his time: The established *fiqh*-training of jurists was preponderant, and the repeated trials of Ibn Taymīyah show that he had influential enemies. Since the Wahhābī movement adopted this view as constitutions for all Saudi states since the 18th century, however, his views have become extremely influential, even in today's scholarship. For the study of Mamluk law it would be interesting to discern by which channels, 'his' idea of restoring Islamic legitimisation to the ruler's just policy (*siyāsah sharʿīyah*) was taken up by later authors, like the Mālikite Ibn Farḥūn (d. 799/1397) in his *Tabṣirat al-Ḥukkām*, and the Ḥanafite al-Tarābulsī (d. 844/1440) in his *Muʿīn al-Ḥukkām*.[72] By discussing the competences of certain 'political charges' (*wilāyāt al-siyāsīyah*), like the *nāẓir al-maẓālim* or the *wālī al-jarā'im*, based on their differences with the *qāḍī*-jurisdiction and according to the terms of Islamic law within the frame of *siyāsah sharʿīyah*, Ibn Farḥūn[73] indirectly affirms the supreme authority of *sharīʿah*-law for these judicial institutions. But jurists distinguish the norm-finding process within *siyāsah sharʿīyah* from school doctrines.[74] Consequently the constitutional relation between jurists' law and Sultanic legislation, within or outside the frame of *sharīʿa*, demands more scholarly attention.

In history, the direct implication of Mamluk authorities in legal matters is attested by a certain type of documents, the *marāsīm sharīfah*, Sultanic decrees. Seen formerly mainly in the context of an extraordinary, even 'secular' *maẓālim*-jurisdiction,[75] they may well be the result of ordinary procedures when individuals solicited Mamluk administration, particularly in cases of unrest, attacks or homicide. A short remark on a legal-report concerning the mortal attack against villagers in the year 795/1393 reveals such a functioning: confronted with repetitive claims by the victims' families, the Viceroy of Jerusalem excuses his inactivity with the fact that, to resolve the case, he needed a '*marsūm sharīf*', which the claimants finally obtained.[76] Several dozens of Sultanic decrees from the Monastery of St Catherine mandate Mamluk officials to act on behalf of the petitioners. Issued within periods of few years only,[77] these decrees may result

71 Ibid., 695a.

72 Cf. Ibid., 695b.

73 Ibn Farḥūn, *Tabṣirat al-Ḥukkām*, 2:146–150.

74 I.e. the Grenadian scholar al-Shāṭibī (d. 790/1388), *Muwāfaqāt*, 4:147 f.

75 Nielsen, *Secular Justice*. With a case survey ibid., 140–158, and difference of *qāḍī* and *maẓālim* jurisdiction in 114 ff.

76 Ḥaram document no. 30, lines 6–7, edited in ʿAsalī, *Waṯāʾiq*, 2:132–4, on this document cf. Müller, *Crimes without criminals?*.

77 On sultans' decrees from St Catherines Monastery see Ernst, *Sultansurkunden*; and, complementarily, orders from levels lower than the sultan cf. Richards, *Administrative Documents*.

from different solicitations of Sultanic justice in various cases,[78] and not the repeated quest for general protection. These documents add a new perspective on the Sultan's personal justice in public,[79] since they reveal its link to the wider aspects of Mamluk administration and its offices. However, more evidence will be necessary to establish whether these quests for intervention in Cairo corresponded to ordinary rules within a highly centralized state administration. The role of state agents as part of the judicial executive, taking the form of an institutionalized collaboration between Mamluk officials and the *qāḍī*-court of law, is now beyond doubt.[80]

Mamluk Legal Institutions

The legal documents introduce a new element to our vision of Mamluk society: the existence of a *qāḍī*-jurisdiction that touched the lives of all persons: The estate-inventories issued by professional witnesses in Jerusalem also concerned Jews and Christians. From a historian's perspective there is a fundamental difference whether *qāḍī*s appear exclusively as parts of the civilian elite (which they also were), or whether they head judicial institutions with a deputy in smaller towns of the Mamluk Empire.[81] This view of judicial institutions counterbalances studies that analyze exclusively historical chronicles with their intrinsic affinity to the spectacular to the detriment of the ordinary. Since Mamluk historians were often trained jurists, sometimes even acting judges, they might have denounced aberrations of the Sultan who usurped his power in legal matters, also with the goal strengthening their own position as sole interprets of Islamic law. Thus, the sultan was not always free to decide against muftīs and judges, if he didn't want to undermine his own authority in the end.[82] In this context several questions merit scholarly attention: Does the privatization of justice by the *ḥājib* reflect an important and widespread phenomenon, or was it limited to the capital and amplified by jealous jurists?[83] With regard to the *muḥtasib*'s role in keeping social order in Cairo on basis of the *ḥisbah*-maxime 'commanding right and forbidding wrong', were his decisions considered to follow Islamic law? As

78 The link between a Sultan's decree and a preceding court-attestation point to this direction. Müller, Pahlitzsch, *Sultan Baybars I*, 268–271.

79 Fuess, *Ẓulm by Maẓālim?*.

80 Müller, *Crimes without criminals?*

81 Biographical dictionaries contain information on judges and their offices. They provide glimpses on judicial administration even in smaller towns, cf. Jokisch, *Socio-Political Factors*, 503–529.

82 Fernandes, *Qadis and Muftis.*

83 Irving, *Privatization of 'Justice'*; and Tyan, *Histoire*, 544, who excludes judiciary functions of the *ḥājib* in provinces.

far as I see from Stilt's case-accounts, the link to practised *fiqh*-norms was not direct.[84] Thus, if *ḥisbah* in its form of applying customary 'right' (*maʿrūf* linked to *ʿurf*) is considered Islamic law, we adopt implicitly the –minority – position of Ibn Taymīyah.[85] But, if *fiqh*-norms constituted the Islamic legal norm-system, as most Mamluk *fuqahāʾ* would embrace, the *ḥisbah* with its rules created outside juridical hermeneutics (*uṣūl*), was guaranteed by the 'open' character of *fiqh* to maintain systems of foreign origin.[86] In such case, jurists determined the limits of *ḥisbah*-application, not the other way round. Another difference is that *fiqh*-norms were validated to last as normative interpretation of Divine law in Islam, whereas *ḥisbah* resided in conservative, but nevertheless, changing social convention. This is why *fiqh*-norms were carefully transmitted throughout centuries in hundreds of manuscripts, and the temporarily important Mamluk *ḥisbah*-manuals survived only in rare exemplars. For some centuries to come, Islamic law stayed the prerogative of Muslim jurists who were trained in the casuistic system of *fiqh*-norms, not in the application of general laws.

Another point of research is, how could jurisdiction by the *ḥājib* and the *muḥtasib* extend beyond immediate conflict resolution towards a lasting legal title, notarized in a way that it was accepted by other authorities? The existence of a 'Mamluk law' in general does not exclude particular laws for specific social groups. If we do not want to disregard Maqrīzī's report on a Mongolian *yāsā* as unfounded,[87] then his informed text may refer to codified Mongol customary law, practised at certain periods among the Mamluk elite. For this we may never find evidence except Maqrīzī's account,[88] since such "private justice" was limited – compared to the *qāḍī*-institution – and needed no widespread propagation.

In sum, Mamluk Law existed and functioned for major fields of law on the basis of a wide range of practised Islamic law-norms. Mamluk juridical thinking was a backbone of Law. Constitutional legitimisation integrated the political power of the sultan, but did not provide an institutionalized system of checks and balances: changes in the head of state were subject to the 'Turks' law' among the elite of Mamluk emirs. Seeing Law as legal system explains why Mamluk Law cannot be reduced to a Sultan's law, despite repeated reports on Sultanic acts of absolute power in legal affairs. At the present state of research, Mamluk legal practice emerges in the form of isolated elements as the top of an iceberg. When *fiqh* turns out to be practised law, then 'Islamic law' is much more than cultural

84 Stilt refers to Islamic rulings and principles, but cites, as far as I see, no *fiqh*-norms in her chapter on the *muḥtasib*'s actions, idem, *Islamic Law*, 73 – 202. On Mamluk *ḥisbah* see now also Lange, *Ḥisba*.

85 Cf. also Johansen, *Perfect Law*, 268 with note 68.

86 On *ḥisbah* throughout Muslim history see Cook, *Commanding Right*.

87 Fuess, *Ẓulm by Maẓālim?*, 132 with note 47.

88 Maqrīzī, *Al-Mawāʿiẓ*, 3:714 – 8.

heritage and religion. The next step then would consist in describing the particularities of Mamluk Law in the light of a legal system.[89] Islamic law then becomes historical fact, not a dreamed of ideal. To achieve this, research should focus on Mamluk authors in order to identify – if possible – the practised norms, and not skim through the totality of Islamic law traditions for generalities. A future task is then to describe Mamluk history in the light of an existing Law, at the service of society and its rulers. This may be key to answering the question of how a group of some thousand foreign military slaves could govern Egypt and Syria for more than two hundred years.

Bibliography

Primary sources

Al-ʿAsalī, Kāmil Jamīl, *Wathā'iq Maqdisīyah Ta'rīkhīya*, 2 vols., Amman 1983 – 1985.

Al-Asyūṭī, Shams al-Dīn: *Jawāhir al-ʿUqūd wa-Muʿīn al-Quḍāh wa-l-Muwaqqiʿīn wa-l-Shuhūd*, ed. Muḥammad al-Fiqqī, 2 vols., Cairo 1955, re-edition Musʿad al-Saʿdanī, Beirut.

Al-ʿAynī, Maḥmūd b. Aḥmad, *Minḥat al-Sulūk Sharḥ Tuḥfat al-Mulūk*, ed. A. al-Kabīsī, Qaṭar 1428/2007.

Ibn Farḥūn, Burhān al-Dīn Ibrāhīm, *Tabṣirat al-ḥukkām fī uṣūl al-aqḍīya wa-manāhiJ al-aḥkām*, ed. Ṭaha ʿAbd al-Ra'ūf Saʿd, 2 vols, Maktabat al-Kulliyyāt al-Azhariyya, Cairo n. d.

Al-Jarawānī, Muḥammad b. ʿAbd al-Munʿim al-Ḥasanī al-Shāfiʿī, *Al-Kawkab al-mushriq fīmā yaḥtāJ ilayhi al-muwaṯṯiq li-ʿālim ash-shurūṭ*. Ed. Souad Saghbini. Bonn 2010.

Al-Kāfiyağī, Abū_ʿAlī Muḥammad, *K. al-Faraḥ wa-l-Surūr*, ed. Ḥasan Ūzār, together with its commentary, *Nashāṭ al-Ṣudūr*, Istanbul, 2011.

Khalīl b. Isḥāq, *Mukhtaṣar*, reprint Dār al-fikr, 1981.

Al-Maqrīzī, *Al-Mawāʿiẓ wa-l-Iʿtibār fī Dhikr al-Khiṭaṭ wa-l-Athār*, ed. Ayman F. Sayyid, 4 vols. and Index volume, London 2002 – 2004.

Al-Nawawī, Yaḥyā, *Minhāj al-Ṭālibīn*, Cairo 1914, reprinted with the commentary of M. al-Zuhrī al-Ghamrāwī, Cairo 1934, reprint with the abridgment by Zakariyā al-Anṣārī (d. 926/1520), Dār al-Fikr 1992 [references to this edition].

Al-Nuʿaymī, ʿAbd al-Qādir, *Kitāb al-Dāris fī Ta'rīkh al-Madāris*, 2 vols. Damascus 1948 – 51.

Al-Nuwayrī, Shihāb al-Dīn Aḥmad, *Nihāyat al-Arab fī Funūn al-Adab*, 33 vols. published until 1997, here vol. 9, Cairo 1351/1933.

Al-Qalqashandī, Aḥmad, *Ṣubḥ al-Aʿshā fī Ṣināʿat al-Inshā'*, 14 vols., Cairo 1913 – 19.

Al-Rāzī, Muḥammad b. Abī Bakr b. ʿAbd al-Qādir [?], *Tuḥfat al-Mulūk*, ed. Dār al-Basha'ir al-Islāmīyah, Beirut 1417. [used from the CD "*al-Fiqh wa-Uṣūlihi*," ed. al-Turāṯ].

89 Cf. Raz, *Concept*, 187 ff.

Ṣāliḥiyya, Muḥammad, *Al-Muʿjam al-Shāmil li-l-Turāth al-ʿArabī al-Maṭbūʿ*, 6 vols., Cairo 1992–98.

Al-Shāṭibī, Ibrāhīm al-Lakhmī al-Mālikī, *Muwāfaqāt fī Uṣūl al-Sharīʿah*, ed. Dār al-Maʿrifah, Beirut n. d., [used from the CD "*al-Fiqh wa-Uṣūlihi*," ed. Al-Turāth].

Secondary sources

Bauer, Thomas, Die Kultur der Ambiguität. Eine andere Geschichte des Islams. Berlin 2011.

Brockelmann, Carl, Geschichte der Arabischen Litteratur, 2 vols. 1898–1902, 3 Supplement volumes published between 1937–42 (S1-S3). References are to volumes and page numbers of the second and, reprinted third edition, Leiden [2]1943–9, [3]1996. [GAL]

Conermann, Stephan and Lucian Reinfandt, "Anmerkungen zu einer mamlūkischen waqf-Urkunde aus dem 9./15. Jahrhundert", in: Die Mamlūken. Studien zu ihrer Geschichte und Kultur. Zum Gedenken an Ulrich Haarmann (1942–1999), eds. Stephan Conermann and Anja Pistor-Hatam, Hamburg, Schenefeld 2003, pp. 179–238.

Cook, Michael, Commanding Right and Forbidding Wrong in Islamic Thought, Cambridge 2000.

El-Rouayeb, Khaled, "From Ibn Ḥajar al-Hayrami (d. 1566) to Khayr asl-Dīn al-Alūsī (d. 1899): Changing views of Ibn Taymiyya among non-Ḥanbalī Sunni scholars," in: Ibn Taymiyya and his Times, eds. Yossef Rappoport and Shahab Ahmed, Oxford, 2010, pp. 269–318.

Ernst, Hans, Die mamlukischen Sultansurkunden des Sinai-Klosters, Wiesbaden 1960.

Fernandes, Leonor, "Between Qadis and Muftis: To Whom Does the Mamluk Sultan Listen," Mamlūk Studies Review 6 (2002), pp. 95–108.

Fuess, Albrecht, "Ẓulm by Maẓālim? The Political Implications of the Use of Maẓālim Jurisdiction by the Mamluk Sultans," Mamlūk Studies Review 13 (2009), pp. 121–147.

Haarmann, Ulrich (ed.), Geschichte der Arabischen Welt, München 1987.

Havemann, Axel, "The Chronicle of Ibn Iyās as a Source for Social and Cultural History from Below," in: Towards a Cultural History of the Mamluk Era, eds. Mahmoud Haddad et al., Beirut 2010, pp. 87–98.

Heinrichs, Wolfhart, "Qawāʿid as a Genre of Legal Literature," in: Studies in Islamic Legal Theory, ed. Bernard. G. Weiss, Leiden et al. 2002, pp. 365–384.

Heinrichs, Wolfhart, "Structuring the Law: Remarks on the Furūq Literature", in: Studies in Honour of Clifford Edmund Bosworth, vol. 1: Hunter of the East: Arabic and Semitistic Studies, ed. Ian Richard Netton, Leiden et al. 2000, pp. 332–344.

Irving, Robert, "The Privatization of 'Justice' Under the Circassian Mamluks," Mamlūk Studies Review 6 (2002), pp. 63–70.

Jackson, Sherman A, "From Prophetic Action to Constitutional Theory: A Novel Chapter in Medieval Muslim jurisprudence", IJMES 25 (1993), 71–90.

Johansen, Baber, "A Perfect Law in an Imperfect Society: Ibn Taymiyya's Concept of "Governance in the Name of the Sacred Law," in: The Law Applied. Contextualizing the Islamic Shariʿa. A Volume in Honor of Frank E. Vogel, eds. Peri Bearman, Wolfhart Heinrichs and Bernard G. Weiss, London/New York 2008, pp. 259–294.

Johansen, Baber, "Casuistry: Between Legal Concept and Social Praxis," Islamic Law and Society 2 (1995), pp. 35–156.

Johansen, Baber, "Legal Literature and the Problem of Change: The Case of the Land Rent," in: Islam and Public Law. Classical and Contemporary Studies, ed. Chibli Mallat, London / Norwell (Ma) 1993, pp. 29 – 47.

Johansen, Baber, "Signs as Evidence: The Doctrine of Ibn Taymiyya (1263 – 1328) and Ibn Qayyim al-Jawziyya (d. 1351) on Proof," Islamic Law and Society 9 (2002), pp. 168 – 193.

Johansen, Baber, "The Muslim fiqh as a Sacred Law," in: Contingency in a Sacred Law, ed. idem, Leiden 1999, pp. 1 – 76.

Johansen, Baber, "Vérité et torture: ius commune et droit musulman entre le Xe et le XIIIe siècle," in: De la violence, ed. Françoise Héritier, Paris 1996, pp. 123 – 169.

Jokisch, Benjamin, "Socio-Political Factors of Qaḍā' in Eight/Fourteenth Century Syria," Al-Qanṭara 20 (1999), pp. 503 – 529.

Lange, Christian, "Ḥisba and the Problem of Overlapping Jurisdictions: An Introduction to, and Translation of, Ḥisba Diplomas in Qalqashandī Ṣubḥ al-Aʿshā," Harvard Middle Eastern and Islamic Review 7 (2006), pp. 85 – 107.

Lange, Christian, Justice, Punishment and the Medieval Muslim Imagination, Cambridge 2008.

Little, Donald, "Documents Related to the Estates of a Merchant and His Wife in Late Fourteenth Century Jerusalem," Mamlūk Studies Review 2 (1998), pp. 93 – 193.

Little, Donald, "Two Fourteenth-Century Court Records from Jerusalem Concerning the Disposition of Slaves by Minors," Arabica 29 (1982), pp. 16 – 49.

Little, Donald, A Catalogue of the Islamic Documents from al-Ḥaram aš-Šarīf in Jerusalem, Beirut 1984.

Martel-Thoumian, "Plaisirs illicites et châtiments dans les sources mamloukes: fin IXe/XVe – début Xe/XVIe siècle," Annales islamologiques 39, (2005), pp. 275 – 323.

Martel-Thoumian, "Voleurs et assassins à Damas et au Caire (fin IXe/XVe – début Xe/XVIe siècle)," Annales islamologiques 35/1 (2001), pp. 193 – 240.

Martel-Thoumian, Bernadette, "Pouvoir et justice sous les derniers sultans circassiens (872 – 922/1468 – 1516)," in: Continuity and Change in the Realms of Islam: Studies in Honour of Professor Urbain Vermeulen, eds. K. D'Hulster and J. van Steenbergen, Leuven 2008, pp. 451 – 467.

Masud, Muhammad Khalid, Brinkley Messick, and David S. Powers (eds.), Islamic Legal Interpretation. Muftis and their Fatwas, Cambridge/Mass et al. 1996.

Masud, Muhammad Khalid, Ruud Peters, and David. S. Powers (eds.), Dispensing Justice in Islam. Qadis and their Judgments, Leiden 2006.

Müller, Christian and Johannes Pahlitzsch, "Sultan Baybars I and the Georgians – in the Light of new Documents related to the Monastery of the Holy Cross in Jerusalem," Arabica 51 (2004), pp. 258 – 290.

Müller, Christian, "Crimes without criminals? 14th-century injury- and homicide-cases from the Ḥaram al-Sharīf-collection in Jerusalem" in: Legal Documents as Sources for the History of Muslim Societies: Studies in Honour of Rudolph Peters, eds. Maaike van Berkel, Léon Buskens and Petra Sijpesteijn (forthcoming)

Müller, Christian, "Écrire pour établir la preuve orale en Islam: la pratique d'un tribunal à Jérusalem au XIVe siècle", in: Les outils de la pensée. Étude historique et comparative des "textes", eds. Akira Saito and Yusuke Nakamura, Paris: Maison des Sciences de l'homme 2010, pp. 63 – 97.

Müller, Christian, "Settling Litigations without Judgment: The Importance of a Ḥukm in Qāḍī Cases of Mamlūk Jerusalem," in: Dispensing Justice in Islam. Qadis and their Judgments, eds. Muhammad Khalid Masud, Rudolph Peters, and David S. Powers, Leiden/Boston 2006, pp. 47 – 69.

Müller, Christian, Der Kadi und seine Zeugen. Studie der mamlūkischen Dokumente des Ḥaram Sharīf, Wiesbaden: Harrassowitz Verlag (forthcoming).

Nielsen, Jørgen, Secular Justice in an Islamic State: Maẓālim under the Baḥrī Mamlūks, 662/1264 – 789/1387, Istanbul 1985.

Northrup, Linda, From Slave to Sultan. The career of al-Manṣūr Qalāwūn and the consolidation of Mamluk rule in Egypt and Syria (678 – 689 A.H./1279 – 1290 A.D.), Stuttgart 1998.

Petry, Carl, "'Quis Custodiet Custodes?' Revisited: The Prosecution of Crime in the Late Mamluk Sultanate," Mamlūk Studies Review 3 (1999), pp. 13 – 30.

Petry, Carl, "The Politics of Insult: The Mamluk Sultanate's Response to Criminal Affronts," Mamlūk Studies Review 15 (2011), pp. 87 – 115.

Pouzet, Luis, Damas au VIIe/XIIIe s. Vie et structures religieuses dans une métropole islamique. Beirut 1988

Rāghib, Yūsuf, Actes de vente d'esclaves et d'animaux d'Égypte médiévale, 2 vols., Cairo 2002 and 2006.

Rapoport, Yossef, "Legal Diversity in the Age of Taqlīd: The Four Chief Qadis under the Mamluks," Islamic Law and Society 10 (2003), pp. 210 – 28.

Raz, Joseph, Practical Reason and Norms, London 1975, reprint Oxford/New York 1999.

Raz, Joseph, The Concept of a Legal System. An Introduction to the Theory of Legal System, Oxford 1970, reprint 1990.

Reinfandt, Lucien, Mamlukische Sultansstiftungen des 9./15. Jahrhunderts, nach den Urkunden der Stifter al-Ashraf Īnāl und al-Mu'ayyad Aḥmad Ibn Īnāl, Berlin 2003.

Richards, Donald, Mamluk Administrative Documents from St Catherine's Monastery, Leuven et al. 2011.

Schacht, Joseph, An introduction to Islamic law, Oxford 1964, reprinted.

Stilt, Kirsten, Islamic Law in Action. Authority, Discretion, and Everyday Experiences in Mamluk Egypt, Oxford 2011.

Tyan, Émile, Histoire de l'Organisation judiciaire en pays d'islam, 2nd ed., Leiden 1960.

Tyan, Émile, Le notariat et le régime de la preuve par écrit dans la pratique du droit musulman, 2nd ed., Beirut 1959.

Vogel, Frank E., "Siyāsa. 3," EI², 9:694 – 696.

Wiederhold, Lutz, "Some Remarks on Mālikī Judges in Mamluk Egypt and Syria," in: Die Mamlūken. Studien zu ihrer Geschichte und Kultur. Zum Gedenken an Ulrich Haarmann (1942 – 1999), eds. Stephan Conermann and Anja Pistor-Hatam, Hamburg, Schenefeld 2003, pp. 403 – 413.

Internet

http://www.ilm-project.net/en/

Lucian Reinfandt

Mamlūk Documentary Studies

The Mamlūk sultanate is a downright documentary era of Islamic history. Whoever occupies himself with Mamlūk Egypt and Syria wallows in an abundance of documentary remnants unknown to other eras and regions of the premodern Islamicate world (with the exceptions of the Ottoman Empire and, perhaps, papyrological Egypt).[1] Moreover, "the issue of documentary material is topical, as the field of Middle Eastern history has experienced in the last decades important and exciting developments that added decisively to the pool of available sources".[2] And lastly, exciting new concepts and questions have been put to the material in recent years that released documentary studies from its binding as a mere auxiliary science of history and evince its potential as a powerful tool towards socio-anthropological approaches. These are reasons enough to contribute a chapter on Mamlūk documentary studies to the present book. In the following, something will be said about written documents in principle (part 1) and then an overview of the latest scholarly output in the field will be given (part 2). The final part is reserved for suggestions of how and for what purpose Mamlūk documents can be used in research, and against the background of current trends in Mamlūk historical and documentary studies (part 3). By this will become evident the role of written documents in a discipline that combines philology with history and cultural studies – a discipline that calls itself *Mamlukology.*

1 Research for this article was conducted under the auspices of the project "The Language of Power II: Official Epistolography in Islamic Egypt (642–969)" funded by the FWF Austrian Science Fund. The project is part of the National Research Network (NFN) "Imperium and Officium: Comparative Studies in Ancient Bureaucracy and Officialdom" (www.univie.ac.at/babylon/drupal/?q=node/12). – Editions of documents are cited according to the *Checklist of Arabic Documents* (www.ori.uzh.ch/isap/isapchecklist.html) and, for convenience, also according to the *Arabic Papyrology Bibliography* (www.ori.uzh.ch/research/papyrology/bibliography.html) [all accessed 11 March 2012].

2 Görke, Hirschler, *Introduction*, 11.

Definitions

Documents, in the classical sense of the word, are everything that has remained as traces from past events. Still useful is Droysen's famous understanding of documents as 'remnants' (*Überreste*) that have been unintentionally preserved and thus are authentic traces of daily life. They stand in opposition to 'traditions' (*Traditionen*) that are of literary character and were intended to be delivered to posterity.[3] With such a maximalist definition in mind, all remnants of human production, textual and non-textual, become 'documents', provided that they have been preserved and found in unintentional contexts. This can comprise everything from papers, parchments and ostraca to coins and inscriptions to archaeological traces to even art and architecture.

Such an understanding of documentary sources as 'remnants' is not free of criticism. In a recent publication, it has even been rejected as insufficient for the historian of Islamicate societies, because it disregards the fact that there are documents that very well have the intention of being preserved for and even used by, later generations, e.g. endowment deeds. Instead a different understanding of documents has been recommended as being everything that is not offering coherent accounts or interpretation but bears witness to specific individual or collective acts.[4] Such an understanding of documents, at least in the textual variant, comes close to the English, French, Italian and Spanish use of the word, meaning any written evidence that is of non-fictional nature and corresponds more or less to what is referred to as (non-legal) *Urkunden* in the German academic tradition.[5]

In the following, we will keep both definitions in mind. The material, however, will be narrowed down to written documents, and these are to be narrowed down even a bit more to texts of a perishable character, written with ink on paper, parchment, or perhaps cloth. The interest is both in high-quality chancery documents and low-quality casual writings of everyday life (*Gebrauchsschreiben*). Their find context, of considerable importance for the interpretation of documents, varies widely between garbage heaps, jugs and leather bags, caves and remains of buildings, monasteries and modern archives. By attention to functionality and content, the documents can be put into five main categories: (A) letters and writings of non-legal character; (B) legal deeds and contracts with or without testimonies; (C) lists, notes and accounts; (D) sacred texts and amulets; (E) writing exercises.[6]

3 Droysen, *Grundriss*, 14.

4 Görke, Hirschler, *Introduction*, 10–11.

5 We follow here the definition made by Diem *Wurzelrepetition*, 25–26.

6 Examples from published original documents may be the following: (A) Letters and writings:

On the other hand, coins and inscriptions, art and archaeology are excluded from our focus. The reason is a practical one, for there are separate contributions in this book devoted to them.[7] As regards the substance, however, it would be more useful not to draw a line between perishable and non-perishable, textual and non-textual 'documents', but rather point out their common potential. Documents can very well confirm, debunk or enhance the information obtained from conventional literary sources. They should not be understood, however, as mere supplements to literary sources but as carriers of textual or non-textual information in which literary sources are deficient. Documents are complex and multilayered information carriers and should be 'read' as such. Philology, semiotics and text anthropology pull together. Copies of documents preserved in literary sources are a welcome gain for the corpus. Yet, mostly bare of context and materiality they misguide and over-accentuate the textual at the expense of other information intrinsic to documents, as has so often been the case in older

---

P.Philad.Arab. 115 (letter written by a Mamlūk officer), 8th/14th c, Egypt (official letter); CPR XXXII 15 (order to prepare a meal for a ceremony), 8th/14th c, Egypt (private letter); P.Vind.Arab. III 1 (decree of Sayfaddīn Khāyir Bak al-Malakī al-Ashrafī to the heads of districts and the local peasants), 875/1470, Egypt (decree); P.GenizahCambr. 60 (court record concerning a surgical operation by a physician), 7th /13th c, al-Fusṭāṭ (court record); P.Vind.Arab. III 50 (petition of two men in the matter of an attack and related decree), 7th/13th c, Egypt (petition). -- (B) Legal deeds and contracts: P.Philad.Arab. 29 (purchase of a house), 8th/14th c, Egypt? (sales contract); P.DiemRechtsurkunden 1 (lease contract for a house), 8th/14th c, Egypt (lease contract); P.Moriscos 39 (labour agreement), 905/1500, al-Andalus (labour contract); P.DiemRechtsurkunden 3 (record of repayment of a debt), 861/1462, Egypt (quittance); P.Diem Rechtsurkunden 2 (financial agreement between married partners), 9th/15th c, Egypt (marriage contract); CPR XXVI 11 (record of assessment of value of a street roofage), 674/1276, Egypt (notarisation); P.HaramCat. 596 (guarantee for a person not to enter a certain district), 707/1308, Jerusalem (warranty); P.HaramCat. 59 (accounting of credits from estates), 793/1391, Jerusalem (loan); CPR XXVI 6 (document dealing with a will), 8th–9th/14th–15th c, Egypt (will); P.Philad.Arab. 34 (acknowledgment of a debt in wheat and clover), 8th/14th c, Egypt? (obligation); P.HaramCat. 80, 793/1391, Jerusalem (inventory); P.GenizahCambr. 68 (question to a jurisconsult concerning the permissibility of a Jewish eye-doctor working among Muslims), 6th–7th/12th–13th c, al-Fusṭāṭ (legal opinion); P.Cair.Archives 7 (deed of *waqf*), 903/1498, Egypt (endowment). -- (C) Lists, notes and accounts: P.QuseirArab. I 34v (a working account or inventory list), 7th/13th c, Egypt (list). Lists, notes and accounts could be subdivided into a myriad of different types due to the individual character of this genre, which is however in the interest of this article. -- (D) Sacred texts and amulets: P.AbbottRise 21 (Quran), 839–40/1435–36, Egypt (Quran); P.Philad.Arab. 158 (fragment of a Christian text), 7th–8th/13th–14th c, Egypt (fragment of codex); P.QuseirArab. I 80r (a prayer with the scribe's motto), 7th/13th c, al-Quṣayr (prayer); P.QuseirArab. 81 (hand-written amulet providing prevention of, and cures for, certain physical ailments), 7th/13th c, al-Quṣayr (amulet); Seidel, *Medizinisches* (recipes for oral and dental medicines), 7th–8th/13th –14th c, Egypt (medical recipe). -- (E) Writing exercises: P.Vind.Arab. III 80 (an official's writing exercise), 744/1343, Egypt (exercise); CPR XXXII 17 (beginning of an official letter), 7th–8th/AD 13th–14th c, Egypt (draft); P.GenizahCambr. 51 (drafts of a testimony concerning the qualifications and good conduct of a physician), 7th/13th c, al-Fusṭāṭ (draft).

7 Cf. the contributions by Bethany Walker on archaeology, Carine Juvin on epigraphy.

research. The present chapter therefore intends to consider only original documents as intrinsic objects of study. Whereas copies of documents in literary sources are welcome for comparative reasons, they should be treated as what they in fact are: literary sources. For the same reason, the present chapter favours the label 'documentary studies' over the more conventional 'diplomatics'. Diplomatics "is the discipline which studies the genesis, forms, and transmission of archival documents, and their relationship with the facts represented in the and with their creator, in order to identify, evaluate and communicate their true nature."[8] Even if this is a relatively wide definition, it still describes a discipline that is after all more concerned with textual aspects than with the physical characteristics of documents.

Take Mamlūk chancery documents as an example. These have been seen by conventional diplomatics as being preserved either as originals or as copies. Original documents are preserved in archive collections (Muslim or non-Muslim, Near Eastern or European), libraries, museums, and private collections, whereas copies of documents can be found abundantly in literary sources, such as chronicles, chancery manuals, administrative encyclopaedias, and literary anthologies, all of them being very numerous in the Mamlūk era.[9] While in the past both original documents and their copies in literary sources have been seen as two sides of the same coin, it will be maintained here that it is by far not the texts of documents alone that bear information for the historian. Rather non-textual components like materiality, *mise en page*, use and storage as well as the find context supply additional and often decisive information that is a unique characteristic of documents as against literary sources. Here Mamlūk documentary studies come close to neighbouring papyrology that is more concerned with aspects of material and find context due to the fragmentary and haphazard conditions of preservation. The unique characteristic of papyrology as an academic discipline is not so much the time window of interest (not going further than the 9th c CE), nor the material of the objects studied (papyrus, leather, potsherd, bone, wood), but a 'holistic' approach towards written documents that exceeds their written content. The present author would go as far as to label it as 'Mamlūk papyrology', were it not so ludicrous in terms of material designation. But it seems to him useful to point out at least what Mamlūk documentary studies should *not* be: a mere reading of Arabic diplomas.[10]

8 Duranti, *Diplomatics*, 45.

9 Bauden, *Mamluk Era*, 19–27.

10 This idea has in fact been advanced already by Frantz-Murphy 1985:34 and Little, *Use of Documents*, 5. There is however the reasonable criticism of Bauden, *Mamluk Era*, 15–16 in terms of the misleading designation of the support material.

State of the art

Already since the late 1940s, the state of the art of research on Mamlūk diplomatics has periodically been summarised in articles and book chapters by Jean Sauvaget,[11] Hans Robert Roemer,[12] Stephen Humphreys,[13] Donald Little,[14] Stephan Conermann,[15] Frédéric Bauden,[16] and Petra Sijpesteijn.[17] None of them settles for simple stock taking but reflects on the value of documents for the research on Middle Eastern history, discusses methodological and epistemological aspects and proposes new directions of research, thereby revealing the particular states of affairs in Mamlūk Studies in the successive decades. The present chapter follows this rule and, in doing so, considerably stands on the shoulders (Bernard of Chartres) of Frédéric Bauden's 2005 study as being the most comprehensive and up to date overview of Mamlūk documentary studies for now. The reader interested in documentary research that is antedating the year 2005 is referred to this excellent and well-informed overview.[18] The present chapter concerns itself with the latest trends, however it is not a simple updating of Bauden's work, but embraces the opportunity to address the subject slightly differently. While Bauden has arranged the material according to internal characteristics and its present-day provenance (collections, archives, libraries), the following will put emphasis on different approaches to working with documents, namely editions, studies, auxiliary tools, and trends and priorities.

Editions in collected volumes

A preferred (and indeed recommendable) way of publishing documents is the form of collected volumes. Since 2005 a number of such volumes have appeared. Werner Diem has published in 2011 a volume of Arabic private, business and

11 Sauvaget, *Introduction* (1946); Sauvaget, *Introduction* (1961); Cahen, *Jean Sauvaget's Introduction*; all of them being partly dedicated to Mamlūk Diplomatics.

12 Roemer, *Urkunden*; idem, *Arabische Herrscherurkunden*; idem, *Sinai-Urkunden*; idem, *Sinai Documents*.

13 Humphreys, *Islamic History*, 40–49.

14 Little, *Use of Documents*.

15 Conermann, *Es boomt*, 14–18.

16 Bauden, *Mamluk Era*.

17 Sijpesteijn, *Arabic Papyri*, 16–17 (on excavations at Quṣayr al-Qadīm).

18 Bauden, *Mamluk Era*. – Frédéric Bauden is currently undertaking a revision of that article as it will become a chapter of a forthcoming book under the title *Mamuk historical sources and how to exploit them (manuscripts and documents)*, based on material from a seminar he gave in Chicago back in 2008 (oral communication from 23 December 2011). This book is conceived as a manual for historians approaching the Mamlūk sultanate and will become the standard introduction into the field.

administrative letters on paper from 10th–16th c CE Egypt that contains, *inter alia*, at least six letters dated to the Mamlūk era (nota bene: the letters are undated and have been ascribed by the editor to the Mamlūk era only on the basis of palaeographical and stylistic aspects): no. 12 (reply to a letter of a higher personality regarding financial matters; 5th–7th/11th–13th c); no. 13 (appeal for advance of salary; 6th–7th/12th–13th c); no. 14 (business letter; 7th–8th/13th–14th c); no. 15 (instruction to prepare a meal for a large ceremonial act; end of 8th/14th c); no. 16 (letter between merchants about a claim for money; 842/1438 – 39 or shortly after); no. 17 (writing exercise: beginning of official letter; 7th–8th/13th–14th c).[19] New Arabic business letters, notes and records on paper excavated at the 13th c Egyptian Red Sea port of al-Quṣayr al-Qadīm are currently being prepared for publication by Andreas Kaplony.[20] Another volume of texts from the same corpus has been finished by Anne Regourd and is going to print.[21] Both resume the work taken up by Li Guo with his edition of 84 documents from al-Quṣayr al-Qadīm already published in 2004.[22]

Among the 45 legal deeds published by Michael Thung are seven from Mamlūk Egypt: no. 11 (report of assessment of value of a street roofage with legal attestations; 674/1276, al-Ushmūnayn; paper); no. 43 (quittance of receipt of two and a half artabas of wheat; 685/1286, Egypt; paper); no. 44 (quittance of the rent of a house; 733/1332 – 33, al-Fusṭāṭ; paper); no. 6 (will; 8th–9th/14th–15th c, Egypt; paper); no. 34 (certificate of debt of 16 dirhams; 8th–9th/14th–15th c, al-Fusṭāṭ; paper); no. 45 (quittance of 150 silver coins; 874/1470, al-Fusṭāṭ; paper); no. 35 (certificate of debt of 4 dinars; 887/1482, Aṭfīḥ/Egypt?; paper).[23] A current reedition of Geoffrey Khan's 1993 volume with papers from the Cambridge Genizah Collections bears witness to the importance of the material. It contains, *inter alia*, nine legal and administrative documents from the Mamlūk period: no. 49 (testimony certifying that a man was a Khaybarī Jew; 654/1256, Cairo; paper); no. 50 (testimony certifying a man with leprosy; 660/1262, Cairo; paper); no. 62 (power of attorney; 5th–7th c, Cairo; paper); no. 67 (question to a jurisconsult concerning a case of medical treatment; 6th–7th/12th–13th c, Cairo; paper); no. 68 (question to a jurisconsult concerning the permissibility of a Jewish eye-doctor working among Muslims; 6th–7th/12th–13th c, Cairo; paper); no. 69 (question to a jurisconsult concerning the permissibility of Jewish

19 CPR XXXII = Diem, *Arabische Briefe*.

20 Kaplony, *Zweiundzwanzig Geschäftsbriefe* (forthcoming).

21 Regourd, *Documents administratives et commerciales de Quṣayr al-Qadīm* (forthcoming). A first report on these letters is idem, Arabic Language Documents.

22 P.QuseirArab. = Guo, *Commerce*. The editions should, however, only be used together with corrections proposed by Werner Diem, Frédéric Bauden, and Mordechai Friedman (cf. n. 55 below).

23 CPR XXVI = Thung, *Arabische juristische Urkunden*.

foundations for the poor; 6th–7th/12th–13th c, Cairo; paper); no. 51 (drafts of a testimony concerning the qualifications and good conduct of a physician; 7th/ 13th c, Cairo; paper); no. 60 (court record concerning a surgical operation by a physician; mid-7th/13th c, Cairo; paper); no. 131 (formulary for reports of death; 7th/13th c, Cairo; paper).[24]

More administrative documents have recently been published by Donald Richards. The 18 Mamlūk decrees on paper are documents of guarantee for the protection of the monks and their ability to carry on commercial activity. Their special value lies in the fact that they are not issued by Mamlūk sultans themselves, as has been the case in other editions so far, but by officials of lower rank, thus demonstrating a secondary level of officials giving effect to orders from the centre not documented before.[25] An Arabic peace treaty between the Marinid sultan Abū l-Ḥasan ʿAlī and the Christian king James III of Majorca from the year 1339 CE has been published by Henry Bresc and Yūsuf Rāghib.[26] Although not from the Mamlūk sultanate, it is important contemporaneous reference material and by its exemplary edition and analysis of considerable profit for the study of Mamlūk diplomatics as well. For similar reasons non-Arabic documents can also be of utmost importance, like the 28 Persian documents from Mongol Iran (Ilkhānid and Jalāyirid, 13th–14th c) found in the archive of the congregation of the Safāvids from 15th c Ardabil and published by Gottfried Hermann;[27] and the 114 official and private letters in Ottoman language from the reign of the sultan Süleymān the Magnificent (1520 – 1566 CE) kept at the Vienna *Haus-, Hof- und Staatsarchiv* and published by Gisela Procházka-Eisl and Claudia Römer.[28]

Editions in articles

Another way of publishing documents is by single articles in journals or volumes. This bears the danger of being overlooked by students willing to work with published documents. The advantage is, on the other hand, to provide material more quickly to the very student than can be done in the course of more time-consuming collected edition volumes (as introduced in part 2.1 above). The following arranges the material according to the provenance of the documents.

Christian Müller has published two legal documents on paper from the Ḥaram collection in Jerusalem, one being a sales contract and the other one an

24 P.GenizahCambr. = Khan, *Arabic Legal.*
25 P.St.Catherine = Richards, *Mamluk administrative documents.*
26 Bresc, Rāghib, *Le sultan.*
27 Herrmann, *Persische Urkunden.* Another volume of documents from the same background is currently prepared by Gronke, *Arabische und persische Urkunden.*
28 Procházka-Eisl, Römer, *Osmanische Beamtenschreiben.*

inventory of possession.[29] Also from Jerusalem are two official documents on paper, one being a protocol of a hearing that took place on 759/1358 at the court of the shāfiʿite judge in Jerusalem and the other being a royal decree.[30] From Damascus have been published two documents, an attestation and a petition from shortly before the reign of the Mamlūks, by Jean-Michel Mouton, Janine Sourdel-Thomine and Dominique Sourdel.[31] At the excavations at the Egyptian Red Sea harbour of al-Quṣayr has been found an ostrich egg from the 13th c CE, containing a poem and a prayer. It has been examined and published by Dionisius Agius in the course of two articles.[32] Three papers from Mamlūk Egypt, including two sales contracts from 818/1415 and 822/1419 and a document of oath (*qasāmah*) from 822/1419, have been published by Frédéric Bauden.[33] An endowment deed from Mamlūk Egypt, Dār al-wathā'iq 247 from 6 Rajab 910 (13 December 1504), has been published by Ḥusayn Muṣṭafā Ḥusayn Ramaḍān,[34] while another one, Dār al-wathā'iq 20/122 from 12 Jumādā II 864 (4 April 1460), has been published by Lucian Reinfandt.[35] From Spain have recently been published the following legal deeds (all on paper): a deed of gift from Toledo from the year 1271 CE,[36] a group of notarial deeds from Granada from the year 1499 CE,[37] seven sales contracts and related documents from 15th c Granada,[38] two more sales contracts from Granada from the years 1439 and 1499,[39] as well as two notarial deeds from the year 1493 and two more from the year 1499, all from Granada.[40] As has been said already in the case of the collected edition volumes, editions of contemporaneous documents serve as welcome comparative and reference material for the study of Mamlūk documents.

Studies on the basis of edited documents

The recent years have seen a certain trend towards the increased use of, or even exclusive use of documents for studies on Islamic history. This is an indicator of a greater awareness of using documents next to literary sources, as well as for the

29 Müller, *Écrire*, 63–97.
30 Pahlitzsch, *Documents*, 373–94.
31 Mouton et al., *À propos*, 99–108.
32 Agius, *Ostrich egg*, 158–160; idem, *Leave*, 355–79.
33 Bauden, *L'achat d'esclaves*, 269–325; idem, *Role of Interpreters*, 33–63.
34 Ramaḍān, *Dirāsah*, 67–99 [Arabic part].
35 Reinfandt, *Beurkundung*, 117–52.
36 Ferrando Frutos, *Donación*, 39–49.
37 Rodríguez Gómez, *Documentos*, 217–25.
38 Rodriguez Gómez, *Les Maṣārī*, 555–94.
39 Rodríguez Gómez, Domínguez Rojas, *La compraventa*, 175–99.
40 Rodríguez Gómez, *La porte*, 235–68; idem, *Al otro lado*, 295–319.

fact that Arabic documentary studies have supported this trend by providing editions of new texts, making them more easily available by electronic research tools. Thus the complex of trade in the Red Sea and the Indian Ocean under the Mamlūks has been subject by studies on Aden in the 11–13c CE[41] and on the Egyptian Red Sea port of al-Quṣayr al-Qadīm.[42] A report on another group of documents, found during the excavations at al-Quṣayr al-Qadīm, inscribed textiles, has been published by Anne Regourd and Fiona Handley.[43] Questions of economic history and agriculture in Egypt have been addressed in studies by Werner Diem and Gladys Frantz-Murphy.[44] Judaeo-Arabic material from the Genizah, also from Mamlūk times, has been dealt with painstakingly by Mark Cohen.[45] The discussion of archives in the pre-modern Islamic world has been resumed by a number of recent studies all dealing with documentary material from Mamlūk Egypt and Syria.[46] More groups of documents have been dealt with by Muḥammad ʿAbd al-Raḥīm Jāzim, Aḥmad Maḥmūd ʿAbd al-Wahhāb al-Miṣrī, Anne Regourd, and Amalia Zomeño.[47] Legal documents from Granada (96 documents edited in 1961 by Luis Seco de Lucena as P.Granada) from between 1421 – 1496 CE have served as basis for a gender-study by Maya Shatzmiller,[48] while a volume devoted to Arabic documents in general has been published that addresses the question of archives again and deals to a significant extent with late medieval documents from Muslim Spain.[49]

Not only the textual contents of Mamlūk documents, but also material, linguistic, stylistic and formulaic aspects have found enhanced interest among scholars. While Armin Schopen has dedicated a whole monograph to the issue of ink(s) for writing the documents,[50] Anne Regourd has drawn noteworthy conclusions in her study on the folding of documents that brings her directly to the already mentioned discussion about archiving practice and archiving culture in

---

41 Margariti, *Aden.*

42 Burke, *Archaeological Texts*; Kaplony, *The interplay*, 94 – 115; Regourd, *Arabic Language*, 339 – 44; Regourd, *Ayyubid.*

43 Regourd, Handley, *Textiles.*

44 Diem, *Terminkauf*; Frantz-Murphy, *Identity*, 253 – 64.

45 Cohen, *Geniza for Islamica*, 129 – 45; idem, *Goitein*, 13:294 – 304; idem, *Geniza documents*, 283 – 341.

46 El-Leithy, *Living Documents*, 389 – 434; Müller, The Ḥaram, 435 – 59; Bauden, *Du destin des archives.*

47 Jāzim, *Un nouveau*, 1 – 5; al-Miṣrī, *Maṣādir*, 25 – 50 [Arabic part]; Regourd, *Nouveau formulaire*; Zomeño, *When death*, 217 – 33; idem, *Private Collections*, 461 – 79.

48 Shatzmiller, *Her day in court.*

49 Cf. the contributions by Francisco Vidal Castro, Amalia Zomeño, Emilio Molina López and María del Carmen Jiménez Mata, Camilo Álvarez de Morales, and Eduardo Manzano Moreno in Sijpesteijn et al., *From al-Andalus to Khurasan.*

50 Schopen, *Tinten.*

the pre-modern Islamic world.[51] Linguistic and stylistic aspects of Arabic letters on paper have been dealt with by Werner Diem in an article and a monograph.[52] Aspects of the formulary of late medieval Arabic documents have been the subject of a whole series of publications,[53] while Werner Diem has contributed a helpful overview of Arabic private and administrative letters through all eras.[54]

Auxiliary tools

A vexing problem for the work with Arabic documents is the lack of an authoritative and generally accessible *Berichtigungsliste* like the one available for Greek Papyrology.[55] Corrections of readings of editions are of utmost importance because they might change whole meanings of documents. False readings are very likely to happen in the course of an editorial work that wrestles with cursive scripts, undotted letters, and fragmentary material. Even more so, a better knowledge of formulaic conventions and the availability of modern research tools enable present-day researchers to improve semi-correct readings in older editions (although older editors sometimes score off their younger colleagues by their better philological skills.) Be that as it may, the historian using Mamlūk documents must feel uncomfortable given the possibility that the textual basis might represent obsolete knowledge, let alone be philologically unreliable. But how be certain? So far, corrections and improved readings of documents are scattered in book reviews,[56] studies on documents,[57] appendices of parallel editions,[58] or on the margins of private copies of editions in the hands of the happy few who regularly work with documents. How can we look systematically for corrections, and, even more importantly perhaps, how can we encourage outsiders in the field to work with documents in spite of this unsatisfactory and even dangerous situation? For this purpose, the *Arabic Papyrology Database* (Zurich) has been created. It is a full-text database containing the

51 Regourd, *Folding*, 13 – 16.

52 Diem, *Arabic allaḏī*, 67 – 112; idem, *Wurzelrepetition.*

53 Grob, *Information packaging*, 277 – 290; Rāghib, *Actes de vente*; Veselý, *Beglaubigungsmittel*, 251 – 261.

54 Diem, *Arabic letters*, 885 – 906.

55 Preisigke et al., *Berichtigungsliste.*

56 An example is Li Guo's 2004 edition of 84 Arabic business letters, shipping notes and account records on paper from the 13th c Egyptian Red Sea port of al-Quṣayr al-Qadīm (P.QuseirArab.; cf. n. 21 above), that has provoked important corrections in book reviews by Werner Diem, Review: Guo, *Commerce*; Friedman, *Quṣayr*, 401 – 09; and Bauden, Review: Guo, *Commerce.*

57 Diem, *Philologisches*, 7 – 67, containing corrections of P.Haram = ʻAsali, *Wathāʼiq*.

58 A recommendable example is CPR XXVI p. 223.

editions of Arabic documents written on different material such as papyrus, parchment or paper between the 7th and 16th c CE as well as all later corrections or variants of the readings. The tool provides the historian working with Mamlūk documents an easy and free online access to the latest state of the art in the field.[59] The texts of the documents (currently 1248 out of about 2,500 Arabic documents published so far) are fully searchable in different regards, thereby also serving as historical dictionary of documentary Arabic. It is meant both as a thesaurus of texts and an active research tool for the work with texts that does not take the place of printed editions but facilitates and even enhances the work with them.

While in the past knowledge used to be privatised and hidden in individual files and slip boxes, electronic research tools make collective knowledge available to the public, be it historians or linguists, beginners or experts. The Zurich *Arabic Papyrology Database* (APD) opens up the whole field of electronic research tools, all of them established in recent years the initiative and hard work of younger scholars, many of them being precariously paid by short term project contracts of very different purpose, and doing this kind of groundwork more or less in their spare time and with considerable idealism. How are we to find documents, and how to decode the often arcane papyrological abbreviations with which to cite text editions? What has been the *Checklist* in Greek papyrology[60] for quite some time is now for Arabic documentary studies the *Checklist of [non-literary] Arabic Documents* of the International Society for Arabic Papyrology (ISAP).[61] An additional tool to the *Arabic Checklist* is the Zurich *(Full) Arabic Papyrology Bibliography*, listing not only entries of editions but of a large number of historical and linguistic studies based on Arabic and other documents from the 7th–16th c CE in some way or other.[62] Another bibliography explicitly dedicated to the Mamlūk Sultanate is the *Mamluk Bibliography Online* of the Middle East Documentation Center at the University of Chicago,[63] while the *Princeton Geniza Project Database* contains large numbers of fully search-

59 Andreas Kaplony and Johannes Thomann, *The Arabic Papyrology Database*, www.ori.uzh.ch/apd [accessed 12 March 2012], being a non-commercial project running under the patronage of the International Society for Arabic Papyrology (ISAP, www.ori.uzh.ch/isap.html, accessed 12 March 2012) and a partner of the *Trismegistos* metadata project (www.trismegistos.org, accessed 12 March 2012) of Greek, Demotic, Coptic, and Arabic documents. Access is free via the Internet.

60 Sosin et al., *Checklist.* A print version from 11 November 2011 is downloadable under www.ori.uzh.ch/isap/isapchecklist/ISAP_Checklist_2011.pdf [accessed 12 March 2012].

61 Sijpesteijn et al., *The Checklist.*

62 Kaplony, *Papyrology Bibliography.*

63 Middle East Documentation Center, *Mamluk Bibliography Online*, http://mamluk.lib.uchicago.edu [accessed 12 March 2012].

able Judaeo-Arabic texts also from the Mamlūk era, constituting a natural complement to the *Arabic Papyrology Database.*[64]

One of the very important collections for Arabic documents from the Mamlūk sultanate in size and stock is the Vienna Papyrus Collection in the Austrian National Library. It contains about 40,000 Arabic papers, many of them from the Mamlūk era (the older papyri not included). A very useful tool for working with this material is the collection's online catalogue providing metadata and digital images of published documents.[65] A checklist of edited Viennese papyri and papers has been prepared by Lucian Reinfandt and Sandra Hodecek,[66] a concordance of Josef Karabacek's still important *PERF Catalogue* by Lucian Reinfandt.[67] Other collections holding *inter alia* Arabic papyri from the Mamlūk era are increasingly present in the internet. The Zurich *List of Major Collections Holding Arabic Documents* gives information about the latest state of affairs.[68]

A central aspect of Mamlūk documentary studies is to keep an eye on the recruitment of younger talent (the discipline often tends to be negligent in this regard, and the young might be more interested in documents than expected). Electronic teaching tools play an important role, and the *Arabic Papyrology School* (APS) has the honour to be the first major achievement in this field.[69] A sister to this is the regular *Arabic Papyrology Webclass* (APW) organised by Andreas Kaplony, which has treated different kinds of documents such as legal deeds, letters, and lists and is currently advertising for the Winter Term 2012/13 a reading of unpublished Arabic documents from Upper-Egyptian Edfu.[70] Another step in this direction has been the *International Summer School in Arabic Papyrology* held in Vienna 2007, organised by Cornelia Römer, Andreas Kaplony and Lucian Reinfandt.[71] An important step towards an institutionalisation of Arabic documentary studies is the establishment of the *International Society for Arabic Papyrology* (ISAP) which is not devoted to papyrology alone but to Arabic documentary studies in the widest sense of the word, involving neighbouring disciplines of Archaeology, Coptology, Semitic Philology, Greek Papyrology and Near and Middle Eastern History. Since its foundation in 2002 it has

64 Cohen, *Geniza Project.*

65 Österreichische Nationalbibliothek, *Katalog der Papyrussammlung. Publizierte Papyri der ÖNB*, http://aleph.onb.ac.at/F?func=file&file_name=login&local_base=ONB08 [accessed 12 March 2012].

66 Reinfandt, Hodecek, *Handlist.*

67 Reinfandt, *Papyrus Erzherzog.*

68 Kaplony, *Major Collections.*

69 Kaplony et al., *Papyrology School.*

70 Kaplony, *Papyrology Webclass.*

71 Römer et al., *International Summer School.*

held regular conferences in Cairo (2002), Granada (2004), Alexandria (2006), Vienna (2009) and Tunis (2012).[72]

Trends and priorities

There has been a considerable increase in the past years in both the use of textual documents by historians of the Mamlūk sultanate and the edition of new material. This increase goes hand in hand with a better methodological awareness of the indispensability of documents for research as well as with a better familiarity with the material among many historians in the field. On a substantive level, new excavations of documents (al-Quṣayr al-Qadīm) have been a stimulus for many studies. Likewise, the long known Mamlūk collections from Jerusalem, Alexandria and Cairo or the contemporaneous material from the archives of Granada have a constant pulling effect on social and legal historians of the late Middle Ages,[73] and it is these collections just mentioned that form the basis on which a comparative long-term project is currently undertaken: *Islamic Law Materialized*, initiated by Christian Müller and funded by the European Research Council (ERC). This project investigates the manifestation of legal practice on the basis of a systematic comparison of legal deeds from these collections.[74] Another major field of research is pious foundations in the Mamlūk sultanate. For this field the many published and still more unpublished Arabic endowment deeds (*waqfīyāt*) from the Cairo and other archives offer a wealth of sources. Working with the unpublished ones, however, is a bit of a challenge with the unclear state of the art of editions (no databases, no publication lists), the lack of photographs available, the originals being sometimes subject to restrictive access policies, and not least the fact that not a few of the deeds might be in legal use still today.[75] Moreover the question of state archives, or rather their disappearance, in pre-modern Islamicate societies regularly arouses interest, and there has been controversial debate in the past decades from let us say Samuel Stern ("too few archives preserved") to Michael Chamberlain ("there are reasons for the lack of archives") to Petra Sijpesteijn ("there was an archival

72 *The International Society for Arabic Papyrology*, www.ori.uzh.ch/isap [accessed 12 March 2012].

73 On the archives in Jerusalem, Alexandria and Cairo cf. Bauden, *Mamluk Era*; on the archives of Granada cf. Álvarez de Morales, *La geografía.*

74 *Islamic Law Materialized*, www.ilm-project.net [accessed 12 March 2012].

75 A recent undertaking devoted to Islamic pious foundations and partly treating the era and territory of the Mamlūk sultanate is Meier et al., *Islamische Stiftungen.*

mentality") to recently and very convincingly Tamer El-Leithy.[76] Finally the discovery of new documents in unsuspected places is a fascinating matter, for it not only enriches the documentary stock itself but highlights such anthropologically meaningful questions like life-cycles of documents, the recycling and reuse of documents as well as strategies for preserving and discarding documents.[77]

Also the genre of written 'document' as such has widened its scope. Andreas Görke and Konrad Hirschler have proposed to consider marginal notes on literary codices as documents, and rightly so.[78] Naming them 'manuscript notes' and defining them as "any written material that is found on a manuscript that does not belong to the main text(s), irrespective of whether it refers to the main text and the legal status of the manuscript or is entirely unrelated to text and manuscript itself", these writings comprise reading notes, certificates of and licences for transmission, ownership statements, statements of praise or disparagement, poetry, endowment attestations, and autobiographical statements.[79] This approach is an auspicious step to introduce again literary sources into the field of documentary studies, not in the conventional way of reading the primary text as a document but in terms of a secondary treatment with manuscript notes. A consequential next step could then be to bring into focus the non-textual traces of use found (or not to be found) on the manuscripts: the dirt from fingers, destruction by use, traces of veneration. Such are telling documents of the human background of codices, of reading habits, the proliferation of texts, and the relevance of texts among their respective clientele, and in fact

76 Stern, *Fāṭimid Decrees*; Chamberlain, *Knowledge*; Sijpesteijn, *The Archival Mind*; El-Leithy, *Living documents.*

77 Cf. Bauden, *Recovery*, for the recovery of lavish Mamlūk chancery documents in a notebook used by the 9th/15th c historian al-Maqrīzī. The chancery documents had been cut and reused as scrap paper for brouillons of his literary production. Very similarly Marina Rustow has recently identified Fāṭimid chancery documents on the back sides of Hebrew literary texts from the Cairo Genizah. These documents had been cut and reused, the Hebrew literary texts thereby giving hints to the modern researcher of how to put together the puzzle of dissected documents on the back. Marina Rustow has recently presented results at the *Fifth International Society for Arabic Papyrology Conference in Tunis, March 28–31, 2012*, see, Rustow, *Life-Cycle.* Another case is the preservation of paper documents as linings and fillings of high caps from the Ayyūbid and Mamlūk eras. The present author has recently presented first results at the *21st Colloquium on the History of Egypt and Syria in the Fatimid, Ayyubid, and Mamluk Eras (10th–15th Centuries), May 9–11, 2012* ("Recycled Documents in Textiles from Ayyūbid and Mamlūk Egypt"). A joint publication with an edition of the documents and an analysis of the textile components is currently prepared by Handley et al., *Catalogue raisonné.* The whole subject of life-cycles and the recycling of medieval Islamic documents has recently been brought forward in a very inspiring way by El-Leithy, *Living Documents.*

78 Görke, Hirschler, *Introduction*, 10,15.

79 Görke, Hirschler, *Introduction*, 9–10.

have been subject of an inspiring study by Kathryn Rudy.[80] A further step yet can be taken with literary sources themselves being understood as documents, when serving matters of identity politics of rulers etc. This goes a little bit into Michael Chamberlain's direction and has recently been taken up again by Jo van Steenbergen.[81] But we have diverged from the original idea of diplomatics more than is our aim.

Despite their indisputable significance, many a historian might refrain from using Mamlūk documents as sources, let alone devoting major energies in editing new ones. That is because of the obvious difficulties that come along with them. The presentation of the texts in editions is sometimes self-sufficient if not plainly arcane. Fragmentary texts show a disposition to opaque meanings, and even the more complete and more intelligible ones are often enough meagre by content when held against the lush information from literary sources. The palaeography of Mamluk documents is a challenge, and travelling to collections scattered all over the world, sometimes offering only restricted access to their stock, does not help matters. Not everybody is willing to shoulder this, and conditions press for specialisation. However, specialisation should not lead to isolation (as has been a tendency in the past), and Mamlūk documentary studies should not settle for accurate editions of texts and expert guardianship of their factual contents. Although being a self-confident auxiliary discipline, it should not forget the larger epistemological background that is key to understanding past societies. On a textual basis documents offer a mass of hard data, while on a material basis they reveal silhouettes of the humans behind and around them. This multi-layered potential makes them a playground for encounters between absolutely essential philology on the one hand and ambitious and more theory-driven Cultural Studies on the other leading towards a kind of text-anthropology. To put it another way: there will always be need for a group of specialists taking care of text editions and interpretation, but they should be aware of the many chances that written documents offer to an academic discipline of *Mamlukology*, and prepare their editions accordingly.

80 Rudy, *Dirty Books*, 20: "The dirt ground into the margins of medieval manuscripts is one of their interpretable features, which can help us to understand the desires, fears, and reading habits of the past."

81 Chamberlain, *Knowledge*; van Steenbergen, *Royal Pilgrimage: Kitāb al-Dhahab*; idem, *Royal Pilgrimage: Social Semiotic.*

Conclusion

To conclude, a few suggestions shall be given of how to proceed with Arabic and especially Mamlūk documentary studies and thereby enhance the unique potential inherent in this key discipline:

(a) First of all, more editions of documents need to be given priority. There is much material in the collections unrecognised so far, and every new text exponentially augments the information value of the documentary stock altogether because documents reveal their information most when read together with as many related documents as possible.[82] On the other hand, the growing electronic infrastructure (databases, auxiliary tools; cf. part 2 above) facilitates edition work and eases access to the material for non-specialists. The benefit of documentary studies for non-specialists can also be demonstrated at regular meetings and conferences of e.g. the *International Society for Arabic Papyrology* (ISAP). This goes along with the need for a certain institutionalisation of Arabic documentary studies inside the Middle Eastern Studies group.

(b) A deliberately wide definition of the traditional discipline of diplomatics as well as the notion of 'document' is favoured. With it can be done justice to the wide range of text genres bearing documentary value. Long-established interest in legal and chancery documents is to be enriched by the inclusion of casual writings (*Gebrauchsschreiben*) preserved in papyrus collections. The potential of the latter has been tapped on a larger scale only from the 1990s on, and here is, in the present author's opinion, the most promising subgroup of Mamlūk documents.[83] The range of documents can further be extended to 'new' genres like notes on the margins of literary codices (manuscript notes) or, if one likes, even to literary texts proper that served a documentary purpose, although the latter tends a bit to overstretch the discipline of documentary studies.

(c) Editions of Mamlūk documents should not settle for mere presentations of the texts alone, but should keep an eye on the 'living background' of documents by incorporating the texts into wider questions of a historical, literary or linguistic nature. A document does not 'speak for itself' anymore and should therefore not be edited for its own sake. On the other hand, with solid research questions as a basis even trivial lists can become very meaningful texts. Mamlūk documents should become attractive for all those who are not per se interested in documents. This however becomes only possible when the philological work of

82 Dietrich, P.Hamb.Arab. II p. 7: "Unsere Papyri sind sozusagen "Massenprodukte" und können infolgedessen nur in der Masse ergiebig und aufschlußreich sein." What holds true for Arabic papyri also holds true for Arabic papers from later periods. The need for more editions is also expressed by Bauden, *Mamluk Era*, 46.

83 Most notably by Werner Diem's editions of letters from the Mamlūk period; cf. his P.Heid.Arab. II; P.Berl.Arab. II; P.Vind.Arab. I–III; CPR XXXII.

editing documents is from the outset bound into the larger discourses in *Mamlukology.*

(d) Although the former items have argued for an enlargement of the documentary corpus by new genres of texts, one should not overemphasise the textual component of documents. There is a certain trap of equating texts with documents, for this would narrow documents too much away from their true information potential. Rather, components other than the text itself have to be 'read' as well, like the support of the document (writing material and its quality), its *mise en page*, the archaeological find context (if available) or traces of use (dirt, destruction, recycling) in order to make the document 'tell its story'. A 'holistic' reading is requested that keeps an open eye not only on positive facts (found in the body text) or on narratological patterns (found in between the lines of the body text) but also on non-textual aspects. These latter should not be neglected for it was those that once transported essential information to the addressees in regards of social formation, identity, ideology or else the role of documents in the resolution of conflict, in other words: the semiotic value of documents.[84] For such an undertaking, however, good editions are essential (and have fortunately become more and more standard in recent years): they should contain detailed formal descriptions of objects, critical transcriptions of the texts,[85] elaborate philological commentaries line by line,[86] accurate historical contextualisation of the documents' contents (the *Sitz im Leben*), and not least good photos.[87]

(e) Documentary studies are transdisciplinary by nature. Documents should be read against a background of literary sources, archaeology, and social anthropology.[88] Not only is the number of experts too small to work in isolation but the obstacles posed by documents too many. Mamlūk documentary experts are therefore well-advised to share their knowledge and hardships with partner disciplines from Islamic Studies both synchronic (Persian and Ottoman Diplomatics, Andalusian archives) and diachronic (Arabic Papyrology, pre-Mamlūk Diplomatics, Ottoman and Persian Diplomatics from the early modern period,

84 El-Leithy, *Living Documents*, 410; Wansbrough, *Lingua Franca*, 79. Cf. also Wenzel, *Reflections*, 15 ("Further interest in manuscript layout may lead to the somewhat embarrassing realization of how incomplete or limited even the most minute studies of this moment are.").

85 The transcriptions of Mamlūk documents should by all means follow the conventions of the so-called "Leiden system" adopted in 1931 and since applied in all subdisciplines of papyrology and slightly modified by Werner Diem (in P.Heid.Arab. II) for the Arabic language group. Cf. Schubert, *Editing a Papyrus*, 202–03.

86 The recent trend back towards lean commentaries observable in the neighbouring discipline of Greek Papyrology is, to my mind, not a fortunate development, for it might encourage again a bit to fetishise the old texts and let them 'speak for themselves'.

87 Cf. also the recommendations for editions compiled in Bauden, *Mamluk Era*, 57–58.

88 El-Leithy, *Living Document*, 432.

Swahili Diplomatics from 19th c East Africa). Chancery and epistolographic conventions are of a conservative character, revealing long continuities over centuries and across language groups and partly reaching back into pre-Islamic era. Elaborate deeds from later periods cannot be understood properly without a view on formulaic developments from previous ones. On the other hand, the often sporadic and fragmentary documents from earlier periods (papyri) leave unanswered many questions in regards of their function in administrative procedures or their social use. These can, however, be understood much better when held against the more comprehensive and more abundantly preserved documentation from later periods.

In recent years there has been some discussion about a 'Return to Philology', about 'New Philology', and even about *Zukunftsphilologie*, the proponents arguing for the value of philology in contemporary scholarship.[89] While in the nineteenth century philology used to be a flourishing discipline, it had been abandoned in the twentieth century on methodological and moral grounds.[90] But while its abandonment is partly justified with regard to method, it still maintains a strong and undeniable influence on scholarly practice.[91] Philology offers powerful hermeneutical tools.[92] This fact has also been underlined by Edward Said in a famous late essay,[93] and it is not without irony that it is the initiator of the *Orientalism* caveat who offers a late remedy for a whole generation of self-paralysed post-Orientalists.[94] The "art of reading slowly" is in fact a quality feature of philology.[95] 'Slow' reading, in the widest sense of the word, is a catchy periphrasis also for the hermeneutical tools of Mamlūk documentary studies. One could understand them accordingly as 'new documentary studies', by which Mamlūk written documents become a central domain of *Mamlukology.*

Bibliography

Agius, Dionisius, "'Leave Your Homeland in Search of Prosperity': The Ostrich Egg in a Burial Site at Quseir al-Qadim in the Mamluk Period," in: *Egypt and Syria in the Fatimid, Ayyubid and Mamluk eras 4. Proceedings of the 9th and 10 International Colloquium Organized at the Katholieke Universiteit Leuven in May 2000 and May 2001*, eds. U. Vermeulen and J. van Steenbergen, Leuven: Peeters 2005, pp. 355–79.

89 De Man, *Return*; Wenzel, *Reflections*; Patterson, *Return*; Restall, *History*; Said, *Return*; Pollock, *Future Philology*; Harpham, *Roots*; Neuwirth, *Zukunftsphilologie.*

90 Harpham, *Roots*, 50.

91 Harpham, *Roots*, 54.

92 Neuwirth, *Zukunftsphilologie*, 3.

93 Said, *Return.*

94 Pollock, *Future Philology*, 960.

95 Pollock, *Future Philology*, 933 with reference to Friedrich Nietzsche.

Agius, Dionisius, "The Inscribed Ostrich Egg," in: *Myos Hormos – Quseir al-Qadim: Roman and Islamic Ports on the Red Sea.* 2 vols., eds. D. Peacock and L. K. Blue, Oxford: Oxbow Books 2006–2009, vol. 1: *Survey and Excavations 1999–2003*, pp. 158–160.

Álvarez de Morales, Camilo, "La geografía documental arábigogranadina," in: *Documentos y manuscritos árabes del Occidente musulmán medieval*, ed. N. Martínez de Castilla, Madrid: Consejo Superior de Investigaciones Científicas 2010, pp. 205–23.

Al-ʿAsali, Kāmil J., *Wathā'iq Maqdisīyah Ta'rīḫīyah*, 2 vols., Amman: Jāmiʿat al-Urdun 1983–85.

Bauden, Frédéric, "Du destin des archives en Islam. Analyse des données et éléments de réponse," in: *Actes du colloque international "La correspondance entre souverains. Rédaction, transmission, modalités d'archivage et ambassades. Approches croisées entre l'Orient musulman, l'Occident latin et Byzance (xiiie-début xvie s.), École pratique des hautes-études, Paris, 2–3 décembre 2008"*, eds. Dénise Aigle and Stephane Péquignot, Brepols (in press).

Bauden, Frédéric, "L'achat d'esclaves et la rédemption des captifs à Alexandrie d'après deux documents arabes d'époque mamelouke conservés aux Archives de l'Etat à Venise (ASVe)," in: *Regards croisés sur le Moyen Âge arabe. Mélanges à la mémoire de Louis Pouzet s.j. (1928–2002)*, eds. A.-M. Eddé and E. Gannagé, Beirut 2005: Université Saint-Joseph Dar El-Machreq, pp. 269–325.

Bauden, Frédéric, "Mamluk Era Documentary Studies: The State of the Art," *Mamlūk Studies Review* 9/1 (2005), pp. 15–60.

Bauden, Frédéric, "Review: Guo, Li, *Commerce, Culture, and Community in a Red Sea Port in the Thirteenth Century*," *Mamlūk Studies Review* 13/1 (2009), pp. 167–71.

Bauden, Frédéric, "The Recovery of Mamluk Chancery Documents in an Unsuspected Place," in: *The Mamluks in Egyptian and Syrian politics and society*, eds. Michael Winter and Amalia Levanoni, Leiden: Brill 2004, pp. 59–76.

Bauden, Frédéric, "The Role of Interpreters in Alexandria in the Light of an Oath (*qasāma*) Taken in the Year 822 A.H./1419 A.D.," in: *Continuity and Change in the Realms of Islam. Studies in Honour of Professor Urbain Vermeulen*, eds. K. d'Hulster and J. van Steenbergen, Leuven: Peeters 2008, pp. 33–63.

Bresc, Henri and Rāġib, Yūsuf, *Le sultan mérinide Abū al-Ḥasan ʿAlī et Jacques III de Majorque: du traité de paix au pacte secret*, Le Caire: Institut français d'archéologie orientale 2011.

Burke, Katherine Strange, *Archaeological Texts and Contexts on the Red Sea: The Sheikh's House at Quseir al-Qadim*, Diss. Chicago 2007.

Cahen, Claude, *Jean Sauvaget's Introduction to the History of the Muslim East: A Bibliographical Guide*, Berkeley, Los Angeles: University of California Press 1965 [reprint 1982].

Chamberlain, Michael, *Knowledge and Social Practice in Medieval Damascus, 1190–1350*, Cambridge: Cambridge University Press 1994.

Cohen, Mark R., "Geniza Documents for the Comparative History of Poverty and Charity," in: *Charity and Giving in Monotheistic Religions*, eds. M. Frenkel and Y. Lev, Berlin–New York: W. de Gruyter 2009, pp. 283–341.

Cohen, Mark R., "Geniza for Islamicists, Islamic Geniza, and the 'New Cairo Geniza'," *Harvard Middle Eastern and Islamic Review* 7 (2006), pp. 129–145.

Cohen, Mark R., "Goitein, Magic, and the Geniza," *Jewish Studies Quarterly* 13 (2006), pp. 294 - 304

Conermann, Stephan, "Es Boomt! Die Mamlūkenforschung (1992 - 2002)," in: *Die Mamlūken, Studien zu ihrer Geschichte und Kultur. Zum Gedenken an Ulrich Haarmann (1942 - 1999)*, eds. Stephan Conermann and Anja Pistor-Hatam, Hamburg: EB-Verlag 2003, pp. 1 - 69.

De Man, Paul, "The Return to Philology," in: *The Resistance to Theory*, ed. Paul De Man, Minneapolis: University of Minnesota Press 1986, pp. 21 - 26.

Diem, Werner, "Arabic *allaḏī* as a Conjunction: An old Problem and a New Approach," in: *Approaches to Arabic linguistics. Presented to Kees Versteegh on the occasion of his sixtieth birthday*, eds. E. Ditters and H. Motzki, Leiden: Brill 2007, pp. 67 - 112.

Diem, Werner, "Arabic Letters in Pre-modern Times: A Survey with Commented Selected bibliographies," in: *Documentary Letters from the Middle East: The Evidence in Greek, Coptic, South Arabian, Pehlevi, and Arabic (1st–15th c CE)*, eds. E. M. Grob and A. Kaplony, Bern: Peter Lang 2008, pp. 671 - 906.

Diem, Werner, "Philologisches zu den mamlūkischen Erlassen, Eingaben und Dienstschreiben des Jerusalemer al-Ḥaram aš-Šarīf," *Zeitschrift für arabische Linguistik* 33 (1997), pp. 7–67.

Diem, Werner, "Review: Guo, Li, *Commerce, Culture and Community in a Red Sea Port in the Thirteenth Century*," *Zeitschrift der Deutschen Morgenländischen Gesellschaft* 158 (2008), pp. 164–70.

Diem, Werner, *Arabische Briefe aus dem 10.–16. Jahrhundert*, Berlin–Boston: De Gruyter 2011.

Diem, Werner, *Arabischer Terminkauf. Ein Beitrag zur Rechts- und Wirtschaftsgeschichte Ägyptens im 8. bis 14. Jahrhundert*, Wiesbaden: Harrassowitz 2006.

Diem, Werner, *Wurzelrepetition und Wunschsatz. Untersuchungen zur Stilgeschichte des arabischen Dokuments des 7. bis 20. Jahrhunderts*, Wiesbaden: Harrassowitz 2005.

Droysen, J.G., *Grundriss der Historik*, Leipzig: Veit 1868.

Duranti, Luciana, *Diplomatics: New Uses for an Old Science*, Lanham, MD: Scarecrow Press 1998.

Ferrando Frutos, Ignacio, "Donación en Totanés (Toledo), año 1271, un documento árabe de los mozárabes de Toledo," *Al-Andalus Magreb: Estudios árabes e islámicos* 14 (2007), pp. 39 - 49.

Frantz-Murphy, Gladys, "Arabic Papyrology and Middle Eastern Studies," *Middle East Studies Association Bulletin* 19 (1985), pp. 34 - 48.

Frantz-Murphy, Gladys, "Identity and Security in the Mediterranean World ca. AD 640 - ca. 1517," in: *Proceedings of the Twenty-Fifth International Congress of Papyrology, Ann Arbor 2007*, eds. T. Gagos and Ann Arbor: University of Michigan Library 2010, pp. 253 - 64.

Friedman, Mordechai A., "Quṣayr and Geniza Documents on the Indian Ocean Trade," *Journal of the American Oriental Society* 126 (2006), pp. 401 - 09.

Görke, Andreas and Konrad Hirschler, "Introduction: Manuscript Notes as Documentary Sources," in: *Manuscript Notes as Documentary Sources*, eds. Andreas Görke and Konrad Hirschler, Beirut, Würzburg: Orient Institut Beirut / Ergon 2011, pp. 9 - 20.

Grob, Eva Mira, "Information Packaging in Arabic Private and Business Letters (8th to 13th c. CE): Templates, Slots and a Cascade of Reduction and Rearrangement," in:

Proceedings of the 25th International Congress of Papyrology, Ann Arbor 2007, eds. T. Gagos and Ann Arbor: University of Michigan Library 2010, pp. 277 – 290.
Gronke, Monika, *Arabische und persische Urkunden der Mongolenzeit*, 3 vols. (forthcoming).
Guo, Li, *Commerce, Culture and Community in a Red Sea Port in the Thirteenth Century: The Arabic Documents from Quseir*, Leiden: Brill 2004.
Harpham, Geoffrey G., "Roots, Races, and the Return to Philology," *Representations* 106 (2009), pp. 34 – 62.
Herrmann, Gottfried, *Persische Urkunden der Mongolenzeit*, Wiesbaden: Harrassowitz 2004.
Humphreys, R. Stephen, *Islamic History: A Framework for Inquiry. Revised Edition*, Princeton: Princeton University Press 1992 [reprint 2009].
Jāzim, Muḥammad ʿAbd al-Raḥīm, "Un nouveau corpus documentaire d'époque rasūlide: les actes des waqf de Taʿizz," *Chroniques du manuscrit au Yémen* 10 (2010), pp. 1 – 5.
Kaplony, Andreas, "The Interplay of Different Kinds of Commercial Documents at the Red Sea Port al-Quṣayr al-Qadīm (13th c CE)," in: *Verbal Festivity in Arabic and Other Semitic Languages. Proceedings of the Workshop at the Universitätsclub Bonn on January 16, 2009*, ed. L. Edzard and St. Guth, Wiesbaden: Harrassowitz 2010, pp. 94 – 115.
Kaplony, Andreas, *Zweiundzwanzig Geschäftsbriefe, Geleitscheine, Laufzettel und Geschäftsjournale aus dem Rotmeer-Hafen al-Quṣayr al-Qadīm (13. Jh.)* (forthcoming).
Khan, Geoffrey, *Arabic Legal and Administrative Documents in the Cambridge Genizah Collections*, (Cambridge Library Geniza Series 10), Cambridge: Press Syndicate of the University of Cambridge 1993, 2nd unaltered ed. Oxford 2007.
Leithy, Tamer El-, "Living Documents, Dying Archives: Towards a Historical Anthropology of Medieval Arabic Archives," *Al-Qanṭara* 32/2 (2011), pp. 389 – 434.
Little, Donald P., "The Use of Documents for the Study of Mamluk History," *Mamlūk Studies Review* 1 (1997), pp. 1 – 13.
Margariti, Roxani Eleni, *Aden and the Indian Ocean Trade: 150 Years in the Life of a Medieval Arabian Port*, Chaplet Hill: University of North Carolina Press 2007 (Islamic Civilization and Muslim Networks).
Meier, Astrid and Pahlitzsch, Johannes and Reinfandt, Lucian, *Islamische Stiftungen zwischen juristischer Norm und sozialer Praxis*, Berlin: Akademie Verlag 2009.
Al-Miṣrī, Aḥmad Maḥmūd ʿAbd al-Wahhāb, "Maṣādir Dirāsat al-Wathā'iq al-ʿArabīyah al-Islāmīyah," *Annales islamologiques* 40 (2006), pp. 25 – 50.
Mouton, Jean-Michel, Sourdel, Dominique, Sourdel-Thomine, Janine, "À propos de la "pauvreté" à Damas à l'époque ayyoubide: deux documents inédits," *Archiv für Papyrusforschung und verwandte Gebiete* 57 (2011), pp. 99 – 108.
Müller, Christian, "Écrire pour établir la preuve orale en Islam: la pratique d'un tribunal à Jérusalem au XIVe siècle," in: *Les outils de la pensée: étude historique et comparative des "textes"*, eds. A. Saito and Y. Nakamura, Paris: Éditions de la Maison des sciences de l'homme 2010, pp. 63 – 97.
Müller, Christian, "The Ḥaram al-Sharīf Collection of Arabic Legal Documents in Jerusalem: A Mamlūk Court Archive?" *Al-Qanṭara* 32/2 (2011), pp. 435 – 59.
Neuwirth, Angelika, *Zukunftsphilologie: Revisiting the Canons of Textual Scholarship*, http://www.forum-transregionale-studien.de/de/revisiting-the-canons-of-textual-

scholarship/profil/langfassung.html?PHPSESSID=76bd4d45a033bcc391ebc9dc9db b088a [accessed 11 March 2012].

Pahlitzsch, Johannes, "Documents on Intercultural Communication in Mamluk Jerusalem: The Georgians under Sultan an-Nasir Hasan in 759 (1358)," in: *Diplomatics in the Eastern Mediterranean 1000 – 1500. Aspects of Cross-Cultural Communication*, (The Medieval Mediterranean 74), eds. A. Beihammer, M. Parani and Ch. Schabel, Leiden: Brill 2008 pp. 373 – 94.

Patterson, Lee, "The Return to Philology," in: *The Past and Future of Medieval Studies*, ed. John van Engen and Notre Dame, IN: University of Notre Dame Press 1994, pp. 231 – 44.

Pollock, Sheldon, "Future Philology? The Fate of a Soft Science in a Hard World," *Critical Inquiry* 35 (2009), pp. 931 – 61.

Preisigke, Friedrich et al., *Berichtigungsliste der Griechischen Papyrusurkunden aus Ägypten*, Berlin–Leipzig et al.: Vereinigung wissenschaftlicher Verleger 1922 ff.

Procházka-Eisl, Gisela and Römer, Claudia, *Osmanische Beamtenschreiben und Privatbriefe der Zeit Süleymāns des Prächtigen aus dem Haus-, Hof- und Staatsarchiv zu Wien*, Wien: Verlag der Österreichischen Akademie der Wissenschaften 2007.

Rāġib, Yūsuf, *Actes de vente d'esclaves et d'animaux d'Égypte médiévale*, 2 vols., Le Caire: Institut français d'archéologie orientale, 2002 – 2006.

Ramaḍān, Ḥusayn Muṣṭafā Ḥusayn, "Dirāsah li-Waqf al-Amīr Qīt al-Rajabī," *Annales islamologiques* 41 (2007), pp. 67 – 99.

Regourd, Anne and Fiona J. L. Handley, "Textiles with Writing from Quseir al-Qadim: Finds from the Southampton Excavations 1999–2003," in: *Connected Hinterlands: Proceedings of the Red Sea Project IV Held at the University of Southampton, September 2008*, (Society for Arabian Studies Monographs 8), eds. L. Blue, J. Cooper, R. Thomas and J. Whitewright, Oxford: Archaeopress 2009, pp. 141 – 54.

Regourd, Anne, "A Late Ayyubid Report of Death Found at Quseir al-Qadim (Egypt)," in: *Documents and the History of the Early Islamic World: Proceedings of the Third international conference of the International Society for Arabic Papyrology (ISAP), Bibliotheca Alexandrina, Alexandria (Egypt), 23–26 March 2006*, eds. P. M. Sijpesteijn and L. Sundelin, Leiden: Brill (forthcoming).

Regourd, Anne, "Arabic Language Documents on Paper," in: *Myos Hormos – Quseir al-Qadim: Roman and Islamic Ports on the Red Sea.* 2 vols., eds. D. Peacock and L. K. Blue, Oxford: Oxbow Books 2006–2009, vol. 2: *The Finds from the 1999 – 2003 Excavations*, pp. 339 – 44.

Regourd, Anne, "Folding of a Paper Document from Quseir al-Qadim: A Method of Archiving?" *Al-ʿUṣūr al-Wusṭā* 20 (2008), pp. 13 – 16.

Regourd, Anne, "Un nouveau formulaire de bon de transport: 15 documents de la collection Rémondon (musée du Louvre, Département des Arts de l'Islam)," in: *From Nubia to Syria: Documents from the Medieval Muslim World. Proceedings of the 4th Conference of the International Society for Arabic Papyrology (ISAP), Vienna, 2009, ed.* Andreas Kaplony, (forthcoming).

Regourd, Anne, *Documents administratives et commerciales de Quṣayr al-Qadîm* (forthcoming).

Reinfandt, Lucian, "Die Beurkundung einer mamlukenzeitlichen Familienstiftung vom 12. Ǧumādā II 864 (4. April 1460)," in: *Islamische Stiftungen zwischen juristischer Norm und sozialer Praxis*, eds. A. Meier, J. Pahlitzsch and L. Reinfandt, Berlin: Akademie Verlag 2009, pp. 117 - 152.

Restall, Matthew, "A History of the New Philology and the New Philology in History," *Latin American Research Review* 38 (2003), pp. 113 - 134.

Richards, Donald S., *Mamluk Administrative Documents from St Catherine's Monastery*, Leuven: Peeters 2011.

Rodríguez Gómez, María Dolores and S. M. Domínguez Rojas, "Al otro lado de la muralla. Dos documentos notariales árabes granadinos de Almanjáyar (Granada 1499)," *Miscelánea de Estudios Arabes y Hebraicos (Sección Árabe)* 57 (2008), pp. 295 - 319.

Rodríguez Gómez, María Dolores and S. M. Domínguez Rojas, "La compraventa de fincas urbanas en la Granada del siglo XV a través de dos documentos notariales árabes," *Anaquel de Estudios Árabes* 19 (2008), pp. 175 - 199.

Rodríguez Gómez, María Dolores and S. M. Domínguez Rojas, "La porte d'al-Murḍī de Grenade à travers deux documents notariaux arabes (1493)," *Arabica* 56 (2009), pp. 235 - 268.

Rodríguez Gómez, María Dolores, "Documentos notariales árabes sobre Almacerías (Mediados S. XV-1499), Edición y traducción," *Revista del Centro de Estudios Históricos de Granada y su Reino* 19 (2007), pp. 217 - 225.

Rodriguez Gómez, María Dolores, "Les Maṣārī de Grenade d'après quelques documents arabes (1442 - 1490)," *Bibliotheca Orientalis* 65 (2008), pp. 555 - 594.

Roemer, Hans Robert, "Arabische Herrscherurkunden aus Ägypten," *Orientalistische Literaturzeitung* 61 (1966), pp. 325 - 344.

Roemer, Hans Robert, "Sinai-Urkunden zur Geschichte der islamischen Welt. Aufgaben und Stand der Forschung," in: *Studien zur Geschichte und Kultur des Vorderen Orients. Festschrift für Bertold Spuler zum siebzigsten Geburtstag*, eds. Albrecht Noth and Hans Robert Roemer, Leiden: Brill 1981, pp. 321 - 36.

Roemer, Hans Robert, "The Sinai Documents and the History of the Islamic World: State of the Art - Future Tasks," in: *Studia Arabica et Islamica: Festschrift for Iḥsān ʿAbbās on His Sixtieth Birthday*, ed. Wadād al-Qāḍī, Beirut: American University of Beirut 1981, pp. 381 - 91.

Roemer, Hans Robert, "Über Urkunden zur Geschichte Ägyptens und Persiens in islamischer Zeit," *Zeitschrift der Deutschen Morgenländischen Gesellschaft* 107 (1957), pp. 519 - 538.

Rudy, Kathryn M., "Dirty Books: Quantifying Patterns of Use in Medieval Manuscripts Using a Densitometer," *Journal of Historians of Netherlandish Art* 2 (2012), http://www.jhna.org/index.php/past-issues/volume-2-issue-1 - 2/129-dirty-books.

Said, Edward W., "The Return to Philology," in: *Humanism and Democratic Criticism*, ed. Edward W. Said, New York: Columbia University Press 2004.

Sauvaget, Jean, *Introduction à l'histoire de l'Orient musulman. Éléments de bibliographie*, Paris: Adrien-Maisonneuve 1946.

Sauvaget, Jean, *Introduction à l'histoire de l'Orient musulman. Éléments de bibliographie. Édition refondue et complétée par Claude Cahen*, Paris: Adrien-Maisonneuve 1961.

Schopen, Armin, *Tinten und Tuschen des arabisch-islamischen Mittelalters. Dokumentation Analyse Rekonstruktion. Ein Beitrag zur materiellen Kultur des Vorderen Orients*, Göttingen: Vandenhoeck & Ruprecht 2006.

Schubert, Paul, "Editing a Papyrus," in: *The Oxford Handbook of Papyrology*, ed. Roger S. Bagnall, Oxford et al.: Oxford University Press 2009, pp. 197–215.

Shatzmiller, Maya, *Her Day in Court: Women's Property Rights in Fifteenth-Century Granada*, Cambridge: Harvard University Press 2007.

Sijpesteijn, Petra M., Lennart Sundelin, Sofia Torallas Tovar, and Amalia Zomeño (eds.), *From al-Andalus to Khurasan: Documents from the Medieval Muslim World*, Leiden–Boston: Brill 2007.

Sijpesteijn, Petra M., "Arabic Papyri and Other Documents from Current Excavations in Egypt, with an Appendix of Arabic Papyri and Some Written Objects in Egyptian Collections," *Al-Bardiyyāt* 2 (2007), pp. 10–23.

Sijpesteijn, Petra M., "Multilingual Archives and Documents in Post-Conquest Egypt," in: *The Multilingual Experience in Egypt, from the Ptolemies to the Abbasids*, ed. A. Papaconstantinou, Farnham-Burlington: Ashgate 2010, pp. 105–24.

Sijpesteijn, Petra, "The Archival Mind in Early Islamic Egypt: Two Arabic Papyri," in: *From al-Andalus to Khurasan: Documents from the Medieval Muslim World*, eds. P. M. Sijpesteijn, L. Sundelin, S. Torallas Tovar, and A. Zomeño, Leiden: Brill 2007, pp. 163–86.

Stern, Samuel M., *Fāṭimid Decrees: Original Documents from the Fāṭimid Chancery*, London: Faber and Faber 1964.

Thung, Michael H., *Arabische juristische Urkunden aus der Papyrussammlung der Österreichischen Nationalbibliothek*, München–Leipzig: K G Saur 2006.

Veselý, Rudolf, "Die richterlichen Beglaubigungsmittel. Ein Beitrag zur Diplomatik arabischer Gerichtsurkunden: 3. 'Imḍāʾ'," in: *Orientalistische Studien zu Sprache und Literatur: Festgabe zum 65. Geburtstag von Werner Diem*, ed. U. Marzolph, Wiesbaden: Harrassowitz 2011, pp. 251–261.

Wansbrough, John E., *Lingua Franca in the Mediterranean*, Richmond, Surrey: Curzon Press 1996.

Wenzel, Siegried, "Reflections on (New) Philology," *Speculum* 65 (1990), pp. 11–18.

Zomeño, Amalia, "'When Death Will Fall Upon Him': Charitable Legacies in 15th Century Granada," in: *Charity and Giving in Monotheistic Religions*, eds. M. Frenkel and Y. Lev, Berlin–New York: W. de Gruyter 2009, pp. 217–233.

Zomeño, Amalia, "From Private Collections to Archives: How Christians Kept Arabic Legal Documents in Granada," *Al-Qanṭara* 32/2 (2011), pp. 461–479.

Internet links

Cohen, Marc, *Princeton University Geniza Project*, updated 3 March 2011, www.princeton.edu/~geniza [accessed 12 March 2012].

Islamic Law Materialized, www.ilm-project.net [accessed 12 March 2012].

Kaplony, Andreas and Arn, David and Thomann, Johannes, *The Arabic Papyrology School (APS): an Interactive Introduction to the Reading of Arabic Documents*, www.ori.uzh.ch/aps [accessed 12 March 2012].

Kaplony, Andreas and Thomann, Johannes, *The Arabic Papyrology Database*, www.ori.uzh.ch/apd [accessed 12 March 2012].

Kaplony, Andreas, *Arabic Papyrology Webclass*, www.ori.uzh.ch/apw [accessed 23 June 2012].

Kaplony, Andreas, *List of Major Collections Holding Arabic Documents*, www.ori.uzh.ch/isap/collections.html [accessed 12 March 2012].

Kaplony, Andreas, *The (Full) Arabic Papyrology Bibliography (of Editions and Research)*, www.ori.uzh.ch/research/papyrology/bibliography.html

Middle East Documentation Center, *Mamluk Bibliography Online*, http://mamluk.lib.uchicago.edu [accessed 12 March 2012].

Österreichische Nationalbibliothek, *Katalog der Papyrussammlung. Publizierte Papyri der ÖNB*, http://aleph.onb.ac.at/F?func=file&file_name=login&local_base=ONB08 [accessed 12 March 2012].

Reinfandt, Lucian and Hodecek, Sandra, *Handlist of Published Arabic Papyri from the Vienna Collection (Austrian National Library)*. Version 05 from May 2011, http://www.onb.ac.at/files/IOWP_reinfandt_hodecek_handlist05.pdf [accessed 12 March 2012].

Reinfandt, Lucian, *Papyrus Erzherzog Rainer, Führer durch die Ausstellung (PERF). Konkordanz*. Version April 2006, http://www.onb.ac.at/files/perf_konkordanz.pdf [accessed 12 March 2012].

Römer, Cornelia and Kaplony, Andreas and Reinfandt, Lucian, *First International Summer School in Arabic Papyrology. 1st– 8th July 2007*, www2.onb.ac.at/sammlungen/papyrus/aktuell/summerschool2007.pdf [accessed 26 October 2011].

Sijpesteijn, Petra M. and Kaplony, Andreas and Youssef-Grob, Eva M., *The Checklist of Arabic Documents*, last updated 3 June 2012, www.ori.uzh.ch/isap/isapchecklist.html [accessed 12 March 2012].

Sosin, Joshua D. And Bagnall, Roger S. and Cowey, James and Depauw, Mark and Wilfong, Terry G. and Worp, Klaas A., *Checklist of Editions of Greek, Latin, Demotic, and Coptic Papyri, Ostraca and Tablets*, last updated 1 June 2011, http://library.duke.edu/rubenstein/scriptorium/papyrus/texts/clist.html [accessed 12 March 2012]. A print version from 11 November 2011 is downloadable under www.ori.uzh.ch/isap/isapchecklist/ISAP_Checklist_2011.pdf [accessed 12 March 2012].

The International Society for Arabic Papyrology, www.ori.uzh.ch/isap [accessed 12 March 2012].

Paper read at a conference

Van Steenbergen, Jo, "On Royal Pilgrimage and Patronage in 15th-Century Egypt: the *Kitāb al-Dhahab al-Masbūk* by Aḥmad b. ʿAlī al-Maqrīzī (d. 1442) and its Documentary Value", paper read at the *Fifth International Society for Arabic Papyrology Conference in Tunis, March 28–31, 2012*;

Van Steenbergen, Jo, "On Royal Pilgrimage and Patronage in 15th-Century Egypt: a Social Semiotic reading of al-Maqrīzī's *Kitāb al-Dhahab al-Masbūk*", paper read at the *21st Colloquium on the History of Egypt and Syria in the Fatimid, Ayyubid, and Mamluk Eras (10th–15th Centuries), May 9–11, 2012.*

Bethany J. Walker

What Can Archaeology Contribute to the New Mamlukology? Where Culture Studies and Social Theory Meet[1]

That archaeology has until recently remained at the margins of Mamluk studies should come as no surprise. Among the subfields of Islamic history, Mamluk studies have perhaps been the most traditionally text-focused in source material, methods of analysis, and scope of inquiry. Art historians have contributed in important ways to Mamluk studies; it has been more difficult for archaeologists and anthropologists, however, to make the same inroads. On the other hand, the field of archaeology has failed to keep pace with developments in Islamic historiography. It also remains the case that archaeologists' use of texts has been generally limited, restricted, for the most part, to those narrative genres that yield the most immediate returns on matters related to space and time. These are namely geographical texts, travelers' accounts, and chronicles, which are useful for locating and dating archaeological sites and tying them to historical events. Archaeologists have not always been the best historians, and why should they?; these are, of course, distinctly different disciplines. Moreover, as generally true of the archaeology of any historical era, the results of archaeological fieldwork have remained "buried" (to use a good trade term) in unfamiliar technical journals and not properly distilled for consumption by historians. The published reports themselves are meant for other archaeologists to read: they are full of technical jargon, tend towards heavy description, and are admittedly opaque as a result. The result has been that a rich body of literature generated by archaeological research on issues that should be of interest to Mamluk historians has for too long remained unknown, and inaccessible, to them.

Mamluk studies has in recent years experienced some important transformations in the kinds of data used, the kinds of questions asked of that data, and in scholarly conversations outside the field. This kind of cross-disciplinary outreach includes a new relationship with, or at least a curiosity about, archaeological research.Increasingly, archaeologists, and the specialists that work

1 In the following article diacriticals have been removed from the names of archaeological sites. The most widely accepted spellings in English of these place names are used, instead.

in the field with them, have been participating in Mamluk-themed conferences[2]; ever more collective volumes in the field are including archaeological contributions and now even collaboratively written ones (where text-based historians and field archaeologists work on a historical problem together)[3]. One important result of these publication trends has been to make archaeological research more accessible and comprehensible. Islamic archaeology as a whole is experiencing important developments, as well, is its approach to texts, with a wider and more intense engagement with the written record and the interrogation of "text" as "artifact", with all of the challenges of context, preservation, and interpretation with which traditional historians struggle when approaching the written record. In this way the "linguistic turn" that has so impacted historiography since the 1980s has also permeated archaeology.

The following essay serves several purposes. On one level, it is a brief and non-technical assessment of the potential of archaeology as a very relevant venue of historical inquiry and one uniquely positioned to provide information about Mamluk society and socio-cultural processes.[4] On another level, the essay aims at predicting the future, by suggesting ways in which the field may develop in coming years and how it could potentially mold tomorrow's Mamlukology.

What is "Mamluk Archaeology?

Technically "Mamluk" archaeology is a chronological specialization within Islamic archaeology. It is a relatively late bloomer within the larger archaeology of Islamic societies, emerging as a distinctive field of study from the late 1970s. One can generally trace its roots in the excavation of multi-period Crusader castles and Early Islamic cities, where investigation of the Mamluk period was of secondary interest. Likewise, the preservation and restoration of Mamluk-era monuments ultimately led to monument-based studies by architectural historians and occasionally archaeologists, whose efforts were largely devoted to documenting architectural construction phases (useful for restoration efforts). In Israel, interest in the Mamluk period has grown slowly out of salvage excavations, where Mamluk strata, laying close to the ground surface, were readily

2 The conference that produced this collection of essays is an excellent example. One would also note the series of conferences launched by "Exercising Power in the Age of the Sultanates" project by the French and American institutes in Cairo and Amman from 2004 to 2006.

3 Such collaboratively written articles will appear in the forthcoming *Oxford Handbook of Islamic Archaeology* (ed. Bethany Walker).

4 For other assessment of the field, from different perspectives see Whitcomb, *Mamluk Archaeological Study*, 97–106 and Walker, *Ceramics*, 109–157.

exposed. In none of these cases were projects designed specifically to explore Mamluk-era strata.

As a form of "historical archaeology", Mamluk archaeology is also a multidisciplinary, anthropologically informed investigation of a textually rich period of human history. The degree to which texts should drive archaeological research has been a heated one, particularly in the United States, where historical archaeology was long considered "the handmaiden of history".[5] The quantity and diversity of textual sources available for the Mamluk period presents a special challenge to archaeologists: should field projects be designed to specifically address the textual narrative, or should texts refine archaeological interpretations? The projects described below illustrate ways in which a deductive approach to research, in which questions about Mamluk society that arise from a complementary "reading" of both the (appropriate) textual and material records, are the basis of research design.

The field is further characterized by the physical realities of the archaeological record. A Mamluk specialization within Islamic archaeology has been slow to develop, much like Ottoman archaeology, because of the very special logistical challenges that study of the most recent historical periods presents. With their shallow and near-surface deposition, Mamluk-era occupational levels suffer poor preservation. Moreover, as many Mamluk sites continued to be occupied into, or were reoccupied in, modern times, many sites are simply not accessible for excavation or their levels contaminated by subsequent rebuilding and reoccupation.[6] Sites with monumental architecture, in the form of urban and defensive structures, suffer a similar fate: continued use of forts, defensive walls, large residences, and caravanserais, as well as the demolishing of the same to reuse building material for other purposes, creates architectural sequences that are difficult to untangle. Mamluk architecture, whether urban or rural, tends towards degeneration and collapse: the fine façades of the multi-purpose complexes on the Bayn al-Qasrayn in Cairo mask rough, rubble cores; many of the rural forts of the Syrian frontier were quickly and haphazardly built, with roughly hewn blocks, irregular use of mortar, and reuse, wherever possible, of ancient structures (Fig. 1). Unless regularly maintained, such construction, particularly when facing stones are removed for building materials, lends itself to collapse, and they weather earthquakes and floods poorly. In the worst of cases, massive rock tumbles result (Fig. 2).

5 This is especially true of specialists of colonial America. For literature on the debates, see Hume, *Handmaiden*, 215–225; Whittenburg, *But What does it Mean*, 49–54; idem, *On Why Historians*, 4–9; and Levy, *Always a Handmaiden*, published online at: http://www.archaeology.org/online/features/history/.

6 Notable exceptions are single-period rural sites, such as those being excavated as salvage projects in Israel, where the stratigraphy is clearer and better preserved.

The artifacts of the period present further complications to archaeological analysis. When one moves beyond the urban centers, the ceramic record, in particular, become less familiar. There are fewer readily recognizable (and datable) imports at rural sites, the ceramic assemblages characterized by local products and handmade wares that changed little in form and surface decoration over time. They are difficult to date, hampering archaeologists' efforts to identify Mamluk-era sites throughout Bilād al-Shām. Furthermore, in the case of the problematic HMGP wares that dominate Syrian assemblages, such coarse wares betray distinctive regionalisms in production and distribution (Fig. 3).[7] One is struck by the marked regionalisms of the material culture (the "minor arts" in art historical parlance) as a whole in the Mamluk-held lands. One could argue the same for the texts of the period, possibly illustrating ways in which the Mamluk "empire" was more a fractured entity, socially and culturally, than a homogenous whole. Archaeological fieldwork of the last decade, in particular, has painted a picture of distinctive cultural regionalisms, localized identities, and networks that are created and maintained quite independently of the actions of the state. In this sense, Mamluk archaeology provides a uniquely localized, and indeed rural, view on Mamluk society (societies) that enriches the cultural narrative drawn from the written record.

The Pioneers

The earliest purposive excavations of Mamluk-era sites, ones designed to specifically explore the Mamluk period and not tied to monument studies or restoration efforts, date to the late 1970s. The seminal project in this regard, unfortunately, never reached the stage of fieldwork. Jean-Claude Garcin's fine textual study, and architectural prospection, of the provincial center of Qus in Upper Egypt was meant to be a precursor to archaeological fieldwork that never materialized.[8] In 1979, three years after the publication of Garcin's monograph on Qus, the University of Chicago began excavations at the Red Sea port connected to that medieval town: Quseir al-Qadim. As arguably the first purposeful,

7 This is an acronym for Handmade Geometric-Painted wares, a ubiquitous form of common pottery used for serving and storage and variety of other purposes throughout Bilād al-Shām. Though it is usually associated with the Ayyubid-Mamluk periods in southern Syria (historical Palestine and Transjordan), it is generally believed that its history of use spans the late eleventh through early twentieth centuries of the Common Era. For debates about this ware, see Johns, *Rise*, 65–93.

8 According to Garcin's report, he was denied an excavation permit, as the Egyptian Antiquities Service, following the discovery a hoard of valuable artifacts at the site, intended to conduct the fieldwork itself. Garcin attributes the failure of the Service to follow through with fieldwork to the Six Day War (Garcin, *Un centre musulman*, xiv).

modern and controlled excavation of a Mamluk-era site, fieldwork at Quseir al-Qadim, directed by Donald Whitcomb and which continued until 1982[9], yielded important information regarding economy and trade, urban structure, and state investment; the project moreover, was not driven by textual narratives (of which there are few that pertain to the site), but by purely archaeological lines of inquiry related to local society and spatial networks. Excavations produced, however, texts of their own: nearly 900 fragments of letters and documents, the paper well preserved in the dry Egyptian climate, which originally belonged to a local man's private files of largely business correspondence. These documents have since been studied and published by Li Guo.[10]

At the same time, interest in the later Islamic periods grew among archaeologists working in Jordan. Buttressed by developments in Islamic ceramic analysis, thanks to the efforts of the ceramicist Jim Sauer at Tall Hisban (discussed below), American archaeologists began exploratory investigations of post-Crusader levels at multi-period sites. Among the earliest in this regard were the single-season excavations at Karak and Shobak castles by Robin Brown, an anthropologically trained archaeologist. The small-scale probes by Brown in the 1980s inside both castles aimed at isolating Mamluk phases of construction and use and were important for their stratigraphic separation of Crusader and what was then called "Ayyubid-Mamluk" material culture.[11]

In many ways, Mamluk archaeology in southern Bilād al-Shām was born at Tall Hisban. Hisban is a small town in the Madaba Plains of central Jordan, located some twenty kilometers south of Amman and near Madaba; on a clear day, one has a view of the Dead Sea, the walls of the Old City of Jerusalem, and Jericho. It is a multi-period site, with evidence of occupation from the Paleolithic through modern times. Andrews University in Michigan began fieldwork there in 1968, making it is arguably the longest-running, foreign-led excavation in the Middle East.[12] Although the site was originally selected for its possible Biblical associations (with the Amorite capital of "Heshbon"), the expedition encountered, instead, a medieval Islamic castle built on top of a Byzantine basilica,

9 The University of Southhampton's subsequent fieldwork at the site (1999–2003) was primarily concerned with the Roman port there and is, thus, not directly relevant to this essay. For a list of both Chicago and Southhampton publications, see Burke, *Quseir al-Qadim*, 125–132.

10 Guo, *Commerce.*

11 Brown, *Summary Report*, 225–245; idem, *Excavation*, 287–304.

12 The first phase of excavations (1968–1976), generally known as the "Heshbon Expedition", was sponsored by the seminary and Institute of Archaeology at Andrews University. The second phase of excavations (1996–2010), led by the Anthropology Department, under the Senior Direction of LaBianca and today called the "Tall Hisban Cultural Heritage Project", is described in detail in the following section. Fieldwork is on-going: the third phase of excavations begins in 2013, under the Directorship of Walker.

constructed into the foundation of an earlier monumental building of the Roman era (possible a temple) (Fig. 4). Only part of the Islamic site on the summit of the tell was excavated and the medieval village below only begun to be explored, when this first phase of excavations went into hiatus for the purpose of publication.[13]

The legacy of the Heshbon Expedition for Mamluk archaeology is two-fold: the ceramic seriation developed there by Sauer has become invaluable for identifying Mamluk sites through southern Bilād al-Shām, and the excavations produced the first evidence for an extensive rural citadel-cum-administrative center in Jordan, one free of any associations with a Crusader castle. In time the Andrews University excavations would become the most important field project in Jordan, and one could argue for Israel and Palestine as well, for archaeological study of the Mamluk period.

The Field Today

Today a rural focus permeates the archaeological study of the Mamluk period. Certainly traditional architectural-archaeological investigation of the major citadels continues, but it is in the excavation of smaller, geographically peripheral sites in southern Syria, and in regional surveys, that new information about Mamluk social history has been brought to light.[14] Rather than survey all archaeological projects related to the Mamluk period in Bilād al-Shām, I highlight those from which we are learning important lessons about the Mamluk hinterland and that best illustrate potential avenues of inquiry in Mamlukology in the future.

The first Andrews University project at Tall Hisban came to an end in 1976, and final publication of those five important field seasons ensued. It was followed in the 1990s with efforts at restoration of buildings and preparation of the site for public viewing. These efforts were spearheaded by Øystein LaBianca, an anthropologist at Andrews University and one of the founding members of the Heshbon Expedition. The 1996 season was limited to probes strategically placed to explore architectural components of the citadel; in 1998 excavations began anew with the second phase of fieldwork, in order to revisit stratigraphic questions left unanswered by the original Expedition (and in support of the final publications) and to further investigate the standing remains of the only par-

13 For a comprehensive bibliography of Heshbon Expedition reports, see LaBianca, Walker, *Tall Hisban*, 111–120.

14 One respectively notes here the fine work done by IFAO in Islamic Cairo and IFPO, in collaboration with Syrian Antiquities, in the Damascus Citadel.

tially explored medieval complex on the summit (Fig. 5).[15] LaBianca invited this author to join the team that season, to bring to the project ceramics expertise honed in Egypt and a Cairo-based background in both Mamluk archaeology and documentary research.

The partnership between anthropology and Mamluk studies has proven to be a fruitful one for the renewed Hisban project, as it has turned to questions related to food systems and political ecology. One important innovation of the new project has been the systematic incorporation of archival (contemporary manuscript-based) research into the larger archaeological research design, enriching the interpretation of both archaeological and written records related to the site.[16] In terms of its contributions to Mamluk studies, the well preserved castle at Hisban, with its largely intact storeroom and private *hammām*, dominating the summit of the tell, the extensive medieval town at its base, unencumbered by modern housing; the citadel's vast water systems; and the "town dump" have presented the perfect laboratory to test models about Mamluk society and to learn more about the realities of the exercise of state power on the eastern frontier. Today Tall Hisban is generally regarded as the "type site" of Mamluk Jordan.

Tall Hisban, however, is not the only site in Jordan with Mamluk remains. Other tell sites in the central Jordanian plains have produced evidence of contemporary village life. The Andrews University-led project at Tall Jalul, also on the Madaba Plains, has recently produced evidence of an extensive village spanning the late Mamluk and Ottoman periods.[17] As at Hisban, the village architecture takes the form of barrel-vaulted stone structures, and its material culture is characterized by HMGP vessels. The western half of the Iron Age site of ancient Dhiban, approximately seventy kilometers south of Amman and sitting astride two adjacent tells in a highland plateau of the same name, is covered by the remains of late Mamluk houses and shared courtyards, once constituting a village of significant size that was only gradually abandoned over the course of the sixteenth century.[18] That such a large village existed here in this period has puzzled the excavators, as the region around Dhiban is water-challenged in the best of times, and there is strong environmental and textual evidence that the late

15 This complex has been identified by the author as the residence of *wāli al-Balqā* during the first half of the fourteenth century CE.

16 The results of much of this work are cited in Walker, *Jordan*.

17 The Tall Hisban and Jalul excavations are part of the larger Madaba Plains Project, formed by a consortium of American universities in 1982. For more information on the MPP, see the project website at http://www.madabaplains.org/. Preliminary reports on the excavations of the Islamic Village at Jalul can be found in the following: al-Shqour, *2008 Excavations*, 641–655 and Gane, Younker, *2009 Excavations*, 1–2.

18 For a complete list of publications related to this project until 2007, see Porter et al., *Power*, 315–322.

Mamluk period experienced lengthy droughts.[19] At both Dhiban and Hisban remains of massive and ancient cisterns (partially in the form of modified caves) and canals bear witness to the local investment in water harvesting. The directors of these three projects continue to coordinate their fieldwork in ways that promote research on these later historical periods. These on-going excavations at Hisban, Jalul, and Dhiban, as they expose more of the remains of the medieval villages, should shed light on village structure (physical and functional), standards of living and diet, participation in economic and social networks, and local patterns of resource management (namely land and water) – components of local society that are difficult to retrieve from texts alone.

Excavations by Ghent University at Aqaba Castle, recently completed, have documented the changing form and functions of a well known Mamluk waterfront fort and identified the location of the town called al-Ayla in this period.[20] The thirteenth and fourteenth-century toll station was built at the location of an early Islamic (ninth through twelfth centuries CE in date) farming community that once occupied the agricultural hinterland of the city of al-Ayla. True to a pattern repeated at sites throughout Jordan, the fort appears to have been abandoned in the fifteenth century, only to be reused as a caravanserai by the Ottomans. The material culture of the fort is richly diverse, displaying the changing trade networks of the Mamluk and Ottoman eras, as well as highlighting the very close economic and administrative relationships between this part of Bilād al-Shām and Egypt.

In Israel, a variety of small-scale projects, while not specifically designed to study the Mamluk period, are producing new information about contemporary rural society. For purposes of illustration only, I cite two projects by the Israel Antiquities Authority. The first was the excavation and architectural restoration project at Khirbat Din'ila, conducted in 2001 – 2002.[21] While the focus of the IAA's efforts was the Byzantine oil presses, it did uncover evidence of what may be considered a typical Galilean village of the fourteenth and fifteenth centuries CE. Analysis of the pottery retrieved from the excavations documented important developments in vessel forms and assemblages in this period – larger bowls and spouted jugs – that suggest changes in diet, cooking, and dining

19 The literature on this topic is extensive. A list of key sources can be found in Lucke et al., *Soils*, 171 – 188.

20 The project was directed by the late Johnny de Meulemeester and completed by Reem al-Shqour following his passing. For preliminary reports on the excavations, see al-Shqour et al., *Aqaba Castle Project*, 641 – 655.

21 Thatcher, *Khirbat Din'ila Final Report*, published on the web at: http://www.hadashot-esi.org.il/report_detail_eng.asp?id=232&mag_id=110.

customs (a shift to communal dining, for example) from previous periods.[22] In a similar vein, during a brief salvage excavation that preceded road construction in 1999 – 2000, evidence of a thirteenth-fourteenth century settlement at Khirbat Burin, in the eastern Sharon, were discovered.[23] The architectural remains suggested a well-built and relatively prosperous village, as did the associated pottery, which came to this inland village through international networks.[24] The ceramic imports alone (with origins in the eastern Mediterranean and in Italy) speak against rural isolation, at least in this part of the Levant.

One of the most pronounced developments in the archaeology of the Mamluk period, as it has been for Mamluk historiography, is the growing interest in environmental history. As rich as contemporary Arabic texts are for reconstructing certain aspects of the agriculture regime and documenting environmental disasters, a comprehensive environmental history of the Mamluk period also requires recourse to archaeological and soil science research. With this in mind, the Northern Jordan Project was launched by the author in 2003, with an emphasis on the Mamluk and Ottoman periods (Fig. 6).[25] This, a multidisciplinary investigation of the northern hill country between Irbid and the Yarmouk River, aims at documenting shifts in settlement and better understanding the complex interplay among social (settlement, land use, economic and political systems) and natural (climate, landscape) systems (Fig. 7). The theoretical reference of the project is that of political ecology, or the study of the struggle for control over natural resources. Changes in land use and climate are documented through a combined use of soil science and textual analysis. The NJP includes a multi-faceted study of paleoclimates and agricultural regimes, led by specialists in pollen, phytolith (plant silica fossils), soil genesis (soil erosion), and geochemical analysis (Figs. 8 and 9).[26] These, in combination with texts, have the potential to reconstruct ancient floral environments, both natural and man-made. The literary study (by the project director) is relevant in this regard. Going beyond the kinds of narrative sources traditionally used by archaeologists in support of fieldwork, the project identifies and explores documentary sources richest in information about land use and land tenure: *waqfiyāt*, court documents, tax registers, and land registration files. This kind of textual analysis is a

22 Edna J. Stern, "Khirbat Din'ila: The Crusader and Mamluk-Period Pottery". I am grateful to Dr. Stern for sharing the manuscript of her article with me. It is forthcoming in *Átiqot.*

23 'Ad, *Khirbat Burin*, published on the web at: http://www.hadashot-esi.org.il/report_detail_eng.asp?id =235&mag_id=110.

24 Kletter, Stern, *Mamluk-Period*, 173 – 214.

25 For a list of publications related to the NJP, see Walker, *Peasants*, 473 – 480, as well as the project website: http://clio.missouristate.edu/bwalker/njp.html.

26 For preliminary results of this kind of analysis, see Lucke et al., *Soils.*; Lucke et al., *Questioning*, 100 – 126; and Walker et al., *Northern Jordan Project*, 55: in press.

novelty for Islamic archaeology and holds promise for Mamluk studies in the future.

Such environmentally driven landscape archaeology is well developed in Greece and Cyprus, where it has been used to trace the rise and fall of village communities, identify a wide range of settlement types (villages – settled year-round or abandoned, seasonal settlements, hamlets, isolated farmsteads, temporary field camps, pastoral camps), trace the transformation of local agricultural production for export markets, and follow the physical movement of communities through the landscape.[27] The Northern Jordan Project follows in this tradition.

What does Archaeology Have to Offer Mamlukology?

When taken on its own terms – functioning as more than a "handmaiden to history" (merely illustrating what we already know from the textual record) or, worse yet, a soft form of historical inquiry (relying on theory and cultural analogy) – archaeology offers distinctly different, but complementary, perspectives on the historical record.

Social theory and anthropological perspectives

Archaeology is the disciplinary bridge between cultural anthropology and traditional history and, as such, is informative about social action, structures, patterns, and networks, most notable rural ones. It can document processes of social change over long periods of time; provide, in a quite visual and convincing manner, evidence of the physical impact of traumatic events, such as earthquakes, droughts, and war on individuals and communities; and describe exchange networks and the ties that bound communities to one another. It can make the textually invisible – village communities, Bedouin, women, the poor, the socially or religiously marginalized, foreigners – "visible" again. When interpretations are carefully informed by modern cultural analogy, the archaeological record can also potentially reveal indigenous and long-term socio-cultural practices that are not readily retrieved from traditional historical sources, such as communal patterns of land and resource management, buffering strat-

27 Most of this work focuses on the Ottoman period. Some key works include: Given, *Agriculture*, 215–236 (for Cyprus) and Sutton, *Contingent Countryside*, and Zarinebaf et al., *Historical* (for Greece).

egies against scarcity and other forms of adaptation, and informal forms of conflict management.

Rural and spatial analysis

Textual historians and archaeologists generally work with different data sets.[28] The archaeological record is cumulative and answers broad questions about social and economic history, recognizing society and economics as components of the same human system. Its lines of inquiry reflect a disciplinary hybridity and a concern with spatial analysis: the themes of trade and consumption, land use and migration, and social organization and settlement are the underpinning of much archaeological scholarship and pull from the fields of political economy, historical geography, and anthropology, respectively. These are certainly worthwhile areas for Mamluk studies as a whole, and tapping the contemporary Arabic sources for information on topics with spatial dimensions, such as these, would enrich textual analysis.

La longue durée and alternative chronologies

One cannot expect from the archaeological record precise chronologies. It is rarely events, but the broad sweep of time that leaves a trace on an archaeological site and in the artifact assemblage. Archaeologically, there is no "Mamluk period". Material culture does not change immediately with conquest and the arrival of a new overlord. People use the same pots they have always used and their houses take the same form during political transitions. The preference for the chronological moniker "Middle Islamic" (roughly twelfth to fifteenth centuries), preferred today by many archaeologists working in Bilād al-Shām, rejects the political periodization used by historians and best reflects the conservatism of material culture, and traditional societies.[29] Specific chronologies can be obtained through a variety of methods; when these are used in combination, they can be instrumental in tracing socio-cultural developments over *la longue durée*. These include, among others, ceramic analysis, numismatics, inscriptions, C14, and dendrochronology.

28 There can be, of course, overlap. Historically trained archaeologists do textual analysis, as well. Many historians today, notably those in Early Islam, make use of the results of archaeological research. This kind of cross-fertilization is healthy and advances the field.

29 The periodization was first promoted by Donald Whitcomb over twenty years ago.

Ties to the natural sciences

Archaeology could potentially make a "science" out of Mamluk studies. Archaeological fieldwork is generally multi-disciplinary in methods, research strategy, and interpretive framework. Three areas of research that offer the most promise for scientific inquiry in Mamluk studies are environmental history (discussed throughout this essay), food systems, and trade. Food systems – which refers to the many activities connected to the procurement, processing, storage, consumption, and disposal of food – can be reconstructed archaeologically through the forms of cooking, serving, and storage vessels; residue analysis of those vessels (to determine what kinds of foodstuffs were used in them); and paleobotanical and paleofaunal analysis obtained through soils and in midden deposits (as proxy data for diet). Written sources are rich in descriptions of urban foodways, but less so for rural ones; archaeological analysis in this regard completes the picture of diet and dining culled from texts and the visual arts. Trade networks can be mapped through laboratory analysis of the clays in ceramics, which determine place of manufacture, and distributions of export wares culled from survey reports.

Alternative historical narratives

The relationship between "text" and "tell" in historical archaeology is a complicated one. The written record produces its own narratives about the state and local society, and this is certainly true for Bilād al-Shām under Mamluk rule. The archaeological record creates its own narratives, enriching or challenging those held so dearly by historians of the Mamluk period. The "nomadization" of the Mamluk period is a case in point. The chroniclers suggest that there was a gradual retreat to pastoralism in much of Syria over the course of the 15th century, and the region as a whole suffered economic decline.[30] This scenario is being challenged be recent archaeological research.

The decline of the countryside in the fifteenth century has dominated the archaeological literature on Mamluk Syria for the last twenty years. Regional surveys in central and southern Jordan, in particular, have documented much fewer and generally smaller sites from this period, suggesting to many archaeologists a return to a more pastoral way of life.[31] Guided by references in Arab

30 For more synthetic studies on this theme for Jordan, see historical studies by Ghawanmeh, *Dimashq*, and Ḥajjah, *al-Tārīkh*; the archaeological/anthropological study by LaBianca, *Sedentarization*; and the survey reports listed below.

31 Important survey reports for this region include Ibach, *Archaeological Survey*; Miller, *Ar-*

chronicles to natural disasters (such as disease, drought, floods, and earthquakes)[32], civil war[33], and the unchecked ravages of "the Bedu" against once productive villages[34], along with a selective reading of Ottoman cadastral surveys[35], the archaeological literature has come to repeatedly assert a marked demographic decline and abandonment of many (though not all) villages for full-time occupation in Jordan.[36] There has been, however, little systematic study of the issue in order to determine to what degree population levels dropped from fourteenth-century level and how many settlements "disappeared". We have no population estimates at all, in fact, for rural regions, and no site numbers from different periods country-wide to compare to one other.[37] Statistics on settlement are impossible to obtain without thorough surveys in other regions of Syria; in Jordan, at least, the projection of survey data from the south to other parts of the country that have been less intensively surveyed presents a picture of demographic decline that simply cannot be sustained there by either the historical or archaeological records. Surveys and excavation in villages in northern Jordan, for example, have indicated not only continuous occupation of the region from the Mamluk period until today but also agricultural productivity and a generally healthy economy. The latter image is supported by parallel research on

chaeological Survey: Southern Moab and Miller, *Archaeological Survey: Kerak Plateau*; Worschech, *Northwest*; MacDonald, *Wadi el-Hasa*; idem, *Southern Ghors*; idem, *Tafila-Busayra* and idem, *Ayl*, 277 – 98; Ji, Lee, *Preliminary Report*, 493 – 506; and Ji, *'Iraq al-Amir*, 137 – 142 and published field reports cited therein. Recent data from the Madaba Plains Project hinterland survey is available on the web at: http://www.casa.arizona.edu/MPP.

32 Dols, *Black Death*; Ghawanmeh, *al-Ṭa'ūn*, 315 – 322, idem, *Earthquake Effects*, 53 – 59; Little, *Date on Earthquake*, 137 – 151.

33 Ḥajja, *Al-Tārīkh.*

34 Ibid.

35 Archaeologists have generally relied on the one English-language study of some of the surveys, with convenient charts and maps (Hütteroth, Abdulfattah, *Historical Geography*). The surveys on which this useful work is based, however, are rather late and when used alone do not document changes in settlement and agricultural production over the century. See below for other, less frequently cited, editions of sixteenth-century tax registers.

36 There appears to have been less disruption of settlement in Palestine during this period (see maps comparing Palestine and Transjordan in Hütteroth, Abdulfattah, *Historical Geography*). A systematic comparison of settlement on both sides of the Jordan River has yet to be done.

37 There are no extant Mamluk-era censuses for this region to compare with the early Ottoman tax registers (that record tax-paying populations). While two formal cadastral surveys were known to have been ordered by Mamluk sultans in their domains, only one is known for southern Syria: the *rawk* of Sultan al-Nāṣir Muḥammad that began in 713/1313 and was completed in 714/1314. Unlike the survey conducted in Egypt (the results of which are preserved by the later Egyptian chronicler, Ibn Ji'an (d. 885/1480) [edited and published as *Kitāb il Tuḥfa il Saniya bi Asmā il Bilād il Masrīya*, ed. B. Moritz. Cairo, 1898]), the survey of southern Syria, which would have included today's Jordan, is no longer extant (Sato, *Evolution*, 99 – 131, and Sato, *Historical Character*, 223 – 225.

late Mamluk and Ottoman-era economic documents and early twentieth-century memoirs and the archives of the Endowments Ministry.

The village of Malka was surveyed in 2003 by the Northern Jordan Project, largely because of a fourteenth-century *waqfīyah* identified in the Dār al-Wathā'iq in Cairo. The document enumerates in detail the urban and rural endowments made by Sultan Barqūq in 796/1393 to support a *madrasah* complex he had built in Cairo.[38] In it Malka is described an agriculturally productive village, where much land was endowed for local benefit and olive oil produced for export markets, and this in a period when most archaeologists describe a countryside in decline. The identification of an industrial-size olive press in a modified cave complex, in use from the Byzantine through Mamluk periods, provided archaeological support for this level of olive oil production. The project estimated the annual production capability of the installation, based on the size and number of the presses, the size of the olive groves as described in the *waqfīyah*, and revenues described in European customs lists, as the equivalent of 1/3 of an average shipment of Spanish olive oil to Alexandria in 1405 – a significant amount for a single village.[39] Surface sherding and a review of tax registers suggest that Malka continued to be a productive and fairly affluent village through the fifteenth and sixteenth centuries, which differentiates it from others in the central and southern plains.[40] Although Malka did decline in population after the sixteenth century, it remained settled and productive. Its demographic and economic revival in the nineteenth was the combined result of the local application of Tanzimat-inspired legislation and the arrival of an Iraqi shaykh of the Qadarīyah Order (Shaykh ʿUmar), who is buried in a cemetery associated with his shrine (*maqām*) in the heart of the modern village. According to the original Ottoman registers in the Bureau of Lands and Surveys in Amman, members of Shaykh ʿUmar's family were among the first to register land, in Malka and nearby Hawar, with the Ottoman authorities in the 1880s, converting their newly gained political and economic capital as land owners to public service, by providing public education and health care in the region, in the absence of state-run facilities.[41]

The village of Hubras has a longer and richer history, reconstructed through Mamluk chronicles and biographical dictionaries, Ottoman tax registers and travelers' accounts, architectural survey, interviews with villagers, and excavation. Excavations of the original village mosque by the NJP in 2006 indicated a relatively uninterrupted settlement from the Umayyad period until today

38 For previously published studies of this document, see Walker, *Northern Jordan Survey 2003*, 71 and idem, *Mamluk Investment*, 119 – 147.

39 Walker, *Sowing*, 192 – 193.

40 Walker, *Mamluk Investment*, 130 – 131.

41 Walker, *Rural Sufism*, 217 – 234.

(Fig. 10). Possibly built in the eighth century, the sanctuary doubled in size in the thirteenth – early fourteenth century, its congregation having outgrown the original structure.[42] In this period, the village was one of the largest in Jordan and hosted an important farmer's market, as well as being home to many successful scholars. In the sixteenth century this may have been one of the two mosques in the village documented by Ottoman authorities, in addition to three shrines *zāwiyahs*. Additional buildings were added to the mosque in the eighteenth century, creating a larger complex that remained in use through the nineteenth century. In a final stage of use, in 1931 a smaller mosque was built inside the sanctuary of the medieval structure. The call to prayer continued to be heard from its roof until 1970, when it was finally abandoned for prayer, making it arguably the oldest, continuously used Muslim sanctuary in the country! As for agricultural productivity, a review of tax registers, combined with pollen analysis, suggests a diversified agricultural regime and uninterrupted production throughout the period under study.[43]

The picture that is emerging from this regional project, then, in many ways contradicts the image of decay, decline, and impoverishment following the collapse of the Mamluk state that has been suggested by archaeological fieldwork in central and southern Jordan. Villages in the north appear to have achieved some level of economic self-sufficiency and productivity throughout the vagaries of imperial rule. What may have been true for other parts of Jordan – demographic and economic decline – was apparently not necessarily the case for the northern hill country. The assumption that Syria experienced widespread decline at the close of Mamluk rule needs to be revisited.

Tomorrow's Mamlukology – Archaeologically-Informed?

Quite independently of one another, Mamluk studies and Mamluk archaeology have developed in similar ways in recent years and are gradually converging. Recently both have cultivated an appreciation for environmental history, global

42 These dates were confirmed by an inscription, C14 analysis, and ceramic and architectural analysis. The inscription originally appeared on the minaret and attributed to Sultan Qalawun the addition of that minaret to the mosque in 686/1287. It was transcribed in the 1880s by Schumacher (idem, *Basan*, 183; Meinecke, *Mamlukische Architektur*, 65, entry 43) and again later by a team of Yarmuk University architecture students in the 1980s (Ghawanmeh, *Madinat Irbid*, 59). For the results of the C14, ceramic, and architectural studies, see Walker et al., *Northern Jordan Project 2006*, 429–470.

43 Walker, *Northern Jordan Survey 2003*; Walker et al., *Northern Jordan Project 2006*; Walker, Kenney, *Rural Islam*, 1–4. This is not to say there wasn't some reduction in agricultural productivity in the early sixteenth century, as both sources indicate was the case. However, fields were not abandoned here as has been argued for other regions of the country.

theory, and questions related to identity and meaning. There is every indication that these strains in scholarship are strong and will continue in the future. As archaeological research enters the mainstream of Mamlukology, it promises to enrich these lines of inquiry, bringing with it its unique methods of data collection and interpretation. Ultimately, archaeology will contribute scientific approaches to tomorrow's Mamlukology: in the natural sciences (ecological approaches and environmental analysis), as well as the social sciences (anthropological approaches and socio-cultural theory).

Illustrations

(All photos by author unless otherwise noted.)

Fig. 1 – Mamluk-era staircase to Hisban Citadel – Note use of rubble fill left of stairs to create a level foundation for makeshift corner tower.

Fig. 2 – Saham mosque – The rubble fill of this nineteenth-century mosque in northern Jordan contributed to the collapse of the northern wall after a recent heavy winter rain.

Fig. 3 – Handmade Geometrically Painted Ware jug from Hisban. (courtesy Andrews University archives)

Fig. 4 – Aerial view of Tall Hisban. Mamluk complex on left side of summit; nave of Byzantine basilica to right. (courtesy of David Kennedy, University of Western Australia)

Fig. 5 – Entrance to the Hisban Citadel.

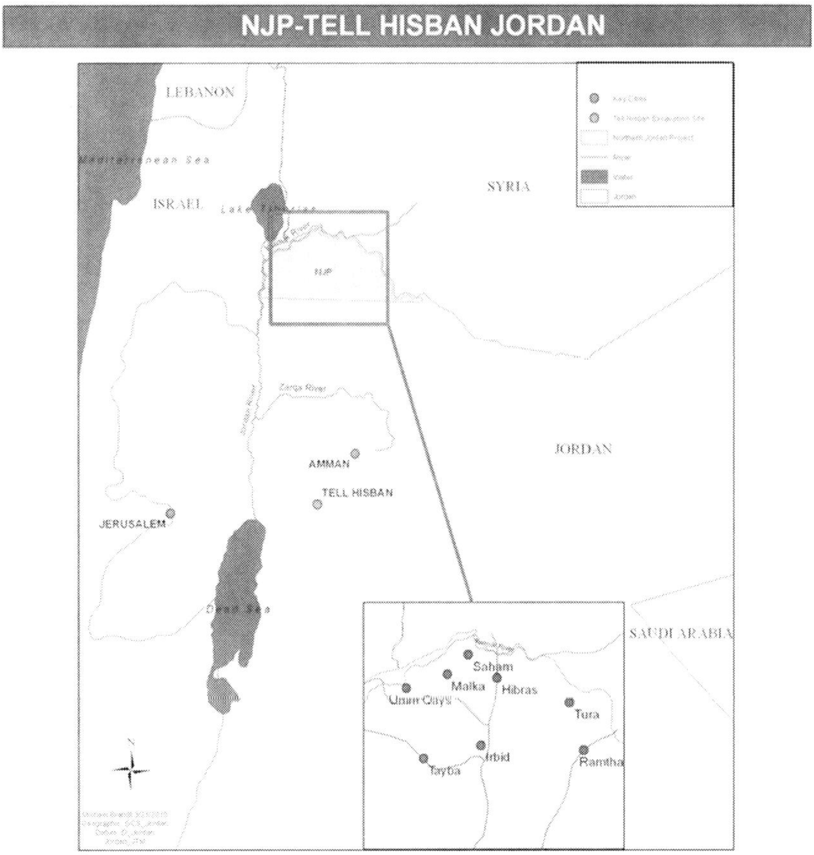

Fig. 6 – Map of author's field projects in Jordan: Tall Hisban excavations and the Northern Jordan Project. (courtesy Michael Brandt, Missouri State University)

Fig. 7 – Upper Wadi Shallaleh, Northern Jordan, focus of fieldwork for the NJP in 2012.

Fig. 8 – Pollen sampling from "dry" contexts – building mortar of a historical building in village of Hubras. Sampling by author.

Fig. 9 – Phytolith sampling from earthen floors inside garrison storeroom at Tall Hisban. Sampling by project specialist Ms. Sofia Laparidou, University College London.

Fig. 10 – Hubras mosque. The *miḥrab* of the Mamluk-period mosque is visible to the right; the British Mandate-era sanctuary appears to the left.

Literature

'Ad, Uzi, "Khirbat Burin", *Hadashot Arkheologiyat* 117 (2005) - published on the web at:

Brown, Robin, "Excavation in the 14th Century AD Mamluk Palace at Kerak," *Annual of the Department of Antiquities of Jordan* 33 (1989), pp. 287 - 304.

Brown, Robin, "Summary Report of the 1986 Excavations: Late Islamic Shobak," *Annual of the Department of Antiquities of Jordan* 32 (1988), pp. 225 - 245.

Burke, Katherine Strange, "Quseir al-Qadim", *Oriental Institute Annual Report* (2003 - 2004), pp. 125 - 132.

Chang-Ho, Ji, "The 'Iraq al-Amir and Dhiban Plateau Regional Surveys", in: Levy et al, *Crossing Jordan*, pp. 137 - 142.

Dols, Michael, *The Black Death in the Middle East*, Princeton: Princeton University Press 1977.

Gane, Constance E. and Randall W. Younker, "The 2009 Excavations at Jalul", *Newsletter of the Institute of Archaeology, Siegfired H. Horn Museum* 30/3 (2010); 1 - 2.

Garcin, Jean-Claude, *Un centre musulman de la Haute-Égypte médiévale: Qūṣ* (Cairo, 1976).

Ghawanmeh, Yousef, "al-Ṭa'ūn wa-l-Jafāf wa-Athruhuma 'ala al-Bi'ah fī Junūb al-Shām (al-Urdunn wa Filisṭīn) fī al-'Asr al-Mamluki," *Studies in the History and Archaeology of Jordan* 2 (1985), pp. 315 - 322.

Ghawanmeh, Yousef, "Earthquake Effects on Bilād ash-Shām Settlements," *Studies in the History and Archaeology of Jordan* 4 (1992), pp. 53 - 59.

Ghawanmeh, Yousef, *Dimashq fī 'Aṣr Dawlat al-Mamālīk al-Thāniyah*, Amman: Dar al-Fikrah 2005.

Ghawanmeh, Yousef, *Madīnat Irbid fī al-'Aṣr al-Islāmī*, Irbid 1986.

Given, Michael, "Agriculture, settlement and landscape in Ottoman Cyprus," Levant 32 (2000), pp.215 - 236.

Guo, Li, *Commerce, culture, and community in a Red Sea port in the thirteenth century: the Arabic documents from Quseir*, Leiden 2004.

Ḥajjah, Shawkat Ramadan, *Al-Tārīkh al-Siyāsī li-Minṭaqat Sharq al-Urdunn (min Junūb al-Shām) fī 'Aṣr Dawlat al-Mamālīk al-Thānīyah*, Irbid 2002.

http://www.hadashot-esi.org.il/report_detail_eng.asp?id=235&mag_id=110.

Hume, Ivor Noel, "Handmaiden to History," *North Carolina Historical Review* 41/2 (1964), pp. 215 - 225.

Hütteroth, Wolf-Dieter and Abdulfattah, Kamal, *Historical Geography of Palestine, Transjordan, and Southern Syria in the Late 16th Century*, Erlangen 1977.

Ibach, R. D. Jr., *Archaeological Survey of the Hesban Region: Catalogue of Sites and Characterization of Periods*, Berrien Springs: 1987.

Ji, Chang-Ho and J. K. Lee, "A Preliminary Report on the Dhiban Plateau Survey Project, 1999: The Versacare Expedition," *Annual of the Department of Antiquities of Jordan* 44 (2000), pp. 493 - 506.

Johns, Jeremy, "The Rise of Middle Islamic Hand-Made Geometrically-Painted Ware in Bilād al-Shām (11th-13th Centuries A.D.)," in: *Colloque international d'archéologie islamique*, ed. Roland-Pierre Gayraud, Cairo 1998, pp. 65 - 93.

Kletter, Raz and Edna J. Stern, "A Mamluk-Period Site at Khirbat Burin in the Eastern Sharon," *'Atiqot* 51 (2006), pp. 173 - 214.

LaBianca, Øystein S. and Bethan J. Walker, "Tall Hisban: Palimpsest of Great and Little Traditions of Transjordan and the Ancient Near East." in: Levy et al, *Crossing Jordan*, 111 - 120.

LaBianca, Øystein S., *Sedentarization and Nomadization: Food System Cycles at Hesban and Vicinity in Transjordan (Hesban 1)*, Berrien Springs/Mich. 1990.

Levy, Philip, "Always a Handmaiden, Never a Bride: The Relationship Between Historians and Historical Archaeologists," *Archaeology* 65/2 (2000), an on-line publication (http://www.archaeology.org/online/features/history/).

Levy, Thomas et al (eds.), *Crossing Jordan: North American Contributions to the Archeology of Jordan*, London 2007.

Little, Donald, "Date on Earthquakes Recorded by Mamluk Historians: An Historiographical Essay," in: *Natural Disasters in the Ottoman Empire*, ed. E. Zachariadou, Rethymnon 1999, pp. 137 - 151.

Lucke, Bernhard and Ziad al-Saad, Michael Schmidt, Rupert Bäumler, S.O. Lorenz, P. Udluft, K.-U. Heussner, and Bethany J. Walker, "Soils and Land Use in the Decapolis Region (Northern Jordan): Implications for landscape development and the Impact of Climate Change," *Zeitschrift der Deutschen Palaestina-Vereins* 124/2 (2008), pp. 171 - 188.

Lucke, Bernhard and Mohammed Shunnaq, Bethany J. Walker, Atef Shiyab, Zeidoun al-Muheisen, Hussein al-Sababha, Rupert Bäumler, and Michael Schmidt, "Questioning Transjordan's Historic Desertification: a Critical Review of the Paradigm of 'Empty Lands'," *Levant* 44/1 (2012), pp. 100 - 126.

MacDonald, Burton, "The Ayl to Ras an-Naqab Archaeological Survey, Southern Jordan, Phase I (2005): Preliminary Report," *ADAJ* 49 (2005), pp. 277 - 98.

MacDonald, Burton, *The Southern Ghors and Northeast 'Arabah Archaeological Survey*, Sheffield 1992.

MacDonald, Burton, *The Tafila-Busayra Archaeological Survey 1999 - 2001, West-Central Jordan*, Boston 2004.

MacDonald, Burton, *The Wadi el-Hasa Archaeological Survey, 1979 - 1983, West-Central Jordan*, Waterloo, Ontario: Wilfrid Laurier University Press 1988.

Meinecke, Michael, *Die Mamlukische Architektur in Ägypten und Syrien (648/1250 bis 923/1517), Part Two: Chronologische Liste der Mamlukischen Baumassnahmen*, Glückstadt 1992.

Miller, J. M., *Archaeological Survey of Central and Southern Moab*, Atlanta 1981.

Miller, J. M., *Archaeological Survey of the Kerak Plateau*, Atlanta 1991.

Porter, Benjamin and Routledge, Bruce and Steen, Danielle, "The Power of Place: The Dhiban Community through the Ages," in: Levy et al, *Crossing Jordan*, pp. 315 - 322.

Sato, Tsugitaka, "Historical Character of al-Rawk al-Nasiri in Mamluk Syria," in: *Proceedings of the First International Conference on Bilad al-Sham*, ed. Muhammad A. al-Bakhit, Amman 1984, pp. 223 - 225.

Sato, Tsugitaka, "The Evolution of the Iqta System under the Mamluks: An Analysis of al-Rawk al-Husami and al-Rawk al-Nasiri," *Memoirs of the Research Department of the Tokyo Bunko* 37 (1979), pp. 99 - 131.

Schumacher, Gottlieb,"Das südliche Basan", *Zeitschrift des Deutschen Palästina-Vereins* 20 (1897), pp. 65 – 227.

Al-Shqour, Reem "2008 Excavations at the Islamic Village at Tall Jalul", *Annual of the Department of Antiquities of Jordan* 53 (2009), pp. 641 – 655.

Al-Shqour, Reem and De Meulemeester, Johnny and Herremans, Davy, "The 'Aqaba Castle Project," *Studies in the History and Archaeology of Jordan* 10 (2009), pp. 641 – 655.

Stern, Edna J., "Khirbat Din'ila: The Crusader and Mamluk-Period Pottery" (forthcoming in *Átiqot).*

Sutton, Susan, *Contingent Countryside: Settlement, Economy, and Land Use in the Southern Argolid since 1700*, Stanford 2000.

Thatcher, Ayelet, "Khirbat Din'ila Final Report," *Hadashot Arkheologiyat* 117 (2005); http://www.hadashot-esi.org.il/report_detail_eng.asp?id=232&mag_id=110.

Walker, Bethany J. "Mamluk Investment in the Transjordan: A 'Boom and Bust' Economy," *Mamluk Studies Review* 8/2 (2004), pp. 119 – 147.

Walker, Bethany J. "The Northern Jordan Survey 2003 – Agriculture in Late Islamic Malkā and Ḥubrāṣ Villages: A Preliminary Report on the First Season," *Bulletin of the American Schools of Oriental Research* 339 (2005), pp. 67 – 111.

Walker, Bethany J. and Kenney, Ellen, "Rural Islam in Late Medieval Jordan: NJP 2006 – the Mosques Project," *Newsletter of the American Center of Oriental Research* 18/2 (2006), pp. 1 – 4.

Walker, Bethany J. and Kenney, Ellen and Holzweg, Laura and Carroll, Lynda and Boulogne, Stéphanie and Lucke, Bernhard, "The Northern Jordan Project 2006: Village Life in Mamluk and Ottoman Ḥubrāṣ and Saḥam: A Preliminary Report," *Annual of the Department of Antiquities of Jordan* 52 (2007), pp. 429 – 470.

Walker, Bethany J. and Shunnaq, Mohammed and Byers, David and al-Bataineh, Muwafaq and Laparidou, Sofia and Lucke, Bernhard and Shiyab, Atef, "Northern Jordan Project 2010: the al-Turra Survey," *Annual of the Department of Antiquities of Jordan* 55 (2011), in press.

Walker, Bethany J., "From Ceramics to Social Theory: Reflections on Mamluk Archaeology Today," *Mamluk Studies Review* 14 (2010), pp. 109 – 157.

Walker, Bethany J., "Peasants, Pilgrims, and the Body Politic: The Northern Jordan Project and the Landscapes of the Islamic Periods," in: Levy et al, *Crossing Jordan*, pp. 473 – 480.

Walker, Bethany J., "Rural Sufism as Channels of Charity in Nineteenth-Century Jordan," in: *Interpreting Welfare and Relief in the Middle East*, ed. Nefissa Naguib and Inger Marie Okkenhaug, Leiden 2007, pp. 217 – 234.

Walker, Bethany J., "Sowing the Seeds of Rural Decline? Agriculture as an Economic Barometer for Late Mamluk Jordan," *Mamluk Studies Review* 11/1 (2007), pp. 173 – 199.

Walker, Bethany J., *Jordan in the Late Middle Ages: Transformation of the Mamluk Frontier*, Chicago 2011.

Whitcomb, Donald, "Mamluk Archaeological Studies: A Review," *Mamluk Studies Review* 1 (1997), pp. 97 – 106.

Whittenburg, James, "But What Does It Mean?: A Historian's View of Historical Archaeology," in: *Contributions to Anthropological Studies 3: Forgotten Places and*

Things: Archaeological Perspectives on American History, ed. Albert E. Ward, Bloomington 1983, pp. 49 – 54.
Whittenburg, James, "On Why Historians Have Failed to Recognize the Potential of Material Culture," *American Archaeology* 6/11 (1987), pp. 4 – 9.
Worschech, U. F., *Northwest Ard el-Kerak 1983 and 1984*, Munich 1985.
Zarinebaf, Fariba and Bennet, John and Davis, Jack L., *A Historical and Economic Geography of Ottoman Greece: The Southwestern Morea in the 18th Century*, Athens 2005.

Torsten Wollina

Ibn Ṭawq's *Taʿlīq*. An Ego-Document for Mamlūk Studies

Introduction

In the late 15th and the early 16th centuries a Damascene notary by the name Aḥmad Ibn Ṭawq kept daily notes of his "his showings-up, and no-shows, at countless appointments and events required by his job, his family, and his community".[1] As far as we know he integrated his writing into his schedule for more than twenty years.[2] This text has received increasing attention in Mamlūk studies since the first volume of the edition by shaykh Jaafar al-Muḥājir was published by the French Institute in Damascus (IFPO) in 2000.[3] Until 2007 the remaining three volumes appeared in print but they cover the text only until the end of 906 (1500 - 1501).[4]

Ibn Ṭawq's journal has been appreciated for its value as a source for social history.[5] However, it has so far not been studied in and for itself. In order to do so, Stephan Conermann and Tilman Seidensticker placed it within a trajectory of Arabic ego-documents of which examples can be found from the 10th to the 19th centuries and which also can be considered historiographical works. From their analysis of this tradition, they express the hope that we will gain the ability "to describe the process of individualization in other terms than the common Eu-

1 Guo, *Review: Ibn Ṭawq, Al-Taʿlīq*, 210.

2 According to Ṣalāh al-Dīn al-Munajjid the surviving manuscript covers the years 885 - 914 (1480 - 1509), until shortly before the author's death; see al-Buṣrawī, *Ta'rīkh*, 11.

3 Two reviews of the first and the second and third volumes respectively appeared in *Mamlūk Studies Review:* Conermann, Seidensticker, *Remarks*; Guo, *Review: Ibn Ṭawq, Al-Taʿlīq*. Furthermore, the text has been used as a source by Yossef Rapoport in a monography and an article on the role of women in the 15th century, see Rapoport, *Women*, and by Miura Toru in an article on urban society in 2006. Finally, Amina Elbandary makes use of it in her upcoming dissertation on "Historiography and Public Protest".

4 The four volumes will be referred to by roman numbers I to IV.

5 Guo also provides lists of passages which are useful for legal, monetary, architectural, natural and environmental history as well as for the study of the Arabic language; see Guo, *Review: Ibn Ṭawq, Al-Taʿlīq*, 215 - 217.

ropean ones".[6] This article follows this approach and analyzes Ibn Ṭawq's journal as a written expression of the author's identity. However, I do not take the text as an honest confession on his behalf but rather as the product of a literary endeavour which was written to certain ends and, therefore, a reconstruction of reality.

It is thus necessary to first address the contexts in which Ibn Ṭawq's journal came into existence. Whereas history has always put emphasis on the social and cultural contextualisation of authors, studies in ego-documents have gained increasing popularity because they also acknowledge the literary nature of the texts and the influence that has on how one's self is presented. Every text is produced at the crossroads between the author's intentions, the literary models available for writing and the expectations of a possible audience towards these models. The character of a text plays a great role in how 'reality' is depicted in it. If we neglect that we would implicitly "assume that it is transparent, which means that it practically explains itself."[7]

The text needs to be contextualized both within the literary tradition in which it is set *as well as* within the social and cultural environment in which the author lived, before Ibn Ṭawq's 'loci of identification' can be judged in the right light. Using a survey of the literature on ego-documents as a starting point, I will then introduce the text and its author in more detail and place them within their respective contexts. Following that I will elaborate on the methodological access to the representation of individuality and identity within the journal. Finally, it will be scrutinized for the representations of its author's identity.

Ego-documents – self-testimonies or self-advertising?

From its beginnings research in ego-documents has dealt with questions of self, identity, and, more than anything else, the paradigm of individualization. The link between autobiographical writing and a heightened awareness of one's own individuality was most prominently established by the German (art) historian Jacob Burckhardt (1818 – 1897).

Burckhardt placed the "Big Bang" of individualization in Renaissance Italy which he thought of as a unique development. To him and his epigones individuality, according to the modern western concept, was the only successful outcome in human development. The number of diaries, autobiographies and other ego-documents in any given literature was the standard by which Burck-

6 Conermann, Seidensticker, *Remarks*, 135, for the survey of the tradition, ibid,123 – 125, 127 – 130.

7 Amelang, *Saving*, 133.

hardt wanted to measure how close the respective society had come to his ideal of individuality.

Therefore the lack in such texts from medieval and Early Modern European as well as non-European societies led researchers to the judgement that the 'oriental' peoples only had collective identities which were diametrically opposed to European individualism.[8] This teleological perspective has cast a long shadow on the history of mentalities and of Islamic cultures in general. For a long time it has been common sense in academia that such texts were missing (despite the existence of a long tradition of biography and autobiography in Arabic literature) because Muslim cultures devaluated the individual vis-à-vis the society.[9] Grunebaum, on the other hand, ascribed the lack of ego-documents to the traditionalism of Arabic literary conventions which were 'set in stone since antiquity'.[10] Any examples to the contrary were necessarily presented as exceptions to the rule and always inferior to their European, especially modern counterparts.

Burckhardt's model is informed by two fundamental flaws. Ironically, it allows for only one kind of individuality and its (almost uniform) expression in only a few literary genres, namely autobiography, memoirs, and to a lesser degree, diaries. The term ego-document was first developed in order to get away from these modern (European) genre categories and their ideological baggage.

In order to address questions of self and self-representation several historians applied looser definitions to the genres. According to Benigna von Krusenstjern ego-documents (in German *Selbstzeugnisse*) encompass all autobiographical writings such as diaries, travelogues, letters and memoirs. Winfried Schulze also includes testimonies given under pain of retribution, such as interrogations by the state or the law.[11] Both definitions have been applied to analyze the worldview or even reconstruct a complete picture of the lives of historical persons.[12]

It might have been Jacob Burckhardt's harsh judgement that "any approximation to western (i.e. individualist culture) must have disastrous consequences for Muslims" to incite so much research in ego-documents to prove the opposite.[13] First, research concentrated on the 'little traditions' of diary-like

8 See Enderwitz, *Public Role*, 77; Faroqhi, *Kultur*, 217.
9 For a survey of the Arabic tradition of autobiography, see Reynolds et al., *Interpreting*.
10 "[U]nverrückbar fest wie in der Antike"; Grunebaum: *Islam*, p. 331.
11 Krusenstjern, *Selbstzeugnisse*; idem, *Buchhalter*; Schulze, *Ego-Dokumente*.
12 To give only two early examples, Carlo Ginzburg used documents of the inquisition as an access to the world and worldview of a miller from the Friaul while Iris Origo in her work on a merchant from medieval Prato could rely on that person's large estate, consisting of account books, contracts and other bills, more than 11.000 private letters and even more about business. See Ginzburg, *Formaggio*; Origo, *Merchant*.
13 "[…] jede Annäherung an die okzidentalische Kultur scheint für die Moslemin [Muslime]

texts. It has gained momentum since the 1980s from new findings in Ottoman archives. It could be established that indeed such ego-documents existed prior to European colonialism.[14]

In the last decades, however, the focus has shifted towards the rules and practices by which ego-documents were produced and received. Texts are to be assessed in relation to the social and cultural context in which the authors lived as well as the literary traditions which provided the models to which the texts adhere. As Philippe Lejeune suggested, literary genres provide a code by which past and contemporary works can be understood and classified and on the basis of which new works are created. But they are in no way timeless and cannot be transferred to the literary landscapes of other times or even cultures.[15] This would not further our understanding of the past but serves only mythological functions. Using the letter as an example, Lejeune argues that no form of writing has no timeless essence, but is only a certain, fluctuating and contingent mode of written communication which only makes sense if its relations to other genres are taken into account.[16]

Lejeune's consideration has inspired a reassessment of the rich Arabic tradition of biographies and autobiographies which heretofore was deemed unoriginal and traditional:[17]

> While these texts at first glance look less 'personal' than modern autobiographies (Arabic or western), they are not therefore less 'individuating'. They are, in fact, each replete precisely with the specific details of an individual life. In many cases, they clearly communicate a strong sense of the author's personality."[18]

Dwight Reynolds argued that these texts cannot be assessed in isolation from the rest of an author's literary work but they should be understood as a key by which the reader should be guided through it.[19] Still, the uniting aspect for the Arabic genre of autobiography lay not in their formal characteristics but in the literary

unbedingt verderblich zu sein." Burckhardt, *Betrachtungen*, 113; with reference to "the Turks", ibid., 344.

14 See e.g. Terzioğlu, *Man*; Sajdi, *Peripheral Vision*; Faroqhi, *Kultur*; Kaidbey, *Historiography*; Masters, *View*; Kafadar, *Self*; Haddad, *Interests.*

15 Lejeune, *Pakt*, 379–82.

16 Lejeune, *Pakt*, 385.

17 Devaluing judgements can be found in Georg Misch's grand history of Autobiography, the works of Grunebaum and also in Stephen Humphrey's Review of Sartain's edition of the autobiography of as-Suyūtī. See Misch, *Geschichte*, Grunebaum, *Islam*, Humphreys, *Review: Sartain, al-Suyūṭī.*

18 Reynolds, *Interpreting*, 243.

19 See Reynolds, *Interpreting*, 247–8. This approach has been applied by Patrick Franke with regard to the works of the Meccan scholar al-Qārī; see Franke, *Querverweis*; idem, *Ego.*

act: "the act of 'interpreting', 'representing', or 'portraying' oneself in written form."[20]

Still, the number of extant autobiographies as well as diaries is limited in Arabic literary history. Moreover, by restricting research to these obvious genres of autobiographical writing, we neglect that they were only part of a literary landscape. One group of scholars has suggested the application of the category ego-document to new literary genres. They find autobiographical material of different sorts in such remote places as colophons or introductions to books.[21] Therefore, they widen the scope of ego-documents to "encompass all texts with an ego talking about himself" – even "texts without an ego speaking can be interpreted as ego-documents, since everything we write reveals something about ourselves."[22]

This definition essentially dismisses the distinction between 'authentic' autobiographical and 'fictional' literary texts and instead concentrates on how literature was produced and received. In this context, virtually every text could be studied as an ego-document. Indeed, no ego-document should be considered as a confession of its author. In the Arabic context they were mostly written by people who also wrote other literature and they could apply the same techniques to the writing of their life stories. Along these lines, Ralf Elger explored how Ibn Baṭṭūṭah may have used several modes of plagiarism in the composition of his famous travelogue. It still became widely read and convinced generations of the accuracy of its descriptions. Shifting the focus from the life to the literary work of Ibn Baṭṭūṭah, who invented some 29 years of his life story does not devalue the text, but makes it even more significant: "If my research develops as I think it is possible, not much will remain of the great researcher and explorer Ibn Baṭṭūṭah, but the literary achievement of IB will shine in brighter light than ever before."[23] He did not choose to write about his life, but to rewrite it, very much like the German author Karl May (1842–1912) did in his numerous works of travel literature.[24]

Despite the fact that not every ego-document attempted a reinvention of the author's life, none of them is independent from motives that lie outside the text itself. The self-image a text presents is created with the expectations of an intended audience in mind and is necessarily shaped to fit into the shared group culture in which they originated The individual is thus represented according to the mutually accepted "autobiographical concepts of self and relations".[25]

20 Reynolds, *Interpreting*, 242.
21 See Elger et al., *Konvention.*
22 Elger, Köse, *Introduction*, 9.
23 Elger, *Lying*, 72.
24 May, *Reiseromane.*
25 See Jancke, *Patronagebeziehungen*, 29.

Therefore, all representations of individuality can only be relational and individuality was rarely a goal in itself but rather a means to other ends.

Ego-documents were never produced in a vacuum. As Denise Klein has argued with regard to the reports from Ottoman embassies, they were written in constant interaction with the intended audience at home, internal Ottoman debates and Ottoman literature in general.[26] For the authors they served different functions in the social competition which led to the construction of very diverse identities. For example, the ambassador Nişli Mehmed Ağa portrayed himself as a professional diplomat "in order to convince his employers, the sultan and the grand vizier, of his professional excellence and thereby secure a job promotion".[27]

The chronicle *Iẓhār al-ʿAṣr li-Asrar fī Ahl al-ʿAṣr* by the Mamluk scholar al-Biqāʿī presents a different case. It is a story of failure, both in the author's public and domestic life. Guo demonstrates in detail how subtle the techniques were which the author employed in order to justify his own actions. But still, the text shows him as a self-righteous a man who did not see any responsibility for his misfortunes on his side: "there were [just] too many battles to fight and too many scores to settle".[28]

It was literature that provided the context within which people could design "self-images according to their respective intentions" within certain boundaries.[29] In order to understand what those boundaries were and how authors moved within them, crossed them or even changed them, research on ego-documents cannot be limited to certain genres but has to address literature – or even language – as a whole.[30] On the other hand, as Robin Ostle has argued, "today any analysis of the self in literary material should not be able to avoid questions of self-identity, of self-reference, of authority, of autonomy, or the whole process of self-constitution."[31] The question of how people perceived of themselves – individually or collectively – should therefore be addressed not only to the historiographical or travel literature of the Mamluk era, but even to arts and architecture which can be read as 'texts' by which rulers articulated their self-image and authority.[32]

According to these presets a contextualization of Ibn Ṭawq and his journal will be attempted. While the author will be situated within the social cosmos of

26 Klein, *Envoys*, 99 – 100.
27 Klein, *Envoys*, 94.
28 Guo, *Tales*, 120.
29 Rutz, *Ego*-Dokument, paragraph 12.
30 Lejeune, *Pakt*, 385.
31 Ostle, *Introduction*, 22.
32 With regard to arts, see the contribution on inscriptions in this volume, for architecture see Al-Harithy, *Concept*.

Damascus, his text will be described with respect to historiographical literature as well as religious learning of the time. The description of author and text must be approached interdependently since the journal is the only extant source on the author's life and social standing.

Text and author

Ibn Ṭawq is not mentioned in any chronicles of his day.[33] Apart from his journal all that is known about his life is to be found in one short entry in Najm al-Dīn al-Ghazzī's biographical dictionary "*Kawākib al-Sā'irah bi-A'yān al-Mi'ah al-'Āshirah*". It is only three lines long and does not go into any detail about his biography:

> Aḥmad b. Ṭawq: Aḥmad b. Muḥammad b. Aḥmad b. Aḥmad b. Aḥmad, the shaykh, the *imām*, the *'ālim*, the pious, the *mutaḥaddith* Shihāb al-Dīn al-Dimashqī al-Shāfi'ī, known as Ibn Ṭawq. He was born in *Rabī'* I of the year 834; he died in Damascus on Sunday, the 3rd or 4th of *Ramaḍān* of the year 915.[34]

Shihāb al-Dīn Aḥmad Ibn Ṭawq was a notary (*shāhid*) and scribe (*kātib*) who lived in the residential neighbourhood around the *Qaṣab* Mosque, just north of the walls of old Damascus.[35] In addition he held at times minor posts as a reciter of the Quran and had a hand in agriculture.[36] He was neither rich nor did he hold an office or administrative post. He did not come from a renowned lineage, either. In fact, his father's family originated in the village *Jarūd*, about a day's journey to the northeast. Although throughout the time covered by the journal Damascus was his place of residence, he maintained links and paid regular visits to this area (*bilād al-jubbah*) on an almost yearly basis.[37] In Damascus, his family networks stem mainly from his mother's family who had been Damascene.[38] Both on these travels and in Damascus Ibn Ṭawq conversed with members of all social strata, although the journal highlights his contacts with the elites.

33 E.g. Buṣrawī, *Ta'rīkh*; Ibn al-Ḥimṣī, *Ḥawādith*.

34 Ġazzī, *Kawākib* 1:126.

35 With regard to the *Qaṣab* Mosque in Ibn Ṭawq's neighbourhood Nu'aymī localises it in *Dabāghah*, the old quarter of the tanners, which lay outside the Thomas Gate (*bāb tūmā*), but also close to the quarter '*Uqaybah*; see Nu'aymī, *Dāris*, II:346. Ibn Ṭawq himself relates that his house was next to a public bath (*ḥammām Burhān al-Dīn*) and not far from one of the city gates (*bāb al-salām*); see, *Ta'līq* I, 9.

36 He owned a garden next to his house and an orchard in the village Saṭrā, rented plantations in Barza and Qābūn as well as a grove of abeles in *Kafr Baṭanā*. *Ta'līq* I:117, 158.

37 He regularly receives visitors from *Jarūd:* a *mubāshir* and a *khaṭīb* as well as one shaykh Muḥammad, and he is still informed about social events in the village; he also travels there himself occasionally; *Ta'līq* I:26, 64, 76; II:543, IV:1911.

38 Ibid. I,:9.

The text meets the formal characteristics of the Arabic chronicle. It is a chronographic account broken down into daily entries. Moreover, the text is structured by month and, even more so, by year. This is emphasized by passages which signal the beginning or the end of a year, giving extensive listings of sultans, emirs, judges and other officials. Usually, after this passage the entry for the first day of *Muḥarram* follows.[39] In addition, entries are often dated according to the Christian months, the signs of the zodiac, or the Syrian agrarian calendar.

Whereas the formal structure of the text is very rigid, its content is the opposite. The entries differ greatly in length. Whereas there are some entries more than thirty lines long, for some days nothing but the date was noted, sometimes with the explanations "today there happened nothing to write about" (*lam yakun fīhi mā yuktabu*) or "I did not go to the old city (*lam adkhul-i l-madīnata*)", his place of work.[40] Ibn Ṭawq used his journal to record everything he deemed important. Weather phenomena, price lists, the author's and others' domestic affairs, and his attendances at the scholarly circles are juxtaposed with news from Cairo and Aleppo, from the front lines during the first Mamluk-Ottoman war, Bedouin raids, appointments of new officials or the punishment of criminals. Ibn Ṭawq furthermore used it to give an account of the manifold legal contracts he witnessed or supervised.[41]

Historiography flourished in 15th-century Egypt and Syria, reaching new readerships, adopting new forms of writing.[42] In Syria, the chronicle remained the first choice for historians. It was turned into a sort of diary-chronicle, a process which continued into Ottoman times.[43] Autobiographical notes became

39 An exception is the introduction to the year 902/1496–7 where the list of notables does not appear before the entry for *Muḥarram* 1st; *Taʿlīq* III:1439 f.

40 For the short entries, see e.g. Muḥarram 7th and 8th 899 (18.–19.10.1493), ibid., 1224 f. Among the longest entries are those for the first day of the year. Including the list of officials these can, as in the case of the year 889 (1484–85), reach a length of 35 lines, or one and a half pages (see *Taʿlīq* I:319–20). Apart from these one of the longest thematically unified entries in the whole journal is the report on the funeral of the *shaykh al-islām*'s Egyptian wife, the important attendants, the suras the shaykh recited and the *dhikr* by which he ended in the ceremony. (*Taʿlīq* IV:1762). Several entries concerning a massacre which mamluk soldiers committed among the followers of the Sufi shaykh Mubārak in Ramaḍān 899 (July 1499) in and around the Umayyad mosque as well as in the village Qābūn where Mubārak had his convent and house have about the same length. Between the two relevant entries Ibn Ṭawq devotes 48 lines to the incident, which is described by Ibn al-Ḥimṣī in 42 but only mentioned in 10 lines by Ibn Ṭūlūn; *Taʿlīq* III:1287–89; Ibn al-Ḥimṣī, *Ḥawādith*, 252–254; Ibn Ṭūlūn, *Mufākahat*, vol. 1, 158.

41 For a list of contracts from the 2nd and 3rd volume, see Guo, *Review: Ibn Ṭawq, Al-Taʿlīq*, 216–17.

42 This process is described e.g. by Irwin, *Mamluk History*, and Haarmann, *Auflösung*.

43 Weintritt, *Geschichtsschreibung*, 19.

almost a standard ingredient of these chronicles[44]: "This was perhaps the symptom of a turbulent age, when individuals felt that their personal experiences of the Crusader wars, the Mongol invasions of the Black Death were worthy of record."[45]

Despite the assumption that Ibn Ṭawq's journal could be proof to a widespread practice, it is "the one and only known work of *yawmiyyāt* from Mamluk times".[46] How to approach such a text of which there exists only one extant example from the Mamluk period? Despite the similarities in the outer form between Ibn Ṭawq's journal and chronicles from the same period, they very much differ in the manner of their production. As was demonstrated by Konrad Hirschler, the chronicle's chronographic structure is not necessarily based on a chronological writing process. And despite appearance, chronicles were often designed according to a plot. After all, narrative texts were of great importance in social competition.[47] Al-Biqāʿī's *Iẓhār* is an edited text, which was compiled with 'publication' in mind.[48] It interprets past events retrospectively emphasizing the impact of events which led to the author's quasi-exile in Damascus. This is also manifest by al-Biqāʿī's use of stylistic elements, such as dream narratives that precede and foreshadow important decisions made by the author.[49]

In the manner of its production Ibn Ṭawq's journal rather resembles the European diary than the Arabic chronicle.[50] I argue here, that due to the unedited state of Ibn Ṭawq's journal it lacks the degree of emplotment that literary chronicles possess, and therefore has to be treated differently with regard to the expression of its author's identity. To do so, one could follow George Makdisi's assessment of the role of the diary in Islamic historiography.[51] Makdisi points out the centrality of *ḥadīth* studies as the cause for the emergence of the genre which evolved around the two activities of dating correctly (*ta'rīkh*) and reporting events (*taʿlīq*). In this sense, historiography's major task was to provide

44 The tendency to record personally important events happened at the same tine in renaissance Italy where traditionally historiographical chronicles were used in a new way to fix personal or family history, such as births, deaths, harvests, celebrations. Holm, *Montag*, 12.

45 Irwin, *Mamluk History*, 160; also Guo, *Chronicle.*

46 Conermann, *Es Boomt*, 11. The practice seems to have been widespread for centuries; Makdisi, *Islamic Historiography*; also Conermann, Seidensticker, *Remarks.*

47 Chamberlain, *Knowledge*, 18–21.

48 Such works were 'published in the context of teaching. They were read to an audience of one's students who, in turn, wrote them down again and made copies of the original text. See Rosenthal, *History*, 173–174; Robinson, *Islamic Historiography*, 181–82.

49 For emplotment and use of stylistic elements in chronicles, see Hirschler, *Arabic Historiography*, chapters 5 (pp. 63–85) and 6 (pp. 86–114); also Reynolds, *Interpreting.*

50 Diary is not to be understood by the common definition that it contains the inner feelings of the author, but rather for its formal characteristics. See Holm, *Montag.*

51 Makdisi, *Diary*; for other examples of such diaries, see his articles on Ibn al-Bannā''s diary (Makdisi, *Autograph Diary I–IV*) and Conermann, Seidensticker, *Remarks.*

later generations with information on the character and reliability of *hadīth* scholars in order to evaluate the traditions they transmitted. Although the many obituaries Ibn Ṭawq inserted in his text might follow this impetus, in no way does the text give hints about it.

Indeed, Ibn Ṭawq's journal shows the formal characteristics and the concern over the correctness of given dates which constitute the Islamic diary. But in content it is neither restricted to the lives and deaths of traditionists nor to the 'stuff of history'. Whatever original motivation may have led him to start his record, in time it developed a life of its own and served the author in other ways than might have been originally intended. Nonetheless, in writing about his life and time, he followed the form of the diary even more rigorously than Ibn al-Bannā' who was studied by Makdisi. One can assume that he chose that form since it suited the ends to which he wrote it. This choice influenced the way in which Ibn Ṭawq's identity is represented. Since entries were usually written on the day the recorded events occurred, the selection of material is not due to its retrospectively recognizable impact but due to the author's interests at the time which go far beyond the science of *ḥadīth* or of history in general.

In order to shed some light on Ibn Ṭawq's motivation for writing and continuing his journal we have to go back to Ghazzī's *Kawākib.* The entry on the author suggests that, at some point in his life, Ibn Ṭawq has achieved full recognition as a learned man. Ghazzī calls him a shaykh, a prayer leader (*imām*), an *'ālim* and a traditionist (*muḥaddith*) – a complete scholar so to speak. If we accept Jonathan Berkey's findings about Mamluk Cairo it appears that the author made some, albeit minor contributions to the *Transmission of Knowledge*, most probable in the field of *ḥadīth* studies.[52] Much more enlightening than Ibn Ṭawq's own entry is the one Ghazzī wrote about the *shaykh al-islām* Taqī al-Dīn Abū Bakr b. Qāḍī 'Ajlūn to whom the author seems to have been very close: "He [i.e. the *shaykh* – TW] issued a lot of judgements (*fatwā*) and the *shaykh* Ibn Ṭawq has collected them and he added an appendix (*dhayl*), as my brother al-Najamī Ibn Shakam said."[53] The *dhayl* he wrote and the collection of legal opinions he compiled were the contributions to the transmission of knowledge Ibn Ṭawq had made and which assured him a place within a biographical dictionary despite the fact that in everyday life he was only a minor cog in the

52 Berkey lists some other low-level *'ulamā'* who did not contribute their whole life to education, mostly for lack of financial security; see Berkey, *Transmission*, 28, 200.

53 Ghazzī, *Kawākib* 1:114 – 18, here p. 115. Ghazzī admits that he had problems reconstructing the shaykh's biography and had to rely mostly on the chronicle "*mufākahat al-khillān fī ḥawādiṯ al-zamān*" by Muḥammad Ibn Ṭūlūn (1480 – 1546). See ibid.

administrative apparatus.[54] I argue that the *dhayl* Ghazzī mentions is nothing else but Ibn Ṭawq's journal.

Although Ibn Ṭawq wrote about the 'stuff of history' he also used his journal as a business calendar, taking note of "his showings-up, and no-shows, at countless appointments and events required by his job, his family, and his community."[55] He himself was aware that his writing had wandered from what was considered historiography. Therefore, he justifies its content in the opening passage for one year: "It will be reported: the events of the year 888 according to the Prophet's Ḥijra [1483 – 4 AD]; who died among the notables and others; also such things the author has knowledge of or witnessed himself."[56] As is obvious from Ghazzī's biography of the *shaykh al-islām*, this explanation was intended for other readers. This led Guo to describe it as being of a "hybrid format: a strange blend of a 'public' text, [...] and a 'private' journal".[57]

Ibn Ṭawq's record was finally integrated into the historiographical discourse when the famous scholar-historian Muḥammad Ibn Ṭūlūn (d. 1546) used it as a source for his famous chronicle "*Mufākahat al-Khillān fī Ḥawādith al-Zamān*".[58] While the chronicles of Aḥmad b. al-Ḥimṣī and 'Alā' al-Dīn al-Buṣrawī were published, Ibn Ṭawq's autograph was never even bound.[59] It is probable that by providing material for a 'proper' chronicle, the journal had done its share within the framework of historiography. Thus, the journal's place within the Syrian school of historiography was at best on the fringes, I the same way its author was described as "a peasant on the fringes of the *'ulamā*'".[60]

Large parts of the journal deal with Ibn Ṭawq's daily activities as well as evidently private affairs of the author and other people he knew which do not seem to have had any obvious value for contemporary historiography. But if we consider the journal as a way to provide firsthand material for a biography of the shaykh and, only secondary, of the author himself, this material had a certain value. As can be seen in al-Biqāʿī's chronicle, a public figure's conduct in his domestic life had indeed some importance for his assessment in the public realm. Furthermore, by demonstrating his knowledge of the *shaykh al-islām*'s private affairs, Ibn Ṭawq emphasized his connection to this eminent figure and thus increased his own social standing. The relationship between him and the

54 The notaries made up the lowest level of the legal system but at the same time were the linking pin between it and the populace; see Petry, *Civilian Elite*, 225 – 27.

55 Guo, *Review: Ibn Ṭawq, Al-Taʿlīq*, 210. One summary of what the subjects of historiography should be was given by Ibn Ṭawq's contemporary Sakhāwī; see Makdisi, *Diary*, 179.

56 *Taʿlīq* I:224.

57 Guo, *Review: Ibn Ṭawq, Al-Taʿlīq*, 210.

58 For the life and work of this scholar, see Conermann, *Ibn Ṭūlūn*.

59 The editor tells us in the introduction to the first volume that he found the manuscript consisting of three packets of paper held together by rubber band; see Ibn Ṭawq: Taʿlīq I:9.

60 *Taʿlīq* I:9.

shaykh al-islām seems to have been one of client and patron. The content of the journal should be viewed with respect to that relationship.

How to approach Identity?

In a 2008 article Astrid Meier provides a definition of the self which defines it as the sum of all relationships one has with oneself (ethical self) as well as with other people (social self). For the subject the constructive processes of identification are "largely or wholly unconscious, identities are lived as if they were 'given' rather than chosen; that is, they are often felt to be fundamental to the subject, as if they have been received whole and constitute the subject's essence."[61] The self is represented and, at the same time, constituted in acts of communication and performance in interaction with external factors such as religious (or political) affiliation, age, gender, occupation, social standing and one's integration within family and other groups. The representation is always aimed at a certain audience, and, therefore, conducted in accordance with norms, values, and conventions the performing subject shares with them. Although the performing subject has to follow these rules, it also can bend them at least to a certain degree.[62]

My approach to the representation of self is to some degree inspired by an article written by Steve Tamari on Ottoman Damascus. In his contribution to the volume "Auto/biography and the construction of identity and community in the Middle East", Tamari studied chronicles by three authors from Ottoman Damascus for "attachments to place and community and in historical consciousness as they determine personal identity in an early modern Arab society."[63] His conclusion was that the authors respectively identified with the international world of Islamic scholarship, the empire in which they lived, and the local community of Damascus.[64] Tamari named the prevalent points of reference "loci of identification".

The expressions of identity which can be found in Ibn Ṭawq's journal are dependent on the different contexts in which the text was produced. On the one hand, they follow the genre of the diary in which events are recorded only shortly after they have occurred which does not allow for a complex emplotment as to be found in biographies (*tarjamah*, *sīrah*) or literary chronicles. It is unclear what constituted the intended audience of the journal but it might be assumed that it

61 Frosh, Baraitser, *Goodbye to Identity*, 158.

62 Meier, *Dimensionen*, 4 f.; for collective group identities, see Assmann, *Kulturelles Gedächtnis*.

63 Tamari, *Biography*, 37.

64 Tamari, *Biography*, 38.

was to be found within the circles of the *ʿulamāʾ* who wrote historiography and biography. On the other hand, these expressions answer to the hierarchies in which the author was embedded and within which he positioned himself. Furthermore, the events he recorded were also dependent on the news the author himself received. Therefore, his journal is foremost concerned with events in Damascus and its immediate hinterland. Reports on other regions are scarcer and resemble much more what can be found in literary chronicles. The local focus is also due to the use of the text as a business calendar. Therefore, the representation of Ibn Ṭawq's identity will be analyzed foremost with respect to his immediate *Lebenswelt*.

Although Tamari acknowledged that patronage was described in these chronicles, he apparently neglects the fact that they were also produced in the context of patronage. After all, autobiographic writing was one means among others which could be used to further one's status and career.[65] Tamari omits the literary nature of the chronicles and the role of the audience in their production and emplotment. I argue here, that Ibn Ṭawq also positioned himself in relation to points of reference, but since entries were usually written on the day they happened, the selection of material is not organized to fit into a retrospectively arranged narrative. But due to the unedited state of Ibn Ṭawq's journal, a multifaceted approach is more applicable since it misses the modes of emplotment that the literary sources studied by Tamari possess.[66] For the sake of brevity, I concentrated on three points: the literate community of the *ʿulamāʾ*, the quarters as "the basic units of society [...], which were social solidarities as well as geographic entities"[67], and the household as "an area of order and unity which is contrasted with the labyrinthine anarchy of the city."[68]

Meier introduces three concepts of how the self can be represented.[69] According to the first concept the self is the product of a finished process of education and socialization and appears as complete in itself and safely embedded within society. It is throughout life stable and cohesive. The second concept depicts this stable self as an illusion which is always in danger of a crisis. It is characterized by fragmentation, inconsistency and instability. In the final concept the idea of one identity is dismissed altogether. The self is ever-changing, oscillating and always in flux because it is reinvented every time anew in a continuing process of identity formations. These occur in different social

65 This understanding of patronage is adapted from an article on 16th-century Europe; Jancke, *Patronagebeziehungen*, 30. With regard to biographical literature, see also Chamberlain, *Knowledge*.
66 For modes of emplotment in medieval Arab chronicles, see Hirschler, *Arabic Historiography*.
67 Lapidus, *Muslim Cities*, 49.
68 Essid, *Critique*, 8.
69 In this discussion, I follow Meier, *Dimensionen*, 8–9.

fields and lead to a divisibility of the self. The self is, according to this concept, never complete, since "allegiances or emotional connections" change throughout one's life.[70]

While the first and second concepts can be found frequently in Arabic literature, the third is evidently absent. Meier argues that this is also due to the genre conventions of biography where negative facts about public figures were often omitted.[71] This is only partly true for the historiographical literature of the Mamluk era. To quote Li Guo once more, al-Biqāʿī appears in his chronicle as "a man full of contradictions: an overzealous moralist, a caring father, a wife abuser, and finally, a big-mouthed jackass."[72] And al-Biqāʿī may not be the only author to present himself according to this model. The "blurring of lines between history and autobiography, and hence the increasing representation of the domestic" which is evident throughout the whole period (with a marked increase in the 15th century) may also have led to a different mode of representation of the self than in Ottoman times.[73] It may be assumed that Ibn Ṭawq's representation would be even more inclined towards the concept of the multiple self since his text is not emplotted in the same way as biographies and shows him in his day-to-day interactions with other people in diverse contexts.

Before this question can be answered, however, we turn to the three points of reference in relation to which Ibn Ṭawq positioned himself: the ʿulamāʾ, his neighbourhood and his household. On the basis of the findings provided in this survey, I will attempt to identify the underlying concept of self.

Point of Reference I: The *ʿulamāʾ*

The Arabic term *ʿālim* denotes a man of knowledge and became the notion for the learned men of religion and law. They perceived themselves as the guardians of the true Islamic society. They transcended all social classes. The judges (*qāḍī*) and high state officials came from their ranks. However, like Ibn Ṭawq most *ʿulamāʾ* had to make a living by drawing on several sources for small amounts of money.[74] They strived to attain posts as teachers, prayer leaders or Koran readers in the many mosques or religious schools (*madrasah*) in the city. Ibn Ṭawq takes

70 See Frosh, Baraitser, *Goodbye to Identity*, 158.

71 Meier, *Dimensionen*, 9 – 10.

72 See Guo, *Tales*, 120.

73 Rapoport, *Women*, 3; he also gives an overview over the historiographical works including information on domestic affairs (pp. 3 – 4).

74 For this and the following see Lapidus, *Muslim Cities*, 139.

note of being appointed to two such posts as a reciter of the Koran.[75] But these stipends were usually rather small. While they might have allowed a modest life for a pious man alone, they were not enough to maintain a family. There was great demand for the services of people who could read and write. They worked for fees as legal experts or professional witnesses. Not all legal business had to be brought before the *qāḍī*. Contracts would be written and notarized in the mosques and schools, and Ibn Ṭawq refers to one he wrote on his own doorstep.[76] In addition, one could still hope for gifts or even small stipends distributed by rich *ʿulamāʾ*, merchants or state officials.[77]

Ibn Ṭawq felt himself to be a member of this group. To be more precise, his allegiance was to the Shāfiʿite rite, which in Damascus was the predominant of the four Sunni law schools (*madhab*). Sexual escapades, excess use of alcohol and other scandals were localised only among the other law schools.[78] His own rite stood above such depravities. Its moral perfection is symbolised by Ibn Ṭawq's patron. Abū Bakr b. Qāḍī ʿAjlūn (841 – 928/1433 – 1521) was member of a family with a long tradition in religious learning and teaching. His brother and his father had held the post of *shaykh al-islām* before him. He allegedly taught more students than any other scholar in his day.[79] To Ibn Ṭawq he was the most important figure in the social and political cosmos of Damascus. He was also a link to the greater world of Islamic scholarship. Ibn Ṭawq introduced each year with a passage where he stated what his record was about, followed by a list of office holders. When the *shaykh* left for Cairo, then the Mamluk capital and the seat of the ruling sultan, Ibn Ṭawq marked it with a new headline in the middle of the year that the following "report is on what happened after the honourable shaykh departed for Cairo. May God let him and his companions arrive in health. May He send back him in health and success, and his companions in wealth and health."[80] The text is often more a tale of the *shaykh*'s life than of its author's. Ibn Ṭawq writes about his patron's troubles with his Egyptian wife or his sons, and records his health problems.[81]

75 He attained the first position in the *Zanjīlīya*-School in 887/1481; the second one was in a mosque in the village *Qābūn* a year later. *Taʿlīq* I:197, 227 – 228.

76 Ibid., p. 227.

77 Shortly before the Feast of Immolation (*ʿīd al-aḍḥa*), animals were even more expensive than usual, and Ibn Ṭawq was jubilant to receive sacrificial animals from his patron, a judge, and another shaykh; *Taʿlīq* I:115.

78 Guo, *Review: Ibn Ṭawq, Al-Taʿlīq*, 213.

79 Ghazzī, *Al-Kawākib*, 115.

80 *Taʿlīq* I:298.

81 Quarrels between the *shaykh* and his wife are frequently mentioned; e.g. ibid., 25, 521 – 2, 533; II:584, 587, 1049. On one occasion the *shaykh* even spoke of divorce, and a couple of days later Ibn Ṭawq asked him if he was going through with it (II:744, 747). For cases of sickness, see I:91, 122 – 3, 126, 522 – 28, 541, 546; II:641, 789, 1009 – 19; III:107 – 8, 1157 – 9; the *shaykh*

The *ʿulamāʾ* were for Ibn Ṭawq the advocates for the cause of the local populace as opposed to the mamluks who abused their power. This role was embodied by the *shaykh* before all others. People came to him to ask for his mediation in their problems with the rulers. He was asked to free people from prison, to make peace in the case of social unrest, or to achieve compensation for a murder.[82]

But Ibn Ṭawq also depicted himself as actively involved in the social activities that held the *ʿulamāʾ* community together. He recorded his attendances at teaching sessions in the Umayyad Mosque and other religious buildings. He also went there for the congregational prayers on Fridays whenever his health and the weather allowed it. Ibn Ṭawq accompanied the *shaykh* on his travels in the hinterland of Damascus and took part in the excursions to the gardens of the *ghūṭa*, the oasis surrounding Damascus. Usually these accounts contain little more than a list of attendees, a short itinerary, and a menu of the meal they had while there. Ibn Ṭawq wrote himself into the *shaykh*'s entourage. And he did more to show off his special links to this prominent figure.

Ibn Ṭawq's contacts to other *ʿulamāʾ* were rarely exclusively professional. He emphasized his overnight stays at the homes of the *shaykh* and other *ʿulamāʾ* he befriended, as well as their visits to his house. Their families mingled, with mutual visits for congratulating on a newborn child, providing help in the case of sickness, or without an explicit reason. Ibn Ṭawq's emphasis on his knowledge of the *shaykh*'s domestic affairs shows the extent of his identification with the latter. His depiction transcends the boundaries of the *ʿulamāʾ*'s public role and connects it to his Ibn Ṭawq's domestic life.

The *shaykh* was Ibn Ṭawq's role model for knowledge, social status, and public posture. In the journal his house appears as a landmark to which the author even refers to localize a neighbourhood mosque.[83] Ibn Ṭawq's intimate knowledge of the *shaykh*'s affairs proved for him that this admiration was not in vain. Why else would the *shaykh* have asked him to sleep in the bed of his soon-to-be-wed son, apparently an age-old tradition in Damascus? It was proof of the author's piety that he was chosen to give blessings (*baraka*) to the newly-weds by spending the three nights prior to their wedding night. It was proof that his patron thought as good of him as he did of the *shaykh*.

---

did not go to the teaching session because he was furious with one of his sons, III:1091. Furthermore, a wife of the shaykh got injured (I:94), another had a miscarriage (I:102).

82 Quarters were fined collectively in cases of murder, rebellion and even adultery. The whole quarter was held responsible for the conduct of each of its members. See Lapidus, *Later Middle Ages*, p. 94.

83 *Taʿlīq* I:30.

Point of reference II: The Neighbourhood

As mentioned above, the neighbourhood was the basic social and spatial unit by which Damascus was organized. In contrast to the *ʿulamāʾ* community which covered all of Damascus and even reached out beyond the frontiers of the empire, the neighbourhood was very much limited to a certain locus. Ibn Ṭawq lived in a residential neighbourhood around the Qaṣab Mosque, just north of the walls of old Damascus.[84] His house was next to a public bath (*ḥammām Burhān al-Dīn*) and not far from one of the city gates (*bāb al-salām*).[85]

Ibn Ṭawq follows literary conventions in his focus on the learned men. People of other occupations are usually invisible. He does not tell where he bought his grains or meat, or who made the pewter ware for his household.[86] Of Ibn Ṭawq's social contacts outside we learn only from obituaries. There appear a farrier, several peasants, craftsmen, and a Jewish ophthalmologist.[87] Ibn Ṭawq knew those people but probably not very well. None of them were ever mentioned as guests in his house.

With regard to his neighbourhood the case is different. Neighbourhoods had mixed populations and were "communities of both rich and poor".[88] All those people seem to have been granted the status of "our neighbour" (*jārunā*). Was it due to this characteristic that Ibn Ṭawq recorded their marriages, deaths, circumcisions and births with the same diligence he usually reserved for the *ʿulamāʾ* and high state officials? One case in point would be that when he wrote the obituary for one of his neighbours, he remarked: "I am not sure if the mother of his children was from the neighbourhood or from elsewhere".[89] It seems that a person's status changed in Ibn Ṭawq's perception when both were neighbours.

This hypothesis is strengthened when we look at the occupational background of the people mentioned by Ibn Ṭawq. Besides several *ʿulamāʾ*, there are a carpenter, two ophthalmologists, a weaver, and a wood turner.[90] Also, Ibn Ṭawq received a miller and his family as guests.[91] The most prominent neighbour,

---

84 Nuʿaymī, *Dāris*, 2:346, 429–30.

85 *Taʿlīq* I:9.

86 Food prices are frequently given and commented throughout the text. Ibn Ṭawq bought pewter ware in 888/1481: "the large cauldron and the large frying pan and [everything] but the large drinking vessel"; ibid., 74. But he mentions the benefactor by name when a *shaykh* sent him two copper drinking vessels; ibid., 124.

87 For the Turcoman farrier, see ibid., 95; peasants are mentioned ibid., 91, 202, 507; the ophthalmologist in *Taʿlīq* II:1048.

88 Lapidus, 1967, p. 87.

89 *Taʿlīq* IV:1714.

90 *Taʿlīq* III:1135, 1131, 1137, 1124; IV:1649.

91 *Taʿlīq* III:1363.

however, was one Great Emir (*amīr kabīr*) called Zāmir. Probably the emir moved to the neighbourhood around the year 901/1495 – 6.

Ibn Ṭawq perceived the quarter as an integrated unit which was to offer all its members protection. As they were held responsible collectively, their actions appear to be collective as well. They are referred to as "the people of the Qaṣab [Mosque]", and as a whole they built gates to guard their neighbourhood from external threats.[92] The emir is valued in this respect. He was approached by two shaykhs in 904/1498 – 9 to have a tavern in the neighbourhood to be closed down. In the following year, the emir's entourage opened a tavern in a nearby garden, while the emir was sick. Back in health the emir closed it immediately.[93] In contrast to almost every other mamluk amir, Zāmir is presented in a good light. This was due to his status as the author's neighbour and his role in peace-keeping.[94] When after a fierce fight between that emir and his son, where even weapons were drawn, the author interceded in order to keep the emir's son from being imprisoned. Finally they reached an agreement between them. The son had to swear to abstain from alcohol and prostitutes, and had to take an oath that he would be obedient to his father.[95]

In his neighbourhood, the author was an important figure. People listened to his advice and came to him for help.[96] On the other side, Ibn Ṭawq depended on his neighbours to safeguard his privacy and, thus, his reputation. They could hear him, as he could hear them. How might it have affected one's reputation when neighbours could hear that a pregnant woman "writhed with pain one day and one night" before giving birth?[97] After all, how could a household live in peace when the quarter was in turmoil?

Point of Reference III: The Household

Within the precincts of one's household the ideal was the Arab man who was the master with absolute power over its members and had to oversee "the domestic function founded on the division of labor according to gender, and implying a

92 For the quote, ibid., 1360; for the gates, II, 510, 599. See also Sack, *Damaskus*, 67 and Lapidus, *Muslim Cities*, 64, footnote 17.

93 *Taʿlīq* III:1374; IV:1662, 1720, 1747.

94 The emir also intervened when a fight broke out between two peasants who had allegedly distilled liquor in an orchard. Ibid., 1849.

95 Ibid., 1843 – 4.

96 When a neighbour was confronted with a high fine, Ibn Ṭawq bargained with the officials until the fine was decisively lower. *Taʿlīq* III:1330 – 1.

97 *Taʿlīq* I:537. What was considered public and what private in premodern societies is often confusing; see Marcus, *Privacy*; Alshech, *Do Not Enter Houses.*

socialization of relations based on education."[98] This differed immensely from Ibn Ṭawq's social reality. At the same time as he juggled his different jobs to provide for his family, he was probably additionally indebted to his wife:

> A fifteenth-century husband would have usually owed his wife the deferred part of the marriage gift, an annual payment for her clothing, a daily allowance, and perhaps the rent for living in her house. In addition, she may have been entitled to demand a due portion of the marriage gift at any point during the marriage.[99]

On a regular basis, Ibn Ṭawq mentions small amounts of money he paid to his wife. One time he comments that "out of tradition (*min al-ʿatīq*) 14 dirham belong to the wife for domestic utensils."[100] She also sold a golden broach of hers through her brother, in order to buy a copy of the Koran.[101] Her husband did not have any say in the sale or in the purchase. She seems to have come from a rather wealthy family, and the broach was probably part of her trousseau.[102] Furthermore, it was she who forced her husband to sell a slave-girl, and bought a new one without asking for his consent.[103] Nonetheless, the relationship between the author and his wife seems to have lasted as long as the record.[104]

With regard to his household Ibn Ṭawq represents himself as a caring husband and father, as a provider for his family, and as the head of the household. Throughout the text he had only one wife: Umm as-Sitt Āmina who was a niece of his patron, the *shaykh al-islām* Taqī al-Dīn.[105] Beside his wife, he entertained several consecutive concubines.[106] Maybe this was preferable to true polygamy

98 Essid, *Critique*, 8.
99 Rapoport, *Marriage*, 28.
100 *Taʿlīq* I:121.
101 Ibid., 237; Conermann, Seidensticker, *Remarks*, 126.
102 Rapoport, *Women*, 17–22; idem, *Marriage*, 12–30. Ibn Ṭawq mentions several instances where his mother-in-law seeks to buy or sell real estate in the city; *Taʿlīq* I:531; II:667.
103 *Taʿlīq* I:288, 290.
104 Rapoport mentions a divorce Ibn Ṭawq issued in agreement with his wife but it was only due to other legal matters. A week later she appears again as his wife. Rapoport, *Marriage*, 7; *Taʿlīq* I:449.
105 *Taʿlīq* II: 1032.
106 Slave-girls who bear their master a child are denoted by the legal term *umm al-walad*; EI2, pp. 857–59 (Bitte ins Literaturverzeichnis vollständig aufführen). Ibn Ṭawq refers to them as *umm al-awlād.* One is identifiable by the name of Mubāraka but she dies in 888/1483–84. One or more appear later on but are not referred to by name. *Taʿlīq* I:277, 489; II:778, 1032–33; IV:1861–64. Although the author applies the legally valid term *umm al-awlād* (mother of children) for these women, it was impossible for me to find out which of his children was not born by his wife. However, a miscarriage or abortion of a baby girl by his then concubine is mentioned in 900/1495. *Taʿlīq* III:1363; see also Guo, *Review: Ibn Ṭawq, Al-Taʿlīq*, 214. This could have happened due to active "birth control", allegedly quite common in 15th-century Syria and Egypt. For this hypothesis, see Musallam, *Sex and Society.*

to both him and his wife.[107] While Ibn Ṭawq rarely gives his wife's name and, instead, calls her "the wife" (*al-zawjah*), he is worried when she gets sick, or has "urges" from her pregnancy.[108] He asked god "for mercy in his judgement" after she had a grave argument with his concubine, and did not speak to him until the evening.[109]

Among his children it is Ibn Ṭawq's son Muḥammad Abū al-Faḍl Raḍḍī al-Dīn for whom the author shows the most affection.[110] He follows every step marking his son's way to adulthood.[111] However, whenever any of his children was sick he stayed home to treat and care or them. The most astonishing accounts are on the everyday life at home. Ibn Ṭawq recorded that his eldest daughter and his son were lying to him.[112] His son was behaving strangely after the author and his wife had an argument, and was hit on the head with a stone by another boy.[113]

Ibn Ṭawq was anxious to be a successful provider for his family. This becomes visible in the many lists of food prices and his notes on his spending we find throughout the journal. It was his obligation to provide for his household. Time and again he struggled with the costs and workload of repairs at least to keep the rain out.[114]

The household was where he scrutinized his body and assessed his health. It was also the place he could not leave when really sick. In this respect it was "a protected sanctuary".[115] Ibn Ṭawq mentions that the *shaykh* hid at home when melancholy overcame him or when the demands of the people were too much for him.[116] At the same time, however, the privacy was not exclusive. As mentioned

107 Among the common people taking a concubine instead of a legal wife became rather common while polygamy was on the retreat. Rapoport, *Women*, 15, 30.

108 Near the end of the record, the wife's health deteriorated. This is a selection from the fourth volume; *Taʿlīq* IV:1704, 1812, 1838 – 9, 1861 – 6; the urges appear in her pregnancy with Ibn Ṭawq's second daughter, Umm Hānī; I:135.

109 Ibid., 133.

110 He also fathered five girls. But only one of them perhaps reached adulthood. Three of his daughters died within the first two years after being born; *Taʿlīq* I:280; II:631; III:1136; his oldest daughter, born before the beginning of the journal, died at the age of thirteen; ibid., p. 1121. Their early deaths certainly had an impact on the amount of how much Ibn Ṭawq wrote about them. For the consolation for child mortality, see Gil'adi 1993.

111 Among these are his birth (I:28), the first shaving of his hair (I:126), his circumcision, and his marriage (II:541 – 2; III:1422). After his first wife died a year later from the plague, he married again (IV:1604, 1855).

112 *Taʿlīq* I:146.

113 Ibid., 135; II:764.

114 Leaks in the roof are mentioned almost every second year. *Taʿlīq* I:159, 309; II:738 – 39, 1004; IV:1587, 1690. An earthquake forced them to run out into the garden barefooted; IV:1560. Repairs in his house were less frequent; I:36, 91, 91, 98, 101, 105 – 107; II:635; III:1482; IV:1785.

115 Marcus, *Privacy*, 169.

116 Ibn Ṭawq calls melancholy "a deviation of temperament" (*inḥirāf mizāj*), *Taʿlīq* III:1107, 1224; the shaykh avoided the people, I:546; II:669; IV:1780.

above, Ibn Ṭawq often entertained guests: his fellow *'ulamā'* from Damascus or his father's hometown Jarūd as well as neighbours, relatives, or even some Christians.[117]

The household can therefore not be analyzed as an isolated sphere. As is illustrated by the author's and his wife's overnight stays in other houses and their hosting of guests, it was integrated into the social cosmos of Damascus.

Conclusions

It has been shown that the three points of reference under study do not exclude but complement each other. They are linked to each other and to other points of reference. They are elements of a complex identity which combined local pride, a consciousness of status, and a sense of duty towards one's job as well as to one's family. Ibn Ṭawq does not follow the model of multiple identities but rather the second model. He depicts himself overcoming adversities in all respective spheres. Furthermore, he saw no contradictions in his duties as a father, as a subordinate to the *shaykh al-islām* or, in fact, between his work as a notary and his agricultural occupations. To him, the different spheres of public and domestic life were not separated but parts of a greater whole.

The emphasis the text puts on the respective spheres shifts only in reaction to external influences. So, during the first Ottoman-Mamluk war (1485–91) imperial politics moved to the fore in the text because Ibn Ṭawq feared a collapse of the Mamluk empire and, at the same time, was worried by its effects on the local level.[118] Food prices sky rocketed and public order deteriorated when Egyptian troops were came through on their way to the front.[119] His coverage of his household decreased under such circumstances, and his view turned outwards. At other times, his concern with his family's business is prevalent in the text. One such case is an intense argument between his wife and his son's wife at the very end of the journal. It lasted for about one and a half months. The author blames his daughter-in-law for her "immorality and maliciousness, bad behaviour and bad upbringing" but then "both parties spoke out of all proportion and without any inhibition". He even recorded that his wife "constantly annoyed" him with

117 The author met with or even hosted dignitaries from Ǧarūd on their visits to Damascus. *Taʿlīq* I:26, 64, 76; II:543, IV:1911. Local *'ulamā'* are hosted regularly as well as members of Ibn Ṭawq's wider family. Some Christian peasants and a priest eat at his place for a couple of days in 890/1485; *Taʿlīq* I:428–430.

118 Guo, *Review: Ibn Ṭawq, Al-Taʿlīq*, 211.

119 So it was in 904/1499 when the already rare meat became even scarcer after Egyptian Mamluks arrived. The situation eased only after they departed. *Taʿlīq* IV:1689–90, 1695, 1697, 1702.

her slander. Only on the penultimate day of the edited record he was able to pacify the situation.[120]

But the author not only wrote about the people around him, he also wrote about himself. First and foremost, he wrote about his body. He tells us that he paid half a dirhem for a shave, that he had his hair cut in the public bath (*ḥammām*), or that he had his tooth pulled, the last one in the lower left jaw.[121] His awareness of having a body increased proportionately to its refusal to obey him. In 897/1492 his hand stopped to work properly.[122] While at the beginning of the journal Ibn Ṭawq used his medical knowledge to treat his children, in the last years he cared mostly for himself.[123] His body had to work or he could follow neither his social nor his religious obligations. He could not attend the prayers when in an impure state. He could not go to work when in pain.

Finally, there are also traces of individuality in the journal. Ibn Ṭawq recorded that he saw some swallows and bats flying over the neighbourhood, that he had eaten the first figs, smelled the blossoms of the moringe (*bān*), or picked some flowers.[124] The greatest indicator, however, is the existence of the journal itself. Ibn Ṭawq deemed his everyday life important enough to put time and money into recording it diligently for two decades. While Ibn Ṭawq's journal presents its author as immersed in social roles and obligations, its existence alone renders him rather exceptional. Even if it follows established literary models, writing a report on one's life is an act of individualisation.[125]

Literature

Primary Sources

Buṣrawī, al-Shaikh 'Alā' ad-Dīn 'Alī b. Yūsif b. Aḥmad al-Dimashqī al-Shāfi'ī al-, *Ta'rīkh al-Buṣrawī. Ṣafaḥāt Majhūlah Tārīkh Dimashq fī 'Aṣr al-Mamālīk*, ed. Akram Ḥasan al-'Ulabī, Damaskus 1988.

Ghazzī, Najm al-Dīn, *Al-Kawākib al-Sā'irah bi-A'yān al-Mi'ah al-'Āshirah*, ed. Jibrā'īl Sulaimān Jabdūd, 2 vols., Beirut 1989.

120 *Ta'līq* IV:1907–1910, 1912, 1915.

121 *Ta'līq* I:144; IV:1679; I:469.

122 *Ta'līq* III:1116.

123 After a visit to the bath house, he found some yellow pimples in his belly button. And scratching them felt delightful. Finally, he cut them open. Meanwhile he could not walk on his left foot anymore, because of an intense pain. He used leeches against that. *Ta'līq* IV, pp. 1889, 1894, 1898, 1899–1904, 1911.

124 *Ta'līq* I, pp. 125,235 (roses); II, pp. 594 (bats and swallows), 787 (figs), 1005 (*bān* tree).

125 Ries, *Individualisierung*, p. 111.

Ibn al-Ḥimṣī, Aḥmad, *Ḥawādith al-Zamān wa-Wafayyāt al-Shuyūkh wa-l-Aqrān*, Beirut: Dar an-Nafa'es 2000.
Ibn Ṭawq, Shihāb al-Dīn Aḥmad, *At-Taʿlīq*, ed. Ja'far al-Muhājir, 4 vol., Damascus 2000-2007.
Ibn Ṭūlūn, Šams ad-Dīn Muḥammad, *Mufākahat al-ḫillān fī ḥawādiṯ al-zamān* [ta'rīḫ miṣr wa-aš-šām] (Edition Muḥammad Muṣṭafā), 2 vol., Cairo 1962.
Nu'aymī, 'Abd al-Qādir b. Muḥammad al-Dimashqī, *Al-Dāris fī Ta'rīkh al-Madāris*, ed. Ja'far al-Ḥusnī, 2 vols., Cairo 1988.

Secondary Sources

Al-Harithy, Howayda, "The Concept of Space in Mamluk Architecture," *Muqarnas* 18 (2001), pp. 73-93.
Alshech, Eli, "'Do Not Enter Houses Other than Your Own'. The Evolution of the Notion of a Private Domestic Sphere in Early Sunnī Islamic Thought," *Islamic Law and Society* 11 (2004), pp. 291-332.
Amelang, James S., "Saving the Self from Autobiography," in: *Selbstzeugnisse in der Frühen Neuzeit. Individualisierungsweisen in interdisziplinärer Perspektive*, Schriften des Historischen Kollegs, Bd. 68, ed. Kaspar von Greyerz, München 2007, pp. 129-140.
Assmann, Jan, "Kollektives Gedächtnis und kulturelle Identität," in: *Kultur und Gedächtnis*, ed. Jan Assmann and Toni Hölscher, Frankfurt 1988, pp. 9-19.
Berkey, Jonathan, *The Transmission of Knowledge in Medieval Cairo*, Princeton 1992.
Burckhardt, Jacob, *Betrachtungen. Historische Fragmente*, Leipzig 1985.
Chamberlain, Michael, *Knowledge and social practice in medieval Damascus, 1190-1350*, Cambridge 1994.
Conermann, Stephan and Seidensticker, Tilman, "Some remarks on Ibn Tawq's (d.915/1509) Journal al-Ta'liq, vol. 1 (885/1480 to 890/1485)," *Mamlūk Studies Review* 11 (2007), pp. 121-135.
Conermann, Stephan, "Es Boomt! Die Mamlūkenforschung (1992-2002)," in: *Die Mamlūken. Studien zu ihrer Geschichte und Kultur. Zum Gedenken an Ulrich Haarmann (1942-1999)*, ed. Stephan Conermann and Anja Pistor-Hatam, Hamburg: EB-Verlag 2003, pp. 1-69.
Conermann, Stephan, "Ibn Ṭūlūn (d. 955/1548): Life and Works," *Mamlūk Studies Review* 8/1 (2004), pp. 115-139.
Elger, Ralf and Köse, Yavuz (ed.), *Many ways of Speaking About the Self. Middle Eastern Ego Documents in Arabic, Persian and Turkish (14th - 20th century)*, Wiesbaden: Harrassowitz 2010.
Elger, Ralf et al. (2007): Konvention und Innovation in Ego-Dokumenten (15.-20. Jahrhundert: Arabisch, Persisch, Türkisch), Konferenzbericht, *HSozKult*, 22.11.
Elger, Ralf, "Lying, Forging, Plagiarism: Some Narrative Techniques in Ibn Baṭṭūṭa's Travelogue," in: *Many Way of Speaking About the Self*, ed. Ralf Elger and Yavuz Köse, Wiesbaden 2010, pp. 71-87.
EI2: The Encyclopedia of Islam. New Edition, 11 vol., Leiden 1960-2000.
Enderwitz, Susanne, "Public Role and Private Self," in: *Writing the Self. Autobiographical*

Writing in Modern Arabic Literature, ed. Robin Ostle, Ed de Moor and Stefan Wild, London 1998, pp. 75 – 81.

Essid, Yassine, *A Critique of the Origins of Islamic Economic Thought*, Leiden, New York, Köln 1995.

Faroqhi, Suraiya, *Kultur und Alltag im Osmanischen Reich. Vom Mittelalter bis zum Anfang des 20. Jahrhunderts*, München 1995.

Franke, Patrick, "Querverweis als Selbstzeugnis – Individualität und Intertextualität in den Schriften des mekkanischen Gelehrten Mullah ʿAlī al-Qārī (st. 1014/1606)," in: *Zwischen Alltag und Schriftkultur: Horizonte des Individuellen in der arabischen Literatur des 17. und 18. Jahrhunderts*, Beiruter Texte und Studien 110, ed. Stefan Reichmuth and Florian Schwarz, Beirut/Würzburg 2008, pp. 131 – 163.

Franke, Patrick, "The Ego of the Mullah: Strategies of Self-Representation in the Works of the Meccan Scholar ʿAli al-Qari (d. 1606)," in: *Many Ways of Speaking about the Self. Middle Eastern Ego-Documents in Arabic, Persian, Turkish (14th-20th century)*, ed. Ralf Elger and Yavuz Köse, Wiesbaden 2010, pp. 185 – 200.

Frosh, Stephen and Baraitser, Lisa, "Goodbye to Identity?," in: *Identity in Question*, ed. Anthony Elliott and Paul Du Gay, Los Angeles 2009, pp. 158 – 169.

Gil'adi, Avner, "The Child Was Small… Not So the Grief for Him': Sources, Structure, and Content of Al-Sakhawi's Consolation Treatise for Bereaved Parents," *Poetics Today* 14/2 (1993), pp. 367 – 386.

Ginzburg, Carlo, *Il formaggio e i vermi. Il cosmo di un mugnaio 1500*, Turin 1976.

Grunebaum, Gustav Edmund von (1963): *Der Islam im Mittelalter*, Zürich/Stuttgart.

Guo, Li, "Al-Biqāʿī's Chronicle: a Fifteenth Century Learned Man's Reflection on his Time and World," in: *The Historiography of Islamic Egypt (c. 950 – 1800)*, ed. Hugh Kennedy, Leiden/Boston/Köln 2001, pp. 121 – 148.

Guo, Li, "Review: Ibn Ṭawq, *Al-Taʿlīq: Yawmīyāt Shihāb al-Dīn Aḥmad Ibn Ṭawq*," *Mamlūk Studies Review* 12/1 (2008), pp. 210 – 218.

Guo, Li, "Tales of a Medieval Cairene Harem: Domestic Life in al-Biqāʿī's Autobiographical Chronicle," *Mamlūk Studies Review* 9/1 (2005), pp. 101 – 121.

Haarmann, Ulrich, "Auflösung und Bewahrung der klassischen Formen arabischer Geschichtsschreibung in der Zeit der Mamluken," *Zeitschrift der Morgenländischen Gesellschaft* 121 (1971), pp. 46 – 60.

Haddad, George, "The Interests of an Eighteenth Century Chronicler of Damascus," *Der Islam* 38/3 (1963), pp. 258 – 271.

Hirschler, Konrad, *Medieval Arabic Historiography. Authors as Actors*, London 2006.

Holm, Christiane, "Montag Ich. Dienstag Ich. Mittwoch Ich. Versuch einer Phänomenologie des Diaristischen," in: *Absolut? privat! Vom Tagebuch zum Weblog*, ed. Helmut Gold and Wolfgang Albrecht, Heidelberg 2008, pp. 10 – 50.

Humphreys, R. Stephen, "Review: Sartain, E. M, *Jalāl al-Dīn al-Suyūṭī*," *Journal of Near Eastern Studies* 38/1 (1979), pp. 74 – 76.

Irwin, Robert, "Mamluk History and Historians," in: *Arabic Literature in the Post-Classical Period*, ed. Richards Allen, Cambridge 2006, pp. 159 – 170.

Jancke, Gabriele, "Patronagebeziehungen in autobiographischen Schriften des 16. Jahrhunderts – Individualisierungsweisen?," in: *Selbstzeugnisse in der Frühen Neuzeit. Individualisierungsweisen in interdisziplinärer Perspektive*, ed. Kaspar von Greyerz, München 2007, pp. 13 – 31.

Kafadar, Cemal, "Self and Others: The Diary of a Dervish in Seventeenth Century Istanbul and First-Person Narratives in Ottoman Literature," *Studia Islamica* 69 (1989), pp. 61-79.

Kaidbey, Naila Takieddine (1995): *Historiography in Bilād al-Shām: The Sixteenth and Seventeenth Centuries* (unpubl. Ph.D. diss., American University of Beirut).

Klein, Denise, "The Sultan's Envoys Speak: The Ego in 18th-Century Ottoman Sefâretnâmes on Russia," in: *Many Ways of Speaking About the Self*, ed. Ralf Elger and Yavuz Köse, Wiesbaden: Harrassowitz 2010, pp. 89-102.

Lapidus, Ira Marvin, "Muslim Cities and Islamic Societies," in: *Middle Eastern Cities. A Symposium on Ancient, Islamic and Contemporary Middle Eastern Urbanism*, ed. Ira Marvin Lapidus, Berkeley, Los Angeles 1969, pp. 47-79.

Lapidus, Ira Marvin, *Muslim Cities in the Later Middle Ages*. Cambridge 1967.

Lejeune, Philippe, *Der autobiographische Pakt*, Frankfurt/Main 1994. [French original 1975].

Makdisi, George, "The Diary in Islamic Historiography: Some Notes," *History and Theory* 25/2 (1986), pp. 173-185.

Makdisi, George, "Autograph Diary of an Eleventh-Century Historian of Baghdād I", in: *Bulletin of the School of Oriental and African Studies* 18 (1956), pp. 9-31.

Makdisi, George, "Autograph Diary of an Eleventh-Century Historian of Baghdād II", in: *Bulletin of the School of Oriental and African Studies* 18 (1956), pp. 239-260.

Makdisi, George, "Autograph Diary of an Eleventh-Century Historian of Baghdād III", in: *Bulletin of the School of Oriental and African Studies* 19 (1957), pp. 13-48.

Makdisi, George, "Autograph Diary of an Eleventh-Century Historian of Baghdād IV", in: *Bulletin of the School of Oriental and African Studies* 19 (1957), pp. 281-303.

Makdisi, George, "Autograph Diary of an Eleventh-Century Historian of Baghdād V", in: *Bulletin of the School of Oriental and African Studies* 19 (1957), pp. 426-443.

Marcus, Abraham, "Privacy in Eighteenth-Century Aleppo: The Limits of Cultural Ideals," *International Journal of Middle Eastern Studies* 18 (1986), pp. 165-183.

Masters, Bruce, "The View from the Province: Syrian Chronicles of the 18th Century," *Journal of the American Oriental Society* 114 (1994), pp. 353-362.

May, Karl, *Carl May's Gesammelte Reiseromane*, 33 vols., Freiburg (1892-1910).

Meier, Astrid, "Dimensionen und Krisen des Selbst in biographischen und historischen Schriften aus Damaskus im 17. und 18. Jahrhundert," in: *Zwischen Alltag und Schriftkultur. Horizonte des Individuellen in der arabischen Literatur des 17. und 18. Jahrhunderts*, ed. Stefan Reichmuth and Florian Schwarz, Beirut (2008), pp. 1-21.

Misch, Georg, *Geschichte der Autobiographie. Band III: Das Mittelalter: Das Hochmittelalter im Anfang*, vol. 2, Frankfurt/Main (1962).

Musallam, Basim F., *Sex and Society in Islam. Birth Control Before the Nineteenth Century*, Cambridge 1983.

Origo, Iris, *The Merchant of Prato. Francesco di Marco Datini*, London 1957.

Ostle, Robin, "Introduction," in: *Writing the Self. Autobiographical Writing in Modern Arabic Literature*, ed. Robin Ostle, Ed de Moor and Stefan Wild, London 1998, pp. 18-24.

Petry, Carl F., *The Civilian Elite of Cairo in the Later Middle Ages*, Princeton 1992.

Rapoport, Yossef, "Women and Gender in Mamluk Society - an Overview," *Mamlūk Studies Review* 11/2 (2007), pp. 1-45.

Rapoport, Yossef, *Marriage, Money and Divorce in Medieval Islamic Society*, Cambridge 2005.

Reynolds, Dwight Fletcher and Brustad, Kristen E., *Interpreting the Self. Autobiography in the Arabic Literary Tradition*, Berkeley 2001.

Ries, Rotraud, "Individualisierung im Spannungsfeld differenter Kulturen: Positionsbestimmungen und experimentelle Neudefinitionen in der jüdischen Minderheit," in: *Selbstzeugnisse in der Frühen Neuzeit. Schriften des Historischen Kollegs*, ed. Kaspar von Greyerz, München 2007, pp. 79–112.

Robinson, Chase F., *Islamic Historiography*, Cambridge 2007.

Rosenthal, Franz, *A History of Muslim Historiography*, 2nd revised edition, Leiden: 1968.

Rutz, Andreas, "Ego-Dokument oder Ich-Konstruktion? Selbstzeugnisse als Quellen zur Erforschung des frühneuzeitlichen Menschen," in: *Das ‚Ich' in der Frühen Neuzeit. Autobiographien – Selbstzeugnisse – Ego-Dokumente in geschichts- und literaturwissenschaftlicher Perspektive*, ed. Stefan Elit, Stephan Kraft, and Andreas Rutz, zeitenblicke. Online-Journal für die Geschichtswissenschaften, vol. 1, no. 2 (http://www.zeitenblicke.de/2002/02/rutz/index.html am 11.08.2007).

Sack, Dorothée, *Damaskus. Entwicklung und Struktur einer orientalisch-islamischen Stadt*, Mainz: 1989.

Sajdi, Dana, *Peripheral Visions: The World and Worldviews of Commoner Chronicles in the 18th Century Ottoman Levant*, unpublished PhD. Thesis, Columbia university 2002.

Schulze, Winfried, "Ego-Dokumente: Annäherung an den Menschen in der Geschichte? Vorüberlegungen für die Tagung ‚Ego-Dokumente'," in: *Ego-Dokumente: Annäherung an den Menschen in der Geschichte?* ed. Winfried Schulze, Berlin 1996, pp. 11–30.

Tamari, Steve, "Biography, autobiography, and identity in early modern Damascus," in: *Auto/biography and the construction of identity and community in the Middle East*, ed. Mary Ann Fay, New York 2002, pp. 37–49.

Terzioğlu, Derin, "Man in the image of God in the image of times, Sufi self-narratives and the diary of Niyāzī-i Miṣrī (1618–94)", *Studia Islamica* 94 (2002), pp. 139–165.

Von Krusenstjern, Benigna, "Buchhalter ihres Lebens. Über Selbstzeugnisse aus dem 17. Jahrhundert," in: *Das dargestellte Ich. Studien zu Selbstzeugnissen des späteren Mittelalters und der frühen Neuzeit*, vol. 1, ed. Klaus Arnold, Sabine Schmolinsky and Urs Martin Zahnd, Bochum 1999, pp. 139–145.

Von Krusenstjern, Benigna, "Was sind Selbstzeugnisse? Begriffskritische und quellenkundliche Überlegungen anhand von Beispielen aus dem 17. Jahrhundert," *Historische Anthropologie* 2/3 (1994), pp. 462–471.

Weintritt, Otfried, *Arabische Geschichtsschreibung in den arabischen Provinzen des Osmanischen Reiches (16.–18. Jahrhundert)*, Hamburg-Schenefeld: 2008.